BIG IDEAS MATH®
Modeling Real Life

Grade 6
Advanced

TEACHING EDITION

Ron Larson
Laurie Boswell

Erie, Pennsylvania
BigIdeasLearning.com

Big Ideas Learning, LLC
1762 Norcross Road
Erie, PA 16510-3838
USA

For product information and customer support, contact Big Ideas Learning at **1-877-552-7766** or visit us at ***BigIdeasLearning.com***.

Cover Image:
Valdis Torms, cobalt88/Shutterstock.com

Front Matter:
xxxii Ryan McVay/DigitalVision/Getty Images; **xxxiii** Blackzheep/ iStock/Getty Images Plus; **xxxiv** janulla/ iStock/ Getty Images Plus; **xxxv** Talaj/iStock/Getty Images Plus; **xxxvii** scotto72/E+/Getty Images; **xxxviii** iZonda/ iStock/ Getty Images Plus; **xxxix** Tal Inbar/Wikipedia; **xl** NASA/Terry Virts; **xli** damedeeso/iStock/Getty Images Plus; **xlii** EMFA16/iStock/Getty Images Plus; **xliii** asiseeit/E+/Getty Images; **xliv** eyfoto/iStock/Getty Images Plus; **xlv** goir/ iStock/Getty Images Plus; **xlvi** clintspencer/iStock/Getty Images Plus

Printed in Mexico

IBSN 13: 978-1-63708-339-0

Print Number: 05 Print Year: 2022

One Voice from Kindergarten Through Algebra 2

Written by renowned authors, Dr. Ron Larson and Dr. Laurie Boswell, *Big Ideas Math* offers a seamless math pedagogy from elementary through high school. Together, Ron and Laurie provide a consistent voice that encourages students to make connections through cohesive progressions and clear instruction. Since 1992, Ron and Laurie have authored over 50 mathematics programs.

"*Each time Laurie and I start working on a new program, we spend time putting ourselves in the position of the reader. How old is the reader? What is the reader's experience with mathematics? The answers to these questions become our writing guides. Our goal is to make the learning targets understandable and to develop these targets in a clear path that leads to student success.*"

Ron Larson

Ron Larson, Ph.D., is well known as lead author of a comprehensive and widely used mathematics program that ranges from elementary school through college. He holds the distinction of Professor Emeritus from Penn State Erie, The Behrend College, where he taught for nearly 40 years. He received his Ph.D. in mathematics from the University of Colorado. Dr. Larson engages in the latest research and advancements in mathematics education and consistently incorporates key pedagogical elements to ensure focus, coherence, rigor, and student self-reflection.

"*My passion and goal in writing is to provide an essential resource for exploring and making sense of mathematics. Our program is guided by research around the learning and teaching of mathematics in the hopes of improving the achievement of all students. May this be a successful year for you!*"

Laurie Boswell, Ed.D., is the former Head of School at Riverside School in Lyndonville, Vermont. In addition to authoring textbooks, she provides mathematics consulting and embedded coaching sessions. Dr. Boswell received her Ed.D. from the University of Vermont in 2010. She is a recipient of the Presidential Award for Excellence in Mathematics Teaching and later served as president of CPAM. Laurie has taught math to students at all levels, elementary through college. In addition, Laurie has served on the NCTM Board of Directors and as a Regional Director for NCSM. Along with Ron, Laurie has co-authored numerous math programs and has become a popular national speaker.

Contributors, Reviewers,

Big Ideas Learning would like to express our gratitude to the mathematics education and instruction experts who served as our advisory panel, contributing specialists, and reviewers during the writing of *Big Ideas Math: Modeling Real Life*. Their input was an invaluable asset during the development of this program.

Contributing Specialists and Reviewers

- **Sophie Murphy**, Ph.D. Candidate, Melbourne School of Education, Melbourne, Australia
  Learning Targets and Success Criteria Specialist and Visible Learning Reviewer
- **Linda Hall**, Mathematics Educational Consultant, Edmond, OK
  Advisory Panel and Teaching Edition Contributor
- **Michael McDowell**, Ed.D., Superintendent, Ross, CA
  Project-Based Learning Specialist
- **Kelly Byrne**, Math Supervisor and Coordinator of Data Analysis, Downingtown, PA
  Advisory Panel and Content Reviewer
- **Jean Carwin**, Math Specialist/TOSA, Snohomish, WA
  Advisory Panel and Content Reviewer
- **Nancy Siddens**, Independent Language Teaching Consultant, Las Cruces, NM
  English Language Learner Specialist
- **Nancy Thiele**, Mathematics Consultant, Mesa, AZ
  Teaching Edition Contributor
- **Kristen Karbon**, Curriculum and Assessment Coordinator, Troy, MI
  Advisory Panel and Content Reviewer
- **Kery Obradovich**, K–8 Math/Science Coordinator, Northbrook, IL
  Advisory Panel and Content Reviewer
- **Jennifer Rollins**, Math Curriculum Content Specialist, Golden, CO
  Advisory Panel
- **Becky Walker**, Ph.D., School Improvement Services Director, Green Bay, WI
  Advisory Panel
- **Anthony Smith**, Ph.D., Associate Professor, Associate Dean, University of Washington Bothell, Seattle, WA
  Reading/Writing Reviewer
- **Nicole Dimich Vagle**, Educator, Author, and Consultant, Hopkins, MN
  Assessment Reviewer
- **Jill Kalb**, Secondary Math Content Specialist, Arvada, CO
  Content Reviewer
- **Janet Graham**, District Math Specialist, Manassas, VA
  Response to Intervention and Differentiated Instruction Reviewer
- **Sharon Huber**, Director of Elementary Mathematics, Chesapeake, VA
  Universal Design for Learning Reviewer

Student Reviewers

- Jackson Currier
- Mason Currier
- Taylor DeLuca
- Ajalae Evans
- Malik Goodwine
- Majesty Hamilton
- Reilly Koch
- Kyla Kramer
- Matthew Lindemuth
- Greer Lippert
- Zane Lippert
- Jeffrey Lobaugh
- Riley Moran
- Zoe Morin
- Deke Patton
- Brooke Smith
- Dylan Throop
- Jenna Urso
- Madison Whitford
- Jenna Wigham

Research

Ron Larson and Laurie Boswell used the latest in educational research, along with the body of knowledge collected from expert mathematics instructors, to develop the *Modeling Real Life* series. By implementing the work of renowned researchers from across the world, *Big Ideas Math* offers at least a full year's growth within a full year's learning while also encouraging a growth mindset in students and teachers. Students take their learning from surface-level to deep-level, then transfer that learning by modeling real-life situations. For more information on how this program uses learning targets and success criteria to enhance teacher clarity, see pages xiv–xv.

The pedagogical approach used in this program follows the best practices outlined in the most prominent and widely accepted educational research, including:

- *Visible Learning*
  John Hattie © 2009
- *Visible Learning for Teachers*
  John Hattie © 2012
- *Visible Learning for Mathematics*
  John Hattie © 2017
- *Principles to Actions: Ensuring Mathematical Success for All*
  NCTM © 2014
- *Adding It Up: Helping Children Learn Mathematics*
  National Research Council © 2001
- *Mathematical Mindsets: Unleashing Students' Potential through Creative Math, Inspiring Messages and Innovative Teaching*
  Jo Boaler © 2015
- *What Works in Schools: Translating Research into Action*
  Robert Marzano © 2003
- *Classroom Instruction That Works: Research-Based Strategies for Increasing Student Achievement*
  Marzano, Pickering, and Pollock © 2001
- *Principles and Standards for School Mathematics*
  NCTM © 2000
- *Rigorous PBL by Design: Three Shifts for Developing Confident and Competent Learners*
  Michael McDowell © 2017
- *Universal Design for Learning Guidelines*
  CAST © 2011
- Rigor/Relevance Framework®
  International Center for Leadership in Education
- *Understanding by Design*
  Grant Wiggins and Jay McTighe © 2005
- Achieve, ACT, and The College Board
- *Elementary and Middle School Mathematics: Teaching Developmentally*
  John A. Van de Walle and Karen S. Karp © 2015
- *Evaluating the Quality of Learning: The SOLO Taxonomy*
  John B. Biggs & Kevin F. Collis © 1982
- *Unlocking Formative Assessment: Practical Strategies for Enhancing Students' Learning in the Primary and Intermediate Classroom*
  Shirley Clarke, Helen Timperley, and John Hattie © 2004
- *Formative Assessment in the Secondary Classroom*
  Shirley Clarke © 2005
- *Improving Student Achievement: A Practical Guide to Assessment for Learning*
  Toni Glasson © 2009

Instructional Design

A single authorship team from Kindergarten through Algebra 2 results in a logical progression of focused topics with meaningful coherence from course to course.

FOCUS

A focused program reflects the balance in grade-level standards while simultaneously supporting and engaging students to develop conceptual understanding of the major work of the grade.

The **Learning Target** and **Success Criteria** for each section focus the learning into manageable chunks, using clear teaching text and Key Ideas within the Student Edition.

Learning Target: Find products of integers.

Success Criteria:
- I can explain the rules for multiplying integers.
- I can find products of integers with the same sign.
- I can find products of integers with different signs.

Key Idea

Ratios

Words A **ratio** is a comparison of two quantities. The **value of the ratio** a to b is the number $\frac{a}{b}$, which describes the multiplicative relationship between the quantities in the ratio.

Examples 2 snails *to* 6 fish

$\frac{1}{2}$ cup of milk *for every* $\frac{1}{4}$ cup of cream

Algebra The ratio of a to b can be written as $a : b$.

Laurie's Notes

Chapter 5 Overview

The study of ratios and proportions in this chapter builds upon and connects to prior work with rates and ratios in the previous course. Students should have an understanding of how ratios are represented and how ratio tables are used to find equivalent ratios. Tape diagrams and double number lines were also used to represent and solve problems involving equivalent ratios.

Laurie's Notes prepare you for the math concepts in each chapter and section and make connections to the threads of major topics for the course.

a Single Authorship Team

COHERENCE

A single authorship team built a coherent program that has intentional progression of content within each grade and between grade levels. Your students will build new understanding on foundations from prior grades and connect concepts throughout the course.

The authors developed content that progresses from prior chapters and grades to future ones. In addition to charts like this one, Laurie's Notes provide point of use insights about where your students have come from and where they are going in their learning progression.

Through the Grades		
Grade 7	**Grade 8**	**High School**
• Use samples to draw inferences about populations. • Compare two populations from random samples using measures of center and variability. • Approximate the probability of a chance event and predict the approximate relative frequency given the probability.	• Construct and interpret scatter plots. • Find and assess lines of fit for scatter plots. • Use equations of lines to solve problems and interpret the slope and the y-intercept. • Construct and interpret a two-way table summarizing data. Use relative frequencies to describe possible association between the two variables.	• Classify data as quantitative or qualitative, choose and create appropriate data displays, and analyze misleading graphs. • Make and use two-way tables to recognize associations in data by finding marginal, relative, and conditional relative frequencies. • Interpret scatter plots, determine how well lines of fit model data, and distinguish between correlation and causation.

One author team thoughtfully wrote each course, creating a seamless progression of content from Kindergarten to Algebra 2.

See pages xxviii and xxix for the K–8 Progressions chart.

Gra			Grade 4	Grade 5	Grade 6	Grade 7	Grade 8
			Operations and Algebraic Thinking		Expressions and Equations		
oblems involving and subtraction 0. roperties of ns. ith addition and ion equations. *s 1–5, 10, 11*	Solve problems involving addition and subtraction within 20. Work with equal groups of objects. *Chapters 1–6, 15*	Solve problems involving multiplication and division within 100. Apply properties of multiplication. Solve problems involving the four operations, and identify and explain patterns in arithmetic. *Chapters 1–5, 8, 9, and 14*	Use the four operations with whole numbers to solve problems. Understand factors and multiples. Generate and analyze patterns. *Chapters 2–6, 12*	Write and interpret numerical expressions. Analyze patterns and relationships. *Chapters 2, 12*	Perform arithmetic with algebraic expressions. *Chapter 5* Solve one-variable equations and inequalities. *Chapters 6, 8* Analyze relationships between dependent and independent variables. *Chapter 6*	Write equivalent expressions. *Chapter 3* Use numerical and algebraic expressions, equations, and inequalities to solve problems. *Chapters 3, 4, 6*	Understand the connections between proportional relationships, lines, and linear equations. *Chapter 4* Solve linear equations and systems of linear equations. *Chapters 1, 5* Work with radicals and integer exponents. *Chapters 8, 9*
							Functions
							Define, evaluate, and compare functions, and use functions to model relationships between quantities.

You have used number lines to find sums of positive numbers, which involve movement to the right. Now you will find sums with negative numbers, which involve movement to the left.

Using Number Lines to Find Sums

a. Find 4 + (−4).

Draw an arrow from 0 to 4 to represent 4. Then draw an arrow 4 units to the left to represent adding −4.

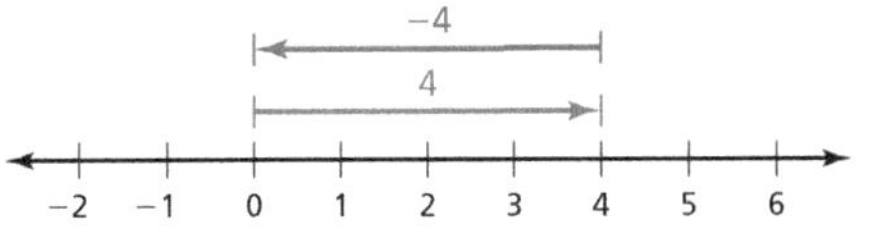

Throughout each course, lessons build on prior learning as new concepts are introduced. Here the students are reminded of the use of number lines with positive numbers.

Rigor in Math: A Balanced Approach

Instructional Design

The authors wrote every chapter and every section to give you a meaningful balance of rigorous instruction.

RIGOR

A rigorous program provides a balance of three important building blocks.

- **Conceptual Understanding** Discovering why
- **Procedural Fluency** Learning how
- **Application** Knowing when to apply

Conceptual Understanding
Students have the opportunity to develop foundational concepts central to the *Learning Target* in each *Exploration* by experimenting with new concepts, talking with peers, and asking questions.

EXPLORATION 1 **Understanding Quotients Involving N**

Work with a partner.

a. Discuss the relationship between multiplication your partner.

b. **INDUCTIVE REASONING** Complete the table. Th for dividing (i) two integers with the same sign a different signs.

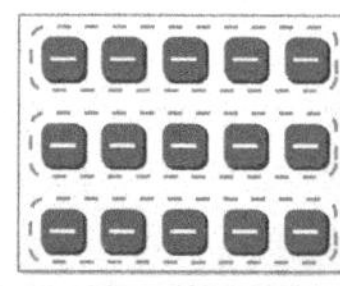

Expression	Type of Quotient	Quoti
$-15 \div 3$	Integers	
$12 \div (-6)$		
$10 \div (-2)$		

Conceptual Thinking
Ask students to think deeply with conceptual questions.

29. **MP NUMBER SENSE** Without solving, determine whether $\frac{x}{4} = \frac{15}{3}$ and $\frac{x}{15} = \frac{4}{3}$ have the same solution. Explain your reasoning.

EXAMPLE 1 **Graphing a Linear Equation in Standard Form**

Graph $-2x + 3y = -6$.

Step 1: Write the equation in slope-intercept form.

$-2x + 3y = -6$ Write the equation.

$3y = 2x - 6$ Add $2x$ to each side.

$y = \frac{2}{3}x - 2$ Divide each side by 3.

Step 2: Use the slope and the y-intercept to graph the equation.

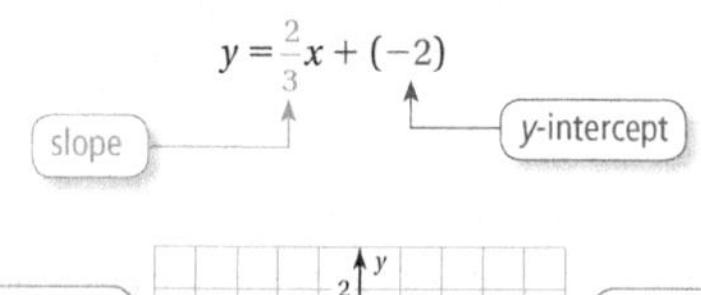

$y = \frac{2}{3}x + (-2)$
slope
y-intercept

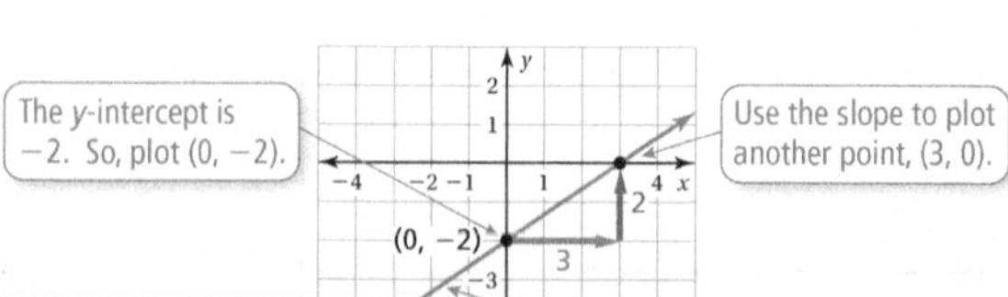

The y-intercept is −2. So, plot (0, −2).
Use the slope to plot another point, (3, 0).
(0, −2)

Procedural Fluency
Solidify learning with clear, stepped-out teaching and examples.

Then shift conceptual understanding into procedural fluency with *Try Its, Self-Assessments, Practice,* and *Review & Refresh.*

STEAM Applications

Students begin every chapter with a fun, engaging STEAM video to see how math applies to everyday life. Students apply what they learn in the chapter with a related *Performance Task*.

Name________________ Date________

Chapter 3 **Performance Task**

Chlorophyll in Plants

What is needed for photosynthesis? How can you use the amount of chlorophyll in a lake to determine the level of biological productivity?

Photosynthesis is the process by which plants acquire energy from the sun. Sunlight, carbon dioxide, and water are used by a plant to produce glucose and dioxygen.

1. You want to make models of the molecules involved in photosynthesis for a science fair project. The table shows the number of each element used for each molecule. Let x, y, and z represent the costs of a model carbon atom, model hydrogen atom, and

	Number of Atoms		
Molecule	**Carbon**	**Hydrogen**	**Oxygen**
Carbon Dioxide	1	0	2
Water	0	2	1

Daily Application Practice

Modeling Real Life, Dig Deeper, Problem Solving, and other non-routine problems help students apply surface-level skills to gain a deeper understanding. These problems lead students to independent problem-solving.

36. **DIG DEEPER!** The *girth* of a package is the distance around the perimeter of a face that does not include the length as a side. A postal service says that a rectangular package can have a maximum combined length and girth of 108 inches.

   a. Write an inequality that represents the allowable dimensions for the package.

   b. Find three different sets of allowable dimensions that are reasonable for the package. Find the volume of each package.

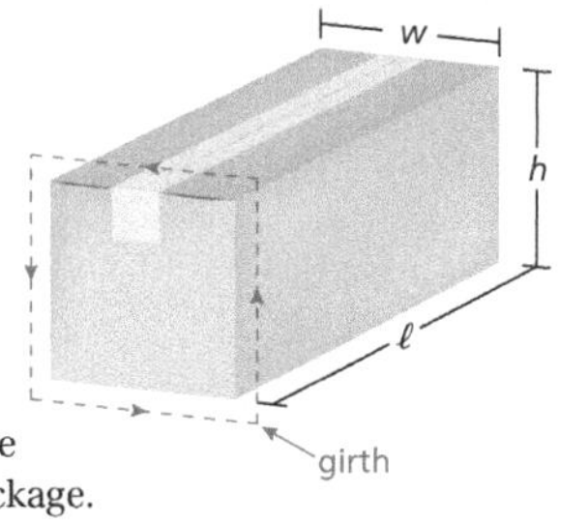

Problem-Solving Plan

Walk students through the Problem-Solving Plan, featured in many examples, to help students make sense of problems with confidence.

THE PROBLEM-SOLVING PLAN

1. **Understand the Problem**
   Think about what the problem is asking, what information you know, and how you might begin to solve.
2. **Make a Plan**
   Plan your solution pathway before jumping in to solve. Identify any relationships and decide on a problem-solving strategy.
3. **Solve and Check**
   As you solve the problem, be sure to evaluate your progress and check your answers. Throughout the problem-solving process, you must continually ask, "Does this make sense?" and be willing to change course if necessary.

Embedded Mathematical Practices

Encouraging Mathematical Mindsets

Developing proficiency in the **Mathematical Practices** is about becoming a mathematical thinker. Students learn to ask why, and to reason and communicate with others as they learn. Use this guide to communicate opportunities in your classroom for students to develop proficiency with the mathematical practices.

1

One way to **Make Sense of Problems and Persevere in Solving Them** is to use the Problem-Solving Plan. Students should take time to analyze the given information and what the problem is asking to help them plan a solution pathway.

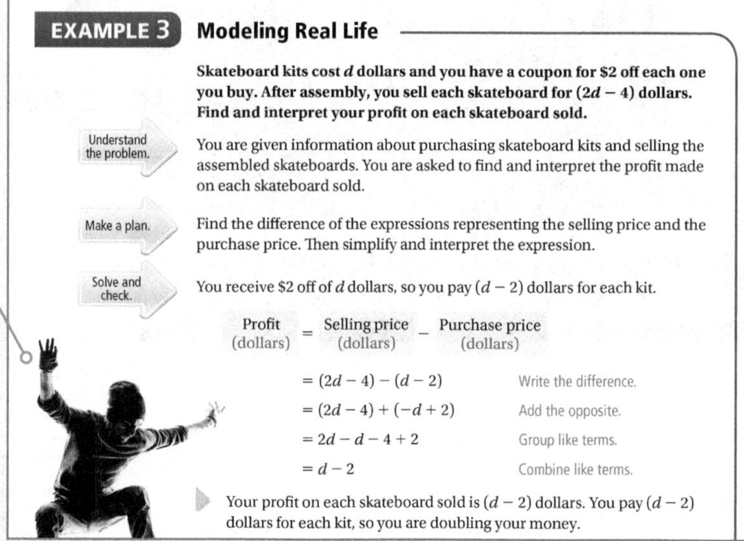

EXAMPLE 3 Modeling Real Life
Skateboard kits cost d dollars and you have a coupon for \$2 off each one you buy. After assembly, you sell each skateboard for $(2d - 4)$ dollars. Find and interpret your profit on each skateboard sold.
Understand the problem.
You are given information about purchasing skateboard kits and selling the assembled skateboards. You are asked to find and interpret the profit made on each skateboard sold.
Make a plan.
Find the difference of the expressions representing the selling price and the purchase price. Then simplify and interpret the expression.
Solve and check.
You receive \$2 off of d dollars, so you pay $(d - 2)$ dollars for each kit.
Profit (dollars) = Selling price (dollars) − Purchase price (dollars)
$= (2d - 4) - (d - 2)$ Write the difference.
$= (2d - 4) + (-d + 2)$ Add the opposite.
$= 2d - d - 4 + 2$ Group like terms.
$= d - 2$ Combine like terms.
Your profit on each skateboard sold is $(d - 2)$ dollars. You pay $(d - 2)$ dollars for each kit, so you are doubling your money.

Look for labels such as:

- Explain the Meaning
- Find Entry Points
- Analyze Givens
- Make a Plan
- Interpret a Solution
- Consider Similar Problems
- Consider Simpler Forms
- Check Progress
- Problem Solving

2

Students **Reason Abstractly** when they explore a concrete example and represent it symbolically. Other times, students **Reason Quantitatively** when they see relationships in numbers or symbols and draw conclusions about a concrete example.

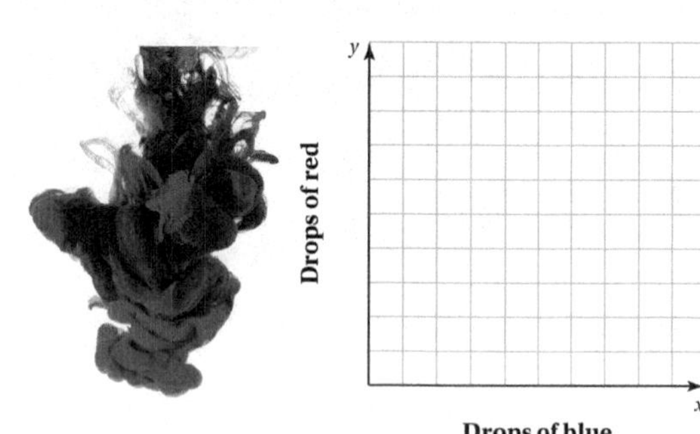

Math Practice

Reasoning

How is the graph of the proportional relationship different from the other graph?

Look for labels such as:

- Make Sense of Quantities
- Use Equations
- Use Expressions
- Understand Quantities
- Use Operations
- Number Sense
- Reasoning

b. Which property can you use to solve each of the equations modeled by the algebra tiles? Solve each equation and explain your method.

46. MP **LOGIC** When you multiply or divide each side of an inequality by the same negative number, you must reverse the direction of the inequality symbol. Explain why.

Math Practice

Make Conjectures

Can you use algebra tiles to solve any equation? Explain your reasoning.

3

When students **Construct Viable Arguments and Critique the Reasoning of Others,** they make and justify conclusions and decide whether others' arguments are correct or flawed.

Look for labels such as:

- Use Assumptions
- Use Definitions
- Use Prior Results
- Make Conjectures
- Build Arguments
- Analyze Conjectures
- Use Counterexamples
- Justify Conclusions
- Compare Arguments
- Construct Arguments
- Listen and Ask Questions
- You Be the Teacher
- Logic

36. MP **APPLY MATHEMATICS** You decide to make and sell bracelets. The cost of your materials is \$84.00. You charge \$3.50 for each bracelet.

a. Write a function that represents the profit P for selling b bracelets.

b. Which variable is independent? dependent? Explain.

c. You will *break even* when the cost of your materials equals your income. How many bracelets must you sell to break even?

Look for labels such as:

- Apply Mathematics
- Simplify a Solution
- Use a Diagram
- Use a Table
- Use a Graph
- Use a Formula
- Analyze Relationships
- Interpret Results
- Modeling Real Life

4

To **Model with Mathematics,** students apply the math they have learned to a real-life problem, and they interpret mathematical results in the context of the situation.

BUILDING TO FULL UNDERSTANDING

Throughout each course, students have opportunities to demonstrate specific aspects of the mathematical practices. Labels throughout the book indicate gateways to those aspects. Collectively, these opportunities will lead students to a full understanding of each mathematical practice. Developing these mindsets and habits will give meaning to the mathematics they learn.

5

To **Use Appropriate Tools Strategically**, students need to know what tools are available and think about how each tool might help them solve a mathematical problem. When students choose a tool to use, remind them that it may have limitations.

Look for labels such as:

- Choose Tools
- Recognize Usefulness of Tools
- Use Other Resources
- Use Technology to Explore
- Using Tools

d. Enter the function $y = \left(\frac{1}{10}\right)^x$ into your graphing calculator. Use the *table* feature to evaluate the function for positive integer values of x until the calculator displays a y-value that is not in standard form. Do the results support your answer in part (c)? Explain.

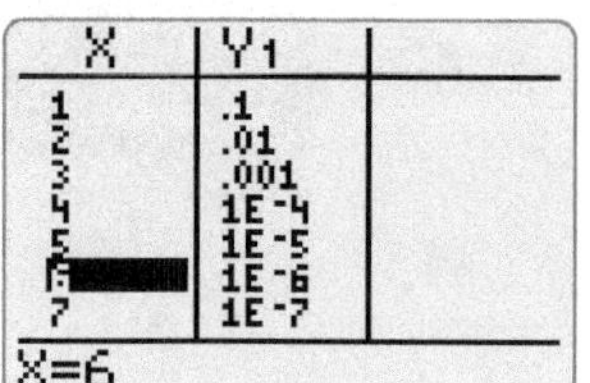

X	Y1
1	.1
2	.01
3	.001
4	1E-4
5	1E-5
6	1E-6
7	1E-7

X=6

Math Practice

Use Technology to Explore

How can writing $\frac{1}{10}$ as a power of 10 help you understand the calculator display?

6

When students **Attend to Precision**, they are developing a habit of being careful in how they talk about concepts, label their work, and write their answers.

Add 1.459 + 23.7.

$$\begin{array}{r} {}^{1} \\ 1.459 \\ +\ 23.700 \\ \hline 25.159 \end{array}$$

Insert zeros so that both numbers have the same number of decimal places.

Math Practice

Calculate Accurately

Why is it important to line up the decimal points when adding or subtracting decimals?

Look for labels such as:

- Communicate Precisely
- Use Clear Definitions
- State the Meaning of Symbols
- Specify Units
- Label Axes
- Calculate Accurately
- Precision

49. MP **PRECISION** Consider the equation $c = ax - bx$, where a, b, and c are whole numbers. Which of the following result in values of a, b, and c so that the original equation has exactly one solution? Justify your answer.

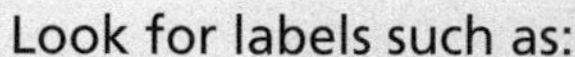

$a - b = 1, c = 0$ $\quad$ $a = b, c \neq 0$ $\quad$ $a = b, c = 0$ $\quad$ $a \neq b, c = 0$

MP STRUCTURE **Tell whether the triangles are similar. Explain.**

14. 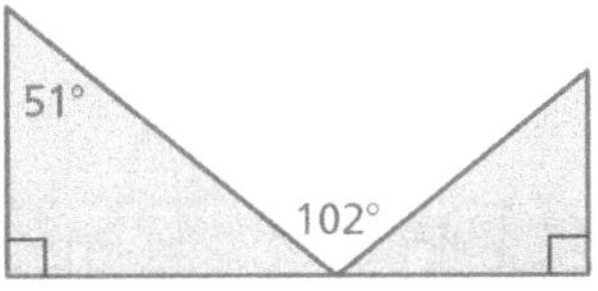

15. 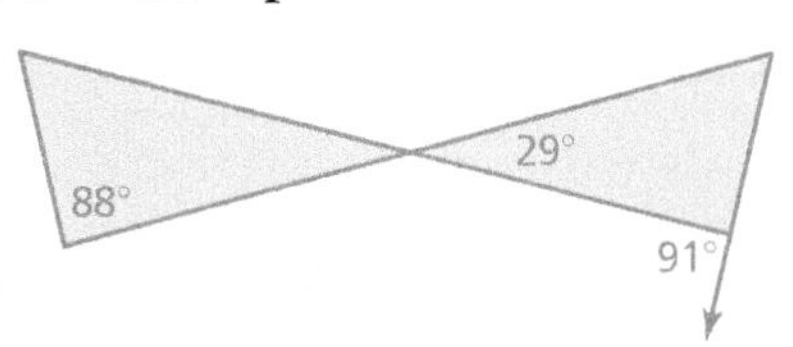

7

Students **Look For and Make Use of Structure** by looking closely to see structure within a mathematical statement, or stepping back for an overview to see how individual parts make one single object.

Find the sum of the areas of the faces.

Surface Area	=	Area of bottom	+	Area of a side	+	Area of a side	+	Area of a side	+	Area of a side	
S	=	49	+	35	+	35	+	35	+	35	= 189

Look for labels such as:

- Look for Structure
- Look for Patterns
- View as Components
- Structure
- Patterns

Math Practice

Look for Patterns

How can you find the surface area of a square pyramid by calculating the area of only two of the faces?

35. **MP REPEATED REASONING** You have been assigned a nine-digit identification number.

a. Should you use the Fundamental Counting Principle or a tree diagram to find the total number of possible identification numbers? Explain.

b. How many identification numbers are possible?

8

When students **Look For and Express Regularity in Repeated Reasoning,** they can notice patterns and make generalizations. Remind students to keep in mind the goal of a problem, which will help them evaluate reasonableness of answers along the way.

Look for labels such as:

- Repeat Calculations
- Find General Methods
- Maintain Oversight
- Evaluate Results
- Repeated Reasoning

Visible Learning Through Learning Targets,

Making Learning Visible

Knowing the learning intention of a chapter or section helps learners focus on the purpose of an activity, rather than simply completing it in isolation. This program supports visible learning through the consistent use of Learning Targets and Success Criteria to ensure positive outcomes for all students.

Every chapter and section shows a **Learning Target** and related **Success Criteria**. These are purposefully integrated into each carefully written lesson.

4.4 Writing and Graphing Inequalities

Learning Target: Write inequalities and represent solutions of inequalities on number lines.

Success Criteria:
- I can write word sentences as inequalities.
- I can determine whether a value is a solution of an inequality.
- I can graph the solutions of inequalities.

Chapter Learning Target:
Understand equations and inequalities.

Chapter Success Criteria:
- I can identify key words and phrases to write equations and inequalities.
- I can write word sentences as equations and inequalities.
- I can solve equations and inequalities using properties.
- I can use equations and inequalities to model and solve real-life problems.

The **Chapter Review** reminds students to rate their understanding of the learning targets.

Chapter Self-Assessment

As you complete the exercises, use the scale below to rate your understanding of the success criteria in your journal.

1	2	3	4
I do not understand.	I can do it with help.	I can do it on my own.	I can teach someone else.

6.1 Writing Equations in One Variable *(pp. 245–250)*

Learning Target: Write equations in one variable and write equations that represent real-life problems.

Write the word sentence as an equation.

. The product of a number m and 2 is 8.

Students review each section with a reminder of that section's learning target.

Icons throughout **Laurie's Notes** suggest ways to target where students are in their learning.

Fist of Five: Ask students to indicate their understanding of the first and second success criterion. Then select students to explain each one.

QUESTIONS FOR LEARNERS

As students progress through a section, they should be able to answer the following questions.

- What are you learning?
- Why are you learning this?
- Where are you in your learning?
- How will you know when you have learned it?
- Where are you going next?

Success Criteria, and Self-Assessment

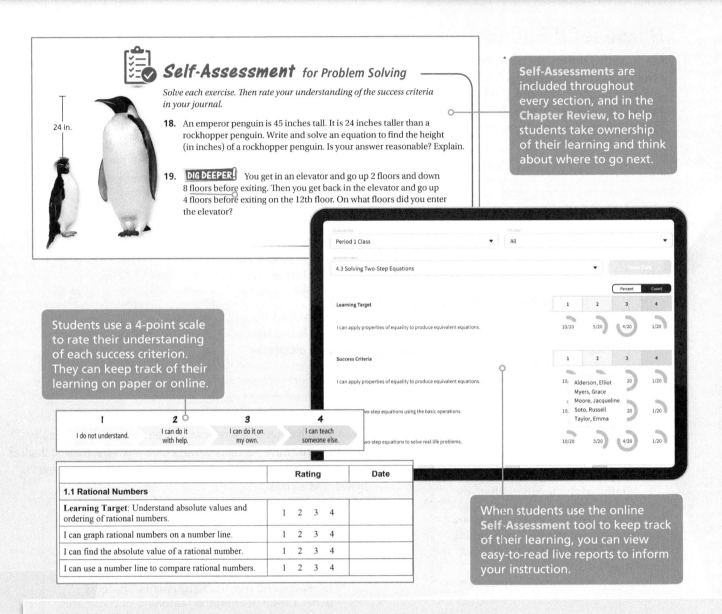

Self-Assessment for Problem Solving

Solve each exercise. Then rate your understanding of the success criteria in your journal.

24 in.

18. An emperor penguin is 45 inches tall. It is 24 inches taller than a rockhopper penguin. Write and solve an equation to find the height (in inches) of a rockhopper penguin. Is your answer reasonable? Explain.

19. DIG DEEPER! You get in an elevator and go up 2 floors and down 8 floors before exiting. Then you get back in the elevator and go up 4 floors before exiting on the 12th floor. On what floors did you enter the elevator?

Self-Assessments are included throughout every section, and in the **Chapter Review**, to help students take ownership of their learning and think about where to go next.

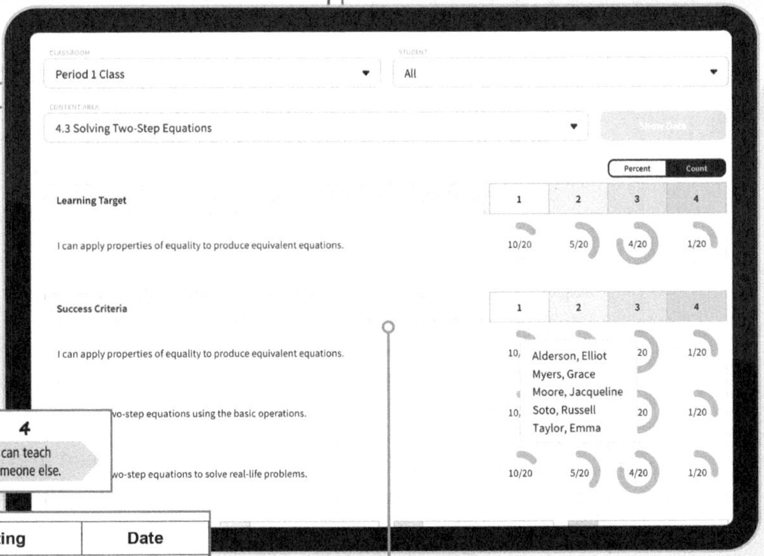

Classroom: Period 1 Class | Student: All

Content Area: 4.3 Solving Two-Step Equations

Percent | Count

Learning Target	1	2	3	4
I can apply properties of equality to produce equivalent equations.	10/20	5/20	4/20	1/20

Success Criteria	1	2	3	4
I can apply properties of equality to produce equivalent equations.	10/		20	1/20
...wo-step equations using the basic operations.	10/		20	1/20
...wo-step equations to solve real-life problems.	10/20	5/20	4/20	1/20

Alderson, Elliot
Myers, Grace
Moore, Jacqueline
Soto, Russell
Taylor, Emma

Students use a 4-point scale to rate their understanding of each success criterion. They can keep track of their learning on paper or online.

1	2	3	4
I do not understand.	I can do it with help.	I can do it on my own.	I can teach someone else.

	Rating	Date
1.1 Rational Numbers		
Learning Target: Understand absolute values and ordering of rational numbers.	1 2 3 4	
I can graph rational numbers on a number line.	1 2 3 4	
I can find the absolute value of a rational number.	1 2 3 4	
I can use a number line to compare rational numbers.	1 2 3 4	

When students use the online **Self-Assessment** tool to keep track of their learning, you can view easy-to-read live reports to inform your instruction.

Ensuring Positive Outcomes

John Hattie's *Visible Learning* research consistently shows that using Learning Targets and Success Criteria can result in two years' growth in one year, ensuring positive outcomes for student learning and achievement.

Sophie Murphy, M.Ed., wrote the chapter-level learning targets and success criteria for this program. Sophie is currently completing her Ph.D. at the University of Melbourne in Australia with Professor John Hattie as her leading supervisor. Sophie completed her Master's thesis with Professor John Hattie in 2015. Sophie has over 20 years of experience as a teacher and school leader in private and public school settings in Australia.

Purposeful Focus

Many of the things we do as educators have a positive effect on student learning, but which ones have the greatest impact? This program purposefully integrates **five key strategies** proven to have some of the highest impact on student achievement.

TEACHER CLARITY

Before starting a new topic, make clear the learning target. As students explore and learn, continue to connect their experiences back to the success criteria so they know where they are in their learning.

 ***Self-Assessment*** **for Concepts & Skills**

- Identify the reasons for incorrect answers for Exercises 9–14. Are the errors computational? Do students complete Exercises 9–12 with ease but struggle with Exercises 13 and 14? Are the negative numbers the issue? Make sure students are aware of the reasons for their mistakes.
- Exercise 15 asks students to explain the relationship between using the Distributive Property to simplify an expression and to factor an expression. Students' responses will provide information about their level of understanding.

FEEDBACK

Actively listen as you probe for student understanding, being mindful of the feedback that you provide. When students provide you with feedback, you see where your students are in their learning and make instructional decisions for where to go next.

Try It

- These exercises provide a review of three additional data displays.
- **Turn and Talk:** Have students discuss their answers. Remind them of *Talk Moves* that they can use in their discussions. Then review the answers as a class.

CLASSROOM DISCUSSION

Encourage your students to talk together! This solidifies understanding while honing their ability to reason and construct arguments. Students benefit from hearing the reasoning of classmates and hearing peers critique their own reasoning.

Daily Support from a Master Educator

In Laurie's Notes, master educator Laurie Boswell uses her professional training and years of experience to help you guide your students to better understanding.

Laurie studied Professor John Hattie's research on *Visible Learning* and met with Hattie on multiple occasions to ensure she was interpreting his research accurately and embedding it effectively. Laurie's expertise continues with an ongoing collaboration with Sophie Murphy, who is pursuing her Ph.D. under Professor Hattie.

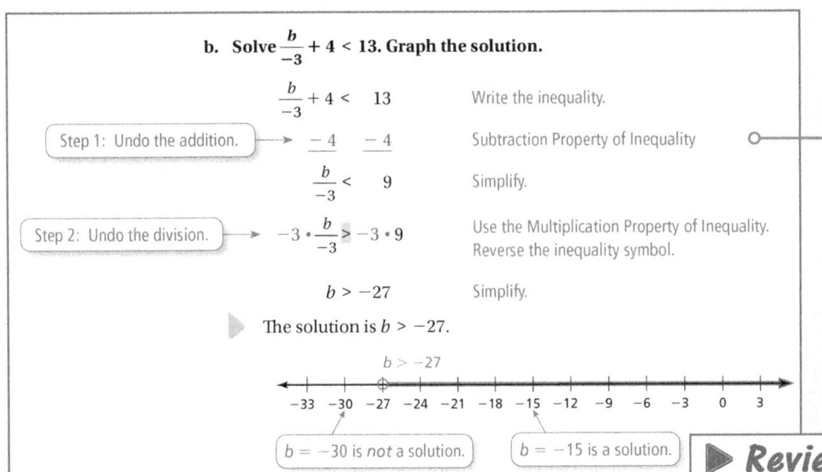

b. Solve $\frac{b}{-3} + 4 < 13$. Graph the solution.

$\frac{b}{-3} + 4 < 13$ Write the inequality.

Step 1: Undo the addition. → $-4 \quad -4$ Subtraction Property of Inequality

$\frac{b}{-3} < 9$ Simplify.

Step 2: Undo the division. → $-3 \cdot \frac{b}{-3} > -3 \cdot 9$ Use the Multiplication Property of Inequality. Reverse the inequality symbol.

$b > -27$ Simplify.

The solution is $b > -27$.

DIRECT INSTRUCTION

Follow exploration and discovery with explicit instruction to build procedural skill and fluency. Teach with clear Key Ideas and powerful stepped-out examples that have been carefully designed to meet the success criteria.

Review & Refresh

Solve the inequality. Graph the solution.

1. $-3x \geq 18$
2. $\frac{2}{3}d > 8$
3. $2 \geq \frac{g}{-4}$

Find the missing values in the ratio table. Then write the equivalent ratios.

4.

Flutes	7		28
Clarinets	4	12	

5.

Boys	6	3	
Girls	10		50

6. What is the volume of the cube?

A. 8 ft^3 B. 16 ft^3

C. 24 ft^3 D. 32 ft^3

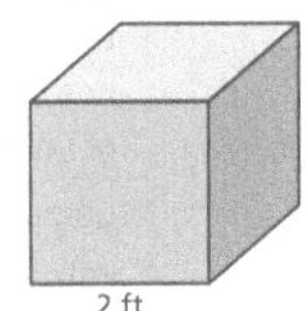

SPACED PRACTICE

Effective practice does not just focus on a single topic of new learning; students must revisit concepts over time so deeper learning occurs. This program cohesively offers multiple opportunities for students to build their conceptual understanding by intentionally revisiting and applying concepts throughout subsequent lessons and chapters. *Review & Refresh* exercises in every section also provide continual practice on the major topics.

We focus on **STRATEGIES** with some of the **HIGHEST IMPACT** on student achievement—up to 2 years of learning for a year of input.

Five Strategies for Purposeful Focus

Professor John Hattie, in his *Visible Learning* network, identified more than 250 influences on student learning, and developed a way of ranking them. He conducted meta-analyses and compared the influences by their **effect size**—the impact the factor had on student learning.

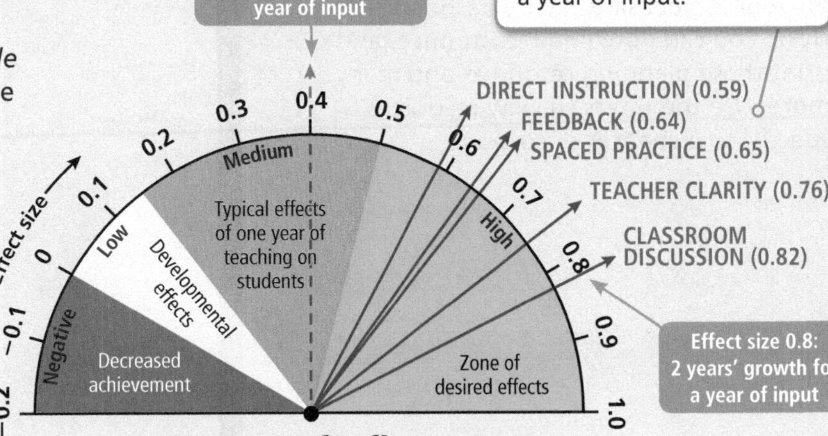

Barometer of Influences

How to Use This Program: Plan

Taking Advantage of Your Resources

You play an indispensable role in your students' learning. This program provides rich resources for learners of all levels to help you **Plan**, **Teach**, and **Assess**.

Plan every chapter and section with tools in the Teaching Edition such as **Suggested Pacing**, **Progression Tables**, and chapter and section **Overviews** written by Laurie Boswell.

Suggested Pacing

Chapter Opener	1 Day
Section 1	2 Days
Section 2	2 Days
Section 3	2 Days
Section 4	2 Days
Section 5	

Preparing to Teach

- Students should be familiar with organizing the results of an **experiment** in a table.
- **Model with Mathematics:** In this exploration, students will gain a conceptual sense of **probability** by performing activities to determine the likelihood of an **event**. They will pursue the concept of possible **outcomes**, which leads to describing the likelihood of an event.

Through the Chapter

Standard	7.1	7.2	7.3	7.4
Understand that a function is a rule that assigns to each input exactly one output. The graph of a function is the set of ordered pairs consisting of an input and the corresponding output.	●	★		
Compare properties of two functions each represented in a different way (algebraically, graphically, numerically in tables, or by verbal descriptions).			★	
Interpret the equation $y = mx + b$ as defining a linear function, whose graph is a straight line; give examples of functions that are not linear.			●	★

Find Your Resources Digitally

Use the resources page that is available on your *BigIdeasMath.com* dashboard. Here, you can download, customize, and print these planning resources and many more. Use the filters to view resources specific to a chapter or section.

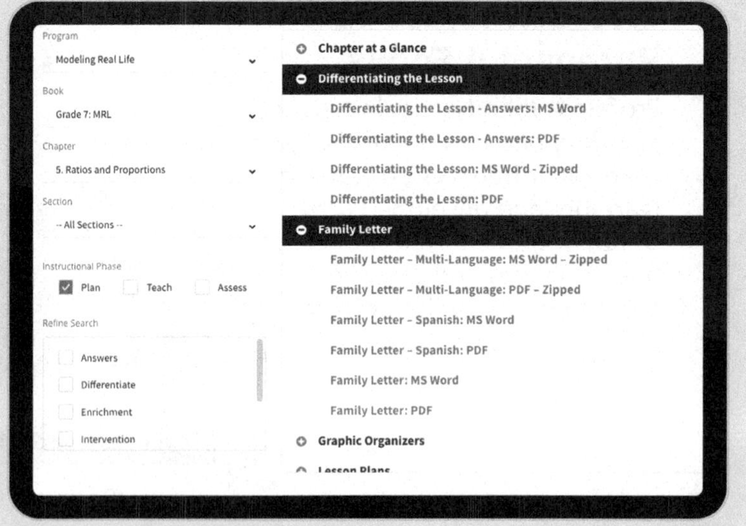

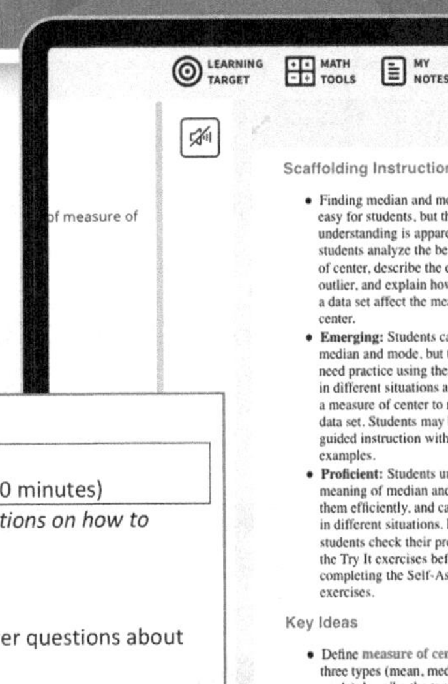

LEARNING TARGET
MATH TOOLS
MY NOTES
LAURIE'S NOTES
Scaffolding Instruction
• Finding median and mode is fairly easy for students, but their depth of understanding is apparent when students analyze the best measure of center, describe the effect of an outlier, and explain how changes to a data set affect the measures of center.
• Emerging: Students can find the median and mode, but they may need practice using these statistics in different situations and choosing a measure of center to represent a data set. Students may benefit from guided instruction with the examples.
• Proficient: Students understand the meaning of median and mode, find them efficiently, and can apply them in different situations. Have students check their progress using the Try It exercises before completing the Self-Assessment exercises.
Key Ideas
• Define measure of center. The three types (mean, median, and mode) describe the typical value of a data set.
• Write the Key Ideas.
• Discuss the median and mode and how each is determined.

Access all planning resources of the Teaching Edition in the **Dynamic Classroom**. Use the customizable **Lesson Plans** to help teach each lesson to meet your specific classroom needs.

Chapter 3 Opener: Angles and Triangles

Materials: STEAM Video from *BigIdeasMath.com*
Pacing: 1 day (minimum: 45 minutes, recommended: 60 minutes)

See Laurie's Notes in the Teaching Edition for her suggestions on how to effectively implement this lesson plan.

STEAM Video
Students will watch a video about honeycomb and answer questions about the shape and volume of a tiling.

Performance Task
Students will preview the Performance Task on angles on turtle shells. This Performance Task can be assigned after completing the chapter.

Chapter Exploration
Students will preview skills taught in the chapter.

- properties of angles formed by a transversal

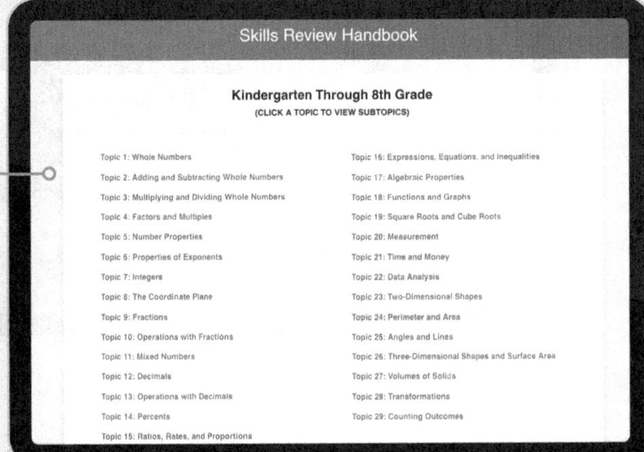

Review topics using the **Skills Review Handbook** to support students. Each topic includes a key concept and vocabulary and contains examples and exercises.

Plan Online

Remember as you are planning, that the *Dynamic Classroom* has the same interactive tools, such as the digital *Sketchpad,* that students will use to model concepts. Plan ahead by practicing these tools to guide students as they use these manipulatives and models.

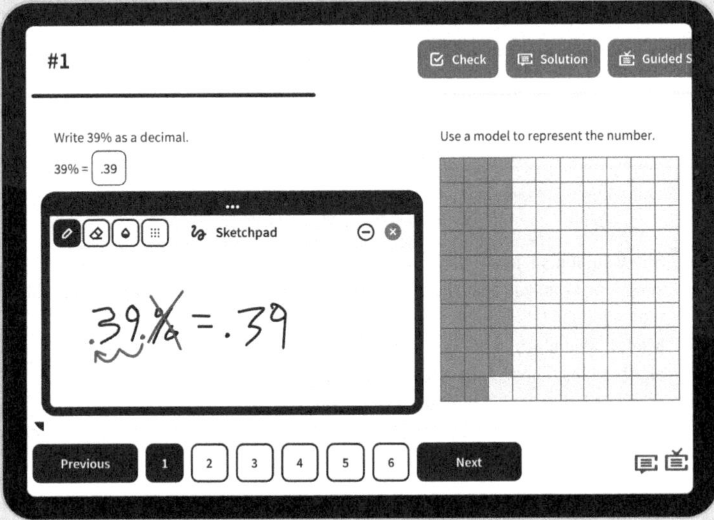

Multiple Pathways for Instruction

Big Ideas Learning provides everything at your fingertips to help you make the best instructional choices for your students.

Present all content digitally using the **Dynamic Classroom**. Send students a page link on-the-fly with **Flip-To** to direct where you want your students to go.

Have students think ahead about chapter concepts in the world around them with a **STEAM video**. Then, students transfer their learning in the **Connecting Concepts** and **Performance Task** at the end of the chapter.

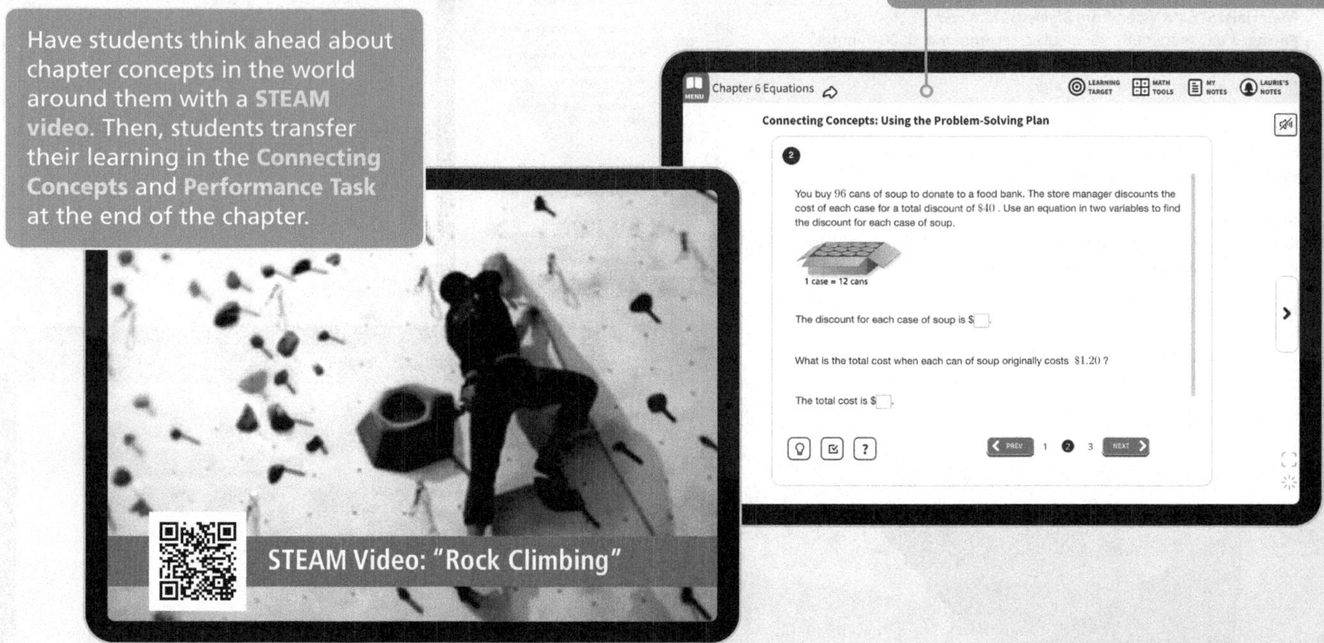

Engage students with a creative hook at the beginning of each section with **Motivate**. This activity, written by master educator Laurie Boswell, provides a conceptual introduction for the section. Then, encourage mathematical discovery with **Exploration**.

Motivate

? Show students a collection of algebra tiles and ask, "Can the collection be simplified? Can you remove zero pairs? What is the expression represented by the collection?"

- **Model:** As a class, model the equations $x + 3 = 7$ and $x + 2 = 5$ using algebra tiles. These do not require a zero pair to solve and will help remind students how to solve equations using algebra tiles.
- Remind students that they need to think of subtracting as *adding the opposite* when using algebra tiles (i.e., $x - 3$ as $x + (-3)$).

? "What does it mean to solve an equation?" To find the value of the variable that makes the equation true.

4.1 Solving Equations Using Addition or Subtraction

Learning Target: Write and solve equations using addition or subtraction.

Success Criteria:
- I can apply the Addition and Subtraction Properties of Equality to produce equivalent equations.
- I can solve equations using addition or subtraction.
- I can apply equations involving addition or subtraction to solve real-life problems.

EXPLORATION 1 **Using Algebra Tiles to Solve Equations**

Work with a partner.

a. Use the examples to explain the meaning of each property.

Addition Property of Equality: $x + 2 = 1$
$x + 2 + 5 = 1 + 5$

Subtraction Property of Equality: $x + 2 = 1$
$x + 2 - 1 = 1 - 1$

Are these properties true for equations involving negative numbers? Explain your reasoning.

b. Write the four equations modeled by the algebra tiles. Explain how you can use algebra tiles to solve each equation. Then find the solutions.

Lead students to procedural fluency with clear **Examples** and **Self-Assessment** opportunities for students to try on their own.

EXAMPLE 1 Determining Whether Two Quantities are Proportional

Tell whether x and y are proportional. Explain your reasoning.

a.

x	1	2	3	4
y	−2	0	2	4

Plot the points. Draw a line through the points.

he line does *not* pass
rough the origin. So,
and y are not proportional.

b.

x	0	2	4	6
y	0	2	4	6

Plot the points. Draw a line through the points.

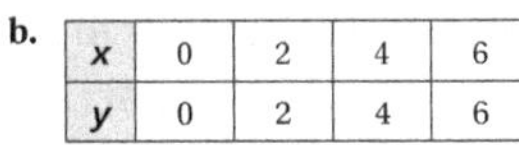

The line passes through the origin. So, x and y are proportional.

EXAMPLE 3 Modeling Real Life

The graph shows the area y (in square feet) that a robotic vacuum cleans in x minutes. Find the area cleaned in 10 minutes.

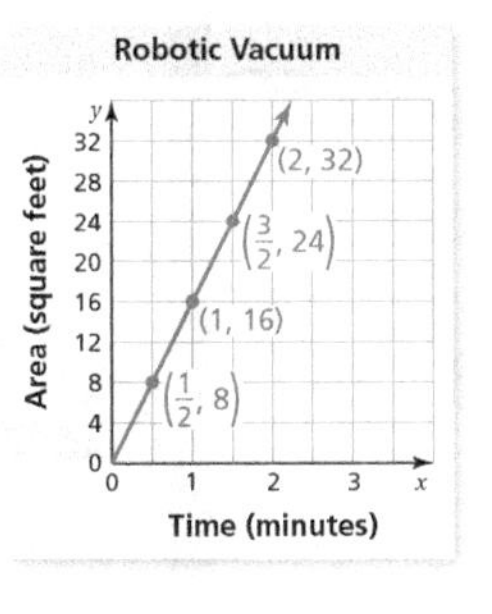

The graph is a line through the origin, so x and y are proportional. You can write an equation to represent the relationship between area and time.

Because the graph passes through the point (1, 16), the unit rate is 16 square feet per minute and the constant of proportionality is $k = 16$. So, an equation of the line is $y = 16x$. Substitute to find the area cleaned in 10 minutes.

$y = 16x$ Write the equation.

$= 16(10)$ Substitute 10 for x.

$= 160$ Multiply.

So, the vacuum cleans 160 square feet in 10 minutes.

Help students apply and problem solve with **Modeling Real Life** applications, **Dig Deeper** problems, and **Math Practice** conceptual problems.

Let **Laurie's Notes** guide your teaching and scaffolding decisions at every step to support and deepen all students' learning. You may want to group students differently as they move in and out of these levels with each skill and concept. Student self-assessment and feedback help guide your instructional decisions about how and when to layer support.

Scaffolding Instruction

- In the exploration, students discussed various methods of solving proportions. They will continue this work in the lesson.
- **Emerging:** Students may be able to create a ratio table but may struggle to write and/or solve the proportion. Students will benefit from close examination of the examples.
- **Proficient:** Students can write and solve proportions using a variety of methods (including tables). Students should review Examples 4 and 5 before proceeding to the Self-Assessment exercises.

Name ____________________ Date ________

Lesson 7.1 Extra Practice

You randomly choose one of the tiles shown.

1 2 3 4 5 6 7 8 9

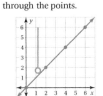

1. How many possible outcomes are there?
2. What are the favorable outcomes of choosing a number greater than 6?
3. In how many ways can choosing a number divisible by 2 occur?

Differentiate and support your learners with **Differentiating the Lesson, Resources by Chapter, English Language Support**, and much more.

How to Use This Program: Assess

Powerful Assessment Tools

Gain insight into your students' learning with these powerful formative and summative assessment tools tailored to every learning target and standard.

Access real-time data and navigate easily through student responses with **Formative Check**.

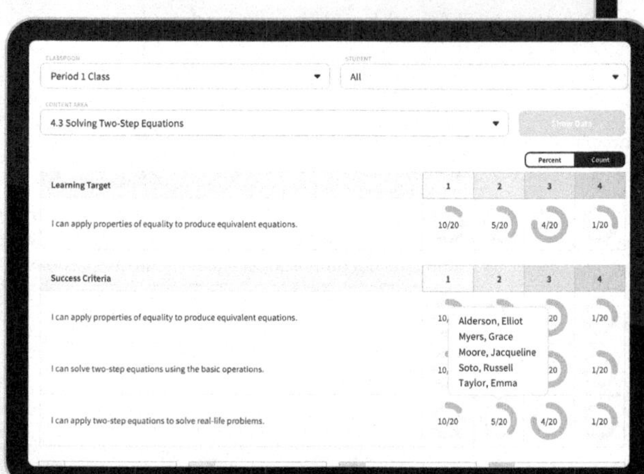

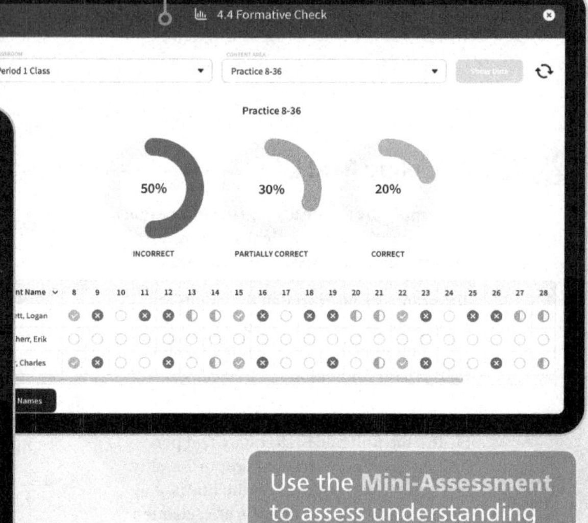

Use the **Mini-Assessment** to assess understanding of lesson concepts.

Scaffold **Practice** from the **Assignment Guide and Concept Check**. Assign print or digital versions, and project answers and solutions in class using the **Answer Presentation Tool**.

Mini-Assessment

Write the word sentence as an inequality.

1. A number a is at least 5. $a \geq 5$
2. Four times a number b is no more than -4.73. $4b \leq -4.73$
3. Tell whether -2 is a solution of $6g - 14 > -21$. not a solution
4. A rollercoaster is at most 45 meters high. Write and graph an inequality that represents the height of the ...

$h \leq 45$; 40 41 42 43 44

Scaffold assignments to support all students in their learning progression. The suggested assignments are a starting point. Continue to assign additional exercises and revisit with spaced practice to move every student toward proficiency.

6.1 Practice

Review & Refresh

Find the missing dimension. Use the scale 1 : 15.

	Item	Model	Actual
1.	Figure skater	Height: ___ in.	Height: 67.5 in.
2.	Pipe	Length: 5 ft	Length: ___ ft

Simplify the expression.

3. $2(3p - 6) + 4p$

4. $5n - 3(4n + 1)$

Assignment Guide and Concept Check

Level	Assignment 1	Assignment 2
Emerging	4, 8, 9, 10, 11, 14, 16, 17, 26, 27, 31	18, 19, 32, 33, 35, 36, 39, 40, 41, 42
Proficient	4, 8, 9, 10, 11, 17, 18, 19, 26, 28, 30, 32, 48	25, 33, 35, 37, 39, 40, 42, 43, 47
Advanced	4, 8, 9, 12, 13, 14, 23, 25, 26, 30, 32, 33, 48	38, 40, 45, 46, 47, 49, 50, 51

- Assignment 1 is for use after students complete the Self-Assessment for Concepts & Skills.
- Assignment 2 is for use after students complete the Self-Assessment for Problem Solving.
- The red exercises can be used as a concept check.

Assign **Quizzes** or **Chapter Tests** to assess understanding of section or chapter content or use **Alternative Assessments** and **Performance Tasks**, which include scoring rubrics.

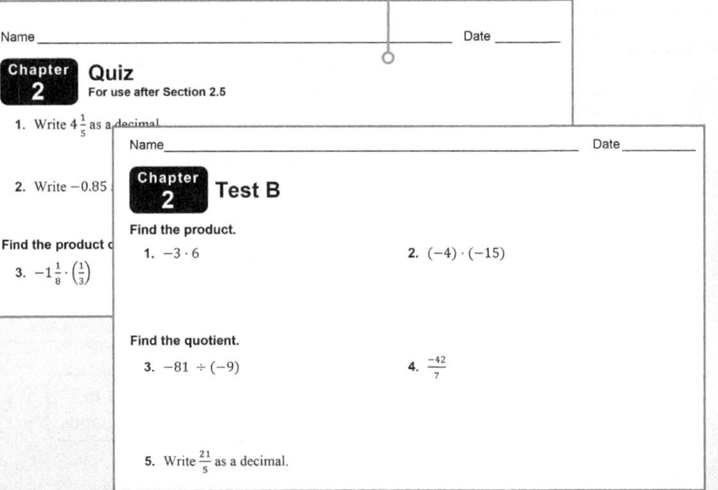

Name________ Date ________

Chapter 2 **Quiz**
For use after Section 2.5

1. Write $4\frac{1}{5}$ as a decimal.
2. Write -0.85 …

Find the product …

3. $-1\frac{1}{8} \cdot \left(\frac{1}{3}\right)$

Name________ Date ________

Chapter 2 **Test B**

Find the product.

1. $-3 \cdot 6$
2. $(-4) \cdot (-15)$

Find the quotient.

3. $-81 \div (-9)$
4. $\frac{-42}{7}$
5. Write $\frac{21}{5}$ as a decimal.

Name________ Date ________

Grade 7 **Course Benchmark 2**
For use after Chapter 5

Find the sum. Write your answer in simplest form.

1. $-\frac{1}{7} + \frac{1}{7}$
2. $-3.2 + (-4.92)$
3. The table shows the change in the water level (in centimeters) of a reservoir for three months. Find the total change in the water level for the three-month period.

Month	1	2	3
Change in Water Level	$-\frac{1}{3}$	$-\frac{2}{21}$	$-\frac{16}{21}$

Find the difference. Write your answer in simplest form.

4. $-\frac{2}{5} - \left(-\frac{9}{5}\right)$
5. $-8.3 - 6.8$
6. At 4 P.M., the total snowfall is 3 centimeters. At 8P.M., the total snowfall is 14 centimeters. What is the mean hourly snowfall?

Assess student learning of standards throughout the year with cumulative **Course Benchmark Tests** to measure progress. Use the results to help plan instruction and intervention.

Measure learning across grades with adaptive **Progression Benchmark Tests.**

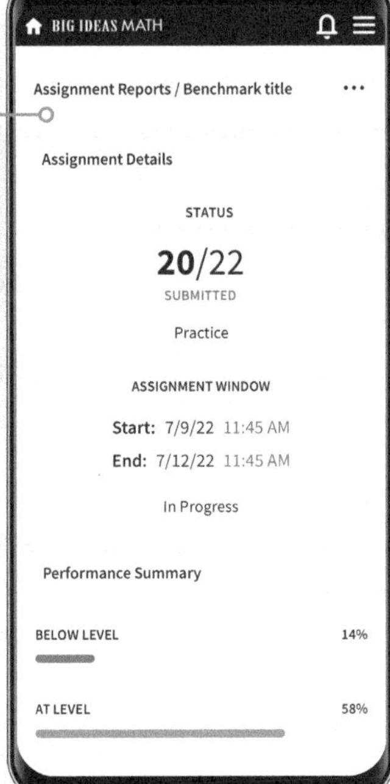

Use the **Assignment Builder** to assign digital versions of the print **Quizzes, Chapter Tests,** and **Course Benchmark Tests.** Receive immediate feedback through robust reporting.

Assessment item point values are weighted. You can customize an item's total point value to fit your needs.

Strategic Support for All Learners

Support for English Language Learners

Big Ideas Learning supports English Language Learners (ELLs) with a blend of print and digital resources available in Spanish. Look to your Teaching Edition for opportunities to support all students with the language development needed for mathematical understanding.

Students' WIDA scores are a starting point. As the year progresses, students may move in and out of language levels with varying language demands of the content and as students change and grow.

Clarify, Connect, and Scaffold

- Clarify language that may be difficult or confusing for ELLs
- Connect new learning to something students already know
- Differentiate student comprehension while completing practice exercises
- Target Beginner, Intermediate, and Advanced ELLs, which correspond to **WIDA** reading, writing, speaking, and listening language mastery levels

Practice Language and Content

- Practice math while improving language skills
- Use language as a resource to develop procedural fluency

Assess Understanding

- Check for development of mathematical reasoning
- Informally assess student comprehension of concepts

ELL Support

After demonstrating Example 1, have students practice language by working in pairs to complete Try It Exercises 1–3. Have one student ask another, "What is the first step? Do you add or subtract? What is the solution?" Have students alternate roles.

WIDA 1: Entering
WIDA 2: Emerging

Beginner: Write the steps and provide one-word answers.

WIDA 3: Developing
WIDA 4: Expanding

Intermediate: Answer with phrases or simple sentences such as, "First, I add five."

WIDA 5: Bridging
WIDA 6: Reaching

Advanced: Answer with detailed sentences such as, "First, I add five to each side of the equation."

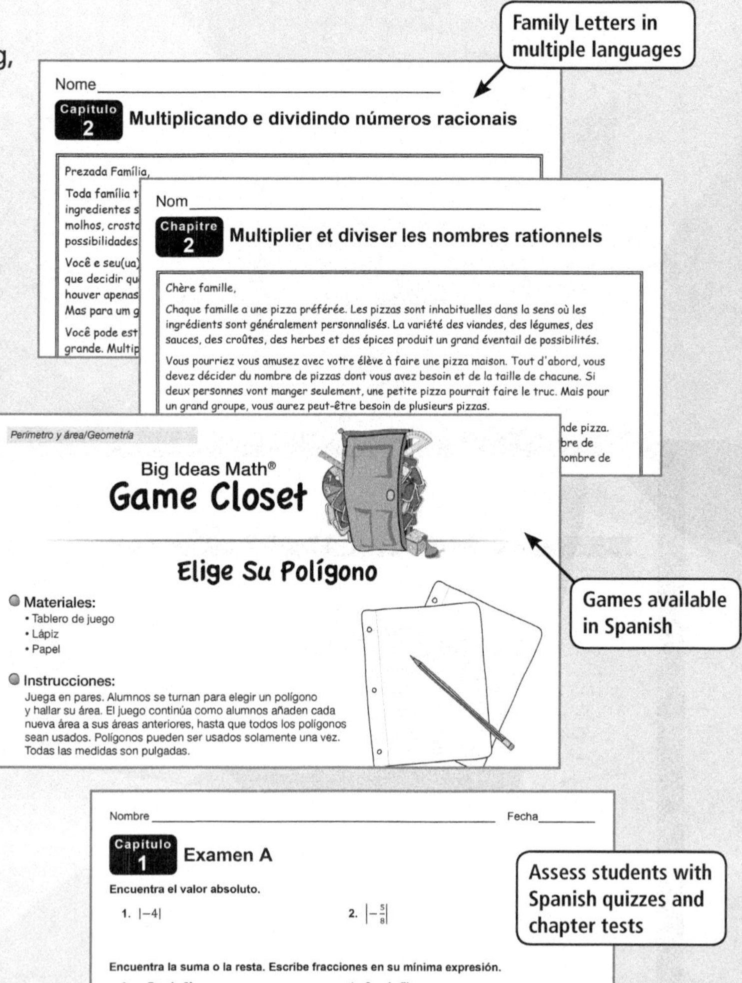

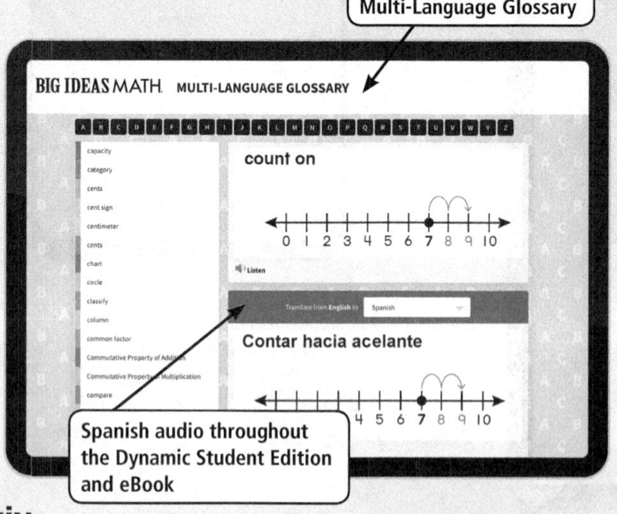

Students Get the Support They Need, When They Need It

There will be times throughout this course when students may need help. Whether students missed a section, did not understand the content, or just want to review, take advantage of the resources provided in the *Dynamic Student Edition*.

Students use the **Self-Assessment** tool to keep track of their understanding of the section's Learning Target and Success Criteria.

Students can take notes throughout the lesson using the **My Notes** function. These notes will be organized for them by chapter and section.

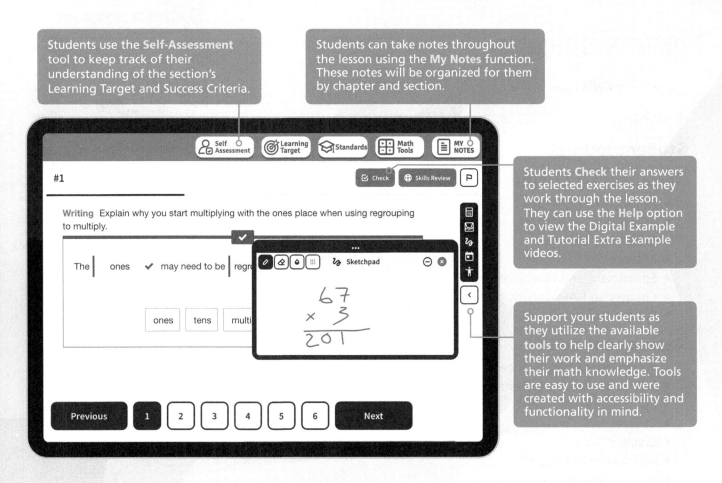

Students **Check** their answers to selected exercises as they work through the lesson. They can use the **Help** option to view the Digital Example and Tutorial Extra Example videos.

Support your students as they utilize the available **tools** to help clearly show their work and emphasize their math knowledge. Tools are easy to use and were created with accessibility and functionality in mind.

USE THESE QR CODES TO EXPLORE ADDITIONAL RESOURCES

Multi-Language Glossary

View definitions and examples of vocabulary words

Skills Trainer

Practice previously learned skills

Interactive Tools

Visualize mathematical concepts

Skills Review Handbook

A collection of review topics

Meeting the Needs of All Learners

Resources at Your Fingertips

This robust, innovative program utilizes a mixture of print and digital resources that allow for a variety of instructional approaches. The program encompasses hands-on activities, interactive explorations, videos, scaffolded instruction, learning support, and many more resources that appeal to students and teachers alike.

PRINT RESOURCES

Student Edition

Teaching Edition

Student Journal

Resources by Chapter

- Family Letter
- Warm-Ups
- Extra Practice
- Reteach
- Enrichment and Extension
- Chapter Self-Assessment
- Puzzle Time

Assessment Book

- Prerequisite Skills Practice
- Pre- and Post-Course Tests
- Course Benchmark Tests
- Quizzes
- Chapter Tests
- Alternative Assessments
- STEAM Performance Tasks

Rich Math Tasks

Skills Review Handbook

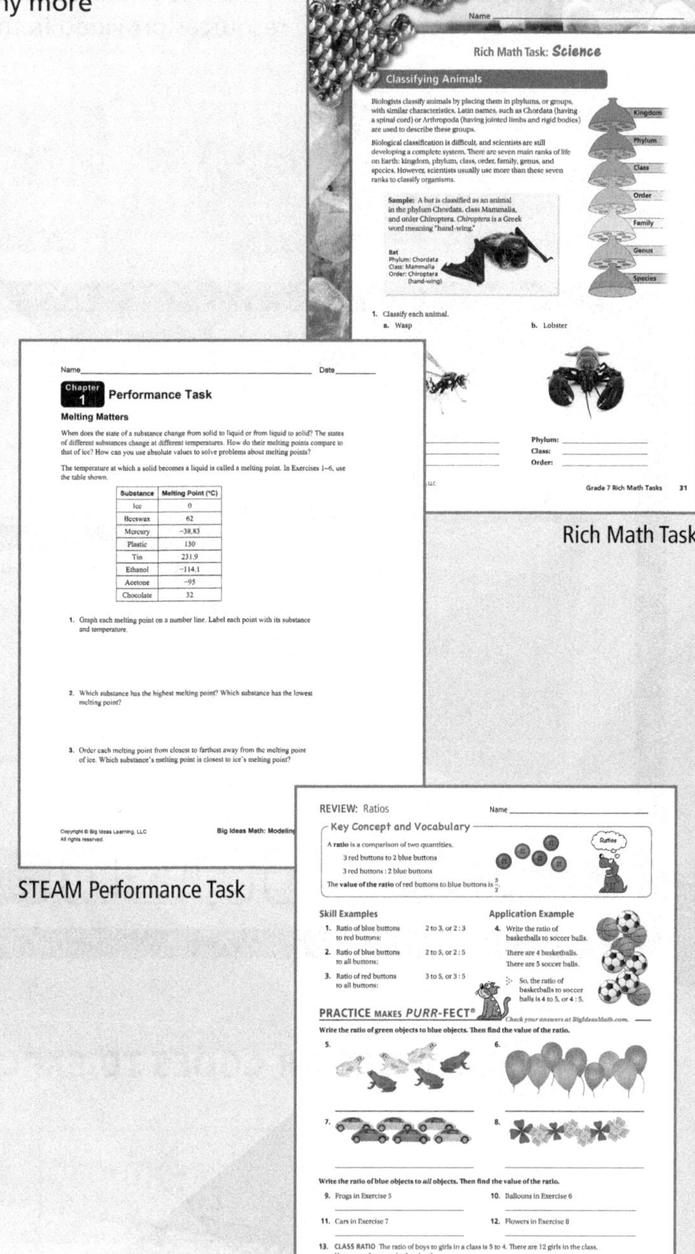

Name ____________

Rich Math Task: *Science*

Classifying Animals

Biologists classify animals by placing them in phylums, or groups, with similar characteristics. Latin names, such as Chordata (having a spinal cord) or Arthropoda (having jointed limbs and rigid bodies) are used to describe these groups.

Biological classification is difficult, and scientists are still developing a complete system. There are seven main ranks of life on Earth: kingdom, phylum, class, order, family, genus, and species. However, scientists usually use more than these seven ranks to classify organisms.

Sample: A bat is classified as an animal in the phylum Chordata, class Mammalia, and order Chiroptera. *Chiroptera* is a Greek word meaning "hand-wing."

Bat
Phylum: Chordata
Class: Mammalia
Order: Chiroptera (hand-wing)

Kingdom
Phylum
Class
Order
Family
Genus
Species

1. Classify each animal.
   a. Wasp
   b. Lobster

Phylum: ____________
Class: ____________
Order: ____________

Grade 7 Rich Math Tasks 31

Rich Math Task

Name____________ Date________

Chapter 1 Performance Task

Melting Matters

When does the state of a substance change from solid to liquid or from liquid to solid? The states of different substances change at different temperatures. How do their melting points compare to that of ice? How can you use absolute values to solve problems about melting points?

The temperature at which a solid becomes a liquid is called a melting point. In Exercises 1–6, use the table shown.

Substance	Melting Point (°C)
Ice	0
Beeswax	62
Mercury	−38.83
Plastic	130
Tin	231.9
Ethanol	−114.1
Acetone	−95
Chocolate	32

1. Graph each melting point on a number line. Label each point with its substance and temperature.
2. Which substance has the highest melting point? Which substance has the lowest melting point?
3. Order each melting point from closest to farthest away from the melting point of ice. Which substance's melting point is closest to ice's melting point?

Copyright © Big Ideas Learning, LLC All rights reserved. Big Ideas Math: Modeling

STEAM Performance Task

REVIEW: Ratios Name ____________

Key Concept and Vocabulary

A **ratio** is a comparison of two quantities.

3 red buttons to 2 blue buttons

3 red buttons : 2 blue buttons

The **value of the ratio** of red buttons to blue buttons is $\frac{3}{2}$.

Ratios

Skill Examples

1. Ratio of blue buttons to red buttons: 2 to 3, or 2 : 3
2. Ratio of blue buttons to all buttons: 2 to 5, or 2 : 5
3. Ratio of red buttons to all buttons: 3 to 5, or 3 : 5

Application Example

4. Write the ratio of basketballs to soccer balls.
   There are 4 basketballs.
   There are 5 soccer balls.
   So, the ratio of basketballs to soccer balls is 4 to 5, or 4 : 5.

PRACTICE MAKES *PURR*-FECT® *Check your answers at BigIdeasMath.com.*

Write the ratio of green objects to blue objects. Then find the value of the ratio.

5.
6.
7.
8.

Write the ratio of blue objects to *all* objects. Then find the value of the ratio.

9. Frogs in Exercise 5
10. Balloons in Exercise 6
11. Cars in Exercise 7
12. Flowers in Exercise 8
13. CLASS RATIO The ratio of boys to girls in a class is 5 to 4. There are 12 girls in the class. How many boys are in the class? ____________

82 Skills Review Topic 15.1 Copyright © Big Ideas Learning, LLC

Skills Review Handbook

Through Program Resources

TECHNOLOGY RESOURCES

Dynamic Student Edition

- Interactive Tools
- Interactive Explorations
- Digital Examples
- Tutorial Extra Example Videos
- Self-Assessments

Dynamic Classroom

- Laurie's Notes
- Interactive Tools
- Interactive Explorations
- Digital Examples with PowerPoints
- Formative Check
- Flip-To
- Digital Warm-Ups and Closures
- Mini-Assessments

Resources

- Answer Presentation Tool
- Chapter at a Glance
- Complete Materials List
- Cross-Curricular Projects
- Skills Trainer
- Vocabulary Flash Cards
- STEAM Videos
- Game Library
- Multi-Language Glossary
- Lesson Plans
- Differentiating the Lesson
- Graphic Organizers
- Pacing Guides
- Worked-Out Solutions Key
- Math Tool Paper
- Family Letters
- Homework App
- Skills Review Handbook

Dynamic Assessment System

- Practice
- Assessments
- Progression Benchmark Tests
- Detailed Reports

Video Support for Teachers

- Life on Earth Videos
- Professional Development Videos
- Concepts and Tools Videos

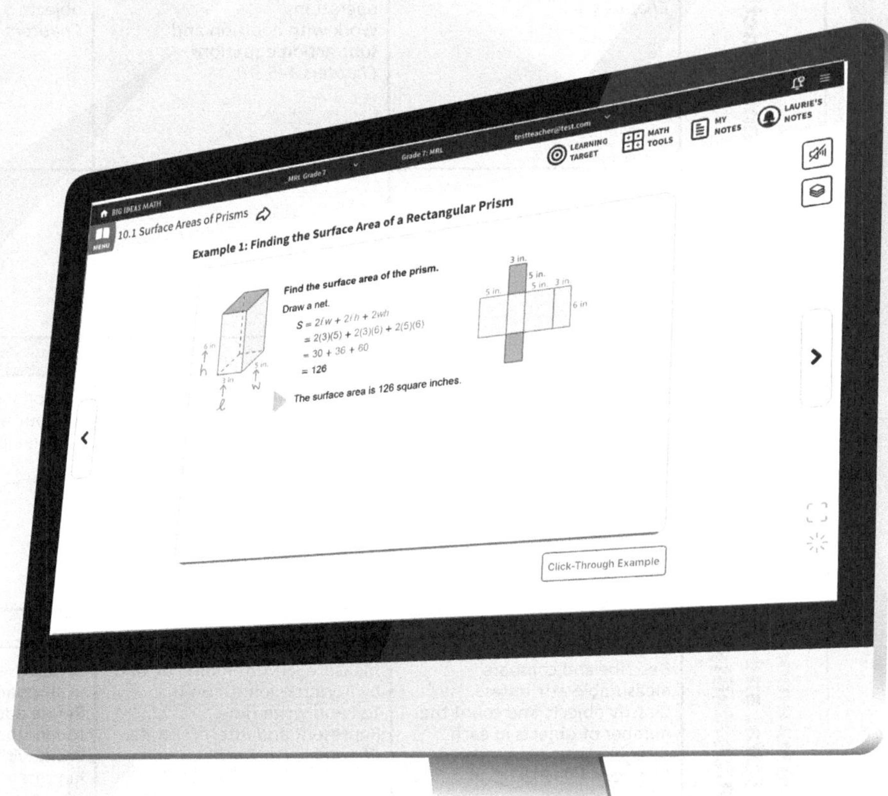

Cohesive Progressions

	Grade K	Grade 1	Grade 2	Grade 3
Number and Quantity	**Counting and Cardinality**			
	Know number names and the count sequence. Count to tell the number of objects. Compare numbers. *Chapters 1–4, 6, 8–10*			
	Number and Operations – Base Ten			
	Work with numbers 11–19 to gain foundations for place value. *Chapter 8*	Extend the counting sequence. Use place value and properties of operations to add and subtract. *Chapters 6–9*	Use place value and properties of operations to add and subtract. *Chapters 2–10, 14*	Use place value and properties of operations to perform multi-digit arithmetic. *Chapters 7–9, 12*
				Num. and Oper. – Fractions
				Understand fractions as numbers. *Chapters 10, 11, 14*
Algebra and Functions	**Operations and Algebraic Thinking**			
	Understand addition as putting together and adding to, and understand subtraction as taking apart and taking from. *Chapters 5–7*	Solve problems involving addition and subtraction within 20. Apply properties of operations. Work with addition and subtraction equations. *Chapters 1–5, 10, 11*	Solve problems involving addition and subtraction within 20. Work with equal groups of objects. *Chapters 1–6, 15*	Solve problems involving multiplication and division within 100. Apply properties of multiplication. Solve problems involving the four operations, and identify and explain patterns in arithmetic. *Chapters 1–5, 8, 9, and 14*
Geometry	**Geometry**			
	Identify and describe shapes. Analyze, compare, create, and compose shapes. *Chapters 11, 12*	Reason with shapes and their attributes. *Chapters 12, 14*	Reason with shapes and their attributes. *Chapter 15*	Reason with shapes and their attributes. *Chapters 10, 13*
Measurement, Data, and Probability	**Measurement and Data**			
	Describe and compare measurable attributes. Classify objects and count the number of objects in each category. *Chapters 4, 11, 13*	Measure lengths indirectly and by iterating length units. Tell and write time. Represent and interpret data. *Chapters 10–12*	Measure and estimate lengths in standard units. Relate addition and subtraction to length. Work with time and money. Represent and interpret data. *Chapters 11–14*	Solve problems involving measurement and estimation of intervals of time, liquid volumes, and masses of objects. Represent and interpret data. Understand the concepts of area and perimeter. *Chapters 6, 12, 14, 15*

Through the Grades

Grade 4	Grade 5	Grade 6	Grade 7	Grade 8
Number and Operations – Base Ten		**The Number System**		
Generalize place value understanding for multi-digit whole numbers. Use place value and properties of operations to perform multi-digit arithmetic. *Chapters 1–5*	Understand the place value system. Perform operations with multi-digit whole numbers and with decimals to hundredths. *Chapters 1, 3–7*	Perform operations with multi-digit numbers and find common factors and multiples. *Chapter 1* Divide fractions by fractions. *Chapter 2* Extend understanding of numbers to the rational number system. *Chapter 8*	Perform operations with rational numbers. *Chapters 1, 2*	Extend understanding of numbers to the real number system. *Chapter 9*
Number and Operations – Fractions		**Ratios and Proportional Relationships**		
Extend understanding of fraction equivalence and ordering. Build fractions from unit fractions. Understand decimal notation for fractions, and compare decimal fractions. *Chapters 7–11*	Add, subtract, multiply, and divide fractions. *Chapters 6, 8–11*	Use ratios to solve problems. *Chapters 3, 4*	Use proportional relationships to solve problems. *Chapters 5, 6*	
Operations and Algebraic Thinking		**Expressions and Equations**		
Use the four operations with whole numbers to solve problems. Understand factors and multiples. Generate and analyze patterns. *Chapters 2–6, 12*	Write and interpret numerical expressions. Analyze patterns and relationships. *Chapters 2, 12*	Perform arithmetic with algebraic expressions. *Chapter 5* Solve one-variable equations and inequalities. *Chapters 6, 8* Analyze relationships between dependent and independent variables. *Chapter 6*	Write equivalent expressions. *Chapter 3* Use numerical and algebraic expressions, equations, and inequalities to solve problems. *Chapters 3, 4, 6*	Understand the connections between proportional relationships, lines, and linear equations. *Chapter 4* Solve linear equations and systems of linear equations. *Chapters 1, 5* Work with radicals and integer exponents. *Chapters 8, 9*
				Functions
				Define, evaluate, and compare functions, and use functions to model relationships between quantities. *Chapter 7*
Geometry				
Draw and identify lines and angles, and classify shapes by properties of their lines and angles. *Chapters 13, 14*	Graph points on the coordinate plane. Classify two-dimensional figures into categories based on their properties. *Chapters 12, 14*	Solve real-world and mathematical problems involving area, surface area, and volume. *Chapter 7*	Draw, construct, and describe geometrical figures and describe the relationships between them. *Chapters 5, 9, 10* Solve problems involving angle measure, area, surface area, and volume. *Chapters 9, 10*	Understand congruence and similarity. *Chapters 2, 3* Use the Pythagorean Theorem. *Chapter 9* Solve problems involving volumes of cylinders, cones, and spheres. *Chapter 10*
Measurement and Data		**Statistics and Probability**		
Solve problems involving measurement and conversion of measurements from a larger unit to a smaller unit. Represent and interpret data. Understand angles and measure angles. *Chapters 10–13*	Convert measurement units within a given measurement system. Represent and interpret data. Understand volume. *Chapters 11, 13*	Develop understanding of statistical variability and summarize and describe distributions. *Chapters 9, 10*	Make inferences about a population, compare two populations, and use probability models. *Chapters 7, 8*	Investigate patterns of association in bivariate data. *Chapter 6*

Suggested Pacing

Chapters 1–E	159 Days

Chapter 1	(9 Days)
Chapter Opener	1 Day
Section 1.1	1 Day
Section 1.2	1 Day
Section 1.3	1 Day
Section 1.4	1 Day
Section 1.5	1 Day
Connecting Concepts	1 Day
Chapter Review	1 Day
Chapter Test	1 Day
Year-To-Date	**9 Days**

Chapter 2	(12 Days)
Chapter Opener	1 Day
Section 2.1	1 Day
Section 2.2	2 Days
Section 2.3	1 Day
Section 2.4	1 Day
Section 2.5	1 Day
Section 2.6	1 Day
Section 2.7	1 Day
Connecting Concepts	1 Day
Chapter Review	1 Day
Chapter Test	1 Day
Year-To-Date	**21 Days**

Chapter 3	(13 Days)
Chapter Opener	1 Day
Section 3.1	1 Day
Section 3.2	1 Day
Section 3.3	2 Days
Section 3.4	2 Days
Section 3.5	1 Day
Section 3.6	2 Days
Connecting Concepts	1 Day
Chapter Review	1 Day
Chapter Test	1 Day
Year-To-Date	**34 Days**

Chapter 4	(9 Days)
Chapter Opener	1 Day
Section 4.1	1 Day
Section 4.2	1 Day
Section 4.3	1 Day
Section 4.4	2 Days
Connecting Concepts	1 Day
Chapter Review	1 Day
Chapter Test	1 Day
Year-To-Date	**43 Days**

Chapter 5	(10 Days)
Chapter Opener	1 Day
Section 5.1	1 Day
Section 5.2	1 Day
Section 5.3	1 Day
Section 5.4	1 Day
Section 5.5	2 Days
Connecting Concepts	1 Day
Chapter Review	1 Day
Chapter Test	1 Day
Year-To-Date	**53 Days**

Chapter 6	(10 Days)
Chapter Opener	1 Day
Section 6.1	2 Days
Section 6.2	1 Day
Section 6.3	1 Day
Section 6.4	2 Days
Connecting Concepts	1 Day
Chapter Review	1 Day
Chapter Test	1 Day
Year-To-Date	**63 Days**

Chapter 7	(11 Days)
Chapter Opener	1 Day
Section 7.1	1 Day
Section 7.2	1 Day
Section 7.3	1 Day
Section 7.4	1 Day
Section 7.5	1 Day
Section 7.6	1 Day
Section 7.7	1 Day
Connecting Concepts	1 Day
Chapter Review	1 Day
Chapter Test	1 Day
Year-To-Date	**74 Days**

Chapter 8	(14 Days)
Chapter Opener	1 Day
Section 8.1	1 Day
Section 8.2	1 Day
Section 8.3	1 Day
Section 8.4	1 Day
Section 8.5	1 Day
Section 8.6	1 Day
Section 8.7	2 Days
Section 8.8	2 Days
Connecting Concepts	1 Day
Chapter Review	1 Day
Chapter Test	1 Day
Year-To-Date	**88 Days**

Chapter 9	(9 Days)
Chapter Opener	1 Day
Section 9.1	1 Day
Section 9.2	1 Day
Section 9.3	1 Day
Section 9.4	1 Day
Section 9.5	1 Day
Connecting Concepts	1 Day
Chapter Review	1 Day
Chapter Test	1 Day
Year-To-Date	**97 Days**

Chapter 10	(9 Days)
Chapter Opener	1 Day
Section 10.1	1 Day
Section 10.2	1 Day
Section 10.3	1 Day
Section 10.4	1 Day
Section 10.5	1 Day
Connecting Concepts	1 Day
Chapter Review	1 Day
Chapter Test	1 Day
Year-To-Date	**106 Days**

Chapter A	(11 Days)
Chapter Opener	1 Day
Section A.1	1 Day
Section A.2	1 Day
Section A.3	2 Days
Section A.4	1 Day
Section A.5	2 Days
Connecting Concepts	1 Day
Chapter Review	1 Day
Chapter Test	1 Day
Year-To-Date	**117 Days**

Chapter B	(11 Days)
Chapter Opener	1 Day
Section B.1	1 Day
Section B.2	1 Day
Section B.3	1 Day
Section B.4	2 Days
Section B.5	2 Days
Connecting Concepts	1 Day
Chapter Review	1 Day
Chapter Test	1 Day
Year-To-Date	**128 Days**

Chapter C	(8 Days)
Chapter Opener	1 Day
Section C.1	1 Day
Section C.2	1 Day
Section C.3	1 Day
Section C.4	1 Day
Connecting Concepts	1 Day
Chapter Review	1 Day
Chapter Test	1 Day
Year-To-Date	**136 Days**

Chapter D	(13 Days)
Chapter Opener	1 Day
Section D.1	1 Day
Section D.2	1 Day
Section D.3	2 Days
Section D.4	2 Days
Section D.5	2 Days
Section D.6	1 Day
Connecting Concepts	1 Day
Chapter Review	1 Day
Chapter Test	1 Day
Year-To-Date	**149 Days**

Chapter E	(10 Days)
Chapter Opener	1 Day
Section E.1	1 Day
Section E.2	1 Day
Section E.3	1 Day
Section E.4	1 Day
Section E.5	1 Day
Section E.6	1 Day
Connecting Concepts	1 Day
Chapter Review	1 Day
Chapter Test	1 Day
Year-To-Date	**159 Days**

An editable version of the Pacing Guide is available in two forms (regular and block scheduling) at *BigIdeasMath.com*.

Numerical Expressions and Factors

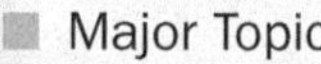

Major Topic
Supporting Topic
Additional Topic

Fractions and Decimals

2

Ratios and Rates

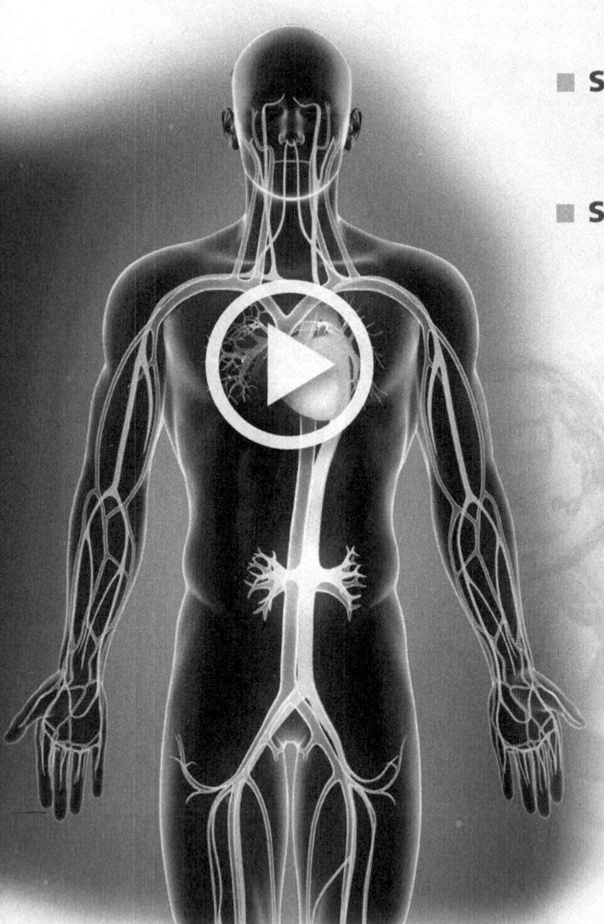

■ Major Topic
■ Supporting Topic
■ Additional Topic

Percents

4

Algebraic Expressions and Properties

■ Major Topic
■ Supporting Topic
■ Additional Topic

Equations

Area, Surface Area, and Volume

Major Topic
Supporting Topic
Additional Topic

Integers, Number Lines, and the Coordinate Plane

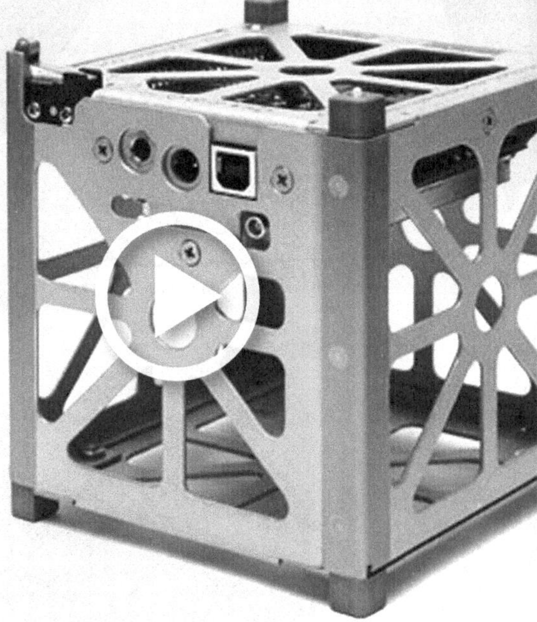

Statistical Measures

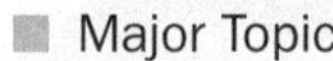

- Major Topic
- Supporting Topic
- Additional Topic

Data Displays

Adding and Subtracting Rational Numbers

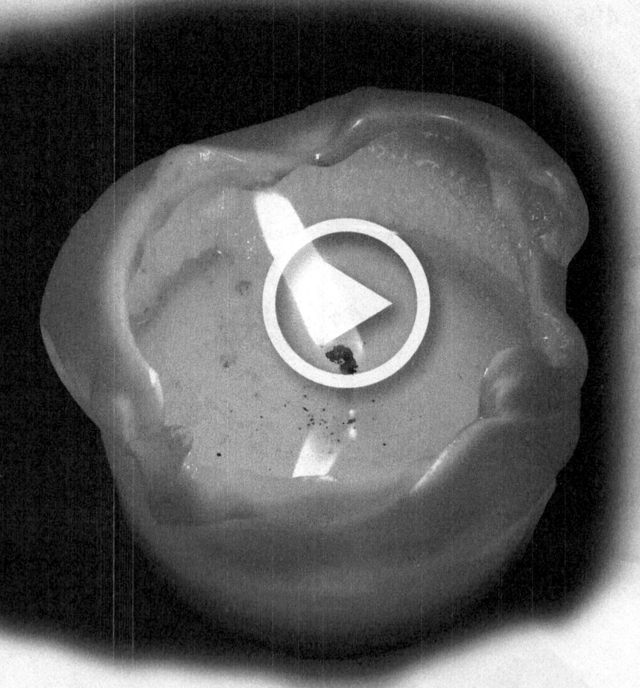

■ Major Topic
■ Supporting Topic
■ Additional Topic

Multiplying and Dividing Rational Numbers

Expressions

■ Major Topic
■ Supporting Topic
■ Additional Topic

Ratios and Proportions

Percents

- Major Topic
- Supporting Topic
- Additional Topic

Adding and Subtracting Rational Numbers

Chapter Learning Target:
Understand adding and subtracting rational numbers.

Chapter Success Criteria:
- I can represent rational numbers on a number line.
- I can explain the rules for adding and subtracting integers using absolute value.
- I can apply addition and subtraction with rational numbers to model real-life problems.
- I can solve problems involving addition and subtraction of rational numbers.

Laurie's Notes

Chapter A Overview

In prior chapters and courses, students learned to order, compare, and perform operations with fractions and decimals. They learned about the connection between these two forms of numbers. In this chapter, rational numbers are introduced and all of the concepts and skills related to positive whole numbers, fractions, and decimals are explored for their opposites (numbers less than zero).

Chapter A begins with an introduction to rational numbers. Number lines are used to explore opposites and absolute values. The geometric interpretation of absolute value, the distance a number is from 0 on a number line, is used to help students make sense of adding and subtracting integers.

The approach used in this chapter and the next is to explore operations with integers using integer counters and/or number lines. You want students to make sense of adding and subtracting integers. The rules students develop are then applied to the set of rational numbers. Help students understand that they are transferring their knowledge of operations on one set of numbers, integers, to another set of numbers, rational numbers.

Encourage students to pause and ask what a reasonable answer would be. For example, a student may say, "I'm adding -3.1 and 6.7. My answer should be somewhere around 3. When you add two numbers with different signs, you use the sign of the number with the greater absolute value. So my answer will be positive. Then you subtract the absolute values: $|6.7| - |-3.1| = 6.7 - 3.1 = 3.6$. My answer is 3.6 and it makes sense."

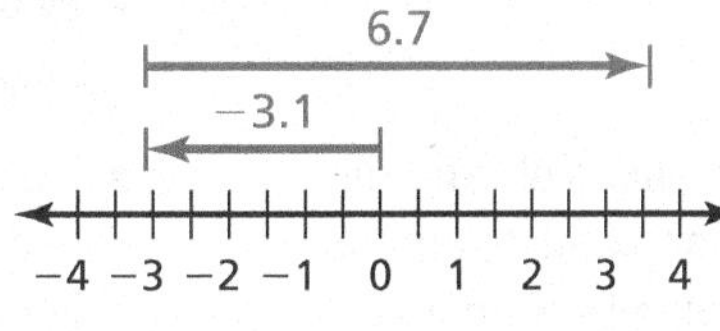

Suggested Pacing

Chapter Opener	1 Day
Section 1	1 Day
Section 2	1 Day
Section 3	2 Days
Section 4	1 Day
Section 5	2 Days
Connecting Concepts	1 Day
Chapter Review	1 Day
Chapter Test	1 Day
Total Chapter A	11 Days
Year-to-Date	118 Days

Chapter Learning Target

Understand adding and subtracting rational numbers.

Chapter Success Criteria

- Represent rational numbers on a number line.
- Explain the rules for adding and subtracting integers using absolute value.
- Apply addition and subtraction with rational numbers to model real-life problems.
- Solve problems involving addition and subtraction of rational numbers.

Chapter A Learning Targets and Success Criteria

Section	Learning Target	Success Criteria
A.1 Rational Numbers	Understand absolute values and ordering of rational numbers.	• Graph rational numbers on a number line. • Find the absolute value of a rational number. • Use a number line to compare rational numbers.
A.2 Adding Integers	Find sums of integers.	• Explain how to model addition of integers on a number line. • Find sums of integers by reasoning about absolute values. • Explain why the sum of a number and its opposite is 0.
A.3 Adding Rational Numbers	Find sums of rational numbers.	• Explain how to model addition of rational numbers on a number line. • Find sums of rational numbers by reasoning about absolute values. • Use properties of addition to efficiently add rational numbers.
A.4 Subtracting Integers	Find differences of integers.	• Explain how subtracting integers is related to adding integers. • Explain how to model subtraction of integers on a number line. • Find differences of integers by reasoning about absolute values.
A.5 Subtracting Rational Numbers	Find differences of rational numbers and find distances between numbers on a number line.	• Explain how to model subtraction of rational numbers on a number line. • Find differences of rational numbers by reasoning about absolute values. • Find distances between numbers on a number line.

Progressions

Through the Grades		
Grade 6	**Grade 7**	**Grade 8**
• Fluently add and subtract multi-digit decimals. • Describe quantities with positive and negative numbers. • Order integers and absolute value numbers.	• Add and subtract integers and rational numbers. • Apply properties of operations as strategies to perform operations with rational numbers. • Solve problems involving the four operations with rational numbers.	• Understand that numbers that are not rational are irrational. • Compare irrational numbers using rational approximations.

Through the Chapter					
Standard	**A.1**	**A.2**	**A.3**	**A.4**	**A.5**
Describe situations in which opposite quantities combine to make 0.	▲	●	★		
Understand $p + q$ as the number located a distance $\|q\|$ from p, in the positive or negative direction depending on whether q is positive or negative. Show that a number and its opposite have a sum of 0 (are additive inverses). Interpret sums of rational numbers by describing real-world contexts.	▲	●	★		
Understand subtraction of rational numbers as adding the additive inverse, $p - q = p + (-q)$. Show that the distance between two rational numbers on the number line is the absolute value of their difference, and apply this principle in real-world contexts.	▲			●	★
Apply properties of operations as strategies to add and subtract rational numbers.	▲	●	●		★
Solve real-world and mathematical problems involving the four operations with rational numbers.	▲	●	●	●	●

Key

▲ = preparing ★ = complete

● = learning ■ = extending

Laurie's Notes

STEAM Video

1. a. *Sample answer*: 53°C; The wax becomes a solid at 53°C.
   b. The temperature of the gas in the smoke is at least 343°C.
   c. liquid
2. gas; solid

Performance Task

They are the same; The temperature is less than 0°C; A substance changes from a liquid to a solid or a solid to a liquid at the same temperature; "Below freezing" means below the freezing point of water.

Mathematical Practices

Students have opportunities to develop aspects of the mathematical practices throughout the chapter. Here are some examples.

1. **Make Sense of Problems and Persevere in Solving Them**
   A.1 Math Practice note, *p. 503*
2. **Reason Abstractly and Quantitatively**
   A.2 Exercise 65, *p. 516*
3. **Construct Viable Arguments and Critique the Reasoning of Others**
   A.2 Math Practice note, *p. 511*
4. **Model with Mathematics**
   A.4 Exercise 45, *p. 528*
5. **Use Appropriate Tools Strategically**
   A.5 Exercises 9 and 10, *p. 534*
6. **Attend to Precision**
   A.1 Math Practice note, *p. 504*
7. **Look for and Make Use of Structure**
   A.3 Math Practice note, *p. 517*
8. **Look for and Express Regularity in Repeated Reasoning**
   A.3 Exercise 37, *p. 522*

STEAM Video

Before the Video

- To introduce the STEAM Video, read aloud the first paragraph of Freezing Solids and discuss the question with your students.
- ? "Why do you think the scale is defined using these two points?"

During the Video

- The video discusses various forms of matter.
- ? Pause the video at 1:00 and ask, "What is matter?" Something that takes up space and is pulled by the force of gravity.
- ? "What are three states of matter?" solid, liquid, and gas
- Watch the remainder of the video.

After the Video

- ? "What is the most common state of matter in the universe?" plasma
- ? "Which two common forms of matter are found in most homes in a solid, liquid, and gaseous form?" water and candle wax
- Have students work with a partner to answer Questions 1 and 2.
- As students discuss and answer the questions, listen for understanding of comparing integers.

Performance Task

- Use this information to spark students' interest and promote thinking about real-life problems.
- ? Ask, "How is the freezing point of a substance related to its melting point? What is meant when someone says it is below freezing outside? Explain."
- After completing the chapter, students will have gained the knowledge needed to complete "Melting Matters."

STEAM Video

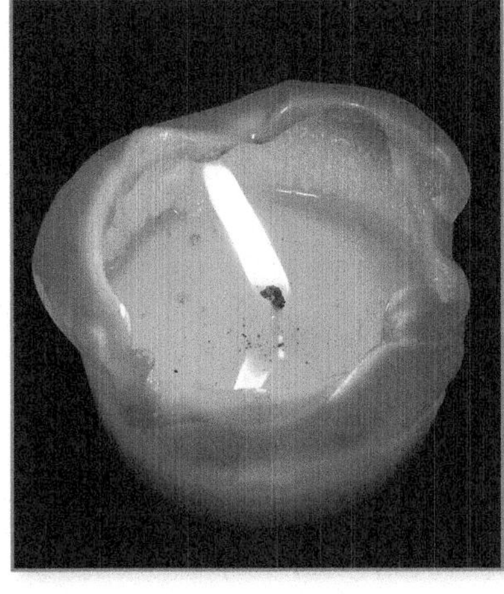

Freezing Solids

The Celsius temperature scale is defined using the freezing point, 0°C, and the boiling point, 100°C, of water. Why do you think the scale is defined using these two points?

Watch the STEAM Video "Freezing Solids." Then answer the following questions.

1. In the video, Tony says that the freezing point of wax is 53°C and the boiling point of wax is 343°C.
    - **a.** Describe the temperature of wax that has just changed from liquid form to solid form. Explain your reasoning.
    - **b.** After Tony blows out the candle, he demonstrates that there is still gas in the smoke. What do you know about the temperature of the gas that is in the smoke?
    - **c.** In what form is wax when the temperature is at 100°C, the boiling point of water?
2. Consider wax in solid, liquid, and gaseous forms. Which is hottest? coldest?

Performance Task

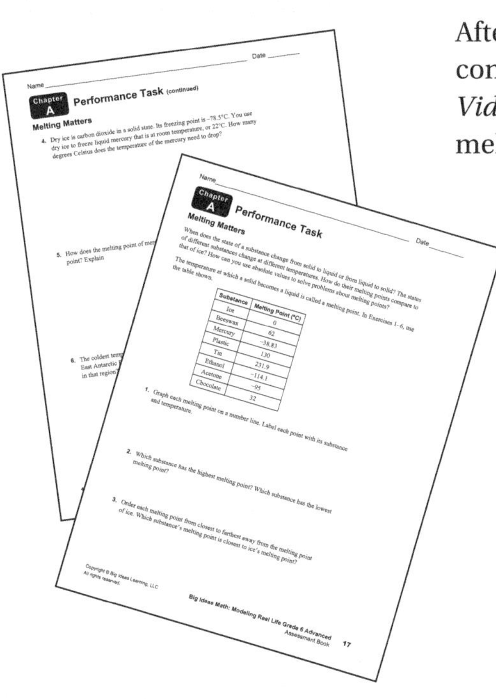

Name ______ Date ______

Chapter A **Performance Task** (continued)

Melting Matters

4. Dry ice is carbon dioxide in a solid state. Its freezing point is −78.5°C. You use dry ice to freeze liquid mercury that is at room temperature, or 22°C. How many degrees Celsius does the temperature of the mercury need to drop?

5. How does the melting point of mer... point? Explain

6. The coldest temp... East Antarctic ... in that region?

Name ______ Date ______

Chapter A **Performance Task**

Melting Matters

When does the state of a substance change from solid to liquid or from liquid to solid? The states of different substances change at different temperatures. How do their melting points compare to that of ice? How can you use absolute values to solve problems about melting points?

The temperature at which a solid becomes a liquid is called a melting point. In Exercises 1–6, use the table shown.

Substance	Melting Point (°C)
Ice	0
Beeswax	62
Mercury	−38.83
Plastic	130
Tin	231.9
Ethanol	−114.1
Acetone	−95
Chocolate	32

1. Graph each melting point on a number line. Label each point with its substance and temperature.

2. Which substance has the highest melting point? Which substance has the lowest melting point?

3. Order each melting point from closest to farthest away from the melting point of ice. Which substance's melting point is closest to ice's melting point?

Copyright © Big Ideas Learning, LLC
All rights reserved.

Big Ideas Math: Modeling Real Life Grade 6 Advanced
Assessment Book 17

Melting Matters

After completing this chapter, you will be able to use the concepts you learned to answer the questions in the *STEAM Video Performance Task*. You will answer questions using the melting points of the substances below.

Ice	**Tin**
Beeswax	**Ethanol**
Mercury	**Acetone**
Plastic	**Chocolate**

You will graph the melting points of the substances on a number line to make comparisons. How is the freezing point of a substance related to its melting point? What is meant when someone says it is below freezing outside? Explain.

Getting Ready for Chapter 

Chapter Exploration

1. Work with a partner. Plot and connect the points to make a picture.

1(1, 11)	2(4, 10)	3(7, 10)	4(11, 9)	5(13, 8)
6(15, 5)	7(15, 3)	8(16, 1)	9(16, −1)	10(15, −1)
11(11, 1)	12(9, 2)	13(7, 1)	14(5, −1)	15(1, −1)
16(0, 0)	17(3, 1)	18(1, 1)	19(−2, 0)	20(−6, −2)
21(−9, −6)	22(−9, −7)	23(−7, −9)	24(−7, −11)	25(−8, −12)
26(−9, −11)	27(−11, −10)	28(−13, −11)	29(−15, −11)	30(−17, −12)
31(−17, −10)	32(−15, −7)	33(−12, −6)	34(−11, −6)	35(−10, −3)
36(−8, 2)	37(−5, 6)	38(−3, 9)	39(−4, 10)	40(−5, 10)
41(−2, 12)				

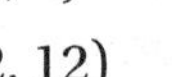

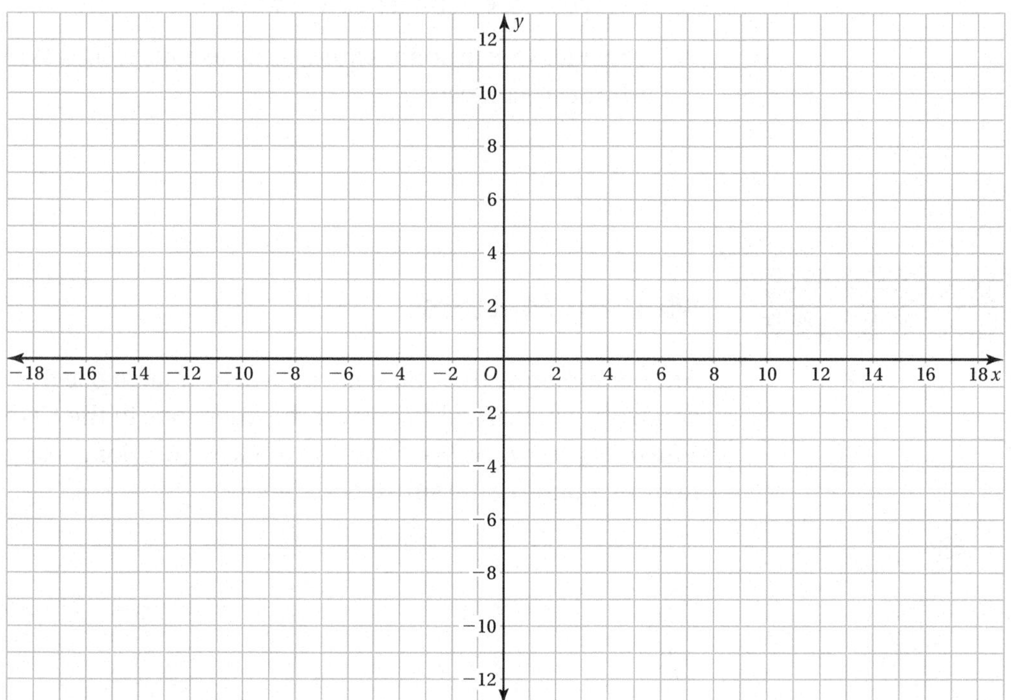

2. Create your own "dot-to-dot" picture. Use at least 20 points.

Vocabulary

The following vocabulary terms are defined in this chapter. Think about what each term might mean and record your thoughts.

integers absolute value rational number additive inverse

Laurie's Notes

Check out the
digital flash cards.
BigIdeasMath.com

Chapter Exploration

- In a previous chapter, students plotted points in all four quadrants of the coordinate plane.
- You may need to review how to plot a point in each of the four quadrants of the coordinate plane. Examples: (4, 5), (−4, 5), (−4, −5), and (4, −5).
- Allow students to work in pairs to complete the exercises.
- Ask volunteers to share their "dot-to-dot" pictures from Exercise 2.
- **Extension:** Have each pair write the coordinates of their "dot-to-dot" picture on a piece of paper and then exchange papers with another pair. Have each pair plot the other pair's points to make a picture.

Vocabulary

- These terms represent some of the vocabulary that students will encounter in Chapter A. Discuss the terms as a class.
- Where have students heard the term *absolute value* of outside of a math classroom? In what contexts? Students may not be able to write the actual definition, but they may write phrases associated with *absolute value*.
- Allowing students to discuss these terms now will prepare them for understanding the terms as they are presented in the chapter.
- When students encounter a new definition, encourage them to write in their *Student Journals*. They will revisit these definitions during the Chapter Review.

ELL Support

Explain that the prefix *in–* can mean "not," "in," or "on." Knowing prefix and root word meanings can help students decipher the meaning of unknown words. The Latin root word *vertere* (to turn) combined with the prefix *in–* means "to turn in the opposite direction." The sum of a number and its additive inverse (or opposite) is zero.

Topics for Review

- Adding and Subtracting Fractions
- Addition Property of Zero
- Commutative and Associative Properties
- Compare and Order Integers
- Operations with Whole Numbers
- Place Value
- Simplifying Fractions

Chapter Exploration

1. See Additional Answers.
2. Check students' work.

Check out the
Dynamic Classroom.
BigIdeasMath.com

Laurie's Notes

Learning Target

Understand absolute values and ordering of rational numbers.

Success Criteria

- Graph rational numbers on a number line.
- Find the absolute value of a rational number.
- Use a number line to compare rational numbers.

Warm Up

Cumulative, vocabulary, and prerequisite skills practice opportunities are available in the *Resources by Chapter* or at *BigIdeasMath.com.*

ELL Support

Students may know the word *rational* as meaning "reasonable or sensible" in everyday language. In math, a rational number is a number that can be written fraction with integers in both the numerator and the denominator, and the denominator cannot be zero. Be aware that students from foreign countries may use atypical phrases to express fractions, such as "two by three" for $\frac{2}{3}$. Explain that in American English "two by three" would signal multiplication, not division.

Exploration 1

a. *Sample answer:* 3 units; the absolute value

b. Answers will vary. The number to the right on the number line is greater.

c. Check students' work.

Preparing to Teach

- In this lesson, students will use integers, absolute values, and number lines, which were all introduced in Chapter 8. It is important that students review these foundational skills because they are necessary for adding and subtracting rational numbers.
- **Attend to Precision:** Students may incorrectly say, "Absolute value just makes the number positive." Be sure that students correctly refer to the absolute value of a number as the distance the number is from zero.

Motivate

- Tell students that positive and negative signs help describe a relationship between amounts. For example, a negative number can represent the time before an event and a positive number can represent the time after the event.
  - 3 hours before a rocket launch can be represented by $T - 3$ and 3 hours after the rocket launch can be represented by $T + 3$.

? "Why is the letter T used?" It represents the time of the rocket launch.

- Solicit other examples of real-life situations involving **integers**.
- Review and discuss the definitions for integers and a **rational number**.

Exploration 1

- Have students use index cards or pieces of paper to label the points on their floor number lines. Check that the tick marks on their number lines are equally spaced and labeled properly. If space is an issue, students can make number lines at their desks using counters or tiles for tick marks.
- As students complete part (a), listen for understanding that the distance between a number and 0 on a number line is the **absolute value**.
- Have students share their reasoning for part (b). Their language may not be precise, but tell students that they will focus on using precise language in this course and it will improve!
- **Construct Viable Arguments and Critique the Reasoning of Others:** Have students share their reasoning for part (c) and ask other students to critique it. For the third bullet, a student might say, "It's not possible. If your number is positive and your partner's number is less than yours, then your partner is between 0 and you. So, you can't be the same distance from 0." Expect other students to listen carefully and critique the reasoning by saying, "Your partner can be at the opposite of your number. For example, if you are standing at 4, your partner can stand at -4." Do not do all the thinking for students.

◉ The reasoning students use in part (c) can help you assess students' initial understanding of comparing rational numbers on a number line.

? "Is the opposite of 2 on the number line?" yes

? "Are integers the only numbers on the number line? Explain." No, rational numbers are also on the number line.

? "Is 5 the only number 4 units from 1 on the number line? Explain." No, -3 is also 4 units from 1 on the number line.

A.1 Rational Numbers

Learning Target: Understand absolute values and ordering of rational numbers.

Success Criteria:
- I can graph rational numbers on a number line.
- I can find the absolute value of a rational number.
- I can use a number line to compare rational numbers.

Recall that **integers** are the set of whole numbers and their opposites. A **rational number** is a number that can be written as $\frac{a}{b}$, where a and b are integers and $b \neq 0$.

EXPLORATION 1

Using a Number Line

Work with a partner. Make a number line on the floor. Include both negative numbers and positive numbers.

a. Stand on an integer. Then have your partner stand on the opposite of the integer. How far are each of you from 0? What do you call the distance between a number and 0 on a number line?

b. Stand on a rational number that is not an integer. Then have your partner stand on any other number. Which number is greater? How do you know?

c. Stand on any number other than 0 on the number line. Can your partner stand on a number that is:

- greater than your number and farther from 0?
- greater than your number and closer to 0?
- less than your number and the same distance from 0?
- less than your number and farther from 0?

For each case in which it was not possible to stand on a number as directed, explain why it is not possible. In each of the other cases, how can you decide where your partner can stand?

Math Practice

Find Entry Points
What are some ways to determine which of two numbers is greater?

A.1 Lesson

Key Vocabulary
integers, *p. 503*
rational number, *p. 503*
absolute value, *p. 504*

Math Practice

Use Clear Definitions

Explain to a classmate why $|4| \neq -4$.

Key Idea

Absolute Value

Words The **absolute value** of a number is the distance between the number and 0 on a number line. The absolute value of a number a is written as $|a|$.

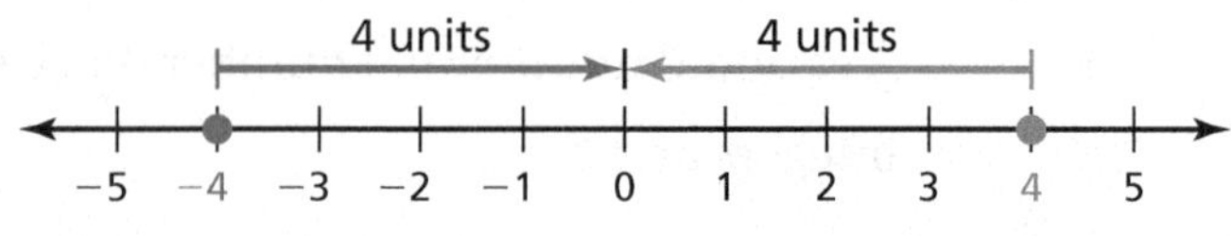

Numbers $|-4| = 4$ $|4| = 4$

EXAMPLE 1 Finding Absolute Values of Rational Numbers

a. Find the absolute value of −3.

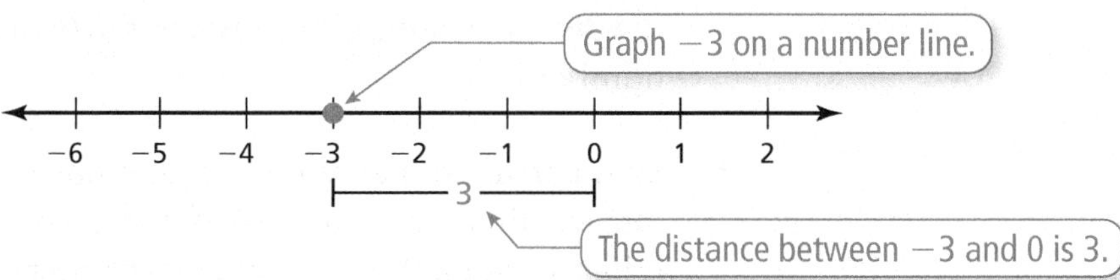

So, $|-3| = 3$.

b. Find the absolute value of $1\frac{1}{4}$.

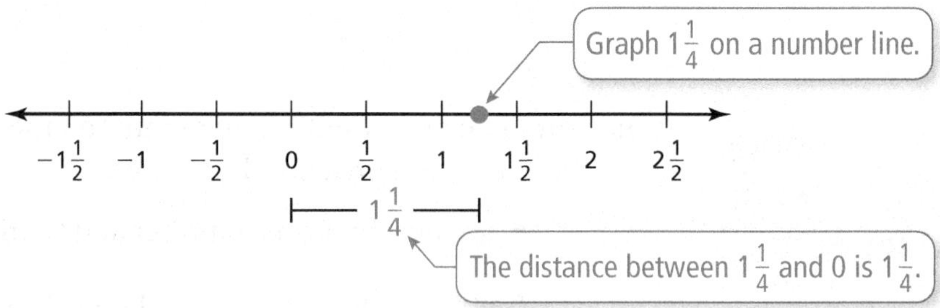

So, $\left|1\frac{1}{4}\right| = 1\frac{1}{4}$.

Try It **Find the absolute value.**

1. $|7|$ **2.** $\left|-\frac{5}{3}\right|$ **3.** $|-2.6|$

Laurie's Notes

Scaffolding Instruction

- Students have used a visual representation, a number line, to find the distance between two points. Now they will use the formal definition of absolute value.
- **Emerging:** Students may be unsure of the language and reasoning associated with positive and negative numbers. Provide guided instruction for the examples. Relate the notation to experiences students had with the number line in the exploration.
- **Proficient:** Students have a clear understanding of absolute value and can find the absolute value of a number without a number line. Have students review the Key Idea to clarify the notation and then proceed to the Self-Assessment for Concepts & Skills exercises.

Key Idea

- Write the Key Idea on the board.
- When students state that "absolute values are always positive," try to clarify the statement. Students may make incorrect assumptions when there are numeric or variable expressions within absolute value symbols.
- At this stage of development, stress the geometric definition of absolute value. **Absolute value** is the distance a number is from zero.

EXAMPLE 1

- Work through each part as shown. Number lines help to develop a visual understanding of absolute value.
- ? When you finish the example, ask, "What is the absolute value of 12?" 12 "What is the absolute value of −8?" 8
- **Common Error:** When students plot −3 on a number line, they may make a scale on the number line and forget to place a closed circle on the number −3. Remind students that plotting a point involves actually placing a closed circle on the number line at the point they are plotting. Remind them that the numbers for the scale are written below the number line, not above it.

Try It

- **Neighbor Check:** Have students work independently and then have their neighbors check their work. Have students discuss any discrepancies.
- **Teaching Tip:** You want to model that your classroom is a safe learning environment. If there are incorrect answers, state without judgement, "I've seen different answers to this problem. That will happen often this year. We can all learn from mistakes and learning is our goal, not just getting a correct answer."
- ◉ Say, "You have found the absolute value of a number. This is the second success criterion. Use *Thumbs Up* to show me how confident you are with finding the absolute value of a number."

Scaffold instruction to support all students in their learning. Learning is individualized and you may want to group students differently as they move in and out of these levels with each skill and concept. Student self-assessment and feedback help guide your instructional decisions about how and when to layer support for all students to become proficient learners.

Formative Assessment Tip

Thumbs Up

This technique asks students to indicate the extent to which they understand a concept, procedure, or even the directions for an activity. It can be a quick way for students to communicate where their learning is with respect to a specific success criterion.

I get it

I don't get it

I'm not sure

Extra Example 1

a Find the absolute value of 6. 6

b. Find the absolute value of $-11\frac{3}{4}$. $11\frac{3}{4}$

ELL Support

After demonstrating Example 1, have students practice language by working in pairs to complete Try It Exercises 1–3. Monitor students' discussions. Expect students at different language levels to perform as described.

Beginner: Write the answer.

Intermediate/Advanced: State the answer. For example, "seven."

Try It

1. 7

2. $\frac{5}{3}$

3. 2.6

Laurie's Notes

Extra Example 2

Compare $\frac{7}{8}$ and $|-0.8|$. $\frac{7}{8} > |-0.8|$

Try It

4. =
5. <
6. >

ELL Support

Allow students to work in pairs on Self-Assessment for Concepts & Skills Exercises 7, 9, and 10. Have each pair display their answers on a whiteboard for your review. Have two pairs form a group to discuss Exercises 8, 11, and 12. Monitor discussions and provide support as needed.

Self-Assessment

for Concepts & Skills

7. 9, −1, 15
8. the distance between the number and zero on a number line
9. =

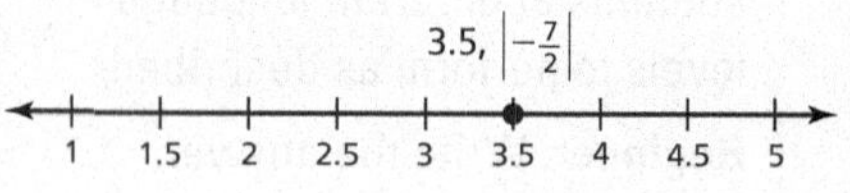

10. <

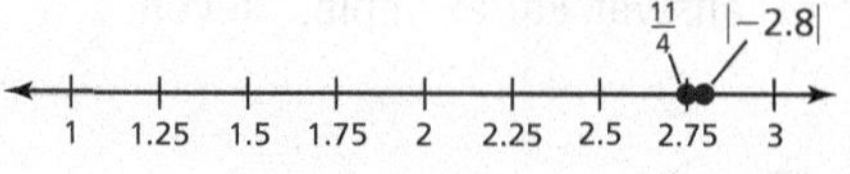

11. b is to the left of a on a number line and farther from 0.
12. −6; All of the other expressions are equal to 6.

EXAMPLE 2

- Students may mix up or forget the meanings of the inequality symbols.
- Graphing rational numbers on a number line helps students visualize the two numbers being compared. Some students may be able to visualize without drawing the number line, but do they know how to use the tool? Can they plot rational numbers on a number line?
- **Common Error:** Students may label the number line left-to-right for both positive and negative integers as shown below. Explain that negative integers are labeled from 0, such that 1 and −1 are both one unit from 0.

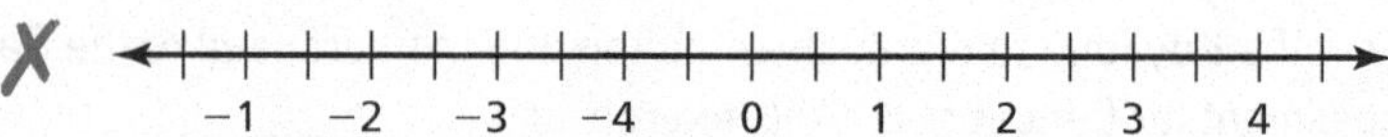

- **Attend to Precision:** When students write their answers, check to see that the absolute value symbols are included. It is incorrect to write $-2.5 > \frac{3}{2}$. The correct answer is $|-2.5| > \frac{3}{2}$.

Try It

- In Exercise 5, remind students that for negative numbers, you work from right to left when labeling a number line. Label 0, $-\frac{1}{4}$, $-\frac{1}{2}$, $-\frac{3}{4}$, −1 from right to left and 0, $\frac{1}{4}$, $\frac{1}{2}$, $\frac{3}{4}$, 1 from left to right.
- Have students display their answers on whiteboards for your review. Select volunteers to explain their reasoning.
- **Teaching Tip:** Use a class roster or seating chart to track students' participation. Put marks next to students' names when they share their reasoning or show their work. This will help you to ensure that all students are being heard. You can laminate the roster, use a washable marker, and wipe it clean every few days.

Self-Assessment for Concepts & Skills

- As students are working through the exercises, encourage them to assess their understanding of the learning target and success criteria, keeping the focus on the learning target. Tell students to rate their understanding of each success criterion.
- Discuss Exercise 11 by asking a volunteer to share his or her thinking. Ask others to critique or clarify the explanation.
- For Exercise 12, remind students to select one expression that does *not* belong *and* to explain their reasoning.

The Success Criteria Self-Assessment chart can be found in the *Student Journal* or online at *BigIdeasMath.com*.

EXAMPLE 2 Comparing Rational Numbers

Compare $|-2.5|$ and $\frac{3}{2}$.

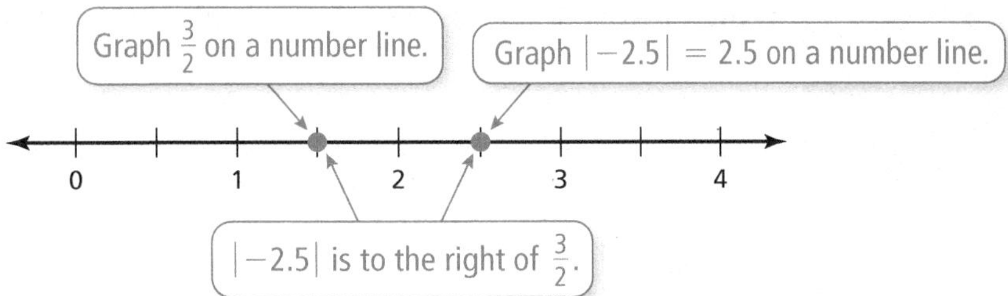

Remember

Two numbers that are the same distance from 0 on a number line, but on opposite sides of 0, are called *opposites*. The opposite of a number a is $-a$.

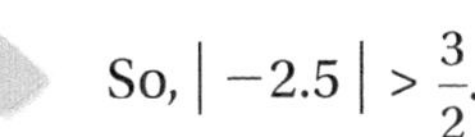

So, $|-2.5| > \frac{3}{2}$.

Try It **Copy and complete the statement using <, >, or =.**

4. $|9|$ ▭ $|-9|$
5. $-\left|\frac{1}{2}\right|$ ▭ $-\frac{1}{4}$
6. 7 ▭ $-|-4.5|$

Self-Assessment *for Concepts & Skills*

Solve each exercise. Then rate your understanding of the success criteria in your journal.

7. **VOCABULARY** Which of the following numbers are integers?

$$9, 3.2, -1, \frac{1}{2}, -0.25, 15$$

8. **VOCABULARY** What is the absolute value of a number?

COMPARING RATIONAL NUMBERS **Copy and complete the statement using <, >, or =. Use a number line to justify your answer.**

9. 3.5 ▭ $\left|-\frac{7}{2}\right|$
10. $\left|\frac{11}{4}\right|$ ▭ $|-2.8|$

11. **WRITING** You compare two numbers, a and b. Explain how $a > b$ and $|a| < |b|$ can both be true statements.

12. **WHICH ONE DOESN'T BELONG?** Which expression does *not* belong with the other three? Explain your reasoning.

$\lvert 6\rvert$	6	-6	$\lvert -6\rvert$

EXAMPLE 3 Modeling Real Life

A moon has an ocean underneath its icy surface. Scientists run tests above and below the surface. The table shows the elevations of each test. Which test is deepest? Which test is closest to the surface?

Test	Temperature	Salinity	Atmosphere	Organics	Ice
Elevation (miles)	−3.8	−5.15	0.3	−4.5	−0.25

To determine which test is deepest, find the least elevation. Graph the elevations on a vertical number line.

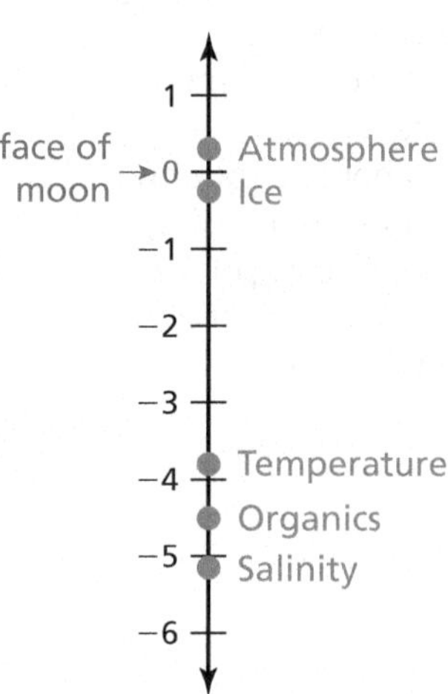

The number line shows that the salinity test is deepest. The number line also shows that the atmosphere test and the ice test are closest to the surface. To determine which is closer to the surface, identify which elevation has a lesser absolute value.

Atmosphere: $|0.3| = 0.3$ **Ice:** $|-0.25| = 0.25$

So, the salinity test is deepest and the ice test is closest to the surface.

Self-Assessment for Problem Solving

Solve each exercise. Then rate your understanding of the success criteria in your journal.

13. An airplane is at an elevation of 5.5 miles. A submarine is at an elevation of −10.9 kilometers. Which is closer to sea level? Explain.

14. The image shows the corrective powers (in *diopters*) of contact lenses for eight people. The farther the number of diopters is from 0, the greater the power of the lens. Positive diopters correct *farsightedness* and negative diopters correct *nearsightedness*. Who is the most nearsighted? the most farsighted? Who has the best eyesight?

Patient	1	2	3	4	5	6	7	8
Power (diopters)	−1.25	0.75	2.5	−3.75	−2.5	−4.75	−7.5	1.5

Laurie's Notes

EXAMPLE 3

- **FYI:** This example is based on Jupiter's moon, Europa. The tests mentioned are fictitious, but NASA is planning a mission to Europa and other moons in the 2030s. Europa is particularly interesting because its surface seems to be covered with ice, leading scientists to believe there is an ocean beneath the surface. At Europa's equator, the warmest temperature is −260°F. At its poles, the warmest temperature is −370°F.
- Pose the problem. Ask students to work with a partner to plot the temperatures on a vertical number line.

? "Why does a vertical number line make sense for this problem?" The numbers refer to elevations above and below the surface of the moon.

- Ask students to explain how the number line helps them answer the questions about greatest and least depths.

Self-Assessment for Problem Solving

- The goal for all students is to feel comfortable with the problem-solving plan. It is important for students to problem-solve in class, where they may receive support from you and their peers. Keep in mind that some students may only be ready to understand the problem.
- Students should work independently on these exercises or in small groups. Circulate and listen to discussions. Support students with probing questions and by providing feedback.

? **Probing Questions:** "What resources do you have available? How can a number line help you? Do your answers make sense? Can you check your solution?"

- Coach students not to solve the problem for their peers. Model what guided questions sound like.
- Before asking volunteers to share their answers for Exercise 14, ask students to share any information they know about nearsightedness and farsightedness.
- Students are again asked to rate their understanding of the success criteria. It is important for students to know what they are learning, where they are in their learning, and what steps are next. The success criteria help students assess their progress.

The Success Criteria Self-Assessment chart can be found in the *Student Journal* or online at *BigIdeasMath.com*.

Closure

- The freezing point of vinegar is −2°C and the freezing point of honey is −3°C. Is the freezing point of vinegar or honey closer to the freezing point of water, 0°C? Explain your reasoning. vinegar; Because $|-2| < |-3|$, the freezing point of vinegar is closer to 0°C, the freezing point of water.

Extra Example 3

The table shows the temperatures recorded at the same location each day for several days. On which day is the temperature coldest? On which day is the temperature closest to the freezing point of water, 0°C?

Day	Temperature (°C)
Monday	−3.5
Tuesday	3.4
Wednesday	−2.1
Thursday	−4.6

Thursday; Wednesday

Self-Assessment for Problem Solving

13. airplane; $|5.5| < |-10.9|$

14. 7; 3; 2

Learning Target

Understand absolute values and ordering of rational numbers.

Success Criteria

- Graph rational numbers on a number line.
- Find the absolute value of a rational number.
- Use a number line to compare rational numbers.

Review & Refresh

1. 6:4
2. 4:6
3. 4:10
4. 10:6
5. 4
6. 6
7. 7
8. 24

Concepts, Skills, & Problem Solving

9. 4; -6; *Sample answer:* 4 is farther right, $|-6| > |4|$
10. $\frac{7}{2}$; $\frac{7}{2}$; *Sample answer:* $\frac{7}{2}$ is farther right, $\left|\frac{7}{2}\right| > |-3.25|$
11. $-\frac{4}{5}$; -1.3; *Sample answer:* $-\frac{4}{5}$ is farther right, $|-1.3| > \left|-\frac{4}{5}\right|$
12. 8
13. 2
14. 10
15. 10
16. 0
17. $\frac{1}{3}$
18. $\frac{7}{8}$
19. $\frac{5}{9}$
20. $\frac{11}{8}$
21. 3.8
22. 5.3
23. $\frac{15}{4}$
24. 7.64
25. 18.26
26. $4\frac{2}{5}$
27. $5\frac{1}{6}$
28. $<$
29. $<$
30. $=$
31. $>$
32. $<$
33. $<$
34. $<$
35. $>$
36. $>$
37. no; The absolute value of a number cannot be negative.
38. yes; $\frac{4}{5} > -\frac{1}{2}$

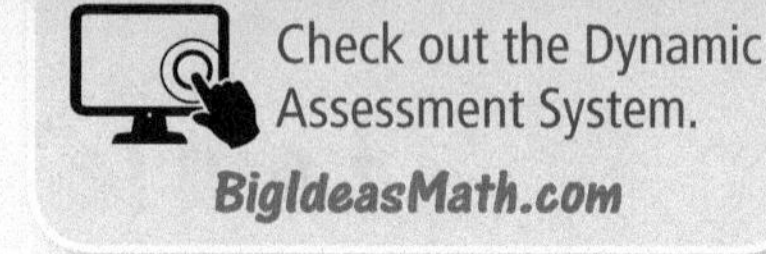
Check out the Dynamic Assessment System.
BigIdeasMath.com

Assignment Guide and Concept Check

Scaffold assignments to support all students in their learning progression. The suggested assignments are a starting point. Continue to assign additional exercises and revisit with spaced practice to move every student toward proficiency.

Level	Assignment 1	Assignment 2
Emerging	4, 8, 9, 13, 15, 17, 25, 29, 31, 33, 37, 38	11, 27, 35, 40, 41, 42, 47
Proficient	4, 8, 10, 12, 16, 20, 22, 30, 32, 34, 37, 38	11, 36, 39, 40, 41, 44, 46, 51
Advanced	4, 8, 11, 16, 24, 27, 30, 33, 36, 37, 38	39, 45, 46, 47, 48, 49, 50, 51

- Assignment 1 is for use after students complete the Self-Assessment for Concepts & Skills.
- Assignment 2 is for use after students complete the Self-Assessment for Problem Solving.
- The red exercises can be used as a concept check.

Review & Refresh Prior Skills

Exercises 1–4 Writing Ratios
Exercises 5–8 Finding the GCF

Common Errors

- **Exercises 12–27** Students may think that the absolute value of a number is its opposite. For example, they may think $|6| = -6$. Use a number line to show students that the absolute value is a number's distance from 0, so it is always a positive number or zero.
- **Exercises 28–36** When comparing absolute values of negative numbers, students may not find the absolute values and instead compare the numbers themselves.
- **Exercises 34–36** Students may misinterpret the opposite of an absolute value as the absolute value of the opposite. For example, they may think $-|4.7| = |-4.7|$, so $-|4.7| = 4.7$. Remind students to use the order of operations and that absolute value bars are a grouping symbol.

A.1 Practice

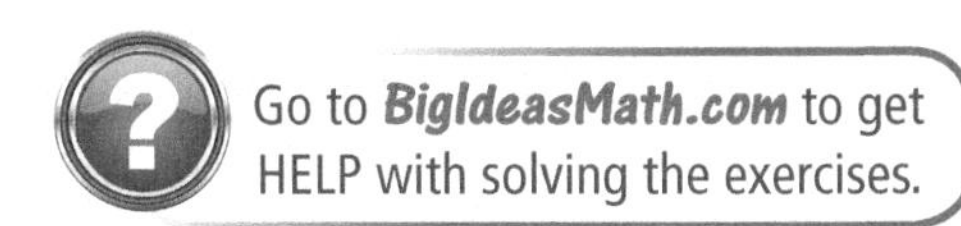
Go to BigIdeasMath.com to get HELP with solving the exercises.

Review & Refresh

Write the ratio.

1. deer to bears
2. bears to deer
3. bears to animals
4. animals to deer

Find the GCF of the numbers.

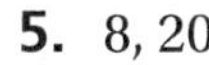

5. 8, 20   6. 12, 30   7. 7, 28   8. 48, 72

Concepts, Skills, & Problem Solving

MP NUMBER SENSE **Determine which number is greater and which number is farther from 0. Explain your reasoning.** (See Exploration 1, p. 503.)

9. $4, -6$ 10. $-3.25, \frac{7}{2}$ 11. $-\frac{4}{5}, -1.3$

FINDING ABSOLUTE VALUES **Find the absolute value.**

12. $|8|$ 13. $|-2|$ 14. $|-10|$ 15. $|10|$

16. $|0|$ 17. $\left|\frac{1}{3}\right|$ 18. $\left|\frac{7}{8}\right|$ 19. $\left|-\frac{5}{9}\right|$

20. $\left|\frac{11}{8}\right|$ 21. $|3.8|$ 22. $|-5.3|$ 23. $\left|-\frac{15}{4}\right|$

24. $|7.64|$ 25. $|-18.26|$ 26. $\left|4\frac{2}{5}\right|$ 27. $\left|-5\frac{1}{6}\right|$

COMPARING RATIONAL NUMBERS **Copy and complete the statement using <, >, or =.**

28. $2 \;\square\; |-5|$ 29. $|-1| \;\square\; |-8|$ 30. $|5| \;\square\; |-5|$

31. $|-2| \;\square\; 0$ 32. $0.4 \;\square\; \left|-\frac{7}{8}\right|$ 33. $|4.9| \;\square\; |-5.3|$

34. $-|4.7| \;\square\; \frac{1}{2}$ 35. $\left|-\frac{3}{4}\right| \;\square\; -\left|\frac{3}{4}\right|$ 36. $-\left|1\frac{1}{4}\right| \;\square\; -\left|-1\frac{3}{8}\right|$

MP YOU BE THE TEACHER **Your friend compares two rational numbers. Is your friend correct? Explain your reasoning.**

37. $|-10| = -10$

38. $\left|-\frac{4}{5}\right| > -\left|\frac{1}{2}\right|$

39. OPEN-ENDED Write a negative number whose absolute value is greater than 3.

40. MP **MODELING REAL LIFE** The *summit elevation* of a volcano is the elevation of the top of the volcano relative to sea level. The summit elevation of Kilauea, a volcano in Hawaii, is 1277 meters. The summit elevation of Loihi, an underwater volcano in Hawaii, is −969 meters. Which summit is higher? Which summit is closer to sea level?

41. MP **MODELING REAL LIFE** The *freezing point* of a liquid is the temperature at which the liquid becomes a solid.

a. Which liquid in the table has the lowest freezing point?

b. Is the freezing point of mercury or butter closer to the freezing point of water, 0°C?

Liquid	Freezing Point (°C)
Butter	35
Airplane fuel	−53
Honey	−3
Mercury	−39
Candle wax	53

ORDERING RATIONAL NUMBERS Order the values from least to greatest.

42. $8, |3|, -5, |-2|, -2$

43. $|-6.3|, -7.2, 8, |5|, -6.3$

44. $|3.5|, |-1.8|, 4.6, 3\frac{2}{5}, |2.7|$

45. $\left|-\frac{3}{4}\right|, \frac{5}{8}, \left|\frac{1}{4}\right|, -\frac{1}{2}, \left|-\frac{7}{8}\right|$

46. MP **PROBLEM SOLVING** The table shows golf scores, relative to *par*.

a. The player with the lowest score wins. Which player wins?

b. Which player is closest to par?

c. Which player is farthest from par?

Player	Score
1	+5
2	0
3	−4
4	−1
5	+2

47. **DIG DEEPER!** You use the table below to record the temperature at the same location each hour for several hours. At what time is the temperature coldest? At what time is the temperature closest to the freezing point of water, 0°C?

Time	10:00 A.M.	11:00 A.M.	12:00 P.M.	1:00 P.M.	2:00 P.M.	3:00 P.M.
Temperature (°C)	−2.6	−2.7	−0.15	1.6	−1.25	−3.4

MP **REASONING Determine whether $n \geq 0$ or $n \leq 0$.**

48. $n + |-n| = 2n$

49. $n + |-n| = 0$

TRUE OR FALSE? Determine whether the statement is *true* or *false*. Explain your reasoning.

50. If $x < 0$, then $|x| = -x$.

51. The absolute value of every rational number is positive.

Mini-Assessment

Find the absolute value.

1. $|16|$ 16
2. $\left|-7\frac{1}{3}\right|$ $7\frac{1}{3}$

Copy and complete the statement using <, >, or =.

3. $|-11|$ ▢ 11 $|-11| = 11$
4. $-\left|-\frac{1}{2}\right|$ ▢ $\left|-\frac{5}{6}\right|$ $-\left|-\frac{1}{2}\right| < \left|-\frac{5}{6}\right|$
5. The table shows the locations of several fish, relative to sea level. Which fish in the table is at the greatest depth? Which fish is closest to sea level?

Fish	Location (meters)
Parrotfish	−3.8
Flying fish	3.2
Mackerel	−10.7
Grouper	−5.4

mackerel; flying fish

Section Resources

Surface Level	Deep Level
Resources by Chapter • Extra Practice • Reteach • Puzzle Time Student Journal • Self-Assessment • Practice Differentiating the Lesson Tutorial Videos Skills Review Handbook Skills Trainer	Resources by Chapter • Enrichment and Extension Graphic Organizers Dynamic Assessment System • Section Practice

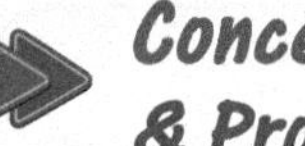

Concepts, Skills, & Problem Solving

39. *Sample answer:* -4
40. Kilauea; Loihi
41. **a.** airplane fuel
    b. butter
42. $-5, -2, |-2|, |3|, 8$
43. $-7.2, -6.3, |5|, |-6.3|, 8$
44. $|-1.8|, |2.7|, 3\frac{2}{5}, |3.5|, 4.6$
45. $-\frac{1}{2}, \left|\frac{1}{4}\right|, \frac{5}{8}, \left|-\frac{3}{4}\right|, \left|-\frac{7}{8}\right|$
46. **a.** Player 3
    b. Player 2
    c. Player 1
47. 3:00 P.M.; 12:00 P.M.
48. $n \geq 0$
49. $n \leq 0$
50. true; If a number x is negative, then its absolute value is its opposite, $-x$.
51. false; The absolute value of zero is zero, which is neither positive nor negative.

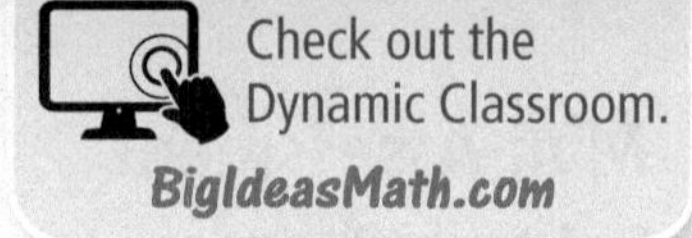
Check out the
Dynamic Classroom.
BigIdeasMath.com

Learning Target

Find sums of integers.

Success Criteria

- Explain how to model addition of integers on a number line.
- Find sums of integers by reasoning about absolute values.
- Explain why the sum of a number and its opposite is 0.

Warm Up

Cumulative, vocabulary, and prerequisite skills practice opportunities are available in the *Resources by Chapter* or at *BigIdeasMath.com.*

ELL Support

Students with beginner language proficiency may confuse homophones, such as *sum* and *some*. Explain the differences. Students may be familiar with the word *model* as a person who wears clothing to show how it looks when worn. Explain that the word *model* can also be used to represent other things visually, such as modeling with clay or modeling a mathematical process.

Exploration 1

a. *Sample answer:* Use integer counters to represent each number; Use the same number of positive and negative counters.

b. $-3 + 2$; -1

c–e. See Additional Answers.

Laurie's Notes

Preparing to Teach

- In this lesson, students will use color integer counters to develop a conceptual understanding of integer addition.
- **Look for and Express Regularity in Repeated Reasoning:** Mathematically proficient students will observe that when the signs are the same, it is a combining process and the sum has the same sign. When the signs are different, it is a combining process *and* you remove some zero pairs.

Motivate

- "What is the net result of an 8-yard loss in football followed by a 10-yard gain?" a 2-yard gain
- "What is the net result of scoring 25 points in a video game and then losing 40 points?" a loss of 15 points
- Tell students that today's exploration is about how integers are added.

Exploration 1

- If this is students' first experience with integer counters, define a yellow counter as positive 1 (+1) and a red counter as negative 1 (−1).
- Counters of opposite color "neutralize" each other, so the net result of such a pair is zero. This is called a *zero pair*.
- **Model:** Show students that there are many ways to model a single integer. For example, the number 2 can be represented by two yellow counters or by three yellow counters with one red counter (2 plus 1 zero pair).
- **Teaching Tip:** Store integer counters in self-locking bags. Put 15–20 counters in each bag for quick distribution.
- Students should use counters even if they say they know the answer.
- In the second exercise of part (c), tell students that the use of parentheses around the integer −3 is for clarity. Although it is not mathematically necessary, it helps to avoid confusion between the negative sign and a subtraction operation. Sometimes people write $-4 + {}^{-}3$, with a raised negative sign to avoid confusion.
- **Attend to Precision:** Students should use correct language in reading the problems. They should say, "Negative 3 plus 2 equals negative 1." If students say "minus 3," remind students that minus is an operation.
- Students should work with partners to complete the table. It is important for students to record the *Type of Sum*.
- The reasoning that students use to answer parts (d) and (e) provides insight into their understanding of the two types of addition problems: integers with the same sign and integers with different signs.
- **Quick Check:** Have students raise their hands if the statement is true.
  - The answer to $-10 + 5$ is a positive number. false
  - The answer to $-6 + 12$ is a positive number. true
  - The answer to $11 + (-11)$ is a negative number. false

A.2 Adding Integers

Learning Target: Find sums of integers.

Success Criteria:
- I can explain how to model addition of integers on a number line.
- I can find sums of integers by reasoning about absolute values.
- I can explain why the sum of a number and its opposite is 0.

EXPLORATION 1 Using Integer Counters to Find Sums

+ = +1
− = −1

Work with a partner. You can use the integer counters shown at the left to find sums of integers.

a. How can you use integer counters to model a sum? a sum that equals 0?

b. What expression is being modeled below? What is the value of the sum?

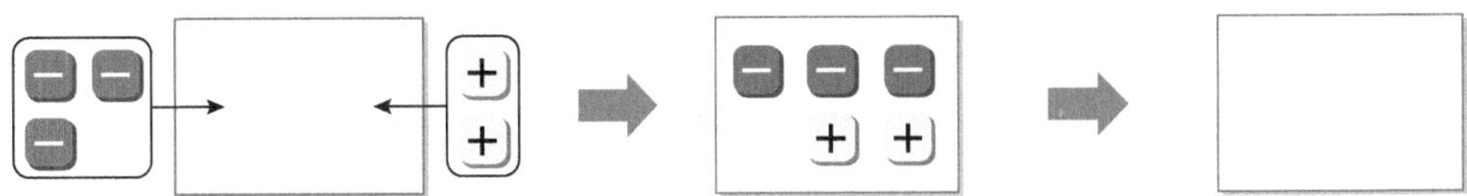

c. **INDUCTIVE REASONING** Use integer counters to complete the table.

Expression	Type of Sum	Sum	Sum: Positive, Negative, or Zero
$-3 + 2$	Integers with different signs		
$-4 + (-3)$			
$5 + (-3)$			
$7 + (-7)$			
$2 + 4$			
$-6 + (-2)$			
$-5 + 9$			
$15 + (-9)$			
$-10 + 10$			
$-6 + (-6)$			
$13 + (-13)$			

d. How can you tell whether the sum of two integers is *positive*, *negative*, or *zero*?

e. Write rules for adding (i) two integers with the same sign, (ii) two integers with different signs, and (iii) two opposite integers.

Math Practice

Make Conjectures

How can absolute values be used to write a rule about the sum of two integers?

A.2 Lesson

Key Vocabulary
additive inverse, *p. 511*

You have used number lines to find sums of positive numbers, which involve movement to the right. Now you will find sums with negative numbers, which involve movement to the left.

EXAMPLE 1 Using Number Lines to Find Sums

The length of each arrow is the absolute value of the number it represents.

a. Find $4 + (-4)$.

Draw an arrow from 0 to 4 to represent 4. Then draw an arrow 4 units to the left to represent adding -4.

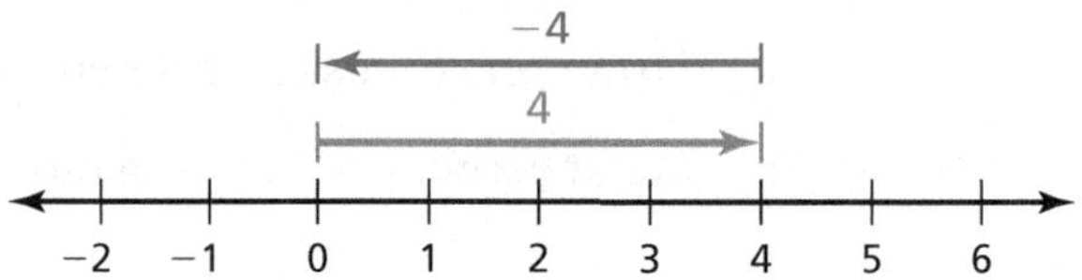

So, $4 + (-4) = 0$.

b. Find $-1 + (-3)$.

Draw an arrow from 0 to -1 to represent -1. Then draw an arrow 3 units to the left to represent adding -3.

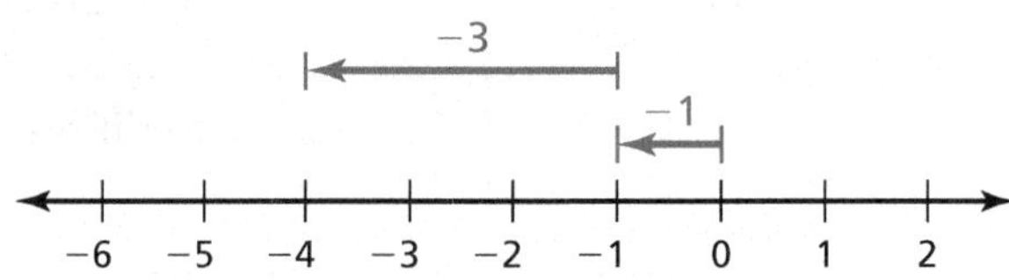

So, $-1 + (-3) = -4$.

c. Find $-2 + 6$.

Draw an arrow from 0 to -2 to represent -2. Then draw an arrow 6 units to the right to represent adding 6.

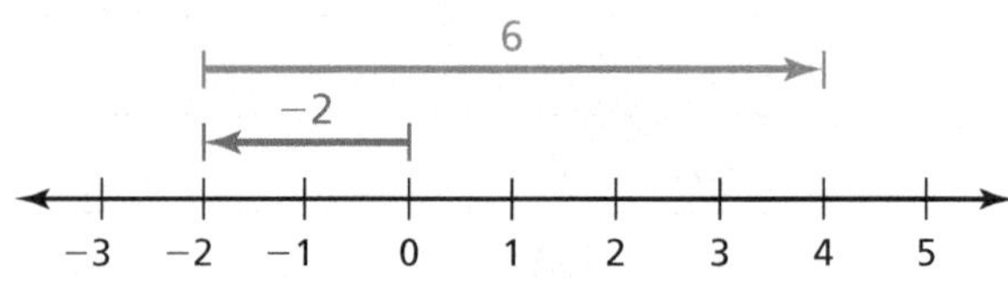

So, $-2 + 6 = 4$.

Try It **Use a number line to find the sum.**

1. $-2 + 2$ **2.** $4 + (-5)$ **3.** $-3 + (-3)$

 Multi-Language Glossary at BigIdeasMath.com

Laurie's Notes

Scaffolding Instruction

- Students explored using integer counters to find sums of two integers and to write the rules for adding integers. Now students will extend this understanding to find sums of integers using number lines and the rules for adding integers.
- **Emerging:** Students may struggle with the process of adding integers. Provide guided instruction for the examples. These students may benefit from using number lines and integer counters to visualize the process.
- **Proficient:** Students observe that when the signs are the same, you "just add" and keep the sign. When the signs are different, the strategy is different. Have students review the Key Ideas to clarify the rules for each type, paying close attention to the Additive Inverse Property. Then have students proceed to the Self-Assessment for Concepts & Skills exercises.

Scaffold instruction to support all students in their learning. Learning is individualized and you may want to group students differently as they move in and out of these levels with each skill and concept. Student self-assessment and feedback help guide your instructional decisions about how and when to layer support for all students to become proficient learners.

EXAMPLE 1

- Work through each part as shown.
- Remind students that the first number is represented on the number line by an arrow starting at 0. The second number starts at the end of that arrow.
- The goal is to develop some understanding about the two types of addition problems: integers with the same sign and integers with different signs.

  ? "When do the arrows go in the same direction on the number line?" when the integers have the same sign

  ? "When do the arrows go in different directions?" when the integers have different signs

  ? "How do you know if the sum is positive or negative?" If the second arrow ends to the right of 0 on the number line, the sum is positive. If the second arrow ends to the left of 0 on the number line, the sum is negative.

Extra Example 1

a. Find $2 + (-2)$. 0

b. Find $-3 + (-12)$. -15

c. Find $-5 + 7$. 2

Try It

- Have students complete the exercises independently and then share their work on whiteboards. If students are struggling, have them use integer counters to demonstrate.

Try It

1. 0

2. -1

3. -6

Laurie's Notes

Key Idea

- Write the first Key Idea on the board.
- **Model:** As you discuss the first Key Idea, ask half the students to model $2 + 5$ using integer counters and the other half to model using number lines. Repeat for $-2 + (-5)$.
  - When the signs are the *same*, the counters will be the *same color*.
  - When the signs are the *same*, both arrows will be going in the same *direction*.
- Write the second Key Idea on the board.
- **? Construct Viable Arguments and Critique the Reasoning of Others:** "When you add two integers with different signs, how do you know if the sum is positive or negative?" Students answered a similar question in Example 1, but now they should be using the concept of absolute value, even if they don't use the precise language. You want to hear something about the size of the number, meaning its absolute value.
- **? Look for and Make Use of Structure:** Write these problems on the board: $14 + (-8) = ?$ and $(-14) + 8 = ?$. Ask, "How are these problems alike? How are they different?" *Sample answers:* They each use the numbers 14 and 8, and both consist of two different signs being added together; In the first problem, 14 is positive and 8 is negative. In the second problem, 14 is negative and 8 is positive.
- Write the third Key Idea on the board. This is a special case of adding integers with different signs.
- **Model:** Ask half the students to model $6 + (-6)$ using integer counters and the other half to model using number lines. Repeat for $-6 + 6$.
  - ? "What happens with the integer counters when finding the sum of additive inverses?" Zero pairs are formed with no counters left over.
  - ? "What happens on the number line?" The second arrow ends at 0 on the number line.

EXAMPLE 2

- **Teaching Tip:** You can complete this example after discussing the first Key Idea, or after discussing all of the Key Ideas.
- If the students seem to have grasped the concepts of adding integers with the same sign, they can go directly to Try It Exercises 4–6 to assess their understanding. If students need more instruction, ask volunteers to explain how $-4 + (-2)$ is computed and modeled.

Try It

- Have students complete the exercises on whiteboards and then share their work with the class.
- If students are not getting correct answers, ask volunteers to demonstrate the problems using integer counters and number lines.

Extra Example 2

Find $-5 + (-3)$. -8

ELL Support

Have students practice language by working in pairs to complete Try It Exercises 4–6. Expect students to perform as follows.

Beginner: Write the answer.

Intermediate: State the answer. For example, "twenty."

Advanced: Explain using a sentence. For example, "The sum of seven and thirteen is twenty."

Try It

4. 20
5. -13
6. -17

Using integer counters and number lines leads to the following rules for adding integers.

Key Ideas

Adding Integers with the Same Sign

Words Add the absolute values of the integers. Then use the common sign.

Numbers $2 + 5 = 7$ $\quad -2 + (-5) = -7$

Adding Integers with Different Signs

Words Subtract the lesser absolute value from the greater absolute value. Then use the sign of the integer with the greater absolute value.

Numbers $8 + (-10) = -2$ $\quad -13 + 17 = 4$

Additive Inverse Property

Words The sum of a number and its **additive inverse,** or opposite, is 0.

Numbers $6 + (-6) = 0$ $\quad -25 + 25 = 0$

Algebra $a + (-a) = 0$

Math Practice

Justify Conclusions

Use a number line to justify the rule for adding integers with the same sign.

Notice that Example 1(a) shows the Additive Inverse Property.

EXAMPLE 2 Adding Integers with the Same Sign

Find $-4 + (-2)$.

$-4 + (-2) = -6$ Add $|-4|$ and $|-2|$.

Use the common sign.

The sum is -6.

Check Use integer counters.

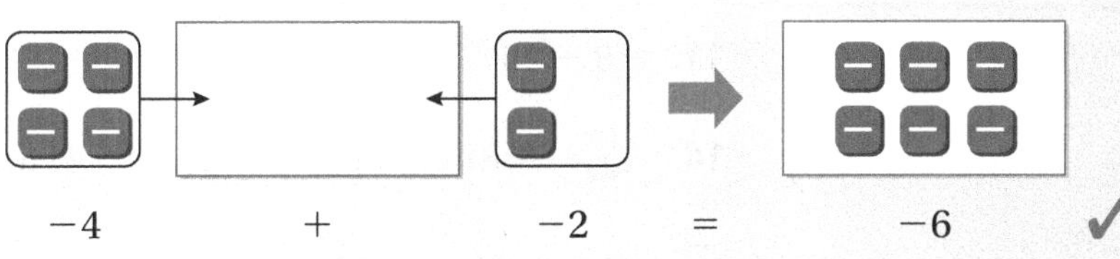

Try It **Find the sum.**

4. $7 + 13$ **5.** $-8 + (-5)$ **6.** $-2 + (-15)$

EXAMPLE 3 Adding Integers with Different Signs

a. Find $5 + (-10)$.

$5 + (-10) = -5$ $\quad$ $|-10| > |5|$. So, subtract $|5|$ from $|-10|$.

Use the sign of -10.

The sum is -5.

b. Find $-3 + 7$.

$-3 + 7 = 4$ $\quad$ $|7| > |-3|$. So, subtract $|-3|$ from $|7|$.

Use the sign of 7.

The sum is 4.

c. Find $-12 + 12$.

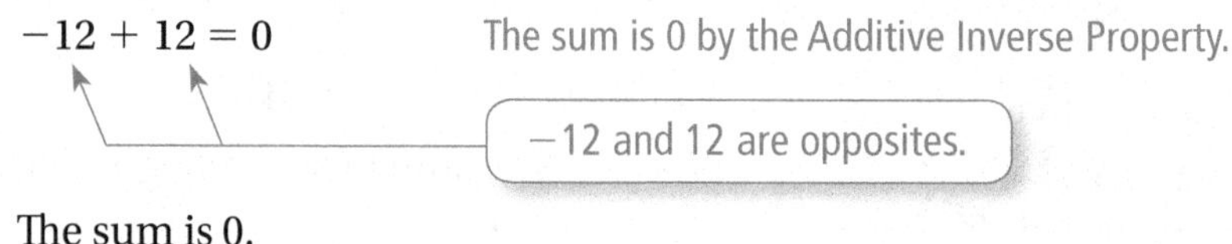

−12 + 12 = 0
The sum is 0 by the Additive Inverse Property.
−12 and 12 are opposites.

The sum is 0.

Try It Find the sum.

7. $-2 + 11$ **8.** $9 + (-10)$ **9.** $-31 + 31$

Self-Assessment for Concepts & Skills

Solve each exercise. Then rate your understanding of the success criteria in your journal.

10. **WRITING** Explain how to use a number line to find the sum of two integers.

ADDING INTEGERS **Find the sum. Use a number line to justify your answer.**

11. $-8 + 20$ **12.** $30 + (-30)$ **13.** $-10 + (-18)$

14. MP **NUMBER SENSE** Is $3 + (-4)$ the same as $-4 + 3$? Explain.

MP **LOGIC** **Tell whether the statement is *true* or *false*. Explain your reasoning.**

15. The sum of two negative integers is always negative.

16. The sum of an integer and its absolute value is always 0.

Laurie's Notes

EXAMPLE 3

- **Teaching Tip:** You can complete this example after discussing the second and third Key Ideas or after discussing all of the Key Ideas.
- In part (a), because 5 has the lesser absolute value, you subtract it from the absolute value of -10. In general, use the sign of the number with the greater absolute value. In this case, the answer will be negative.
- **Model:** Be sure students understand that the subtraction of the two absolute values is connected to the zero pairs that are removed when using integer counters, or it is the overlapping distance when a number line is used.
- If the students seem to have grasped the concepts of adding integers with different signs, they can go directly to Try It Exercises 7–9 to assess their understanding.

Try It

- Have students complete the exercises on whiteboards and then share for a quick check of understanding.
- If students are not getting correct answers, ask volunteers to demonstrate the problems using integer counters and number lines.

Self-Assessment for Concepts & Skills

- Students should use these examples to assess their progress with all three success criteria.
- Discuss Exercise 10 by asking a volunteer to share his or her thinking. Ask others to critique or clarify the explanation.
- For Exercise 14, have students stand if they agree. Select a standing student to explain.
- Exercises 15 and 16 provide a quick check of students' understanding. After students complete Exercise 15, have them write T or F on whiteboards. Solicit explanations. Repeat for Exercise 16.
- If time permits, you can ask students to solve a problem such as $47 + (-58)$. Clearly, you do not want to model this with integer counters. Students should be able to describe the strategy of putting 47 yellow and 58 red together. There will be 47 zero pairs with 11 red counters remaining, representing a sum of -11.

The Success Criteria Self-Assessment chart can be found in the *Student Journal* or online at *BigIdeasMath.com*.

Extra Example 3

a. Find $-11 + 6$. -5

b. Find $12 + (-5)$. 7

c. Find $9 + (-9)$. 0

Try It

7. 9

8. -1

9. 0

ELL Support

Allow students to work in pairs on Self-Assessment for Concepts & Skills Exercises 11–13. Check comprehension by asking each pair to display their answers on a whiteboard for your review. Have pairs discuss and answer Exercises 10 and 14–16 and then compare their answers with another pair. Each group should come to agreement if their answers differ. Monitor discussions and provide support.

Self-Assessment for Concepts & Skills

10. Draw an arrow from zero to the first integer. Draw a second arrow from the first integer the length of the absolute value of the second integer toward the right if it is positive or toward the left if it is negative.

11–13. See Additional Answers.

14. yes; The sums are the same by the Commutative Property of Addition.

15. true; To add integers with the same sign, add the absolute values and use the common sign.

16. false; The sum of a positive integer and its absolute value is double the integer.

Laurie's Notes

Discuss

- Review the properties of addition (associative, commutative, zero) from Chapter 5. Explain to students that these rules also apply to integers.
- **Make Sense of Problems and Persevere in Solving Them:** Ask students to explain what a withdrawal and a deposit mean in banking. A *deposit* is when you add money to an account, and a *withdrawal* is when you take money out of an account. Checkbooks are one context where addition of opposites occurs. Depositing $100 and writing a check for $100 results in a zero change in the balance.

EXAMPLE 4

- Work through the example as shown.
- ? "Can you think of another way to write the sum?" Students may state several correct sums. Continue asking, "Is there another way?" until grouping the deposits and grouping the withdrawals surfaces.
- ? "What is the advantage of writing the sum as $(-40) + 75 + 50 + (-50)$?" 50 and -50 are opposites, so their sum is 0.

Self-Assessment for Problem Solving

- Allow time in class for students to practice using the problem-solving plan. Remember, some students may only be able to complete the first step.
- Have students work with a partner. Assign half the class Exercise 17 and the other half Exercise 18. After students finish, select one pair for each problem to explain their answer and reasoning to the class.

The Success Criteria Self-Assessment chart can be found in the *Student Journal* or online at *BigIdeasMath.com.*

Formative Assessment Tip

Exit Ticket

This technique asks students to respond to a question at the end of a lesson, activity, or learning experience. The *Exit Ticket* allows you to collect evidence of student learning. I cut scrap paper into smaller pieces so that "exit tickets" can be distributed quickly to students.

The *Exit Ticket* is helpful in planning instruction. During the class there may be students you have not heard from. They may not have raised their hands, or they may have been less vocal when working with partners. The *Exit Ticket* helps you gauge the ability of all students to answer a particular type of question. Collect the *Exit Tickets* and use the responses to inform subsequent instruction.

Closure

- **Exit Ticket:** Two integers have different signs. Their sum is -8. What are possible values for the two integers? *Sample answer:* -9 and 1

Extra Example 4

The list shows account transactions made in August. Find the change in the account balance for August.

August Transactions	
Deposit	$35
Deposit	$40
Withdrawal	−$25

increased $50

Self-Assessment for Problem Solving

17. 377 lb/in.^{2}

18. 8414 ft

Learning Target

Find sums of integers.

Success Criteria

- Explain how to model addition of integers on a number line.
- Find sums of integers by reasoning about absolute values.
- Explain why the sum of a number and its opposite is 0.

You can use the Commutative and Associative Properties of Addition to find sums of integers.

EXAMPLE 4 Modeling Real Life

The list shows four account transactions. Find the change in the account balance.

JULY TRANSACTIONS	
Withdrawal	-$40
Deposit	$50
Deposit	$75
Withdrawal	-$50

Understand the problem.

You are given amounts of two withdrawals and two deposits. You are asked to find how much the balance in the account changed.

Make a plan.

Find the sum of the transactions. Notice that 50 and −50 are opposites and combine to make 0. So, use properties of addition to first group those terms.

Solve and check.

$$-40 + 50 + 75 + (-50) = -40 + 75 + 50 + (-50) \quad \text{Comm. Prop. of Add.}$$
$$= -40 + 75 + [50 + (-50)] \quad \text{Assoc. Prop. of Add.}$$
$$= -40 + 75 + 0 \quad \text{Add. Inv. Prop.}$$
$$= 35 + 0 \quad \text{Add } -40 \text{ and } 75.$$
$$= 35 \quad \text{Add. Prop. of Zero}$$

So, the account balance increased $35.

Another Method Find the sum by grouping the first two terms and the last two terms.

$$-40 + 50 + 75 + (-50) = (-40 + 50) + [75 + (-50)]$$
$$= 10 + 25 = 35 \checkmark$$

Self-Assessment for Problem Solving

Solve each exercise. Then rate your understanding of the success criteria in your journal.

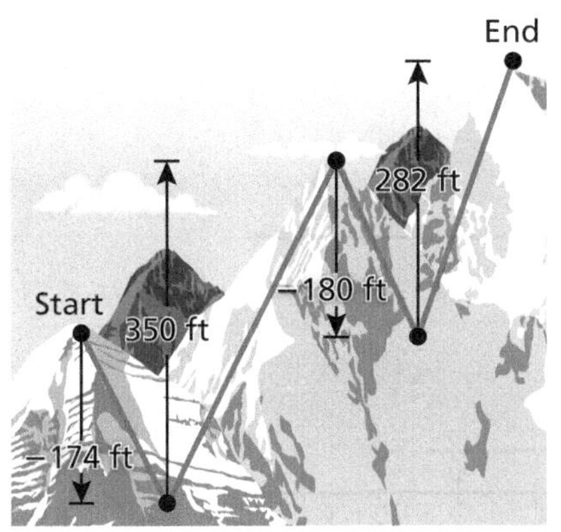

17. At 12:00 P.M., the water pressure on a submarine is 435 pounds per square inch. From 12:00 P.M. to 12:30 P.M., the water pressure increases 58 pounds per square inch. From 12:30 P.M. to 1:00 P.M., the water pressure decreases 116 pounds per square inch. What is the water pressure at 1:00 P.M.?

18. The diagram shows the elevation changes between checkpoints on a trail. The trail begins at an elevation of 8136 feet. What is the elevation at the end of the trail?

A.2 Practice

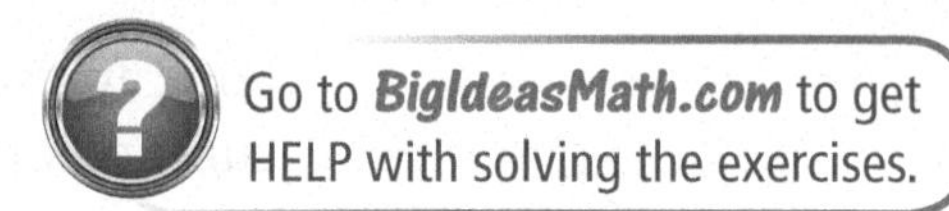

Review & Refresh

Copy and complete the statement using $<$, $>$, or $=$.

1. $5 \ \square \ |-7|$
2. $|-2.6| \ \square \ |-2.06|$
3. $\left|-\frac{3}{5}\right| \ \square \ -\left|\frac{5}{8}\right|$

Add.

4. $8.43 + 5.21$
5. $2.316 + 4.09$
6. $\frac{5}{9} + \frac{3}{9}$
7. $\frac{1}{2} + \frac{1}{8}$
8. The regular price of a photograph printed on a canvas is \$18. You have a coupon for 15% off. How much is the discount?

   A. \$2.70 **B.** \$3 **C.** \$15 **D.** \$15.30

9. Represent the ratio relationship using a graph.

Time (hours)	1	2	3
Distance (miles)	55	110	165

Concepts, Skills, & Problem Solving

USING INTEGER COUNTERS Use integer counters to complete the table. (See Exploration 1, p. 509.)

	Expression	Type of Sum	Sum	Sum: Positive, Negative, or Zero
10.	$-5 + 8$			
11.	$-3 + (-7)$			

USING NUMBER LINES Write an addition expression represented by the number line. Then find the sum.

12.
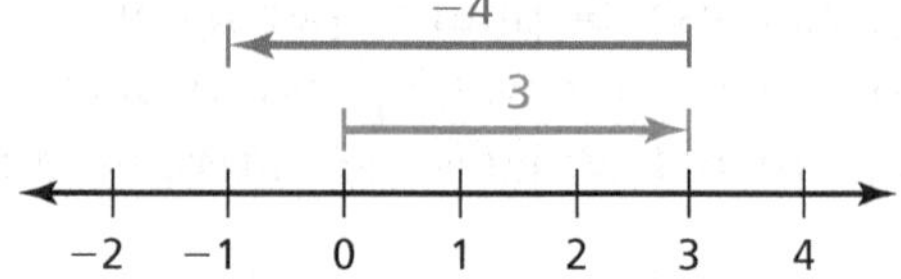

13.
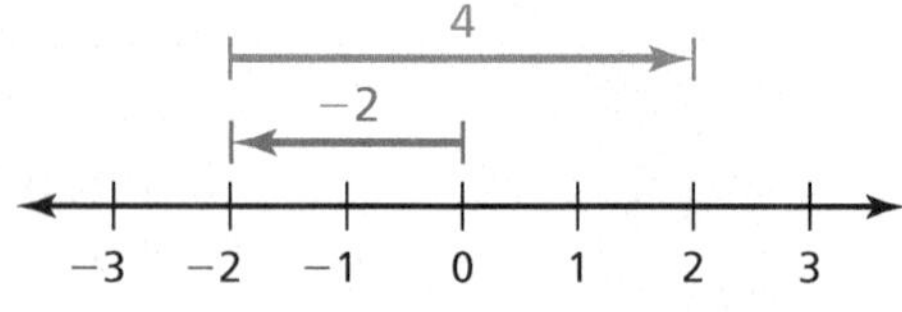

14.
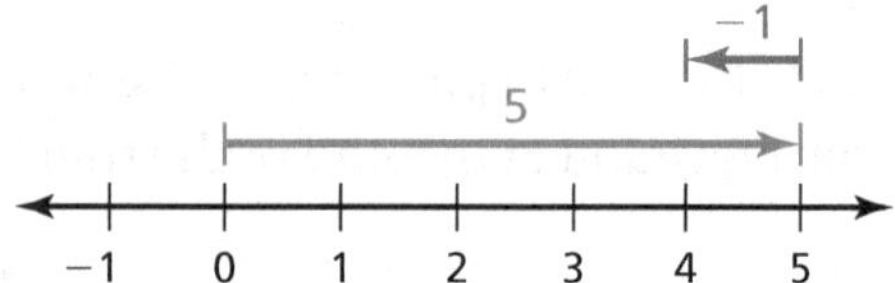

15.
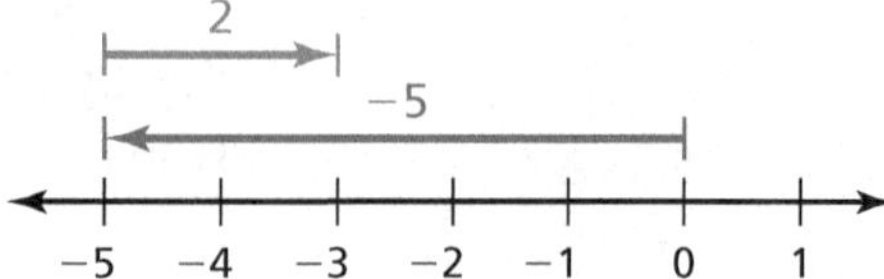

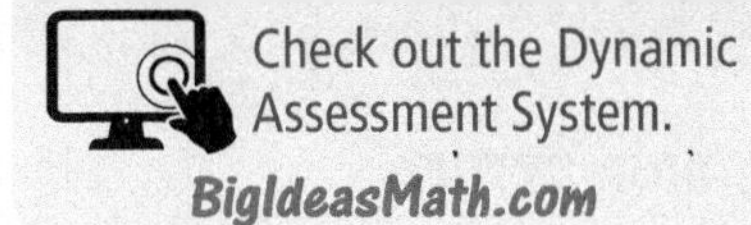

Check out the Dynamic Assessment System.

BigIdeasMath.com

Assignment Guide and Concept Check

Scaffold assignments to support all students in their learning progression. The suggested assignments are a starting point. Continue to assign additional exercises and revisit with spaced practice to move every student toward proficiency.

Level	Assignment 1	Assignment 2
Emerging	3, 5, 7, 8, 9, 10, 12, 17, 19, 21, 32, 39, 45	11, 14, 26, 28, 33, 34, 35, 46, 54, 62, 64
Proficient	3, 5, 7, 8, 9, 10, 13, 22, 24, 30, 32, 40, 46	11, 28, 33, 35, 36, 37, 48, 50, 55, 57, 58, 62, 64
Advanced	3, 5, 7, 8, 9, 10, 14, 26, 28, 30, 32, 42, 48	33, 36, 37, 53, 56, 57, 60, 63, 64, 65, 66

- Assignment 1 is for use after students complete the Self-Assessment for Concepts & Skills.
- Assignment 2 is for use after students complete the Self-Assessment for Problem Solving.
- The red exercises can be used as a concept check.

Review & Refresh Prior Skills

Exercises 1–3 Comparing Rational Numbers
Exercises 4 and 5 Adding Decimals
Exercises 6 and 7 Adding Fractions
Exercise 8 Finding the Percent of a Number
Exercise 9 Graphing Ratios

Review & Refresh

1. <
2. >
3. >
4. 13.64
5. 6.406
6. $\frac{8}{9}$
7. $\frac{5}{8}$
8. A
9. 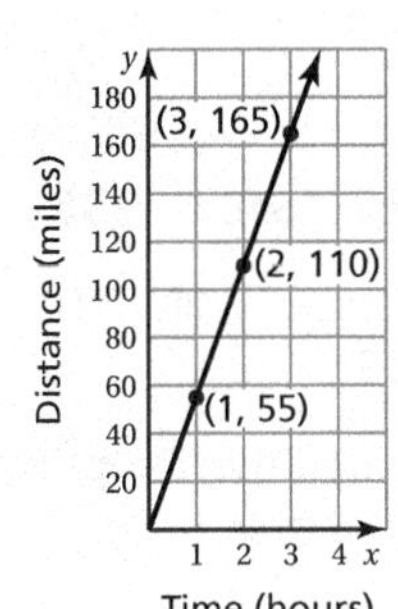

Concepts, Skills, & Problem Solving

10. integers with different signs; 3; positive
11. integers with the same sign; -10; negative
12. $3 + (-4); -1$
13. $(-2) + 4; 2$
14. $5 + (-1); 4$
15. $-5 + 2; -3$

Concepts, Skills, & Problem Solving

16. 10 **17.** -10

18. -5 **19.** 7

20. -2 **21.** 0

22. -2 **23.** 10

24. -20 **25.** -4

26. 9 **27.** -11

28. -25 **29.** -4

30. 0 **31.** -34

32. yes; The sum is correct.

33. no; $-10 + (-10) = -20$

34. 18°F **35.** \$48 **36.** 0

37. *Sample answer:* $-26 + 1$; $-12 + (-13)$

38. Use the Associative Property to add 6 and -6 first. 9

39. Use the Associative Property to add 13 and -13 first. -8

40. *Sample answer:* Use the Commutative Property to switch the last two terms. -17

41. *Sample answer:* Use the Commutative Property to switch the last two terms. -12

42. *Sample answer:* Use the Commutative Property to switch the last two terms. -2

43. *Sample answer:* Use the Commutative Property to switch the last two terms. 11

44. 8 **45.** -4

46. -4 **47.** 21

48. -7 **49.** -85

50. 3 units to the right of p

51. 7 units to the left of p

52. at p

53. a distance of q units away from p

54. -1 **55.** -3

56. 9

Common Errors

- **Exercises 16–31 and 38–49** Students may ignore the signs and just add the absolute values. Make sure they understand that they should use the sign of the number that is farther from zero. Also remind students of the Key Ideas and how the signs of the integers determine if they need to find the sum or difference of the absolute values.

ADDING INTEGERS **Find the sum. Use integer counters or a number line to verify your answer.**

16. $6 + 4$ **17.** $-4 + (-6)$ **18.** $-2 + (-3)$ **19.** $-5 + 12$

20. $5 + (-7)$ **21.** $8 + (-8)$ **22.** $9 + (-11)$ **23.** $-3 + 13$

24. $-4 + (-16)$ **25.** $-3 + (-1)$ **26.** $14 + (-5)$ **27.** $0 + (-11)$

28. $-10 + (-15)$ **29.** $-13 + 9$ **30.** $18 + (-18)$ **31.** $-25 + (-9)$

MP YOU BE THE TEACHER **Your friend finds the sum. Is your friend correct? Explain your reasoning.**

32. $9 + (-6) = 3$

33. $-10 + (-10) = 0$

34. **MP MODELING REAL LIFE** The temperature is $-3°$F at 7:00 A.M. During the next 4 hours, the temperature increases 21°F. What is the temperature at 11:00 A.M.?

35. **MP MODELING REAL LIFE** Your bank account has a balance of $-\$12$. You deposit \$60. What is your new balance?

Lithium Atom

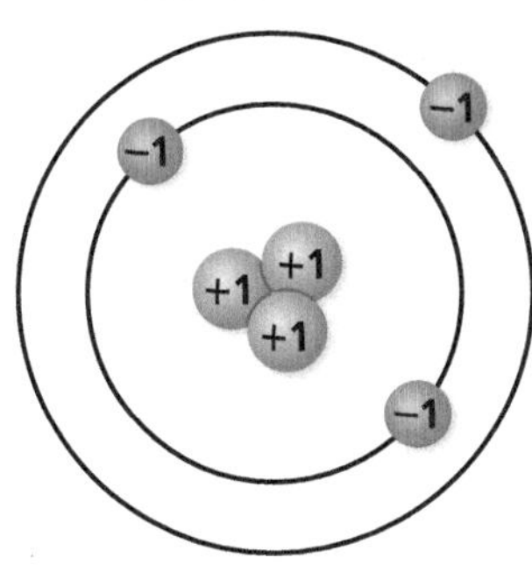

36. **MP PROBLEM SOLVING** A lithium atom has positively charged protons and negatively charged electrons. The sum of the charges represents the charge of the lithium atom. Find the charge of the atom.

37. **OPEN-ENDED** Write two integers with different signs that have a sum of -25. Write two integers with the same sign that have a sum of -25.

USING PROPERTIES **Tell how the Commutative and Associative Properties of Addition can help you find the sum using mental math. Then find the sum.**

38. $9 + 6 + (-6)$ **39.** $-8 + 13 + (-13)$ **40.** $9 + (-17) + (-9)$

41. $7 + (-12) + (-7)$ **42.** $-12 + 25 + (-15)$ **43.** $6 + (-9) + 14$

ADDING INTEGERS **Find the sum.**

44. $13 + (-21) + 16$ **45.** $22 + (-14) + (-12)$ **46.** $-13 + 27 + (-18)$

47. $-19 + 26 + 14$ **48.** $-32 + (-17) + 42$ **49.** $-41 + (-15) + (-29)$

DESCRIBING A SUM **Describe the location of the sum, relative to p, on a number line.**

50. $p + 3$ **51.** $p + (-7)$ **52.** $p + 0$ **53.** $p + q$

ALGEBRA **Evaluate the expression when $a = 4$, $b = -5$, and $c = -8$.**

54. $a + b$ **55.** $-b + c$ **56.** $|a + b + c|$

57. MP **MODELING REAL LIFE** The table shows the income and expenses for a school carnival. The school's goal was to raise \$1100. Did the school reach its goal? Explain.

Games	Concessions	Donations	Flyers	Decorations
\$650	\$530	\$52	−\$28	−\$75

OPEN-ENDED Write a real-life story using the given topic that involves the sum of an integer and its additive inverse.

58. income and expenses

59. the amount of water in a bottle

60. the elevation of a blimp

MENTAL MATH Use mental math to solve the equation.

61. $d + 12 = 2$

62. $b + (-2) = 0$

63. $-8 + m = -15$

64. **DIG DEEPER!** Starting at point *A*, the path of a dolphin jumping out of the water is shown.

a. Is the dolphin deeper at point *C* or point *E*? Explain your reasoning.

b. Is the dolphin higher at point *B* or point *D*? Explain your reasoning.

c. What is the change in elevation of the dolphin from point *A* to point *E*?

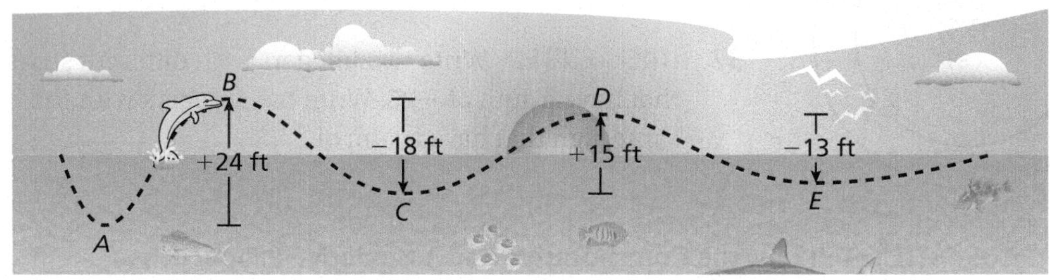

65. MP **NUMBER SENSE** Consider the integers p and q. Describe all of the possible values of p and q for each circumstance. Justify your answers.

a. $p + q = 0$

b. $p + q < 0$

c. $p + q > 0$

66. **PUZZLE** According to a legend, the Chinese Emperor Yu-Huang saw a magic square on the back of a turtle. In a *magic square*, the numbers in each row and in each column have the same sum. This sum is called the *magic sum*.

Copy and complete the magic square so that each row and each column has a magic sum of 0. Use each integer from −4 to 4 exactly once.

Common Errors

- **Exercise 64** Students may not realize that each height measurement is given in reference to the previous point. Tell them to determine the measurement in relation to point A, which would be zero on a number line.

Mini-Assessment

Find the sum.

1. $10 + (-12)$ -2
2. $-7 + (-5)$ -12
3. $-17 + 25$ 8
4. $65 + (-99)$ -34
5. The temperature is −2°F at 6 A.M. During the next three hours, the temperature increases 15°F. What is the temperature at 9 A.M.? 13°F

Section Resources

Surface Level	Deep Level
Resources by Chapter • Extra Practice • Reteach • Puzzle Time Student Journal • Self-Assessment • Practice Differentiating the Lesson Tutorial Videos Skills Review Handbook Skills Trainer	Resources by Chapter • Enrichment and Extension Graphic Organizers Dynamic Assessment System • Section Practice

Concepts, Skills, & Problem Solving

57. yes; $650 + 530 + 52 + (-28) + (-75) = 1129$

58. *Sample answer:* Ticket sales at a professional baseball game generated $2300 in income. The expenses to pay the baseball players was $2300.

59. *Sample answer:* You filled your water bottle with 12 ounces of water this morning and then drank 12 ounces.

60. *Sample answer:* After liftoff of the blimp, it ascended 1300 feet in the air. Two hours later, it descended 1300 feet to the ground.

61. $d = -10$ **62.** $b = 2$

63. $m = -7$

64. **a.** C; E is $15 + (-13) = 2$ higher than C, so C is deeper.

b. B; D is $-18 + 15 = -3$ from B, so D is 3 units lower than B.

c. 8 ft

65. **a.** $p = -q$; *Sample answer:* Subtract q from each side.

b. $p < -q$; *Sample answer:* Subtract q from each side.

c. $p > -q$; *Sample answer:* Subtract q from each side.

66.

−1	4	−3
−2	0	2
3	−4	1

Check out the
Dynamic Classroom.
BigIdeasMath.com

Learning Target

Find sums of rational numbers.

Success Criteria

- Explain how to model addition of rational numbers on a number line.
- Find sums of rational numbers by reasoning about absolute values.
- Use properties of addition to efficiently add rational numbers.

Warm Up

Cumulative, vocabulary, and prerequisite skills practice opportunities are available in the *Resources by Chapter* or at *BigIdeasMath.com.*

ELL Support

Students may be familiar with the word *property* as it applies to a person owning a home or possessions. Explain that a property in math is a rule that is always true. You may want to review the three properties listed in part (c) with students.

Exploration 1

a. *Sample answer:* $\frac{1}{7}$; $\frac{1}{7}+\frac{3}{7}$; $-\frac{2}{7}+\left(-\frac{3}{7}\right)$; $-\frac{4}{7}+\frac{5}{7}$; $\frac{4}{7}+\left(-\frac{5}{7}\right)$; $\frac{4}{7}$, $-\frac{5}{7}$, $\frac{1}{7}$, $-\frac{1}{7}$

b. yes; *Sample answer:* Use absolute values and a number line to add any numbers.

c. yes; *Sample answer:* Rational numbers are added the same way integers are added, so the properties would still apply.

Laurie's Notes

Preparing to Teach

- Students should be comfortable adding positive fractions, positive decimals, and integers. Now students will extend their understanding of addition to rational numbers.
- **Reason Abstractly and Quantitatively:** Mathematically proficient students are able to use a number line to represent the sum of two rational numbers. Representing a sum on a number line means students must attend to the meaning of addition and to the meaning of a rational number.

Motivate

? Pose a series of contextual questions to help students think about negative rational numbers. These questions should suggest why you need to be able to add rational numbers. Examples:

- "If finding a dollar and a quarter is represented as 1.25, how is losing a dollar and a quarter represented?" -1.25
- "If a half mile above sea level is represented as $\frac{1}{2}$, how is a half mile below sea level represented?" $-\frac{1}{2}$
- "Represent a loss of $5\frac{1}{2}$ yards during a play in a football game." $-5\frac{1}{2}$
- "Represent a drop in temperature of 4.2°F." -4.2

Exploration 1

- Remind students that a *rational number* is a number that can be written as the ratio of two integers.
- **Reason Abstractly and Quantitatively:** The number line helps students see that the rules for adding rational numbers shouldn't be different from the rules for adding integers.
- Work through the first number line with students. Choose $\frac{1}{2}$ as the unit fraction and label the tick marks.

? "What is the length of the first arrow? the second arrow?" $\frac{1}{2}$ unit; $1\frac{1}{2}$ units

? "What is the length of the sum?" 2 units

- For each of the remaining number lines, you can tell students to use the same unit fraction or have them select different unit fractions.

? "When adding rational numbers with different signs, can you predict the sign of the sum? Explain." Yes, the sum has the same sign as the number with the greater absolute value.

- For part (b), have students stand if they answer "yes" and solicit explanations.
- ◉ For part (c), divide the class into three groups and assign each group one of the properties. Ask each group to find three examples that demonstrate why the property works. Have groups present and explain their examples.

A.3 Adding Rational Numbers

Learning Target: Find sums of rational numbers.

Success Criteria:
- I can explain how to model addition of rational numbers on a number line.
- I can find sums of rational numbers by reasoning about absolute values.
- I can use properties of addition to efficiently add rational numbers.

EXPLORATION 1 Adding Rational Numbers

Work with a partner.

a. Choose a unit fraction to represent the space between the tick marks on each number line. What addition expressions are being modeled? What are the sums?

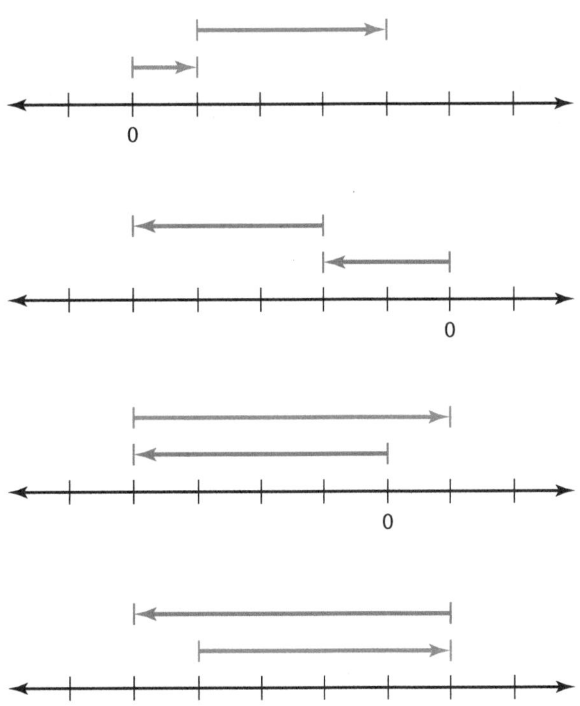

Math Practice

Look for Structure

How do the lengths and directions of the arrows determine the sign of the sum?

b. Do the rules for adding integers apply to all rational numbers? Explain your reasoning.

c. You have used the following properties to add integers. Do these properties apply to all rational numbers? Explain your reasoning.

- Commutative Property of Addition
- Associative Property of Addition
- Additive Inverse Property

A.3 Lesson

Key Idea

Adding Rational Numbers

Words To add rational numbers, use the same rules as you used for adding integers.

Numbers

$$\frac{3}{5} + \left(-\frac{1}{5}\right) = \left|\frac{3}{5}\right| - \left|-\frac{1}{5}\right|$$

$$= \frac{3}{5} - \frac{1}{5}$$

$$= \frac{2}{5}$$

Model

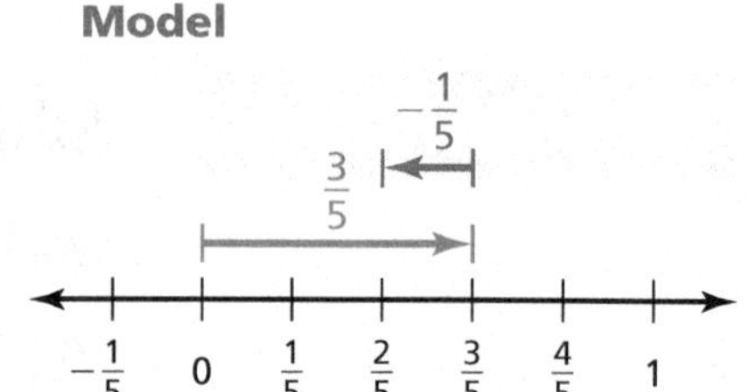

EXAMPLE 1 Adding Rational Numbers

Find $-\frac{8}{3} + \frac{5}{6}$. **Estimate** $-3 + 1 = -2$

Because the signs are different and $\left|-\frac{8}{3}\right| > \left|\frac{5}{6}\right|$, subtract $\left|\frac{5}{6}\right|$ from $\left|-\frac{8}{3}\right|$.

$$\left|-\frac{8}{3}\right| - \left|\frac{5}{6}\right| = \frac{8}{3} - \frac{5}{6}$$ Find the absolute values.

$$= \frac{16}{6} - \frac{5}{6}$$ Rewrite $\frac{8}{3}$ as $\frac{16}{6}$.

$$= \frac{16 - 5}{6}$$ Write the difference of the numerators over the common denominator.

$$= \frac{11}{6}, \text{ or } 1\frac{5}{6}$$ Simplify.

Because $\left|-\frac{8}{3}\right| > \left|\frac{5}{6}\right|$, use the sign of $-\frac{8}{3}$.

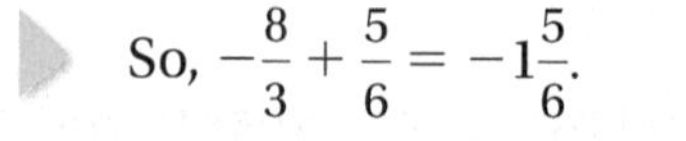

So, $-\frac{8}{3} + \frac{5}{6} = -1\frac{5}{6}$. **Reasonable?** $-1\frac{5}{6} \approx -2$ ✓

Try It **Find the sum. Write your answer in simplest form.**

1. $-\frac{1}{2} + \left(-\frac{3}{2}\right)$ **2.** $-1\frac{3}{8} + \frac{3}{4}$ **3.** $4 + \left(-\frac{7}{2}\right)$

Laurie's Notes

Scaffolding Instruction

- In the exploration, students used number lines to add rational numbers and determined that the same rules for adding integers apply to adding rational numbers.
- **Emerging:** Students are uncertain that the rules for adding integers apply to all rational numbers. They may also need to review adding fractions and mixed numbers. These students will benefit from guided instruction for Examples 1 and 2.
- **Proficient:** Students can add and subtract fractions and mixed numbers with unlike denominators. They can also apply the rules for adding rational numbers. Have students review the Key Idea before proceeding to the Self-Assessment for Concepts & Skills exercises.

Scaffold instruction to support all students in their learning. Learning is individualized and you may want to group students differently as they move in and out of these levels with each skill and concept. Student self-assessment and feedback help guide your instructional decisions about how and when to layer support for all students to become proficient learners.

Key Idea

- Write the Key Idea on the board.
- ? Work through the problem in the Model. Then show $3 + (-1)$ on a number line. "How are the two problems related?" *Sample answer:* The problem in the Model represents $\frac{1}{5}$ of $3 + (-1)$.

EXAMPLE 1

- ? "What type of fraction is $-\frac{8}{3}$?" improper
- ? "What is $-\frac{8}{3}$ as a mixed number?" $-2\frac{2}{3}$
- Be sure to tell students to check their answers for reasonableness.

Extra Example 1

Find $\frac{4}{5} + \left(-\frac{3}{10}\right)$. $\frac{1}{2}$

Try It

- Have three pairs of students complete one of the exercises at the board, while the other students try the problems at their desks. Have the students at the board explain their work.
- ? Ask questions such as, "How do you know your answer is reasonable?"

ELL Support

Have students work in pairs to discuss and complete Exercises 1–3.

Beginner: Write the sum.

Intermediate: State the sum.

Advanced: Explain the process used to find the sum.

Try It

1. -2
2. $-\frac{5}{8}$
3. $\frac{1}{2}$

Extra Example 2

Find $-3.92 + (-6.89)$. -10.81

Try It

4. -6
5. -1.35
6. 0.75

Self-Assessment for Concepts & Skills

7. Draw an arrow from zero to the first number. Draw a second arrow from the first number the length of the absolute value of the second number toward the right or left depending on the sign.
8. $-\frac{1}{2}$
9. $-1\frac{1}{12}$
10. 1.7
11. What is the distance between -4.5 and 3.5?; 8; -1

Laurie's Notes

EXAMPLE 2

? Write the problem and ask, "Will the final answer be *positive* or *negative*? Why?" negative; Because both numbers are negative.

Try It

- Have three pairs of students complete one of the exercises at the board, while the other students try the problems at their desks. Have the students at the board explain their work.

Formative Assessment Tip

Paired Verbal Fluency (PVF)

This technique is used between two partners where each person takes a turn speaking, uninterrupted, for a specified period of time. The roles reverse and the listener then speaks, uninterrupted, for the same amount of time. Verbalizing their understanding and being attentive listeners will activate student thinking and should help identify areas of difficulty or uncertainty.

Paired Verbal Fluency can be used at the beginning, middle, or end of instruction. Used at the beginning of instruction, students share their prior knowledge about a particular topic, skill, or concept. Used at the end of instruction, students reflect on learning that occurred during the lesson or at the end of a connected group of lessons.

Self-Assessment for Concepts & Skills

- After completing the exercises independently, students should use *Paired Verbal Fluency* to discuss Exercises 7 and 11.

ELL Support

Provide students with extra support and language practice by having them work in groups. Check comprehension of Exercises 8–10 by having groups hold up their answers for your review. Have intermediate and advanced speakers use a structured form of *Paired Verbal Fluency* to discuss Exercises 7 and 11. Provide sentence starters as support. *PVF* may be too challenging for beginner speakers. Then discuss Exercises 7 and 11 as a class.

The Success Criteria Self-Assessment chart can be found in the *Student Journal* or online at *BigIdeasMath.com.*

EXAMPLE 2 Adding Rational Numbers

Find $-0.75 + (-1.5)$. **Estimate** $-1 + (-1.5) = -2.5$

Because the signs are the same, add $|-0.75|$ and $|-1.5|$.

$$|-0.75| + |-1.5| = 0.75 + 1.5 \quad \text{Find the absolute values.}$$

$$= 2.25 \quad \text{Add.}$$

Because -0.75 and -1.5 are both negative, use a negative sign in the sum.

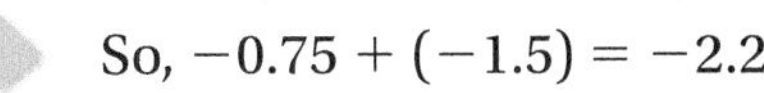

So, $-0.75 + (-1.5) = -2.25$. **Reasonable?** $-2.25 \approx -2.5$ 

Check

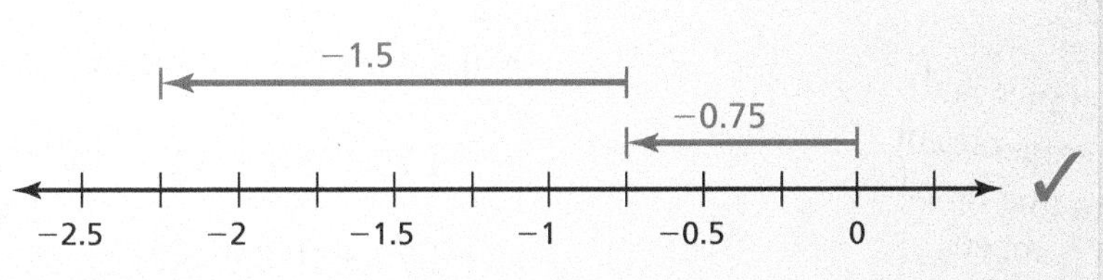

Try It Find the sum.

4. $-3.3 + (-2.7)$

5. $-5.35 + 4$

6. $1.65 + (-0.9)$

Self-Assessment for Concepts & Skills

Solve each exercise. Then rate your understanding of the success criteria in your journal.

7. WRITING Explain how to use a number line to find the sum of two rational numbers.

ADDING RATIONAL NUMBERS **Find the sum.**

8. $-\frac{7}{10} + \frac{1}{5}$

9. $-\frac{3}{4} + \left(-\frac{1}{3}\right)$

10. $-2.6 + 4.3$

11. DIFFERENT WORDS, SAME QUESTION Which is different? Find "both" answers.

Add -4.5 and 3.5.	What is the distance between -4.5 and 3.5?
What is -4.5 increased by 3.5?	Find the sum of -4.5 and 3.5.

EXAMPLE 3 Modeling Real Life

Year	Profit (millions of dollars)
2013	-1.7
2014	-4.75
2015	1.7
2016	0.8
2017	3.2

The table shows the annual profits (in millions of dollars) of an online gaming company from 2013 to 2017. Positive numbers represent *gains*, and negative numbers represent *losses*. Which statement describes the profit over the five-year period?

A. gain of $0.75 million **B.** gain of $75,000

C. loss of $75,000 **D.** loss of $750,000

To determine the amount of the gain or loss, find the sum of the profits.

five-year profit	$= -1.7 + (-4.75) + 1.7 + 0.8 + 3.2$	Write the sum.
	$= -1.7 + 1.7 + (-4.75) + 0.8 + 3.2$	Comm. Prop. of Add.
	$= 0 + (-4.75) + 0.8 + 3.2$	Additive Inv. Prop.
	$= -4.75 + 0.8 + 3.2$	Add. Prop. of Zero
	$= -4.75 + (0.8 + 3.2)$	Assoc. Prop. of Add.
	$= -4.75 + 4$	Add 0.8 and 3.2.
	$= -0.75$	Add -4.75 and 4.

The Commutative and Associative Properties of Addition are true for all rational numbers.

The five-year profit is $-\$0.75$ million. So, the company has a five-year loss of $0.75 million, or $750,000.

 The correct answer is **D**.

Self-Assessment for Problem Solving

Solve each exercise. Then rate your understanding of the success criteria in your journal.

12. A bottle contains 10.5 cups of orange juice. You drink 1.2 cups of the juice each morning and 0.9 cup of the juice each afternoon. How much total juice do you drink each day? When will you run out of juice?

Day	Change in elevation (miles)
1	$-\frac{1}{4}$
2	$\frac{1}{2}$
3	$-\frac{1}{5}$
4	?

13. **DIG DEEPER!** The table shows the changes in elevation of a hiker each day for three days. How many miles of elevation must the hiker gain on the fourth day to gain $\frac{1}{4}$ mile of elevation over the four days?

Laurie's Notes

EXAMPLE 3

- Before beginning, remind students that the properties of addition also apply to rational numbers.
- Ask a volunteer to read the problem. Check to see that students are comfortable with the vocabulary.

? "What is the relationship between -1.7 and 1.7?" They are opposites.

- Explain how -1.7 and 1.7 represent a loss and a gain of $1.7 million, which combine to make $0. Discuss other quantities that combine to make 0.
- **Attend to Precision:** When students finish the computation they will have −$0.75 million. Students need to convert −$0.75 million to thousands.

Self-Assessment for Problem Solving

- Encourage students to use a Four Square to complete these exercises. Until students become comfortable with the problem-solving plan, they may only be ready to complete the first square.

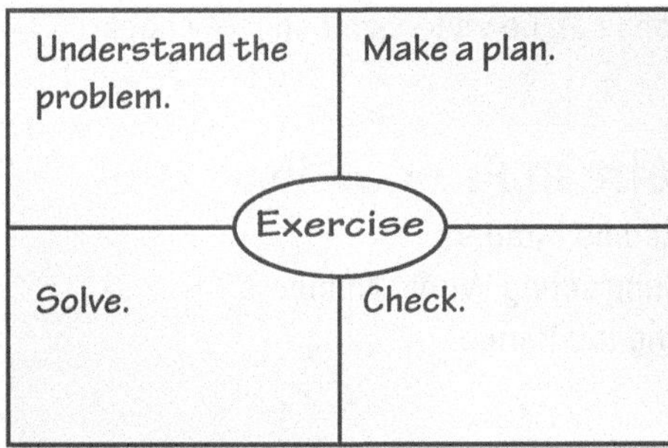

- **Paired Verbal Fluency:** After students complete the exercises independently, ask them to explain their work and reasoning for Exercise 12 to a partner. Pairs should reverse roles for Exercise 13.
- There are different strategies students may use in solving Exercise 12. Ask volunteers to share their work at the board or document camera. How do they know when they will run out of juice?
- **Use Appropriate Tools Strategically:** For Exercise 13, a vertical number line may be used to show the change in elevation each day. Some students may find it easier to rewrite the fractions as decimals.

The Success Criteria Self-Assessment chart can be found in the *Student Journal* or online at *BigIdeasMath.com*.

Closure

- Ask students to explain how addition of rational numbers is similar to addition of integers. *Sample answer:* When the numbers have the same sign, the sign of the sum is the common sign. When the numbers have different signs, the sign of the sum is the sign of the number with the greater absolute value.

Extra Example 3

The table shows the changes in the value of a stock during one week. Positive numbers represent *gains*, and negative numbers represent *losses*. Which statement describes the change in value over the week?

Day	Change in Value (dollars)
Monday	3.45
Tuesday	−12.90
Wednesday	−5.02
Thursday	29.31
Friday	−9.44

A. loss of $60.12
B. loss of $5.40
C. gain of $5.40
D. gain of $60.12
C

Self-Assessment for Problem Solving

12. 2.1 cups; 5 days

13. $\frac{1}{5}$

Learning Target

Find sums of rational numbers.

Success Criteria

- Explain how to model addition of rational numbers on a number line.
- Find sums of rational numbers by reasoning about absolute values.
- Use properties of addition to efficiently add rational numbers.

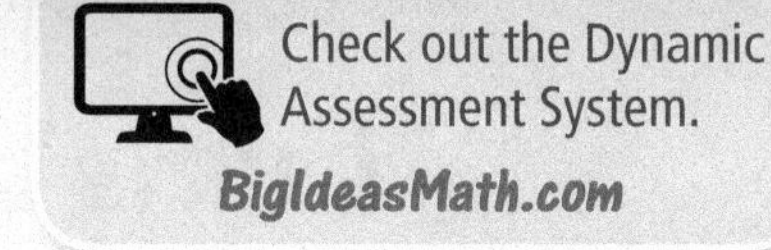
Check out the Dynamic Assessment System.
BigIdeasMath.com

Review & Refresh

1. 15
2. -2
3. -5
4. 0
5. 31
6. 8
7. 114
8. 183
9. D

Concepts, Skills, & Problem Solving

10. *Sample answer:* $\frac{1}{5}$; $-\frac{2}{5}+\frac{5}{5}=\frac{3}{5}$
11. *Sample answer:* $\frac{1}{3}$; $\frac{5}{3}+\left(-\frac{4}{3}\right)=\frac{1}{3}$
12. $\frac{1}{3}$
13. $-1\frac{4}{5}$
14. -0.9
15. $-\frac{5}{14}$
16. 1.844
17. $-2\frac{5}{6}$
18. -4.539
19. -57.19
20. $-\frac{7}{12}$
21. no; The sum is -3.95.
22. *Sample answer:* The water level of a lake drops $\frac{5}{3}$ feet during a drought, then rises $\frac{2}{3}$ foot during a storm to 1 foot below its original level.
23. *Sample answer:* You earn \$1.25 doing chores and buy a sandwich for \$1.25. You have no money left.

Assignment Guide and Concept Check

Scaffold assignments to support all students in their learning progression. The suggested assignments are a starting point. Continue to assign additional exercises and revisit with spaced practice to move every student toward proficiency.

Level	Assignment 1	Assignment 2
Emerging	2, 8, 9, 10, 12, 13, 14, 21, 27	17, 19, 22, 24, 25, 29, 32, 36
Proficient	2, 8, 9, 10, 14, 15, 17, 19, 21, 22, 26, 27	20, 24, 25, 28, 30, 33, 36
Advanced	2, 8, 9, 11, 17, 18, 19, 20, 21, 23, 26, 27	25, 28, 31, 34, 35, 36, 37

- Assignment 1 is for use after students complete the Self-Assessment for Concepts & Skills.
- Assignment 2 is for use after students complete the Self-Assessment for Problem Solving.
- The red exercises can be used as a concept check.

Review & Refresh Prior Skills

Exercises 1–4 Adding Integers
Exercises 5–8 Subtracting Whole Numbers
Exercise 9 Finding the Range

Common Errors

- **Exercises 15 and 20** Students may try to identify the sign of the answer before finding a common denominator. Remind students that they need to find a common denominator first.
- **Exercises 14, 16, 18, and 19** Students may forget to line up the decimal points when adding decimals. Remind students that the decimal points must be lined up before adding. Students may benefit from using grid paper to help keep the numbers and decimal points aligned.

A.3 Practice

Go to BigIdeasMath.com to get
HELP with solving the exercises.

Review & Refresh

Find the sum. Use a number line to verify your answer.

1. $3 + 12$ **2.** $5 + (-7)$ **3.** $-4 + (-1)$ **4.** $-6 + 6$

Subtract.

5. $69 - 38$ **6.** $82 - 74$ **7.** $177 - 63$ **8.** $451 - 268$

9. What is the range of the numbers below?

12, 8, 17, 12, 15, 18, 30

A. 12 **B.** 15 **C.** 18 **D.** 22

Concepts, Skills, & Problem Solving

MP USING TOOLS **Choose a unit fraction to represent the space between the tick marks on the number line. Write the addition expression being modeled. Then find the sum.** (See Exploration 1, p. 517.)

10.

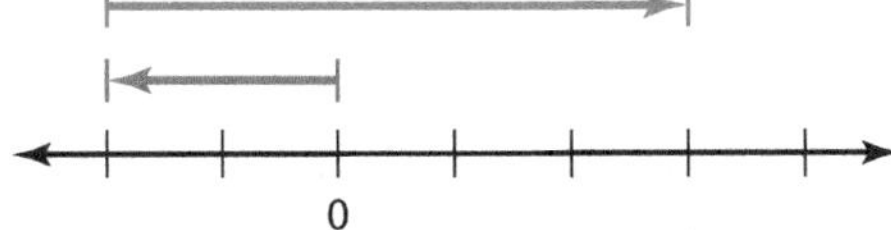
0

11.

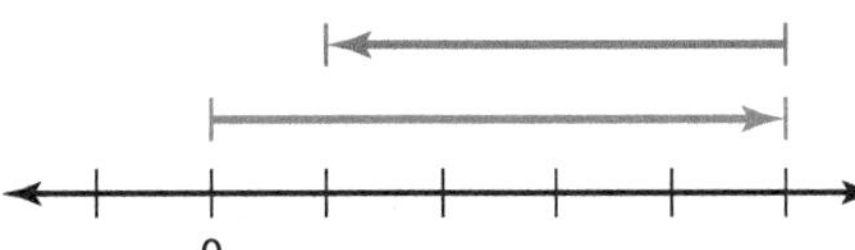
0

ADDING RATIONAL NUMBERS **Find the sum. Write fractions in simplest form.**

12. $\frac{11}{12} + \left(-\frac{7}{12}\right)$ **13.** $-1\frac{1}{5} + \left(-\frac{3}{5}\right)$ **14.** $-4.2 + 3.3$

15. $-\frac{9}{14} + \frac{2}{7}$ **16.** $12.48 + (-10.636)$ **17.** $-2\frac{1}{6} + \left(-\frac{2}{3}\right)$

18. $-20.25 + 15.711$ **19.** $-32.306 + (-24.884)$ **20.** $\frac{15}{4} + \left(-4\frac{1}{3}\right)$

21. MP YOU BE THE TEACHER Your friend finds the sum. Is your friend correct? Explain your reasoning.

$$-3.7 + (-0.25) = |-3.7| + |-0.25|$$
$$= 3.7 + 0.25$$
$$= 3.95$$

OPEN-ENDED **Describe a real-life situation that can be represented by the addition expression modeled on the number line.**

22.

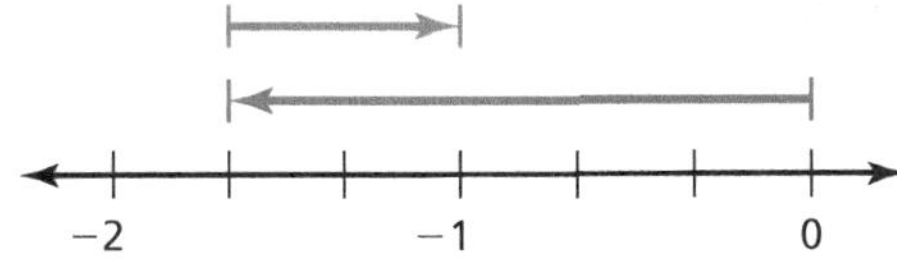
−2
−1
0

23.

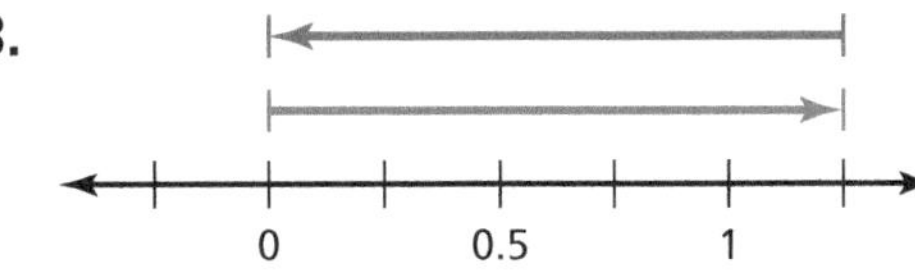
0
0.5
1

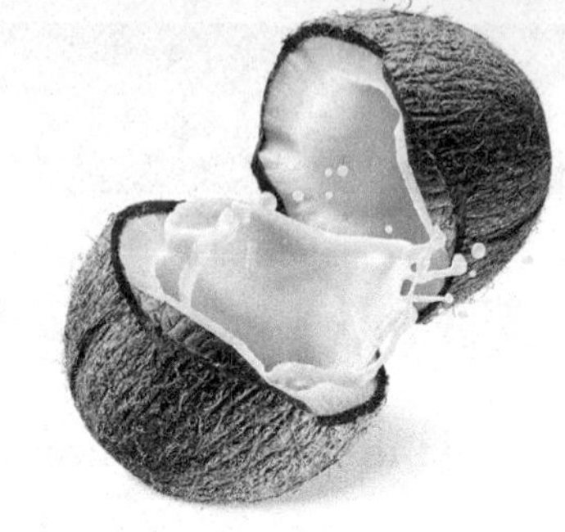

24. **MODELING REAL LIFE** You eat $\frac{3}{10}$ of a coconut. Your friend eats $\frac{1}{5}$ of the coconut. What fraction of the coconut do you and your friend eat?

25. **MODELING REAL LIFE** Your bank account balance is $-\$20.85$. You deposit \$15.50. What is your new balance?

26. **NUMBER SENSE** When is the sum of two negative mixed numbers an integer?

June	July	August
$-2\frac{1}{8}$	$1\frac{1}{4}$	$-\frac{7}{8}$

27. **WRITING** You are adding two rational numbers with different signs. How can you tell if the sum will be *positive, negative,* or *zero*?

28. **DIG DEEPER!** The table at the left shows the water level (in inches) of a reservoir for three months compared to the yearly average. When you include May and September, the water level for the five-month period is greater than the yearly average. Given that the level in September is below the yearly average, what can you determine about the level in May compared to the other four months? Justify your answer.

USING PROPERTIES Tell how the Commutative and Associative Properties of Addition can help you find the sum using mental math. Then find the sum.

29. $4.5 + (-6.21) + (-4.5)$

30. $\frac{1}{3} + \left(\frac{2}{3} + \frac{5}{8}\right)$

31. $8\frac{1}{2} + \left[4\frac{1}{10} + \left(-8\frac{1}{2}\right)\right]$

ADDING RATIONAL NUMBERS Find the sum. Explain each step.

32. $6 + 4\frac{3}{4} + (-2.5)$

33. $-4.3 + \frac{4}{5} + 12$

34. $5\frac{1}{3} + 7.5 + \left(-3\frac{1}{6}\right)$

35. **PROBLEM SOLVING** The table at the right shows the annual profits (in thousands of dollars) of a county fair from 2013 to 2016. What must the 2017 profit be (in hundreds of dollars) to break even over the five-year period?

Year	Profit (thousands of dollars)
2013	2.5
2014	1.4
2015	−3.3
2016	−1.4
2017	?

36. **REASONING** Is $|a + b| = |a| + |b|$ true for all rational numbers a and b? Explain.

37. **REPEATED REASONING** Evaluate the expression.

$$\frac{19}{20} + \left(-\frac{18}{20}\right) + \frac{17}{20} + \left(-\frac{16}{20}\right) + \cdots + \left(-\frac{4}{20}\right) + \frac{3}{20} + \left(-\frac{2}{20}\right) + \frac{1}{20}$$

Mini-Assessment

Find the sum. Write fractions in simplest form.

1. $2\frac{4}{5} + \left(-\frac{12}{15}\right)$ 2
2. $-\frac{3}{4} + \left(-\frac{8}{9}\right)$ $-1\frac{23}{36}$
3. $15.48 + (-17.23)$ -1.75
4. $-3.89 + (-5.34)$ -9.23
5. Your bank account balance is −\$15.50. You deposit \$75. What is your new balance? \$59.50

Section Resources

Surface Level	Deep Level
Resources by Chapter • Extra Practice • Reteach • Puzzle Time Student Journal • Self-Assessment • Practice Differentiating the Lesson Tutorial Videos Skills Review Handbook Skills Trainer	Resources by Chapter • Enrichment and Extension Graphic Organizers Dynamic Assessment System • Section Practice
Transfer Level	
Dynamic Assessment System • Mid-Chapter Quiz	Assessment Book • Mid-Chapter Quiz

Concepts, Skills, & Problem Solving

24. $\frac{1}{2}$

25. −\$5.35

26. when the fractional parts add up to an integer

27. The sum will be positive when the addend with the greater absolute value is positive. The sum will be negative when the addend with the greater absolute value is negative. The sum will be zero when the numbers are opposites.

28. greater than the other four months;
June through August:
$-2\frac{1}{8} + 1\frac{1}{4} + \left(-\frac{7}{8}\right) = -1\frac{3}{4}$
June through September:
less than $-1\frac{3}{4}$
May through September:
greater than 0
So, the value for May must be greater than $1\frac{3}{4}$, which is greater than the other four months.

29. *Sample answer:* Use the Commutative Property to switch the last two terms; −6.21

30. Use the Associative Property to add $\frac{1}{3}$ and $\frac{2}{3}$ first; $1\frac{5}{8}$

31. *Sample answer:* Use the Commutative Property to switch the last two terms and the Associative Property to regroup; $4\frac{1}{10}$

32–34. See Additional Answers.

35. 8

36. no; This is only true when a and b have the same sign.

37. $\frac{1}{2}$

Check out the
Dynamic Classroom.
BigIdeasMath.com

Learning Target

Find differences of integers.

Success Criteria

- Explain how subtracting integers is related to adding integers.
- Explain how to model subtraction of integers on a number line.
- Find differences of integers by reasoning about absolute values.

Warm Up

Cumulative, vocabulary, and prerequisite skills practice opportunities are available in the *Resources by Chapter* or at *BigIdeasMath.com.*

ELL Support

Point out that when you compare things, you look for differences. This is a common use of the word *difference* in everyday language. Explain that a common direction line in mathematics is, "Find the difference." This direction line asks for one number to be subtracted from another. When one number is subtracted from another, the answer is known as the *difference*.

Exploration 1

a. 2; 2; The answers are the same.

b. Place 3 negative counters in the box and then place a zero pair in the box. Remove the positive counter of the zero pair and the result is the sum.

c. See Additional Answers.

d. *Sample answer:* When subtracting two integers, add the opposite of the subtracted integer.

Laurie's Notes

Preparing to Teach

- **Look for and Express Regularity in Repeated Reasoning:** Students will develop a conceptual understanding of integer subtraction. They will recognize that each subtraction problem has a related addition problem. Modeling each problem with integer counters helps students make sense of subtraction.

Motivate

- Hand a student a collection of objects (8 pencils, 12 index cards, 9 paper clips) and ask another student to take some of the objects (5 pencils, 7 index cards, 3 paper clips).
- ? "What expressions represent this situation?" $8 - 5, 12 - 7, 9 - 3$
- ? "One way to think about subtraction: you have some amount and you take away another amount. Does this still work when you begin with negative amounts like –3 (owe a friend \$3)?" yes
- Tell students that today's exploration investigates subtraction of integers.

Exploration 1

- ? "How can you model $4 + (-2)$ using integer counters?" Combine 4 yellow counters with 2 red counters, and then remove 2 zero pairs. Students should model the problem using their counters even if they say they know the answer.
- Have partners discuss how $4 - 2$ is like $4 + (-2)$. Have students share their ideas with the class.
- Before working on part (b), have students model $2 - 4$ with integer counters. It will remind students that subtraction is *not* commutative.
- ? "How can you model $2 - 4$ using integer counters?" Some students may say that this is not possible, because you should subtract the lesser number from the greater number. This model will remind students that subtraction is *not* commutative.
- ? Show the class two yellow counters and ask, "How can you take 4 yellow counters away?" Add two zero pairs and then take away 4 yellow counters. 2 red counters are left, so $2 - 4 = -2$.

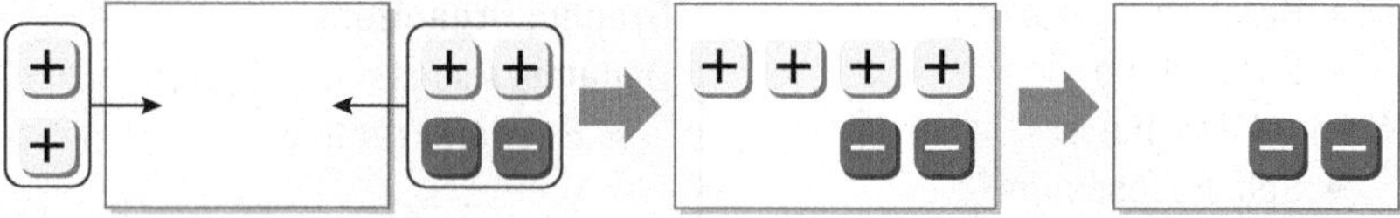

- ? "4 – 2 has the related problem $4 + (-2)$. What is the related addition problem for $2 - 4$?" $2 + (-4)$
- After modeling $2 - 4$ using integer counters, students should be able to use a similar method to complete part (b).
- For part (c), pairs should use integer counters to complete the table.
- ◉ The reasoning students use in part (d) provides insight into students' understanding of how subtracting integers and adding integers are related.

A.4 Subtracting Integers

Learning Target: Find differences of integers.

Success Criteria:
- I can explain how subtracting integers is related to adding integers.
- I can explain how to model subtraction of integers on a number line.
- I can find differences of integers by reasoning about absolute values.

EXPLORATION 1 Using Integer Counters to Find Differences

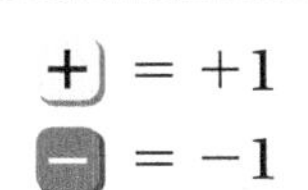

Work with a partner.

a. Use integer counters to find the following sum and difference. What do you notice?

$$4 + (-2) \qquad 4 - 2$$

b. In part (a), you *removed* zero pairs to find the sums. How can you use integer counters and zero pairs to find $-3 - 1$?

c. **INDUCTIVE REASONING** Use integer counters to complete the table.

Expression	Operation: Add or Subtract	Answer
$4 - 2$	Subtract 2.	
$4 + (-2)$		
$-3 - 1$		
$-3 + (-1)$		
$3 - 8$		
$3 + (-8)$		
$9 - 13$		
$9 + (-13)$		
$-6 - (-3)$		
$-6 + 3$		
$-5 - (-12)$		
$-5 + 12$		

Math Practice

Interpret Results
What do the results tell you about the relationship between subtracting integers and adding integers?

d. Write a general rule for subtracting integers.

A.4 Lesson

Subtracting Integers

Words To subtract an integer, add its opposite.

Numbers $3 - 4 = 3 + (-4) = -1$

Models

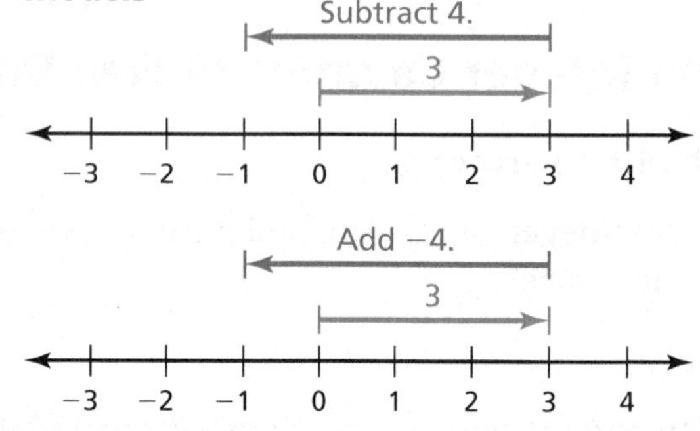

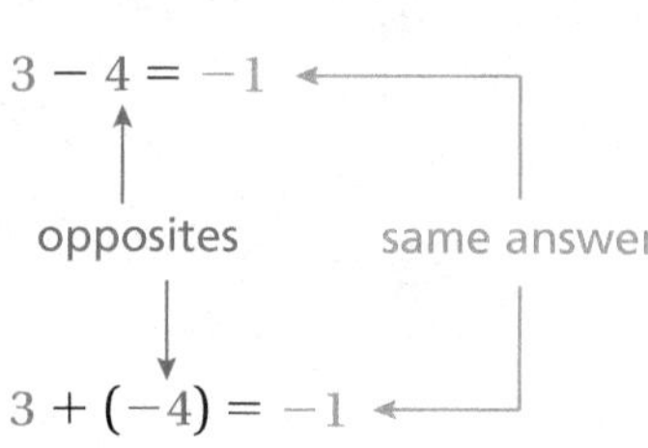

EXAMPLE 1 Using Number Lines to Find Differences

a. Find $-2 - 4$.

Draw an arrow from 0 to -2 to represent -2. Then draw an arrow 4 units to the left to represent subtracting 4, or adding -4.

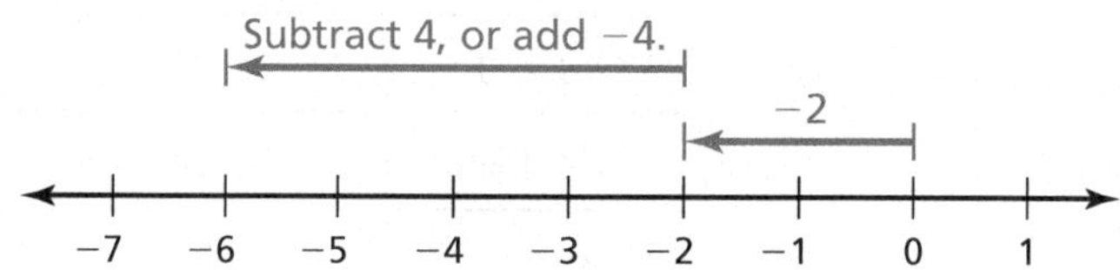

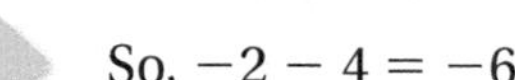

So, $-2 - 4 = -6$.

b. Find $-3 - (-7)$.

Draw an arrow from 0 to -3 to represent -3. Then draw an arrow 7 units to the right to represent subtracting -7, or adding 7.

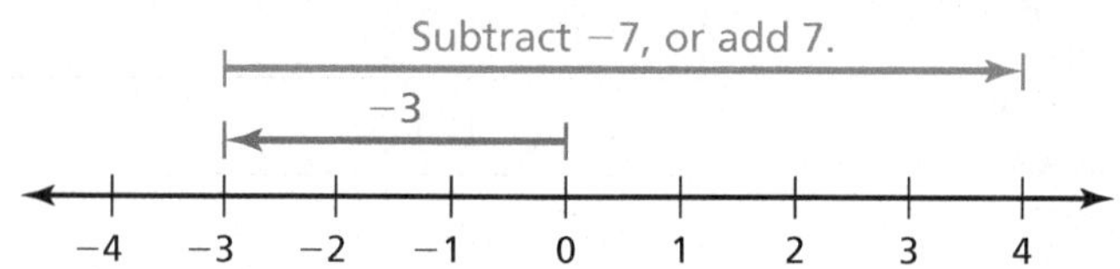

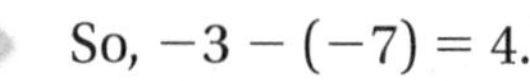

So, $-3 - (-7) = 4$.

Try It **Use a number line to find the difference.**

1. $1 - 4$

2. $-5 - 2$

3. $6 - (-5)$

Laurie's Notes

Scaffolding Instruction

- Students have used integer counters as a visual representation of subtracting integers.
- **Emerging:** Students may be uncertain of the relationship between adding and subtracting integers. Provide guided instruction for the examples. Relate the use of number lines to using integer counters in the exploration.
- **Proficient:** Students have a clear understanding of the relationship between adding and subtracting integers and the general rule for subtracting integers. Students should review the Key Idea to clarify how number lines can be used to subtract integers. Then students can proceed to the Self-Assessment for Concepts & Skills exercises.

Scaffold instruction to support all students in their learning. Learning is individualized and you may want to group students differently as they move in and out of these levels with each skill and concept. Student self-assessment and feedback help guide your instructional decisions about how and when to layer support for all students to become proficient learners.

Key Idea

- Write the Words and Numbers on the board.
- **Model:** To model $3 - 4$, draw an arrow pointing to the right from 0 to 3. Then move left 4 because you are subtracting positive 4. Model $3 + (-4)$ for students and compare the two models.

EXAMPLE 1

- **Reason Abstractly and Quantitatively:** To subtract a positive number, move to the left. To subtract a negative number, move to the right. To help students make sense of subtracting a negative quantity, use the context of money and owing someone $2. If you subtract away a debt of $2, you are moving 2 units in the positive direction, to the right.
- Work through each part of the example as shown.

Extra Example 1

a. Find $-4 - 5$. -9

b. Find $-3 - (-6)$. 3

Try It

- **Neighbor Check:** Students should complete the exercises independently. Then have students share with a partner and discuss any discrepancies.
- ◉ Say, "You have modeled subtraction of integers on a number line. This is the second success criterion. Use *Thumbs Up* to show me how confident you are with modeling subtraction of integers on a number line."

Try It

1. -3

2. -7

3. 11

ELL Support

Have students practice language by working in groups to complete Exercises 1–3. Expect students to perform as follows.

Beginner: Draw the number line.

Intermediate: Describe the arrows and the difference.

Advanced: Explain the process used to find the difference.

Extra Example 2

a. Find $8 - 10$. -2

b. Find $-7 - 8$. -15

c. Find $2 - (-4)$. 6

Try It

4. 5 **5.** −8

6. −6 **7.** −23

8. 18 **9.** 0

Self-Assessment
for Concepts & Skills

10. Draw an arrow from zero to the first integer. Draw a second arrow from the first integer the length of the absolute value of the second integer toward the left if it is positive or toward the right if it is negative.

11. D; Add the opposite.

12. C; Add the opposite.

13. A; Add the opposite.

14. B; Add the opposite.

15. −2

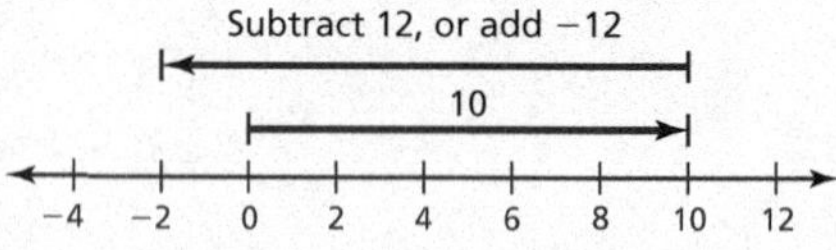

16. 14

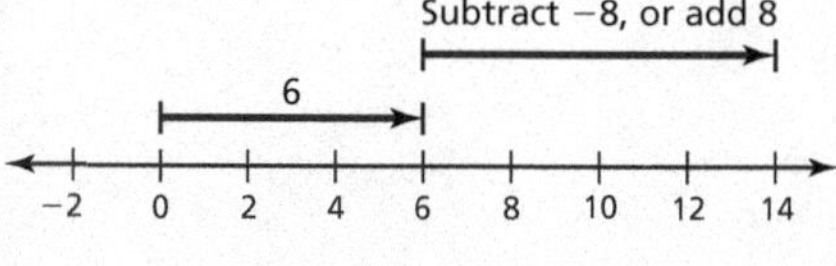

17. −3

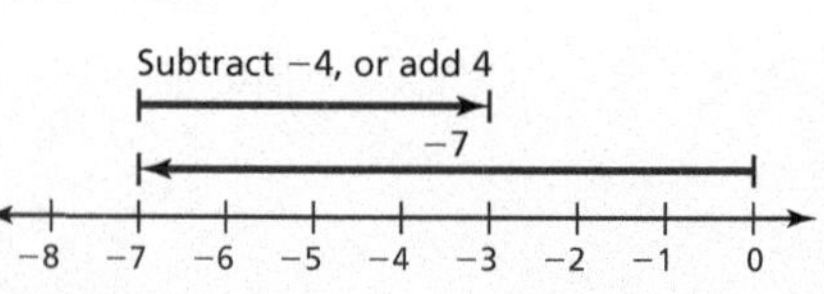

Laurie's Notes

EXAMPLE 2

- Work through each part of the example with students.
- For students who are having difficulty, have them record the problems on whiteboards. They should say aloud, "add the opposite," and state what that means for the particular problem.
- Discuss the Math Practice note. Point students who are struggling to the first step in part (c).
- **Construct Viable Arguments and Critique the Reasoning of Others:** Ask students if it is possible to determine when the difference of two negative numbers will be positive and when the difference of two negative numbers will be negative.

Try It

- Caution students to work slowly.
- **Neighbor Check:** Students should complete the exercises independently. Then have students share with a partner and discuss any discrepancies.

Formative Assessment Tip

Popsicle Sticks
This technique ensures that any student can be called on during questioning time in class. Write the name of each student on a Popsicle stick. Place the sticks in a cup (or can). When questions are posed in class during *No-Hands Questioning*, each student should think and be prepared to answer. If you only call on students who raise their hands, students can then opt out of being engaged. All students think they have an equal chance of being called on when a stick is pulled randomly, so they engage more in the lesson.
If there are certain students that you want to hear from, the cup could have an inner cylinder where select sticks are placed. It will appear that the process is still random and the voices you have not heard much from will still have the opportunity to prepare and formulate their answers.

Self-Assessment for Concepts & Skills

- **Popsicle Sticks:** Select students to share their answers.

ELL Support

Allow students to work in groups to discuss and answer Exercise 10. Monitor discussions and provide support. Check comprehension of Exercises 11–14 by having students hold up 1 finger for A, 2 fingers for B, 3 fingers for C, and 4 fingers for D. Have groups hold up their answers for Exercises 15–17 for your review.

The Success Criteria Self-Assessment chart can be found in the *Student Journal* or online at *BigIdeasMath.com*.

EXAMPLE 2 Subtracting Integers

a. Find 3 − 12.

$3 - 12 = 3 + (-12)$ Add the opposite of 12.

$= -9$ Add.

The difference is −9.

b. Find −8 − (−13).

$-8 - (-13) = -8 + 13$ Add the opposite of −13.

$= 5$ Add.

The difference is 5.

c. Find 5 − (−4).

$5 - (-4) = 5 + 4$ Add the opposite of −4.

$= 9$ Add.

The difference is 9.

Math Practice

Construct Arguments

Let p and q be integers. How can you write $p + q$ as a subtraction expression? Explain your reasoning.

Try It **Find the difference.**

4. $8 - 3$ **5.** $9 - 17$ **6.** $-3 - 3$

7. $-14 - 9$ **8.** $10 - (-8)$ **9.** $-12 - (-12)$

Self-Assessment for Concepts & Skills

Solve each exercise. Then rate your understanding of the success criteria in your journal.

10. WRITING Explain how to use a number line to find the difference of two integers.

MATCHING Match the subtraction expression with the corresponding addition expression. Explain your reasoning.

11. $9 - (-5)$ **12.** $-9 - 5$ **13.** $-9 - (-5)$ **14.** $9 - 5$

A. $-9 + 5$ **B.** $9 + (-5)$ **C.** $-9 + (-5)$ **D.** $9 + 5$

SUBTRACTING INTEGERS Find the difference. Use a number line to justify your answer.

15. $10 - 12$ **16.** $6 - (-8)$ **17.** $-7 - (-4)$

EXAMPLE 3 Modeling Real Life

Which continent has the greater range of elevations?

	North America	Africa
Highest Elevation	6198 m	5895 m
Lowest Elevation	−86 m	−155 m

Understand the problem.

You are given the highest and lowest elevations in North America and Africa. You are asked to find the continent with the greater difference between its highest and lowest elevations.

Make a plan.

Find the range of elevations for each continent by subtracting the lowest elevation from the highest elevation. Then compare the ranges.

Solve and check.

North America

$$\text{range} = 6198 - (-86)$$
$$= 6198 + 86$$
$$= 6284 \text{ m}$$

Africa

$$\text{range} = 5895 - (-155)$$
$$= 5895 + 155$$
$$= 6050 \text{ m}$$

Because 6284 meters is greater than 6050 meters, North America has the greater range of elevations.

Another Method North America's highest elevation is $6198 - 5895 = 303$ meters higher than Africa's highest elevation. Africa's lowest elevation is $|-155| - |-86| = 69$ meters lower than North America's lowest elevation. Because $303 > 69$, North America has the greater range of elevations. ✓

Self-Assessment for Problem Solving

Solve each exercise. Then rate your understanding of the success criteria in your journal.

18. A polar vortex causes the temperature to decrease from 3°C at 3:00 P.M. to −2°C at 4:00 P.M. The temperature continues to change by the same amount each hour until 8:00 P.M. Find the total change in temperature from 3:00 P.M. to 8:00 P.M.

19. **DIG DEEPER!** The table shows record high and low temperatures for three countries. Sweden has the greatest range of temperatures of the three countries. Describe the possible record low temperatures for Sweden.

	Norway	Sweden	Finland
High	96.1°F	100.4°F	99.0°F
Low	−60.5°F		−60.7°F

Laurie's Notes

EXAMPLE 3

- **Vocabulary:** You may need to review the meanings of *elevation* and *range*.
- **Fun Fact:** The highest point in Hawaii is Mauna Kea at 4208 meters above sea level. The lowest points in Hawaii are at sea level, where the coast of Hawaii meets the Pacific Ocean.

Self-Assessment for Problem Solving

- Students may benefit from trying the exercises independently and then working with peers to refine their work. It is important to provide time in class for problem solving, so that students become comfortable with the problem-solving plan.
- **FYI:** A polar vortex is a pocket of very cold air that sits over a polar region. There is one over each of the north and south poles. A polar vortex can expand and send cold air into the northern United States.
- **Popsicle Sticks:** Select students to present their solutions.

The Success Criteria Self-Assessment chart can be found in the *Student Journal* or online at *BigIdeasMath.com.*

Closure

- **Writing:** Your friend is home sick today. Imagine you are video chatting with him or her. How will you explain how to subtract integers? Be sure to use an example.

Extra Example 3

Which continent has the greater range of elevations?

	South America	Europe
Highest Elevation	6960 m	5642 m
Lowest Elevation	−40 m	−92 m

South America

Self-Assessment for Problem Solving

18. −25°C

19. less than −59.3°F

Learning Target

Find differences of integers.

Success Criteria

- Explain how subtracting integers is related to adding integers.
- Explain how to model subtraction of integers on a number line.
- Find differences of integers by reasoning about absolute values.

Review & Refresh

1. $\frac{1}{3}$
2. -6.32
3. $-5\frac{1}{2}$
4. 9.191
5. 19.923
6. 32.7456
7. $-1 + (-3)$
8. $2 + (-5)$

Concepts, Skills, & Problem Solving

9. 2
10. -3
11. 4
12. $4 + (-3)$; $4 - 3$; 1
13. $-2 + 5$; $-2 - (-5)$; 3
14. -3
15. 13
16. 1
17. -5
18. -3
19. -10
20. -5
21. 3
22. -21
23. 17
24. 4
25. 1
26. 0
27. -22
28. 38
29. 20
30. yes; The addition is correct.

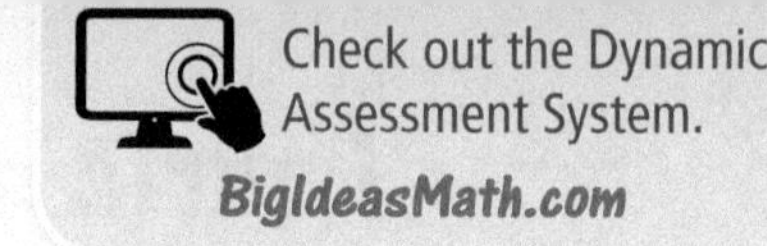

Check out the Dynamic Assessment System.
BigIdeasMath.com

Assignment Guide and Concept Check

Scaffold assignments to support all students in their learning progression. The suggested assignments are a starting point. Continue to assign additional exercises and revisit with spaced practice to move every student toward proficiency.

Level	Assignment 1	Assignment 2
Emerging	2, 3, 6, 7, 10, 14, 15, 16, 17, 30, 41, 46	22, 23, 26, 29, 31, 32, 33, 35, 42, 47
Proficient	2, 3, 6, 7, 11, 18, 22, 23, 24, 30, 42, 47	26, 29, 32, 33, 34, 36, 44, 48, 51
Advanced	2, 3, 6, 7, 11, 26, 27, 28, 29, 30, 44, 47	32, 34, 40, 45, 48, 50, 51

- Assignment 1 is for use after students complete the Self-Assessment for Concepts & Skills.
- Assignment 2 is for use after students complete the Self-Assessment for Problem Solving.
- The red exercises can be used as a concept check.

Review & Refresh Prior Skills

Exercises 1–3 Adding Rational Numbers
Exercises 4–6 Adding Decimals
Exercises 7 and 8 Using Number Lines to Add Integers

Common Errors

- **Exercises 14–29** Students may change the sign of the first number or forget to change the problem from subtraction to addition when changing the sign of the second number. Remind them that the first number is a starting point and will never change, but the sign of the second number and the operation will change.

A.4 Practice

Review & Refresh

Find the sum. Write fractions in simplest form.

1. $\frac{5}{9} + \left(-\frac{2}{9}\right)$
2. $-8.75 + 2.43$
3. $-3\frac{1}{8} + \left(-2\frac{3}{8}\right)$

Add.

4. $2.48 + 6.711$
5. $12.807 + 7.116$
6. $18.7126 + 14.033$

Write an addition expression represented by the number line. Then find the sum.

7. 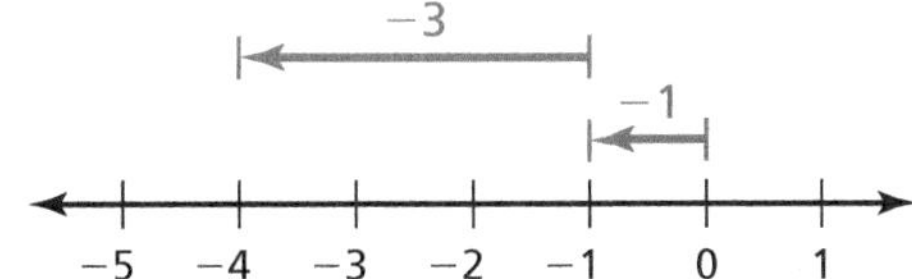

8. 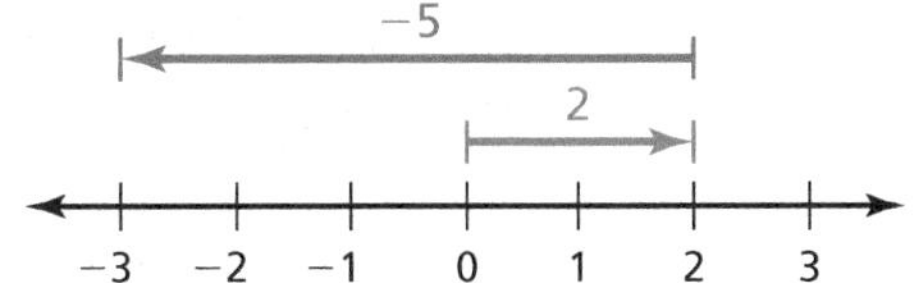

Concepts, Skills, & Problem Solving

USING INTEGER COUNTERS **Use integer counters to find the difference.** (See Exploration 1, p. 23.)

9. $5 - 3$
10. $1 - 4$
11. $-2 - (-6)$

USING NUMBER LINES **Write an addition expression and write a subtraction expression represented by the number line. Then evaluate the expressions.**

12. 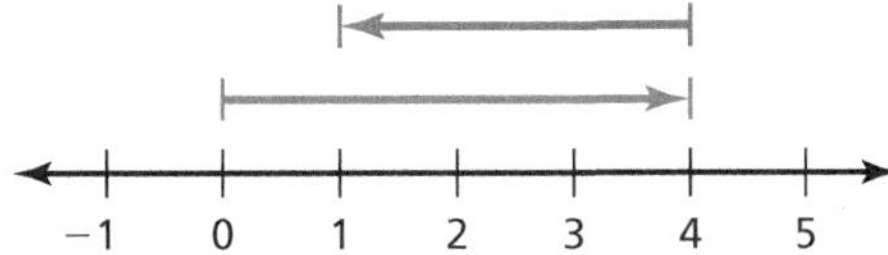

13. 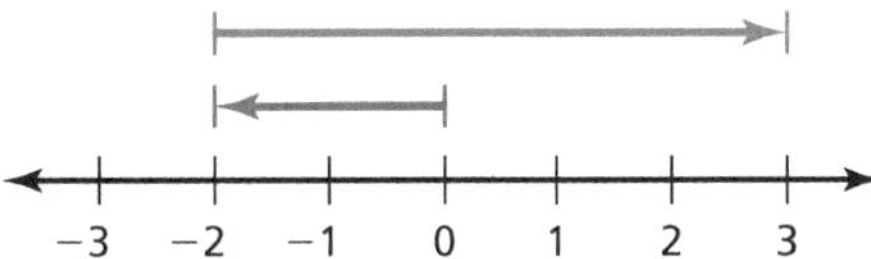

SUBTRACTING INTEGERS **Find the difference. Use a number line to verify your answer.**

14. $4 - 7$
15. $8 - (-5)$
16. $-6 - (-7)$
17. $-2 - 3$
18. $5 - 8$
19. $-4 - 6$
20. $-8 - (-3)$
21. $10 - 7$
22. $-8 - 13$
23. $15 - (-2)$
24. $-9 - (-13)$
25. $-7 - (-8)$
26. $-6 - (-6)$
27. $-10 - 12$
28. $32 - (-6)$
29. $0 - (-20)$

30. **MP YOU BE THE TEACHER** Your friend finds the difference. Is your friend correct? Explain your reasoning.

$$7 - (-12) = 7 + 12 = 19$$

31. MP **STRUCTURE** A scientist records the water temperature and the air temperature in Antarctica. The water temperature is $-2°C$. The air is $9°C$ colder than the water. Which expression can be used to find the air temperature? Explain your reasoning.

$-2 + 9$ $\quad$ $-2 - 9$ $\quad$ $9 - 2$

32. MP **MODELING REAL LIFE** A shark is 80 feet below the surface of the water. It swims up and jumps out of the water to a height of 15 feet above the surface. Find the vertical distance the shark travels. Justify your answer.

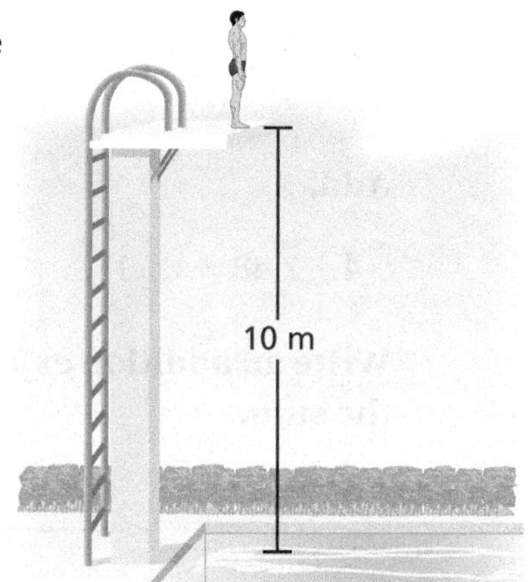

33. MP **MODELING REAL LIFE** The figure shows a diver diving from a platform. The diver reaches a depth of 4 meters. What is the change in elevation of the diver?

34. **OPEN-ENDED** Write two different pairs of negative integers, x and y, that make the statement $x - y = -1$ true.

USING PROPERTIES **Tell how the Commutative and Associative Properties of Addition can help you evaluate the expression using mental math. Then evaluate the expression.**

35. $2 - 7 + (-2)$

36. $-6 - 8 + 6$

37. $8 + (-8 - 5)$

38. $-39 + 46 - (-39)$

39. $[13 + (-28)] - 13$

40. $-2 + (-47 - 8)$

ALGEBRA **Evaluate the expression when $k = -3$, $m = -6$, and $n = 9$.**

41. $4 - n$

42. $m - (-8)$

43. $-5 + k - n$

44. $|m - k|$

45. MP **MODELING REAL LIFE** The table shows the record monthly high and low temperatures for a city in Alaska.

	Jan	Feb	Mar	Apr	May	Jun	Jul	Aug	Sep	Oct	Nov	Dec
High (°F)	56	57	56	72	82	92	84	85	73	64	62	53
Low (°F)	−35	−38	−24	−15	1	29	34	31	19	−6	−21	−36

a. Which month has the greatest range of temperatures?

b. What is the range of temperatures for the year?

MP **REASONING** **Tell whether the difference of the two integers is *always*, *sometimes*, or *never* positive. Explain your reasoning.**

46. two positive integers

47. a positive integer and a negative integer

48. two negative integers

49. a negative integer and a positive integer

MP **NUMBER SENSE** **For what values of a and b is the statement true?**

50. $|a - b| = |b - a|$

51. $|a - b| = |a| - |b|$

Common Errors

- **Exercise 33** Students may try to add $-4 + 10$ instead of subtracting $-4 - 10$ because they do not recognize that *change in elevation* means a range (subtraction). Use a vertical number line to help students see the meaning of change in elevation.
- **Exercises 35 and 36** Students may try to complete the addition first instead of working from left to right. Remind students that the order of operations does *not* put addition before subtraction, but that addition *and* subtraction are performed from left to right.

Mini-Assessment

Find the difference.

1. $6 - 10$ -4
2. $-14 - 16$ -30
3. $-9 - (-4)$ -5
4. $26 - (-35)$ 61
5. The top of a flag pole is 15 feet high. The base is at -3 feet. Find the length of the flag pole. 18 feet

Section Resources

Surface Level	Deep Level
Resources by Chapter • Extra Practice • Reteach • Puzzle Time Student Journal • Self-Assessment • Practice Differentiating the Lesson Tutorial Videos Skills Review Handbook Skills Trainer	Resources by Chapter • Enrichment and Extension Graphic Organizers Dynamic Assessment System • Section Practice

Concepts, Skills, & Problem Solving

31. $-2 - 9$; *Sample answer:* The air temperature is 9°C colder, so subtract 9.

32. 95 ft; *Sample answer:* The difference of the elevations is $15 - (-80)$.

33. -14 m

34. *Sample answer:* $x = -2, y = -1$; $x = -3, y = -2$

35. *Sample answer:* Write the subtraction as addition. Then use the Commutative Property to switch the last two terms; -7

36. *Sample answer:* Write the subtraction as addition. Then use the Commutative Property to switch the last two terms; -8

37. Use the Associative Property to add 8 and -8 first; -5

38. *Sample answer:* Use the Commutative Property to switch the first two terms; 46

39. *Sample answer:* Use the Commutative Property to switch the first two terms and the Associative Property to regroup; -28

40. *Sample answer:* Write the subtraction as addition. Then use the Commutative Property to switch the last two terms and the Associative Property to regroup; -57

41. -5 **42.** 2

43. -17 **44.** 3

45. **a.** February
b. 130°F

46. sometimes; It's positive only if the first integer is greater.

47. always; It's always positive because the first integer is always greater.

48. sometimes; It's positive only if the first integer is greater.

49–51. See Additional Answers.

Check out the
Dynamic Classroom.
BigIdeasMath.com

Learning Target

Find differences of rational numbers and find distances between numbers on a number line.

Success Criteria

- Explain how to model subtraction of rational numbers on a number line.
- Find differences of rational numbers by reasoning about absolute values.
- Find distances between numbers on a number line.

Warm Up

Cumulative, vocabulary, and prerequisite skills practice opportunities are available in the *Resources by Chapter* or at *BigIdeasMath.com.*

ELL Support

Remind students that in math a rational number is a number that can be written as a fraction $\frac{a}{b}$ where a and b are integers and b is not zero. Point out that the word *rational* is often used to mean "reasonable or logical" in everyday language, but that is not its meaning in math.

Exploration 1

a. *Sample answer:* $\frac{1}{7}; \frac{2}{7} - \frac{5}{7}; -\frac{4}{7} - \left(-\frac{1}{7}\right); -\frac{3}{7}; -\frac{3}{7}$

b. yes; *Sample answer:* Use absolute values and a number line to subtract any numbers.

c. *Sample answer:* yes; Rewrite the subtraction as addition first, then apply the properties.

Exploration 2

a. 5

b–c. See Additional Answers.

Laurie's Notes

Preparing to Teach

- **Reason Abstractly and Quantitatively:** Mathematically proficient students can use a number line to represent the difference of two rational numbers. Representing a difference on a number line means students must attend to the meaning of subtraction and to the meaning of a rational number.
- In this lesson, students will apply the rules of subtracting integers to subtracting rational numbers.

Motivate

- Draw two "dots" on the board (locate them horizontally) and ask students about the distance between them. They may say to measure it with a ruler.
- Draw a line through the points, extending the line beyond the points. Put a tick mark to the left of both dots and label it 0.
- ? "Besides using a ruler, is there another way to find the distance between the two points?" Listen for scaling the number line and then subtracting the lesser number from the greater number.
- ? "Will this work if 0 is between the two points? If 0 is to the right of both points?" Students will be less certain that subtraction will work. You may need to try simple integer values where students can count.
- Tell students that they will return to distance on a number line later in the lesson.

Exploration 1

- **Reason Abstractly and Quantitatively:** The number line helps students see that the rules for subtracting rational numbers shouldn't be different from the rules for subtracting integers.
- **Teaching Tip:** Suggest to students that they use the tick marks on the number line to help them perform the moves in stages.
- For part (a), you can tell students to use the same unit fraction, or have them select different unit fractions for each number line. Each of these problems involves subtracting a positive number.
- When students have finished part (a), ask volunteers to share their work. Display work at a document camera, if possible.
- **Agree-Disagree Statement:** Have students share their answers for parts (b) and (c). As each answer is presented, ask students if they agree or disagree and to explain why or why not. See page T-530 for a description of *Agree-Disagree Statement*.

Exploration 2

- In this exploration, students will use absolute value to find distances on a number line.
- When students have finished, use *Popsicle Sticks* to select students to share their work and reasoning.

A.5 Subtracting Rational Numbers

Learning Target: Find differences of rational numbers and find distances between numbers on a number line.

Success Criteria:
- I can explain how to model subtraction of rational numbers on a number line.
- I can find differences of rational numbers by reasoning about absolute values.
- I can find distances between numbers on a number line.

EXPLORATION 1 Subtracting Rational Numbers

Work with a partner.

a. Choose a unit fraction to represent the space between the tick marks on each number line. What expressions involving subtraction are being modeled? What are the differences?

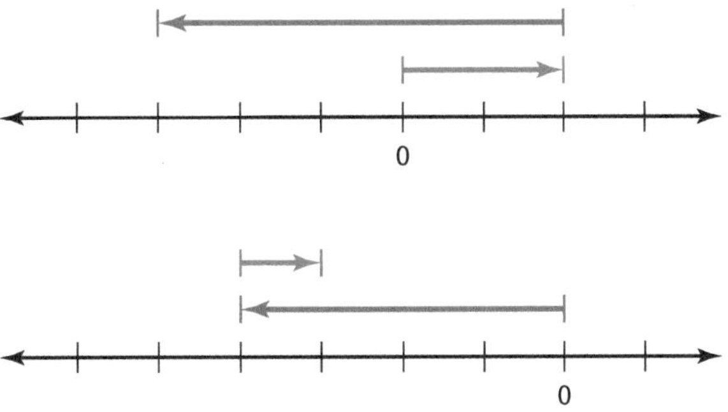

b. Do the rules for subtracting integers apply to all rational numbers? Explain your reasoning.

c. You have used the commutative and associative properties to add integers. Do these properties apply in expressions involving subtraction? Explain your reasoning.

EXPLORATION 2 Finding Distances on a Number Line

Work with a partner.

a. Find the distance between 3 and -2 on a number line.

b. The distance between 3 and 0 is the absolute value of 3, because $|3 - 0| = |3| = 3$. How can you use absolute values to find the distance between 3 and -2? Justify your answer.

c. Choose any two rational numbers. Use your method in part (b) to find the distance between the numbers. Use a number line to check your answer.

Math Practice

Find General Methods

How can you find the distance between any two rational numbers on a number line?

A.5 Lesson

Key Idea

Subtracting Rational Numbers

Words To subtract rational numbers, use the same rules as you used for subtracting integers.

Numbers $\frac{1}{5} - \left(-\frac{4}{5}\right) = \frac{1}{5} + \frac{4}{5}$

$= \frac{5}{5}$

$= 1$

Model

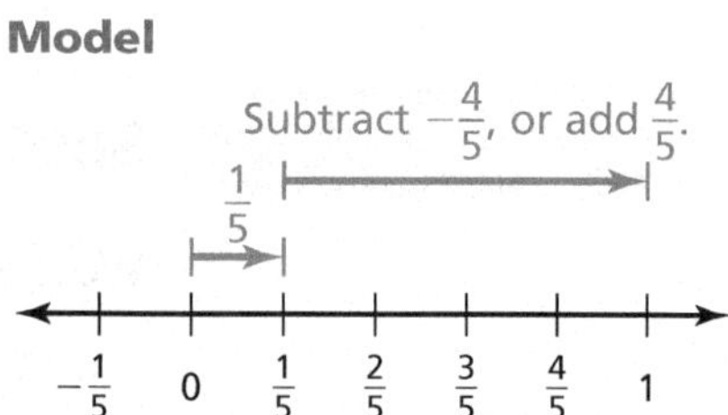

EXAMPLE 1 Subtracting Rational Numbers

Find $-4\frac{1}{7} - \frac{5}{7}$. **Estimate $-4 - 1 = -5$**

Rewrite the difference as a sum by adding the opposite.

$$-4\frac{1}{7} - \frac{5}{7} = -4\frac{1}{7} + \left(-\frac{5}{7}\right)$$

Because the signs are the same, add $\left|-4\frac{1}{7}\right|$ and $\left|-\frac{5}{7}\right|$.

$\left|-4\frac{1}{7}\right| + \left|-\frac{5}{7}\right| = 4\frac{1}{7} + \frac{5}{7}$ Find the absolute values.

$= 4 + \frac{1}{7} + \frac{5}{7}$ Write $4\frac{1}{7}$ as $4 + \frac{1}{7}$.

$= 4 + \frac{6}{7}$, or $4\frac{6}{7}$ Add fractions and simplify.

Because $-4\frac{1}{7}$ and $-\frac{5}{7}$ are both negative, use a negative sign in the difference.

So, $-4\frac{1}{7} - \frac{5}{7} = -4\frac{6}{7}$. **Reasonable?** $-4\frac{6}{7} \approx -5$ ✓

Try It **Find the difference. Write your answer in simplest form.**

1. $\frac{1}{3} - \left(-\frac{1}{3}\right)$
2. $-3\frac{1}{3} - \frac{2}{3}$
3. $4 - 5\frac{1}{2}$

Laurie's Notes

Scaffolding Instruction

- In the exploration, students used a number line to subtract rational numbers and find distances.
- **Emerging:** Students may need more concrete information to master the success criteria. These students will benefit from guided instruction for the Key Ideas and examples.
- **Proficient:** Students can use a number line to represent the difference of two rational numbers and use absolute value to find the distance between two points on a number line. Have students review the Key Ideas and then proceed to the Self-Assessment for Concepts & Skills exercises.

Key Idea

- Write the Key Idea. Work through the example shown.
- **Teaching Tip:** Use a different color when you *add the opposite.*

EXAMPLE 1

? "How do you subtract integers?" The statement "add the opposite" should be familiar. Once the problem is written as an addition problem, students should recall the rules for integer addition.

? "The problem is now $-4\frac{1}{7} + \left(-\frac{5}{7}\right)$. Will the sum be positive or negative? Explain." negative; The signs are the same, so you use the common sign.

- **FYI:** Some students may choose to solve by first rewriting $-4\frac{1}{7}$ as $-3\frac{8}{7}$ because they think they need to rename so that they can subtract the fractions. Renaming is not necessary for this problem because after changing from subtraction to addition, students need to find the sum; however, the result will be the same.
- **Connection:** The rule for subtracting rational numbers is the same as the rule for subtracting integers. The challenge will be working with fractions!

Try It

- **Neighbor Check:** Have students work independently and then have their neighbors check their work. Have students discuss any discrepancies.

Scaffold instruction to support all students in their learning. Learning is individualized and you may want to group students differently as they move in and out of these levels with each skill and concept. Student self-assessment and feedback help guide your instructional decisions about how and when to layer support for all students to become proficient learners.

Formative Assessment Tip

Agree-Disagree Statement

This technique has two parts. First, students are given a statement with which they may agree or disagree, or they can indicate that they need additional information to decide. Students are then asked to explain why they agree or disagree, or why they need additional information. The second part of the technique involves students describing how they can investigate, figure out, or test their thinking. *Agree-Disagree Statement* gives students the opportunity to think about their own understanding of a concept or process. It helps students practice the skill of actively investigating their own thinking. In listening to their own words, and in listening to the thinking of others, students can solidify or modify their beliefs.

Extra Example 1

Find $-8\frac{2}{3} - 6\frac{1}{6}$. $-14\frac{5}{6}$

Try It

1. $\frac{2}{3}$
2. -4
3. $-1\frac{1}{2}$

Extra Example 2

Find $-3.75 - (-0.96)$. -2.79

Try It

4. -6
5. 0
6. 0.5

Extra Example 3

Evaluate $6 - 8\frac{1}{2} - \left(-2\frac{3}{4}\right)$. $\frac{1}{4}$

Try It

7. $-\frac{4}{5}$
8. 10

Laurie's Notes

EXAMPLE 2

- Write the problem. Students should see that the difference will be negative. Rewrite the problem by "adding the opposite."
- Continue to work through the problem as shown.
- Encourage students to estimate the answer to check for reasonableness: $2.4 - 5.6 \approx 2 - 6 = -4$ and -3.2 is close to -4, so the answer is reasonable.

Try It

- **Neighbor Check:** Have students work independently and then have their neighbors check their work. Have students discuss any discrepancies.

EXAMPLE 3

- **Construct Viable Arguments and Critique the Reasoning of Others:** Mathematically proficient students will make conjectures about which properties of addition justify their work.
- Review the Commutative and Associative Properties of Addition with students.
- Work through the example as shown. Point out the properties as they are used.
- Encourage students to estimate the answer to check for reasonableness: $-1\frac{3}{8} - 8\frac{1}{2} - \left|-6\frac{7}{8}\right| \approx -1 - 9 - (-7) = -1 + (-9) + 7 = -10 + 7 = -3$ and -3 is equal to -3, so the answer is reasonable.

Try It

- **Neighbor Check:** Have students work independently and then have their neighbors check their work. Have students discuss any discrepancies.

ELL Support

Have students practice language by working in groups to complete Exercises 7 and 8. Expect students to perform as follows.

Beginner: Write each step.

Intermediate: Describe each step.

Advanced: Explain the process used to evaluate the expression.

EXAMPLE 2 Subtracting Rational Numbers

Find 2.4 − 5.6.

Rewrite the difference as a sum by adding the opposite.

$$2.4 - 5.6 = 2.4 + (-5.6)$$

Because the signs are different and $|-5.6| > |2.4|$, subtract $|2.4|$ from $|-5.6|$.

$|-5.6| - |2.4| = 5.6 - 2.4$ Find the absolute values.

$= 3.2$ Subtract.

Because $|-5.6| > |2.4|$, use the sign of −5.6.

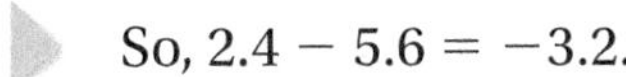

So, $2.4 - 5.6 = -3.2$.

Check

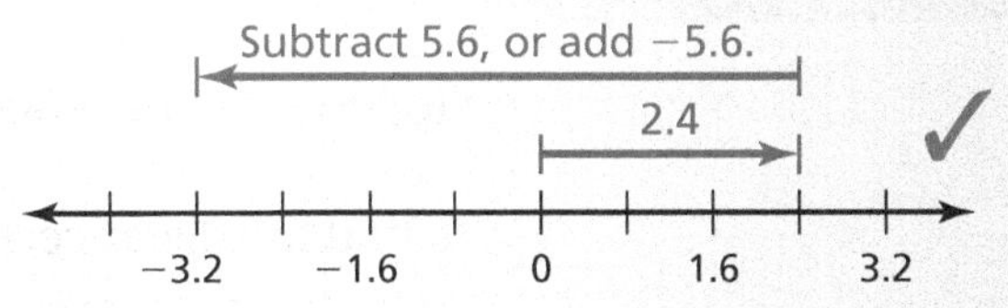

Try It **Find the difference.**

4. $-2.1 - 3.9$ **5.** $-8.8 - (-8.8)$ **6.** $0.45 - (-0.05)$

EXAMPLE 3 Using Properties of Addition

Evaluate $-1\frac{3}{8} - 8\frac{1}{2} - \left(-6\frac{7}{8}\right)$.

Use properties of addition to group the mixed numbers that include fractions with the same denominator.

$-1\frac{3}{8} - 8\frac{1}{2} - \left(-6\frac{7}{8}\right) = -1\frac{3}{8} + \left(-8\frac{1}{2}\right) + 6\frac{7}{8}$ Rewrite as a sum of terms.

$= -1\frac{3}{8} + 6\frac{7}{8} + \left(-8\frac{1}{2}\right)$ Comm. Prop. of Add.

$= 5\frac{1}{2} + \left(-8\frac{1}{2}\right)$ Add $-1\frac{3}{8}$ and $6\frac{7}{8}$.

$= -3$ Add $5\frac{1}{2}$ and $-8\frac{1}{2}$.

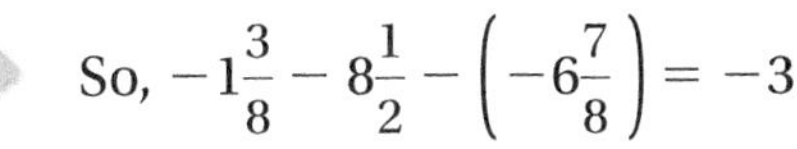

So, $-1\frac{3}{8} - 8\frac{1}{2} - \left(-6\frac{7}{8}\right) = -3$.

Try It **Evaluate the expression. Write fractions in simplest form.**

7. $-2 - \frac{2}{5} + 1\frac{3}{5}$ **8.** $7.8 - 3.3 - (-1.2) + 4.3$

Key Idea

Distance between Numbers on a Number Line

Words The distance between any two numbers on a number line is the absolute value of the difference of the numbers.

Model

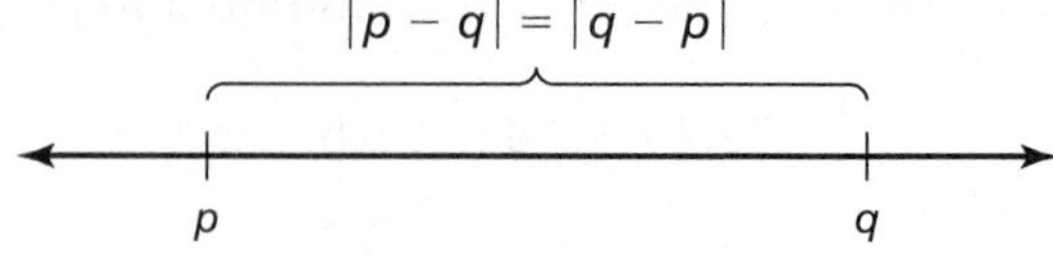

EXAMPLE 4 Finding Distance on a Number Line

Find the distance between $-\frac{1}{3}$ and -2 on a number line.

To find the distance, find the absolute value of the difference of the numbers.

$$\left|-2-\left(-\frac{1}{3}\right)\right| = \left|-2+\frac{1}{3}\right| \quad \text{Add the opposite of } -\frac{1}{3}.$$

$$= \left|-1\frac{2}{3}\right| \quad \text{Add } -2 \text{ and } \frac{1}{3}.$$

$$= 1\frac{2}{3} \quad \text{Find the absolute value.}$$

So, the distance between $-\frac{1}{3}$ and -2 is $1\frac{2}{3}$.

Try It **Find the distance between the two numbers on a number line.**

9. -3 and 9 **10.** -7.5 and -15.3 **11.** $1\frac{1}{2}$ and $-\frac{2}{3}$

Self-Assessment for Concepts & Skills

Solve each exercise. Then rate your understanding of the success criteria in your journal.

12. WRITING Explain how to use a number line to find the difference of two rational numbers.

SUBTRACTING RATIONAL NUMBERS Find the difference. Use a number line to justify your answer.

13. $4.9 - 1.6$ **14.** $\frac{7}{8} - \left(-\frac{3}{4}\right)$ **15.** $\frac{1}{3} - 2\frac{1}{6}$

Laurie's Notes

Key Idea

- Write the Key Idea on the board.
- This Key Idea connects subtraction to finding distances on a number line, an idea that was investigated in the Motivate.
- ? "When finding the distance between two points, does the order in which you subtract matter?" Listen for students to state that subtraction is *not* commutative, however, because you take the absolute value, you can subtract in either order. The differences will be opposites and the absolute values of opposites are the same value.
- Demonstrate a few examples by replacing *p* and *q* with integers and then fractions.

EXAMPLE 4

- Work through the problem, referring to the number line as you work.
- Remind students that the order of the numbers does not matter because you find the absolute value of the difference. Demonstrate the alternate method: $\left|-\frac{1}{3}-(-2)\right| = \left|-\frac{1}{3}+2\right| = \left|1\frac{2}{3}\right| = 1\frac{2}{3}$ and encourage students to think about the order in which they will subtract the numbers. Some calculations are more efficient than others.

Try It

- Have students complete the exercises on whiteboards.

Self-Assessment for Concepts & Skills

These exercises will help students assess their understanding of all three success criteria.

? "How does absolute value help in finding the distance between two numbers on a number line?" *Sample answer:* Absolute value represents the distance between a number and 0 on a number line, so finding the absolute value of the difference of two numbers represents the distance between the two numbers.

ELL Support

Have students work in pairs to complete Exercises 12–15 and display their answers to Exercises 13–15 for your review. For Exercise 12, have two pairs discuss their ideas and reach an agreement for the answer. Have groups present their answers to the class.

The Success Criteria Self-Assessment chart can be found in the *Student Journal* or online at *BigIdeasMath.com*.

Extra Example 4

Find the distance between $-3\frac{1}{4}$ and $2\frac{1}{4}$ on a number line. $5\frac{1}{2}$

Try It

9. 12

10. 7.8

11. $2\frac{1}{6}$

Self-Assessment for Concepts & Skills

12. Draw an arrow from zero to the first number. Draw a second arrow from the first number the length of the absolute value of the second number toward the left if it is positive or toward the right if it is negative.

13. 3.3

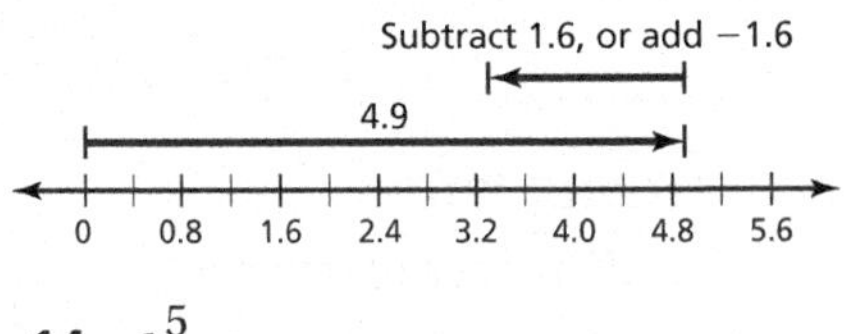

14. $1\frac{5}{8}$

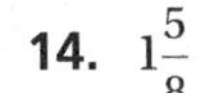

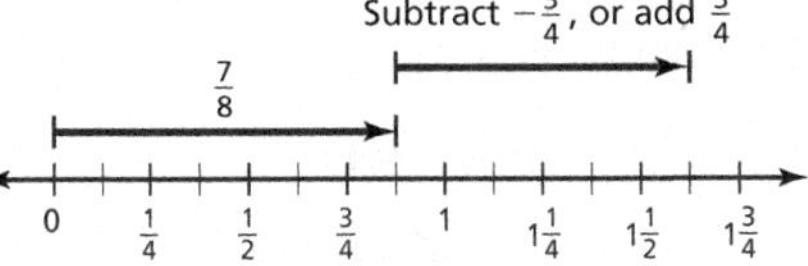

15. $-1\frac{5}{6}$

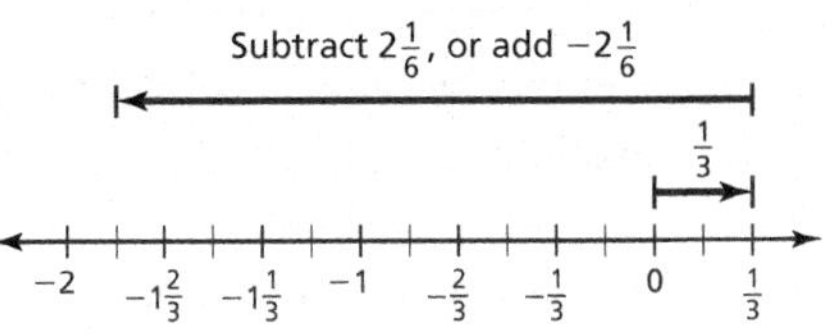

Extra Example 5

The number line shows the daily high and low temperatures. Find and interpret the distance between the points.

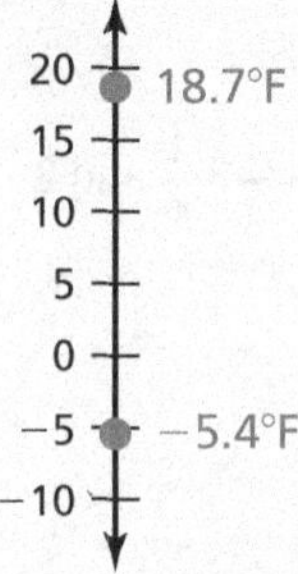

24.1°F; The daily high temperature is 24.1°F warmer than the daily low temperature.

Self-Assessment for Problem Solving

16. $-\frac{1}{100}$ mi; The parasail fell $\frac{1}{100}$ mile.

17. **a.** \$31.50; You deposit \$31.50.

b. \$29.68

Learning Target

Find differences of rational numbers and find distances between numbers on a number line.

Success Criteria

- Explain how to model subtraction of rational numbers on a number line.
- Find differences of rational numbers by reasoning about absolute values.
- Find distances between numbers on a number line.

Laurie's Notes

EXAMPLE 5

- **Model with Mathematics:** The vertical number line provides a visual model that helps students make a reasonable estimate.
- "How can you find the distance between the points?" Students will probably say, "Add 185 and 388." Remind students that they are really subtracting −388 from 185 and then finding the absolute value. It is also acceptable to subtract the 185 from −388 and then find the absolute value.
- "What does the distance represent?" Students will likely say, "The hot side is 573°F hotter than the cold side." It is also acceptable to say, "The cold side is 573°F colder than the hot side."

Self-Assessment for Problem Solving

- The goal for all students is to feel comfortable with the problem-solving plan. It is important for students to problem-solve in class, where they may receive support from you and their peers. Keep in mind that some students may only be ready for the first step.
- Review the success criteria with students. Then have students complete the exercises. Discuss any common errors that may arise.

The Success Criteria Self-Assessment chart can be found in the *Student Journal* or online at *BigIdeasMath.com.*

Closure

- **Exit Ticket:** Explain how subtraction of rational numbers is similar to subtraction of integers. *Sample answer:* To subtract an integer or a rational number, you add its opposite.

EXAMPLE 5 Modeling Real Life

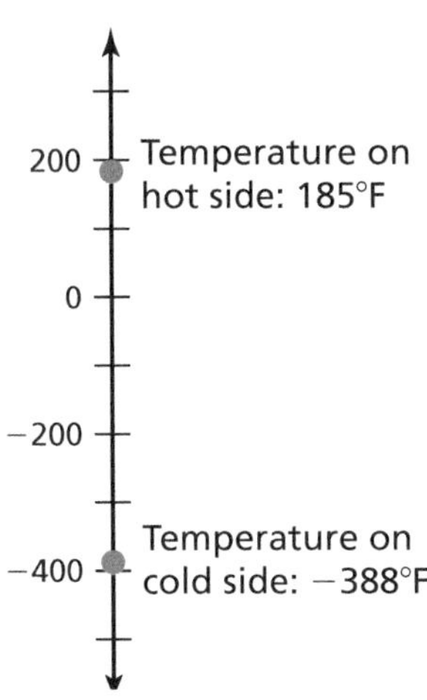

The number line shows the temperatures on each side of the James Webb telescope when in Earth's orbit. Find and interpret the distance between the points.

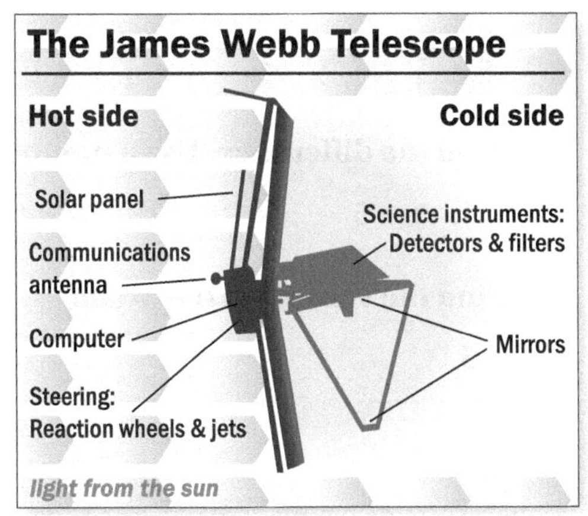

The number line shows that the temperature on the hot side is 185°F and the temperature on the cold side is −388°F.

To find the distance between the points, find the absolute value of the difference of the numbers.

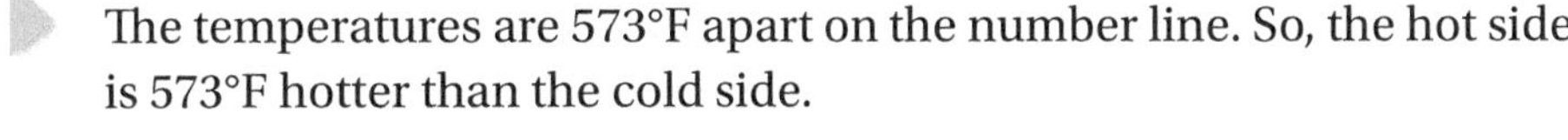

$|185 - (-388)| = |185 + 388|$ Add the opposite of −388.

$= |573|$ Add 185 and 388.

$= 573$ Find the absolute value.

The temperatures are 573°F apart on the number line. So, the hot side is 573°F hotter than the cold side.

Self-Assessment for Problem Solving

Solve each exercise. Then rate your understanding of the success criteria in your journal.

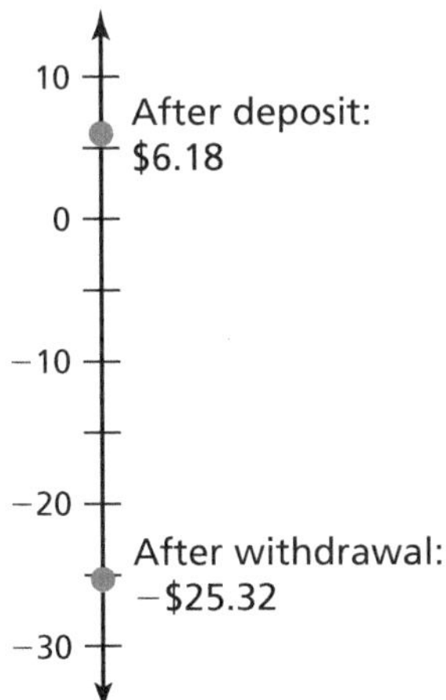

16. A parasail is $\frac{3}{100}$ mile above the water. After 5 minutes, the parasail is $\frac{1}{50}$ mile above the water. Find and interpret the change in height of the parasail.

17. DIG DEEPER! You withdraw $55 from a bank account to purchase a game. Then you make a deposit. The number line shows the balances of the account after each transaction.

a. Find and interpret the distance between the points.

b. How much money was in your account before buying the game?

A.5 Practice

Go to *BigIdeasMath.com* to get HELP with solving the exercises.

Review & Refresh

Find the difference. Use a number line to verify your answer.

1. $9 - 5$ **2.** $-8 - (-8)$ **3.** $-12 - 7$ **4.** $12 - (-3)$

Find the volume of the prism.

5.

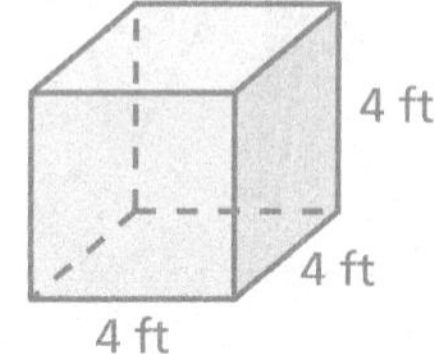

6.

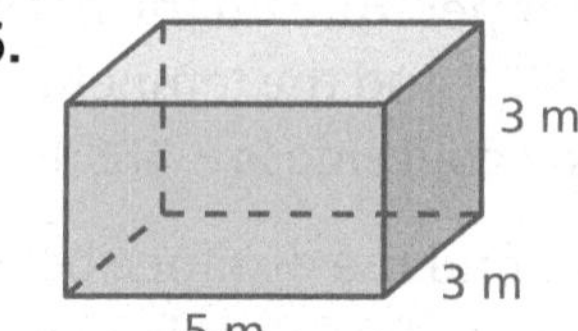

Order the values from least to greatest.

7. $6, |3|, |-4|, 1, -2$

8. $|4.5|, -3.6, 2, |-1.8|, 1.2$

Concepts, Skills, & Problem Solving

MP USING TOOLS **Choose a unit fraction to represent the space between the tick marks on the number line. Write an expression involving subtraction that is being modeled. Then find the difference.** (See Exploration 1, p. 529.)

9.

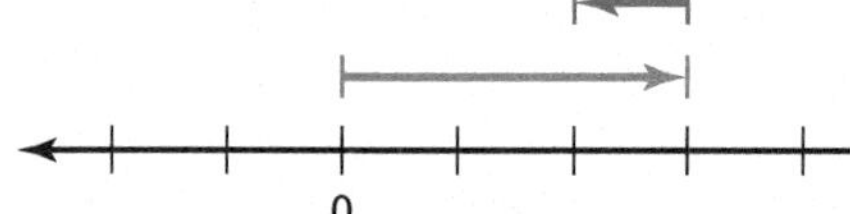

10.

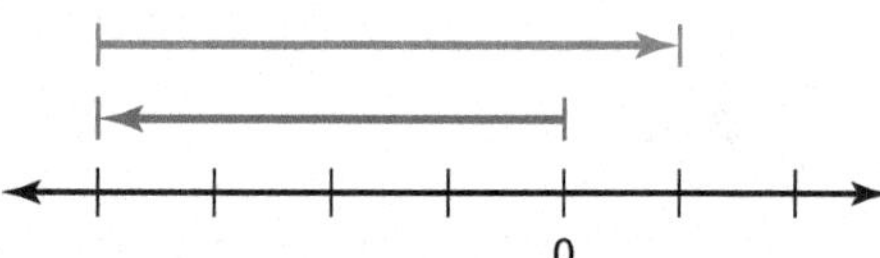

SUBTRACTING RATIONAL NUMBERS **Find the difference. Write fractions in simplest form.**

11. $\frac{5}{8} - \left(-\frac{7}{8}\right)$ **12.** $-1\frac{1}{3} - 1\frac{2}{3}$ **13.** $-1 - 2.5$

14. $\frac{4}{5} - \left(-\frac{3}{10}\right)$ **15.** $5.5 - 8.1$ **16.** $-5 - \frac{5}{3}$

17. $-8\frac{3}{8} - 10\frac{1}{6}$ **18.** $-4.62 - 3.51$ **19.** $-\frac{1}{2} - \left(-\frac{5}{9}\right)$

20. $-7.34 - (-5.51)$ **21.** $6.673 - (-8.29)$ **22.** $12\frac{2}{5} - 17\frac{1}{3}$

23. **MP YOU BE THE TEACHER** Your friend finds the difference. Is your friend correct? Explain your reasoning.

$$\frac{3}{2} - \frac{9}{2} = \left|\frac{3}{2}\right| + \left|\frac{9}{2}\right| = \frac{12}{2} = 6$$

Assignment Guide and Concept Check

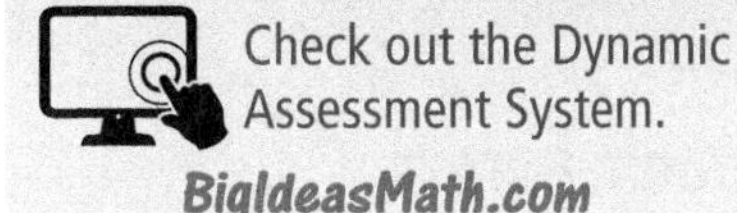
Check out the Dynamic Assessment System.
BigIdeasMath.com

Scaffold assignments to support all students in their learning progression. The suggested assignments are a starting point. Continue to assign additional exercises and revisit with spaced practice to move every student toward proficiency.

Level	Assignment 1	Assignment 2
Emerging	3, 6, 8, 9, 11, 13, 15, 23, 29, 35, 36	18, 19, 24, 26, 27, 30, 39, 40, 44, 46, 55, 56
Proficient	3, 6, 8, 9, 14, 16, 18, 23, 30, 36, 37, 55, 56	21, 22, 24, 27, 28, 32, 41, 44, 45, 48, 52, 57
Advanced	3, 6, 8, 9, 20, 21, 22, 23, 34, 41, 42, 55, 56	24, 27, 28, 43, 44, 45, 50, 51, 52, 53, 54, 57

- Assignment 1 is for use after students complete the Self-Assessment for Concepts & Skills.
- Assignment 2 is for use after students complete the Self-Assessment for Problem Solving.
- The red exercises can be used as a concept check.

Review & Refresh Prior Skills

Exercises 1–4 Subtracting Integers
Exercises 5 and 6 Finding the Volume of a Rectangular Prism
Exercises 7 and 8 Ordering Rational Numbers

Common Errors

- **Exercises 13, 15, 18, 20, and 21** Students may forget to line up the decimal points when they subtract decimals. Remind students that the decimal points must be lined up before subtracting. Students may benefit from using grid paper to help keep the numbers and decimal points aligned.

Review & Refresh

1. 4
2. 0
3. -19
4. 15
5. 64 ft^3
6. 45 m^3
7. $-2, 1, |3|, |-4|, 6$
8. $-3.6, 1.2, |-1.8|, 2, |4.5|$

Concepts, Skills, & Problem Solving

9. $\frac{1}{9}; \frac{3}{9} - \frac{1}{9}; \frac{2}{9}$
10. $\frac{1}{5}; -\frac{4}{5} - (-1); \frac{1}{5}$
11. $1\frac{1}{2}$
12. -3
13. -3.5
14. $1\frac{1}{10}$
15. -2.6
16. $-6\frac{2}{3}$
17. $-18\frac{13}{24}$
18. -8.13
19. $\frac{1}{18}$
20. -1.83
21. 14.963
22. $-4\frac{14}{15}$
23. no; $\frac{3}{2} - \frac{9}{2} = \frac{3}{2} + \left(-\frac{9}{2}\right) = -3$

Concepts, Skills, & Problem Solving

24. *Sample answer:* The temperature rose by 4.5°F and then dropped 6°F for a total change of −1.5°F.

25. *Sample answer:* A judge deducts $\frac{5}{8}$ point from an athlete's score, then removes the deduction after watching a tape of the athlete from another angle.

26. $\frac{11}{24}$ bottle **27.** no; $\frac{1}{12}$ oz

28. when the decimals have the same sign and the digits to the right of the decimal point are the same, or the decimals have different signs and the sum of the decimal parts is 1

29. *Sample answer:* Use the Commutative Property to switch the first two numbers; $\frac{2}{3}$

30. *Sample answer:* Write the subtraction as addition. Then use the Commutative Property to switch the last two numbers; $\frac{3}{10}$

31–34. See Additional Answers.

35. 3.2 **36.** $\frac{5}{9}$

37. 10.6 **38.** $\frac{5}{8}$

39. 9.21 **40.** $3\frac{1}{3}$

41. 5.556 **42.** $3\frac{1}{4}$

43. $13\frac{11}{12}$

44. 51°F; From 2:00 A.M. to 2:00 P.M., the temperature in the Gobi Desert changes by 51°F.

Common Errors

- **Exercises 35–43** Students may find the difference of the numbers but forget to take the absolute value of the difference. Remind students that distance is a positive number or 0.

OPEN-ENDED **Describe a real-life situation that can be represented by the subtraction expression modeled on the number line.**

24.

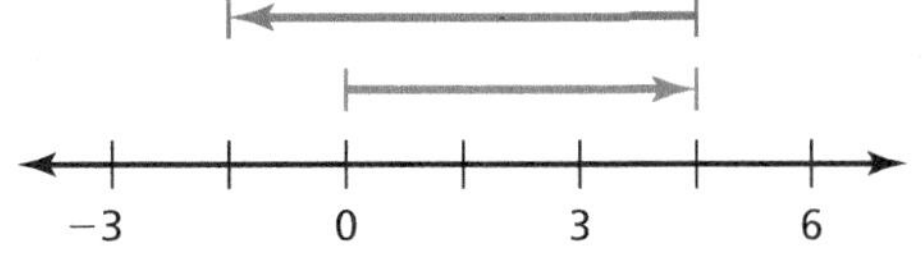

25.

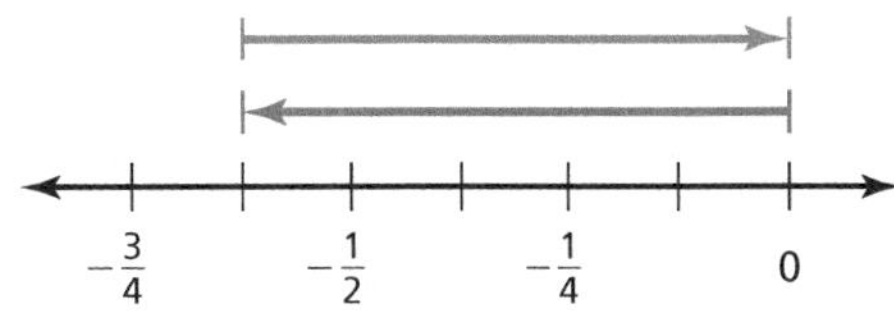

26. MP **MODELING REAL LIFE** Your water bottle is $\frac{5}{6}$ full. After tennis practice, the bottle is $\frac{3}{8}$ full. How much of the water did you drink?

27. MP **MODELING REAL LIFE** You have $2\frac{2}{3}$ ounces of sodium chloride. You want to replicate an experiment that uses $2\frac{3}{4}$ ounces of sodium chloride. Do you have enough sodium chloride? If not, how much more do you need?

28. MP **REASONING** When is the difference of two decimals an integer? Explain.

USING PROPERTIES **Tell how the Commutative and Associative Properties of Addition can help you evaluate the expression. Then evaluate the expression.**

29. $\frac{3}{4} + \frac{2}{3} - \frac{3}{4}$

30. $\frac{2}{5} - \frac{7}{10} - \left(-\frac{3}{5}\right)$

31. $8.5 + 3.4 - 6.5 - (-1.6)$

32. $-1\frac{3}{4} - \left(-8\frac{1}{3}\right) - \left(-4\frac{1}{4}\right)$

33. $2.1 + (5.8 - 4.1)$

34. $2\frac{3}{8} - 4\frac{1}{2} + 3\frac{1}{8} - \left(-\frac{1}{2}\right)$

FINDING DISTANCE ON A NUMBER LINE **Find the distance between the two numbers on a number line.**

35. 2.7 and 5.9

36. $-\frac{7}{9}$ and $-\frac{2}{9}$

37. −2.2 and 8.4

38. $\frac{3}{4}$ and $\frac{1}{8}$

39. −1.85 and 7.36

40. −7 and $-3\frac{2}{3}$

41. 2.491 and −3.065

42. $-2\frac{1}{2}$ and $-5\frac{3}{4}$

43. $-1\frac{1}{3}$ and $12\frac{7}{12}$

44. MP **MODELING REAL LIFE** The number line shows the temperatures at 2:00 A.M. and 2:00 P.M. in the Gobi Desert. Find and interpret the distance between the points.

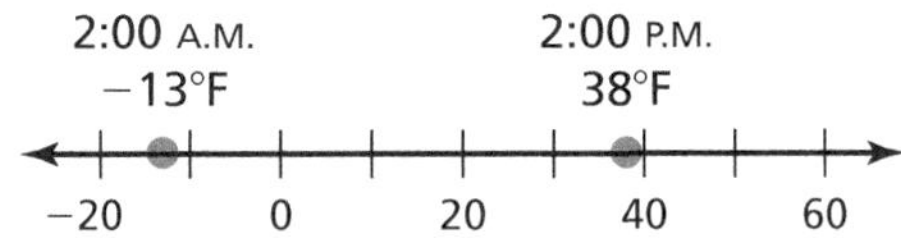

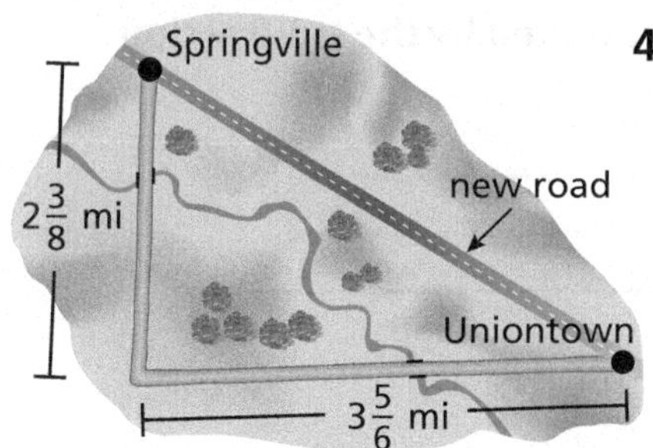

45. **MP PROBLEM SOLVING** A new road that connects Uniontown to Springville is $4\frac{1}{3}$ miles long. What is the change in distance when using the new road instead of the dirt roads?

FINDING DISTANCE IN A COORDINATE PLANE **Find the distance between the points in a coordinate plane.**

46. $(-4, 7.8), (-4, -3.5)$

47. $(-2.63, 7), (1.85, 7)$

48. $\left(-\frac{1}{2}, -1\right), \left(\frac{5}{8}, -1\right)$

49. $\left(6, 2\frac{1}{3}\right), \left(6, -5\frac{2}{9}\right)$

50. $(-6.2, 1.4), (8.9, 1.4)$

51. $\left(7\frac{1}{7}, 1\frac{4}{5}\right), \left(7\frac{1}{7}, -\frac{9}{10}\right)$

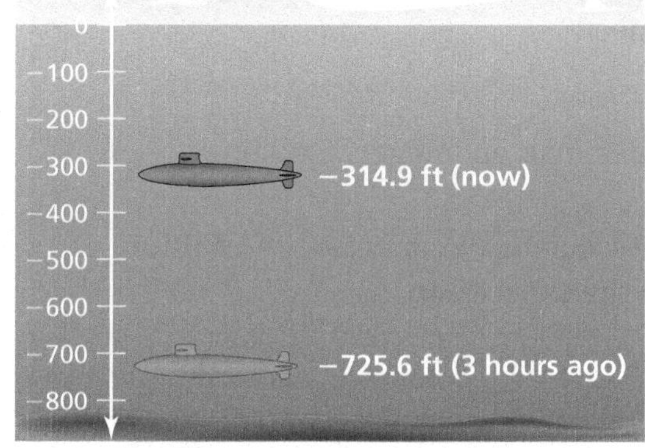

52. **DIG DEEPER!** The figure shows the elevations of a submarine.

a. Find the vertical distance traveled by the submarine.

b. Find the mean hourly vertical distance traveled by the submarine.

53. **MP LOGIC** The bar graph shows how each month's rainfall compares to the historical average.

a. What is the difference in rainfall of the wettest month and the driest month?

b. What do you know about the total amount of rainfall for the year?

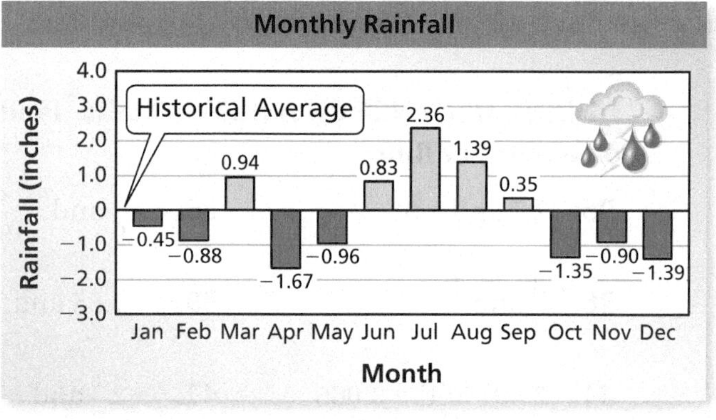

54. **OPEN-ENDED** Write two different pairs of negative decimals, x and y, that make the statement $x - y = 0.6$ true.

MP REASONING **Tell whether the difference of the two numbers is *always, sometimes,* or *never* positive. Explain your reasoning.**

55. two negative fractions

56. a positive decimal and a negative decimal

57. **MP STRUCTURE** Fill in the blanks to complete the decimals.

$$5.\square 4 - \square.\square = -3.61$$

Common Errors

- **Exercises 46–51** Students may find the difference of the coordinates that are different but forget to take the absolute value of the difference. Remind students that distance is a positive number or 0.

Mini-Assessment

Find the difference. Write fractions in simplest form.

1. $\frac{1}{2} - \frac{3}{4}$ $-\frac{1}{4}$
2. $2\frac{2}{5} - \left(-\frac{6}{5}\right)$ $3\frac{3}{5}$
3. $-12.55 - (-23.08)$ 10.53
4. Find the distance between -2.4 and 6.7. 9.1
5. The temperature in a town is -4.7°C. The temperature decreases 5.4°C. What is the new temperature? -10.1°C

Section Resources

Surface Level	Deep Level
Resources by Chapter • Extra Practice • Reteach • Puzzle Time Student Journal • Self-Assessment • Practice Differentiating the Lesson Tutorial Videos Skills Review Handbook Skills Trainer	Resources by Chapter • Enrichment and Extension Graphic Organizers Dynamic Assessment System • Section Practice
Transfer Level	
Dynamic Assessment System • End-of-Chapter Quiz	Assessment Book • End-of-Chapter Quiz

Concepts, Skills, & Problem Solving

45. $-1\frac{7}{8}$ mi
46. 11.3
47. 4.48
48. $1\frac{1}{8}$
49. $7\frac{5}{9}$
50. 15.1
51. $2\frac{7}{10}$
52. **a.** 410.7 ft
    b. 136.9 ft/h
53. **a.** 4.03 in.
    b. The rainfall is 1.73 inches below the historical average for the year.
54. *Sample answer:* $x = -1.8$ and $y = -2.4$; $x = -5.5$ and $y = -6.1$
55. sometimes; It is positive only if the first fraction is greater.
56. always; It is always positive because the first decimal is always greater.
57. 2; 8; 85

Skills Needed

Exercise 1

- Drawing a Polygon in the Coordinate Plane
- Finding the Area of a Parallelogram
- Finding Distance in a Coordinate Plane
- Subtracting Rational Numbers

Exercise 2

- Adding Rational Numbers
- Solving Inequalities
- Subtracting Rational Numbers
- Writing Inequalities

ELL Support

For Exercise 2, tell ELLs that in the U.S. height is typically measured in feet and inches. The metric system is not the standard. Explain that 1 meter is approximately 3.28 feet and 1 inch is $\frac{1}{12}$ of a foot. Point out that the plural of foot is feet, not foots.

Using the Problem-Solving Plan

1. 15.9375 mi^2

2. $x + 5\frac{1}{4} \geq 5\frac{1}{3}$; at least $\frac{1}{12}$ foot or 1 inch taller

Performance Task

The *STEAM Video Performance Task* provides the opportunity for additional enrichment and greater depth of knowledge as students explore the mathematics of the chapter within a context tied to the chapter STEAM Video. The performance task and a detailed scoring rubric are provided at *BigIdeasMath.com.*

Laurie's Notes

Scaffolding Instruction

- The goal of this lesson is to help students become more comfortable with problem solving. These exercises combine adding and subtracting rational numbers with prior skills from other chapters. The solution for Exercise 1 is worked out below, to help you guide students through the problem-solving plan. Use the remaining class time to have students work on the other exercise.
- **Emerging:** The goal for these students is to feel comfortable with the problem-solving plan. Allow students to work in pairs to write the beginning steps of the problem-solving plan for Exercise 2. Keep in mind that some students may only be ready to do the first step.
- **Proficient:** Students may be able to work independently or in pairs to complete Exercise 2.
- Visit each pair to review their plan. Ask students to describe their plans.

Using the Problem-Solving Plan

Exercise 1

Understand the problem. You know the vertices of a parallelogram-shaped park and that each unit represents 1 mile. You are asked to find the area of the park.

Make a plan. Use a coordinate plane to draw a map of the park. Then find the height and base length of the park. Find the area by using the formula for the area of a parallelogram.

Solve and check. Use the plan to solve the problem. Then check your solution.

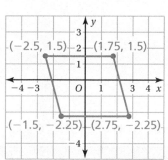

- Draw a map of the park.
- Find the height of the park.
  $h = |1.5 - (-2.25)| = |1.5 + 2.25|$
  $= |3.75| = 3.75$
  So, the height of the park is 3.75 miles.
- Find the base length of the park.
  $b = |2.75 - (-1.5)| = |2.75 + 1.5|$
  $= |4.25| = 4.25$
  So, the base length of the park is 4.25 miles.
- Find the area of the park.
  $A = (4.25)(3.75)$
  $= 15.9375 \text{ mi}^2$
  So, the area of the park is 15.9375 square miles.
- **Check:** Count the grid squares to estimate the area of the park.
  There are about 16 grid squares.
  Each grid square represents $(1.0 \text{ mi})(1.0 \text{ mi}) = 1.0 \text{ mi}^2$ and $16 \times 1.0 = 16 \text{ mi}^2$, which is about 15.9375 mi^2. ✓

A Connecting Concepts

Problem-Solving Strategies

Using an appropriate strategy will help you make sense of problems as you study the mathematics in this course. You can use the following strategies to solve problems that you encounter.

- Use a verbal model.
- Draw a diagram.
- Write an equation.
- Solve a simpler problem.
- Sketch a graph or number line.
- Make a table.
- Make a list.
- Break the problem into parts.

Using the Problem-Solving Plan

1. A land surveyor uses a coordinate plane to draw a map of a park, where each unit represents 1 mile. The park is in the shape of a parallelogram with vertices $(-2.5, 1.5)$, $(-1.5, -2.25)$, $(2.75, -2.25)$, and $(1.75, 1.5)$. Find the area of the park.

Understand the problem. You know the vertices of the parallelogram-shaped park and that each unit represents 1 mile. You are asked to find the area of the park.

Make a plan. Use a coordinate plane to draw a map of the park. Then find the height and base length of the park. Find the area by using the formula for the area of a parallelogram.

Solve and check. Use the plan to solve the problem. Then check your solution.

2. The diagram shows the height requirement for driving a go-cart. You are $5\frac{1}{4}$ feet tall. Write and solve an inequality to represent how much taller you must be to drive a go-cart.

Performance Task

Melting Matters

At the beginning of this chapter, you watched a STEAM Video called "Freezing Solids." You are now ready to complete the performance task related to this video, available at ***BigIdeasMath.com***. Be sure to use the problem-solving plan as you work through the performance task.

A Chapter Review

Review Vocabulary

Write the definition and give an example of each vocabulary term.

integers, *p. 503*
rational number, *p. 503*
absolute value, *p. 504*
additive inverse, *p. 511*

Graphic Organizers

You can use a **Definition and Example Chart** to organize information about a concept. Here is an example of a Definition and Example Chart for the vocabulary term ***absolute value***.

Absolute value: the distance between a number and 0 on a number line

Example
$|3| = 3$

Example
$|-5| = 5$

Example
$|0| = 0$

Choose and complete a graphic organizer to help you study the concept.

1. integers
2. rational numbers
3. adding integers
4. Additive Inverse Property
5. adding rational numbers
6. subtracting integers
7. subtracting rational numbers

"I made a Definition and Example Chart to give my owner ideas for my birthday next week."

Review Vocabulary

- As a review of the chapter vocabulary, have students revisit the vocabulary section in their *Student Journals* to fill in any missing definitions and record examples of each term.

Graphic Organizers

Sample answers:

1.

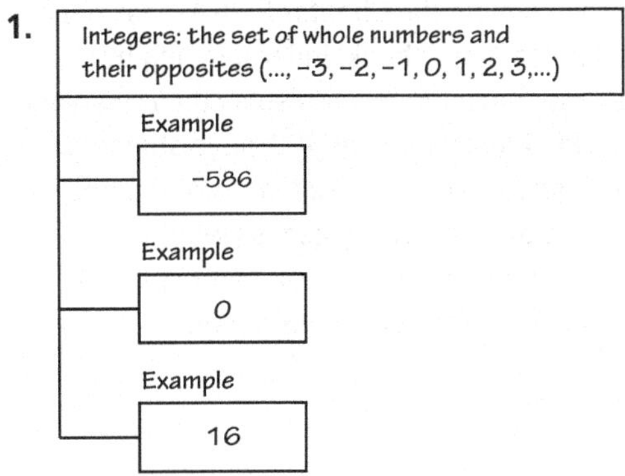

Integers: the set of whole numbers and their opposites (..., −3, −2, −1, 0, 1, 2, 3,...)
Example
−586
Example
0
Example
16

2.

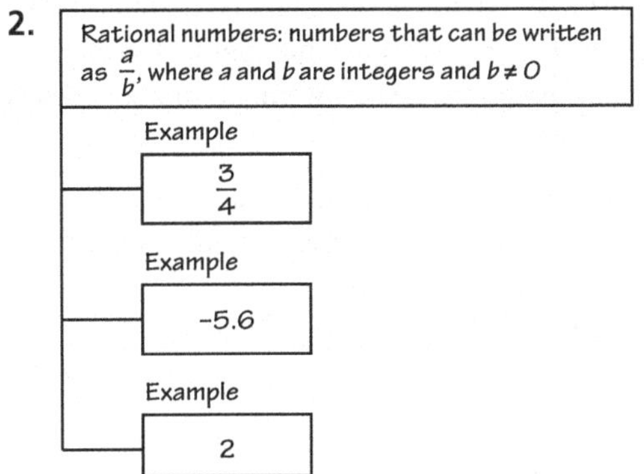

Rational numbers: numbers that can be written as $\frac{a}{b}$, where a and b are integers and $b \neq 0$
Example
$\frac{3}{4}$
Example
−5.6
Example
2

3.

Adding integers: To add integers with the same sign, add the absolute values of the integers. Then use the common sign. To add integers with different signs, subtract the lesser absolute value from the greater absolute value. Then use the sign of the integer with the greater absolute value.

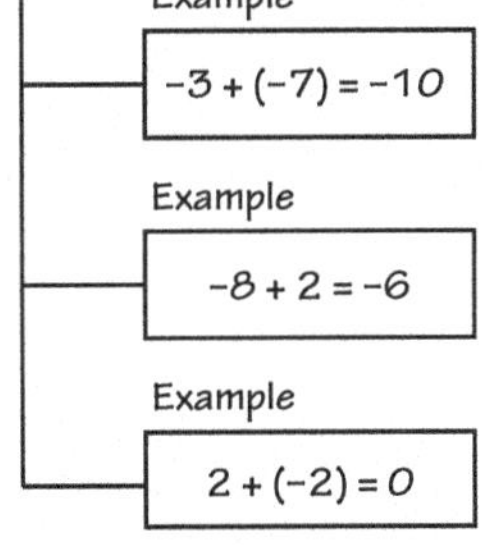

Example
$-3 + (-7) = -10$
Example
$-8 + 2 = -6$
Example
$2 + (-2) = 0$

4–7. Answers at *BigIdeasMath.com.*

List of Organizers

Available at *BigIdeasMath*.com

Definition and Example Chart

Example and Non-Example Chart

Four Square

Information Frame

Summary Triangle

About this Organizer

A **Definition and Example Chart** can be used to organize information about a concept. Students fill in the top rectangle with a term and its definition or description. Students fill in the rectangles that follow with examples to illustrate the term. Each sample answer shows three examples, but students can show more or fewer examples. Definition and Example Charts are useful for concepts that can be illustrated with more than one type of example.

Chapter Self-Assessment

1. 3
2. 9
3. $\frac{3}{4}$
4. 5.2
5. $\frac{6}{7}$
6. 4.15
7. >
8. <
9. =
10. $-2, 1\frac{1}{4}, |-1.5|, |2.25|, \left|2\frac{1}{2}\right|$
11. you
12. *Sample answer:* $a = -5, b = 4$
13. Nairobi

The Success Criteria Self-Assessment chart can be found in the *Student Journal* or online at *BigIdeasMath.com.*

ELL Support

Allow students to work in pairs to complete the Chapter Self-Assessment. Once pairs have completed the first section, check understanding by asking for answers to each exercise. Have each pair display their answers on a whiteboard for your review. To check Exercises 7–9, have students use thumbs up for *greater than*, thumbs down for *less than*, and thumbs sideways for *equal to*. You should be able to quickly assess whether the majority of students understand the concepts. Use these techniques to check the remaining sections of the Chapter Self-Assessment.

Common Errors

- **Exercises 1–6** Students may think that the absolute value of a number is its opposite. For example, they may think $|6| = -6$. Use a number line to show students that the absolute value is a number's distance from 0, so it is always a positive number or zero.
- **Exercises 7–10** When comparing or ordering absolute values of negative numbers, students may not find the absolute values and instead compare or order the numbers themselves.

Chapter Self-Assessment

As you complete the exercises, use the scale below to rate your understanding of the success criteria in your journal.

1	2	3	4
I do not understand.	I can do it with help.	I can do it on my own.	I can teach someone else.

A.1 Rational Numbers *(pp. 503–508)*

Learning Target: Understand absolute values and ordering of rational numbers.

Find the absolute value.

1. $|3|$

2. $|-9|$

3. $\left|\frac{3}{4}\right|$

4. $|-5.2|$

5. $\left|-\frac{6}{7}\right|$

6. $|4.15|$

Copy and complete the statement using <, >, or =.

7. $|-2|$ ▢ -2

8. $\left|-\frac{1}{3}\right|$ ▢ $\left|-\frac{5}{6}\right|$

9. $-|1.7|$ ▢ -1.7

10. Order $|2.25|$, $|-1.5|$, $1\frac{1}{4}$, $\left|2\frac{1}{2}\right|$, and -2 from least to greatest.

11. Your friend is in Death Valley, California, at an elevation of -282 feet. You are near the Mississippi River in Illinois at an elevation of 279 feet. Who is closer to sea level?

12. Give values for a and b so that $a < b$ and $|a| > |b|$.

13. The map shows the longitudes (in degrees) for Salvador, Brazil, and Nairobi, Kenya. Which city is closer to the Prime Meridian?

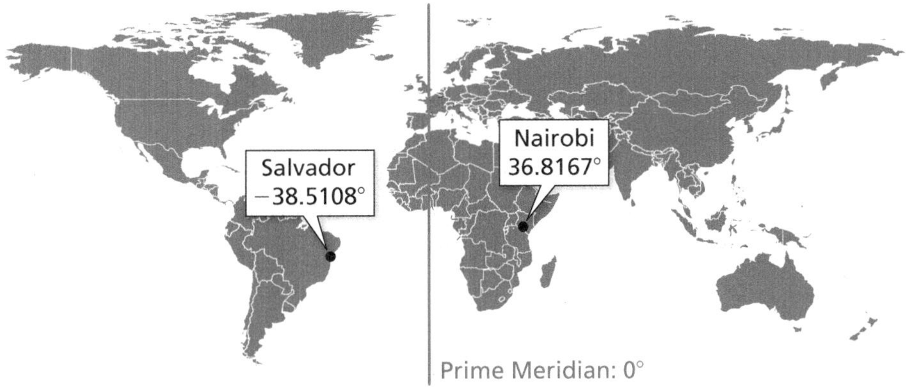

A.2 Adding Integers (pp. 509–516)

Learning Target: Find sums of integers.

14. Write an addition expression represented by the number line. Then find the sum.

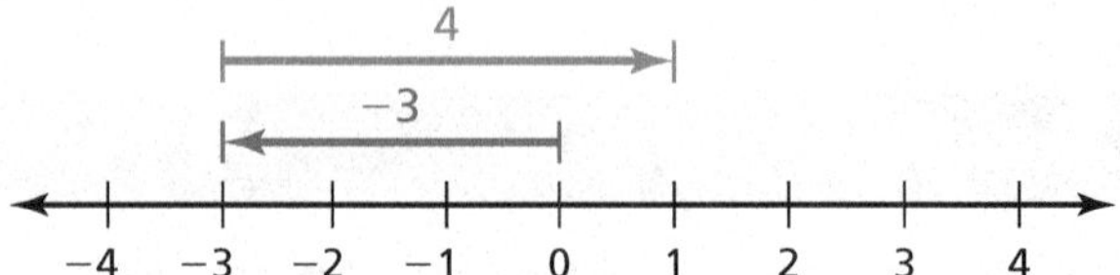

Find the sum. Use a number line to verify your answer.

15. $-16 + (-11)$ **16.** $-15 + 5$ **17.** $100 + (-75)$

18. $-32 + (-2)$ **19.** $-2 + (-7) + 15$ **20.** $9 + (-14) + 3$

21. During the first play of a football game, you lose 3 yards. You gain 7 yards during the second play. What is your total gain of yards for these two plays?

22. Write an addition expression using integers that equals -2. Use a number line to justify your answer.

23. Describe a real-life situation that uses the sum of the integers -8 and 12.

A.3 Adding Rational Numbers (pp. 517–522)

Learning Target: Find sums of rational numbers.

Find the sum. Write fractions in simplest form.

24. $\frac{9}{10} + \left(-\frac{4}{5}\right)$ **25.** $-4\frac{5}{9} + \frac{8}{9}$ **26.** $-1.6 + (-2.4)$

27. Find the sum of $-4 + 6\frac{2}{5} + (-2.7)$. Explain each step.

28. You open a new bank account. The table shows the activity of your account for the first month. Positive numbers represent deposits and negative numbers represent withdrawals. What is your balance (in dollars) in the account at the end of the first month?

Date	Amount (dollars)
3/5	100
3/12	−12.25
3/16	25.82
3/21	14.95
3/29	−18.56

- **Exercises 15–20** Students may ignore the signs and just add the absolute values. Make sure they understand that they should use the sign of the number that is farther from zero. Also remind them of how the signs of the integers determine if they need to find the sum or difference of the absolute values.
- **Exercise 24** Students may try to identify the sign of the answer before finding a common denominator. Remind students that they need to find a common denominator first.

Chapter Self-Assessment

14. $-3 + 4; 1$

15. -27

16. -10

17. 25

18. -34

19. 6

20. -2

21. 4 yd

22. *Sample answer:* $2 + (-4)$

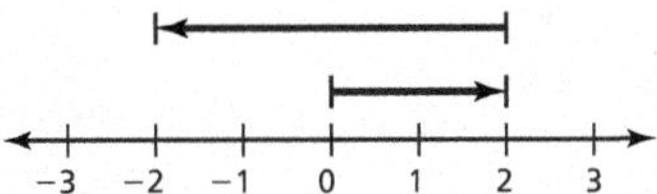

23. *Sample answer:* A team loses the first round of a competition by 8 points and wins the second round by 12 points, winning by 4 points totaled.

24. $\frac{1}{10}$

25. $-3\frac{2}{3}$

26. -4

27. *Sample answer:*

$-4 + 6\frac{2}{5} + (-2.7)$

$= -4 + (-2.7) + 6\frac{2}{5}$

Comm. Prop. of Add.

$= -6.7 + 6\frac{2}{5}$

Add -4 and -2.7.

$= -6.7 + 6.4$

Write $6\frac{2}{5}$ as a decimal.

$= -0.3$ Add.

28. $109.96

Chapter Self-Assessment

29. -10

30. -11

31. -25

32. 15

33. -700 points

34. -36°C

35. $6

36. *Sample answer:* $-10 - (-4)$

37. *Sample answer:* $-6, (-8)$

38. $-\frac{43}{60}$

39. $2\frac{7}{8}$

40. 11.25

41. 1.12

42. $-11\frac{5}{12}$ in.

43. 145.9°C

Common Errors

- **Exercises 29–32** Students may change the sign of the first number or forget to change the problem from subtraction to addition when changing the sign of the second number. Remind them that the first number is a starting point and will never change, but the sign of the second number and the operation will change.
- **Exercise 40** Students may forget to line up the decimal points when they subtract decimals. Remind students that the decimal points must be lined up before subtracting. Students may benefit from using grid paper to help keep the numbers and decimal points aligned.
- **Exercise 41** Students may find the difference of the numbers but forget to take the absolute value of the difference. Remind students that distance is a positive number or 0.

Chapter Resources

Surface Level	Deep Level
Resources by Chapter • Extra Practice • Reteach • Puzzle Time Student Journal • Practice • Chapter Self-Assessment Differentiating the Lesson Tutorial Videos Skills Review Handbook Skills Trainer Game Library	Resources by Chapter • Enrichment and Extension Graphic Organizers Game Library
Transfer Level	
STEAM Video Dynamic Assessment System • Chapter Test	Assessment Book • Chapter Tests A and B • Alternative Assessment • STEAM Performance Task

A.4 Subtracting Integers *(pp. 523–528)*

Learning Target: Find differences of integers.

Find the difference. Use a number line to verify your answer.

29. $8 - 18$ **30.** $-16 - (-5)$ **31.** $-18 - 7$ **32.** $-12 - (-27)$

33. Your score on a game show is -300. You answer the final question incorrectly, so you lose 400 points. What is your final score?

34. Oxygen has a boiling point of $-183°C$ and a melting point of $-219°C$. What is the temperature difference of the melting point and the boiling point?

35. In one month, you earn \$16 for mowing the lawn, \$15 for babysitting, and \$20 for allowance. You spend \$12 at the movie theater. How much more money do you need to buy a \$45 video game?

36. Write a subtraction expression using integers that equals -6.

37. Write two negative integers whose difference is positive.

A.5 Subtracting Rational Numbers *(pp. 529–536)*

Learning Target: Find differences of rational numbers and find distances between numbers on a number line.

Find the difference. Write fractions in simplest form.

38. $-\frac{5}{12} - \frac{3}{10}$ **39.** $3\frac{3}{4} - \frac{7}{8}$ **40.** $3.8 - (-7.45)$

41. Find the distance between -3.71 and -2.59 on a number line.

42. A turtle is $20\frac{5}{6}$ inches below the surface of a pond. It dives to a depth of $32\frac{1}{4}$ inches. What is the change in the turtle's position?

43. The lowest temperature ever recorded on Earth was $-89.2°C$ at Soviet Vostok Station in Antarctica. The highest temperature ever recorded was $56.7°C$ at Greenland Ranch in California. What is the difference between the highest and lowest recorded temperatures?

Practice Test

Find the absolute value.

1. $\left| -\frac{4}{5} \right|$

2. $|6.43|$

3. $|-22|$

Copy and complete the statement using <, >, or =.

4. $4 \; \square \; |-8|$

5. $|-7| \; \square \; -12$

6. $-7 \; \square \; |3|$

Add or subtract. Write fractions in simplest form.

7. $-6 + (-11)$

8. $2 - (-9)$

9. $-\frac{4}{9} + \left(-\frac{23}{18}\right)$

10. $\frac{17}{12} - \left(-\frac{1}{8}\right)$

11. $9.2 + (-2.8)$

12. $2.86 - 12.1$

13. Write an addition expression and write a subtraction expression represented by the number line. Then evaluate the expressions.

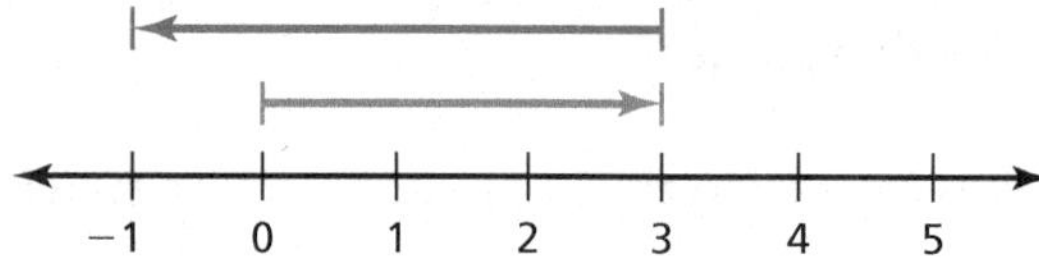

14. The table shows your scores, relative to *par*, for nine holes of golf. What is your total score for the nine holes?

Hole	1	2	3	4	5	6	7	8	9
Score	+1	−2	−1	0	−1	+3	−1	−3	+1

15. The elevation of a fish is −27 feet. The fish descends 32 feet, and then rises 14 feet. What is its new elevation?

16. The table shows the rainfall (in inches) for three months compared to the yearly average. Is the total rainfall for the three-month period greater than or less than the yearly average? Explain.

October	November	December
−0.86	2.56	−1.24

17. Bank Account A has \$750.92, and Bank Account B has \$675.44. Account A changes by -\$216.38, and Account B changes by −\$168.49. Which account has the greater balance? Explain.

18. On January 1, you recorded the lowest temperature as 23°F and the highest temperature as 6°C. A formula for converting from degrees Fahrenheit F to degrees Celsius C is $C = \frac{5}{9}F - \frac{160}{9}$. What is the temperature range (in degrees Celsius) for January 1?

Practice Test Item References

Practice Test Questions	Section to Review
1, 2, 3, 4, 5, 6	A.1
7, 14	A.2
9, 11, 16, 17	A.3
8, 13, 15	A.4
10, 12, 18	A.5

Test-Taking Strategies

Remind students to quickly look over the entire test before they start so that they can budget their time. They should not spend too much time on any single problem. Urge students to try to work on a part of each problem, because partial credit is better than no credit. When students hurry on a test dealing with positive and negative numbers, they often make "sign" errors. Sometimes it helps to represent each problem with a number line to ensure that they are thinking through the process. Teach students to use the **Stop** and **Think** strategy before answering. **Stop** and carefully read the problem and **Think** about what the answer should look like.

Common Errors

- **Exercises 1–3** Students may think that the absolute value of a number is its opposite. For example, they may think $|6| = -6$. Use a number line to show students that the absolute value is a number's distance from 0, so it is always a positive number or zero.
- **Exercises 4–6** When comparing absolute values of negative numbers, students may not find the absolute values and instead compare the numbers themselves.
- **Exercises 7, 9, and 11** Students may ignore the signs and just add the absolute values. Make sure they understand that they should use the sign of the number that is farther from zero. Also remind them of how the signs of the numbers determine if they need to find the sum or difference of the absolute values.
- **Exercises 8, 10, and 12** Students may change the sign of the first number or forget to change the problem from subtraction to addition when changing the sign of the second number. Remind them that the first number is a starting point and will never change. Also remind students that the sign of the second number and the operation change.

Practice Test

1. $\frac{4}{5}$
2. 6.43
3. 22
4. $<$
5. $>$
6. $<$
7. -17
8. 11
9. $-1\frac{13}{18}$
10. $1\frac{13}{24}$
11. 6.4
12. -9.24
13. $3 + (-4); 3 - 4; -1$
14. -3
15. -45 ft
16. greater than; The sum of the rainfalls for the three months is 0.46 inch.
17. Bank Account A; Bank Account A has $534.54 while Bank Account B only has $506.95.
18. 11°C

Test-Taking Strategies

Available at *BigIdeasMath.com*

After Answering Easy Questions, Relax

Answer Easy Questions First

Estimate the Answer

Read All Choices before Answering

Read Question before Answering

Solve Directly or Eliminate Choices

Solve Problem before Looking at Choices

Use Intelligent Guessing

Work Backwards

About this Strategy

When taking a multiple-choice test, be sure to read each question carefully and thoroughly. Before answering a question, determine exactly what is being asked, then eliminate the wrong answers and select the best choice.

Cumulative Practice

1. C
2. H
3. C
4. 25
5. I

Item Analysis

1. **A.** The student treats all numbers as gains and finds the sum.
   B. The student finds the correct total but thinks it is a gain instead of a loss.
   C. Correct answer
   D. The student treats all numbers as losses and finds the sum.

2. **F.** The student does not perform the operation correctly.
   G. The student does not perform the operation correctly.
   H. Correct answer
   I. The student does not perform the operation correctly.

3. **A.** The student finds the sum of -2 and -2.5 instead of finding the difference and forgets to find the absolute value of the result.
   B. The student correctly simplifies the expression inside the absolute value bars but finds the opposite of 0.5 instead of the absolute value.
   C. Correct answer
   D. The student finds the absolute value of each number inside the absolute value bars instead of simplifying the expression inside the absolute value bars and then finds the sum of 2 and 2.5.

4. **Gridded Response:** Correct answer: 25

   Common error: The student thinks that $17 - (-8)$ is equivalent to $17 - 8$ and gets an answer of 9.

5. **F.** The student correctly finds the difference of the numbers but forgets to find the absolute value.
   G. The student finds the sum of the numbers instead of the difference and then forgets to find the absolute value.
   H. The student finds the sum of the numbers instead of the difference.
   I. Correct answer

Cumulative Practice

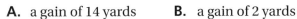

Test-Taking Strategy

Solve Directly or Eliminate Choices

Three swamp cats meet for lunch. One disappears. How many swamp cats are left?

Ⓐ 3 + 1 Ⓑ 3 + (−1)

Ⓒ 2 + 2 Ⓓ −17

What happened? Now I won't be able to sleep.

"You can eliminate C and D. Then solve directly to determine that the correct answer is B."

1. A football team gains 2 yards on the first play, loses 5 yards on the second play, loses 3 yards on the third play, and gains 4 yards on the fourth play. What is the team's total gain or loss?

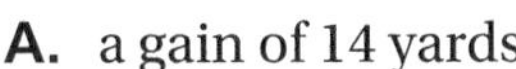

A. a gain of 14 yards **B.** a gain of 2 yards

C. a loss of 2 yards **D.** a loss of 14 yards

2. Which expression is *not* equal to 0?

F. $5 - 5$ **G.** $-7 + 7$

H. $6 - (-6)$ **I.** $-8 - (-8)$

3. What is the value of the expression?

$$|-2 - (-2.5)|$$

A. -4.5 **B.** -0.5

C. 0.5 **D.** 4.5

4. What is the value of the expression?

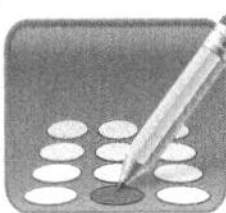

$$17 - (-8)$$

5. What is the distance between the two numbers on the number line?

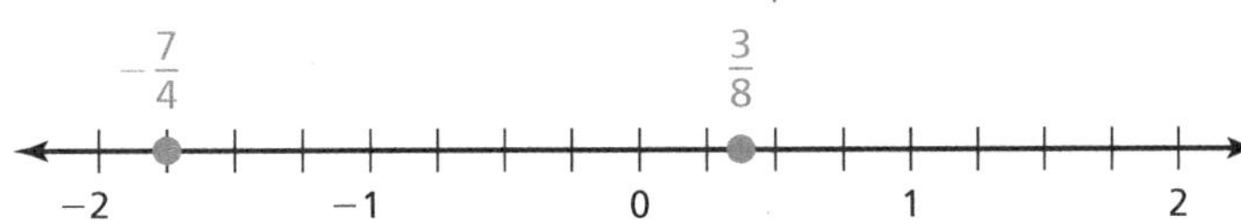

F. $-2\frac{1}{8}$ **G.** $-1\frac{3}{8}$

H. $1\frac{3}{8}$ **I.** $2\frac{1}{8}$

6. What is the value of the expression when $a = 8$, $b = 3$, and $c = 6$?

$$\left| a^2 - 2ac + 5b \right|$$

A. -65

B. -17

C. 17

D. 65

7. What is the value of the expression?

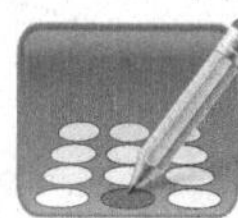

$$-9.74 + (-2.23)$$

8. Four friends are playing a game using the spinner shown. Each friend starts with a score of 0 and then spins four times. When you spin blue, you add the number to your score. When you spin red, you subtract the number from your score. The highest score after four spins wins. Each friend's spins are shown. Which spins belong to the winner?

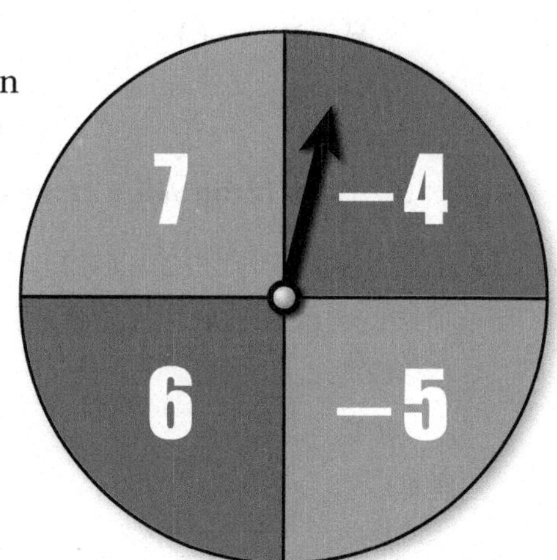

F. 6, 7, 7, 6

G. $-4, -4, 7, -5$

H. $6, -5, -4, 7$

I. $-5, 6, -5, 6$

9. What number belongs in the box to make the equation true?

$$3\frac{1}{2} \div 5\frac{2}{3} = \frac{7}{2} \times \square$$

A. $\frac{3}{17}$

B. $\frac{3}{2}$

C. $\frac{17}{3}$

D. $\frac{13}{2}$

10. What is the value of the expression?

$$\frac{5.2 - 2.25}{0.05}$$

F. -346

G. 0.59

H. 5.9

I. 59

Item Analysis (continued)

6. **A.** The student multiplies the value of a by 2 instead of squaring the value of a and then forgets to find the absolute value.

   B. The student evaluates the expression inside the absolute value bars correctly but forgets to find the absolute value.

   C. Correct answer

   D. The student multiplies the value of a by 2 instead of squaring the value of a.

7. **Gridded Response:** Correct answer: -11.97

   Common error: The student subtracts the two numbers instead of adding and gets -7.51.

8. **F.** The student adds the red values instead of subtracting.

   G. Correct answer

   H. The student adds the absolute values of the numbers for this spin but calculates the values of other spins correctly.

   I. The student chooses the spin with the greatest absolute value, not the greatest value.

9. **A.** Correct answer

   B. The student only finds the reciprocal of the fractional part of the divisor and ignores the whole number.

   C. The student rewrites the divisor as $\frac{17}{3}$ but does not find the reciprocal.

   D. The student only finds the reciprocal of the fractional part of the divisor and rewrites it as $5\frac{3}{2}$, which the student then rewrites as $\frac{13}{2}$.

10. **F.** The student subtracts 5.2 from 2.25 instead of subtracting 2.25 from 5.2.

    G. The student divides by 5 instead of dividing by 0.05.

    H. The student divides by 0.5 instead of dividing by 0.05.

    I. Correct answer

Cumulative Practice

6. C
7. -11.97
8. G
9. A
10. I

Cumulative Practice

11. D

12. G

13. D

14. a. -5

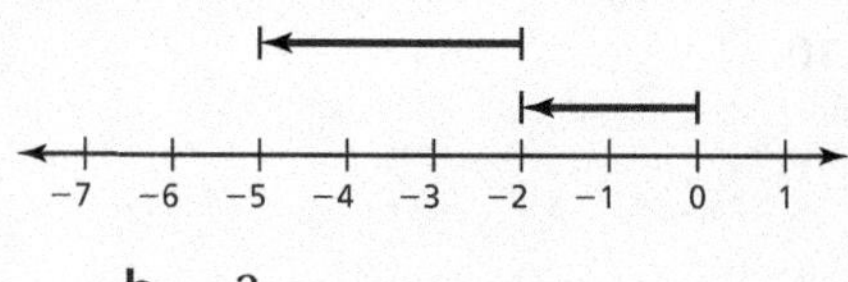

b. -3

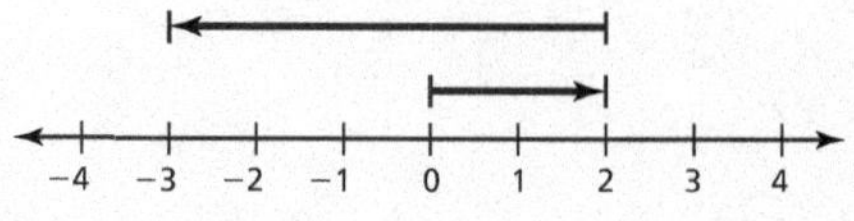

15. F

Item Analysis (continued)

11. A. The student finds the difference instead of finding the sum of the distances.

B. The student finds the product of the distances instead of finding the sum.

C. The student does not line up the decimal points correctly when finding the sum.

D. Correct answer

12. F. The student misidentifies the property as the Commutative Property of Addition.

G. Correct answer

H. The student misidentifies the property as the Additive Inverse Property.

I. The student misidentifies the property as the Addition Property of Zero.

13. A. The student identifies the two negative points that are the greatest distance apart instead of finding the greatest sum.

B. The student identifies the two points that are the greatest distance apart instead of finding the greatest sum.

C. The student misidentifies point S as a positive point and then identifies the two "positive" points that are the greatest distance apart instead of finding the greatest sum.

D. Correct answer

14. 2 points The student's explanations demonstrate a thorough understanding of adding and subtracting integers using a number line. The student demonstrates how to add using a number line, writes the expression, and gets the correct answer $-2 + (-3) = -5$. The student demonstrates how to subtract using a number line, writes the expression, and gets the correct answer $2 - 5 = -3$.

1 point The student's explanations demonstrate a partial but limited understanding of adding and subtracting integers using a number line. The student shows some knowledge of adding and subtracting integers but is not successful in determining the correct answers.

0 points The student provides no response, a completely incorrect or incomprehensible response, or a response that demonstrates insufficient understanding of adding and subtracting integers using a number line.

15. F. Correct answer

G. The student does not find the absolute values in answer choices F or G.

H. The student does not find the absolute value in answer choice F and finds the opposites in answer choice H instead of finding the absolute values.

I. The student does not find the absolute value in answer choices F and I.

11. You leave school and walk 1.237 miles west. Your friend leaves school and walks 0.56 mile east. How far apart are you and your friend?

A. 0.677 mile

B. 0.69272 mile

C. 1.293 miles

D. 1.797 miles

12. Which property does the equation represent?

$$-80 + 30 + (-30) = -80 + [30 + (-30)]$$

F. Commutative Property of Addition

G. Associative Property of Addition

H. Additive Inverse Property

I. Addition Property of Zero

13. The values of which two points have the greatest sum?

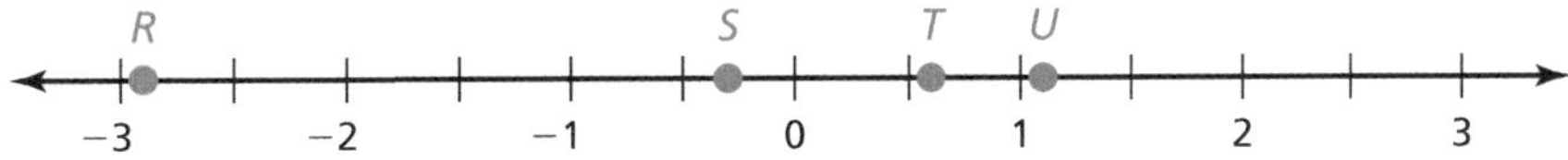

A. R and S

B. R and U

C. S and T

D. T and U

14. Consider the number line shown.

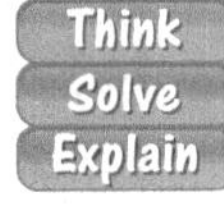

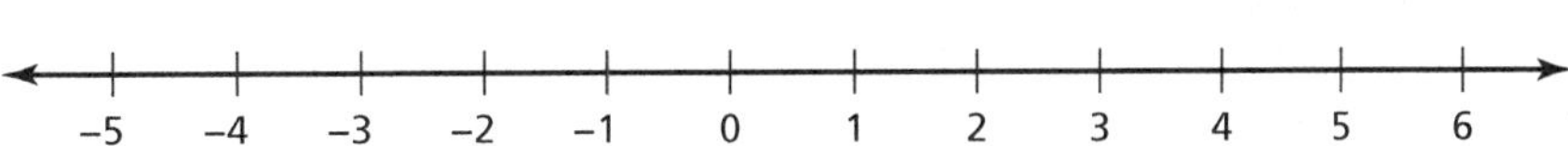

Part A Use the number line to explain how to add −2 and −3.

Part B Use the number line to explain how to subtract 5 from 2.

15. Which expression represents a *negative* value?

F. $2 - |-7 + 3|$

G. $|-12 + 9|$

H. $|5| + |11|$

I. $|8 - 14|$

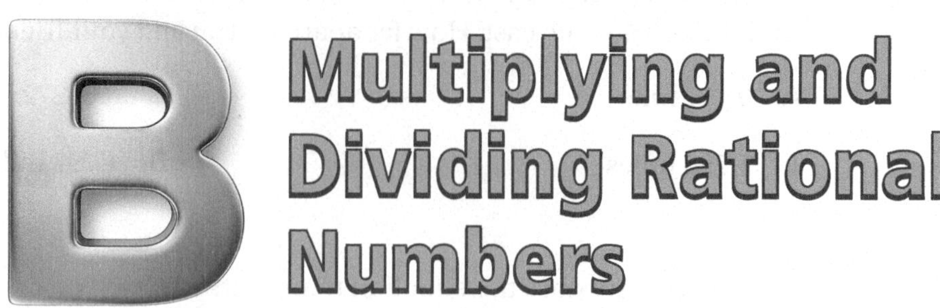

B Multiplying and Dividing Rational Numbers

Chapter Learning Target:
Understand multiplying and dividing rational numbers.

Chapter Success Criteria:
- I can explain the rules for multiplying integers.
- I can explain the rules for dividing integers.
- I can evaluate expressions involving rational numbers.
- I can solve real-life problems involving multiplication and division of rational numbers.

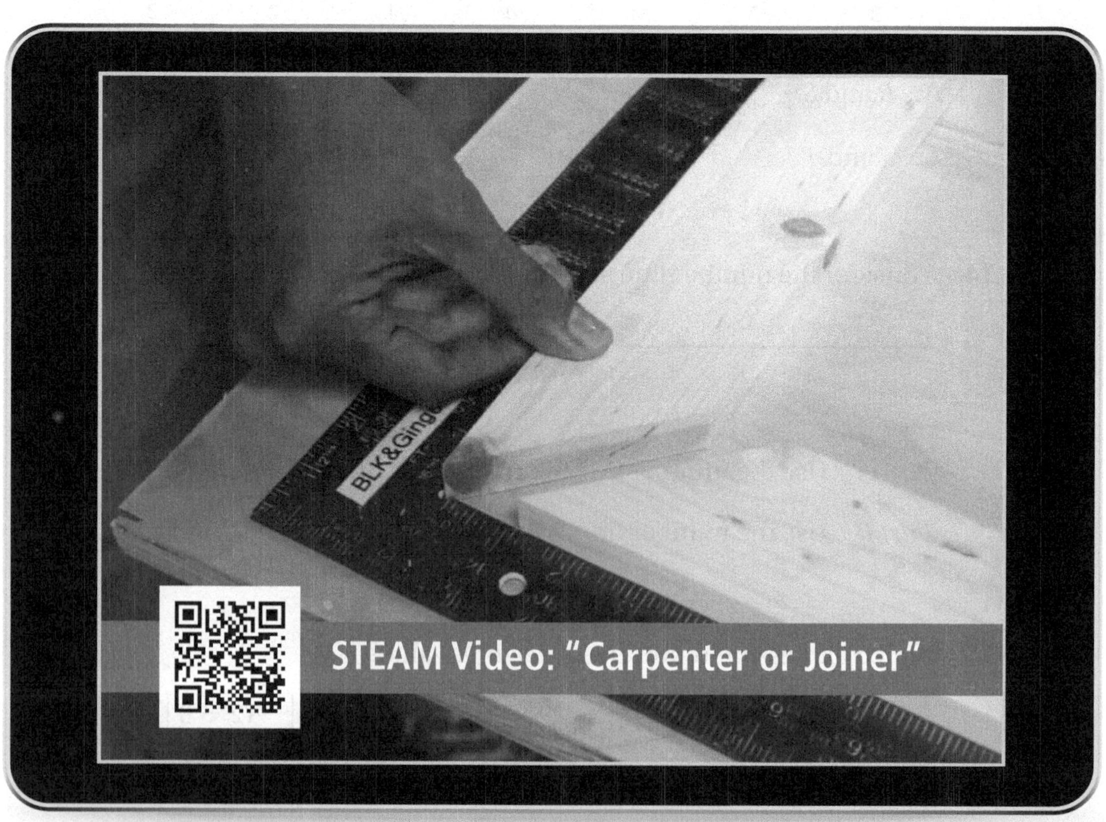

Laurie's Notes

Chapter B Overview

In the previous chapter, students learned to add and subtract integers and applied that understanding to add and subtract rational numbers. The lessons in that chapter provided a review of adding and subtracting fractions and decimals, which was the last time that these skills will be formally taught. The same type of review is presented in this chapter for multiplying and dividing fractions and decimals. First, students will investigate multiplication and division of integers and then they will apply that understanding to rational numbers.

The explorations help students make sense of multiplying and dividing rational numbers by using number lines, integer counters, and inductive reasoning. Students generally make sense of the rules for multiplying and dividing signed numbers, however, they may begin to make errors when adding and subtracting signed numbers. They often confuse the rules, so it is important to refer to all four operations and include problems that integrate several operations.

Notation and representations of signed numbers and operations can be confusing to students. Be sure to address the following cases with students.

Multiplication: In the expression $8 \cdot (-4)$, the -4 is enclosed in parentheses to help clarify the operation. If it was written as $8 \cdot -4$, students might read it as "8 times minus 4."

Evaluating Exponents: Squaring a positive number and then finding the opposite is *not* the same as squaring a negative number (i.e., $-3^2 \neq (-3)^2$). The order of operations says to evaluate exponents before multiplying. For -3^2, you square 3 before finding the opposite (or multiplying by -1).

Division: Whether you think of $\frac{3}{4}$ as a fraction or as *3 divided by 4,* the rational number is the same. There are three equivalent ways to represent the opposite of $\frac{3}{4}$: $\frac{-3}{4} = \frac{3}{-4} = -\frac{3}{4}$, with $-\frac{3}{4}$ being most common.

The third lesson reminds students that fractions and decimals are two ways of representing a quantity. The language of repeating and terminating decimals is introduced as well. Converting between benchmark fractions and decimals is helpful and provides an alternate approach to a computation.

Example: $-2.5 \times 3.6 \longrightarrow -2\frac{1}{2} \times 3\frac{3}{5}$

$$\begin{array}{r} 2.5 \\ \times\ 3.6 \\ \hline 150 \\ +\ 750 \\ \hline 9.00 \end{array} \qquad -2\frac{1}{2} \times 3\frac{3}{5} = -\frac{5}{2} \times \frac{18}{5} = -\frac{\overset{1}{\cancel{5}} \cdot \overset{9}{\cancel{18}}}{\underset{1}{\cancel{2}} \cdot \underset{1}{\cancel{5}}} = -\frac{9}{1} = -9$$

So, $-2.5 \times 3.6 = -9$.

Suggested Pacing

Chapter Opener	1 Day
Section 1	1 Day
Section 2	1 Day
Section 3	1 Day
Section 4	2 Days
Section 5	2 Days
Connecting Concepts	1 Day
Chapter Review	1 Day
Chapter Test	1 Day
Total Chapter B	11 Days
Year-to-Date	129 Days

Chapter Learning Target

Understand multiplying and dividing rational numbers.

Chapter Success Criteria

- Explain the rules for multiplying integers.
- Explain the rules for dividing integers.
- Evaluate expressions involving rational numbers.
- Solve real-life problems involving multiplication and division of rational numbers.

Chapter B Learning Targets and Success Criteria

Section	Learning Target	Success Criteria
B.1 Multiplying Integers	Find products of integers.	• Explain the rules for multiplying integers. • Find products of integers with the same sign. • Find products of integers with different signs.
B.2 Dividing Integers	Find quotients of integers.	• Explain the rules for dividing integers. • Find quotients of integers with the same sign. • Find quotients of integers with different signs.
B.3 Converting Between Fractions and Decimals	Convert between different forms of rational numbers.	• Explain the difference between terminating and repeating decimals. • Write fractions and mixed numbers as decimals. • Write decimals as fractions and mixed numbers.
B.4 Multiplying Rational Numbers	Find products of rational numbers.	• Explain the rules for multiplying rational numbers. • Find products of rational numbers with the same sign. • Find products of rational numbers with different signs.
B.5 Dividing Rational Numbers	Find quotients of rational numbers.	• Explain the rules for dividing rational numbers. • Find quotients of rational numbers with the same sign. • Find quotients of rational numbers with different signs.

Progressions

Through the Grades		
Grade 6	**Grade 7**	**Grade 8**
• Fluently multiply and divide multi-digit decimals. • Describe quantities with positive and negative numbers.	• Multiply and divide rational numbers. • Apply properties of operations as strategies to perform operations with rational numbers. • Convert a rational number to a decimal using long division. • Solve problems involving the four operations with rational numbers.	• Understand that numbers that are not rational are irrational. • Compare irrational numbers using rational approximations.

Through the Chapter					
Standard	**B.1**	**B.2**	**B.3**	**B.4**	**B.5**
Understand that multiplication is extended from fractions to rational numbers by requiring that operations continue to satisfy the properties of operations, particularly the distributive property, leading to products such as $(-1)(-1) = 1$ and the rules for multiplying signed numbers. Interpret products of rational numbers by describing real-world contexts.	●			★	
Understand that integers can be divided, provided that the divisor is not zero, and every quotient of integers (with non-zero divisor) is a rational number. If p and q are integers, then $-(p/q) = (-p)/q = p/(-q)$. Interpret quotients of rational numbers by describing real-world contexts.		●	●		★
Apply properties of operations as strategies to multiply and divide rational numbers.	●			★	
Convert a rational number to decimal using long division; know that the decimal form of a rational number terminates in 0s or eventually repeats.			★		
Solve real-world and mathematical problems involving the four operations with rational numbers.	●	●		●	★

Key

▲ = preparing ★ = complete

● = learning ■ = extending

Laurie's Notes

STEAM Video

1. *Sample answer:* The width changes more than the length.
2. *Sample answer:* Cut wide, short pieces and long, narrow pieces.

Performance Task

Sample answer: Different machines have different levels of precision.

Mathematical Practices

Students have opportunities to develop aspects of the mathematical practices throughout the chapter. Here are some examples.

1. **Make Sense of Problems and Persevere in Solving Them**
   B.4 Math Practice note, *p. 567*
2. **Reason Abstractly and Quantitatively**
   B.1 Exercise 47, *p. 554*
3. **Construct Viable Arguments and Critique the Reasoning of Others**
   B.3 Exercise 26, *p. 565*
4. **Model with Mathematics**
   B.5 Math Practice note, *p. 573*
5. **Use Appropriate Tools Strategically**
   B.2 Math Practice note, *p. 555*
6. **Attend to Precision**
   B.2 Math Practice note, *p. 558*
7. **Look for and Make Use of Structure**
   B.2 Exercise 42, *p. 560*
8. **Look for and Express Regularity in Repeated Reasoning**
   B.5 Math Practice note, *p. 575*

STEAM Video

Before the Video

- To introduce the STEAM Video, read aloud the first paragraph of Carpenter or Joiner and discuss the question with your students.

? "In what other real-life situations must measurements be precise?"

During the Video

- The video shows Tory and Robert discussing the difference between a carpenter and a joiner.

? Pause the video at 2:08 and ask, "How precise must carpenters' measurements be?" within $\frac{1}{16}$ of an inch

? "Why can carpenters' measurements vary within $\frac{1}{16}$ of an inch?"
Sample answer: Because the wood can expand and shrink.

- Watch the remainder of the video.

After the Video

? "How precise are joiners' measurements?" usually within $\frac{5}{1000}$ of an inch

? "Why do joiners have to be more precise than carpenters?" *Sample answer:* Because they cut at an angle, so differences are more noticeable.

- Have students work with a partner to answer Questions 1 and 2.
- As students discuss and answer the questions, listen for understanding of the importance of precise measurements.

Performance Task

- Use this information to spark students' interest and promote thinking about real-life problems.

? Ask, "Why do different telescopes have different accuracies?"

- After completing the chapter, students will have gained the knowledge needed to complete "Precisely Perfect."

STEAM Video

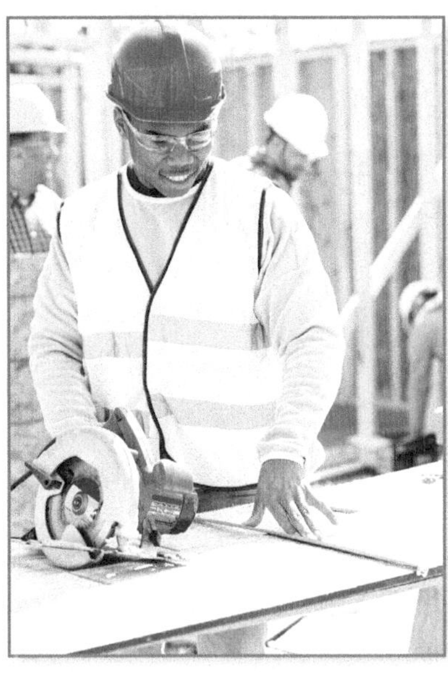

Carpenter or Joiner

Carpenters and joiners must be precise with their measurements when building structures. In what other real-life situations must measurements be precise?

Watch the STEAM Video "Carpenter or Joiner." Then answer the following questions.

1. Robert says that changes in water content cause wood to shrink or expand *across* the grain more than *along* the grain. What does this mean?
2. Describe how you can cut a log so that the pieces shrink in different ways as they dry out.

Performance Task

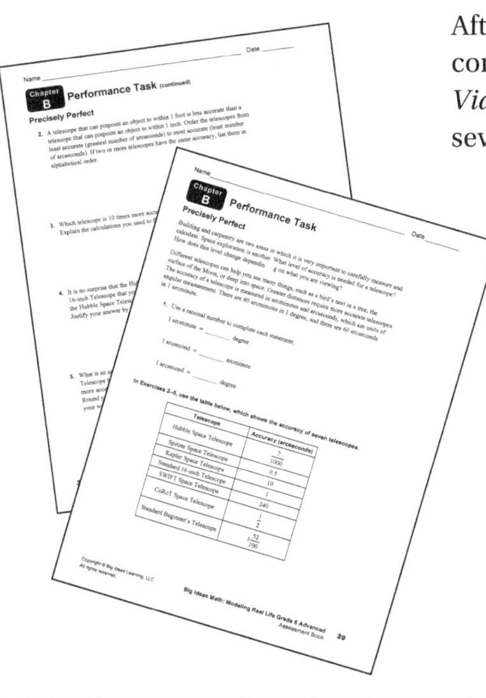

Name ______ Date ______

Chapter B **Performance Task** (continued)

Precisely Perfect

2. A telescope that can pinpoint an object to within 1 foot is less accurate than a telescope that can pinpoint an object to within 1 inch. Order the telescopes from least accurate (greatest number of arcseconds) to most accurate (least number of arcseconds). If two or more telescopes have the same accuracy, list them in alphabetical order.

3. Which telescope is 10 times more accu… Explain the calculations you used to f…

4. It is no surprise that the Hu… 16-inch Telescope that yo… the Hubble Space Telesc… Justify your answer by…

5. What is an a… Telescope… more acc… Round y… your w…

Name ______ Date ______

Chapter B **Performance Task**

Precisely Perfect

Building and carpentry are two areas in which it is very important to carefully measure and calculate. Space exploration is another. What level of accuracy is needed for a telescope? How does this level change depending on what you are viewing?

Different telescopes can help you see many things, such as a bird's nest in a tree, the surface of the Moon, or deep into space. Greater distances require more accurate telescopes. The accuracy of a telescope is measured in arcminutes and arcseconds, which are units of angular measurement. There are 60 arcminutes in 1 degree, and there are 60 arcseconds in 1 arcminute.

1. Use a rational number to complete each statement.

   1 arcminute = ______ degree

   1 arcsecond = ______ arcminute

   1 arcsecond = ______ degree

In Exercises 2–5, use the table below, which shows the accuracy of seven telescopes.

Telescope	Accuracy (arcseconds)
Hubble Space Telescope	$\frac{7}{1000}$
Spitzer Space Telescope	0.5
Kepler Space Telescope	10
Standard 16-inch Telescope	1
SWIFT Space Telescope	240
CoRoT Space Telescope	$\frac{1}{2}$
Standard Beginner's Telescope	$1\frac{52}{100}$

Big Ideas Math: Modeling Real Life Grade 6 Advanced Assessment Book 29

Precisely Perfect

After completing this chapter, you will be able to use the concepts you learned to answer the questions in the *STEAM Video Performance Task*. You will be given the accuracies of seven telescopes. For example:

Accuracy (arcseconds)

Hubble Space Telescope:	$\frac{7}{1000}$
Kepler Space Telescope:	10
Standard Beginner's Telescope:	$1\frac{52}{100}$

You will be asked to compare the accuracies of the telescopes. Why do different telescopes have different accuracies?

Getting Ready for Chapter B

Chapter Exploration

$+ = +1$

$- = -1$

1. Work with a partner. Use integer counters to find each product.

a. $(+3) \times (-2)$

$(+3) \times (-2)$

Add 3 groups of -2.

$(+3) \times (-2) =$ ______

b. $(-2) \times (-2)$

$(-2) \times (-2)$

Remove 2 groups of -2.

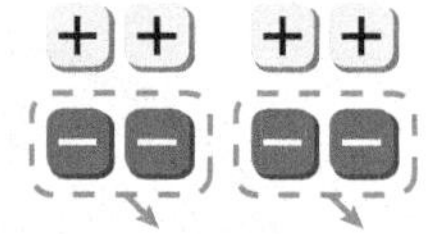

Start with enough zero pairs so you can remove 2 groups of -2.

$(-2) \times (-2) =$ ______

c. $(-2) \times (+3)$

$(-2) \times (+3)$

Remove 2 groups of 3.

Start with enough zero pairs so you can remove 2 groups of 3.

$(-2) \times (+3) =$ ______

Work with a partner. Use integer counters to find the product.

2. $(+3) \times (+2)$ **3.** $(+3) \times (-1)$ **4.** $(+2) \times (-4)$

5. $(-3) \times (+2)$ **6.** $(-2) \times (-3)$ **7.** $(-1) \times (-4)$

8. $(-1) \times (-2)$ **9.** $(+3) \times (+1)$ **10.** $(-3) \times (-2)$

11. $(-2) \times (+2)$ **12.** $(-2) \times (+4)$ **13.** $(-4) \times (-2)$

14. MP **MAKE CONJECTURES** Use your results in Exercises 1–13 to determine the sign of each product.

a. negative integer and a positive integer

b. two negative integers

c. two positive integers

Vocabulary

The following vocabulary terms are defined in this chapter. Think about what each term might mean and record your thoughts.

terminating decimal repeating decimal complex fraction

Laurie's Notes

Check out the
digital flash cards.
BigIdeasMath.com

Chapter Exploration

- Students used integer counters in the previous chapter to find sums and differences. They will now use integer counters to find products.
- **Reason Abstractly and Quantitatively:** Integer counters can help students make sense of multiplying integers. Integer counters are a concrete representation, deepening student understanding of what it means to find products of integers.
- Work through Exercise 1 as a class.
- In part (a), explain that the *positive* 3 tells you to *add* 3 groups of the next factor. Because the next factor is *negative* 2, each group will be made of 2 *negative* counters. Use integer counters to model adding 3 groups of -2. There are 6 negative counters in the model, so $(+3) \times (-2) = -6$.
- **Attend to Precision:** Students should use correct language in reading the problems. They should say, "3 times negative 2 equals negative 6." If students say "minus 2," remind students that minus is an operation.

? "How do you represent the product of negative 2 and negative 2 using integer counters?" Students may not know how to begin the model when the first factor is negative. Prompt them by asking, "What is the opposite of addition?" subtraction Relate subtraction to its visual representation, removing counters.

? "How can you begin by removing counters?" Start with zero pairs. Students should be familiar with this process from finding sums and differences in the previous chapter.

- **Model:** The first factor tells you to *remove* 2 groups and the next factor tells you that each group will be made of 2 *negative* counters. So, you need to start with 4 zeros pairs. After removing 2 groups of -2, there are 4 positive counters remaining, so $(-2) \times (-2) = 4$.
- Work through part (c) and then have students complete the remaining exercises with a partner. Have each pair compare their answers with another pair. Discuss any discrepancies as a class.
- **Popsicle Sticks:** Solicit responses for Exercise 14, which asks students to formalize the sign rules for products of integers.

Vocabulary

- These terms represent some of the vocabulary that students will encounter in Chapter B. Discuss the terms as a class.
- Where have students heard the term *terminating decimal* outside of a math classroom? In what contexts? Students may not be able to write the actual definition, but they may write phrases associated with a *terminating decimal.*
- Allowing students to discuss these terms now will prepare them for understanding the terms as they are presented in the chapter.
- When students encounter a new definition, encourage them to write in their *Student Journals.* They will revisit these definitions during the Chapter Review.

Topics for Review

- Commutative and Associative Properties
- Distributive Property
- Dividing Numbers Using the Standard Algorithm
- Multiplication Property of One
- Multiplication Property of Zero
- Multiplying and Dividing Fractions
- Operations with Whole Numbers
- Place Value
- Simplifying Fractions
- Writing Decimals as Fractions
- Writing Mixed Numbers as Improper Fractions

ELL Support

Students should be familiar with decimals from prior courses. Remind students that the root word *dec–* refers to 10 and each digit that appears to the right of a decimal point represents one tenth of the value of the digit to its left. Review the meanings of the words *terminating* (ending) and *repeating* (appearing over and over). Have students guess the meanings of the terms *terminating decimal* and *repeating decimal.*

Chapter Exploration

1. a. -6 b. 4 c. -6
2. 6
3. -3
4. -8
5. -6
6. 6
7. 4
8. 2
9. 3
10. 6
11. -4
12. -8
13. 8
14. a. negative b. positive c. positive

Check out the
Dynamic Classroom.
BigIdeasMath.com

Learning Target

Find products of integers.

Success Criteria

- Explain the rules for multiplying integers.
- Find products of integers with the same sign.
- Find products of integers with different signs.

Warm Up

Cumulative, vocabulary, and prerequisite skills practice opportunities are available in the *Resources by Chapter* or at *BigIdeasMath.com.*

ELL Support

Students may know the word *product* from everyday language. Explain that in the context of math it has a very specific meaning. In everyday life, a product is something that is made to be sold. In math, a product is the result of multiplication.

Exploration 1

a. *Sample answer:* Use three groups of two negative counters

b. −6; 6; *Sample answer:* Subtract 2 from each row in the first table. Subtract −3 from each row in the second table.

c. See Additional Answers.

Laurie's Notes

Preparing to Teach

- **Look for and Express Regularity in Repeated Reasoning:** In this lesson, students will use the repeated addition model of multiplication and inductive reasoning to develop a conceptual understanding of integer multiplication.

Motivate

- Play *Guess My Rule.* Write the first four terms of a sequence on the board. Ask students to give the next few terms and guess the rule. Here are some possibilities.
  - 2, 4, 8, 16, . . . 32, 64, 128; The rule is to multiply by 2, powers of 2, or doubling (any one of these responses is acceptable).
  - 0, 4, 8, 12, . . . 16, 20, 24; The rule is adding 4, multiples of 4, or counting by 4s (any one of these responses is acceptable).
  - −6, −3, 0, 3, . . . 6, 9, 12; The rule is adding 3.
- Ask students if any of the patterns seem different than the others. In the sequences above, students may recognize that the third one involves negative numbers.

Exploration 1

- **Vocabulary Review:** Ask students to define *factor, product,* and *Commutative Property of Multiplication.*
- In part (a), students explore the *repeated addition model* of multiplication.
- In part (b), make sure that students recognize the patterns.
  - In the first table, students can use integer counters or number lines for most of the products, or as justification for the pattern. The first factor is decreasing by 1, the second factor is constant, and the product is decreasing by 2.
  - In the second table, integer counters or number lines can be used but students may have difficulty observing the pattern from the models. The first factor is constant, the second factor is decreasing by 1, and the product is increasing by 3.
- In part (c), the goal is for students to recognize the overall pattern. When both factors have the same sign, the product is positive. When both factors have different signs, the product is negative.
- Note that the first four problems were in parts (a) and (b).
- **Look for and Express Regularity in Repeated Reasoning:** It is important for students to record the *Type of Product.* Mathematically proficient students will use the pattern in the table to write general rules for multiplying.
- Have students share their rules with the class.
- **Extension:** Have students use the rules they developed to find the product of three numbers, such as 3(−2)(−4). 24

B.1 Multiplying Integers

Learning Target: Find products of integers.

Success Criteria:
- I can explain the rules for multiplying integers.
- I can find products of integers with the same sign.
- I can find products of integers with different signs.

EXPLORATION 1 Understanding Products Involving Negative Integers

Work with a partner.

a. The number line and integer counters model the product $3 \bullet 2$. How can you find $3 \bullet (-2)$? Explain.

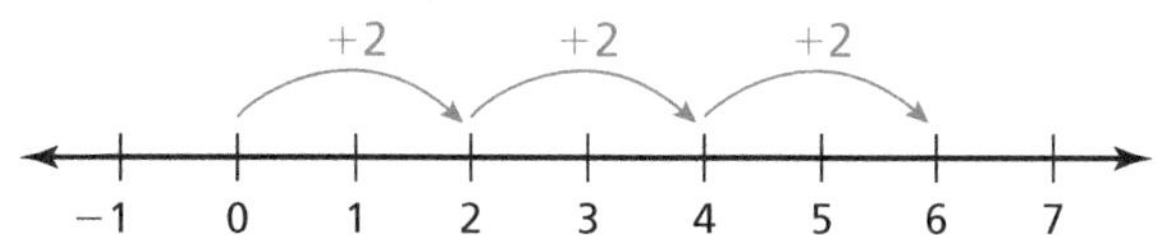

b. Use the tables to find $-3 \bullet 2$ and $-3 \bullet (-2)$. Explain your reasoning.

2	•	2	=	4
1	•	2	=	2
0	•	2	=	0
−1	•	2	=	
−2	•	2	=	
−3	•	2	=	

−3	•	3	=	−9
−3	•	2	=	−6
−3	•	1	=	−3
−3	•	0	=	
−3	•	−1	=	
−3	•	−2	=	

c. **INDUCTIVE REASONING** Complete the table. Then write general rules for multiplying (i) two integers with the same sign and (ii) two integers with different signs.

Expression	Type of Product	Product	Product: Positive or Negative
$3 \bullet 2$	Integers with the same sign		
$3 \bullet (-2)$			
$-3 \bullet 2$			
$-3 \bullet (-2)$			
$6 \bullet 3$			
$2 \bullet (-5)$			
$-6 \bullet 5$			
$-5 \bullet (-3)$			

Math Practice

Construct Arguments

Construct an argument that you can use to convince a friend of the rules you wrote in Exploration 1(c).

B.1 Lesson

Consider the following methods for evaluating $3(-2+4)$.

Evaluate in parentheses:

$$3(-2+4) = 3(2)$$
$$= 6$$

Use the Distributive Property:

$$3(-2+4) = 3(-2) + 3(4)$$
$$= ? + 12$$

For the Distributive Property to be true, $3(-2)$ must equal -6. This leads to the following rules for multiplying integers.

Key Ideas

Multiplying Integers with the Same Sign

Words The product of two integers with the same sign is positive.

Numbers $2 \cdot 3 = 6$ $\quad -2 \cdot (-3) = 6$

Multiplying Integers with Different Signs

Words The product of two integers with different signs is negative.

Numbers $2 \cdot (-3) = -6$ $\quad -2 \cdot 3 = -6$

EXAMPLE 1 Multiplying Integers

Find each product.

a. $-5 \cdot (-6)$

The integers have the same sign.

$$-5 \cdot (-6) = 30$$

The product is positive.

The product is 30.

b. $3(-4)$

The integers have different signs.

$$3(-4) = -12$$

The product is negative.

The product is -12.

Try It **Find the product.**

1. $5 \cdot 5$ **2.** $-1(-9)$ **3.** $-7 \cdot (-8)$

4. $12 \cdot (-2)$ **5.** $4(-6)$ **6.** $-25(0)$

Laurie's Notes

Scaffolding Instruction

- In the exploration, students used inductive reasoning to write general rules for multiplying integers. Now students will apply those rules.
- **Emerging:** Students may confuse the rules for multiplying integers with the rules for adding integers. Use integer counters to remind students that addition of two negative integers results in a negative sum. These students will benefit from guided instruction for the Key Ideas and examples.
- **Proficient:** Students can explain and apply the rules for multiplying integers. They should proceed to Example 2 to review evaluating exponents and expressions.

Discuss

- Work through both methods for evaluating $3(-2 + 4)$ with students. Explain that the ? must equal -6 because $? + 12 = 6$ and $-6 + 12 = 6$.
- Show an expression that leads to the product of two negative numbers.

$$-5(-2 + 4) = -5(2) = -10 \qquad -5(-2 + 4) = -5(-2) + (-5)(4) = ? + (-20)$$

For the Distributive Property to be true, $-5(-2)$ must equal 10.

Key Ideas

- Write the rules for the two cases of multiplying integers.
- Discuss how the multiplication dots represent multiplication and the parentheses surround negative integers. The parentheses are used for clarity, so that the negative sign is not confused with the operation of subtraction.

EXAMPLE 1

- Work through each part of the example.
- Say, "You know that 5 times 6 is 30 and both integers in this example are negative (-5 and -6), so the product is positive 30."
- **Attend to Precision:** Students should use correct language in reading the problems. They should say, "Negative 5 times negative 6 equals 30." If students say "minus 5," remind students that minus is an operation.
- **Look for and Make Use of Structure:** Point out to students how multiplication is represented differently in the two problems. Ask students to write each problem another way. *Sample answers:* $(-5)(-6)$; $3 \cdot (-4)$ The goal is for students to be comfortable with all multiplication representations.

Try It

- Students should work independently and check their work.
- ? Alternately, you could write the problems on index cards. Then ask two students to sort the cards into two piles: integers with the same sign and integers with different signs. Ask, "What is true about all of the products (or answers) in this pile?" Point to one of the piles and then repeat the same question for the other pile. Ask volunteers to explain the problems.

Scaffold instruction to support all students in their learning. Learning is individualized and you may want to group students differently as they move in and out of these levels with each skill and concept. Student self-assessment and feedback help guide your instructional decisions about how and when to layer support for all students to become proficient learners.

Extra Example 1

Find each product.

a. $-8 \cdot (-12)$ 96

b. $-6 \cdot 6$ -36

ELL Support

Point out that *negative* and *positive* are opposites. After demonstrating Example 1, have students practice language by working in pairs to complete Try It Exercises 1–6. Have one student ask another, "What is the product of five and five?" Have partners alternate roles.

Beginner: State the product.

Intermediate: Answer with a simple sentence such as, "The product is twenty-five."

Advanced: Answer with a detailed sentence such as, "The product of five and five is twenty-five."

Try It

1. 25 **2.** 9
3. 56 **4.** -24
5. -24 **6.** 0

Extra Example 2

a. Find $(-8)^2$. 64

b. Find -9^2. −81

c. Find $-3 \cdot (-12) \cdot 4$. 144

d. Find $4(5 - 11) + 2$. −22

Try It

7. 0 **8.** −3

9. 24

Formative Assessment Tip

Always-Sometimes-Never True (AT-ST-NT)

This strategy is useful in assessing whether students overgeneralize or under generalize a particular concept. When answering, a student should be asked to justify his or her answer and other students listening should critique the reasoning.

AT-ST-NT statements help students practice the habit of checking validity when a statement (or conjecture) is made. Are there different cases that need to be checked? Is there a counterexample that would show the conjecture to be false?

To develop these statements for a lesson, consider the common errors or misconceptions that students have relating to the success criteria of the lesson. Allow private think time before students share their thinking with partners or the whole class.

Self-Assessment for Concepts & Skills

10. **a.** They have the same sign.

b. They have different signs.

11. −32 **12.** 35

13. 30

14–15. See Additional Answers.

Laurie's Notes

Discuss

- Students should know the meaning of exponents. Write the expression 5^2 on the board and ask students to tell you what it means.
- **Vocabulary Review:** 5 is the *base* and 2 is the *exponent.* The exponent of a power indicates the number of times the base is used as a factor. So, $5^2 = 5 \times 5 = 25$ and it is read as "5 raised to the second power" or "5 squared."
- Review the order of operations and properties of multiplication with students.

EXAMPLE 2

- Part (a) shows how to raise a negative integer to a power.
- **Common Error:** When a negative number is raised to a power, the number must be written within parentheses. In part (b), the expression is read as "the opposite of 2 squared." If you wanted to raise −2 to the second power, it would be written as $(-2)^2$. For part (b), the order of operations says to square the number and then take its opposite.
- ? **Extension:** "When you raise a negative number to a power is the answer always positive?" No, if the exponent is odd the answer is negative.
- In part (c), make sure students recognize that using the Commutative Property of Multiplication allows them to multiply only positive numbers in the last step.

Try It

- Have students work with a partner and display their answers on whiteboards.

Self-Assessment for Concepts & Skills

- Exercise 10 will help students assess their understanding of the first success criterion.
- Have students work in pairs for Exercises 10–13. Ask volunteers to write their answers on the board.
- Use *Always-Sometimes-Never True* for Exercises 14 and 15. Students should explain their reasoning and give examples.

ELL Support

Proceed as described in Laurie's Notes for the exercises and allow students to work in pairs. Have each pair display their answers for Exercises 11–13 on a whiteboard for your review. Have two pairs form a group to discuss Exercises 10, 14, and 15. Monitor discussions and provide support as needed. Then use *Always-Sometimes-Never True* for Exercises 14 and 15.

The Success Criteria Self-Assessment chart can be found in the *Student Journal* or online at *BigIdeasMath.com.*

EXAMPLE 2 Evaluating Expressions

The expression $(-2)^2$ indicates to multiply the number in parentheses, -2, by itself.

The expression -2^2, however, indicates to find the opposite of 2^2.

a. Find $(-2)^2$.

$(-2)^2 = (-2) \cdot (-2)$ Write $(-2)^2$ as repeated multiplication.

$= 4$ Multiply.

b. Find -2^2.

$-2^2 = -(2 \cdot 2)$ Write 2^2 as repeated multiplication.

$= -4$ Multiply 2 and 2.

c. Find $-2 \cdot 17 \cdot (-5)$.

$-2 \cdot 17 \cdot (-5) = -2 \cdot (-5) \cdot 17$ Commutative Property of Multiplication

$= 10 \cdot 17$ Multiply -2 and -5.

$= 170$ Multiply 10 and 17.

Remember

Use order of operations when evaluating an expression.

d. Find $-6(-3 + 4) + 6$.

$-6(-3 + 4) + 6 = -6(1) + 6$ Perform operation in parentheses.

$= -6 + 6$ Multiplication Property of 1

$= 0$ Additive Inverse Property

Try It **Evaluate the expression.**

7. $8 \cdot (-15) \cdot 0$ **8.** $24 - 3^3$ **9.** $10 - 7(3 - 5)$

Self-Assessment for Concepts & Skills

Solve each exercise. Then rate your understanding of the success criteria in your journal.

10. WRITING What can you conclude about two integers whose product is (a) positive and (b) negative?

EVALUATING AN EXPRESSION **Evaluate the expression.**

11. $4(-8)$ **12.** $-5(-7)$ **13.** $12 - 3^2 \cdot (-2)$

MP REASONING **Tell whether the statement is *true* or *false*. Explain your reasoning.**

14. The product of three positive integers is positive.

15. The product of three negative integers is positive.

EXAMPLE 3 Modeling Real Life

You solve a number puzzle on your phone. You start with 250 points. You finish the puzzle in 8 minutes 45 seconds and make 3 mistakes. What is your score?

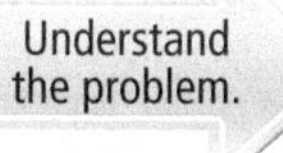

You are given ways to gain points and lose points when completing a puzzle. You are asked to find your score after finishing the puzzle.

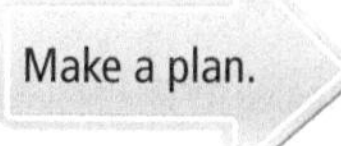

Use a verbal model to solve the problem. Find the sum of the starting points, mistake penalties, and time bonus.

Solve and check.

Score = Starting points + Number of mistakes • Penalty per mistake + Time bonus

$= 250 + 3(-50) + 75$

10 min − 8 min 45 sec = 1 min 15 sec
= 75 sec

$= 250 + (-150) + 75$

$= 100 + 75$

$= 175$

So, your score is 175 points.

Another Method

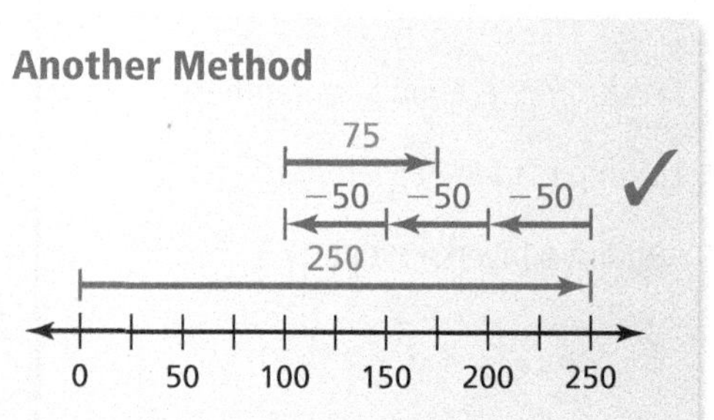

Self-Assessment for Problem Solving

Solve each exercise. Then rate your understanding of the success criteria in your journal.

16. On a mountain, the temperature decreases by 18°F for each 5000-foot increase in elevation. At 7000 feet, the temperature is 41°F. What is the temperature at 22,000 feet? Justify your answer.

17. DIG DEEPER! Players in a racing game earn 3 points for each coin and lose 5 points for each second later than the fastest time. The table shows results of a race. Can Player E finish with the third-best time and have the second-most points? Justify your answer.

Player	Coins	Time
A	31	0:02:03
B	18	0:01:55
C	24	0:01:58
D	27	0:02:01
E		

Laurie's Notes

EXAMPLE 3

- Ask a volunteer to read the problem.
- Use *Popsicle Sticks* to select students to explain the problem. Simply re-reading the problem is not an explanation. Responses should be similar to, "You are solving a puzzle. You start with a certain number of points and then gain or lose points depending on what happens. You are asked to find your final score."
- Write the verbal model on the board.
- ? "Where does the verbal model come from?" *Sample answer:* From the given information in the problem and the cell phone.
- Ask students how the verbal model helps to solve the problem.
- Demonstrate substituting numbers for the words in the verbal model.

Self-Assessment for Problem Solving

- The goal for all students is to feel comfortable with the problem-solving plan. It is important for students to problem-solve in class, where they may receive support from you and their peers. Keep in mind that some students may only be ready for the first step.
- Have students work in pairs to complete these exercises. Have each student write the verbal model independently and then compare verbal models. After pairs reach a consensus about the verbal model, have students use whiteboards to substitute and solve.
- Have students assess their understanding of the success criteria.
- Use *Popsicle Sticks* to solicit explanations for each exercise.

The Success Criteria Self-Assessment chart can be found in the *Student Journal* or online at *BigIdeasMath.com*.

Closure

- Write the number −4 on the board. Ask students to write a problem to represent each of the following statements. Select students to share their responses.
  - "A multiplication problem that has −4 as one of the factors and has a negative product." *Sample answer:* $(-4)(2) = -8$
  - "A second multiplication problem that has −4 as one of the factors and has a positive product." *Sample answer:* $(-4)(-2) = 8$

Extra Example 3

A roller coaster starts at a height of 45 meters. From the starting position, the roller coaster descends 3 meters per second for 5 seconds. How high is the roller coaster 5 seconds after the ride begins? 30 meters

Self-Assessment for Problem Solving

16. −13°F; $(22{,}000 - 7000) \div 5000 = 3$, $3(-18) = -54$

17. yes; *Sample answer:* If Player E finishes at 0:01:59 with 25 coins, they will have the third best time and second most points, 55 points.

Learning Target

Find products of integers.

Success Criteria

- Explain the rules for multiplying integers.
- Find products of integers with the same sign.
- Find products of integers with different signs.

Review & Refresh

1. 5.1
2. 1.3
3. $1\frac{3}{5}$
4. 3
5. 8
6. 14
7. 19.125
8. D

Concepts, Skills, & Problem Solving

9. -8
10. -18
11. -20
12. 24
13. -21
14. -16
15. 12
16. -42
17. 27
18. -40
19. 12
20. -50
21. 0
22. -81
23. -30
24. -110
25. 78
26. -98
27. 121
28. -200
29. $-320{,}000$
30. 16
31. -36
32. 30
33. 0
34. -700
35. -59
36. -100
37. 54
38. 0
39. 12
40. 900
41. -3

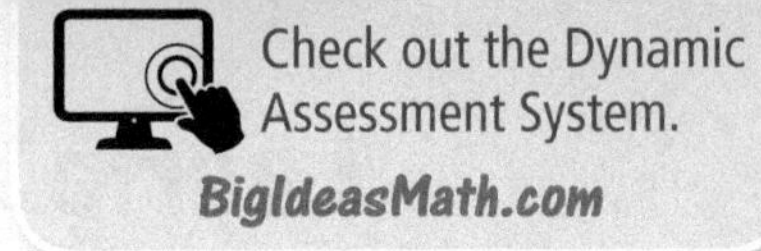

Check out the Dynamic Assessment System.
BigIdeasMath.com

Assignment Guide and Concept Check

Scaffold assignments to support all students in their learning progression. The suggested assignments are a starting point. Continue to assign additional exercises and revisit with spaced practice to move every student toward proficiency.

Level	Assignment 1	Assignment 2
Emerging	3, 7, 8, 9, 13, 15, 17, 30, 31, 32, 42, 43	21, 27, 28, 29, 35, 41, 45, 49
Proficient	3, 7, 8, 10, 20, 26, 27, 30, 35, 37, 38, 42, 43	29, 39, 41, 44, 46, 47, 49
Advanced	3, 7, 8, 11, 24, 25, 26, 39, 40, 41, 42, 43	44, 46, 47, 48, 49, 50

- Assignment 1 is for use after students complete the Self-Assessment for Concepts & Skills.
- Assignment 2 is for use after students complete the Self-Assessment for Problem Solving.
- The red exercises can be used as a concept check.

Review & Refresh Prior Skills

Exercises 1–3 Finding Distance on a Number Line
Exercises 4–7 Dividing Whole Numbers
Exercise 8 Writing a Prime Factorization

Common Errors

- **Exercises 31 and 36** Students may incorrectly interpret -6^2 as $(-6)(-6)$ instead of $-1(6^2)$. Remind them that the negative sign means multiplication by -1 and that exponents are evaluated before multiplication.
- **Exercises 32 and 34** Students may multiply all the numbers together ignoring the signs and then place the incorrect sign in front. For example, a student might say $-7(-3)(-5) = 105$. Tell students to multiply only two integers at a time, determine the sign, and then multiply by the last number.

B.1 Practice

Go to *BigIdeasMath.com* to get HELP with solving the exercises.

Review & Refresh

Find the distance between the two numbers on a number line.

1. -4.3 and 0.8

2. -7.7 and -6.4

3. $-2\frac{3}{5}$ and -1

Divide.

4. $27 \div 9$

5. $48 \div 6$

6. $56 \div 4$

7. $153 \div 8$

8. What is the prime factorization of 84?

A. $2^2 \times 3^2$ **B.** $2^3 \times 7$ **C.** $3^3 \times 7$ **D.** $2^2 \times 3 \times 7$

Concepts, Skills, & Problem Solving

MP **CHOOSE TOOLS** **Use a number line or integer counters to find the product.** (See Exploration 1, p. 549.)

9. $2(-4)$

10. $-6(3)$

11. $4(-5)$

MULTIPLYING INTEGERS **Find the product.**

12. $6 \cdot 4$

13. $7(-3)$

14. $-2(8)$

15. $-3(-4)$

16. $-6 \cdot 7$

17. $3 \cdot 9$

18. $8 \cdot (-5)$

19. $-1 \cdot (-12)$

20. $-5(10)$

21. $-13(0)$

22. $-9 \cdot 9$

23. $15(-2)$

24. $-10 \cdot 11$

25. $-6 \cdot (-13)$

26. $7(-14)$

27. $-11 \cdot (-11)$

28. MP **MODELING REAL LIFE** You burn 10 calories each minute you jog. What integer represents the change in your calories after you jog for 20 minutes?

29. MP **MODELING REAL LIFE** In a four-year period, about 80,000 acres of coastal wetlands in the United States are lost each year. What integer represents the total change in coastal wetlands?

EVALUATING EXPRESSIONS **Evaluate the expression.**

30. $(-4)^2$

31. -6^2

32. $-5 \cdot 3 \cdot (-2)$

33. $3 \cdot (-12) \cdot 0$

34. $-5(-7)(-20)$

35. $5 - 8^2$

36. $-5^2 \cdot 4$

37. $-2 \cdot (-3)^3$

38. $2 + 1 \cdot (-7 + 5)$

39. $4 - (-2)^3$

40. $4 \cdot (25 \cdot 3^2)$

41. $-4(3^2 - 8) + 1$

MP YOU BE THE TEACHER **Your friend evaluates the expression. Is your friend correct? Explain your reasoning.**

42. $-2(-7) = -14$

43. $-10^2 = -100$

MP PATTERNS **Find the next two numbers in the pattern.**

44. $-12, 60, -300, 1500, \ldots$

45. $7, -28, 112, -448, \ldots$

46. **MP PROBLEM SOLVING** In a scavenger hunt, each team earns 25 points for each item that they find. Each team loses 15 points for every minute after 4:00 P.M. that they report to the city park. The table shows the number of items found by each team and the time that each team reported to the park. Which team wins the scavenger hunt? Justify your answer.

Team	Items	Time
A	13	4:03 P.M.
B	15	4:07 P.M.
C	11	3:56 P.M.
D	12	4:01 P.M.

47. **MP REASONING** The height of an airplane during a landing is given by $22{,}000 + (-480t)$, where t is the time in minutes. Estimate how many minutes it takes the plane to land. Explain your reasoning.

48. **MP PROBLEM SOLVING** The table shows the price of a bluetooth speaker each month for 4 months.

Month	Price (dollars)
June	165
July	$165 + (-12)$
August	$165 + 2(-12)$
September	$165 + 3(-12)$

a. Describe the change in the price of the speaker.

b. The table at the right shows the amount of money you save each month. When do you have enough money saved to buy the speaker? Explain your reasoning.

Amount Saved	
June	$35
July	$55
August	$45
September	$18

49. **DIG DEEPER!** Two integers, a and b, have a product of 24. What is the least possible sum of a and b?

50. **MP NUMBER SENSE** Consider two integers p and q. Explain why $p \times (-q) = (-p) \times q = -pq$.

Mini-Assessment

Find the product.

1. $-4(-5)$ 20
2. $-2(15)$ -30

Evaluate the expression.

3. $-7(-3)(-1)$ -21
4. $-4^2 - 3$ -19
5. You have $900 in a checking account. You pay a $60 cell phone bill each month using this account. The account balance is given by $900 + (-60t)$, where t is the time in months. What is the balance of the account after 4 months? $660

Section Resources

Surface Level	Deep Level
Resources by Chapter • Extra Practice • Reteach • Puzzle Time Student Journal • Self-Assessment • Practice Differentiating the Lesson Tutorial Videos Skills Review Handbook Skills Trainer	Resources by Chapter • Enrichment and Extension Graphic Organizers Dynamic Assessment System • Section Practice

Concepts, Skills, & Problem Solving

42. no; The product should be positive.
43. yes; The opposite of 10^2 is -100.
44. $-7500, 37{,}500$
45. $1792, -7168$
46. D; Team A has 280 points, Team B has 270 points, Team C has 275 points, Team D has 285 points
47. about 45.83 min; *Sample answer:* Solve $22{,}000 + (-480t) = 0$.
48. **a.** The price drops $12 every month.

    b. September; In August, you have $135 but the cost is $141. In September, you have $153 and the cost is only $129.
49. -25
50. $$p \times (-q) = p \times (0 - q) = 0 - pq = -pq = (0 - p) \times q$$

Check out the
Dynamic Classroom.
BigIdeasMath.com

Learning Target

Find quotients of integers.

Success Criteria

- Explain the rules for dividing integers.
- Find quotients of integers with the same sign.
- Find quotients of integers with different signs.

Warm Up

Cumulative, vocabulary, and prerequisite skills practice opportunities are available in the *Resources by Chapter* or at *BigIdeasMath.com*.

ELL Support

Point out that the word *divide* can mean a gulf or separation, or the action of separating things. In math, when you divide one number by another, you find how many times a number is contained in another. A *quotient* is the answer to a division problem. The answer to an addition problem is the *sum*, the answer to a subtraction problem is the *difference*, and the answer to a multiplication problem is the *product*.

Exploration 1

a. They are inverse operations.

b. See Additional Answers.

c. -2; -2; -2; They are the same; yes, when $b \neq 0$; The quotients have the same value and the same sign.

d. yes, when the divisor is nonzero; The quotient can be written as a fraction.

Laurie's Notes

Preparing to Teach

- **Look for and Express Regularity in Repeated Reasoning:** In this lesson, students will use the relationship between multiplication and division to develop a conceptual understanding of integer division.
- Students will use inductive reasoning to write general rules for dividing integers. They will reason that when the signs of the dividend and the divisor are the same, the quotient is positive; when the signs of the dividend and the divisor are different, the quotient is negative.

Motivate

? "What do you know about football?" Guide students to discuss the length of the field. A football field is 100 yards long, plus two 10-yard end zones, for a total length of 120 yards.

? "If I told you the area of the football field, could you tell me the width of the football field?" The goal is to have students think about the area formula ($A = lw$) and realize that if they know the area and one dimension, they can divide to find the other dimension.

? "The area is 6400 square yards and the length is 120 yards. What is the width?" $53\frac{1}{3}$ yd

Discuss

- **Vocabulary Review:** Ask students to define *dividend, divisor, quotient, Commutative Property,* and *division involving zero.*

? What are fact families? Give some examples for multiplication and division." Fact families show the inverse relationship between multiplication and division. *Sample answer:* $2 \times 3 = 6$, $3 \times 2 = 6$, $6 \div 2 = 3$, and $6 \div 3 = 2$

Exploration 1

- After discussing part (a), partners should complete part (b). It is important for students to record the *Type of Quotient*. The goal is for the students to observe that there is a pattern in the table. When the dividend and the divisor have the same signs, the quotient is positive. When the dividend and the divisor have different signs, the quotient is negative.

? "How do fact families help you determine the sign of the quotient?" *Sample answer:* You can determine the sign of the quotient using the related multiplication expression.

- Have students share their explanations for parts (c) and (d) with the class. Use fact families to remind students that division by zero is undefined. For example, if $6 \div 0 = ?$, then $0 \times ? = 6$.
- **Extension:**
  - ? "Is division commutative, meaning do $18 \div 9$ and $9 \div 18$ have the same quotient?" no
  - ? "What is the relationship between the two quotients?" They are reciprocals.

B.2 Dividing Integers

Learning Target: Find quotients of integers.

Success Criteria:
- I can explain the rules for dividing integers.
- I can find quotients of integers with the same sign.
- I can find quotients of integers with different signs.

EXPLORATION 1 Understanding Quotients Involving Negative Integers

Work with a partner.

a. Discuss the relationship between multiplication and division with your partner.

b. **INDUCTIVE REASONING** Complete the table. Then write general rules for dividing (i) two integers with the same sign and (ii) two integers with different signs.

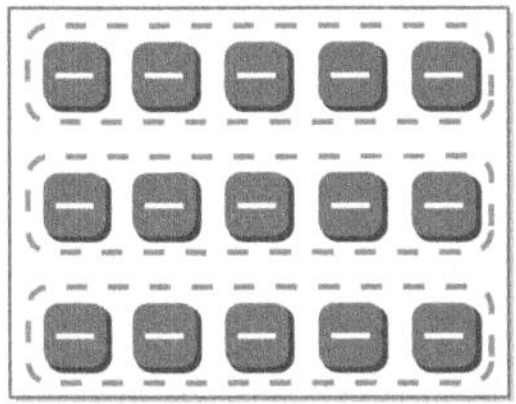

Expression	Type of Quotient	Quotient	Quotient: Positive, Negative, or Zero
$-15 \div 3$	Integers with different signs		
$12 \div (-6)$			
$10 \div (-2)$			
$-6 \div 2$			
$-12 \div (-12)$			
$-21 \div (-7)$			
$0 \div (-15)$			
$0 \div 4$			
$-5 \div 4$			
$5 \div (-4)$			

Math Practice

Recognize Usefulness of Tools

Can you use number lines or integer counters to reach the same conclusions as in part (b)? Explain why or why not.

c. Find the values of $-\frac{8}{4}$, $\frac{-8}{4}$, and $\frac{8}{-4}$. What do you notice? Is this true for $-\frac{a}{b}$, $\frac{-a}{b}$, and $\frac{a}{-b}$ when a and b are integers? Explain.

d. Is every quotient of integers a rational number? Explain your reasoning.

B.2 Lesson

Key Ideas

Remember

Division by 0 is undefined.

Dividing Integers with the Same Sign

Words The quotient of two integers with the same sign is positive.

Numbers $8 \div 2 = 4$ $\quad -8 \div (-2) = 4$

Dividing Integers with Different Signs

Words The quotient of two integers with different signs is negative.

Numbers $8 \div (-2) = -4$ $\quad -8 \div 2 = -4$

EXAMPLE 1 Dividing Integers with the Same Sign

Find $-18 \div (-6)$.

The integers have the same sign.

$$-18 \div (-6) = 3$$

The quotient is positive.

The quotient is 3.

Try It **Find the quotient.**

1. $14 \div 2$ **2.** $-32 \div (-4)$ **3.** $-40 \div (-8)$

EXAMPLE 2 Dividing Integers with Different Signs

Find each quotient.

a. $75 \div (-25)$ **b.** $\dfrac{-54}{6}$

If a and b are integers, then $-\dfrac{a}{b} = \dfrac{-a}{b} = \dfrac{a}{-b}$. So, you can also think of $\dfrac{-54}{6}$ as $-\dfrac{54}{6} = -9$.

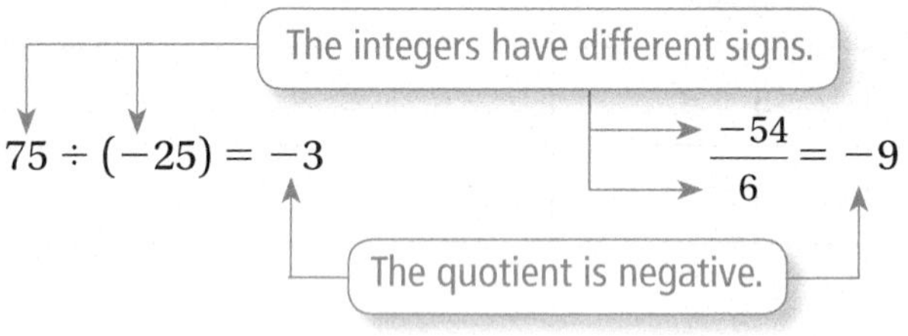

The quotient is -3.

The quotient is -9.

Try It **Find the quotient.**

4. $0 \div (-6)$ **5.** $\dfrac{-49}{7}$ **6.** $\dfrac{21}{-3}$

Laurie's Notes

Scaffolding Instruction

- Students used inductive reasoning to develop general rules for dividing two integers. Although students may have a good sense of how to predict the sign of the quotient, they often use language (as they do with multiplication) such as: "two positives make a positive" and "two negatives make a positive." This language should be avoided.
- **Emerging:** These students may benefit from guided instruction. Examples 1 and 2 provide additional practice for dividing integers.
- **Proficient:** Students are confident in dividing integers and can work through Examples 1–3 in pairs. Have students check their understanding of evaluating expressions using the Try It exercises before proceeding to the Self-Assessment for Concepts & Skills exercises.

Key Ideas

- Students should know that to check a division problem, you multiply the quotient by the divisor and the answer is the dividend.
- Summary of division involving zero: You can divide 0 by a nonzero number and the answer is 0. You cannot divide a number by 0. Later in this lesson, connect this concept to "0 cannot be in the denominator when division is represented in fraction form."

EXAMPLE 1

- Say, "You know that 18 divided by 6 is 3 and both integers are negative, so the quotient is positive 3."
- **Attend to Precision:** Be sure that students use correct language in reading the problems. When they read the problem they should say, "Negative 18 divided by negative 6 equals 3." If students say, "minus 18," remind them that minus is an operation.

Try It

- Have students complete the exercises on whiteboards.

EXAMPLE 2

- Draw attention to the push-pin note. This is helpful for integer division but it can also make addition and subtraction of rational numbers more efficient.
- **Look for and Make Use of Structure:** Point out to students how division is represented differently in the two problems. Before starting part (a), you may want to ask if the problem could be written another way.
- The goal is for students to be comfortable with all of the ways that division is represented.

Try It

- Students should work independently and check their work.

Scaffold instruction to support all students in their learning. Learning is individualized and you may want to group students differently as they move in and out of these levels with each skill and concept. Student self-assessment and feedback help guide your instructional decisions about how and when to layer support for all students to become proficient learners.

Extra Example 1

Find $-48 \div (-6)$. 8

Try It

1. 7 **2.** 8

3. 5

Extra Example 2

Find each quotient.

a. $\frac{84}{-4}$ -21

b. $-39 \div 3$ -13

ELL Support

After demonstrating Examples 1 and 2, have students practice language by working in pairs to complete Try It Exercises 4–6. Have one student ask another, "What is the quotient of zero and negative six?" Have students alternate roles.

Beginner: State the quotient.

Intermediate: Answer with a simple sentence such as, "The quotient is zero."

Advanced: Answer with a detailed sentence such as, "The quotient of zero and negative six is zero."

Try It

4. 0 **5.** -7

6. -7

Extra Example 3

Find the value of each expression when $x = 4$ and $y = -2$.

a. $-x \div y\ 2$

b. $\frac{x-8}{y^2} - 1$

Try It

7. 3
8. −4
9. 2

Formative Assessment Tip

Fact-First Questioning

This is a higher-order questioning technique that goes beyond asking straight recall questions. Instead, this strategy allows you to assess students' growing understanding of a concept or skill.

First, state a fact. Then ask students why, or how, or to explain. Student thinking is activated and you gain insight into the depth of students' conceptual understanding.

Example: Make the statement, "The quotient of two integers with the same sign is positive." Then ask, "Why is this true?"

Self-Assessment for Concepts & Skills

10. a. They have the same sign.
    b. They have different signs.
    c. The dividend is zero.
11. −3
12. 3
13. −5
14. $\frac{-10}{-5}$; The other quotients are negative.

Laurie's Notes

EXAMPLE 3

- Students should know the order of operations and the meaning of exponents. Students will need to use the order of operations to evaluate these expressions. Instead of telling students, "remember the order of operations," wait to see what they remember without prompting.
- Write the problem in part (a) and ask what it means to "evaluate." To evaluate a numerical expression means to perform the operations to find the value of the expression.
- Solve each problem as shown.
- In part (b), be sure that students correctly evaluate $-x^2$. Students often find the opposite of 8 and then square −8 instead of squaring 8 and then finding the opposite of 64. Remind students to write the power as repeated multiplication before finding the opposite.
- **Common Error:** If students forget the order of operations, they may perform the operations from left to right. Solicit explanations of the order in which the operations should be completed and why.

Try It

- Have students work with partners.

Extension: "Can Exercise 8 be rewritten as $a + 6 \div 3$?" No, there is an implied order of operations by the division bar and it would need to be written as $(a + 6) \div 3$.

Self-Assessment for Concepts & Skills

- Review the success criteria with students. Ask students to use whiteboards to indicate how well they have met the criteria using a percent (100%, 80%, 50%, etc.).
- Have students complete the exercises independently. Then use *Fact-First Questioning* to evaluate their answers for Exercises 10 and 14.

ELL Support

Allow students to work in pairs to complete Exercises 11–13. Check comprehension by having each pair write their answers on a whiteboard for your review. Have pairs discuss and answer Exercises 10 and 14. Then have each pair compare their answers with another pair. Each group should come to agreement if their answers differ. Monitor discussions and provide support.

The Success Criteria Self-Assessment chart can be found in the *Student Journal* or online at *BigIdeasMath.com*.

EXAMPLE 3 Evaluating Expressions

Find the value of each expression when $x = 8$ and $y = -4$.

a. $\dfrac{x}{2y}$

$\dfrac{x}{2y} = \dfrac{8}{2(-4)}$ — Substitute 8 for x and -4 for y.

$= \dfrac{8}{-8}$ — Multiply 2 and -4.

$= -1$ — Divide 8 by -8.

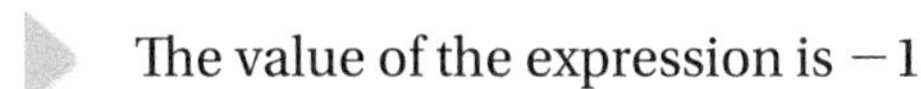

The value of the expression is -1.

b. $-x^2 + 12 \div y$

$-x^2 + 12 \div y = -8^2 + 12 \div (-4)$ — Substitute 8 for x and -4 for y.

$= -(8 \cdot 8) + 12 \div (-4)$ — Write 8^2 as repeated multiplication.

$= -64 + 12 \div (-4)$ — Multiply 8 and 8.

$= -64 + (-3)$ — Divide 12 by -4.

$= -67$ — Add.

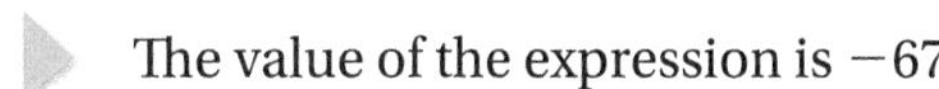

The value of the expression is -67.

Try It **Evaluate the expression when $a = -18$ and $b = -6$.**

7. $a \div b$

8. $\dfrac{a+6}{3}$

9. $\dfrac{b^2}{a} + 4$

Self-Assessment for Concepts & Skills

Solve each exercise. Then rate your understanding of the success criteria in your journal.

10. WRITING What can you conclude about two integers whose quotient is (a) positive, (b) negative, or (c) zero?

DIVIDING INTEGERS **Find the quotient.**

11. $-12 \div 4$

12. $\dfrac{-6}{-2}$

13. $15 \div (-3)$

14. WHICH ONE DOESN'T BELONG? Which expression does *not* belong with the other three? Explain your reasoning.

$\dfrac{10}{-5}$ $\dfrac{-10}{5}$ $\dfrac{-10}{-5}$ $-\dfrac{10}{5}$

EXAMPLE 4 Modeling Real Life

You measure the height of the tide using the support beams of a pier. What is the mean hourly change in the height?

To find the mean hourly change in the height of the tide, divide the change in the height by the elapsed time.

$$\text{mean hourly change} = \frac{\text{final height} - \text{initial height}}{\text{elapsed time}}$$

The elapsed time from 2 P.M. to 8 P.M. is 6 hours.

$$= \frac{8 - 59}{6} \qquad \text{Substitute.}$$

$$= \frac{-51}{6} \qquad \text{Subtract.}$$

$$= -8\frac{1}{2} \qquad \text{Divide.}$$

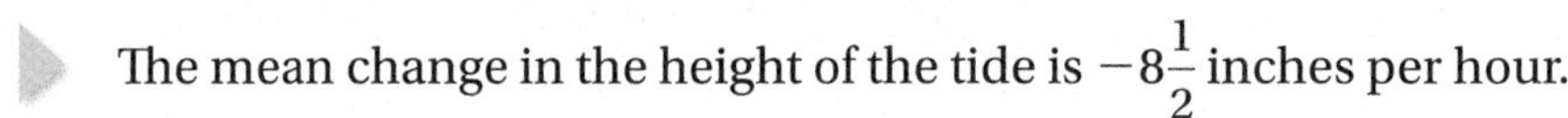

The mean change in the height of the tide is $-8\frac{1}{2}$ inches per hour.

Math Practice

Communicate Precisely

Explain to a classmate why the change in height is represented by 8 − 59 rather than 59 − 8.

Self-Assessment for Problem Solving

Solve each exercise. Then rate your understanding of the success criteria in your journal.

15. A female grizzly bear weighs 500 pounds. After hibernating for 6 months, she weighs only 350 pounds. What is the mean monthly change in weight?

16. The table shows the change in the number of crimes committed in a city each year for 4 years. What is the mean yearly change in the number of crimes?

Year	2014	2015	2016	2017
Change in Crimes	215	−321	−185	95

17. **DIG DEEPER!** At a restaurant, when a customer buys 4 pretzels, the fifth pretzel is free. Soft pretzels cost \$3.90 each. You order 12 soft pretzels. What is your mean cost per pretzel?

Laurie's Notes

EXAMPLE 4

- **Model with Mathematics:** Discuss how the word *mean* is used in this context. Students often only think of computing a mean by adding values and then dividing by the number of values. So, if students think of *mean* as adding values, they may not solve this problem correctly.
- **Construct Viable Arguments and Critique the Reasoning of Others:** Have students discuss the Math Practice note in pairs. After several minutes, discuss the results as a class. Make sure students understand why you find the total change in height by finding the difference between the final height and the initial height.

Self-Assessment for Problem Solving

- Students may benefit from trying the exercises independently and then working with peers to refine their work. It is important to provide time in class for problem solving, so that students become comfortable with the problem-solving plan. Support students with probing questions and by providing feedback.
- **Probing Questions:** What information do you need before dividing? What tool(s) can be used to help answer Exercise 17? Do your answers make sense?
- "How did you use the success criteria to solve these problems?" *Sample answer:* All of these problems use the rules for dividing integers with the same sign or different signs.

The Success Criteria Self-Assessment chart can be found in the *Student Journal* or online at *BigIdeasMath.com.*

Closure

- **Exit Ticket:** How are the rules for multiplication and division of integers related? Why are they related? The rules are the same, because the operations are inverses. You can use fact families to rewrite a division problem as a multiplication problem and vice versa.

Extra Example 4

The morning high tide at a beach is 57 inches. Six hours later, the afternoon low tide is 12 inches. What is the mean hourly change in the height of the tide? −7.5 inches

Self-Assessment for Problem Solving

15. −25 lb/mo

16. −49 crimes/yr

17. $3.25

Learning Target

Find quotients of integers.

Success Criteria

- Explain the rules for dividing integers.
- Find quotients of integers with the same sign.
- Find quotients of integers with different signs.

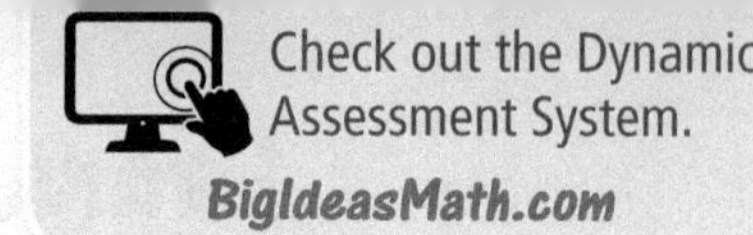
Check out the Dynamic Assessment System.
BigIdeasMath.com

Review & Refresh

1. 80
2. −54
3. 28
4. 72
5. 0.24, $\frac{1}{4}$, 28%
6. $\frac{2}{5}$, 42%, 0.45
7. 0.69, $\frac{7}{10}$, 71%, 0.84, $\frac{9}{10}$
8. $5 + (-1); 5 - 1; 4$
9. $-3 + 3; -3 - (-3); 0$

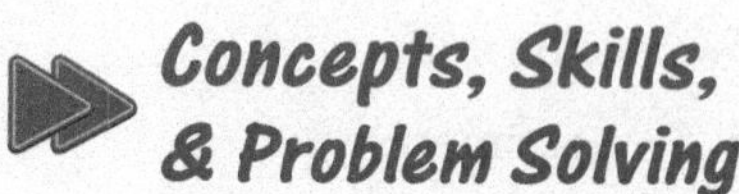

Concepts, Skills, & Problem Solving

10. integers with different signs; −7; negative
11. integers with different signs; −2; negative
12. integers with the same sign; 11; positive
13. −2
14. −3
15. −5
16. 6
17. −7
18. 0
19. 3
20. −6
21. −3
22. 7
23. 0
24. −10
25. −4
26. undefined
27. −13
28. 12
29. no; The quotient should be positive.
30. no; The quotient should be 0.

Assignment Guide and Concept Check

Scaffold assignments to support all students in their learning progression. The suggested assignments are a starting point. Continue to assign additional exercises and revisit with spaced practice to move every student toward proficiency.

Level	Assignment 1	Assignment 2
Emerging	4, 7, 8, 10, 13, 15, 17, 19, 29, 30, 32, 35, 37	12, 26, 27, 28, 31, 33, 39, 40, 42, 43, 47
Proficient	4, 7, 8, 11, 18, 20, 22, 29, 30, 32, 36, 38, 42	12, 26, 27, 28, 31, 40, 41, 43, 44, 47
Advanced	4, 7, 8, 12, 25, 26, 28, 29, 30, 33, 40, 41, 42	43, 44, 45, 46, 47

- Assignment 1 is for use after students complete the Self-Assessment for Concepts & Skills.
- Assignment 2 is for use after students complete the Self-Assessment for Problem Solving.
- The red exercises can be used as a concept check.

Review & Refresh Prior Skills

Exercises 1–4 Multiplying Integers
Exercises 5–7 Ordering Numbers
Exercises 8 and 9 Using Number Lines to Add and Subtract Integers

Common Errors

- **Exercises 18, 23, and 26** For the exercises involving zero, students may just say that the quotient is undefined. Remind students that when 0 is the dividend, it means 0 is the quotient. For example, $0 \div (-2) = 0$ because $0 \cdot (-2) = 0$. Remind students that when 0 is the divisor, it means the quotient is undefined. For example, $18 \div 0$ is undefined because there is no number that when multiplied to 0 equals 18.

B.2 Practice

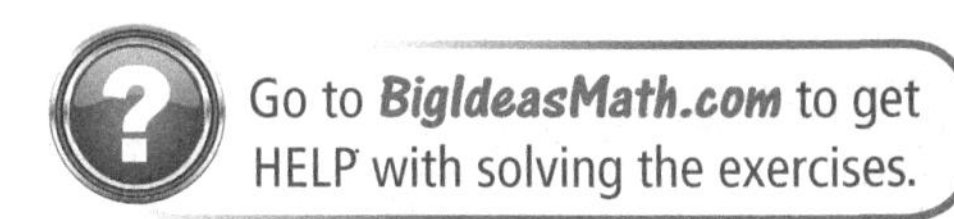

Review & Refresh

Find the product.

1. $8 \cdot 10$
2. $-6(9)$
3. $4(7)$
4. $-9(-8)$

Order the numbers from least to greatest.

5. $28\%, \frac{1}{4}, 0.24$
6. $42\%, 0.45, \frac{2}{5}$
7. $\frac{7}{10}, 0.69, 71\%, \frac{9}{10}, 0.84$

Write an addition expression and write a subtraction expression represented by the number line. Then evaluate the expressions.

8. 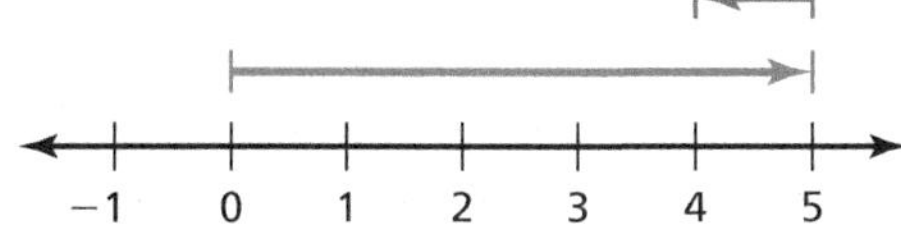

9. 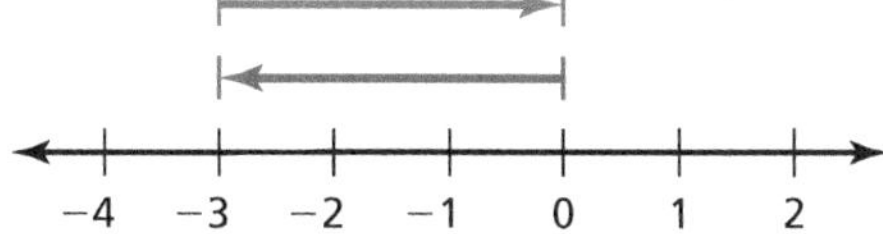

Concepts, Skills, & Problem Solving

MP **CHOOSE TOOLS** **Complete the table.** (See Exploration 1, p. 555.)

	Expression	Type of Quotient	Quotient	Quotient: Positive, Negative, or Zero
10.	$14 \div (-2)$			
11.	$-24 \div 12$			
12.	$-55 \div (-5)$			

DIVIDING INTEGERS **Find the quotient, if possible.**

13. $4 \div (-2)$
14. $21 \div (-7)$
15. $-20 \div 4$
16. $-18 \div (-3)$
17. $\frac{-14}{2}$
18. $\frac{0}{6}$
19. $\frac{-15}{-5}$
20. $\frac{54}{-9}$
21. $-\frac{33}{11}$
22. $-49 \div (-7)$
23. $0 \div (-2)$
24. $\frac{60}{-6}$
25. $\frac{-56}{14}$
26. $\frac{18}{0}$
27. $-\frac{65}{5}$
28. $\frac{-84}{-7}$

MP **YOU BE THE TEACHER** **Your friend finds the quotient. Is your friend correct? Explain your reasoning.**

29. $\frac{-63}{-9} = -7$

30. $0 \div (-5) = -5$

31. **MP MODELING REAL LIFE** You read 105 pages of a novel over 7 days. What is the mean number of pages you read each day?

USING ORDER OF OPERATIONS **Evaluate the expression.**

32. $-8 - 14 \div 2 + 5$

33. $24 \div (-4) + (-2) \cdot (-5)$

EVALUATING EXPRESSIONS **Evaluate the expression when $x = 10$, $y = -2$, and $z = -5$.**

34. $x \div y$

35. $12 \div (3y)$

36. $\frac{2z}{y}$

37. $\frac{-x + y}{6}$

38. $100 \div (-z^2)$

39. $\frac{10y^2}{z}$

40. $\left|\frac{xz}{-y}\right|$

41. $\frac{-x^2 + 6z}{y}$

42. **MP PATTERNS** Find the next two numbers in the pattern $-128, 64, -32, 16, \ldots$. Explain your reasoning.

43. **MP MODELING REAL LIFE** The Detroit-Windsor Tunnel is an underwater highway that connects the cities of Detroit, Michigan, and Windsor, Ontario. How many times deeper is the roadway than the bottom of the ship?

44. **MP MODELING REAL LIFE** A snowboarder descends from an elevation of 2253 feet to an elevation of 1011 feet in 3 minutes. What is the mean change in elevation per minute?

45. **MP REASONING** The table shows a golfer's scores relative to *par* for three out of four rounds of a tournament.

Scorecard	
Round 1	+1
Round 2	−4
Round 3	−3
Round 4	?

a. What was the golfer's mean score per round for the first 3 rounds?

b. The golfer's goal for the tournament is to have a mean score no greater than −3. Describe how the golfer can achieve this goal.

46. **MP PROBLEM SOLVING** The regular admission price for an amusement park is \$72. For a group of 15 or more, the admission price is reduced by \$25 per person. How many people need to be in a group to save \$500?

47. **DIG DEEPER!** Write a set of five different integers that has a mean of −10. Explain how you found your answer.

Common Errors

- **Exercises 32–41** Students may forget to follow the order of operations. Review the order of operations, especially the left-to-right rules of evaluating multiplication/division and addition/subtraction.
- **Exercise 45** Students may not remember how to find the mean of several numbers. They may get confused by the negative numbers and subtract instead of add. Remind students of the definition for *mean*.

Mini-Assessment

Find the quotient, if possible.

1. $-16 \div (-4)$ 4
2. $\frac{35}{-5}$ -7

Evaluate the expression when $x = -3$, $y = 9$, and $z = -2$.

3. $y \div x$ -3
4. $\frac{yz}{x}$ 6
5. You play a video game for 15 minutes. You lose 75 points. What is the mean change in points per minute? -5 points

Section Resources

Surface Level	Deep Level
Resources by Chapter • Extra Practice • Reteach • Puzzle Time Student Journal • Self-Assessment • Practice Differentiating the Lesson Tutorial Videos Skills Review Handbook Skills Trainer	Resources by Chapter • Enrichment and Extension Graphic Organizers Dynamic Assessment System • Section Practice
Transfer Level	
Dynamic Assessment System • Mid-Chapter Quiz	Assessment Book • Mid-Chapter Quiz

Concepts, Skills, & Problem Solving

31. 15 **32.** -10

33. 4 **34.** -5

35. -2 **36.** 5

37. -2 **38.** -4

39. -8 **40.** 25

41. 65

42. –8, 4; Divide the previous number by -2 to obtain the next number.

43. 5

44. -414 ft/min

45. **a.** -2

b. Score -6 or less in round 4.

46. 20

47. *Sample answer:* $-20, -15, -10, -5, 0$; Start with -10, then pair -15 with -5 and -20 with 0. The sum of the integers must be $5(-10) = -50$.

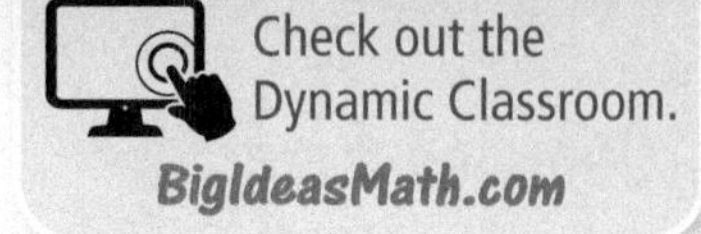
Check out the
Dynamic Classroom.
BigIdeasMath.com

Learning Target

Convert between different forms of rational numbers.

Success Criteria

- Explain the difference between terminating and repeating decimals.
- Write fractions and mixed numbers as decimals.
- Write decimals as fractions and mixed numbers.

Warm Up

Cumulative, vocabulary, and prerequisite skills practice opportunities are available in the *Resources by Chapter* or at *BigIdeasMath.com*.

ELL Support

Explain that the word *convert* means "to change or transform." Its Latin parts mean "together" (*con*) and "to turn" (*vertere*), so *convert* roughly means "turning together." In everyday life, convert is often associated with a person changing his or her view about something or changing a substance into a different form. In math, however, it means changing a quantity expressed in one form into another, such as changing a fraction into a decimal.

Exploration 1

a. $\frac{7}{10}$; $1\frac{29}{100}$; $12\frac{831}{1000}$; $\frac{41}{10,000}$;

b. *Sample answer:* The factors (other than 1) are multiples of 2 and 5; yes

Exploration 2

a–c. See Additional Answers.

Laurie's Notes

Preparing to Teach

- In prior courses, students divided decimals that terminated or they rounded the results. Now students will write fractions and mixed numbers as decimals, including repeating decimals. In the next course, students will expand this understanding to write repeating decimals as fractions.
- **Reason Abstractly and Quantitatively:** In this lesson, students will write fractions as decimals and vice versa. Students should always check the reasonableness of their answers. For instance, $\frac{7}{11}$ is greater than $\frac{1}{2}$. So, when you write $\frac{7}{11}$ as a decimal, the result should be greater than 0.5.

Motivate

- Ask students to form a "name fraction," where the numerator is the number of letters in the student's first name and the denominator is the number of letters in the student's last name.
- Before class, go through your class roster and select two students whose name fractions are nearly equivalent, but one is a **terminating decimal** and the other is a **repeating decimal**. Discuss writing the fractions as decimals.
- When you discuss the repeating decimal, share that today's lesson is about writing rational numbers, which may be repeating decimals.

Exploration 1

- ? Tell students that *decimal fractions* are those with powers of 10 in the denominator, such as $\frac{3}{10}$ or $\frac{21}{100}$.
- Review the proper way to read decimals using place value. For example, 0.9 is *not* read as "point nine." It is read as "nine-tenths" and written as $\frac{9}{10}$.
- Discuss part (b). Students should notice that the denominators of decimal fractions are always powers of 10.
- ? "What are *prime numbers*?" Numbers greater than 1 whose only factors are 1 and itself. Examples: 2, 3, 5, 23, 41.
- ? "What are the *prime factors* of the denominators of decimal fractions?" 2 and 5

Exploration 2

- Students should recognize some of the decimals *terminate* and others *repeat*.
- Discuss the question in the Math Practice note. Have students use equivalent fractions to convert some of the fractions to decimals.
- ? "Will equivalent fractions work for all of the fractions? Explain." No, some of the fractions have denominators that are not powers or factors of 10.

B.3 Converting Between Fractions and Decimals

Learning Target: Convert between different forms of rational numbers.

Success Criteria:
- I can explain the difference between terminating and repeating decimals.
- I can write fractions and mixed numbers as decimals.
- I can write decimals as fractions and mixed numbers.

EXPLORATION 1 Analyzing Denominators of Decimal Fractions

Work with a partner.

a. Write each decimal as a fraction or mixed number.

0.7 1.29 12.831 0.0041

b. What do the factors of the denominators of the fractions you wrote have in common? Is this always true for decimal fractions?

EXPLORATION 2 Exploring Decimal Representations

Work with a partner.

a. A fraction $\frac{a}{b}$ can be interpreted as $a \div b$. Use a calculator to convert each unit fraction to a decimal. Do some of the decimals look different than the others? Explain.

$\frac{1}{2}$ $\frac{1}{3}$ $\frac{1}{4}$ $\frac{1}{5}$

$\frac{1}{6}$ $\frac{1}{7}$ $\frac{1}{8}$

$\frac{1}{9}$ $\frac{1}{10}$ $\frac{1}{11}$ $\frac{1}{12}$

b. Compare and contrast the fractions in part (a) with the fractions you wrote in Exploration 1. What conclusions can you make?

c. Does every fraction have a decimal form that either *terminates* or *repeats*? Explain your reasoning.

Math Practice

Use Technology to Explore

How do calculators help you learn about different types of decimals? How can you find decimal forms of fractions without using a calculator?

B.3 Lesson

Key Vocabulary
terminating decimal, *p. 562*
repeating decimal, *p. 562*

Because you can divide any integer by any nonzero integer, you can use long division to write fractions and mixed numbers as decimals. These decimals are rational numbers and will either *terminate* or *repeat.*

A **terminating decimal** is a decimal that ends.

1.5, −0.25, 10.824

A **repeating decimal** is a decimal that has a pattern that repeats.

$-1.333\ldots = -1.\overline{3}$

$0.151515\ldots = 0.\overline{15}$

Use *bar notation* to show which of the digits repeat.

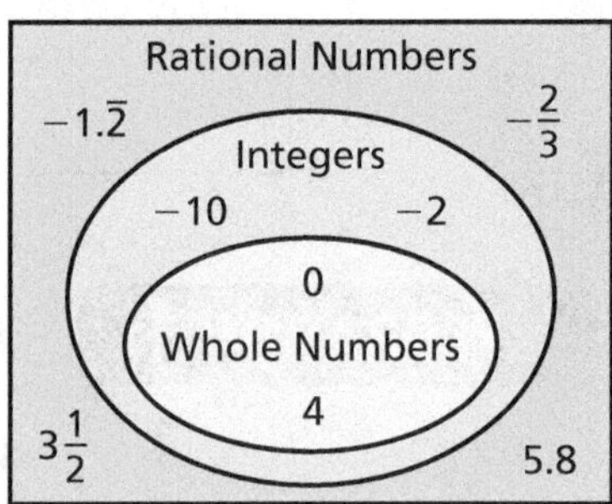

EXAMPLE 1 Writing Fractions and Mixed Numbers as Decimals

a. Write $-2\frac{1}{4}$ as a decimal.

Notice that $-2\frac{1}{4} = -\frac{9}{4}$.

Use long division to divide 9 by 4.

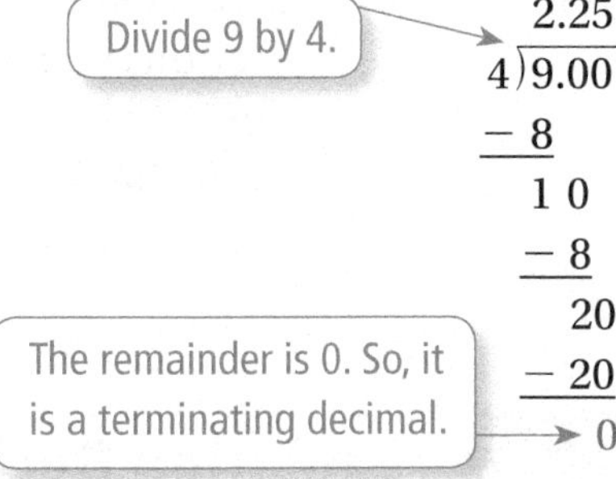

$$\begin{array}{r} 2.25 \\ 4\overline{)9.00} \\ -8 \\ 1\,0 \\ -8 \\ 20 \\ -20 \\ 0 \end{array}$$

The remainder is 0. So, it is a terminating decimal.

So, $-2\frac{1}{4} = -2.25$.

Another Method
Use equivalent fractions.

$\frac{1}{4} = \frac{1 \times 25}{4 \times 25} = \frac{25}{100}$

So, $-2\frac{1}{4} = -2\frac{25}{100}$
$= -2.25$. ✓

b. Write $\frac{5}{11}$ as a decimal.

Use long division to divide 5 by 11.

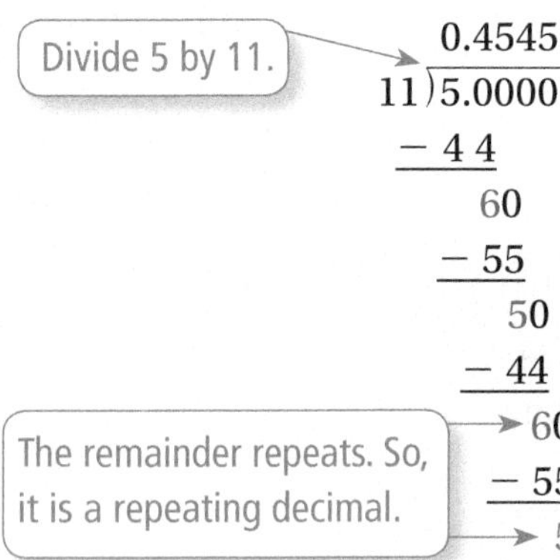

$$\begin{array}{r} 0.4545 \\ 11\overline{)5.0000} \\ -4\,4 \\ 60 \\ -55 \\ 50 \\ -44 \\ 60 \\ -55 \\ 5 \end{array}$$

The remainder repeats. So, it is a repeating decimal.

So, $\frac{5}{11} = 0.\overline{45}$.

Try It **Write the fraction or mixed number as a decimal.**

1. $-\frac{6}{5}$
2. $-7\frac{3}{8}$
3. $-\frac{3}{11}$
4. $1\frac{5}{27}$

Laurie's Notes

Scaffolding Instruction

- Students should understand that rational numbers can be written as decimals and as fractions. They should also understand that rational numbers in decimal form will either terminate or repeat.
- **Emerging:** Students may understand that rational numbers can be written in different forms but struggle to convert between the forms. Provide guided instruction for Examples 1 and 2. Then have students complete the Try It exercises before proceeding to the Self-Assessment exercises.
- **Proficient:** Students can convert between the forms of rational numbers and explain the difference between terminating and repeating decimals. After discussing the Key Vocabulary, these students can proceed to the Self-Assessment exercises.

Discuss

- All students should discuss the information at the top of the page, paying close attention to the diagram showing the relationships between whole numbers, integers, and rational numbers.

? "Are whole numbers also rational numbers?" yes "Are integers also rational numbers?" yes

? "What is the difference between integers and rational numbers?" Rational numbers contain the set of integers, but they also include fractions, mixed numbers, and decimals.

EXAMPLE 1

? "How do you write a fraction as a decimal?" Listen for 3 methods: using benchmark fractions that you know, writing the fraction as an equivalent fraction with a denominator that is a power of 10 and use the place value, or divide the numerator by the denominator.

- **Make Sense of Problems and Persevere in Solving Them:** Mathematically proficient students are able to plan a solution. Choosing between methods may help students be more efficient and accurate when writing fractions as decimals.
- Complete part (a) as a class. The first step is to write the mixed number as an equivalent improper fraction. Then divide the numerator by the denominator. Point out that the negative sign is simply placed in the answer after the calculations are complete.
- Discuss the Another Method note with students. Point out that to find an equivalent fraction with a denominator that is a power of 10, you multiply the numerator and denominator by powers of 2 or 5. This is not possible for repeating decimals.
- Complete part (b) as a class. Remind students to always divide the numerator by the denominator, regardless of the size of the numbers!

Try It

- **Neighbor Check:** Have students work independently and then have their neighbors check their work. Have students discuss any discrepancies.

Scaffold instruction to support all students in their learning. Learning is individualized and you may want to group students differently as they move in and out of these levels with each skill and concept. Student self-assessment and feedback help guide your instructional decisions about how and when to layer support for all students to become proficient learners.

Extra Example 1

a. Write $4\frac{3}{16}$ as a decimal. 4.1875

b. Write $-\frac{4}{9}$ as a decimal. $-0.\overline{4}$

ELL Support

After demonstrating Example 1, have students practice language by working in pairs to complete Try It Exercises 1–4. Have one student ask another, "What is negative six-fifths as a decimal?" Have students alternate roles.

Beginner: State the decimal.

Intermediate: Answer with a simple sentence such as, "The decimal is negative one and two tenths."

Advanced: Answer with a detailed sentence such as, "Negative six-fifths is equivalent to negative one and two tenths."

Try It

1. -1.2
2. -7.375
3. $-0.\overline{27}$
4. $1.\overline{185}$

Extra Example 2

Write −2.625 as a mixed number in simplest form. $-2\frac{5}{8}$

Try It

5. $-\frac{3}{10}$
6. $\frac{1}{8}$
7. $-3\frac{1}{10}$
8. $-10\frac{1}{4}$

ELL Support

Allow students to work in pairs to complete the Self-Assessment for Concepts & Skills exercises. Discuss students' responses to Exercise 9 as a class. Check comprehension of Exercises 10–15 by having each pair display their answers on a whiteboard for your review.

Self-Assessment for Concepts & Skills

9. *Sample answer:* Terminating decimals end, repeating decimals have a pattern that repeats.
10. 0.1875
11. $-0.4\overline{6}$
12. 6.85
13. $\frac{3}{5}$
14. $-12\frac{12}{25}$
15. $\frac{51}{125}$

Laurie's Notes

EXAMPLE 2

- ? "How do you write a terminating decimal as a fraction?" Use the place value of the last digit in the decimal as the denominator.
- Work through the example as shown.
- ? "How do you simplify the fraction $-\frac{26}{100}$?" Divide both the numerator and the denominator by a common factor of 2.
- Be sure to discuss the Reading note.
- **Extension:** Write −0.026 and −2.6 as fractions. $-\frac{26}{1000} = -\frac{13}{500}$ and $-2\frac{6}{10} = -2\frac{3}{5}$ This helps students focus on the importance of place value and where the last digit is located.

Try It

- **Neighbor Check:** Have students work independently and then have their neighbors check their work. Have students discuss any discrepancies.
- ? "How did you handle the whole-number parts in Exercises 7 and 8?" *Sample answer:* The whole number is the same in both the decimal and mixed number form.

Formative Assessment Tip

Response Cards

This technique is used as a quick check to see whether students' knowledge of a skill, technique, or procedure is correct. Students are given cards at the beginning of class that are held up in front of them in response to a question. The cards are prepared in advance with particular responses, such as: A, B, C, and D; or 1, 2, and 3; or True and False. The cards can also be left blank for students to write their responses on. If you plan to use the cards multiple times, consider laminating them. *Response Cards* give all students the opportunity to participate in the lesson, because you are soliciting information from everyone and not just those who raise their hands. Because the cards are held facing the teacher, it is a private way to gather quick information about students' understanding.

Self-Assessment for Concepts & Skills

- Before students begin these exercises, distribute *Response Cards* with *terminating* and *repeating* to students. "Will the decimal be *terminating* or *repeating* in Exercise 10? Exercise 11? Exercise 12?" Solicit explanations.
- Students may understand the process of converting fractions to decimals and decimals to fractions, but make errors in calculations. Remind students to check their work and check their answers for reasonableness.

The Success Criteria Self-Assessment chart can be found in the *Student Journal* or online at *BigIdeasMath.com*.

Math Practice

Look for Structure
Explain why these two representations for simplifying fractions have the same result. Which do you prefer?

Any terminating decimal can be written as a fraction whose denominator is a power of 10. You can often simplify the resulting fraction by *dividing out* any common factors, which is the same as removing the common factor from the numerator and denominator.

$$0.48 = \frac{48}{100} = \frac{48 \div 4}{100 \div 4} = \frac{12}{25} \quad \text{or} \quad 0.48 = \frac{48}{100} = \frac{12 \bullet \cancel{4}}{25 \bullet \cancel{4}} = \frac{12}{25}$$

EXAMPLE 2 Writing a Terminating Decimal as a Fraction

Write -0.26 as a fraction in simplest form.

$$-0.26 = -\frac{26}{100}$$

Write the digits after the decimal point in the numerator.

The last digit is in the hundredths place. So, use 100 in the denominator.

$$= -\frac{13 \bullet \cancel{2}}{50 \bullet \cancel{2}}$$ Divide out the common factor, 2.

$$= -\frac{13}{50}$$ Simplify.

So, $-0.26 = -\frac{13}{50}$.

Reading

-0.26 is read as "negative twenty-six hundredths."

Try It **Write the decimal as a fraction or mixed number in simplest form.**

5. -0.3 **6.** 0.125 **7.** -3.1 **8.** -10.25

Self-Assessment for Concepts & Skills

Solve each exercise. Then rate your understanding of the success criteria in your journal.

9. **WRITING** Compare and contrast terminating decimals and repeating decimals.

WRITING A FRACTION OR MIXED NUMBER AS A DECIMAL **Write the fraction or mixed number as a decimal.**

10. $\frac{3}{16}$ **11.** $-\frac{7}{15}$ **12.** $6\frac{17}{20}$

WRITING A DECIMAL AS A FRACTION OR MIXED NUMBER **Write the decimal as a fraction or mixed number in simplest form.**

13. 0.6 **14.** -12.48 **15.** 0.408

EXAMPLE 3 Modeling Real Life

Creature	Elevation (kilometers)
Anglerfish	$-\frac{13}{10}$
Shark	$-\frac{2}{11}$
Squid	$-2\frac{1}{5}$
Whale	-0.8

The table shows the elevations of four sea creatures relative to sea level. Which of the sea creatures are deeper than the whale? Explain.

One way to compare the depths of the creatures is to use a number line. First, write each fraction or mixed number as a decimal.

$$-\frac{13}{10} = -1.3$$

$$-\frac{2}{11} = -0.\overline{18}$$

Divide 2 by 11.

$$\begin{array}{r} 0.1818 \\ 11\overline{)2.0000} \\ -1\,1 \\ \hline 90 \\ -88 \\ \hline 20 \\ -11 \\ \hline 90 \\ -88 \\ \hline 2 \end{array}$$

The remainder repeats. So, it is a repeating decimal.

$$-2\frac{1}{5} = -2\frac{2}{10} = -2.2$$

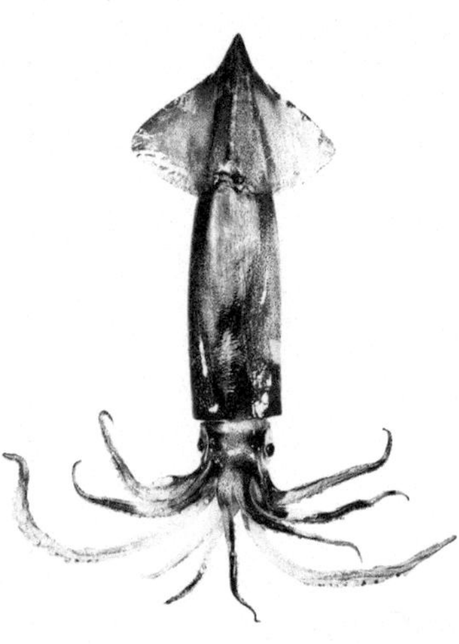

Then graph each decimal on a number line.

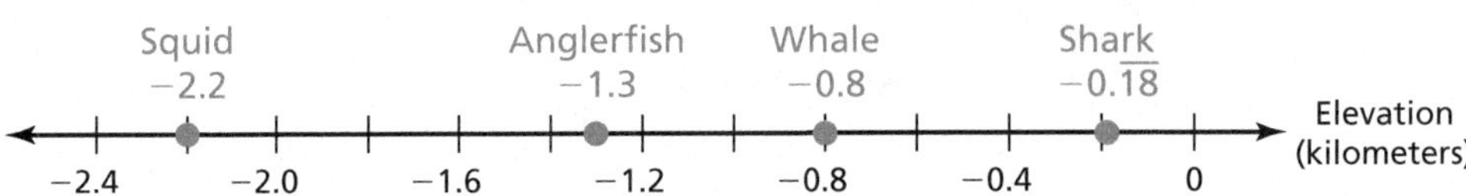

Both -2.2 and -1.3 are less than -0.8. So, the squid and the anglerfish are deeper than the whale.

Self-Assessment for Problem Solving

Solve each exercise. Then rate your understanding of the success criteria in your journal.

16. A box turtle hibernates in sand at an elevation of -1.625 feet. A spotted turtle hibernates at an elevation of $-1\frac{7}{12}$ feet. Which turtle hibernates deeper in the sand? How much deeper?

17. A *red sprite* is an electrical flash that occurs in Earth's upper atmosphere. The table shows the elevations of four red sprites. What is the range of the elevations?

Elevation (miles)	
50.6	$50\frac{13}{25}$
$50\frac{8}{15}$	$\frac{155}{3}$

Laurie's Notes

EXAMPLE 3

- Discuss the unit of measure, kilometers.
- Work through the problem with the class. Draw the number line vertically and identify sea level.

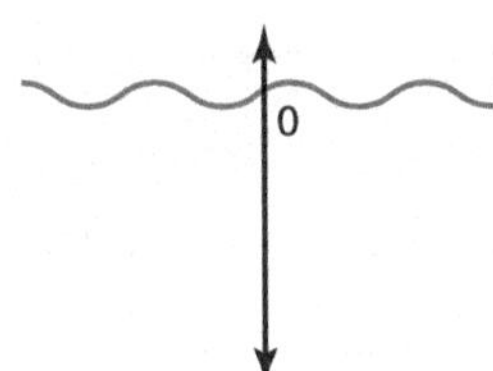

Self-Assessment for Problem Solving

- The goal for all students is to feel comfortable with the problem-solving plan. It is important for students to problem-solve in class where they may receive support from you and their peers. Keep in mind that some students may only be ready for the first step.
- Have students work in pairs to complete the exercises. Ask volunteers to present their work and answers using a document camera, if possible.

The Success Criteria Self-Assessment chart can be found in the *Student Journal* or online at *BigIdeasMath.com*.

Closure

- **Exit Ticket:**
  - Write $-\frac{5}{6}$ as a decimal. $-0.8\overline{3}$
  - Write -0.56 as a fraction in simplest form. $-\frac{56}{100} = -\frac{14}{25}$

Extra Example 3

The table shows the elevations of four animals relative to ground level. Which of the animals are deeper than the rabbit? Explain.

Animal	Elevation (feet)
Rabbit	$-\frac{19}{10}$
Mole	-2.9
Chipmunk	$-1\frac{7}{9}$
Groundhog	$-2\frac{7}{8}$

mole and groundhog; Both -2.9 and -2.875 are less than -1.9.

Self-Assessment for Problem Solving

16. box turtle; $\frac{1}{24}$ ft

17. $1\frac{11}{75}$ mi

Learning Target

Convert between different forms of rational numbers.

Success Criteria

- Explain the difference between terminating and repeating decimals.
- Write fractions and mixed numbers as decimals.
- Write decimals as fractions and mixed numbers.

Review & Refresh

1. -2
2. -6
3. 6
4. 11
5. 35.28
6. 8.014
7. 74.16441
8. 0.0030018
9.

Hours	2	8	$\frac{4}{3}$
Dollars Earned	18	72	12

$2:18;\ 8:72;\ \frac{4}{3}:12$

Concepts, Skills, & Problem Solving

10. terminates; 8 is a factor of 1000
11. repeats; 7 is not a factor of a power of 10
12. terminates; 40 is a factor of 1000
13. repeats; 24 is not a factor of a power of 10
14. 0.875
15. $0.\overline{09}$
16. -3.5
17. $-0.\overline{7}$
18. -0.425
19. $1.8\overline{3}$
20. $4.1\overline{3}$
21. $1.041\overline{6}$
22. $-1.\overline{18}$
23. $-2.9\overline{4}$
24. $-5.58\overline{3}$
25. $8.6\overline{81}$
26. no; The bar should be over both 6 and 3.
27. $-\frac{9}{10}$
28. $\frac{9}{20}$
29. $-\frac{129}{500}$
30. $-\frac{39}{125}$
31. $-2\frac{8}{25}$
32. $-1\frac{16}{25}$
33. $6\frac{3}{250}$
34. $-12\frac{81}{200}$
35. a. 0.55

    b. $\frac{11}{20}$

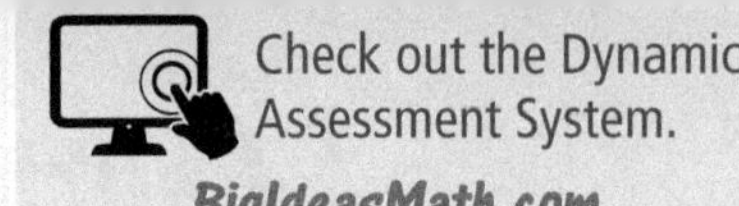
Check out the Dynamic Assessment System.
BigIdeasMath.com

Assignment Guide and Concept Check

Scaffold assignments to support all students in their learning progression. The suggested assignments are a starting point. Continue to assign additional exercises and revisit with spaced practice to move every student toward proficiency.

Level	Assignment 1	Assignment 2
Emerging	4, 8, 9, 10, 11, 14, 16, 17, 26, 27, 31, 48	18, 19, 32, 33, 35, 36, 39, 40, 41, 42
Proficient	4, 8, 9, 10, 11, 17, 18, 19, 26, 28, 30, 32, 48	25, 33, 35, 37, 39, 40, 42, 43, 47
Advanced	4, 8, 9, 12, 13, 14, 23, 25, 26, 30, 32, 33, 48	38, 40, 45, 46, 47, 49, 50, 51

- Assignment 1 is for use after students complete the Self-Assessment for Concepts & Skills.
- Assignment 2 is for use after students complete the Self-Assessment for Problem Solving.
- The red exercises can be used as a concept check.

Review & Refresh Prior Skills

Exercises 1–4 Dividing Integers
Exercises 5 and 6 Multiplying Decimals and Whole Numbers
Exercises 7 and 8 Multiplying Decimals
Exercise 9 Completing Ratio Tables and Writing Equivalent Ratios

Common Errors

- **Exercises 16–18 and 22–24** Students may forget to carry the negative sign through the division operation. Tell them to create a space for the final answer and to write the sign of the answer in the space at the beginning.
- **Exercises 27–34** Students may try to put the decimal number over the denominator. Remind students to remove the decimal point before they write it as a fraction.

B.3 Practice

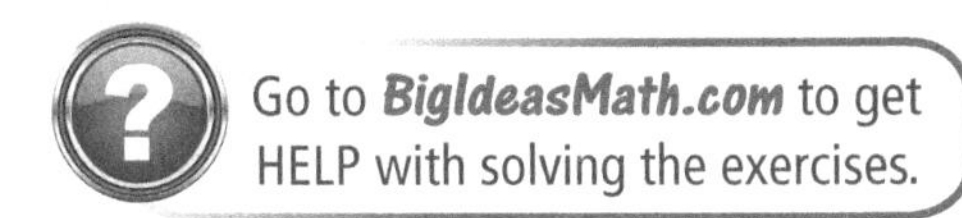
Go to BigIdeasMath.com to get HELP with solving the exercises.

Review & Refresh

Find the quotient.

1. $12 \div (-6)$
2. $-48 \div 8$
3. $-42 \div (-7)$
4. $-33 \div (-3)$

Find the product.

5. 5.88×6
6. $2.0035 \cdot 4$
7. 5.49×13.509
8. 1.0006×0.003

9. Find the missing values in the ratio table. Then write the equivalent ratios.

Hours	2		$\frac{4}{3}$
Dollars Earned	18	72	

Concepts, Skills, & Problem Solving

MP STRUCTURE **Without dividing, determine whether the decimal form of the fraction *terminates* or *repeats*. Explain.** (See Explorations 1 & 2, p. 561.)

10. $\frac{3}{8}$
11. $\frac{5}{7}$
12. $\frac{11}{40}$
13. $\frac{5}{24}$

WRITING A FRACTION OR MIXED NUMBER AS A DECIMAL **Write the fraction or mixed number as a decimal.**

14. $\frac{7}{8}$
15. $\frac{1}{11}$
16. $-3\frac{1}{2}$
17. $-\frac{7}{9}$
18. $-\frac{17}{40}$
19. $1\frac{5}{6}$
20. $4\frac{2}{15}$
21. $\frac{25}{24}$
22. $-\frac{13}{11}$
23. $-2\frac{17}{18}$
24. $-5\frac{7}{12}$
25. $8\frac{15}{22}$

26. **MP YOU BE THE TEACHER** Your friend writes $-\frac{7}{11}$ as a decimal. Is your friend correct? Explain your reasoning.

$$-\frac{7}{11} = -0.6\overline{3}$$

WRITING A DECIMAL AS A FRACTION OR MIXED NUMBER **Write the decimal as a fraction or mixed number in simplest form.**

27. -0.9
28. 0.45
29. -0.258
30. -0.312
31. -2.32
32. -1.64
33. 6.012
34. -12.405

35. **MP MODELING REAL LIFE** You find one quarter, two dimes, and two nickels.

    a. Write the dollar amount as a decimal.

    b. Write the dollar amount as a fraction or mixed number in simplest form.

COMPARING RATIONAL NUMBERS **Copy and complete the statement using < or >.**

36. $-4\frac{6}{10}$ ☐ -4.65 **37.** $-5\frac{3}{11}$ ☐ $-5.\overline{2}$ **38.** $-2\frac{13}{16}$ ☐ $-2\frac{11}{14}$

39. **MP MODELING REAL LIFE** Is the half pipe deeper than the skating bowl? Explain.

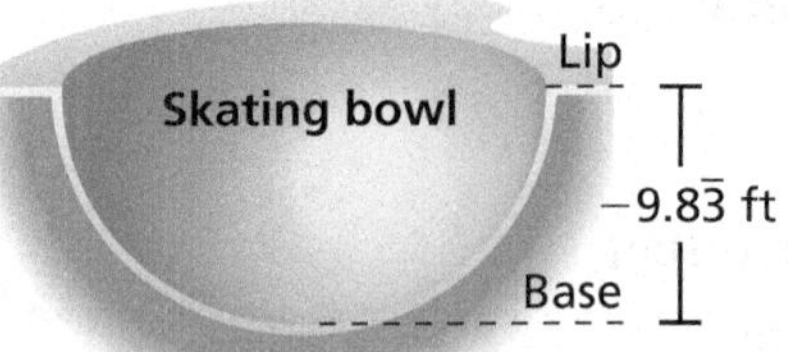

Player	Hits	At Bats
1	42	90
2	38	80

40. **MP MODELING REAL LIFE** In softball, a batting average is the number of hits divided by the number of times at bat. Does Player 1 or Player 2 have the greater batting average?

ORDERING RATIONAL NUMBERS **Order the numbers from least to greatest.**

41. $-\frac{3}{4}, 0.5, \frac{2}{3}, -\frac{7}{3}, 1.2$ **42.** $\frac{9}{5}, -2.5, -1.1, -\frac{4}{5}, 0.8$ **43.** $-1.4, -\frac{8}{5}, 0.6, -0.9, \frac{1}{4}$

44. $2.1, -\frac{6}{10}, -\frac{9}{4}, -0.75, \frac{5}{3}$ **45.** $-\frac{7}{2}, -2.8, -\frac{5}{4}, \frac{4}{3}, 1.3$ **46.** $-\frac{11}{5}, -2.4, 1.6, \frac{15}{10}, -2.25$

47. **MP MODELING REAL LIFE** The table shows the changes in the water level of a pond over several weeks. Order the numbers from least to greatest.

Week	1	2	3	4
Change (inches)	$-\frac{7}{5}$	$-1\frac{5}{11}$	-1.45	$-1\frac{91}{200}$

48. **OPEN-ENDED** Find one terminating decimal and one repeating decimal between $-\frac{1}{2}$ and $-\frac{1}{3}$.

49. **MP PROBLEM SOLVING** You miss 3 out of 10 questions on a science quiz and 4 out of 15 questions on a math quiz. On which quiz did you have a greater percentage of correct answers?

50. **CRITICAL THINKING** A hackberry tree has roots that reach a depth of $6\frac{5}{12}$ meters. The top of the tree is $18.2\overline{8}$ meters above the ground. Find the total height from the bottom of the roots to the top of the tree.

51. **DIG DEEPER!** Let a and b be integers.

a. When can $-\frac{1}{a}$ be written as a positive, repeating decimal?

b. When can $\frac{1}{ab}$ be written as a positive, terminating decimal?

Common Errors

- **Exercises 41–46** Students may order the numbers without the negative signs. Remind students that some numbers are negative and will be less than the positive numbers.

Mini-Assessment

Write the fraction or mixed number as a decimal.

1. $\frac{8}{9}$ $0.\overline{8}$
2. $-\frac{11}{10}$ -1.1

Write the decimal as a fraction or mixed number in simplest form.

3. -0.032 $-\frac{4}{125}$
4. 2.86 $2\frac{43}{50}$
5. When your cousin was born, she was $21\frac{4}{5}$ inches long. When your friend was born, he was $21\frac{5}{6}$ inches long. Who was longer at birth? your friend

Section Resources

Surface Level	Deep Level
Resources by Chapter • Extra Practice • Reteach • Puzzle Time Student Journal • Self-Assessment • Practice Differentiating the Lesson Tutorial Videos Skills Review Handbook Skills Trainer	Resources by Chapter • Enrichment and Extension Graphic Organizers Dynamic Assessment System • Section Practice

Concepts, Skills, & Problem Solving

36. $>$
37. $<$
38. $<$
39. no; $9\frac{5}{6} = 9.8\overline{3}$
40. Player 2
41. $-\frac{7}{3}, -\frac{3}{4}, 0.5, \frac{2}{3}, 1.2$
42. $-2.5, -1.1, -\frac{4}{5}, 0.8, \frac{9}{5}$
43. $-\frac{8}{5}, -1.4, -0.9, \frac{1}{4}, 0.6$
44. $-\frac{9}{4}, -0.75, -\frac{6}{10}, \frac{5}{3}, 2.1$
45. $-\frac{7}{2}, -2.8, -\frac{5}{4}, 1.3, \frac{4}{3}$
46. $-2.4, -2.25, -\frac{11}{5}, \frac{15}{10}, 1.6$
47. $-1\frac{91}{200}, -1\frac{5}{11}, -1.45, -\frac{7}{5}$
48. *Sample answer:* $-0.4, -0.\overline{45}$
49. math quiz
50. $24\frac{127}{180}$ m
51. **a.** when a is negative, and a is not a factor of a power of 10

    b. when a and b have the same sign, $a \neq 0 \neq b$, and a and b are factors of a power of 10

Check out the
Dynamic Classroom.
BigIdeasMath.com

Learning Target

Find products of rational numbers.

Success Criteria

- Explain the rules for multiplying rational numbers.
- Find products of rational numbers with same sign.
- Find products of rational numbers with different signs.

Warm Up

Cumulative, vocabulary, and prerequisite skills practice opportunities are available in the *Resources by Chapter* or at *BigIdeasMath.com.*

ELL Support

Remind students that in math, a rational number is a number that can be written as a fraction $\frac{a}{b}$ where a and b are integers and b is not zero. Point out that the word *rational* is often used to mean "reasonable" or "logical" in everyday language, but that is not its meaning in math.

Exploration 1

a. *Sample answer:* $0.2 \cdot 0.9$; $0.3 \cdot 0.5$; 0.18; 0.15

b. **i.** 0.18; −0.18

ii. 0.15; −0.15

iii. $\frac{1}{8}$; $-\frac{1}{8}$

iv. 0.48; 0.48

v. $\frac{3}{25}$; $\frac{3}{25}$

vi. 1.08; −1.08

vii. $3\frac{1}{8}$; $3\frac{1}{8}$

c. yes; *Sample answer:* $-a$ is the opposite of a for any number.

Laurie's Notes

Preparing to Teach

- **Make Sense of Problems and Persevere in Solving Them:** The area model for multiplication is a visual tool used to help students make sense of multiplying rational numbers. The dimensions of the area model represent the denominators and the purple shading represents the product.
- In the exploration, students will extend their understanding of multiplying fractions and integers to rational numbers.

Motivate

- Before beginning the formal lesson, it would be helpful to review the rules for multiplying integers.
  - same signs ⟶ product is positive
  - different signs ⟶ product is negative
- **Paired Verbal Fluency:** Have students explain how the rules were developed.

? "Do you think the same rules apply to rational numbers? Explain."

Exploration 1

- **Use Appropriate Tools Strategically:** Students should have experience using area models. If they do not, have students use a piece of paper to multiply $\frac{2}{3} \times \frac{3}{5}$. Fold the paper into fifths and shade three of the sections. Fold the paper the other way into thirds and shade two sections.

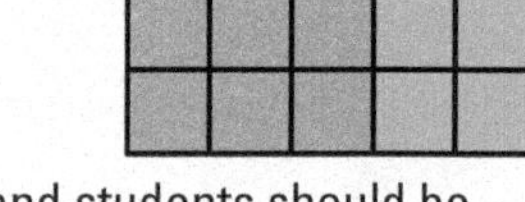

? "How many total squares are there?" 15
"How many squares are shaded with both colors?" 6 "What is the product?" $\frac{6}{15} = \frac{2}{5}$

- In part (b), completing the second column is review and students should be able to make a reasonable conjecture about the values in the last column.

Formative Assessment Tip

Turn and Talk

This technique allows all students in the class to have a voice. Using a three-foot voice, students turn and talk to their partners about a problem or discuss a question. There may be different roles that I ask partners to assume, so I refer to Partner A and Partner B. In discussing a procedure or explaining an answer, I might ask Partner A to talk uninterrupted for a fixed period of time. Then Partner B might be asked to repeat back what he or she heard, or to ask a question about what has been shared. Example: "*Turn and Talk*, so that Partner A explains how multiplying integers is similar to multiplying rational numbers." It is important to establish norms: three-foot voices should be expected when students are doing partner work. Discuss with students the difference between *authentic listening* and just being quiet while your partner is speaking.

- Have students *Turn and Talk* to discuss part (c) and the questions in the Math Practice note. Use *Popsicle Sticks* to solicit responses.

B.4 Multiplying Rational Numbers

Learning Target: Find products of rational numbers.

Success Criteria:
- I can explain the rules for multiplying rational numbers.
- I can find products of rational numbers with the same sign.
- I can find products of rational numbers with different signs.

EXPLORATION 1 Finding Products of Rational Numbers

Work with a partner.

a. Write a multiplication expression represented by each area model. Then find the product.

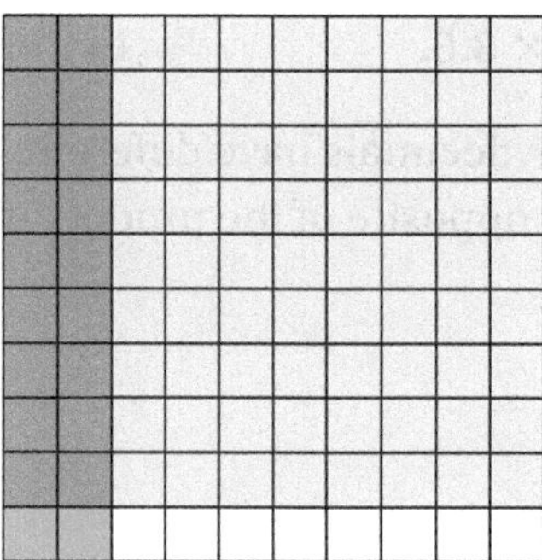

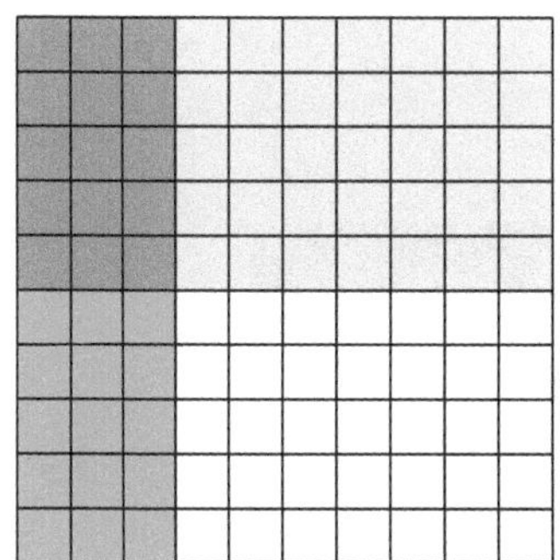

b. Complete the table.

	Expression	Product	Expression	Product
i.	0.2×0.9		-0.2×0.9	
ii.	$0.3(0.5)$		$0.3(-0.5)$	
iii.	$\frac{1}{4} \bullet \frac{1}{2}$		$\frac{1}{4} \bullet \left(-\frac{1}{2}\right)$	
iv.	$1.2(0.4)$		$-1.2(-0.4)$	
v.	$\frac{3}{10}\left(\frac{2}{5}\right)$		$-\frac{3}{10}\left(-\frac{2}{5}\right)$	
vi.	0.6×1.8		-0.6×1.8	
vii.	$1\frac{1}{4} \bullet 2\frac{1}{2}$		$-1\frac{1}{4} \bullet \left(-2\frac{1}{2}\right)$	

c. Do the rules for multiplying integers apply to all rational numbers? Explain your reasoning.

Math Practice

Consider Similar Problems

How is multiplying integers similar to multiplying other rational numbers? How is it different?

B.4 Lesson

When the signs of two numbers are different, their product is negative. When the signs of two numbers are the same, their product is positive.

Key Idea

Multiplying Rational Numbers

Words To multiply rational numbers, use the same rules for signs as you used for multiplying integers.

Numbers $-\frac{2}{7} \bullet \frac{1}{3} = -\frac{2}{21}$ $\qquad -\frac{2}{7} \bullet \left(-\frac{1}{3}\right) = \frac{2}{21}$

EXAMPLE 1 Multiplying Rational Numbers

a. Find -2.5×3.6. **Estimate** $-2.5 \bullet 4 = -10$

Because the decimals have different signs, the product is negative. So, find the opposite of the product of 2.5 and 3.6.

Math Practice

Justify Conclusions

Explain each step in multiplying 2.5 and 3.6.

```
   2.5  ←——  1 decimal place
 × 3.6  ←——  + 1 decimal place
  1 5 0
  7 5 0
  9.0 0 ←——  2 decimal places
```

So, $-2.5 \times 3.6 = -9$. **Reasonable?** $-9 \approx -10$ ✓

b. Find $-\frac{1}{3}\left(-2\frac{3}{4}\right)$. **Estimate** $-\frac{1}{3} \bullet (-3) = 1$

Because the numbers have the same sign, the product is positive. So, find the product of $\frac{1}{3}$ and $2\frac{3}{4}$.

$\frac{1}{3}\left(2\frac{3}{4}\right) = \frac{1}{3}\left(\frac{11}{4}\right)$ Write the mixed number as an improper fraction.

$= \frac{11}{12}$ Multiply the numerators and the denominators.

So, $-\frac{1}{3}\left(-2\frac{3}{4}\right) = \frac{11}{12}$. **Reasonable?** $\frac{11}{12} \approx 1$ ✓

Try It **Find the product. Write fractions in simplest form.**

1. -5.1×1.8 **2.** $-6.3(-0.6)$ **3.** $-\frac{4}{5}\left(-\frac{2}{3}\right)$ **4.** $4\frac{1}{2} \bullet \left(-2\frac{1}{3}\right)$

Laurie's Notes

Scaffolding Instruction

- **Look for and Express Regularity in Repeated Reasoning:** Students have explored how the rules of multiplying integers extend to multiplying rational numbers, as expressed in the first success criterion. Mathematically proficient students recognize that the same rules for signs are used to multiply both integers and rational numbers.
- **Emerging:** Students can explain the rules for multiplying rational numbers but will benefit from guided practice. Review the Key Idea with students and provide guided instruction for the examples.
- **Proficient:** Students understand the rules and successfully apply the rules as they multiply rational numbers. Have students proceed to Example 2 to practice using properties to multiply rational numbers.

Key Idea

- Discuss the Key Idea with students.
- **Response Cards:** Distribute cards with *positive* and *negative* to students. Display a variety of problems involving multiplication of rational numbers (you could use Practice Exercises 13–21). Ask, "Will the answer be *positive* or *negative*?"

EXAMPLE 1

- **Make Sense of Problems and Persevere in Solving Them:** Mathematically proficient students continually ask themselves, "Does this make sense?"
- Before starting part (a), take time to discuss estimating products and how students can tell if an answer makes sense. When finding the product of two fractions such as $-\frac{1}{2}$ and $\frac{5}{9}$, the answer should be fairly small. Remind students to always check the sign of the answer and to estimate before beginning problem.
- Work through each part with students. Do not skip the initial estimate.
- In part (b), remind students that when multiplying fractions, mixed numbers must be written as improper fractions.

Try It

- Students should work independently on these problems. Ask volunteers to present their work and solutions.

Scaffold instruction to support all students in their learning. Learning is individualized and you may want to group students differently as they move in and out of these levels with each skill and concept. Student self-assessment and feedback help guide your instructional decisions about how and when to layer support for all students to become proficient learners.

Extra Example 1

a. Find $-0.6 \times (-2.4)$. 1.44

b. Find $\frac{3}{5}\left(-4\frac{2}{3}\right)$. $-2\frac{4}{5}$

ELL Support

After demonstrating Example 1, have students practice language by working in pairs to complete Try It Exercises 1–4. Have one student ask another, "What is the product of negative five and one tenth and positive one and eight tenths?" Have students alternate roles.

Beginner: State the product.

Intermediate: Answer with a simple sentence such as, "The product is negative nine and eighteen hundredths."

Advanced: Answer with a detailed sentence such as, "The product of negative five and one tenth and positive one and eight tenths is negative nine and eighteen hundredths."

Try It

1. -9.18
2. 3.78
3. $\frac{8}{15}$
4. $-10\frac{1}{2}$

Laurie's Notes

Discuss

- Review the paragraph at the top of the page with students and discuss the different placements of the negative sign.
  - You know that $-\frac{a}{b} \cdot b = -a$. Divide both sides of the equation by b, $\frac{-\frac{a}{b} \cdot \cancel{b}}{\cancel{b}} = \frac{-a}{b}$ to show $-\frac{a}{b} = \frac{-a}{b}$.
  - You know that $-\frac{a}{b} \cdot -b = a$. Divide both sides of the equation by $-b$, $\frac{-\frac{a}{b} \cdot \cancel{-b}}{\cancel{-b}} = \frac{a}{-b}$ to show $-\frac{a}{b} = \frac{a}{-b}$.
- Review the Properties of Multiplication: Associative, Commutative, and Multiplicative Inverse.

EXAMPLE 2

- **Look for and Make Use of Structure:** Write the problem. Discuss possible strategies for performing the computation. Students should recognize that algebraic properties can be used to perform the operations in a more efficient manner than how the problem is presented.
- Encourage students to justify their ideas using the properties. The more frequently you refer to these properties by name, the more fluent students become in using them.
- Once the problem is rewritten, you can "cross out" factors common to both the numerator and the denominator. It is not necessary to write out the factors before "crossing out" common factors. Review the push-pin note with students.

Try It

- Have two pairs of students choose one exercise to complete at the board. Have the other students try these problems on whiteboards. Have the pairs of students explain their work at the board.

? "How can you check that your answer is reasonable?" Use estimation.

Self-Assessment for Concepts & Skills

- Each student should work independently before comparing answers with a neighbor. Students should show all work, including their checks.
- ◉ Have students display their answers on whiteboards so you can quickly assess their progress with the success criteria. Offer feedback as needed.

The Success Criteria Self-Assessment chart can be found in the *Student Journal* or online at *BigIdeasMath.com.*

Extra Example 2

Find $\frac{10}{3} \cdot \left(-3\frac{3}{5}\right) \cdot (-3)$. 36

Try It

5. $-7\frac{7}{8}$ 6. 702

ELL Support

Proceed as described in Laurie's Notes for the Self-Assessment for Concept & Skills exercises, but allow students to work in pairs. Monitor discussions of Exercise 7 and provide support as needed. Review answers to Exercises 8–11 as described.

Self-Assessment for Concepts & Skills

7. *Sample answer:* The product is positive when the numbers have the same sign and negative when the numbers have different signs.

8. $\frac{4}{25}$ 9. $-\frac{8}{9}$

10. 4.76 11. -6

The properties of multiplication you have used apply to all rational numbers. You can also write $-\frac{a}{b}$ as $\frac{-a}{b}$ or $\frac{a}{-b}$ when performing operations with rational numbers.

EXAMPLE 2 Using Properties to Multiply Rational Numbers

Find $\left(-\frac{1}{7}\cdot\frac{4}{5}\right)\cdot(-7)\cdot\left(-\frac{1}{2}\right)$.

You can use properties of multiplication to find the product.

$\left(-\frac{1}{7}\cdot\frac{4}{5}\right)\cdot(-7)\cdot\left(-\frac{1}{2}\right) = -7\cdot\left(-\frac{1}{7}\cdot\frac{4}{5}\right)\cdot\left(-\frac{1}{2}\right)$	Commutative Property of Multiplication
$= \left[-7\cdot\left(-\frac{1}{7}\right)\right]\cdot\frac{4}{5}\cdot\left(-\frac{1}{2}\right)$	Associative Property of Multiplication
$= 1\cdot\frac{4}{5}\cdot\left(-\frac{1}{2}\right)$	Multiplicative Inverse Property
$= \frac{4}{5}\cdot\left(\frac{-1}{2}\right)$	Multiplication Property of One
$= \frac{\overset{2}{\cancel{4}}\cdot(-1)}{5\cdot\underset{1}{\cancel{2}}}$	Multiply. Divide out the common factor, 2.
$= \frac{-2}{5}$, or $-\frac{2}{5}$	Simplify.

Notice that Example 2 uses different notation to demonstrate the following.

$$\frac{4\cdot(-1)}{5\cdot 2} = \frac{2\cdot\overset{1}{\cancel{2}}\cdot(-1)}{5\cdot\underset{1}{\cancel{2}}}$$

Try It **Find the product. Write fractions in simplest form.**

5. $-\frac{2}{3}\cdot 7\frac{7}{8}\cdot\frac{3}{2}$

6. $-7.02(0.1)(100)(-10)$

Self-Assessment for Concepts & Skills

Solve each exercise. Then rate your understanding of the success criteria in your journal.

7. WRITING Explain how to determine whether a product of two rational numbers is *positive* or *negative.*

MULTIPLYING RATIONAL NUMBERS **Find the product. Write fractions in simplest form.**

8. $-\frac{3}{10}\times\left(-\frac{8}{15}\right)$

9. $-\frac{2}{3}\cdot 1\frac{1}{3}$

10. $-2.8(-1.7)$

11. $1\frac{3}{5}\cdot\left(-3\frac{3}{4}\right)$

EXAMPLE 3 Modeling Real Life

A school record for the 40-meter dash is 15.24 seconds. Predict the school record after 15 years when the school record decreases by about 0.06 second per year.

Use a verbal model to solve the problem. Because the school record *decreases* by about 0.06 second per year, the change in the school record each year is -0.06 second.

School record after 15 years = Current school record + Number of years • Average yearly change

$= 15.24 + 15(-0.06)$ Substitute.

$= 15.24 + (-0.9)$ Multiply 15 and -0.06.

$= 14.34$ Add 15.24 and -0.9.

You can predict that the school record will be about 14.34 seconds after 15 years.

Check Reasonableness

Because $0.06 < 0.1$, the school record decreases by less than $0.1 \cdot 15 = 1.5$ seconds. So, the school record is greater than $15.24 - 1.5 = 13.74$ seconds.

Because $14.34 > 13.74$, the answer is reasonable. ✓

Self-Assessment for Problem Solving

Solve each exercise. Then rate your understanding of the success criteria in your journal.

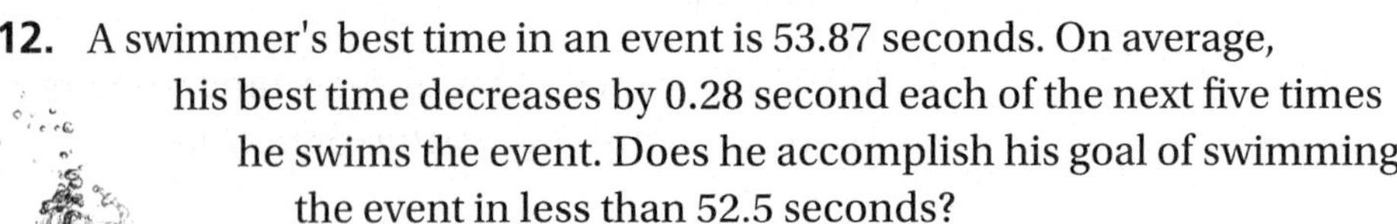

12. A swimmer's best time in an event is 53.87 seconds. On average, his best time decreases by 0.28 second each of the next five times he swims the event. Does he accomplish his goal of swimming the event in less than 52.5 seconds?

13. **DIG DEEPER!** *Terminal velocity* is the fastest speed that an object can fall through the air. A skydiver reaches a terminal velocity of 120 miles per hour. What is the change in elevation of the skydiver after falling at terminal velocity for 15 seconds? Justify your answer.

Laurie's Notes

EXAMPLE 3

- Work through the problem as shown.
- Remind students that verbal models are often helpful in solving real-life problems.
- **Turn and Talk:** Have students discuss the Check Reasonableness note.

? "Is there another way to check your answer?" *Sample answer:* Replace *Record after 15 years* in the verbal model with 14.34 and solve for a known value.

Self-Assessment for Problem Solving

- Allow time in class for students to practice using the problem-solving plan. Remember, some students may only be able to complete the first step.
- Have students work with a partner to write verbal models for the exercises. Ask volunteers to share their verbal models at the board or document camera. Then ask other students to provide feedback. After students reach a consensus, have students solve the problems independently.

The Success Criteria Self-Assessment chart can be found in the *Student Journal* or online at *BigIdeasMath.com.*

Closure

- **Exit Ticket:** Find the product. Write fractions in simplest form.

a. $-2\frac{1}{3} \times 3\frac{2}{3}$ $-8\frac{5}{9}$

b. $(-0.5)(-4.2) \times 0.2$ 0.42

Extra Example 3

The value of a stock is \$65.34. Predict the value of the stock after 8 years when the stock decreases by about \$1.22 per year. about \$55.58

Self-Assessment for Problem Solving

12. yes

13. $-\frac{1}{2}$ mi; 15 sec $= \frac{1}{240}$ h,

$$-120 \times \frac{1}{240} = -\frac{1}{2}$$

Learning Target

Find products of rational numbers.

Success Criteria

- Explain the rules for multiplying rational numbers.
- Find products of rational numbers with same sign.
- Find products of rational numbers with different signs.

Review & Refresh

1. 0.3125
2. $-0.4\overline{09}$
3. $6.\overline{72}$
4. $-1.08\overline{3}$
5. 36 in.^{2}
6. 9 m^2
7. 121 ft^2

Concepts, Skills, & Problem Solving

8. *Sample answer:* 0.8 • 0.9; 0.72
9. *Sample answer:* 0.7 • 0.5; 0.35
10. negative; The numbers have different signs.
11. negative; The numbers have different signs.
12. positive; The numbers have the same sign.
13. $\frac{1}{3}$
14. $-\frac{4}{9}$
15. $2\frac{1}{2}$
16. 9
17. -0.012
18. 0.025
19. 0.36
20. $8\frac{1}{4}$
21. $-4\frac{17}{27}$

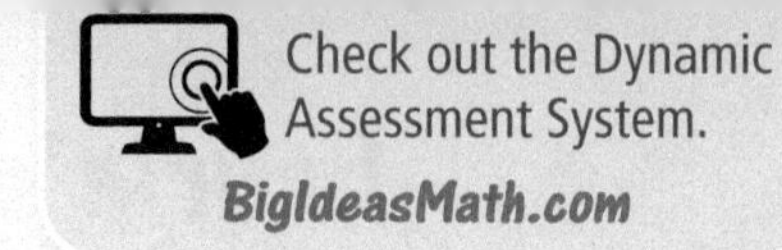
Check out the Dynamic Assessment System.
BigIdeasMath.com

Assignment Guide and Concept Check

Scaffold assignments to support all students in their learning progression. The suggested assignments are a starting point. Continue to assign additional exercises and revisit with spaced practice to move every student toward proficiency.

Level	Assignment 1	Assignment 2
Emerging	4, 6, 7, 9, 10, 13, 14, 17, 22, 23, 27, 34	11, 16, 19, 24, 25, 28, 35, 38, 41
Proficient	4, 6, 7, 9, 11, 15, 16, 17, 22, 23, 28, 35	19, 21, 24, 25, 26, 32, 33, 36, 39, 41
Advanced	4, 6, 7, 9, 12, 19, 20, 21, 22, 23, 31, 37	24, 25, 26, 32, 33, 40, 41

- Assignment 1 is for use after students complete the Self-Assessment for Concepts & Skills.
- Assignment 2 is for use after students complete the Self-Assessment for Problem Solving.
- The red exercises can be used as a concept check.

Review & Refresh Prior Skills

Exercises 1–4 Writing a Fraction or Mixed Number as a Decimal
Exercises 5 and 7 Finding the Area of a Trapezoid
Exercise 6 Finding Areas by Decomposition

B.4 Practice

Go to *BigIdeasMath.com* to get HELP with solving the exercises.

Review & Refresh

Write the fraction or mixed number as a decimal.

1. $\frac{5}{16}$ **2.** $-\frac{9}{22}$ **3.** $6\frac{8}{11}$ **4.** $-\frac{26}{24}$

Find the area of the figure.

5.

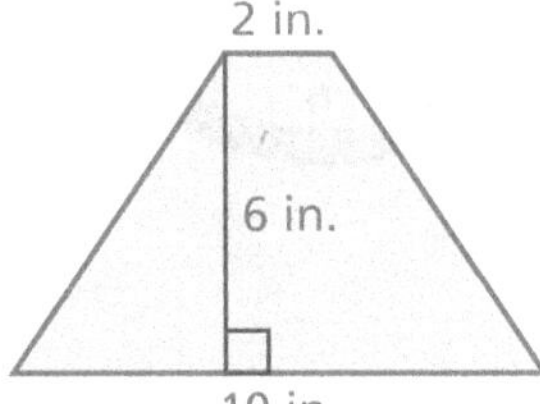

6.

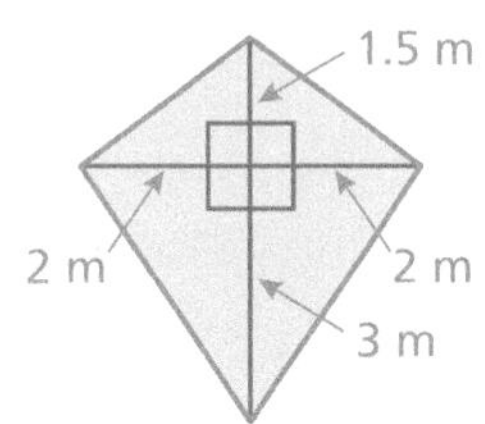

7.

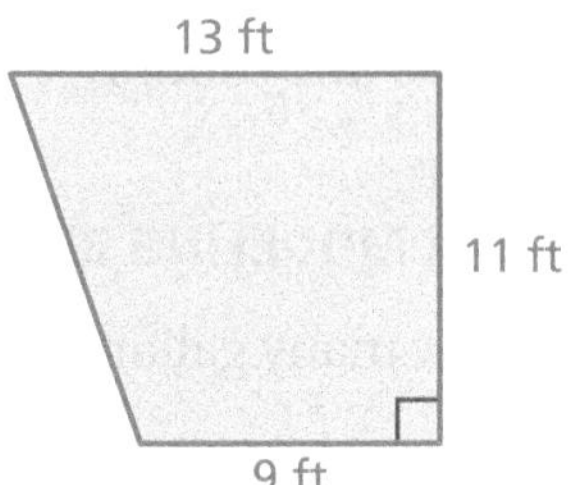

Concepts, Skills, & Problem Solving

FINDING PRODUCTS OF RATIONAL NUMBERS **Write a multiplication expression represented by the area model. Then find the product.** (See Exploration 1, p. 567.)

8.

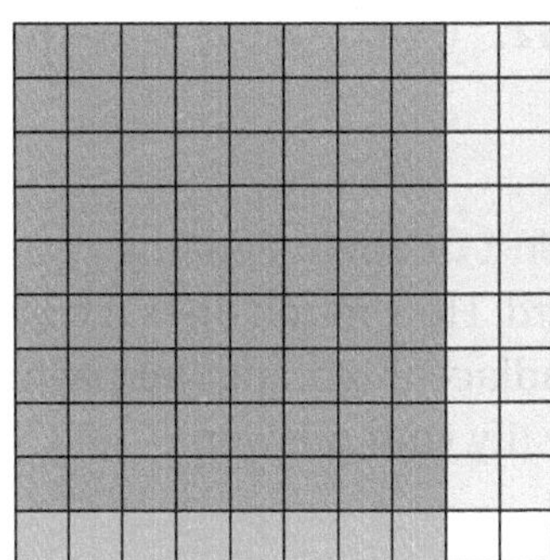

9.

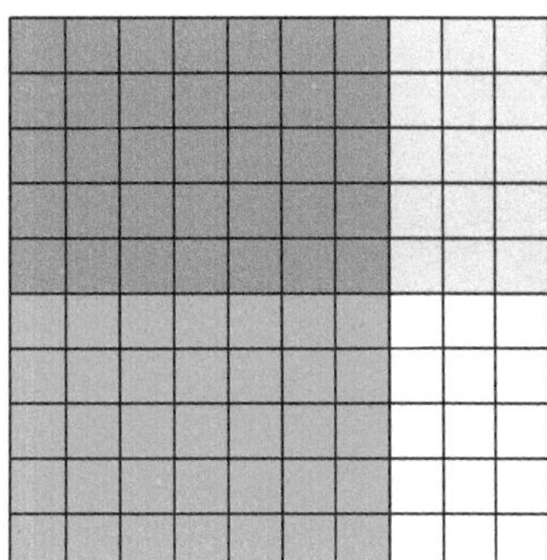

MP REASONING **Without multiplying, tell whether the value of the expression is positive or negative. Explain your reasoning.**

10. $-1\left(\frac{4}{5}\right)$ **11.** $\frac{4}{7} \cdot \left(-3\frac{1}{2}\right)$ **12.** $-0.25(-3.659)$

MULTIPLYING RATIONAL NUMBERS **Find the product. Write fractions in simplest form.**

13. $-\frac{1}{4} \times \left(-\frac{4}{3}\right)$ **14.** $\frac{5}{6}\left(-\frac{8}{15}\right)$ **15.** $-2\left(-1\frac{1}{4}\right)$

16. $-3\frac{1}{3} \cdot \left(-2\frac{7}{10}\right)$ **17.** $0.4 \times (-0.03)$ **18.** $-0.05 \times (-0.5)$

19. $-8(0.09)(-0.5)$ **20.** $\frac{5}{6} \cdot \left(-4\frac{1}{2}\right) \cdot \left(-2\frac{1}{5}\right)$ **21.** $\left(-1\frac{2}{3}\right)^3$

MP YOU BE THE TEACHER **Your friend evaluates the expression. Is your friend correct? Explain your reasoning.**

22. $-\frac{1}{4} \times \frac{3}{2} = \frac{-1}{4} \times \frac{3}{2}$

$= \frac{-3}{8}$

23. $-2.2 \times (-3.7) = -8.14$

24. **MP MODELING REAL LIFE** The hour hand of a clock moves −30° every hour. How many degrees does it move in $2\frac{1}{5}$ hours?

25. **MP MODELING REAL LIFE** A 14.5-gallon gasoline tank is $\frac{3}{4}$ full. How many gallons will it take to fill the tank?

26. **OPEN-ENDED** Write two fractions whose product is $-\frac{3}{5}$.

USING PROPERTIES **Find the product. Write fractions in simplest form.**

27. $\frac{1}{5} \cdot \frac{3}{8} \cdot (-5)$

28. $0.01(4.6)(-200)$

29. $(-17.2 \times 2.5) \times 4$

30. $\left(-\frac{5}{9} \times \frac{2}{7}\right) \times \left(-\frac{7}{2}\right)$

31. $\left[-\frac{2}{3} \cdot \left(-\frac{5}{7}\right)\right] \cdot \left(-\frac{9}{4}\right)$

32. $(-4.5 \cdot 8.61) \cdot \left(-\frac{2}{9}\right)$

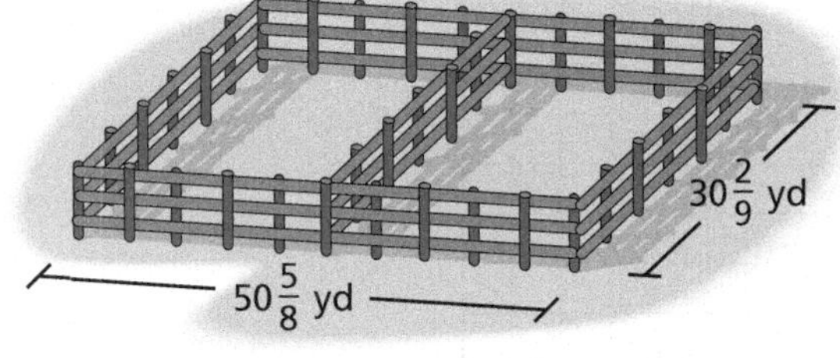

33. **MP PROBLEM SOLVING** Fencing costs \$25.80 per yard. How much does it cost to enclose two adjacent rectangular pastures as shown? Justify your answer.

ALGEBRA **Evaluate the expression when $x = -2$, $y = 3$, and $z = -\frac{1}{5}$.**

34. $x \cdot z$

35. xyz

36. $\frac{1}{3} + x \cdot z$

37. $\frac{1}{2}z - \frac{2}{3}y$

EVALUATING AN EXPRESSION **Evaluate the expression. Write fractions in simplest form.**

38. $-4.2 + 8.1 \times (-1.9)$

39. $-3\frac{3}{4} \times \frac{5}{6} - 2\frac{1}{3}$

40. $\left(-\frac{2}{3}\right)^2 - \frac{3}{4}\left(2\frac{1}{3}\right)$

41. **DIG DEEPER!** Use positive or negative integers to fill in the blanks so that the product is $\frac{1}{4}$. Justify your answer.

$$\frac{\square}{2} \times \left(-\frac{5}{\square}\right) \times \frac{\square}{\square}$$

Common Errors

- **Exercises 34–40** Students may forget to follow the order of operations. Remind students about the order of operations and have them use parentheses to help remember which parts to evaluate first.

Mini-Assessment

Find the product. Write fractions in simplest form.

1. $-\frac{6}{7} \cdot \left(-\frac{5}{2}\right)$ $2\frac{1}{7}$
2. $3.5(-7.65)$ -26.775
3. $(-2.78)(-0.06)$ 0.1668
4. $-\frac{4}{5} \cdot 2\frac{1}{2} \cdot 3\frac{1}{7}$ $-6\frac{2}{7}$
5. The cell phone company will add −\$2.74 to your next bill for each of the 4 months you were overcharged. How much will be added to your next bill? −\$10.96

Section Resources

Surface Level	Deep Level
Resources by Chapter • Extra Practice • Reteach • Puzzle Time Student Journal • Self-Assessment • Practice Differentiating the Lesson Tutorial Videos Skills Review Handbook Skills Trainer	Resources by Chapter • Enrichment and Extension Graphic Organizers Dynamic Assessment System • Section Practice

Concepts, Skills, & Problem Solving

22. yes; The multiplication is correct.
23. no; $-2.2 \times (-3.7) = 8.14$
24. $-66°$
25. $3\frac{5}{8}$ gal
26. *Sample answer:* $-\frac{9}{10}, \frac{2}{3}$
27. $-\frac{3}{8}$
28. -9.2
29. -172
30. $\frac{5}{9}$
31. $-1\frac{1}{14}$
32. 8.61
33. \$4951.45; The total length is $191\frac{11}{12}$ yards.
34. $\frac{2}{5}$
35. $1\frac{1}{5}$
36. $\frac{11}{15}$
37. $-2\frac{1}{10}$
38. -19.59
39. $-5\frac{11}{24}$
40. $-1\frac{11}{36}$
41. *Sample answer:* $\frac{1}{2} \times \left(-\frac{5}{4}\right) \times \frac{-2}{5}$

Check out the Dynamic Classroom.
BigIdeasMath.com

Laurie's Notes

Learning Target

Find quotients of rational numbers.

Success Criteria

- Explain the rules for dividing rational numbers.
- Find quotients of rational numbers with the same sign.
- Find quotients of rational numbers with different signs.

Warm Up

Cumulative, vocabulary, and prerequisite skills practice opportunities are available in the *Resources by Chapter* or at *BigIdeasMath.com.*

ELL Support

Remind students that a quotient is the answer to a division problem. As a review, ask students to identify the names for the answers to an addition problem, a subtraction problem, and a multiplication problem. sum; difference; product

Exploration 1

a. *Sample answer:* $0.9 \div 0.6$; $0.9 \div 1.5$; 1.5; 0.6

b. **i.** 0.6; -0.6

ii. 2; -2

iii. 8; -8

iv. 0; 0

v. $\frac{1}{2}$; $\frac{1}{2}$

vi. 8; 8

c. yes; *Sample answer:* $-a$ is the opposite of a for any number.

d. *Sample answer:* Stock values dropped \$0.75 in 3 days. The stock values fell \$0.25 per day.

Preparing to Teach

- **Look for and Express Regularity in Repeated Reasoning:** Students understand how to divide fractions and integers. In this lesson, students will extend their understanding of division to rational numbers.

Motivate

- Students often ask, "Who uses this stuff?" Provide the following example.
  - Some jobs cannot be performed in extreme temperatures. For instance, a snowplow company may require their employees to stop spreading salt on roadways when the temperature is -16°F or below because the salt will have no effect.
  - ? "The current temperature is -2°F and drops 3.5°F every 0.5 hour. How much time do the drivers have to salt the roadways? Explain." 2 hours; $-16-(-2)=-14$ and $-14 \div (-3.5 \div 0.5) = -14 \div (-7) = 2$.
- Ask students to think of other jobs that require understanding of dividing rational numbers.

Exploration 1

- **Make Sense of Problems and Persevere in Solving Them:** Students used area models to find products in the previous section. They will now use an area model to find quotients.
- ? "How can the fact that multiplication and division are inverse operations help you interpret the area model for division?" *Sample answer:* The area model represents $1.5 \times 0.6 = 0.9$. So, there are two related division equations: $0.9 \div 0.6 = 1.5$ and $0.9 \div 1.5 = 0.6$.
- In part (b), completing the second column is review and students should be able to make a reasonable conjecture about the values in the last column.
- Have pairs *Turn and Talk* to discuss parts (c) and (d) and the Math Practice note. Use *Popsicle Sticks* to select students to share.

B.5 Dividing Rational Numbers

Learning Target: Find quotients of rational numbers.

Success Criteria:
- I can explain the rules for dividing rational numbers.
- I can find quotients of rational numbers with the same sign.
- I can find quotients of rational numbers with different signs.

EXPLORATION 1 Finding Quotients of Rational Numbers

Work with a partner.

a. Write two division expressions represented by the area model. Then find the quotients.

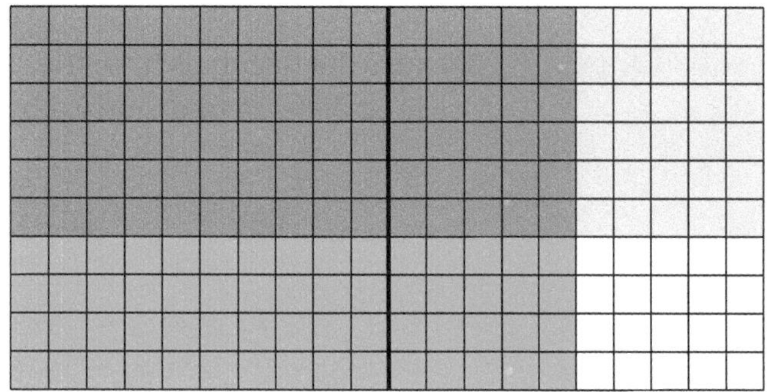

b. Complete the table.

	Expression	Quotient	Expression	Quotient
i.	$0.9 \div 1.5$		$-0.9 \div 1.5$	
ii.	$1 \div \frac{1}{2}$		$-1 \div \frac{1}{2}$	
iii.	$2 \div 0.25$		$2 \div (-0.25)$	
iv.	$0 \div \frac{4}{5}$		$0 \div \left(-\frac{4}{5}\right)$	
v.	$1\frac{1}{2} \div 3$		$-1\frac{1}{2} \div (-3)$	
vi.	$0.8 \div 0.1$		$-0.8 \div (-0.1)$	

c. Do the rules for dividing integers apply to all rational numbers? Explain your reasoning.

d. Write a real-life story involving the quotient $-0.75 \div 3$. Interpret the quotient in the context of the story.

Math Practice

Apply Mathematics

How does interpreting a division expression in a real-life story help you make sense of the quotient?

B.5 Lesson

Key Vocabulary
complex fraction, *p. 575*

Key Idea

Dividing Rational Numbers

Words To divide rational numbers, use the same rules for signs as you used for dividing integers.

Numbers $-\frac{1}{2} \div \frac{4}{9} = -\frac{1}{2} \cdot \frac{9}{4} = -\frac{9}{8}$ $\qquad -\frac{1}{2} \div \left(-\frac{4}{9}\right) = -\frac{1}{2} \cdot \left(-\frac{9}{4}\right) = \frac{9}{8}$

EXAMPLE 1 Dividing Rational Numbers

a. Find −8.4 ÷ (−3.6).

Because the decimals have the same sign, the quotient is positive. Use long division to divide 8.4 by 3.6.

$$3.6\overline{)8.4} \longrightarrow 36\overline{)84.00}$$

```
       2.33
 36)84.00
   −72
    12 0
   −10 8
     1 20
    −1 08
       12
```

The remainder repeats. So, it is a repeating decimal.

So, $-8.4 \div (-3.6) = 2.\overline{3}$.

Another Method Write the division expression as a fraction.

$$\frac{-8.4}{-3.6} = \frac{84}{36} = \frac{7}{3} = 2\frac{1}{3}, \text{ or } 2.\overline{3} \ \checkmark$$

b. Find $\frac{6}{5} \div \left(-\frac{4}{3}\right)$.

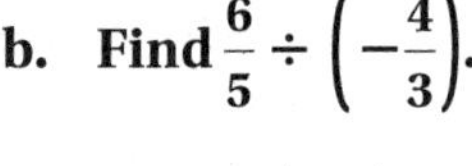

$\frac{6}{5} \div \left(-\frac{4}{3}\right) = \frac{6}{5} \cdot \left(-\frac{3}{4}\right)$ Multiply by the reciprocal of $-\frac{4}{3}$.

$= \frac{\overset{3}{\cancel{6}} \cdot (-3)}{5 \cdot \underset{2}{\cancel{4}}}$ Multiply the numerators and the denominators. Divide out the common factor, 2.

$= \frac{-9}{10}$, or $-\frac{9}{10}$ Simplify.

So, $\frac{6}{5} \div \left(-\frac{4}{3}\right) = -\frac{9}{10}$.

Remember

The *reciprocal* of $\frac{a}{b}$ is $\frac{b}{a}$.

Try It **Find the quotient. Write fractions in simplest form.**

1. $-2.4 \div 3.2$ **2.** $-6 \div (-1.1)$ **3.** $-\frac{6}{5} \div \left(-\frac{1}{2}\right)$ **4.** $-\frac{1}{3} \div 2\frac{2}{3}$

Laurie's Notes

Scaffolding Instruction

- **Look for and Express Regularity in Repeated Reasoning:** Students have explored how the rules of dividing integers extend to dividing rational numbers, as expressed in the first success criterion. Mathematically proficient students recognize that the same rules for signs are used to divide both integers and rational numbers.
- **Emerging:** Students may understand the rules for dividing rational numbers but will benefit from guided practice. Review the Key Idea with students and provide guided instruction for the examples.
- **Proficient:** Students understand the rules and successfully apply the rules as they divide rational numbers. Have students review the definition of a complex fraction before working through Example 2.

Key Idea

- Write the Numbers on the board. This is a good time to point out the Remember note in Example 1(b).

? "Is the quotient of two negative rational numbers *positive* or *negative*?" positive "Is the quotient of a negative rational number and a positive rational number *positive* or *negative*?" negative

EXAMPLE 1

- In part (a), the division is completed first and then the appropriate sign is applied. In part (b), the sign is carried throughout the problem. Discuss why both methods work.
- For part (a), students may need to review how to divide by a decimal. Remind students to make the divisor a whole number by multiplying each number by a power of 10. Students may say, "move the decimal points", but they need to understand what they are really doing.
- Discuss the difference between terminating and repeating decimals.

Try It

- Have students use *Think-Pair-Share* to complete these exercises.

ELL Support

After demonstrating Example 1, have students practice language by working in pairs to complete Exercises 1–4. Have one student ask another, "What is the quotient of negative two and four tenths and positive three and two tenths?" Have students alternate roles.

Beginner: State the quotient.

Intermediate: Answer with a simple sentence such as, "The quotient is negative seventy-five hundredths."

Advanced: Answer with a detailed sentence such as, "The quotient of negative two and four tenths and three and two tenths is negative seventy-five hundredths."

Scaffold instruction to support all students in their learning. Learning is individualized and you may want to group students differently as they move in and out of these levels with each skill and concept. Student self-assessment and feedback help guide your instructional decisions about how and when to layer support for all students to become proficient learners.

Formative Assessment Tip

Think-Pair-Share

This technique allows students to share their thinking about a problem with their partners after they have had time to consider the problem alone. Once partners have discussed the problem, small groups or the whole class should discuss the problem.

The initial time working alone is important for students to develop their own understanding of the mathematics. "Private think time" is what I call it. Once students have engaged in the problem, sharing with partners helps confirm their understanding or perhaps the need to modify their thinking. Sharing their thinking with the whole class is more comfortable for students when they have had the chance to discuss their thinking with partners.

Extra Example 1

a. Find $-6.8 \div 3.2$. -2.125

b. Find $3\frac{1}{4} \div \left(-1\frac{1}{8}\right)$. $-2\frac{8}{9}$

Try It

1. -0.75 **2.** $5.\overline{45}$

3. $2\frac{2}{5}$ **4.** $-\frac{1}{8}$

Laurie's Notes

Discuss

- Define a **complex fraction** and give examples. Remind students to use the order of operations to evaluate complex fractions.
- Remind students that anything above the fraction bar is a group and everything below the fraction bar is another group. For example,

$$\frac{-\frac{3}{5}}{-5+\frac{3}{10}} = -\frac{3}{5} \div \left(-5+\frac{3}{10}\right), \text{ which is } \textit{not} \text{ equivalent to } -\frac{3}{5} \div -5 + \frac{3}{10}.$$

EXAMPLE 2

- Work through the example as shown.
- Discuss the Math Practice note. Make sure students understand why the negative sign can be written in front of the fraction, in the numerator, or in the denominator.
- **Common Error:** Students may try to divide out factors common to $-\frac{10}{9}$ and $-\frac{1}{6}$. Remind students that to "cross out" common factors the factors must be common to both the *entire* numerator and the *entire* denominator.
- ? **Extension:** "What happens when you multiply the complex fraction by $\frac{18}{18}$?"

The fraction is no longer complex:

$$\frac{-\frac{10}{9}}{-\frac{1}{6}+1} \cdot \frac{18}{18} = \frac{-\frac{10}{9}\cdot 18}{\left(-\frac{1}{6}+1\right)18} = \frac{-20}{-3+18} = \frac{-20}{15} = -\frac{4}{3}.$$ "Why can you do this?"

$\frac{18}{18}$ is equivalent to 1 and multiplying by 1 does not change the value.

Try It

- Have students work in pairs. Ask three pairs of students to choose one exercise to complete at the board.

Self-Assessment for Concepts & Skills

- Have students use *Think-Pair-Share* to complete these exercises.
- Ask students to share any confusion they may have about the success criteria. This may be less intimidating if students write their responses on index cards.

ELL Support

Have students work in pairs to complete Exercises 8–11. Check answers to Exercises 9–11 by having each pair display their answers on a whiteboard for your review. For Exercise 8, have two pairs discuss their ideas and come to an agreement on an answer. Have groups present their answer to the class.

The Success Criteria Self-Assessment chart can be found in the *Student Journal* or online at *BigIdeasMath.com*.

Extra Example 2

Evaluate $\frac{\frac{2}{3}}{-\frac{4}{5}-\frac{1}{3}}$. $-\frac{10}{17}$

Try It

5. $-\frac{1}{12}$
6. $3\frac{1}{3}$
7. 9

Self-Assessment for Concepts & Skills

8. *Sample answer:* The quotient is positive when the numbers have the same sign and negative when the numbers have different signs.
9. $-\frac{5}{24}$
10. $1.\overline{8}$
11. $-\frac{5}{54}$

You can represent division involving fractions using *complex fractions*. A **complex fraction** has at least one fraction in the numerator, denominator, or both.

EXAMPLE 2 Evaluating a Complex Fraction

Evaluate $\dfrac{-\dfrac{10}{9}}{-\dfrac{1}{6}+1}$.

Rewrite the complex fraction as a division expression.

$$-\frac{10}{9} \div \left(-\frac{1}{6}+1\right) = -\frac{10}{9} \div \left(\frac{-1}{6}+\frac{6}{6}\right)$$ Rewrite $-\frac{1}{6}$ as $\frac{-1}{6}$ and 1 as $\frac{6}{6}$.

$$= -\frac{10}{9} \div \frac{5}{6}$$ Add fractions.

$$= -\frac{10}{9} \bullet \frac{6}{5}$$ Multiply by the reciprocal of $\frac{5}{6}$.

$$= -\frac{\overset{2}{\cancel{10}} \bullet \overset{2}{\cancel{6}}}{\underset{3}{\cancel{9}} \bullet \underset{1}{\cancel{5}}}$$ Multiply. Divide out common factors.

$$= -\frac{4}{3}$$ Simplify.

Math Practice

Maintain Oversight

Why can you write $-\frac{1}{6}$ as $\frac{-1}{6}$? Why is it helpful when evaluating the expression?

Try It **Evaluate the expression. Write fractions in simplest form.**

5. $\dfrac{-\frac{1}{2}}{6}$

6. $\dfrac{-2\frac{1}{2}}{-\frac{3}{4}}$

7. $\dfrac{-1\frac{2}{3} \bullet \left(-\frac{3}{5}\right)}{\left(\frac{1}{3}\right)^2}$

Self-Assessment for Concepts & Skills

Solve each exercise. Then rate your understanding of the success criteria in your journal.

8. **WRITING** Explain how to determine whether a quotient of two rational numbers is *positive* or *negative*.

EVALUATING AN EXPRESSION Evaluate the expression. Write fractions in simplest form.

9. $\frac{3}{8} \div \left(-\frac{9}{5}\right)$

10. $-6.8 \div (-3.6)$

11. $\dfrac{-\frac{2}{9}}{2\frac{2}{5}}$

EXAMPLE 3 Modeling Real Life

A restaurant launches a mobile app that allows customers to rate their food on a scale from −5 to 5. So far, customers have given the lasagna scores of 2.25, −3.5, 0, −4.5, 1.75, −1, 3.5, and −2.5. Should the restaurant consider changing the recipe? Explain.

Understand the problem.

You are given eight scores for lasagna. You are asked to determine whether the restaurant should make changes to the lasagna recipe.

Make a plan.

Use the mean score to determine whether people generally like the lasagna. Then decide whether the recipe should change.

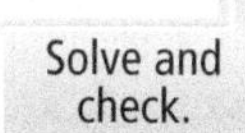

Divide the sum of the scores by the number of scores. Group together scores that are convenient to add.

$$\text{mean} = \frac{0 + (-3.5 + 3.5) + (2.25 + 1.75) + [(-4.5) + (-2.5) + (-1)]}{8}$$

$$= \frac{0 + 0 + 4 + (-8)}{8}$$

$$= \frac{-4}{8}, \text{ or } -0.5$$

The mean score is below the “mediocre” score of 0.

So, the restaurant should consider changing the recipe.

Look Back

Only 3 of the 8 scores were better than “mediocre.” So, it makes sense to conclude that the restaurant should change the recipe. ✓

Self-Assessment for Problem Solving

Solve each exercise. Then rate your understanding of the success criteria in your journal.

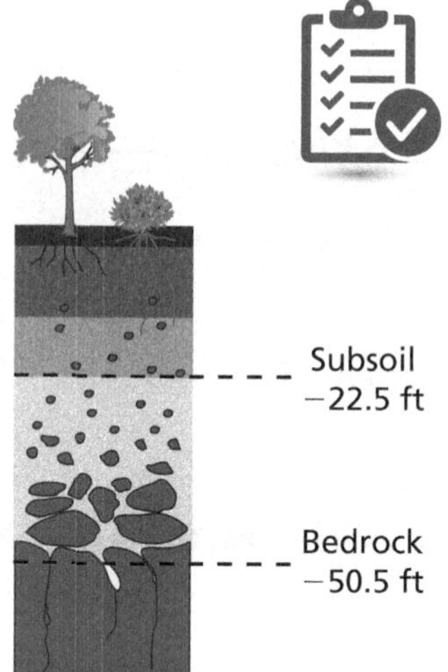

12. **DIG DEEPER!** Soil is composed of several layers. A geologist measures the depths of the *subsoil* and the *bedrock*, as shown. Find and interpret two quotients involving the depths of the subsoil and the bedrock.

13. The restaurant in Example 3 receives additional scores of −0.75, −1.5, −1.25, 4.75, −0.25, −0.5, 5, and −0.5 for the lasagna. Given the additional data, should the restaurant consider changing the recipe? Explain.

Laurie's Notes

EXAMPLE 3

- Ask a volunteer to read the problem.
- Ask students to share different methods for determining whether the restaurant should change the lasagna recipe. Suggestions may include: using a number line, finding the median, finding the mean, etc.
- Some students may say that a few scores are high, so the restaurant should not make a change. Others may say that because most of the scores are low, the restaurant should change the recipe.
- You can extend this discussion to scratch the surface of statistics. Should you make a conclusion from a sample this small? Could there be reasons for the low scores that are not related to the recipe (i.e., bad cook, rotten ingredients, customers upset about service)?

Self-Assessment for Problem Solving

- Students may benefit from trying the exercises independently and then working with peers to refine their work. It is important to provide time in class for problem solving, so that students become comfortable with the problem-solving plan.
- Have students write the rules for multiplying and dividing rational numbers on whiteboards. Discuss any discrepancies.

The Success Criteria Self-Assessment chart can be found in the *Student Journal* or online at *BigIdeasMath.com*.

Closure

- How do the rules for dividing rational numbers compare to the rules for adding, subtracting, and multiplying rational numbers? *Sample answer:* The rules for dividing rational numbers are not related to the rules for adding or subtracting rational numbers. Dividing rational numbers and multiplying rational numbers use the same rules for signs.

Extra Example 3

A pizzeria asks customers to rate a new crust on a scale from −10 to 10, where −10 is "awful", 0 is "mediocre", and 10 is "amazing." So far, customers have given the crust scores of −3.5, 0, 8.25, 7.5, −9.5, −1.5, −3.25, and −5.5. Should the pizzeria keep using the recipe? Explain. No, the mean score (−0.9375) is below the "mediocre" score of 0.

Self-Assessment for Problem Solving

12. The subsoil is $0.\overline{4455}$ times as deep as the bedrock; The bedrock is $2.2\overline{4}$ times deeper than the subsoil.
13. *Sample answer:* no; The mean score is 0.0625.

Learning Target

Find quotients of rational numbers.

Success Criteria

- Explain the rules for dividing rational numbers.
- Find quotients of rational numbers with the same sign.
- Find quotients of rational numbers with different signs.

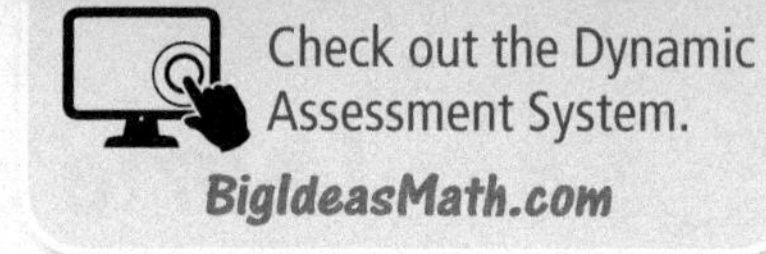
Check out the Dynamic Assessment System.
BigIdeasMath.com

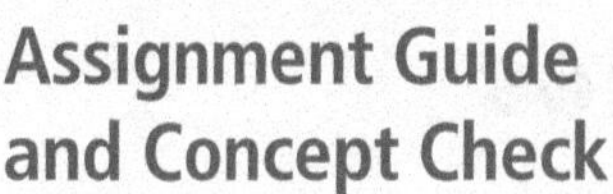

Review & Refresh

1. -0.655

2. $-1\frac{1}{8}$ 3. $\frac{1}{8}$

4. Terms: $3b$, 12; Coefficient: 3; Constant: 12

5. Terms: 14, z, $6f$; Coefficients: 1, 6; Constant: 14

6. Terms: $8g$, 14, $5c$, 7; Coefficients: 8, 5; Constants: 14, 7

7. Terms: $42m$, 18, $12c^2$; Coefficients: 42, 12; Constant: 18

Concepts, Skills, & Problem Solving

8. *Sample answer:* $0.2 \div 0.4$; $0.2 \div 0.5$; 0.5; 0.4

9. *Sample answer:* $0.06 \div 0.6$; $0.06 \div 0.1$; 0.1; 0.6

10. $-1\frac{3}{4}$ 11. -6

12. 0.23 13. $3.\overline{63}$

14. $-\frac{2}{3}$ 15. -2.45

16. -2.5875 17. $\frac{2}{5}$

18. $2\frac{5}{14}$

19. no; $-\frac{2}{3} \div \frac{4}{5} = -\frac{2}{3} \times \frac{5}{4}$

20. no; $-4.25 \div 1.7 = -2.5$

Assignment Guide and Concept Check

Scaffold assignments to support all students in their learning progression. The suggested assignments are a starting point. Continue to assign additional exercises and revisit with spaced practice to move every student toward proficiency.

Level	Assignment 1	Assignment 2
Emerging	1, 3, 5, 8, 10, 11, 12, 14, 19, 20, 22, 24, 31	16, 17, 21, 23, 25, 28
Proficient	1, 3, 5, 8, 14, 16, 17, 19, 20, 22, 25, 31	18, 21, 23, 26, 28, 29
Advanced	1, 3, 5, 9, 14, 15, 18, 19, 20, 23, 25, 31	26, 27, 28, 29, 30

- Assignment 1 is for use after students complete the Self-Assessment for Concepts & Skills.
- Assignment 2 is for use after students complete the Self-Assessment for Problem Solving.
- The red exercises can be used as a concept check.

Review & Refresh Prior Skills

Exercises 1–3 Multiplying Rational Numbers
Exercises 4–7 Identifying Parts of Algebraic Expressions

Common Errors

- **Exercises 10, 14, 17, and 18** Students may use the reciprocal of the first fraction or mixed number instead of the second or they may forget to write a mixed number as an improper fraction before finding the reciprocal. Review the rules for dividing fractions and mixed numbers and the definition of reciprocal.
- **Exercises 11–13, 15, and 16** Students may mix up the dividend and the divisor. Remind students that the first number is the dividend and the second number is the divisor.
- **Exercises 11–13, 15, and 16** Students may forget to move the decimal point when dividing by a decimal or they may move the decimal points the wrong number of places. Remind students to use estimation to check their answers and the placement of decimal points.

B.5 Practice

Go to BigIdeasMath.com to get HELP with solving the exercises.

Review & Refresh

Find the product. Write fractions in simplest form.

1. $-0.5(1.31)$
2. $\frac{9}{10}\left(-1\frac{1}{4}\right)$
3. $-\frac{7}{12}\left(-\frac{3}{14}\right)$

Identify the terms, coefficients, and constants in the expression.

4. $3b + 12$
5. $14 + z + 6f$
6. $8g + 14 + 5c + 7$
7. $42m + 18 + 12c^2$

Concepts, Skills, & Problem Solving

 USING TOOLS **Write two division expressions represented by the area model. Then find the quotients.** (See Exploration 1, p. 573.)

8. 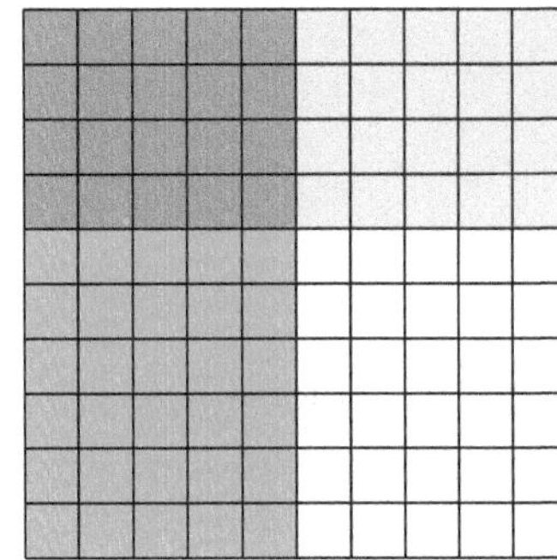

9. 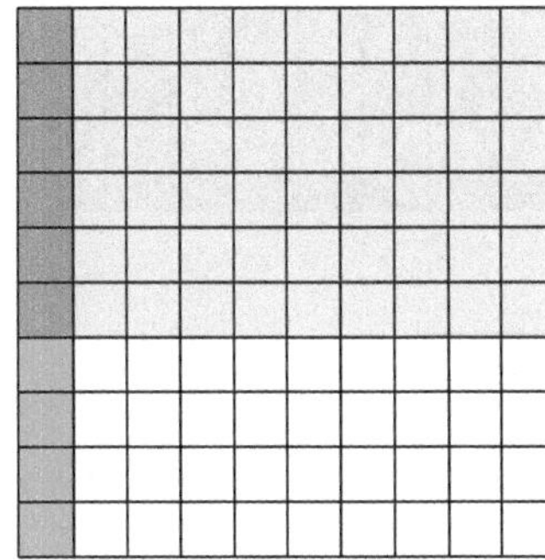

DIVIDING RATIONAL NUMBERS **Find the quotient. Write fractions in simplest form.**

10. $-\frac{7}{10} \div \frac{2}{5}$
11. $-0.18 \div 0.03$
12. $-3.45 \div (-15)$
13. $-8 \div (-2.2)$
14. $\frac{1}{4} \div \left(-\frac{3}{8}\right)$
15. $8.722 \div (-3.56)$
16. $12.42 \div (-4.8)$
17. $-2\frac{4}{5} \div (-7)$
18. $-10\frac{2}{7} \div \left(-4\frac{4}{11}\right)$

MP YOU BE THE TEACHER **Your friend evaluates the expression. Is your friend correct? Explain your reasoning.**

19.
$$-\frac{2}{3} \div \frac{4}{5} = \frac{-3}{2} \times \frac{4}{5}$$
$$= \frac{-12}{10}$$
$$= -\frac{6}{5}$$

20.
$$-4.25 \div 1.7 = 2.5$$

21. **MP MODELING REAL LIFE** How many 0.75-pound packages can you make with 4.5 pounds of sunflower seeds?

EVALUATING AN EXPRESSION **Evaluate the expression. Write fractions in simplest form.**

22. $\dfrac{\frac{14}{9}}{-\frac{1}{3}-\frac{1}{6}}$

23. $\dfrac{-\frac{12}{5}+\frac{3}{10}}{\frac{11}{14}-\left(-\frac{9}{14}\right)}$

24. $-0.42 \div 0.8 + 0.2$

25. $2.85 - 6.2 \div 2^2$

26. $\frac{3}{4}+\frac{7}{10}-\frac{1}{8}\div\left(-\frac{1}{2}\right)$

27. $\dfrac{\frac{7}{6}}{\left(-\frac{11}{5}\right)\left(10\frac{1}{2}\right)\left(-\frac{5}{11}\right)}$

28. **MP PROBLEM SOLVING** The section of the boardwalk shown is made using boards that are each $9\frac{1}{4}$ inches wide. The spacing between each board is equal. What is the width of the spacing between each board?

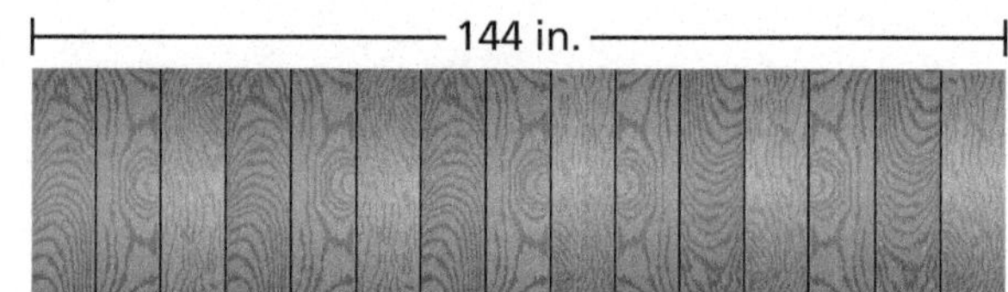

Day	Change in pressure
Monday	−0.05
Tuesday	0.09
Wednesday	−0.04
Thursday	−0.08

29. **MP REASONING** The table shows the daily changes in the barometric pressure (in inches of mercury) for four days.

a. What is the mean change?

b. The mean change for Monday through Friday is −0.01 inch. What is the change in the barometric pressure on Friday? Explain.

30. **MP LOGIC** In an online survey, gym members react to the statement shown by adjusting the position of the needle. The responses have values of −4.2, 1.6, 0.4, 0, 2.1, −5.0, −4.7, 0.6, 1.1, 0.8, 0.4, and 2.1. Explain how two people can use the results of the survey to reach different conclusions about whether the gym should adjust its membership prices.

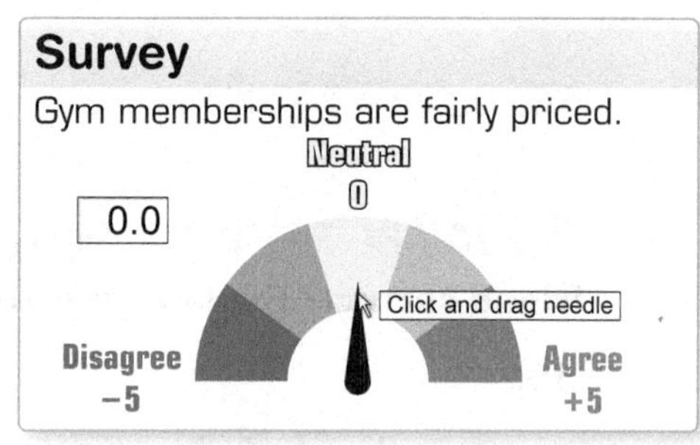

31. **CRITICAL THINKING** Determine whether the statement is *sometimes, always,* or *never* true. Explain your reasoning.

a. The product of two terminating decimals is a terminating decimal.

b. The quotient of two terminating decimals is a terminating decimal.

Common Errors

- **Exercises 22–27** Students may forget to follow the order of operations. Remind students about the order of operations and have them use parentheses to help remember which parts to evaluate first.

Mini-Assessment

Find the quotient. Write fractions in simplest form.

1. $6\frac{1}{2} \div \left(-2\frac{3}{4}\right)$ $-2\frac{4}{11}$
2. $-0.25 \div (-0.05)$ 5

Evaluate the expression. Write fractions in simplest form.

3. $\dfrac{-\frac{8}{9} + \frac{2}{3}}{-\frac{4}{5}}$ $\frac{5}{18}$
4. $-0.64 \div 2^2 - 3.4$ -3.56
5. How many 0.25-pound hamburgers can you make with 5.5 pounds of ground beef? 22 hamburgers

Section Resources

<table>
<tr><th>Surface Level</th><th>Deep Level</th></tr>
<tr><td>Resources by Chapter
• Extra Practice
• Reteach
• Puzzle Time
Student Journal
• Self-Assessment
• Practice
Differentiating the Lesson
Tutorial Videos
Skills Review Handbook
Skills Trainer</td><td>Resources by Chapter
• Enrichment and Extension
Graphic Organizers
Dynamic Assessment System
• Section Practice</td></tr>
<tr><th colspan="2">Transfer Level</th></tr>
<tr><td>Dynamic Assessment System
• End-of-Chapter Quiz</td><td>Assessment Book
• End-of-Chapter Quiz</td></tr>
</table>

Concepts, Skills, & Problem Solving

21. 6 **22.** $-3\frac{1}{9}$

23. $-1\frac{47}{100}$ **24.** -0.325

25. 1.3 **26.** $1\frac{7}{10}$

27. $\frac{1}{9}$ **28.** $\frac{3}{8}$ in.

29. **a.** -0.02 in.

b. 0.03 in.;

$$\frac{-0.05 + 0.09 + (-0.04) + (-0.08) + 0.03}{5} = -0.01$$

30. *Sample answer:* One person could decide not to change prices because only 3 of 12 results are negative. Another person could decide to change prices because the average rating is -0.4.

31. **a.** always; *Sample answer:* The number of decimal places in the product is the sum of the numbers of decimal places in the factors.

b. sometimes; *Sample answer:* $0.5 \div 0.25 = 2$, $0.5 \div 0.3 = 1.\overline{6}$

Skills Needed

Exercise 1

- Adding Rational Numbers
- Choosing Appropriate Measures
- Dividing Rational Numbers
- Interpreting Data

Exercise 2

- Adding Rational Numbers
- Evaluating an Expression
- Subtracting Rational Numbers

Exercise 3

- Finding the Percent of a Number
- Multiplying Rational Numbers
- Subtracting Decimals

ELL Support

Point out that in the United States, weight is often measured in ounces, pounds, and tons. Explain that 1 kilogram is approximately 2.2 pounds. There are 16 ounces in a pound and 2000 pounds in a ton. Review the abbreviations for pounds (lb) and ounces (oz).

Using the Problem-Solving Plan

1. *Sample answer:* -0.07 oz
2. $-\frac{4}{9}$
3. -39.42 in.

Performance Task

The *STEAM Video Performance Task* provides the opportunity for additional enrichment and greater depth of knowledge as students explore the mathematics of the chapter within a context tied to the chapter STEAM Video. The performance task and a detailed scoring rubric are provided at *BigIdeasMath.com.*

Laurie's Notes

Scaffolding Instruction

- The goal of this lesson is to help students become more comfortable with problem solving. These exercises combine multiplying and dividing rational numbers with prior skills from the previous chapter and other courses. The solution for Exercise 1 is worked out below, to help you guide students through the problem-solving plan. Use the remaining class time to have students work on the other exercises.
- **Emerging:** The goal for these students is to feel comfortable with the problem-solving plan. Allow students to work in pairs to write the beginning steps of the problem-solving plan for Exercise 2. Keep in mind that some students may only be ready to do the first step.
- **Proficient:** Students may be able to work independently or in pairs to complete Exercises 2 and 3.
- Visit each pair to review their plan for each problem. Ask students to describe their plans.

Using the Problem-Solving Plan

Exercise 1

Understand the problem. You know the weight changes of 15 hamsters. You want to use this information to find the typical weight change.

Make a plan. Display the data in a dot plot to see the distribution of the data. Then use the distribution to determine the most appropriate measure of center.

Solve and check. Use the plan to solve the problem. Then check your solution.

- Display the data in a dot plot.

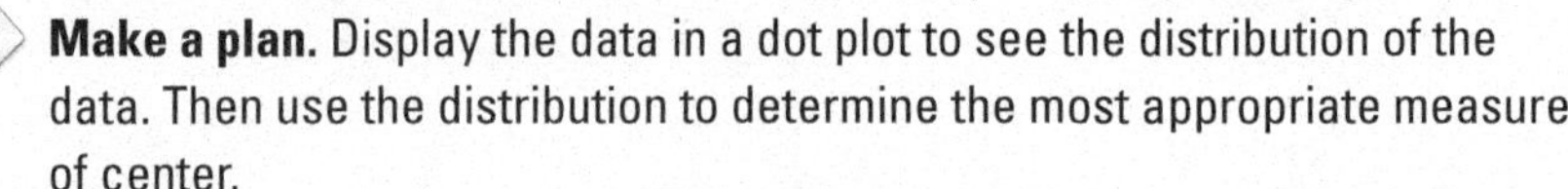

- The distribution is skewed right, so the median is the most appropriate measure to describe the center. The median is -0.07.
- So, a hamster that is fed the new recipe typically loses 0.07 ounce.
- **Check:** Compare the median to the mean and the mode to check for reasonableness.

  Total weight change $= (-0.07) + 0.02 + (-0.11) + (-0.03) + (-0.08) + (-0.1) + (-0.11) + (-0.08) + 0 + (-0.04) + (-0.06) + (-0.07) + (-0.08) + (-0.05) + (-0.08) = -0.94$

  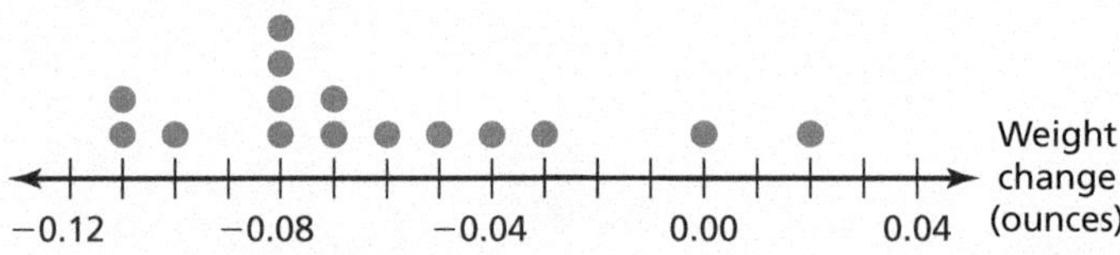

  Mean: $\frac{-0.94}{15} \approx -0.06$ Mode: -0.08

  The median is -0.07 which is close to both -0.06 and -0.08, so the answer is reasonable. ✓

Connecting Concepts

Using the Problem-Solving Plan

1. You feed several adult hamsters equal amounts of a new food recipe over a period of 1 month. You record the changes in the weights of the hamsters in the table. Use the data to answer the question "What is the typical weight change of a hamster that is fed the new recipe?"

Weight Change (ounces)				
−0.07	−0.03	−0.11	−0.04	−0.08
0.02	−0.08	−0.08	−0.06	−0.05
−0.11	−0.1	0	−0.07	−0.08

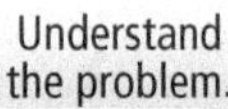
Understand the problem.

You know the weight changes of 15 hamsters. You want to use this information to find the typical weight change.

Make a plan.

Display the data in a dot plot to see the distribution of the data. Then use the distribution to determine the most appropriate measure of center.

Solve and check.

Use the plan to solve the problem. Then check your solution.

2. Evaluate the expression shown at the right. Write your answer in simplest form.

$$\frac{-\frac{1}{2}+\frac{2}{3}}{\frac{3}{5}\left(\frac{3}{4}-\frac{11}{8}\right)}$$

3. You drop a racquetball from a height of 60 inches. On each bounce, the racquetball bounces to a height that is 70% of its previous height. What is the change in the height of the racquetball after 3 bounces?

Performance Task

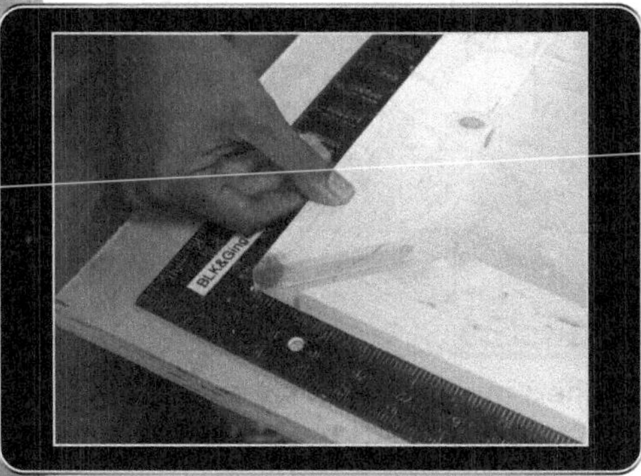

Precisely Perfect

At the beginning of this chapter, you watched a STEAM Video called "Carpenter or Joiner." You are now ready to complete the performance task related to this video, available at ***BigIdeasMath.com***. Be sure to use the problem-solving plan as you work through the performance task.

B Chapter Review

Review Vocabulary

Write the definition and give an example of each vocabulary term.

terminating decimal, *p. 562* repeating decimal, *p. 562* complex fraction, *p. 575*

Graphic Organizers

You can use an **Information Frame** to help organize and remember a concept. Here is an example of an Information Frame for ***multiplying integers***.

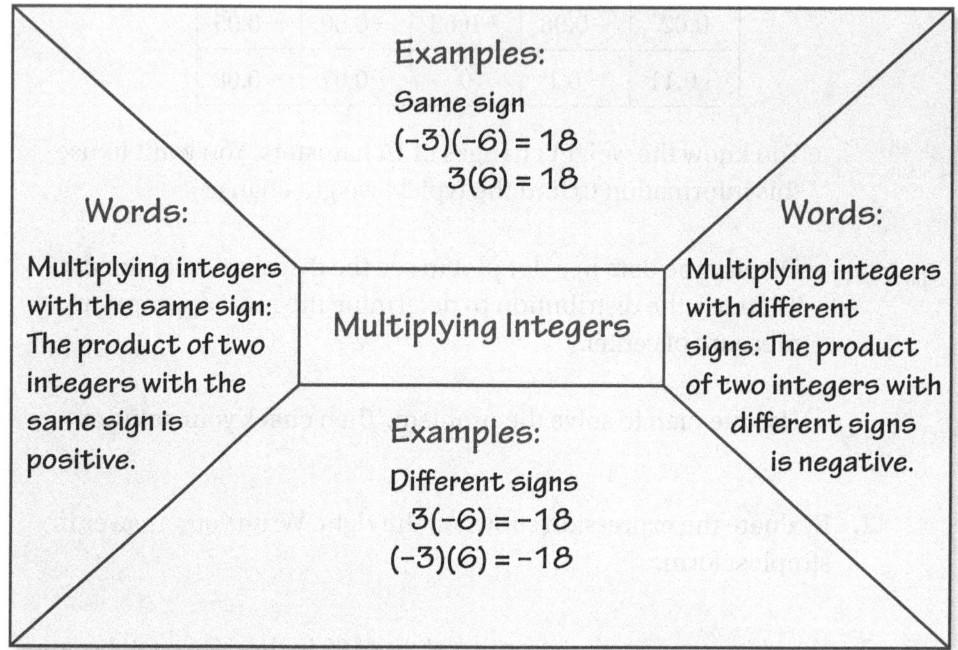

Examples:
Same sign
(−3)(−6) = 18
3(6) = 18
Words:
Multiplying integers with the same sign: The product of two integers with the same sign is positive.
Multiplying Integers
Words:
Multiplying integers with different signs: The product of two integers with different signs is negative.
Examples:
Different signs
3(−6) = −18
(−3)(6) = −18

Choose and complete a graphic organizer to help you study the concept.

1. dividing integers
2. writing fractions or mixed numbers as decimals
3. writing decimals as fractions or mixed numbers
4. multiplying rational numbers
5. dividing rational numbers

"I finished my Information Frame about rainforests. It makes me want to visit Costa Rica. How about you?"

Review Vocabulary

- As a review of the chapter vocabulary, have students revisit the vocabulary section in their *Student Journals* to fill in any missing definitions and record examples of each term.

Graphic Organizers

Sample answers:

1. 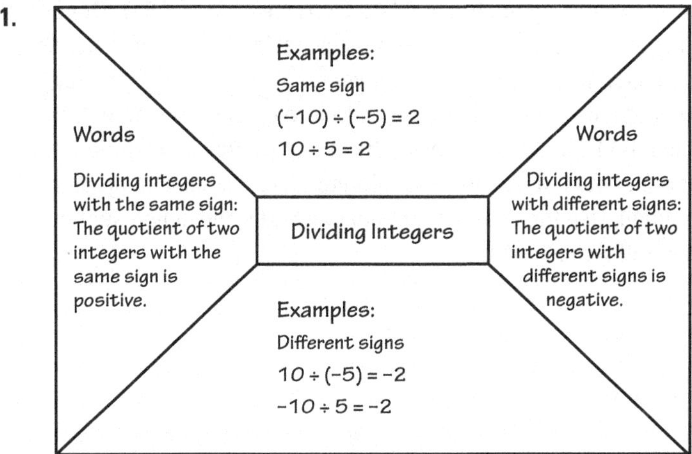

2. 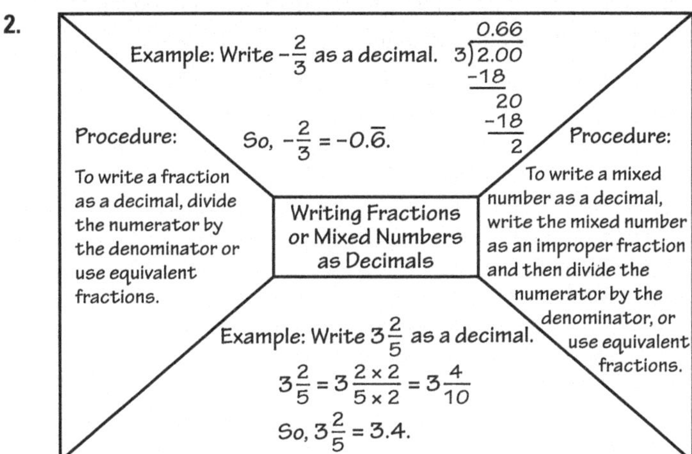

3. 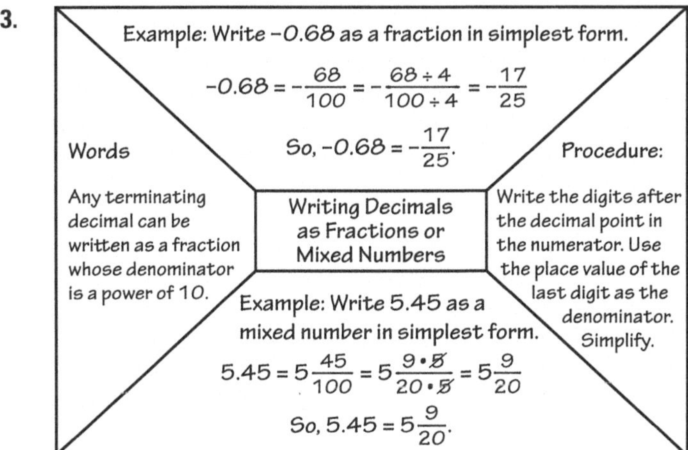

4 and 5. Answers at *BigIdeasMath.com*.

List of Organizers

Available at *BigIdeasMath.com*
Definition and Example Chart
Example and Non-Example Chart
Four Square
Information Frame
Summary Triangle

About this Organizer

An **Information Frame** can be used to help students organize and remember concepts. Students write the concept in the middle rectangle. Then students write related categories in the spaces around the rectangle. Related categories may include: words, numbers, algebra, example, definition, non-example, visual, procedure, details, or vocabulary. Students can place their Information Frames on note cards to use as a quick study reference.

Chapter Self-Assessment

1. -48
2. -70
3. 18
4. -10 min
5. -27
6. 120
7. 66
8. *Sample answer:* $-2, -3, -4$
9. 727 points
10. 0 or 2; *Sample answer:* If a product is positive, then an even number of factors are negative.
11. 5

Chapter Self-Assessment

The Success Criteria Self-Assessment chart can be found in the *Student Journal* or online at *BigIdeasMath.com*.

ELL Support

Allow students to work in pairs to complete Exercises 1–3 and 5–7. Once pairs have finished, check for understanding by asking for answers to each exercise. Have each pair display their answers on a whiteboard for your review. Allow students to work in groups of four to discuss and complete Exercises 4 and 8–11. To check answers, have two groups come together and reach agreement on their answers. Monitor discussions and provide support as needed. Use these techniques to check the remaining sections of the Chapter Self-Assessment.

Common Errors

- **Exercises 1–3 and 5–7** Students may not remember that a negative number multiplied by a negative number is positive. Tell them that it is similar to multiplying by -1, which means to take the opposite. For example, $-6(-13) = (-1 \cdot 6)(-13) = -1[6 \cdot (-13)] = -1(-78) = 78$.

Chapter Self-Assessment

As you complete the exercises, use the scale below to rate your understanding of the success criteria in your journal.

1	2	3	4
I do not understand.	I can do it with help.	I can do it on my own.	I can teach someone else.

B.1 Multiplying Integers *(pp. 549–554)*

Learning Target: Find products of integers.

Find the product.

1. $-8 \cdot 6$
2. $10(-7)$
3. $-3 \cdot (-6)$

4. You and a group of friends participate in a game where you must use clues to escape from a room. You have a limited amount of time to escape and are allowed 3 free clues. Additional clues may be requested, but each removes 5 minutes from your remaining time. What integer represents the total change in the time when you use 5 clues?

Evaluate the expression.

5. $(-3)^3$
6. $(-3)(-4)(10)$
7. $24 - 3(2 - 4^2)$

8. Write three integers whose product is negative.

9. You are playing laser tag. The table shows how many points you gain or lose when you tag or are tagged by another player in different locations. You are tagged three times on the back, twice on the shoulder, and twice on the laser. You tag two players on the front, four players on the back, and one player on the laser. What is your score?

Tag Locations	Points Gained	Points Lost
Front	200	50
Back	100	25
Shoulder	50	12
Laser	50	12

10. The product of three integers is positive. How many of the integers can be negative? Explain.

11. Two integers, c and d, have a product of -6. What is the *greatest* possible sum of c and d?

B.2 Dividing Integers (pp. 555–560)

Learning Target: Find quotients of integers.

Find the quotient.

12. $-18 \div 9$ **13.** $\frac{-42}{-6}$ **14.** $\frac{-30}{6}$ **15.** $84 \div (-7)$

Evaluate the expression when $x = 3$, $y = -4$, and $z = -6$.

16. $z \div x$ **17.** $\frac{xy}{z}$ **18.** $\frac{z - 2x}{y}$

Find the mean of the integers.

19. $-3, -8, 12, -15, 9$ **20.** $-54, -32, -70, -25, -65, -42$

21. The table shows the weekly profits of a fruit vendor. What is the mean profit for these weeks?

Week	1	2	3	4
Profit	−\$125	−\$86	\$54	−\$35

B.3 Converting Between Fractions and Decimals (pp. 561–566)

Learning Target: Convert between different forms of rational numbers.

Write the fraction or mixed number as a decimal.

22. $-\frac{8}{15}$ **23.** $\frac{5}{8}$ **24.** $-\frac{13}{6}$ **25.** $1\frac{7}{16}$

Write the decimal as a fraction or mixed number in simplest form.

26. -0.6 **27.** -0.35 **28.** -5.8 **29.** 24.23

30. The table shows the changes in the average yearly precipitation (in inches) in a city for several months. Order the numbers from least to greatest.

February	March	April	May
-1.75	$\frac{3}{11}$	0.3	$-1\frac{7}{9}$

Common Errors

- **Exercises 17 and 18** Students may forget to follow the order of operations. Review the order of operations, especially the left-to-right rules of evaluating multiplication/division and addition/subtraction.
- **Exercises 19 and 20** Students may not remember how to find the mean of several numbers. They may get confused by the negative numbers and subtract instead of adding. Remind students of the definition for *mean*.
- **Exercises 22 and 24** Students may forget to carry the negative sign through the division operation. Tell them to create a space for the final answer and to write the sign of the answer in the space at the beginning.
- **Exercises 26–29** Students may try to put the decimal number over the denominator. Remind students to remove the decimal point before they write it as a fraction.
- **Exercise 30** Students may order the numbers without the negative signs. Remind students that some numbers are negative and will be less than the positive numbers.

Chapter Self-Assessment

12. -2 **13.** 7

14. -5 **15.** -12

16. -2 **17.** 2

18. 3 **19.** -1

20. -48 **21.** $-\$48$

22. $-0.5\overline{3}$ **23.** 0.625

24. $-2.1\overline{6}$ **25.** 1.4375

26. $-\frac{3}{5}$

27. $-\frac{7}{20}$

28. $-5\frac{4}{5}$

29. $24\frac{23}{100}$

30. $-1\frac{7}{9}, -1.75, \frac{3}{11}, 0.3$

Chapter Self-Assessment

31. $\frac{28}{81}$ **32.** $-\frac{16}{45}$

33. 57.23 **34.** -23.67

35. 5 **36.** 16

37. -75 ft

38. *Sample answer:* $-\frac{1}{3}, -\frac{3}{4}$

39. $-\frac{3}{4}$ **40.** $-1\frac{3}{11}$

41. $2\frac{1}{10}$

42. -2 **43.** 6.16

44. -4.25 **45.** 5

46. $-\frac{1}{2}$

Common Errors

- **Exercises 39–41** Students may use the reciprocal of the first fraction or mixed number instead of the second or they may forget to write a mixed number as an improper fraction before finding the reciprocal. Review the rules for dividing fractions and mixed numbers and the definition of reciprocal.
- **Exercises 42–44** Students may mix up the dividend and the divisor. Remind students that the first number is the dividend and the second number is the divisor.
- **Exercises 42–44** Students may forget to move the decimal point when dividing by a decimal or they may move the decimal points the wrong number of places. Remind students to use estimation to check their answers and the placement of decimal points.
- **Exercise 46** Students may forget to follow the order of operations. Remind students about the order of operations and have them use parentheses to help remember which parts to evaluate first.

Chapter Resources

Surface Level	Deep Level
Resources by Chapter • Extra Practice • Reteach • Puzzle Time Student Journal • Practice • Chapter Self-Assessment Differentiating the Lesson Tutorial Videos Skills Review Handbook Skills Trainer Game Library	Resources by Chapter • Enrichment and Extension Graphic Organizers Game Library
Transfer Level	
STEAM Video Dynamic Assessment System • Chapter Test	Assessment Book • Chapter Tests A and B • Alternative Assessment • STEAM Performance Task

B.4 Multiplying Rational Numbers (pp. 567–572)

Learning Target: Find products of rational numbers.

Find the product. Write fractions in simplest form.

31. $-\frac{4}{9}\left(-\frac{7}{9}\right)$

32. $\frac{8}{15}\left(-\frac{2}{3}\right)$

33. $-5.9(-9.7)$

34. $4.5(-5.26)$

35. $-\frac{2}{3}\left(2\frac{1}{2}\right)(-3)$

36. $-1.6(0.5)(-20)$

37. The elevation of a sunken ship is -120 feet. You are in a submarine at an elevation that is $\frac{5}{8}$ of the ship's elevation. What is your elevation?

38. Write two fractions whose product is between $\frac{1}{5}$ and $\frac{1}{2}$, and whose sum is negative.

B.5 Dividing Rational Numbers (pp. 573–578)

Learning Target: Find quotients of rational numbers.

Find the quotient. Write fractions in simplest form.

39. $\frac{9}{10} \div \left(-\frac{6}{5}\right)$

40. $-\frac{4}{11} \div \frac{2}{7}$

41. $-\frac{7}{8} \div \left(-\frac{5}{12}\right)$

42. $6.4 \div (-3.2)$

43. $-15.4 \div (-2.5)$

44. $-23.8 \div 5.6$

45. You use a debit card to purchase several shirts. Your account balance after buying the shirts changes by $-\$30.60$. For each shirt you purchased, the change in your account balance was $-\$6.12$. How many shirts did you buy?

46. Evaluate $\frac{z}{y - \frac{3}{4} + x}$ when $x = 4$, $y = -3$, and $z = -\frac{1}{8}$.

B Practice Test

Evaluate the expression. Write fractions in simplest form.

1. $-9 \cdot 2$
2. $-72 \div (-3)$
3. $3\frac{9}{10} \times \left(-\frac{8}{3}\right)$
4. $-1\frac{5}{6} \div 4\frac{1}{6}$
5. $-4.4 \times (-6.02)$
6. $-5 \div 1.5$

Write the fraction or mixed number as a decimal.

7. $\frac{7}{40}$
8. $-\frac{1}{9}$
9. $-1\frac{5}{16}$

Write the decimal as a fraction or mixed number in simplest form.

10. -0.122
11. 0.33
12. -7.09

Evaluate the expression when $x = 5$, $y = -3$, and $z = -2$.

13. $\frac{y + z}{x}$
14. $\frac{x - 5z}{y}$
15. $\frac{\frac{1}{3}x}{\frac{y}{z}}$

16. Find the mean of 11, -7, -14, 10, and -5.

17. A driver receives -25 points for each rule violation. What integer represents the change in points after 4 rule violations?

18. How many 2.25-pound containers can you fill with 24.75 pounds of almonds?

19. In a recent 10-year period, the change in the number of visitors to U.S. national parks was about $-11{,}150{,}000$ visitors.
    a. What was the mean yearly change in the number of visitors?
    b. During the seventh year, the change in the number of visitors was about 10,800,000. Explain how the change for the 10-year period can be negative.

20. You have a $50 gift card to go shopping for school supplies. You buy 2 packs of pencils, 5 notebooks, 6 folders, 1 pack of pens, 3 packs of paper, 1 pack of highlighters, and 2 binders.
    a. What number represents the change in the value of the gift card after buying your school supplies?
    b. What percentage of the value remains on your gift card?

Practice Test Item References

Practice Test Questions	Section to Review
1, 17	B.1
2, 13, 14, 16, 19	B.2
7, 8, 9, 10, 11, 12, 20	B.3
3, 5, 20	B.4
4, 6, 15, 18	B.5

Test-Taking Strategies

Remind students to quickly look over the entire test before they start so that they can budget their time. On tests, it is really important for students to **Stop** and **Think**. When students hurry on a test dealing with positive and negative numbers, they often make "sign" errors.

Common Errors

- **Exercise 4** Students may use the reciprocal of the first mixed number instead of the second or they may forget to write the mixed numbers as improper fractions before finding the reciprocal. Review the rules for dividing mixed numbers and the definition of reciprocal.
- **Exercises 13–15** Students may forget to follow the order of operations. Remind students about the order of operations and have them use parentheses to help remember which parts to evaluate first.
- **Exercise 16** Students may not remember how to find the mean of several numbers. They may get confused by the negative numbers and subtract instead of add. Remind students of the definition for *mean*.

Practice Test

1. -18 **2.** 24

3. $-10\frac{2}{5}$ **4.** $-\frac{11}{25}$

5. 26.488 **6.** $-3.\overline{3}$

7. 0.175 **8.** $-0.\overline{1}$

9. -1.3125 **10.** $-\frac{61}{500}$

11. $\frac{33}{100}$ **12.** $-7\frac{9}{100}$

13. -1 **14.** -5

15. $1\frac{1}{9}$ **16.** -1

17. -100 **18.** 11

19. **a.** $-1{,}115{,}000$ visitors

b. During other years, there were more significant changes in visitors in the negative direction.

20. **a.** -38

b. 24%

Test-Taking Strategies

Available at *BigIdeasMath.com*
After Answering Easy Questions, Relax
Answer Easy Questions First
Estimate the Answer
Read All Choices before Answering
Read Question before Answering
Solve Directly or Eliminate Choices
Solve Problem before Looking at Choices
Use Intelligent Guessing
Work Backwards

About this Strategy

When taking a multiple-choice test, be sure to read each question carefully and thoroughly. After reading the question, estimate the answer before trying to solve it.

Cumulative Practice

1. A
2. F
3. $\frac{9}{16}$
4. C
5. G

Item Analysis

1. **A.** Correct answer

   B. The student correctly finds José's height at 5 years old, which was 41 inches, but then reverses the relationship between José and Sean.

   C. When multiplying the rate of growth by the number of elapsed years, the student multiplies only the whole-number parts to get $16\frac{3}{4}$ inches.

   D. When multiplying the rate of growth by the number of elapsed years, the student multiplies only the whole-number parts to get $16\frac{3}{4}$ inches. Then the student uses $16\frac{3}{4}$ inches to find José's height at 5 years old and reverses the relationship between José and Sean.

2. **F.** Correct answer

   G. The student adds 5 and -7 instead of adding -5 and -7.

   H. The student subtracts -7 from -5 instead of adding.

   I. The student adds the absolute values and forgets the common sign.

3. **Gridded Response:** Correct answer: $\frac{9}{16}$

   Common error: The student forgets to find a common denominator before adding and gets 0.

4. **A.** The student does not evaluate a^2 correctly and does not find the absolute value.

   B. The student does not find the absolute value.

   C. Correct answer

   D. The student does not evaluate a^2 correctly.

5. **F.** The student thinks that $-(-5) = -5$.

   G. Correct answer

   H. The student does not subtract from left to right.

   I. When adding different integers with different signs, the student finds the sum of the absolute values instead of finding the difference of the absolute values.

B Cumulative Practice

Test-Taking Strategy
Estimate the Answer

One-fourth of the 36 cats in our town are tabbies. How many are not tabbies?
Ⓐ 9 Ⓑ 18 Ⓒ 27 Ⓓ 36

IC.

"Using estimation you can see that there are about 10 tabbies. So about 30 are not tabbies."

1. When José and Sean were each 5 years old, José was $1\frac{1}{2}$ inches taller than Sean. Then José grew at an average rate of $2\frac{3}{4}$ inches per year until he was 13 years old. José was 63 inches tall when he was 13 years old. How tall was Sean when he was 5 years old?

A. $39\frac{1}{2}$ in. **B.** $42\frac{1}{2}$ in.

C. $44\frac{3}{4}$ in. **D.** $47\frac{3}{4}$ in.

2. What is the value of $-5 + (-7)$?

F. -12 **G.** -2

H. 2 **I.** 12

3. What is the value of the expression?

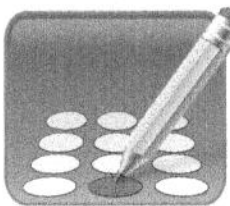

$$-\frac{9}{16} + \frac{9}{8}$$

4. What is the value of $|a^2 - 2ac + 5b|$ when $a = -2$, $b = 3$, and $c = -5$?

A. -9 **B.** -1

C. 1 **D.** 9

5. Your friend evaluated the expression.

$$\begin{aligned} 2 - 3 - (-5) &= -5 - (-5) \\ &= -5 + 5 \\ &= 0 \end{aligned}$$

What should your friend do to correct the error that he made?

F. Subtract 5 from -5 instead of adding.

G. Rewrite $2 - 3$ as -1.

H. Subtract -5 from 3 before subtracting 3 from 2.

I. Rewrite $-5 + 5$ as -10.

6. What is the value of $-1\frac{1}{2} - \left(-1\frac{3}{4}\right)$?

A. $-3\frac{1}{4}$

B. $\frac{1}{4}$

C. $\frac{6}{7}$

D. $2\frac{5}{8}$

7. What is the value of the expression when $q = -2$, $r = -12$, and $s = 8$?

$$\frac{-q^2 - r}{s}$$

F. -2

G. -1

H. 1

I. 2

8. You are stacking wooden blocks with the dimensions shown. How many blocks do you need to stack vertically to build a block tower that is $7\frac{1}{2}$ inches tall?

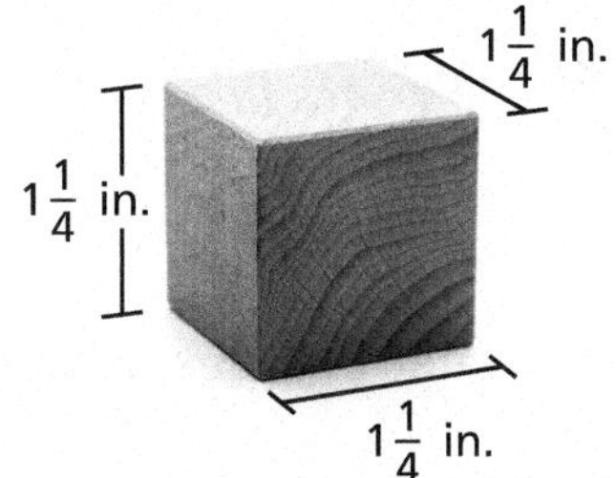

9. Your friend evaluated an expression.

$$\begin{aligned} -4\frac{3}{4} + 2\frac{1}{5} &= -\frac{19}{4} + \frac{11}{5} \\ &= -\frac{95}{20} + \frac{44}{20} \\ &= \frac{-95 + 44}{20} \\ &= \frac{-139}{20} \\ &= -6\frac{19}{20} \end{aligned}$$

What should your friend do to correct the error that she made?

A. Rewrite $-\frac{19}{4} + \frac{11}{5}$ as $\frac{-19 + 11}{4 + 5}$.

B. Rewrite $-95 + 44$ as -51.

C. Rewrite $\frac{-95 + 44}{20}$ as $\frac{51}{20}$.

D. Rewrite $-4\frac{3}{4}$ as $-\frac{13}{4}$.

Item Analysis (continued)

6. **A.** The student finds the sum of the absolute values instead of the difference.

   B. Correct answer

   C. The student finds the quotient of the absolute values instead of the difference.

   D. The student finds the product of the absolute values instead of the difference.

7. **F.** The student subtracts 12 in the numerator instead of adding.

   G. The student thinks $-4 + 12 = -8$ instead of 8.

   H. Correct answer

   I. The student thinks that the opposite of the square of -2 is 4.

8. **Gridded Response:** Correct answer: 6

   Common error: The student divides the whole-number parts and the fractional parts of the mixed numbers and gets $7 + 2 = 9$.

9. **A.** The student does not find a common denominator before adding.

   B. Correct answer

   C. The student subtracts 44 from 95, but does not use the sign of the number with the greater absolute value.

   D. The student incorrectly converts the first mixed number to an improper fraction.

Cumulative Practice

6. B

7. H

8. 6

9. B

Cumulative Practice

10. G

11. *Part A* 2.5; T and U are farthest right; *Part B* 4.85; R and S are farthest apart; *Part C* 2.06; The only positive products are $R \times S$ and $T \times U$, and $R \times S$ has a greater value; *Part D* 5.25; The only positive quotients involve R and S or U and T, $U \div T$ has the greatest value.

12. C

13. H

14. B

15. G

Item Analysis (continued)

10. **F.** The student substitutes 2 instead of -2 for x.

G. Correct answer

H. The student chooses the smallest positive value instead of the greatest value.

I. The student misinterprets xy as addition instead of multiplication.

11. **4 points** The student's work and explanations demonstrate a thorough understanding of rational-number operations using a number line. In Part A, the student recognizes that the two greatest values T and U, have the greatest sum (about 2.5). In Part B, the student recognizes that the two values that are the farthest apart, U and R, have the greatest difference (about 4.85). In Part C, the student recognizes that the two values with the same sign and greatest magnitudes, R and S, have the greatest product (about 2.06). In Part D, the student recognizes that the two values with the same sign and greatest ratio, U and T, have the greatest quotient (about 5.25). The student provides accurate work with clear and complete explanations.

3 points The student's work and explanations demonstrate an essential but less than thorough understanding of rational-number operations using a number line.

2 points The student's work and explanations demonstrate a partial but limited understanding of rational-number operations using a number line.

1 point The student's work and explanations demonstrate a very limited understanding of rational-number operations using a number line.

0 points The student provides no response, a completely incorrect or incomprehensible response, or a response that demonstrates insufficient understanding of rational-number operations using a number line.

12. **A.** The student thinks that the quotient of two negative numbers is negative and that $-0.4 + 0.8 = -1.2$.

B. The student thinks that the quotient of two negative numbers is negative.

C. Correct answer

D. The student thinks that $-0.4 + 0.8 = -1.2$.

13. **F.** The student substitutes 4 instead of -4 for x in choices F and H.

G. The student switches the values for x and y in choices G and H.

H. Correct answer

I. The student substitutes 4 instead of -4 for x in choices H and I.

14. **A.** The student finds half of the sum of the base and the height.

B. Correct answer

C. The student finds the sum of the base and the height.

D. The student finds the product of the base and the height.

15. **F.** The student rounds the decimal to the tenths place instead of finding the repeating decimal.

G. Correct answer

H. The student uses the numerator as the value of the tenths place and the denominator as the value of the hundredths place.

I. The student divides 9 by 2 instead of dividing 2 by 9.

10. Which expression has the greatest value when $x = -2$ and $y = -3$?

F. $-xy$ **G.** xy

H. $x - y$ **I.** $-x - y$

11. Four points are graphed on the number line.

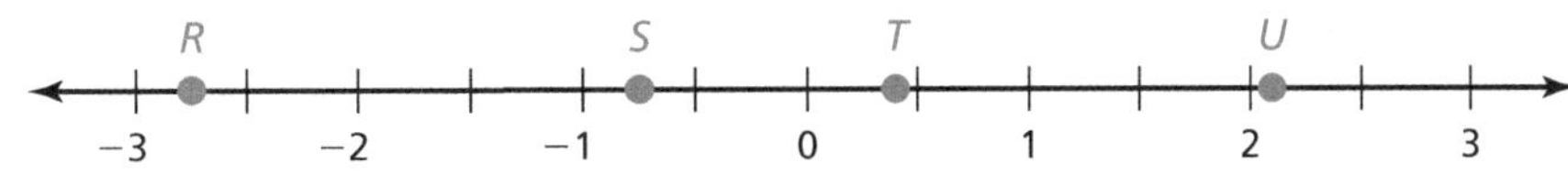

Part A Choose the two points whose values have the greatest sum. Approximate this sum. Explain your reasoning.

Part B Choose the two points whose values have the greatest difference. Approximate this difference. Explain your reasoning.

Part C Choose the two points whose values have the greatest product. Approximate this product. Explain your reasoning.

Part D Choose the two points whose values have the greatest quotient. Approximate this quotient. Explain your reasoning.

12. What number belongs in the box to make the equation true?

$$\frac{-0.4}{\square} + 0.8 = -1.2$$

A. -1 **B.** -0.2

C. 0.2 **D.** 1

13. Which expression has a negative value when $x = -4$ and $y = 2$?

F. $-x + y$ **G.** $y - x$

H. $x - y$ **I.** $-x - y$

14. What is the area of a triangle with a base of $2\frac{1}{2}$ inches and a height of 2 inches?

A. $2\frac{1}{4}$ in.^{2} **B.** $2\frac{1}{2}$ in.^{2}

C. $4\frac{1}{2}$ in.^{2} **D.** 5 in.^{2}

15. Which decimal is equivalent to $\frac{2}{9}$?

F. 0.2 **G.** $0.\overline{2}$

H. 0.29 **I.** 4.5

C Expressions

C.1 Algebraic Expressions

C.2 Adding and Subtracting Linear Expressions

C.3 The Distributive Property

C.4 Factoring Expressions

Chapter Learning Target:
Understand algebraic expressions.

Chapter Success Criteria:
- I can identify parts of an algebraic expression.
- I can write algebraic expressions.
- I can solve problems using algebraic expressions.
- I can interpret algebraic expressions in real-life problems.

Laurie's Notes

Chapter C Overview

In Chapter 5, students were introduced to algebraic expressions. That introduction included related vocabulary (i.e., term, coefficient, exponent, etc.) and writing and evaluating algebraic expressions. That said, it is common for students to see $1.5x + 0.06(1.5x)$ as just a bunch of symbols that have little meaning. Students find it difficult to appreciate that an algebraic expression can model a real-life situation, one that can be interpreted and explored with *what if* questions.

In $1.5x + 0.06(1.5x)$, x can represent the wholesale price of an item. The item is marked up 50%, $1.5x$, and there is a 6% sales tax, $0.06(1.5x)$. The sum of the two terms is the retail price (the price the consumer pays) and the expression can be simplified to show that the consumer pays 59% more than the wholesale price.

$$\begin{aligned} 1.5x + 0.06(1.5x) &= 1(1.5x) + 0.06(1.5x) \\ &= (1 + 0.06)(1.5x) \\ &= 1.06(1.5x) \\ &= 1.59x \end{aligned}$$

What is the retail price if the wholesale price is \$60? If the wholesale price doubles ($x = \$120$), does the retail price double? If the wholesale price increases by 10 dollars ($x = \$70$), does the retail price increase by 10 dollars?

Students will work with percents later in this course, but the skills for writing and simplifying algebraic expressions are in the first two lessons of this chapter. Algebra tiles and area models are used to model operations on linear expressions.

$(2x - 8) + (-3x + 5)$

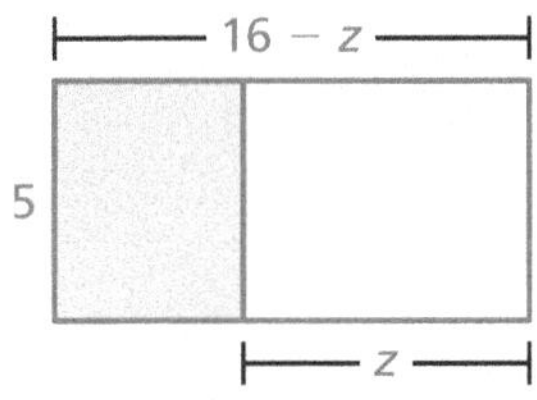

The area of the shaded region is

$(16 - z - z)5$ square units.

The Distributive Property is used to find the product of expressions such as $5(16 - z) = 90 - 5z$. The Distributive Property is also used to factor expressions, as in the real-life situation above represented by $1.5x + 0.06(1.5x) = (1 + 0.06)(1.5x)$. The last two lessons of the chapter look at expanding and factoring expressions. Students' understanding and recognition of the Distributive Property is essential to understanding both of these lessons.

Suggested Pacing

Chapter Opener	1 Day
Section 1	1 Day
Section 2	1 Day
Section 3	1 Day
Section 4	1 Day
Connecting Concepts	1 Day
Chapter Review	1 Day
Chapter Test	1 Day
Total Chapter C	8 Days
Year-to-Date	137 Days

Chapter Learning Target

Understand algebraic expressions.

Chapter Success Criteria

- Identify parts of an algebraic expression.
- Write algebraic expressions.
- Solve problems using algebraic expressions.
- Interpret algebraic expressions in real-life problems.

Chapter C Learning Targets and Success Criteria

Section	Learning Target	Success Criteria
C.1 Algebraic Expressions	Simplify algebraic expressions.	• Identify terms and like terms of algebraic expressions. • Combine like terms to simplify algebraic expressions. • Write and simplify algebraic expressions to solve real-life problems.
C.2 Adding and Subtracting Linear Expressions	Find sums and differences of linear expressions.	• Explain the difference between linear and nonlinear expressions. • Find opposites of terms that include variables. • Apply properties of operations to add and subtract linear expressions.
C.3 The Distributive Property	Apply the Distributive Property to generate equivalent expressions.	• Explain how to apply the Distributive Property. • Use the Distributive Property to simplify algebraic expressions.
C.4 Factoring Expressions	Factor algebraic expressions.	• Identify the greatest common factor of terms, including variable terms. • Use the Distributive Property to factor algebraic expressions. • Write a term as a product involving a given factor.

Progressions

Through the Grades		
Grade 6	**Grade 7**	**Grade 8**
• Use the distributive property to factor algebraic expressions. • Write and evaluate algebraic expressions. • Apply the properties of operations to show expressions are equivalent.	• Add, subtract, factor, and expand linear expressions with rational coefficients. • Understand that rewriting expressions in different forms can show how the quantities are related.	• Use the properties of integer exponents to generate equivalent expressions. • Solve linear equations with rational number coefficients, including equations whose solutions require expanding expressions using the distributive property and collecting like terms.

Through the Chapter				
Standard	**C.1**	**C.2**	**C.3**	**C.4**
Apply properties of operations as strategies to add, subtract, factor, and expand linear expressions with rational coefficients.	●	●	●	★
Understand that rewriting an expression in different forms in a problem context can shed light on the problem and how the quantities in it are related.	●	●	●	★

Key

▲ = preparing ★ = complete

● = learning ■ = extending

Laurie's Notes

STEAM Video

1. *Sample answer:* Fish and plants are biotic components because they are living. Air and sunlight are abiotic because they are non-living.
2. *Sample answer:* Let b, s, and f represent the energy gained from eating the banana, the spinach, and the fish, respectively. The expression $b + s + f$ represents the total energy gained by eating the items.

Performance Task

Multiply the cost of an individual object by the number of objects you buy.

Mathematical Practices

Students have opportunities to develop aspects of the mathematical practices throughout the chapter. Here are some examples.

1. **Make Sense of Problems and Persevere in Solving Them**
   C.2 Math Practice note, *p. 597*
2. **Reason Abstractly and Quantitatively**
   C.3 Exercise 38, *p. 608*
3. **Construct Viable Arguments and Critique the Reasoning of Others**
   C.1 Math Practice note, *p. 591*
4. **Model with Mathematics**
   C.2 Exercise 30, *p. 602*
5. **Use Appropriate Tools Strategically**
   C.3 Math Practice note, *p. 605*
6. **Attend to Precision**
   C.1 Exercise 29, *p. 596*
7. **Look for and Make Use of Structure**
   C.4 Exercise 48, *p. 614*
8. **Look for and Express Regularity in Repeated Reasoning**
   C.3 Math Practice note, *p. 603*

STEAM Video

Before the Video

- To introduce the STEAM Video, read aloud the first paragraph of Trophic Status and discuss the question with your students.
- ? "What is an example of an ecosystem?"

During the Video

- The video shows two people discussing an ecosystem and its various components.
- ? Pause the video at 1:06 and ask, "What are biotic components?" living parts of an ecosystem "What are abiotic components?" non-living parts of an ecosystem
- Watch the remainder of the video.

After the Video

- ? "What components of an ecosystem add energy? plants and algae
- Have students work with a partner to answer Questions 1 and 2.
- As students discuss and answer the questions, listen for understanding of writing an algebraic expression to represent a real-life situation.

Performance Task

- Use this information to spark students' interest and promote thinking about real-life problems.
- ? Ask, "How can you find the total cost of purchasing several identical objects?"
- After completing the chapter, students will have gained the knowledge needed to complete "Chlorophyll in Plants."

STEAM Video

Trophic Status

In an ecosystem, energy and nutrients flow between *biotic* and *abiotic* components. Biotic components are the living parts of an ecosystem. Abiotic components are the non-living parts of an ecosystem. What is an example of an ecosystem?

Watch the STEAM video "Trophic Status." Then answer the following questions.

1. Give examples of both biotic and abiotic components in an ecosystem. Explain.

2. When an organism is eaten, its energy flows into the organism that consumes it. Explain how to use an expression to represent the total energy that a person gains from eating each of the items shown.

Performance Task

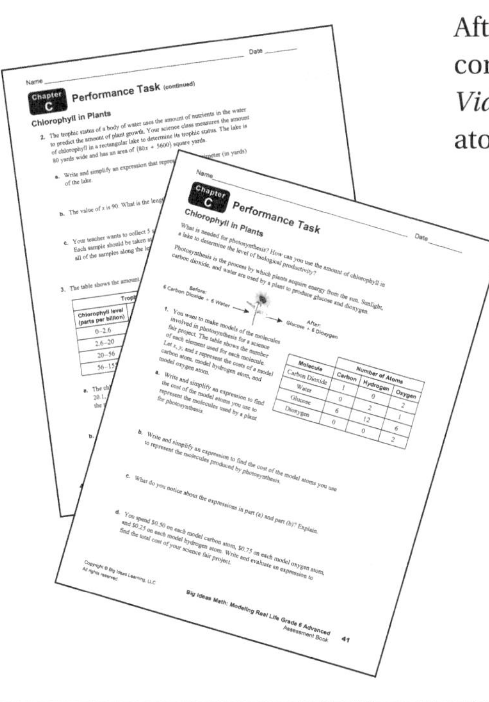

Name ______ Date ______

Chapter C **Performance Task** (continued)

Chlorophyll in Plants

2. The trophic status of a body of water uses the amount of nutrients in the water to predict the amount of plant growth. Your science class measures the amount of chlorophyll in a rectangular lake to determine its trophic status. The lake is 80 yards wide and has an area of $(80x + 5600)$ square yards.

a. Write and simplify an expression that repre... ...meter (in yards) of the lake.

b. The value of x is 90. What is the leng...

c. Your teacher wants to collect 5 ... Each sample should be taken a... all of the samples along the le...

3. The table shows the amount...

Chlorophyll level (parts per billion)
0–2.6
2.6–20
20–56
56–15...

Name ______ Date ______

Chapter C **Performance Task**

Chlorophyll in Plants

What is needed for photosynthesis? How can you use the amount of chlorophyll in a lake to determine the level of biological productivity?

Photosynthesis is the process by which plants acquire energy from the sun. Sunlight, carbon dioxide, and water are used by a plant to produce glucose and dioxygen.

Before: 6 Carbon Dioxide + 6 Water → After: Glucose + 6 Dioxygen

1. You want to make models of the molecules involved in photosynthesis for a science fair project. The table shows the number of each element used for each molecule. Let x, y, and z represent the costs of a model carbon atom, model hydrogen atom, and model oxygen atom.

Molecule	Number of Atoms: Carbon	Hydrogen	Oxygen
Carbon Dioxide	1	0	2
Water	0	2	1
Glucose	6	12	6
Dioxygen	0	0	2

a. Write and simplify an expression to find the cost of the model atoms you use to represent the molecules used by a plant for photosynthesis.

b. Write and simplify an expression to find the cost of the model atoms you use to represent the molecules produced by photosynthesis.

c. What do you notice about the expressions in part (a) and part (b)? Explain.

d. You spend \$0.50 on each model carbon atom, \$0.75 on each model oxygen atom, and \$0.25 on each model hydrogen atom. Write and evaluate an expression to find the total cost of your science fair project.

Big Ideas Math: Modeling Real Life Grade 6 Advanced
Assessment Book 41

Chlorophyll in Plants

After completing this chapter, you will be able to use the concepts you learned to answer the questions in the *STEAM Video Performance Task*. You will be given the numbers of atoms found in molecules involved in photosynthesis.

Glucose Molecule

6 carbon atoms

12 hydrogen atoms

6 oxygen atoms

You will be asked to determine the total cost for a model of a molecule given the costs of different types of atom models. How can you find the total cost of purchasing several identical objects?

Getting Ready for Chapter 

Chapter Exploration

Work with a partner. Rewrite the algebraic expression so that it has fewer symbols but still has the same value when evaluated for any value of x.

	Original Expression	Simplified Expression		Original Expression	Simplified Expression
1.	$2x + 4 + x$		**2.**	$3(x + 1) - 4$	
3.	$x - (3 - x)$		**4.**	$5 + 2x - 3$	
5.	$x + 3 + 2x - 4$		**6.**	$2x + 2 - x + 3$	

7. WRITING GUIDELINES Work with a partner. Use your answers in Exercises 1–6 to write guidelines for simplifying an expression.

Simplifying an Algebraic Expression

Key Idea Use the following steps to simplify an algebraic expression.
1.
2.
3.

APPLYING A DEFINITION Work with a partner. Two expressions are equivalent if they have the same value when evaluated for any value of x. Decide which two expressions are equivalent. Explain your reasoning.

	Expression A	Expression B	Expression C
8.	$x - (2x + 1)$	$-x + 1$	$-x - 1$
9.	$2x + 3 - x + 4$	$x + 7$	$x - 1$
10.	$3 + x - 2(x + 1)$	$-x + 1$	$-x + 5$
11.	$2 - 2x - (x + 2)$	$-3x$	$-3x + 4$

Vocabulary

The following vocabulary terms are defined in this chapter. Think about what each term might mean and record your thoughts.

like terms | linear expression | factoring an expression

Laurie's Notes

Check out the digital flash cards.
BigIdeasMath.com

Chapter Exploration

- Students simplified algebraic expressions in Chapter 5 and performed operations on integers in the last two chapters. This exploration reviews the process of simplifying expressions but extends it to expressions involving integers.
- Have students complete Exercises 1–6 with a partner. Then have each pair compare their answers with another pair. Discuss any discrepancies as a class.
- Have pairs complete Exercise 7. Then ask several pairs to share their ideas with the class. Write a set of guidelines on the board using student responses. Discuss similarities and differences between each pair's guidelines. Change the guidelines on the board as students offer revisions or improvements.
- Have students complete Exercises 8–11 with their partners. Then have each pair compare their answers with another pair. Discuss any discrepancies as a class.

ELL Support

Students have learned that if two expressions have the same value, they are equivalent. Introduce the phrase *like terms*. Ask students what they think it might mean. Explain that it is not the same as *equivalent expressions* and is more closely related to the word *alike*, meaning "similar," than the word *like*, meaning "enjoy." It refers to terms within an expression that have the same variables raised to the same exponents. For example, in the expression $a^2 + 7a - 2a^2 + a$, the terms a^2 and $-2a^2$ are like terms. Other like terms are $7a$ and a.

Vocabulary

- These terms represent some of the vocabulary that students will encounter in Chapter C. Discuss the terms as a class.
- Where have students heard the term *like terms* outside of a math classroom? In what contexts? Students may not be able to write the actual definition, but they may write phrases associated with *like terms*.
- Allowing students to discuss these terms now will prepare them for understanding the terms as they are presented in the chapter.
- When students encounter a new definition, encourage them to write in their *Student Journals*. They will revisit these definitions during the Chapter Review.

Topics for Review

- Distributive Property
- Evaluating Expressions
- Greatest Common Factor (GCF)
- Order of Operations
- Powers and Exponents
- Writing Algebraic Expressions

Chapter Exploration

1. $3x + 4$
2. $3x - 1$
3. $2x - 3$
4. $2x + 2$
5. $3x - 1$
6. $x + 5$
7. *Sample answer:* 1. Use the Distributive Property to eliminate parentheses. 2. Use the Commutative and Associative Properties of Addition to get the variable terms together and the terms without variables together. 3. Combine the variable terms and combine the terms without variables.
8. Expressions A, C; These expressions have the same value when evaluated for any value of x.
9. Expressions A, B; These expressions have the same value when evaluated for any value of x.
10. Expressions A, B; These expressions have the same value when evaluated for any value of x.
11. Expressions A, B; These expressions have the same value when evaluated for any value of x.

Check out the
Dynamic Classroom.
BigIdeasMath.com

Learning Target

Simplify algebraic expressions.

Success Criteria

- Identify terms and like terms of algebraic expressions.
- Combine like terms to simplify algebraic expressions.
- Write and simplify algebraic expressions to solve real-life problems.

Warm Up

Cumulative, vocabulary, and prerequisite skills practice opportunities are available in the *Resources by Chapter* or at *BigIdeasMath.com*.

ELL Support

Students may know the word *expression* from everyday language. It can be used to describe the look on a person's face or the words used to communicate something. Explain that in the context of math, an algebraic expression is a mathematical phrase containing numbers, operations, and/or variables.

Exploration 1

a. See Additional Answers.

b. *Sample answer:* Use the Commutative and Associative Properties of Addition to move and group terms to simplify the expressions.

c. yes; *Sample answer:* An algebraic term represents a number, so to subtract an algebraic term, you can add the opposite of that term.

Laurie's Notes

Preparing to Teach

- **Look for and Make Use of Structure:** Mathematically proficient students are able to see an algebraic expression being composed of several terms. In this lesson, students will simplify algebraic expressions by combining like terms.

Motivate

- **Target Math Game Time!** Write the following problem on the board.

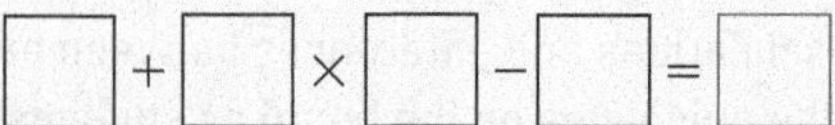

- **Directions:** Tell students that you are going to randomly generate four numbers from −8 to 8 and *as you generate the numbers*, they are to place the numbers in the four boxes to the left of the equal sign. After the fourth number is generated, students should evaluate the expression and write their answers in the red box. The goal is to get as close to the target number of 24 as possible without going over.
- To generate the random numbers, you can use the random number generator on a calculator or write the numbers on slips of paper and draw numbers. When generating random numbers, do not use the same number twice.
- **Extensions:** Play this more than once by changing the target number, changing the range of numbers used, or changing the original expression. The goal is for students to evaluate expressions using the order of operations.

Exploration 1

- **Discuss:** Ask students to recall that an *algebraic expression* is an expression that may contain numbers, operations, and one or more symbols (variables).
- ? "What are *equivalent expressions*?" Expressions that result in the same number for any values of their variables.
- When completing the table, students should use the same value for x in the third column for each expression. Encourage students to write the expression and then rewrite it with the value of the variable substituted.
- Remind students to use the order of operations and show their work.
- **Look for and Express Regularity in Repeated Reasoning:** Share the results of part (a) as a class. Ask if any conclusions can be drawn. You may need to guide students' thinking to draw conclusions about equivalent expressions.
- ? "How do you know which expressions are equivalent?" *Sample answer:* The expressions have the same values when $x = 0$, when $x = 1$, and when $x = ?$.
- Use *Popsicle Sticks* to solicit responses to part (b).
- ? Ask, "What do you think it means to simplify an expression?" Students should say that the expression has fewer terms. They should also say that variable terms have been combined and numeric terms have been combined.
- Use *Think-Pair-Share* for part (c) and to discuss the Math Practice note. Students should provide examples to support their reasoning. Ask students if they found any examples that did not work. If necessary, have students substitute 2 for x in the expressions in the Math Practice note.

C.1 Algebraic Expressions

Learning Target: Simplify algebraic expressions.

Success Criteria:
- I can identify terms and like terms of algebraic expressions.
- I can combine like terms to simplify algebraic expressions.
- I can write and simplify algebraic expressions to solve real-life problems.

EXPLORATION 1 Simplifying Algebraic Expressions

Work with a partner.

a. Choose a value of x other than 0 or 1 for the last column in the table. Complete the table by evaluating each algebraic expression for each value of x. What do you notice?

	Expression	Value When $x = 0$	Value When $x = 1$	Value When $x = ?$
A.	$-\frac{1}{3} + x + \frac{7}{3}$			
B.	$0.5x + 3 - 1.5x - 1$			
C.	$2x + 6$			
D.	$x + 4$			
E.	$-2x + 2$			
F.	$\frac{1}{2}x - x + \frac{3}{2}x + 4$			
G.	$-4.8x + 2 - x + 3.8x$			
H.	$x + 2$			
I.	$-x + 2$			
J.	$3x + 2 - x + 4$			

Math Practice

Analyze Conjectures

A student says that x and x^3 are equivalent because they have the same value when $x = -1$, $x = 0$, and $x = 1$. Explain why the student is or is not correct.

b. How can you use properties of operations to justify your answers in part (a)? Explain your reasoning.

c. To subtract a number, you can add its opposite. Does a similar rule apply to the terms of an algebraic expression? Explain your reasoning.

C.1 Lesson

Key Vocabulary
like terms, *p. 592*
simplest form, *p. 592*

In an algebraic expression, **like terms** are terms that have the same variables raised to the same exponents. Constant terms are also like terms. To identify terms and like terms in an expression, first write the expression as a sum of its terms.

EXAMPLE 1 Identifying Terms and Like Terms

Identify the terms and like terms in each expression.

a. $9x - 2 + 7 - x$

Rewrite as a sum of terms.

$$9x + (-2) + 7 + (-x)$$

Terms: $9x,\quad -2,\quad 7,\quad -x$

Like terms: $9x$ and $-x$, -2 and 7

b. $z^2 + 5z - 3z^2 + z$

Rewrite as a sum of terms.

$$z^2 + 5z + (-3z^2) + z$$

Terms: $z^2,\quad 5z,\quad -3z^2,\quad z$

Like terms: z^2 and $-3z^2$, $5z$ and z

Try It **Identify the terms and like terms in the expression.**

1. $y + 10 - \frac{3}{2}y$ **2.** $2r^2 + 7r - r^2 - 9$ **3.** $7 + 4p - 5 + p + 2q$

An algebraic expression is in **simplest form** when it has no like terms and no parentheses. To *combine* like terms that have variables, use the Distributive Property to add or subtract the coefficients.

EXAMPLE 2 Simplifying Algebraic Expressions

a. Simplify $6n - 10n$.

$6n - 10n = (6 - 10)n$ Distributive Property

$= -4n$ Subtract.

b. Simplify $-8.5w + 5.2w + w$.

$-8.5w + 5.2w + w = -8.5w + 5.2w + 1w$ Multiplication Property of 1

$= (-8.5 + 5.2 + 1)w$ Distributive Property

$= -2.3w$ Add.

Remember

The Distributive Property states
$a(b + c) = ab + ac$
and
$a(b - c) = ab - ac$.

Try It **Simplify the expression.**

4. $-10y + 15y$ **5.** $\frac{3}{8}b - \frac{3}{4}b$ **6.** $2.4g - 2.4g - 9.8g$

Laurie's Notes

Scaffolding Instruction

- Students explored simplifying algebraic expressions by evaluating two expressions for more than one value of the variable. Now students will simplify algebraic expressions by combining like terms.
- **Emerging:** Students may struggle with the idea of like terms as well as simplifying expressions. Examples 1–3 offer practice for both of these concepts. Provide guided instruction for all three examples.
- **Proficient:** Students can use like terms to simplify algebraic expressions. They should work through Example 3 before proceeding to the Self-Assessment for Concepts & Skills exercises.

Discuss

- Ask students if they have ever heard the phrase "you can't add apples and oranges." Some students may have heard this phrase in reference to needing common denominators when adding fractions. Ask how they think the phrase applies to simplifying expressions.
- Review the definition for *term*: a number or variable by itself, or a product of numbers and variables in an algebraic expression.
- **Attend to Precision:** **Like terms** are also referred to as *similar terms*. Be sure to note that in the definition of like terms, the same variables are raised to the same exponents.

EXAMPLE 1

- Terms are separated by addition. The expression $9x - 2 + 7 - x$ can be written as $9x + (-2) + 7 + (-x)$, so it has four terms. This form will help students simplify because they can see the sign associated with each term.
- **Common Error:** When identifying and writing the terms, make sure students include the sign of the term.
- Make sure students understand that the coefficient of $-x$ is -1. Similarly, the exponent of the variable in the terms $5z$ and z is 1.

Try It

- Have students use whiteboards to identify the terms. Be certain that they remember to include the sign of the term.

Teaching Strategy

When discussing the Distributive Property, students may only think of the property as being used to distribute terms: $n(5 + 3) = 5n + 3n$. Review the reverse of the process for simplifying like terms: $5n + 2n = n(5 + 2)$.

EXAMPLE 2

- Discuss: **simplest form**, coefficient, constant terms, and combining like terms.
- **Teaching Strategy:** Discuss the Remember note.
- Ask students to identify the coefficient of each term and any constant terms.
- Have students show the step that uses the Distributive Property until they become proficient in combing like terms.

Extra Example 1

Identify the terms and like terms in each expression.

a. $3y - 2 - 4y + 6$
Terms: $3y, -2, -4y, 6$
Like terms: $3y$ and $-4y$, -2 and 6

b. $w + 5w^2 + 2w^2 - 7w$
Terms: $w, 5w^2, 2w^2, -7w$
Like terms: w and $-7w$, $5w^2$ and $2w^2$

ELL Support

After demonstrating Example 1, have students practice language by working in pairs to complete Try It Exercises 1–3. Have one student ask another, "What are the terms in the expression? the like terms?" Have students alternate roles.

Beginner: Name the terms.

Intermediate/Advanced: Answer with sentences. For example, "The terms are y, 10, and $-\frac{3}{2}y$. The like terms are y and $-\frac{3}{2}y$."

Try It

1. Terms: $y, 10, -\frac{3}{2}y$; Like terms: y and $-\frac{3}{2}y$
2. Terms: $2r^2, 7r, -r^2, -9$; Like terms: $2r^2$ and $-r^2$
3. Terms: $7, 4p, -5, p, 2q$; Like terms: 7 and -5, $4p$ and p

Extra Example 2

a. Simplify $4y - 12y$. $-8y$

b. Simplify $-3.7h + h - 13.5h$. $-16.2h$

Try It

4. $5y$
5. $-\frac{3}{8}b$
6. $-9.8g$

Laurie's Notes

Extra Example 3

a. Simplify $8u + 5u - 7u$. $6u$

b. Simplify $6d - 5 - 4d + 6$. $2d + 1$

Try It

7. $-2z + 22$

8. $6.8x - 5$

9. $-7s + 7t$

Self-Assessment
for Concepts & Skills

10. Terms of an expression are separated by addition. Rewrite the expression as $3y + (-4) + (-5y)$. The terms in the expression are $3y$, -4, and $-5y$. Like terms of an expression have the same variables raised to the same exponents. The like terms in the expression are $3y$ and $-5y$.

11. $13p$

12. $\frac{3}{2}n - 3$

13. $-5w + 2g$

14. no; The like terms $3x$ and $2x$ should be combined.

$$3x + 2x - 4 = (3 + 2)x - 4$$
$$= 5x - 4$$

15. $5x - 10 - 2x$; *Sample answer:* All other expressions simplify to $3x + 2$.

EXAMPLE 3

- Remind students about the Commutative Property.
- Demonstrate how completing one step at a time helps organize work and prevent errors.
- In part (a), students may ask if $\frac{1}{4}y + 6$ can be written as $6 + \frac{1}{4}y$. Tell them that both expressions are correct, but $\frac{1}{4}y + 6$ is more common. Caution students that when rearranging terms, they must move the signs with their corresponding terms. In part (b), $-8y + 13z$ can be written as $13z - 8y$, but not $-13z + 8y$.

Try It

- Students should write the original expression followed by each step in the simplifying process and the justification for each step.
- **Neighbor Check:** Have students work independently and then have their neighbors check their work. Have students discuss any discrepancies.
- Prepare index cards ahead of time each with a different term. Examples: $2x$, $-3x$, $4y$, 6, -7, etc. Make sure there is one card for each student. Randomly distribute the cards. Ask students to gather the like terms together in different areas of the room. Then have each group simplify their "expression" by combining the like terms.

Self-Assessment for Concepts & Skills

- Have students use *Think-Pair-Share* to complete the exercises. Each partner should have an opportunity to share their thinking before you ask a few students to share with the class.
- Students have progressed through the first two success criteria. Have students use *Thumps Up* to indicate their understanding of each success criterion.

ELL Support

Use the instructions provided in Laurie's Notes to allow students to work in pairs and practice language. Have each pair write their answer to Exercises 11–15 on a whiteboard for your review. Have two pairs form a group to discuss explanations for Exercises 10, 14, and 15. Monitor discussions and provide support as needed.

The Success Criteria Self-Assessment chart can be found in the *Student Journal* or online at *BigIdeasMath.com.*

EXAMPLE 3 Simplifying Algebraic Expressions

a. Simplify $\frac{3}{4}y + 12 - \frac{1}{2}y - 6$.

$$\frac{3}{4}y + 12 - \frac{1}{2}y - 6 = \frac{3}{4}y + 12 + \left(-\frac{1}{2}y\right) + (-6)$$ Rewrite as a sum.

$$= \frac{3}{4}y + \left(-\frac{1}{2}y\right) + 12 + (-6)$$ Commutative Property of Addition

$$= \left[\frac{3}{4} + \left(-\frac{1}{2}\right)\right]y + 12 + (-6)$$ Distributive Property

$$= \frac{1}{4}y + 6$$ Combine like terms.

b. Simplify $-3y - 5y + 4z + 9z$.

$$-3y - 5y + 4z + 9z = (-3 - 5)y + (4 + 9)z$$ Distributive Property

$$= -8y + 13z$$ Simplify.

Try It **Simplify the expression.**

7. $14 - 3z + 8 + z$

8. $2.5x + 4.3x - 5$

9. $2s - 9s + 8t - t$

Self-Assessment for Concepts & Skills

Solve each exercise. Then rate your understanding of the success criteria in your journal.

10. **WRITING** Explain how to identify the terms and like terms of $3y - 4 - 5y$.

SIMPLIFYING ALGEBRAIC EXPRESSIONS **Simplify the expression.**

11. $7p + 6p$

12. $\frac{4}{5}n - 3 + \frac{7}{10}n$

13. $2w - g - 7w + 3g$

14. **VOCABULARY** Is the expression $3x + 2x - 4$ in simplest form? Explain.

15. **WHICH ONE DOESN'T BELONG?** Which expression does *not* belong with the other three? Explain your reasoning.

$-4 + 6 + 3x$	$3x + 9 - 7$
$5x - 10 - 2x$	$5x - 4 + 6 - 2x$

EXAMPLE 4 Modeling Real Life

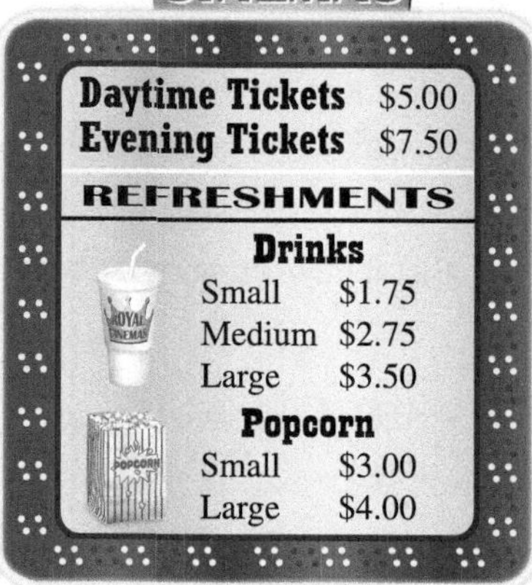

ROYAL CINEMAS
Daytime Tickets $5.00
Evening Tickets $7.50
REFRESHMENTS
Drinks
Small $1.75
Medium $2.75
Large $3.50
Popcorn
Small $3.00
Large $4.00

Each person in a group buys an evening ticket, a medium drink, and a large popcorn. How much does the group pay when there are 5 people in the group?

Write an expression that represents the sum of the costs of the items purchased. Use a verbal model.

Verbal Model	Number of tickets	•	Cost per ticket	+	Number of medium drinks	•	Cost per medium drink	+	Number of large popcorns	•	Cost per large popcorn

Variable The same number of each item is purchased. So, x can represent the number of tickets, the number of medium drinks, and the number of large popcorns.

Expression $7.50x \quad + \quad 2.75x \quad + \quad 4x$

$$7.50x + 2.75x + 4x = (7.50 + 2.75 + 4)x \qquad \text{Distributive Property}$$

$$= 14.25x \qquad \text{Add coefficients.}$$

The expression $14.25x$ indicates that the cost per person is \$14.25. To find the cost for a group of 5 people, evaluate the expression when $x = 5$.

$$14.25(5) = 71.25$$

▶ The total cost for a group of 5 people is \$71.25.

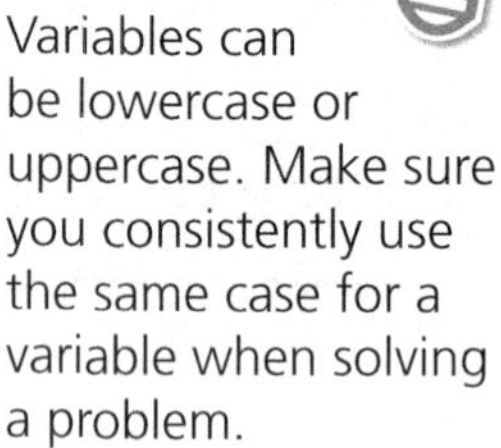

Remember

Variables can be lowercase or uppercase. Make sure you consistently use the same case for a variable when solving a problem.

Self-Assessment for Problem Solving

Solve each exercise. Then rate your understanding of the success criteria in your journal.

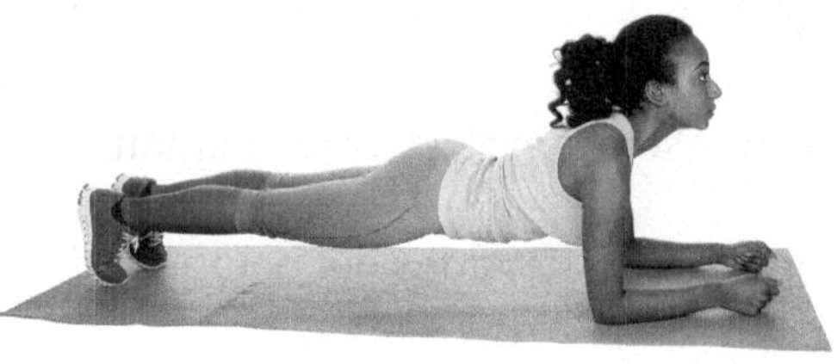

16. **MP MODELING REAL LIFE** An exercise mat is 3.3 times as long as it is wide. Write expressions in simplest form that represent the perimeter and the area of the exercise mat.

17. **DIG DEEPER!** A group of friends visits the movie theater in Example 4. Each person buys a daytime ticket and a small drink. The group buys 1 large popcorn for every 2 people in the group. What is the average cost per person when there are 4 people in the group?

Laurie's Notes

EXAMPLE 4

- Discuss the information in the picture. You might ask how these prices compare to the prices at a local movie theater.
- **Model with Mathematics:** In this example, students write an algebraic expression that models a real-life situation. Ask students to identify what the variable represents in the problem. Do not skip this step!
- Discuss the Remember note. Remind students that they have seen capital letters as variables before. A variable is just a symbol that represents a value and it can be lowercase or uppercase, as long as you are consistent! Just avoid any letter that can be confused with a number (e.g., O, I).
- **Note:** In the Dynamic Assessment System, variable entry is case sensitive.

? **Extension:** "What would the total cost be for a group of 4 people?" $57

Self-Assessment for Problem Solving

- The goal for all students is to feel comfortable with the problem-solving plan. It is important for students to problem-solve in class, where they may receive support from you and their peers. Keep in mind that some students may only be ready for the first step.
- Have students work independently. Allow enough time for students to write a verbal model and an expression for each problem. When students have completed the exercises, place students into groups of four to discuss their solutions and reach a consensus.
- If time permits, select two groups to share their verbal models for one of each of the problems. Select another two groups to simplify the expressions. Be certain to select groups that you know have done the work correctly.

The Success Criteria Self-Assessment chart can be found in the *Student Journal* or online at *BigIdeasMath.com*.

Closure

- **Exit Ticket:** Which of the following expressions simplify to $3x + 4$? If the expression does not simplify to $3x + 4$, write its simplified form.

A. $-6 + 3x + 10$ **B.** $3(x + 4)$

C. $2x + 8 + x - 2$ **D.** $-5x + 4 + 8x$

A and D; B: $3x + 12$, C: $3x + 6$

Extra Example 4

Each person in Example 4 buys an evening ticket, a small drink, and a small popcorn. How much does the group of 5 people pay? $61.25

Self-Assessment for Problem Solving

16. perimeter: $8.6w$
area: $3.3w^2$

17. $8.75

Learning Target

Simplify algebraic expressions.

Success Criteria

- Identify terms and like terms of algebraic expressions.
- Combine like terms to simplify algebraic expressions.
- Write and simplify algebraic expressions to solve real-life problems.

Review & Refresh

1. $-\frac{1}{2}$
2. $\frac{3}{5}$
3. $-6\frac{1}{2}$
4. $\frac{3}{4}$, 78%, 0.85, 87%, $\frac{7}{8}$
5. 15%, 1450%, 14.8, $15\frac{4}{5}$
6. C

Concepts, Skills, & Problem Solving

7. no; Expression 2 simplifies to $-5x$.
8. yes; Expression 1 simplifies to $2x + 1$.
9. Terms: t, 8, $3t$;
Like terms: t and $3t$
10. Terms: $3z$, 4, 2, $4z$;
Like terms: $3z$ and $4z$, 4 and 2
11. Terms: $2n$, $-n$, -4, $7n$;
Like terms: $2n$, $-n$ and $7n$
12. Terms: $-x$, $-9x^2$, $12x^2$, 7;
Like terms: $-9x^2$ and $12x^2$
13. Terms: $1.4y$, 5, -4.2, $-5y^2$, z;
Like terms: 5 and -4.2
14. Terms: $\frac{1}{2}s$, -4, $\frac{3}{4}s$, $\frac{1}{8}$, $-s^3$;
Like terms: $\frac{1}{2}s$ and $\frac{3}{4}s$, -4 and $\frac{1}{8}$
15. no; The terms are $3x$, -5, $-2x$, and $9x$ and the like terms are $3x$, $-2x$, and $9x$.
16. $21g$
17. $11x + 2$
18. $3s$
19. $4b - 5$
20. $-31p$
21. $-2.3v - 5$
22. $14.2 - 5a$
23. $3 - \frac{1}{2}y$
24. $13\frac{1}{3}c - 1\frac{1}{2}$

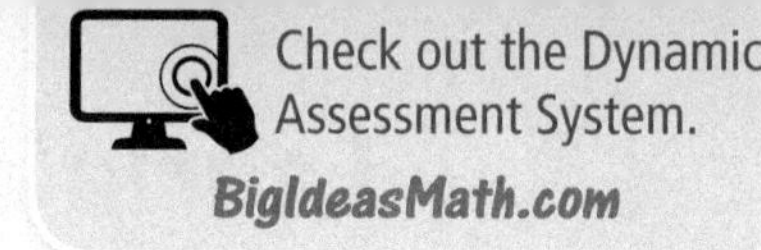
Check out the Dynamic Assessment System.
BigIdeasMath.com

Assignment Guide and Concept Check

Scaffold assignments to support all students in their learning progression. The suggested assignments are a starting point. Continue to assign additional exercises and revisit with spaced practice to move every student toward proficiency.

Level	Assignment 1	Assignment 2
Emerging	3, 5, 6, 7, 9, 11, 15, 16, 17, 19	8, 10, 12, 20, 21, 23, 25, 26, 29
Proficient	3, 5, 6, 8, 10, 12, 15, 16, 18, 19	14, 21, 24, 25, 26, 27, 28, 30
Advanced	3, 5, 6, 8, 12, 14, 15, 20, 22, 24	25, 26, 27, 28, 29, 30, 31, 32

- Assignment 1 is for use after students complete the Self-Assessment for Concepts & Skills.
- Assignment 2 is for use after students complete the Self-Assessment for Problem Solving.
- The red exercises can be used as a concept check.

Review & Refresh Prior Skills

Exercises 1 and 2 Multiplying Fractions
Exercise 3 Dividing with Mixed Numbers
Exercises 4 and 5 Ordering Numbers
Exercise 6 Converting Measures and Subtracting Integers

Common Errors

- **Exercises 11–14** When identifying and writing terms, make sure students include the sign of the term. Students may find it helpful to write the original problem using addition. For example, $2n - n - 4 + 7n = 2n + (-n) + (-4) + 7n$.
- **Exercises 12–14** Students may confuse like variables with like terms. Remind students that the same variables must be raised to the same exponents for terms to be like terms. The terms $-x$ and $-9x^2$ are not like terms because one has an exponent of 1 and the other has an exponent of 2.
- **Exercises 21–24** The subtraction operation can confuse students. It is not obvious to them why it is okay to rewrite $4.2v - 5 - 6.5v$ as $4.2v - 6.5v - 5$. Tell students to write the original problem using addition and then use the Commutative Property.

$$\begin{aligned}4.2v - 5 - 6.5v &= 4.2v + (-5) + (-6.5v)\\ &= 4.2v + (-6.5v) + (-5)\\ &= 4.2v - 6.5v - 5\\ &= -2.3v - 5\end{aligned}$$

C.1 Practice

Go to **BigIdeasMath.com** to get HELP with solving the exercises.

Review & Refresh

Find the product or quotient. Write fractions in simplest form.

1. $-\frac{2}{7} \times \frac{7}{4}$

2. $-\frac{2}{3}\left(-\frac{9}{10}\right)$

3. $1\frac{4}{9} \div \left(-\frac{2}{9}\right)$

Order the numbers from least to greatest.

4. $\frac{7}{8}$, 0.85, 87%, $\frac{3}{4}$, 78%

5. 15%, 14.8, $15\frac{4}{5}$, 1450%

6. A bird's nest is 12 feet above the ground. A mole's den is 12 inches below the ground. What is the difference in height of these two positions?

A. 24 in. **B.** 11 ft **C.** 13 ft **D.** 24 ft

Concepts, Skills, & Problem Solving

MP REASONING Determine whether the expressions are equivalent. Explain your reasoning. (See Exploration 1, p. 591.)

7.

Expression 1	$3 - 5x$
Expression 2	$4.25 - 5x - 4.25$

8.

Expression 1	$1.25x + 4 + 0.75x - 3$
Expression 2	$2x + 1$

IDENTIFYING TERMS AND LIKE TERMS Identify the terms and like terms in the expression.

9. $t + 8 + 3t$

10. $3z + 4 + 2 + 4z$

11. $2n - n - 4 + 7n$

12. $-x - 9x^2 + 12x^2 + 7$

13. $1.4y + 5 - 4.2 - 5y^2 + z$

14. $\frac{1}{2}s - 4 + \frac{3}{4}s + \frac{1}{8} - s^3$

15. **MP YOU BE THE TEACHER** Your friend identifies the terms and like terms in the expression $3x - 5 - 2x + 9x$. Is your friend correct? Explain your reasoning.

$3x - 5 - 2x + 9x$

Terms: $3x$, 5, $2x$, and $9x$

Like Terms: $3x$, $2x$, and $9x$

SIMPLIFYING ALGEBRAIC EXPRESSIONS Simplify the expression.

16. $12g + 9g$

17. $11x + 9 - 7$

18. $8s - 11s + 6s$

19. $4b - 24 + 19$

20. $4p - 5p - 30p$

21. $4.2v - 5 - 6.5v$

22. $8 + 4a + 6.2 - 9a$

23. $\frac{2}{5}y - 4 + 7 - \frac{9}{10}y$

24. $-\frac{2}{3}c - \frac{9}{5} + 14c + \frac{3}{10}$

25. **MP MODELING REAL LIFE** On a hike, each hiker carries the items shown. Write and interpret an expression in simplest form that represents the weight carried by x hikers. How much total weight is carried when there are 4 hikers?

26. **MP STRUCTURE** Evaluate the expression $-8x + 5 - 2x - 4 + 5x$ when $x = 2$ before and after simplifying. Which method do you prefer? Explain.

27. **OPEN-ENDED** Write an expression with five different terms that is equivalent to $8x^2 + 3x^2 + 3y$. Justify your answer.

28. **MP STRUCTURE** Which of the following shows a correct way of simplifying $6 + (3 - 5x)$? Explain the errors made in the other choices.

A. $6 + (3 - 5x) = (6 + 3 - 5)x = 4x$

B. $6 + (3 - 5x) = 6 + (3 - 5)x = 6 + (-2)x = 6 - 2x$

C. $6 + (3 - 5x) = (6 + 3) - 5x = 9 - 5x$

D. $6 + (3 - 5x) = (6 + 3 + 5) - x = 14 - x$

29. **MP PRECISION** Two comets orbit the Sun. One comet travels 30,000 miles per hour and the other comet travels 28,500 miles per hour. What is the most efficient way to calculate the difference of the distances traveled by the comets for any given number of minutes? Justify your answer.

	Car	Truck
Wash	\$8	\$10
Wax	\$12	\$15

30. **MP MODELING REAL LIFE** Find the earnings for washing and waxing 12 cars and 8 trucks. Justify your answer.

31. **CRITICAL THINKING** You apply gold foil to a piece of red poster board to make the design shown.

   a. Find the area of the gold foil when $x = 3$. Justify your answer.

   b. The pattern at the right is called "St. George's Cross." Find a country that uses this pattern as its flag.

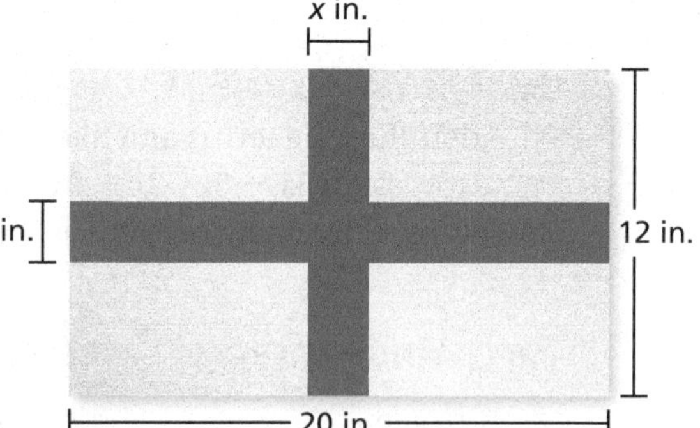

32. **GEOMETRY** Two rectangles have different dimensions. Each rectangle has a perimeter of $(7x + 5)$ inches. Draw and label diagrams that represent possible dimensions of the rectangles.

Mini-Assessment

Identify the terms and like terms in the expression.

1. $4r + 2 - 6 + 3r$
   Terms: $4r$, 2, -6, $3r$
   Like terms: $4r$ and $3r$, 2 and -6

2. $5h^2 - 3h^2 - 4h + 3h + 7$
   Terms: $5h^2$, $-3h^2$, $-4h$, $3h$, 7
   Like terms: $5h^2$ and $-3h^2$, $-4h$ and $3h$

Simplify the expression.

3. $6m + 7 - 3m - 1$ $3m + 6$

4. $9.7 - 4.2g + 2.1 + 7.4g$ $3.2g + 11.8$

5. Find the perimeter of the polygon.

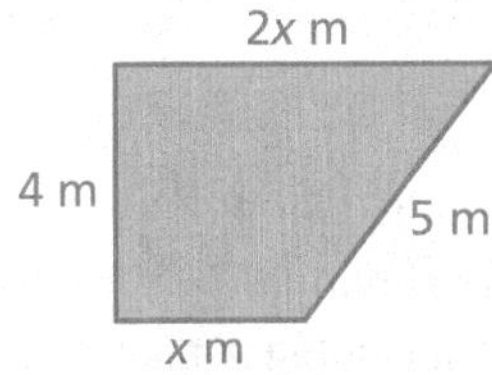

$(3x + 9)$ meters

Section Resources

Surface Level	Deep Level
Resources by Chapter • Extra Practice • Reteach • Puzzle Time Student Journal • Self-Assessment • Practice Differentiating the Lesson Tutorial Videos Skills Review Handbook Skills Trainer	Resources by Chapter • Enrichment and Extension Graphic Organizers Dynamic Assessment System • Section Practice

Concepts, Skills, & Problem Solving

25. $10.2x$; each hiker carries 10.2 pounds of equipment; 40.8 lbs

26. -9; -9; *Sample answer:* Simplifying the expression first is easier because you only have to substitute once instead of substituting three times.

27. *Sample answer:*
$15x^2 - 6x^2 + 2x^2 + 2y + y$;
$$15x^2 - 6x^2 + 2x^2 + 2y + y = [15x^2 + (-6x^2) + 2x^2] + (2y + y) = 11x^2 + 3y,$$
and $8x^2 + 3x^2 + 3y = 11x^2 + 3y$

28. C;

    A. Incorrectly factored an x from every term: $6 + (3 - 5x) \neq (6 + 3 - 5)x$

    B. Incorrectly factored an x from $(3 - 5x)$

    D. Incorrectly added like terms: $6 + (3 - 5x) \neq (6 + 3 + 5) - x$

29. Find the difference of the two distances. Divide the difference by 60 minutes to determine the distance per minute. This difference of the distances traveled in miles per minute can be multiplied by the number of minutes to find the difference of the distances traveled.

30. \$440; 12 cars: $12(8 + 12) = \$240$
8 trucks: $8(10 + 15) = \$200$

31. **a.** 153 in.^{2};
$$\text{Area} = 240 - 32x + x^2 = 240 - 32(3) + 3^2 = 240 - 96 + 9 = 153 \text{ in.}^2$$

    b. *Sample answer:* England

32. See Additional Answers.

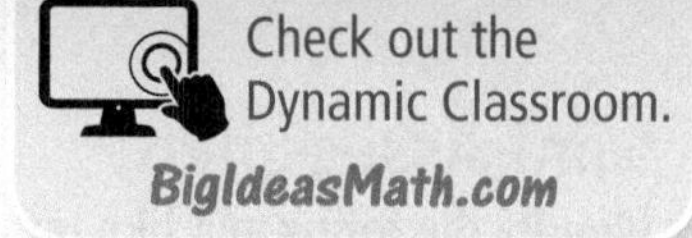
Check out the
Dynamic Classroom.
BigIdeasMath.com

Learning Target

Find sums and differences of linear expressions.

Success Criteria

- Explain the difference between linear and nonlinear expressions.
- Find opposites of terms that include variables.
- Apply properties of operations to add and subtract linear expressions.

Warm Up

Cumulative, vocabulary, and prerequisite skills practice opportunities are available in the *Resources by Chapter* or at *BigIdeasMath.com.*

ELL Support

The word *linear* has related meanings in everyday language and in math. When something is *linear*, it means that it proceeds in a straight line. It may be used literally or figuratively. For example, if someone has linear thinking, he or she thinks in one straight direction. In math, however, a linear expression is an algebraic expression in which the exponent of each variable is 1.

Exploration 1

a. *Sample answer:* By having the same number of positive and negative variable tiles and the same number of positive and negative number tiles, the sum of these values would equal 0.

b–c. See Additional Answers.

Exploration 2

a. See Additional Answers.

b. See Additional Answers.

Laurie's Notes

Preparing to Teach

- **Reason Abstractly and Quantitatively:** Algebra tiles help students make sense of algebraic expressions by modeling them and finding sums and differences. Algebra tiles are a concrete representation, deepening student understanding of the meaning of each expression.

Motivate

- **FYI:** Show students a collection of yellow integer-tiles and one green variable-tile. Define the yellow integer-tile as having dimensions 1 by 1 with an area of 1 square unit and the variable-tile as having dimensions 1 by x with an area of x square units. Algebra tiles are available at *BigIdeasMath.com* and they are also available commercially. Be sure to point out to students that the variable-tile is *not* an integral length, meaning you should not be able to *measure* the length of the variable-tile by lining up yellow integer-tiles. The length of the tile is a variable—x!
- Display a collection of tiles. For example, 1 variable-tile, 3 yellow integer-tiles (+3), and 2 red integer-tiles (−2). Say, "These algebra tiles represent an algebraic expression and just as you simplify algebraic expressions, you are going to simplify expressions modeled by the algebra tiles."

Exploration 1

- **Management Tip:** Distribute a set of algebra tiles to each pair of students. Presort them in baggies for easy distribution and collection.
- Even though the tiles are shown, encourage students to make the display with their own algebra tiles.
- For each addition model in part (b), have one partner make the first expression and the other partner make the second expression. Then have partners combine their tiles in the common work space and simplify by removing any zero pairs. To subtract, students begin by representing the first expression in the common work space and then find the difference by removing the tiles in the second expression from the first expression. For the last model, students will need to add zero pairs to subtract the expressions.
- **Reason Abstractly and Quantitatively:** Handling the tiles helps students understand that $x + x + x = 3x$ and *not* x^3. Students who have worked with algebra tiles should not make that mistake.

? Some students may write expressions that represent each algebra tile, such as $x + 1 + 1 + 1 + 1 + 1 + x + x - 1 - 1 - 1$ for the first model in part (b). Ask, "Is your expression in simplest form? If not, how can you write it in simplest form?" no; $3x + 2$

- Ask volunteers to explain how they used the tiles to simplify and share their results.

Exploration 2

- Remind students that any letter or symbol can be used to represent a variable.
- Have students use *Paired Verbal Fluency* for each part. This will give each partner the opportunity to express his or her ideas.

C.2 Adding and Subtracting Linear Expressions

Learning Target: Find sums and differences of linear expressions.

Success Criteria:
- I can explain the difference between linear and nonlinear expressions.
- I can find opposites of terms that include variables.
- I can apply properties of operations to add and subtract linear expressions.

EXPLORATION 1 Using Algebra Tiles

+ = +1
− = −1
+ = variable
− = −variable

Work with a partner. You can use the algebra tiles shown at the left to find sums and differences of algebraic expressions.

a. How can you use algebra tiles to model a sum of terms that equals 0? Explain your reasoning.

b. Write each sum or difference modeled below. Then use the algebra tiles to simplify the expression.

Math Practice

Consider Similar Problems

How is using integer counters to find sums and differences of integers similar to using algebra tiles to find sums and differences of algebraic expressions?

c. Write two algebraic expressions of the form $ax + b$, where a and b are rational numbers. Find the sum and difference of the expressions.

EXPLORATION 2 Using Properties of Operations

Work with a partner.

a. Do algebraic expressions, such as $2x$, $-3y$, and $3z + 1$ have additive inverses? How do you know?

b. How can you find the sums and differences modeled in Exploration 1 without using algebra tiles? Explain your reasoning.

C.2 Lesson

Key Vocabulary
linear expression, p. 598

A **linear expression** is an algebraic expression in which the exponent of each variable is 1.

Linear Expressions	$-4x$	$3x + 5y$	$5 - \frac{1}{6}x$
Nonlinear Expressions	$\frac{1}{2}x^2$	$-7x^3 + x$	$x^5 + 1$

You can use either a vertical or a horizontal method to add linear expressions.

EXAMPLE 1 Adding Linear Expressions

Find each sum.

a. $(x - 2) + (3x + 8)$

Vertical method: Align like terms vertically and add.

$$\begin{array}{r} x - 2 \\ + \; 3x + 8 \\ \hline 4x + 6 \end{array}$$

Linear expressions are usually written with the variable term first.

The sum is $4x + 6$.

b. $(-4y + 3) + (11y - 5)$

Horizontal method: Use properties of operations to group like terms and simplify.

$(-4y + 3) + (11y - 5) = -4y + 3 + 11y - 5$ Rewrite the sum.

$= -4y + 11y + 3 - 5$ Commutative Property of Addition

$= (-4y + 11y) + (3 - 5)$ Group like terms.

$= 7y - 2$ Combine like terms.

The sum is $7y - 2$.

Try It **Find the sum.**

1. $(x + 3) + (2x - 1)$

2. $(-8z + 4) + (8z - 7)$

3. $(4.5 - n) + (-10n + 6.5)$

4. $\left(\frac{1}{2}w - 3\right) + \left(\frac{1}{4}w + 3\right)$

Multi-Language Glossary at BigIdeasMath.com

Laurie's Notes

Scaffolding Instruction

- Students have used algebra tiles to develop an understanding of how to add and subtract algebraic expressions.
- **Emerging:** Students may struggle with the concept of adding zero pairs to subtract or with the idea that $1x = x$. These students may benefit from using algebra tiles and the vertical method for adding and subtracting linear expressions. Review the definition of linear expressions and provide guided instruction for Examples 1 and 2.
- **Proficient:** Students are able to add and subtract algebraic expressions with and without algebra tiles. These students should work with a partner to discuss the definition of a linear expression and a nonlinear expression before proceeding to the Self-Assessment exercises.

Discuss

- Discuss the definition of a **linear expression**.

? "What is the difference between linear and nonlinear expressions?" In a linear expression, the exponent of each variable is 1. A nonlinear expression contains a variable with an exponent other than 1.

- Remind students that they can use algebra tiles to simplify expressions, such as $3z - 2z = 1z$, or z. Also, remind students of using zero pairs to subtract. For example,

$$\begin{aligned}(-2x + 5) - (x - 1) &= (-2x + (-x + x) + 5 + (1 + (-1))) - (x - 1)\\ &= -3x + 6.\end{aligned}$$

? "When are zero pairs useful?" *Sample answer:* When you are subtracting a greater number from a lesser number.

EXAMPLE 1

- **Connection:** When you add (or subtract) whole numbers, you use the place values of the numbers. The same is true when you add (or subtract) decimals—lining up the decimal points assures that this happens. Lining up place values is similar to lining up like terms. Make this connection for students as you begin to work through these problems.
- Using the vertical method, students should see the connection to adding two whole numbers.
- **Teaching Tip:** Before adding, rewrite $x - 2$ as $x + (-2)$.
- In part (b), the Commutative Property of Addition is used to change the order of the terms so that like terms are adjacent to each other.
- **Note:** In this section, the Distributive Property step is not shown when combining like terms.

Try It

- Each student should work independently before sharing with a partner. Allow students to use algebra tiles if needed. Select four pairs to share their work for one of each of the exercises. Choose pairs that you know have completed the exercises correctly.

Scaffold instruction to support all students in their learning. Learning is individualized and you may want to group students differently as they move in and out of these levels with each skill and concept. Student self-assessment and feedback help guide your instructional decisions about how and when to layer support for all students to become proficient learners.

Extra Example 1

Find each sum.

a. $(-2x + 2) + (4x - 7)$ $2x - 5$

b. $(7y - 5) + (3y + 8)$ $10y + 3$

ELL Support

After demonstrating Example 1, have students practice language by working in groups to complete Try It Exercises 1–4. Provide guiding questions for discussion: How do you begin the vertical method? What are the steps of the horizontal method? Expect students to perform as described.

Beginner: State sum and write the steps.

Intermediate: Use simple sentences to answer the guiding questions.

Advanced: Use detailed sentences to answer the guiding questions and help guide discussion.

Try It

1. $3x + 2$
2. -3
3. $-11n + 11$
4. $\frac{3}{4}w$

Extra Example 2

Find each difference.

a. $(-3x + 7) - (4x - 8)$ $-7x + 15$

b. $(-6y + 18) - (-5y + 4)$ $-y + 14$

Try It

5. $2m - 15$

6. $-8.3c - 15$

Self-Assessment for Concepts & Skills

7. *Sample answer:* All variables in a linear expression have an exponent of 1, while some variables in a nonlinear expression have exponents greater than or less than 1. linear: $3x + 2$; nonlinear: $2x^2 + 3x + 1$

8. What is x more than $3x - 1$?; $4x - 1$; $2x - 1$

Laurie's Notes

EXAMPLE 2

? "How do you think you should subtract linear expressions?" Subtract like terms.

? Write part (a) and ask, "Can you subtract the quantity $(-x + 6)$ by removing the parentheses?" No, you must subtract each term in the linear expression. So, you add the opposite.

- *Add the opposite of the expression* means to add the opposite of each term in the expression. Students often forget to distribute the negative sign.
- My experience is that students make more errors when subtracting linear expressions using the vertical method, unless they take the time to rewrite the problem as shown where *adding the opposite* is obvious.
- **Reason Abstractly and Quantitatively:** It may be helpful to rewrite $(5x + 6) - (-x + 6)$ as $(5x + 6) + [-(-x + 6)]$ and then $(5x + 6) + (-1)(-x + 6)$. This is the Multiplication Property of -1.

? "Do you prefer the vertical or horizontal method? Why?" Answers will vary.

Try It

- Remind students that it is important to subtract each term in the second expression.
- Have students use *Think-Pair-Share* to complete the exercises.

Self-Assessment for Concepts & Skills

- Students should work independently on the exercises.
- Discuss students' descriptions in Exercise 7. Then draw a vertical line on the middle of your board. On the left side write *Nonlinear* and on the right side write *Linear*. Ask students to go to the board and write an appropriate expression on each side. Discuss any discrepancies.

ELL Support

Allow students to work in groups to practice language as they discuss the exercises. After each group has answered both questions and constructed their explanations, have them present their answers to another group. The two groups must reach agreement if their ideas differ. Monitor discussions and provide support.

The Success Criteria Self-Assessment chart can be found in the *Student Journal* or online at *BigIdeasMath.com*.

To subtract one linear expression from another, add the opposite of each term in the expression. You can use a vertical or a horizontal method.

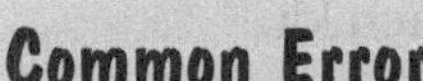

EXAMPLE 2 Subtracting Linear Expressions

Find each difference.

a. $(5x+6)-(-x+6)$

Vertical method: Align like terms vertically and subtract.

$$\begin{array}{r} (5x+6) \\ -\ (-x+6) \\ \hline \end{array} \quad \text{Add the opposite.} \quad \begin{array}{r} 5x+6 \\ +\quad x-6 \\ \hline 6x \end{array}$$

The difference is $6x$.

Common Error

When subtracting an expression, make sure you add the opposite of each term in the expression, not just the first term.

b. $(7y+5)-(8y-6)$

Horizontal method: Use properties of operations to group like terms and simplify.

$(7y+5)-(8y-6) = (7y+5)+(-8y+6)$ Add the opposite.

$= 7y+(-8y)+5+6$ Commutative Property of Addition

$= [7y+(-8y)]+(5+6)$ Group like terms.

$= -y+11$ Combine like terms.

The difference is $-y+11$.

Try It **Find the difference.**

5. $(m-3)-(-m+12)$

6. $(-2c+5)-(6.3c+20)$

Self-Assessment for Concepts & Skills

Solve each exercise. Then rate your understanding of the success criteria in your journal.

7. WRITING Describe how to distinguish a linear expression from a nonlinear expression. Give an example of each.

8. DIFFERENT WORDS, SAME QUESTION Which is different? Find "both" answers.

What is x more than $3x-1$?	Find $3x-1$ decreased by x.
What is the difference of $3x-1$ and x?	Subtract $(x+1)$ from $3x$.

EXAMPLE 3 Modeling Real Life

Skateboard kits cost d dollars and you have a coupon for \$2 off each one you buy. After assembly, you sell each skateboard for $(2d - 4)$ dollars. Find and interpret your profit on each skateboard sold.

Understand the problem.

You are given information about purchasing skateboard kits and selling the assembled skateboards. You are asked to find and interpret the profit made on each skateboard sold.

Make a plan.

Find the difference of the expressions representing the selling price and the purchase price. Then simplify and interpret the expression.

Solve and check.

You receive \$2 off of d dollars, so you pay $(d - 2)$ dollars for each kit.

Profit (dollars) = Selling price (dollars) − Purchase price (dollars)

$= (2d - 4) - (d - 2)$ Write the difference.

$= (2d - 4) + (-d + 2)$ Add the opposite.

$= 2d - d - 4 + 2$ Group like terms.

$= d - 2$ Combine like terms.

Your profit on each skateboard sold is $(d - 2)$ dollars. You pay $(d - 2)$ dollars for each kit, so you are doubling your money.

Look Back Assume each kit is \$40. Verify that you double your money.

When $d = 40$: You pay $d - 2 = 40 - 2 = \$38$.

You sell it for $2d - 4 = 2(40) - 4 = 80 - 4 = \$76$.

Because $\$38 \cdot 2 = \$76$, you double your money. ✓

Self-Assessment for Problem Solving

Solve each exercise. Then rate your understanding of the success criteria in your journal.

9. **DIG DEEPER!** In a basketball game, the home team scores $(2m + 39)$ points and the away team scores $(3m + 40)$ points, where m is the number of minutes since halftime. Who wins the game? What is the difference in the scores m minutes after halftime? Explain.

10. Electric guitar kits originally cost d dollars online. You buy the kits on sale for 50% of the original price, plus a shipping fee of \$4.50 per kit. After painting and assembly, you sell each guitar online for $(1.5d + 4.5)$ dollars. Find and interpret your profit on each guitar sold.

Laurie's Notes

EXAMPLE 3

- Have a quick discussion about how to calculate the profit when buying something and reselling it.
- Ask a volunteer to read the problem. Remind students that the variable d is unknown and they are not writing an expression for the selling price.
- Ask volunteers to explain what the problem is about. Do not let them just re-read the problem. Encourage students to describe it in their own words.
- ? "How is the value of the coupon used?" It is subtracted from the original price.
- ? Ask students to make a plan. "What operation will you use?" subtraction
- Write the verbal model and substitute the linear expressions.
- ? "This is a subtraction problem. What is the next step?" Add the opposite.
- ? "If you pay $(d - 2)$ dollars for an item and earn $(d - 2)$ dollars back, what does this mean?" Your profit on each item sold is $(d - 2)$ dollars. If students are having difficulty, substitute a value for d, such as \$20, and then explain.

Formative Assessment Tip

Partner Speaks

This strategy provides the opportunity for students to share their thinking about a problem or concept. Pair students and ask one person to speak. When the speaker is finished, the listener asks for clarification or gives feedback. Then the listener shares this thinking with the whole class. Thinking through a problem with a partner is less intimidating for many students than sharing it with an entire class. For the listener, he or she needs to pay attention to the thoughts of the speaker and set aside his or her own thinking about the problem. As students are engaged in dialogue, circulate to hear the discussion and gain an understanding of how students are thinking about the problem or concept. *Partner Speaks* should not be used for simple, less challenging problems.

Self-Assessment for Problem Solving

- Encourage students to use a Four Square to complete these exercises. Until students become comfortable with the problem-solving plan, they may only be ready to complete the first square.
- **Partner Speaks:** After students have had time to complete the exercises, pair students. One partner should speak about his or her solution method for Exercise 9. Then the listener asks for clarification or gives feedback. Ask the listener to describe the solution method used by his or her partner. Partners should reverse roles for Exercise 10.

The Success Criteria Self-Assessment chart can be found in the *Student Journal* or online at *BigIdeasMath.com*.

Closure

- **Exit Ticket:** Find the sum or difference.

  a. $(6x - 8) + (2x - 5)$ $8x - 13$

  b. $(6x - 8) - (2x - 5)$ $4x - 3$

Extra Example 3

The original price of a coffee table is d dollars. You use a coupon and buy the table for $(d - 4)$ dollars. You paint the table and sell it for $(3d + 1)$ dollars. Find and interpret your profit on the coffee table. You earn $(2d + 5)$ dollars.

Self-Assessment for Problem Solving

9. away team; $m + 1$; The away team wins because they had more points at halftime and score more points per minute after halftime.

Difference in points
$= $ winning team points
$-$ losing team points
$= (3m + 40) - (2m + 39)$
$= m + 1$

10. d dollars; The profit is equal to the original price of the kit.

Learning Target

Find sums and differences of linear expressions.

Success Criteria

- Explain the difference between linear and nonlinear expressions.
- Find opposites of terms that include variables.
- Apply properties of operations to add and subtract linear expressions.

Review & Refresh

1. $15f$
2. $-4b$
3. $-11z - 3$
4. $-\frac{7}{15}$
5. $\frac{2}{5}$
6. $2\frac{2}{15}$
7. D

Concepts, Skills, & Problem Solving

8. $(2x - 6) + (x + 5) = 3x - 1$
9. $(2x + 7) - (2x - 4) = 11$
10. $2n - 4$
11. $2b + 9$
12. $-2w - 14$
13. $6x - 18$
14. $-0.4k + 14$
15. $-3\frac{3}{10}z - 11$
16. $-2.7h - 1.3j + 2$
17. $\frac{3}{2}x + 2y - 3.5$
18. a. $7m + 19$;
    $(3m + 13) + (4m + 6)$
    $= 7m + 19$

    b. you;
    You: $3(3) + 13 = 22$ fireflies
    Friend: $4(3) + 6 = 18$ fireflies

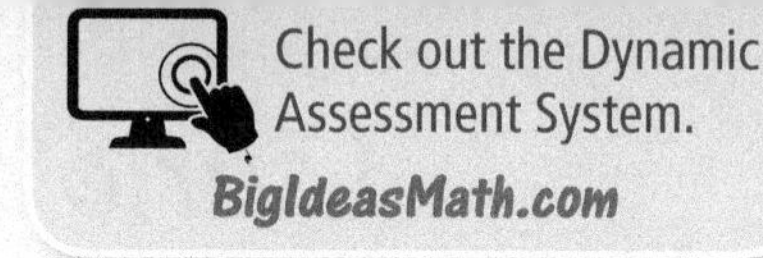
Check out the Dynamic Assessment System.
BigIdeasMath.com

Assignment Guide and Concept Check

Scaffold assignments to support all students in their learning progression. The suggested assignments are a starting point. Continue to assign additional exercises and revisit with spaced practice to move every student toward proficiency.

Level	Assignment 1	Assignment 2
Emerging	3, 6, 7, 8, 9, 10, 11, 14, 19, 21, 27	12, 15, 18, 22, 24, 28, 29
Proficient	3, 6, 7, 8, 9, 11, 12, 16, 22, 24, 27	17, 18, 25, 26, 28, 29, 30, 31
Advanced	3, 6, 7, 8, 9, 11, 12, 17, 24, 26, 27	25, 28, 29, 30, 31, 32

- Assignment 1 is for use after students complete the Self-Assessment for Concepts & Skills.
- Assignment 2 is for use after students complete the Self-Assessment for Problem Solving.
- The red exercises can be used as a concept check.

Review & Refresh Prior Skills

Exercises 1–3 Simplifying Algebraic Expressions
Exercises 4–6 Evaluating Expressions
Exercise 7 Finding the Surface Area of a Prism

C.2 Practice

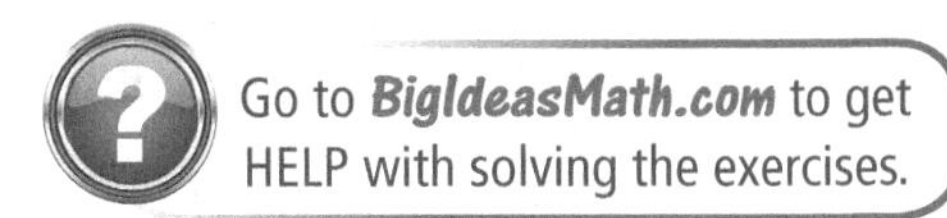
Go to BigIdeasMath.com to get
HELP with solving the exercises.

Review & Refresh

Simplify the expression.

1. $4f + 11f$

2. $b + 4b - 9b$

3. $-4z - 6 - 7z + 3$

Evaluate the expression when $x = -\frac{4}{5}$ and $y = \frac{1}{3}$.

4. $x + y$

5. $2x + 6y$

6. $-x + 4y$

7. What is the surface area of a cube that has a side length of 5 feet?

A. 25 ft^2 **B.** 75 ft^2 **C.** 125 ft^2 **D.** 150 ft^2

Concepts, Skills, & Problem Solving

USING ALGEBRA TILES **Write the sum or difference modeled by the algebra tiles. Then use the algebra tiles to simplify the expression.** (See Exploration 1, p. 597.)

8.

9.

ADDING LINEAR EXPRESSIONS **Find the sum.**

10. $(n + 8) + (n - 12)$

11. $(7 - b) + (3b + 2)$

12. $(2w - 9) + (-4w - 5)$

13. $(2x - 6) + (4x - 12)$

14. $(-3.4k - 7) + (3k + 21)$

15. $\left(-\frac{7}{2}z + 4\right) + \left(\frac{1}{5}z - 15\right)$

16. $(6 - 2.7h) + (-1.3j - 4)$

17. $\left(\frac{7}{4}x - 5\right) + (2y - 3.5) + \left(-\frac{1}{4}x + 5\right)$

18. MP MODELING REAL LIFE While catching fireflies, you and a friend decide to have a competition. After m minutes, you have $(3m + 13)$ fireflies and your friend has $(4m + 6)$ fireflies.

a. How many total fireflies do you and your friend catch? Explain your reasoning.

b. The competition lasts 3 minutes. Who has more fireflies? Justify your answer.

SUBTRACTING LINEAR EXPRESSIONS **Find the difference.**

19. $(-2g + 7) - (g + 11)$

20. $(6d + 5) - (2 - 3d)$

21. $(4 - 5y) - (2y - 16)$

22. $(2n - 9) - (-2.4n + 4)$

23. $\left(-\frac{1}{8}c + 16\right) - \left(\frac{3}{8} + 3c\right)$

24. $\left(\frac{9}{4}x + 6\right) - \left(-\frac{5}{4}x - 24\right)$

25. $\left(\frac{1}{3} - 6m\right) - \left(\frac{1}{4}n - 8\right)$

26. $(1 - 5q) - (2.5s + 8) - (0.5q + 6)$

27. **MP YOU BE THE TEACHER** Your friend finds the difference $(4m + 9) - (2m - 5)$. Is your friend correct? Explain your reasoning.

$$(4m + 9) - (2m - 5) = 4m + 9 - 2m - 5$$
$$= 4m - 2m + 9 - 5$$
$$= 2m + 4$$

28. **GEOMETRY** The expression $17n + 11$ represents the perimeter of the triangle. What is the length of the third side? Explain your reasoning.

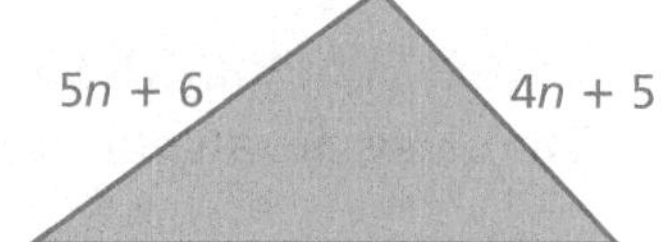

29. **MP LOGIC** Your friend says the sum of two linear expressions is always a linear expression. Is your friend correct? Explain.

30. **MP MODELING REAL LIFE** You burn 265 calories running and then 7 calories per minute swimming. Your friend burns 273 calories running and then 11 calories per minute swimming. You each swim for the same number of minutes. Find and interpret the difference in the amounts of calories burned by you and your friend.

265
calories burned
HR BPM 72

31. **DIG DEEPER!** You start a new job. After w weeks, you have $(10w + 120)$ dollars in your savings account and $(45w + 25)$ dollars in your checking account.

a. What is the total amount of money in the accounts? Explain.

b. How much money did you have before you started your new job? How much money do you save each week?

c. You want to buy a new phone for \$150, and still have \$500 left in your accounts afterwards. Explain how to determine when you can buy the phone.

32. **MP REASONING** Write an expression in simplest form that represents the vertical distance between the two lines shown. What is the distance when $x = 3$? when $x = -3$?

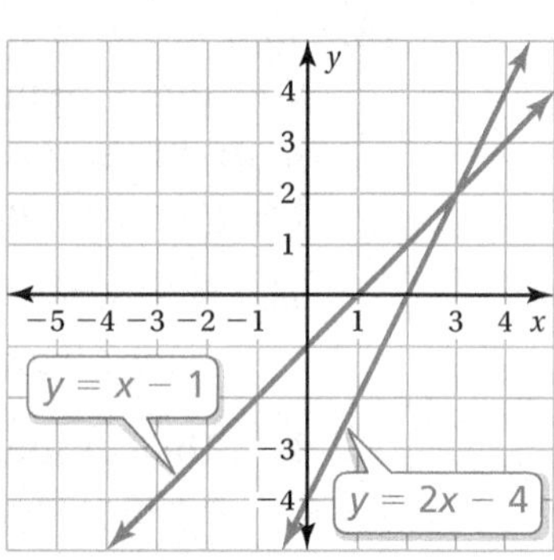

Common Errors

- **Exercises 19–26** Students may forget to subtract each term in the parentheses. Remind students to rewrite the problem so that *adding the opposite* is obvious.
- **Exercise 32** Students may make the distance negative. Remind students that distance is always positive or zero.

Mini-Assessment

Find the sum.

1. $(5m + 3) + (-8m + 8)$ $-3m + 11$
2. $(4 - x) + (2x + 5)$ $x + 9$

Find the difference.

3. $(8x - 3) - (2x + 6)$ $6x - 9$
4. $(2 - 7y) - (3y - 18)$ $-10y + 20$
5. A rectangle has side lengths $(x + 5)$ meters and $(2x - 1)$ meters. Find the perimeter of the rectangle. $(6x + 8)$ meters

Section Resources

Surface Level	Deep Level
Resources by Chapter • Extra Practice • Reteach • Puzzle Time Student Journal • Self-Assessment • Practice Differentiating the Lesson Tutorial Videos Skills Review Handbook Skills Trainer	Resources by Chapter • Enrichment and Extension Graphic Organizers Dynamic Assessment System • Section Practice
Transfer Level	
Dynamic Assessment System • Mid-Chapter Quiz	Assessment Book • Mid-Chapter Quiz

Concepts, Skills, & Problem Solving

19. $-3g - 4$
20. $9d + 3$
21. $-7y + 20$
22. $4.4n - 13$
23. $-3\frac{1}{8}c + 15\frac{5}{8}$
24. $3\frac{1}{2}x + 30$
25. $-6m - \frac{1}{4}n + 8\frac{1}{3}$
26. $-5.5q - 2.5s - 13$
27. no; Your friend dropped the second set of parentheses instead of adding the opposite of the second expression.
28. $8n$; The length of the third side is equal to the perimeter minus the lengths of the other 2 sides, $(17n + 11) - (5n + 6) - (4n + 5)$.
29. no; If the variable terms are opposites, the sum is a numerical expression.
30. $4m + 8$; Your friend will burn $4m + 8$ more calories than you for m minutes swam.
31. **a.** $(55w + 145)$ dollars;
    $(10w + 120) + (45w + 25)$
    $= 55w + 145$

    b. \$145; \$55

    c. *Sample answer:* You would need to have a total of \$650 in the accounts.
    $55w + 145 = 650$; $55w = 505$;
    $w = 9.\overline{18}$

    After 10 weeks, you can buy the new phone.
32. $|x - 3|$, or equivalently $|-x + 3|$; 0; 6

Check out the
Dynamic Classroom.
BigIdeasMath.com

Learning Target

Apply the Distributive Property to generate equivalent expressions.

Success Criteria

- Explain how to apply the Distributive Property.
- Use the Distributive Property to simplify algebraic expressions.

Warm Up

Cumulative, vocabulary, and prerequisite skills practice opportunities are available in the *Resources by Chapter* or at *BigIdeasMath.com*.

ELL Support

Explain that when you distribute flyers, you give a flyer to each person among many people. The term *Distributive Property* is related to the word *distribute*. The Distributive Property states that you can multiply each term in the parentheses by the factor outside the parentheses and then add or subtract. The multiplication process is distributed among each of the terms, instead of adding or subtracting first and then multiplying.

Exploration 1

a. See Additional Answers.

b. Answers will vary. The area of the shaded region can be found by either subtracting the areas of the nonshaded regions from the total area of the figure or by finding the dimensions of the shaded region. Expressions will be either unsimplified or simplified.

Laurie's Notes

Preparing to Teach

- Students have used the Distributive Property in previous courses. They will extend their understanding to include algebraic expressions involving rational numbers. This property is very important to algebraic work in future courses.
- **Make Sense of Problems and Persevere in Solving Them:** Mathematically proficient students can use pictures to help conceptualize and solve a problem. In the exploration, students will use area models to demonstrate the Distributive Property.

Motivate

- ? "Why might you find area in everyday life?" Answers will vary.
- Draw the rectangle on the board.

2

5

- ? Ask, "How do you find the area of this rectangle?" Multiply the length and width.
- ? "If you didn't know the length, how could you write the area?" 2ℓ square units
- ? "If the length was $(3x - 4)$ units, what would the area be?" $2(3x - 4)$ square units
- ? "Does the process for finding the area change when the length changes?" no

Exploration 1

- Discuss the first figure.
- ? "What is the width of the shaded region?" 5 units
- ? "What is the length of the shaded region?" $(16 - 2z)$ units Students should reason that because the length of the larger rectangle is $16 - z$ and the length of the unshaded region is z, the length of the shaded region is $(16 - z) - z = (16 - 2z)$ units.
- ? "How do you find the area of the shaded region?" Multiply the length and width. "What is the area?" $(16 - 2z)5$ square units or $(80 - 10z)$ square units
- ? "Can you think of another way to find the area of the shaded region?" *Sample answer:* Find the area of the larger rectangle, $(16 - z)5 = (80 - 5z)$ square units, find the area of the unshaded rectangle, $z(5) = 5z$ square units, and then find the difference, $80 - 5z - 5z = (80 - 10z)$ square units.
- Students may or may not simplify their area expressions.
- Have partners finish part (a). While students are working, circulate to find pairs with expressions for each figure that look different but are correct. Divide the board into three sections and label the sections: *Figure 1, Figure 2,* and *Figure 3.* Ask pairs with correct expressions to write them in the appropriate sections of the board.
- ? Refer to the Figure 1 section of the board and ask, "Are these expressions equivalent?" yes "How do you know?" Listen for students recognizing that the expressions simplify to the same expression. Students may also suggest evaluating the expression for multiple values of the variables to see if they are equivalent. Repeat this questioning for the other two figures.

C.3 The Distributive Property

Learning Target: Apply the Distributive Property to generate equivalent expressions.

Success Criteria:
- I can explain how to apply the Distributive Property.
- I can use the Distributive Property to simplify algebraic expressions.

EXPLORATION 1 Using Models to Write Expressions

Work with a partner.

a. Write an expression that represents the area of the shaded region in each figure.

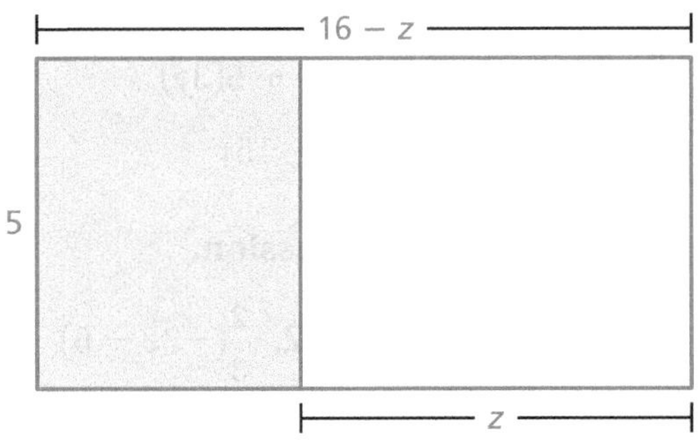

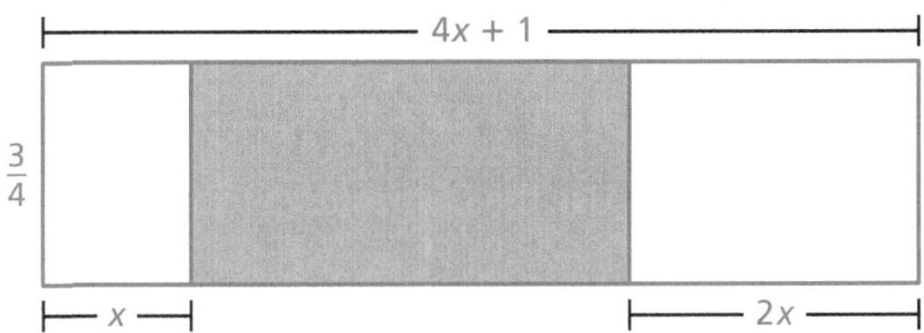

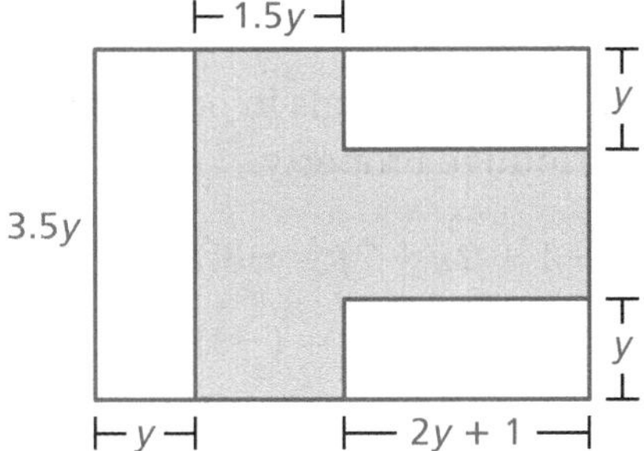

b. Compare your expressions in part (a) with other groups in your class. Did other groups write expressions that look different than yours? If so, determine whether the expressions are equivalent.

Math Practice

Find General Methods

Let a, b, and c be rational numbers. How can you write $a(bx + c)$ as a sum of two terms?

C.3 Lesson

You can use the Distributive Property to simplify expressions involving variable terms and rational numbers.

EXAMPLE 1 Using the Distributive Property

Simplify each expression.

a. $-\frac{1}{3}(3n - 6)$

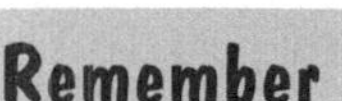

Remember

The Distributive Property states
$a(b + c) = ab + ac$
and
$a(b - c) = ab - ac$.

$$-\frac{1}{3}(3n - 6) = -\frac{1}{3}(3n) - \left(-\frac{1}{3}\right)(6) \quad \text{Distributive Property}$$

$$= -n - (-2) \quad \text{Multiply.}$$

$$= -n + 2 \quad \text{Add the opposite.}$$

b. $5(-x + 3y)$

$$5(-x + 3y) = 5(-x) + 5(3y) \quad \text{Distributive Property}$$

$$= -5x + 15y \quad \text{Multiply.}$$

Try It **Simplify the expression.**

1. $-1(x + 9)$

2. $\frac{2}{3}(-3z - 6)$

3. $-1.5(8m - n)$

EXAMPLE 2 Simplifying Expressions

Simplify $-3(-1 + 2x + 7)$.

Common Error

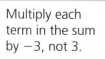

Multiply each term in the sum by −3, not 3.

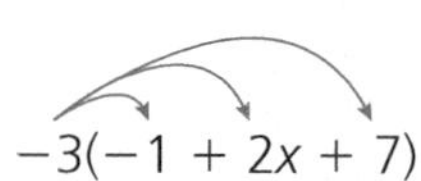

$-3(-1 + 2x + 7)$

Method 1: Use the Distributive Property before combining like terms.

$$-3(-1 + 2x + 7) = -3(-1) + (-3)(2x) + (-3)(7) \quad \text{Distributive Property}$$

$$= 3 + (-6x) + (-21) \quad \text{Multiply.}$$

$$= -6x - 18 \quad \text{Combine like terms.}$$

Method 2: Combine like terms in parentheses before using the Distributive Property.

$$-3(-1 + 2x + 7) = -3(2x + 6) \quad \text{Combine like terms.}$$

$$= (-3)(2x) + (-3)(6) \quad \text{Distributive Property}$$

$$= -6x - 18 \quad \text{Multiply.}$$

Try It **Simplify the expression.**

4. $2(-3s + 1 - 5)$

5. $-\frac{3}{2}(a - 4 - 2a)$

Laurie's Notes

Scaffolding Instruction

- In the exploration, students built upon their experiences with the Distributive Property to include rational numbers.
- **Emerging:** Students may understand that there is an order for distributing over the parentheses but make computational errors or neglect to multiply all parts in the parentheses. These students will benefit from guided instruction for the examples.
- **Proficient:** Students can use the Distributive Property to expand and then simplify expressions. These students should work with a partner on Examples 1–3 and the Try It exercises before proceeding to the Self-Assessment exercises.

EXAMPLE 1

- Work through the example one step at a time, asking students what they should do next.
- In the first steps, point out that you are *expanding* the expression using the Distributive Property. The remaining step(s) are the simplification process.
- Remind students to include negative signs when necessary.

Try It

- Have students use whiteboards to complete the exercises. Tell students to show all their steps and justifications.
- Ask volunteers to share their work with the class.

EXAMPLE 2

- After demonstrating Method 1, have students work through Method 2 with a partner.

? "What is the difference between the two methods?" In Method 1, you use the Distributive Property before combining like terms. In Method 2, you combine like terms before using the Distributive Property.

Try It

- Have students complete the exercises independently. Circulate and look for any misunderstandings.

ELL Support

After demonstrating Examples 1 and 2, have students practice language by working in groups to complete Exercises 4 and 5. Have each group use both methods. Provide guiding questions for discussion: What are the steps for Method 1? What are the steps for Method 2? Expect students to perform as described.

Beginner: State the answer and write the steps.

Intermediate: Use simple sentences to answer the guiding questions.

Advanced: Use detailed sentences to answer the guiding questions and help guide discussion.

Scaffold instruction to support all students in their learning. Learning is individualized and you may want to group students differently as they move in and out of these levels with each skill and concept. Student self-assessment and feedback help guide your instructional decisions about how and when to layer support for all students to become proficient learners.

Extra Example 1

Simplify each expression.

a. $-2.4(4y - 9)$ $-9.6y + 21.6$

b. $\frac{1}{2}(-10m + 4n)$ $-5m + 2n$

Try It

1. $-x - 9$
2. $-2z - 4$
3. $-12m + 1.5n$

Extra Example 2

Simplify $-4(-5d - 11 + 8d)$. $-12d + 44$

Try It

4. $-6s - 8$
5. $1\frac{1}{2}a + 6$

Extra Example 3

Simplify each expression.

a. $\frac{2}{3}(9g + 3) - 5g$ $g + 2$

b. $(2.4a - 5) - 2.5(3a - 4)$ $-5.1a + 5$

Try It

6. $2m + 15$
7. $6w - 22$

Self-Assessment

for Concepts & Skills

8. *Sample answer:* Distribute the number on the outside of the parentheses to each term on the inside of the parentheses. Multiply when necessary and combine like terms if needed.
9. $-1\frac{2}{3}y + 2\frac{1}{2}$
10. $-12s - 15$
11. $10\frac{1}{5}m - 2\frac{2}{5}$
12. $8h - 12.75$
13. $\frac{3}{2}(4x - 8) + 3x$

$$= \frac{3}{2}(4x) - \frac{3}{2}(8) + 3x$$
$$= 6x - 12 + 3x$$
$$= 9x - 12$$

Laurie's Notes

EXAMPLE 3

- Students have not had a lot of practice with a fractional factor in the Distributive Property.
- **Teaching Tip:** Use arrows to show the $-\frac{1}{2}$ being distributed over the $6n$ and the 4.

$$-\frac{1}{2}(6n + 4)$$

- As you work through each part on the board, ask students to supply the justifications.
- **Use Appropriate Tools Strategically:** As students use technology to explore the equivalence of the expressions in part (a), ask students what methods they are using and why. Have other students critique their reasoning.
- Note the use of the Additive Inverse Property and the Addition Property of Zero in part (b).

Try It

- Have students work with a partner to complete the exercises. Find students that have correctly simplified the expressions to share their work and answers at the board or document camera.

Self-Assessment for Concepts & Skills

- Have students work independently. Use *Popsicle Sticks* to select students to share.
- Ask, "How do you apply the Distributive Property?" Multiply each term in the parentheses by the factor outside the parentheses.

ELL Support

Allow students to work in pairs to practice language as they answer Exercises 9–13. Check comprehension by having each pair display their answers on a whiteboard for your review. Discuss students' explanations for Exercise 8 as a class.

The Success Criteria Self-Assessment chart can be found in the *Student Journal* or online at *BigIdeasMath.com*.

EXAMPLE 3 Simplifying Expressions

Math Practice

Use Technology to Explore
Use technology to explore the equivalence of the original and simplified expressions in part (a).

Simplify each expression.

a. $-\frac{1}{2}(6n + 4) + 2n$

$-\frac{1}{2}(6n + 4) + 2n = -\frac{1}{2}(6n) + \left(-\frac{1}{2}\right)(4) + 2n$ — Distributive Property

$= -3n + (-2) + 2n$ — Multiply.

$= -n - 2$ — Combine like terms.

b. $(6d - 5) - 8\left(\frac{3}{4}d - 1\right)$

You can multiply an expression by −1 to find the opposite of the expression.

$(6d - 5) - 8\left(\frac{3}{4}d - 1\right) = (6d - 5) - \left[8\left(\frac{3}{4}d\right) - 8(1)\right]$ — Distributive Property

$= (6d - 5) - (6d - 8)$ — Multiply.

$= (6d - 5) + (-6d + 8)$ — Add the opposite.

$= [6d + (-6d)] + (-5 + 8)$ — Group like terms.

$= 3$ — Combine like terms.

Try It **Simplify the expression.**

6. $3.5m - 1.5(m - 10)$

7. $\frac{4}{5}(10w - 5) - 2(w + 9)$

Self-Assessment for Concepts & Skills

Solve each exercise. Then rate your understanding of the success criteria in your journal.

8. WRITING Explain how to use the Distributive Property when simplifying an expression.

USING THE DISTRIBUTIVE PROPERTY **Simplify the expression.**

9. $\frac{5}{6}(-2y + 3)$

10. $6(3s - 2.5 - 5s)$

11. $\frac{3}{10}(4m - 8) + 9m$

12. $2.25 - 2(7.5 - 4h)$

8	$3x$
$\frac{3}{2}$	$4x$

13. MP STRUCTURE Use the terms at the left to complete the expression below so that it is equivalent to $9x - 12$. Justify your answer.

$\square(\square - \square) + \square$

EXAMPLE 4 Modeling Real Life

A square pool has a side length of *s* feet. How many 1-foot square tiles does it take to tile the border of the pool?

Understand the problem.

You are given information about a square pool and square tiles. You are asked to find the number of tiles it takes to tile the border of the pool.

Make a plan.

Draw a diagram that represents the situation. Use the diagram to write an expression for the number of tiles needed.

Solve and check.

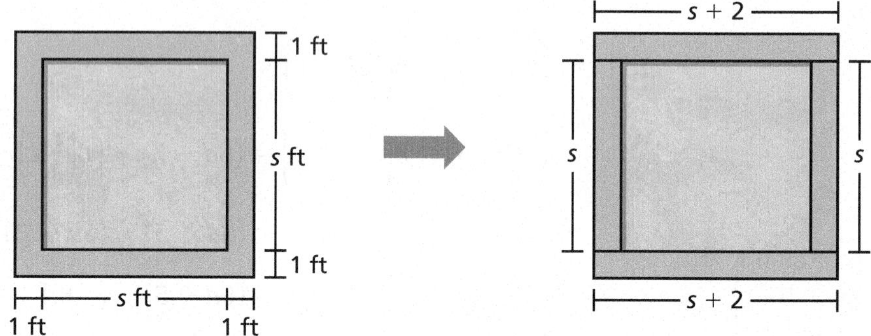

The diagram shows that the tiled border can be divided into two sections that each require $s + 2$ tiles and two sections that each require s tiles. So, the number of tiles can be represented by $2(s + 2) + 2s$. Simplify the expression.

$2(s + 2) + 2s = 2(s) + 2(2) + 2s$ Distributive Property

$= 4s + 4$ Simplify.

The expression $4s + 4$ represents the number of tiles that are needed.

Another Method
Draw a different diagram.

$4(s + 1) = 4(s) + 4(1)$

$= 4s + 4$ ✓

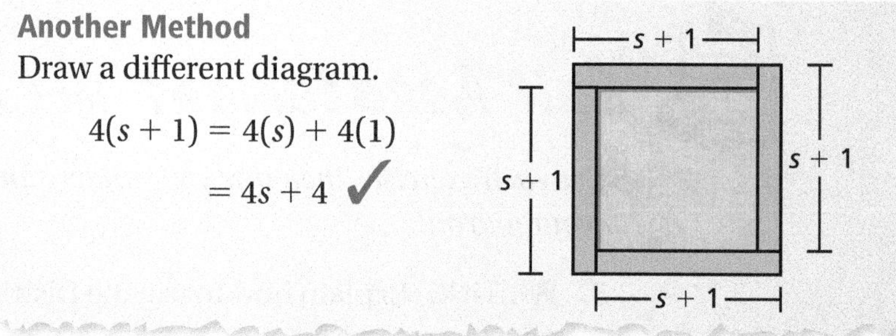

Self-Assessment for Problem Solving

Solve each exercise. Then rate your understanding of the success criteria in your journal.

14. How many 2-foot square tiles does it take to tile the border of the pool in Example 4? Explain.

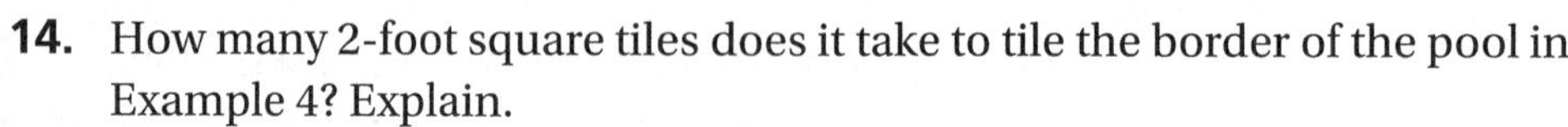

15. DIG DEEPER! The length of a handwoven Peruvian rug is 1 foot greater than its width. The perimeter of the rug is 14 feet. What is the least number of these rugs needed to form a square without any rugs overlapping?

Laurie's Notes

EXAMPLE 4

- Ask a volunteer to read the problem. Then ask another student to explain what the question is asking. To find the number of tiles it takes to tile the border of the pool (the perimeter).
- Draw the diagram on the board.
- Ask students to write their expressions for the number of tiles needed on whiteboards. Compare different expressions and ask students to explain the differences. Although there are different ways to write the original expression, when the expressions are simplified it should be obvious that the expressions are equivalent.
- Represent the solution, $4s + 4$, using a diagram.

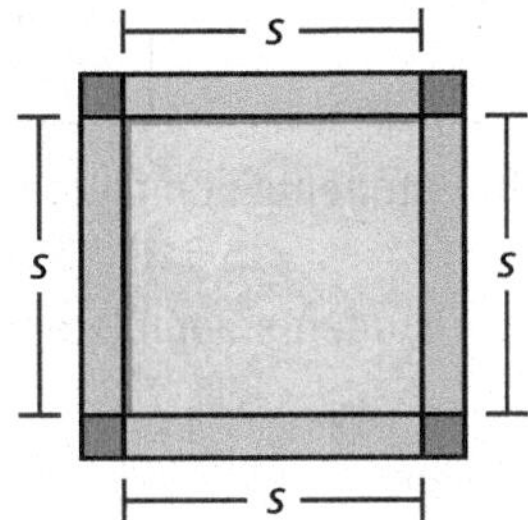

- **Look for and Make Use of Structure:** Discuss other possibilities for the original expression. For example, $4(s + 2) - 4$ is formed by counting each corner twice, so you have to subtract 4 tiles.

Self-Assessment for Problem Solving

- Students may benefit from trying the exercises independently and then working with peers to refine their work. It is important to provide time in class for problem solving, so that students become comfortable with the problem solving plan.

The Success Criteria Self-Assessment chart can be found in the *Student Journal* or online at *BigIdeasMath.com*.

Formative Assessment Tip

One-Minute Card
This technique provides a quick assessment of students' understanding of a concept. Write a short prompt on the board and allow 1 minute for students to consider the prompt. Give each student an index card and allow 1 minute for students to write their responses. When time is up, collect the cards and review the responses. The next day, spend a few minutes discussing any misconceptions or exceptional responses.

Closure

- **One-Minute Card:** Explain how to simplify $-6(-4d - 8.3 + 3d)$.

Extra Example 4

A rectangular garden has a length of 12 feet and a width of w feet. How many 2-foot square blocks are needed to make a path around the garden?
$(2w + 16)$ blocks

Self-Assessment for Problem Solving

14. $2s + 4$; *Sample answer:* The tiled border can be divided into two sections that each require $\left(\frac{s}{2} + 2\right)$ tiles and two sections that each require $\frac{s}{2}$ tiles.

15. 12 rugs

Learning Target

Apply the Distributive Property to generate equivalent expressions.

Success Criteria

- Explain how to apply the Distributive Property.
- Use the Distributive Property to simplify algebraic expressions.

Check out the Dynamic Assessment System.
BigIdeasMath.com

Review & Refresh

1. $6b - 1$
2. $8m - 1$
3. $-6z - 5$
4. $7g + 3n - 2$
5. -36
6. -243
7. -56
8. $11 = |-11|$
9. $|3.5| < |-5.8|$
10. $|-3.5| > \left|\frac{17}{5}\right|$

Concepts, Skills, & Problem Solving

11. $6.5(3x + 4) - 6.5(x + 2)$, $6.5(2x + 2)$;
$6.5(3x + 4) - 6.5(x + 2) = 19.5x + 26 - 6.5x - 13 = 13x + 13$;
$6.5(2x + 2) = 13x + 13$
12. $1.5m(2m) - m(0.5m + 2)$, $1.5m(m) + (m - 2)(m)$;
$1.5m(2m) - m(0.5m + 2) = 3m^2 - 0.5m^2 - 2m = 2.5m^2 - 2m$;
$1.5m(m) + (m - 2)(m) = 1.5m^2 + m^2 - 2m = 2.5m^2 - 2m$
13. $3a - 21$
14. $-6x - 12$
15. $-15m + 20$
16. $36c + 45$
17. $13.5s + 27$
18. $-9.8g + 7$
19. $-2p + 2\frac{2}{5}$
20. $-4q + 13\frac{1}{3}$
21. $8y + 16$
22. $-54n - 36$
23. $6d + 49.8$
24. $-2.3hk + 13.8h$
25. $1\frac{1}{2}y - \frac{3}{8}z$
26. $-4w + 14x - 2.4$
27. $3\frac{1}{3}a + 15b$
28. no; $-2(h + 8k) = -2h - 2(8k) = -2h - 16k$
29. no; $-3(4 - 5b + 7) = -3(11 - 5b) = -3(11) - (-3)(5b) = -33 + 15b$

Assignment Guide and Concept Check

Scaffold assignments to support all students in their learning progression. The suggested assignments are a starting point. Continue to assign additional exercises and revisit with spaced practice to move every student toward proficiency.

Level	Assignment 1	Assignment 2
Emerging	4, 6, 10, 11, 13, 15, 17, 19, 28, 31, 32	20, 22, 26, 29, 33, 34, 36, 37, 39
Proficient	4, 6, 10, 12, 16, 18, 20, 22, 28, 30, 32	24, 26, 29, 33, 34, 36, 37, 39, 41
Advanced	4, 6, 10, 12, 18, 20, 22, 26, 28, 34, 35	27, 29, 33, 37, 38, 39, 40, 41, 42

- Assignment 1 is for use after students complete the Self-Assessment for Concepts & Skills.
- Assignment 2 is for use after students complete the Self-Assessment for Problem Solving.
- The red exercises can be used as a concept check.

Review & Refresh Prior Skills

Exercises 1 and 3 Adding Linear Expressions
Exercises 2 and 4 Subtracting Linear Expressions
Exercises 5–7 Evaluating Expressions
Exercises 8–10 Comparing Rational Numbers

Common Errors

- **Exercises 13–27** Students may forget to distribute to each term in the parentheses, especially when there are more than two terms. Tell students to write the expression in the parentheses on their papers and draw arrows from the number being distributed to each term.

C.3 Practice

Find the sum or difference.

1. $(5b - 9) + (b + 8)$
2. $(3m + 5) - (6 - 5m)$
3. $(1 - 9z) + 3(z - 2)$
4. $(7g - 6) - (-3n - 4)$

Evaluate the expression.

5. -6^2
6. $-9^2 \cdot 3$
7. $(-7) \cdot (-2) \cdot (-4)$

Copy and complete the statement using <, >, or =.

8. $11 \;\square\; |-11|$
9. $|3.5| \;\square\; |-5.8|$
10. $|-3.5| \;\square\; \left|\frac{17}{5}\right|$

Concepts, Skills, & Problem Solving

USING MODELS **Write two different expressions that represent the area of the shaded region. Show that the expressions are equivalent.** (See Exploration 1, p. 603.)

11. 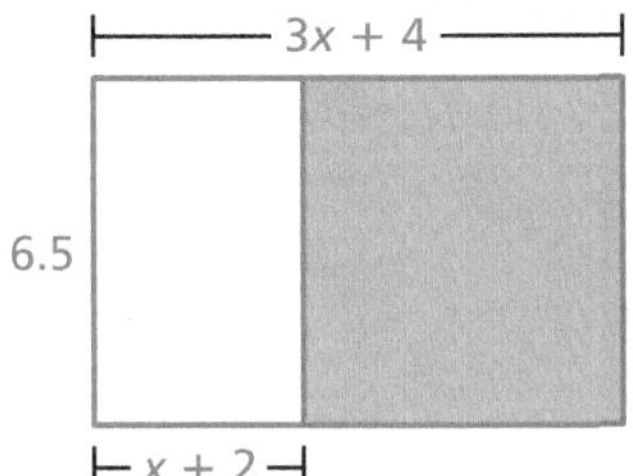

12. 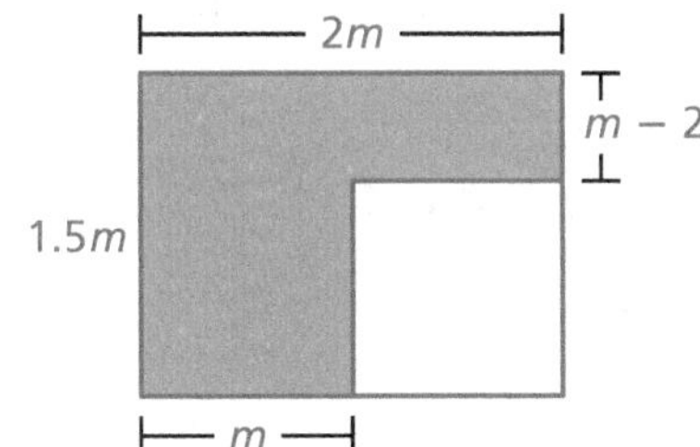

USING THE DISTRIBUTIVE PROPERTY **Simplify the expression.**

13. $3(a - 7)$
14. $-6(2 + x)$
15. $-5(3m - 4)$
16. $-9(-5 - 4c)$
17. $4.5(3s + 6)$
18. $-1.4(-5 + 7g)$
19. $\frac{2}{5}(6 - 5p)$
20. $-\frac{4}{3}(3q - 10)$
21. $2(3 + 4y + 5)$
22. $-9(8 + 6n - 4)$
23. $-6(-4d - 8.3 + 3d)$
24. $2.3h(6 - k)$
25. $-\frac{3}{8}(-4y + z)$
26. $2(-2w - 1.2 + 7x)$
27. $\frac{5}{3}\left(\frac{4}{3}a + 9b + \frac{2}{3}a\right)$

MP YOU BE THE TEACHER **Your friend simplifies the expression. Is your friend correct? Explain your reasoning.**

28.
$$-2(h + 8k) = -2(h) + 2(8k)$$
$$= -2h + 16k$$

29.
$$-3(4 - 5b + 7) = -3(11 - 5b)$$
$$= -3(11) + (-3)(5b)$$
$$= -33 - 15b$$

SIMPLIFYING EXPRESSIONS Simplify the expression.

30. $-3(5g + 1) + 8g$

31. $-6a + 7(-2a - 4)$

32. $9 - 3(5 - 4x)$

33. $-\frac{3}{4}(5p - 12) + 2\left(8 - \frac{1}{4}p\right)$

34. $c(4 + 3c) - 0.75(c + 3)$

35. $-1 - \frac{2}{3}\left(\frac{6}{7} - \frac{3}{7}n\right)$

36. MP **MODELING REAL LIFE** The cost (in dollars) of a custom-made sweatshirt is represented by $3.5n + 29.99$, where n is the number of different colors in the design. Write and interpret a simplified expression that represents the cost of 15 sweatshirts.

37. MP **MODELING REAL LIFE** A ski resort makes snow using a snow fan that costs \$1200. The fan has an average daily operation cost of \$9.50. Write and interpret a simplified expression that represents the cost to purchase and operate 6 snow fans.

38. MP **NUMBER SENSE** Predict whether the instructions below will produce equivalent expressions. Then show whether your prediction is correct.

- Subtract 3 from n, add 3 to the result, and then triple that expression.
- Subtract 3 from n, triple the result, and then add 3 to that expression.

USING A MODEL Draw a diagram that shows how the expression can represent the area of a figure. Then simplify the expression.

39. $5(2 + x + 3)$

40. $(4 + 1)(x + 2x)$

41. DIG DEEPER! A square fire pit with a side length of s feet is bordered by 1-foot square stones as shown.

a. How many stones does it take to border the fire pit with two rows of stones? Use a diagram to justify your answer.

b. You border the fire pit with n rows of stones. How many stones are in the nth row? Explain your reasoning.

42. **PUZZLE** Your friend asks you to perform the following steps.

1) Pick any number except 0.
2) Add 2 to your number.
3) Multiply the result by 3.
4) Subtract 6 from the result.
5) Divide the result by your original number.

Your friend says, "The final result is 3!" Is your friend correct? If so, explain how your friend knew the final result. If not, explain why not.

Mini-Assessment

Simplify the expression.

1. $5(x - 9)$ $5x - 45$
2. $-\frac{2}{3}(3b - 1)$ $-2b + \frac{2}{3}$
3. $-3(8m - 4 + 7m)$ $-45m + 12$
4. $-2(5 - 4c) + 0.6(5c - 2)$ $11c - 11.2$
5. The cost (in dollars) of a scooter rental is represented by $2.5m + 25$, where m is the number of miles traveled. Write and interpret a simplified expression that represents the cost for a family of four to each rent a scooter.
   $(10m + 100)$ dollars; The cost for a family of four to rent scooters is \$100 plus \$10 for each mile traveled.

Section Resources

Surface Level	Deep Level
Resources by Chapter • Extra Practice • Reteach • Puzzle Time Student Journal • Self-Assessment • Practice Differentiating the Lesson Tutorial Videos Skills Review Handbook Skills Trainer	Resources by Chapter • Enrichment and Extension Graphic Organizers Dynamic Assessment System • Section Practice

Concepts, Skills, & Problem Solving

30. $-7g - 3$ **31.** $-20a - 28$

32. $12x - 6$ **33.** $-4\frac{1}{4}p + 25$

34. $3c^2 + 3.25c - 2.25$

35. $\frac{2}{7}n - 1\frac{4}{7}$

36. $52.5n + 449.85$; For the 15 sweatshirts, it costs \$52.50 for each color in the design plus an additional \$449.85.

37. $7200 + 57d$; For the 6 snow fans, it costs \$7200 to buy them and \$57 per day to operate them.

38. *Sample answer:* Due to the first instruction being tripled at the end of the expression, the results will not be equivalent.

Expression 1:
$[(n - 3) + 3]3 = (n)3 = 3n$

Expression 2:
$3(n - 3) + 3 = 3n - 9 + 3$
$= 3n - 6$

$3n - 6 \neq 3n$

39. *Sample answer:*

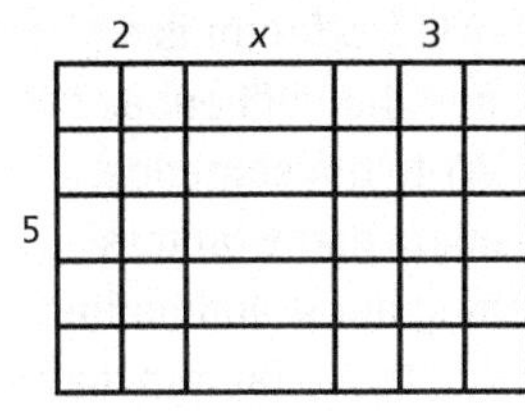

$5x + 25$

40. *Sample answer:*

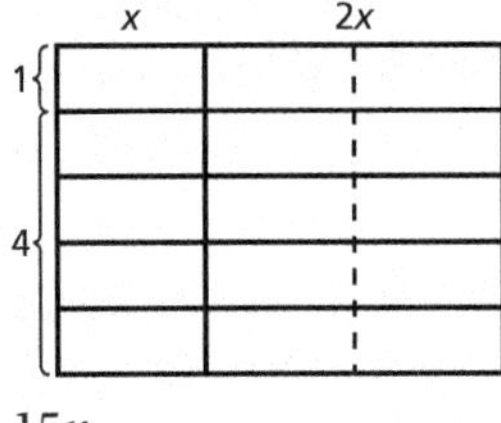

$15x$

41–42. See Additional Answers.

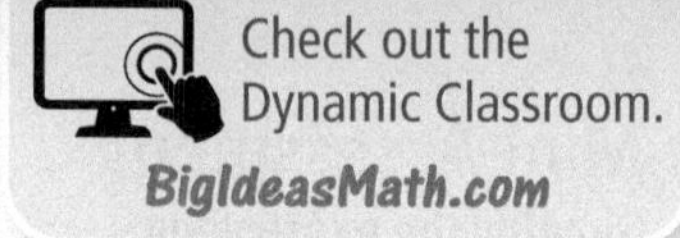

Check out the Dynamic Classroom.
BigIdeasMath.com

Learning Target

Factor algebraic expressions.

Success Criteria

- Identify the greatest common factor of terms, including variable terms.
- Use the Distributive Property to factor algebraic expressions.
- Write a term as a product involving a given factor.

Warm Up

Cumulative, vocabulary, and prerequisite skills practice opportunities are available in the *Resources by Chapter* or at *BigIdeasMath.com.*

ELL Support

Explain that the word *factor* has a special meaning in math. In everyday life, a factor is a circumstance that influences an outcome. Write the sentence, "She considers many factors before visiting her grandmother." Discuss what those factors may be. Explain that in math, a factor is a whole number other than zero that when multiplied with another factor makes a product.

Exploration 1

a. See Additional Answers.

b. yes; *Sample answer:* The Distributive Property can be used to show that the expressions are equivalent.

c. *Sample answer:* Write each term as a product of factors and then you can factor out any rational number.

Laurie's Notes

Preparing to Teach

- Students have used the Distributive Property to simplify algebraic expressions. Now they will extend that understanding to use the Distributive Property to factor algebraic expressions. The connection you want them to make is that the Distributive Property states there is an equality between two expressions: $a(b + c) = ab + ac$.

Motivate

- ? "How many of you have heard the saying, 'Work smarter, not harder?'" Answers will vary. Tell students that this idea is used frequently in math. For example, you may not be able to multiply 15 by 16 in your head, but you can think about it as $15(10 + 6)$, which is the same as $15 \times 10 + 15 \times 6$. Now the problem is more manageable: $15 \times 10 = 150$ and $15 \times 6 = 90$, so $15(10 + 6) = 150 + 90 = 240$.
- Remind students that the greatest common factor is the largest number that divides evenly into all the numbers. For example, 9 is the GCF of 18 and 27.

Exploration 1

- Begin working through the first model as a class. Remind students that they cannot rely on the appearance of the model, but they must use the known information.
- ? Ask, "Which number can represent the width of the larger rectangle?" *Sample answers:* $\frac{1}{5}$, $\frac{2}{5}$, $\frac{4}{5}$, or 1
- **Note:** Remind students that when factoring, they should not use 1 as a common factor because it will not change the expression in the parentheses. Although 1 is a possible width of the larger rectangle, students should choose a number other than 1 to use in their expressions.
- Once students choose the width, have them fill in the other question marks in the model. Do students know where to place the numbers in the expression? Encourage students to ask themselves, "What can I do?" Frequently if students do not know *what* to do, asking what they *can* do will help. Students should recognize that they can replace the question mark outside of the parentheses with the width they choose for the larger rectangle.
- Compare the different expressions that surface: $\frac{1}{5}(4 + 8)$, $\frac{2}{5}(2 + 4)$, $\frac{4}{5}(1 + 2)$, etc.
- **Construct Viable Arguments and Critique the Reasoning of Others:** Have students work with their partners to finish part (a). Group pairs of students together to compare their answers and critique their reasoning.
- Listen to conversations as students complete parts (b) and (c). Use *Popsicle Sticks* to solicit responses for parts (b) and (c). The goal is for students to see that the Distributive Property works in both directions.

C.4 Factoring Expressions

Learning Target: Factor algebraic expressions.

Success Criteria:
- I can identify the greatest common factor of terms, including variable terms.
- I can use the Distributive Property to factor algebraic expressions.
- I can write a term as a product involving a given factor.

EXPLORATION 1 Finding Dimensions

Work with a partner.

a. The models show the areas (in square units) of parts of rectangles. Use the models to find the missing values that complete the expressions. Explain your reasoning.

? ?

? $\frac{4}{5}$ $\frac{8}{5}$

$$\frac{4}{5} + \frac{8}{5} = ?(? + ?)$$

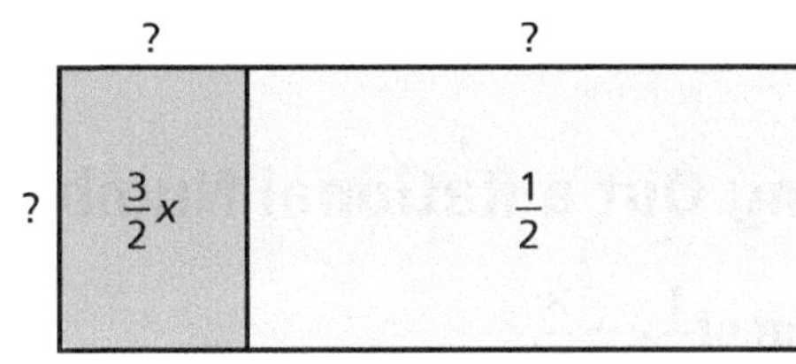

$$\frac{3}{2}x + \frac{1}{2} = ?(? + ?)$$

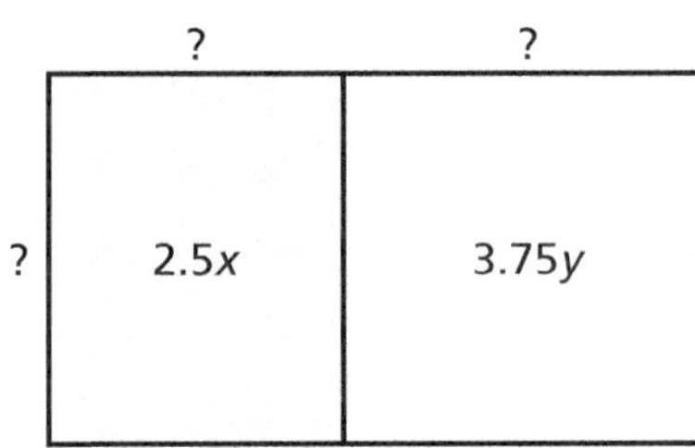

$$2.5x + 3.75y = ?(? + ?)$$

Math Practice

View as Components

How does viewing each rectangle as two distinct parts help you complete the expressions?

b. Are the expressions you wrote in part (a) equivalent to the original expressions? Explain your reasoning.

c. Explain how you can use the Distributive Property to find rational number factors of an expression.

C.4 Lesson

Key Vocabulary
factoring an expression, *p. 610*

When **factoring an expression**, you write the expression as a product of factors. You can use the Distributive Property to factor any rational number from an expression.

EXAMPLE 1 Factoring Out the GCF

Factor $24x - 18$ using the GCF.

Find the GCF of $24x$ and 18.

$$24x = 2 \cdot 2 \cdot 2 \cdot 3 \cdot x$$
$$18 = 2 \cdot 3 \cdot 3$$

Circle the common prime factors.

Math Practice

Communicate Precisely
Help a classmate recall how to find the GCF of two numbers.

So, the GCF of $24x$ and 18 is $2 \cdot 3 = 6$. Use the GCF to factor the expression.

$$24x - 18 = 6(4x) - 6(3)$$ Rewrite using GCF.

$$= 6(4x - 3)$$ Distributive Property

Try It **Factor the expression using the GCF.**

1. $15x + 25$ **2.** $4y - 20$ **3.** $36c + 24d$

EXAMPLE 2 Factoring Out a Rational Number

Factor $\frac{1}{2}$ out of $\frac{1}{2}x + \frac{3}{2}$.

Write each term as a product of $\frac{1}{2}$ and another factor.

$$\frac{1}{2}x = \frac{1}{2} \cdot x$$ Think: $\frac{1}{2}x$ is $\frac{1}{2}$ times what?

$$\frac{3}{2} = \frac{1}{2} \cdot 3$$ Think: $\frac{3}{2}$ is $\frac{1}{2}$ times what?

Use the Distributive Property to factor out $\frac{1}{2}$.

$$\frac{1}{2}x + \frac{3}{2} = \frac{1}{2} \cdot x + \frac{1}{2} \cdot 3$$ Rewrite the expression.

$$= \frac{1}{2}(x + 3)$$ Distributive Property

Try It **Factor out the coefficient of the variable term.**

4. $\frac{1}{2}n - \frac{1}{2}$ **5.** $\frac{3}{4}p - \frac{3}{2}$ **6.** $5 + 2.5q$

Multi-Language Glossary at *BigIdeasMath.com*

Laurie's Notes

Scaffolding Instruction

- In the exploration, students built upon experiences with the Distributive Property from prior courses. Now they have a sense of how the Distributive Property can be used to factor expressions involving rational numbers.
- **Emerging:** Students understand that the Distributive Property can be used to factor common factors, but they may make computational errors or neglect to factor all the parts. Students will benefit from guided instruction for the examples.
- **Proficient:** Students understand the models and are confident in applying the Distributive Property to factor expressions. Have students self-assess using the Try It exercises.

EXAMPLE 1

? "Do $24x$ and 18 have any common factors?" 1, 2, 3, and 6

- Students may find it odd that you did not just ask about 24 and 18. Instead you included the variable factor. Explain that an algebraic term has factors, just like numbers.
- Write the prime factorizations of $24x$ and 18. Students will be comfortable seeing 6 as the GCF of $24x$ and 18. The variable x has not changed that.
- Say, "You want to rewrite $24x - 18$ as a product." Get students started by writing $24x - 18 =$ _____ (______ − ______).

? "How can you use the Distributive Property?" Listen for students to mention that the GCF is the factor you want to remove.

- **Look for and Make Use of Structure:** Students often view the equal sign in the Distributive Property as an arrow pointing to the right. When you finish, be sure that students recognize that this is the Distributive Property, with the arrow pointing left!

Expanding: $6(4x - 3) = 24x - 18$ Distributive Property →
Factoring: $24x - 18 = 6(4x - 3)$ Distributive Property ←

Try It

- Have students complete the exercises on whiteboards.

EXAMPLE 2

- Point out that this example asks you to factor out the coefficient of the variable term.
- **Look for and Make Use of Structure:** Writing each term as a product helps students see the common factor. This is particularly true with fractions.

? "How can you write $\frac{1}{2}x$ as a product?" *Sample answer:* $\frac{1}{2} \cdot x$

? "How can you write $\frac{3}{2}$ as a product?" *Sample answer:* $\frac{1}{2} \cdot 3$

- Because there is a common factor of $\frac{1}{2}$ in each term, you can factor it out.

Expanding: $\frac{1}{2}(x + 3) = \frac{1}{2}x + \frac{3}{2}$ Distributive Property →

Factoring: $\frac{1}{2}x + \frac{3}{2} = \frac{1}{2}(x + 3)$ Distributive Property ←

Scaffold instruction to support all students in their learning. Learning is individualized and you may want to group students differently as they move in and out of these levels with each skill and concept. Student self-assessment and feedback help guide your instructional decisions about how and when to layer support for all students to become proficient learners.

Extra Example 1

Factor $6x - 27$ using the GCF. $3(2x - 9)$

ELL Support

After demonstrating Example 1, have students practice language by working in pairs to complete Try It Exercises 1–3. Have each student factor one number and compare factors to find the GCF.

Beginner: State the factored expression.

Intermediate: Answer with a simple sentence. For example, "The factored form of the expression is $5(3x + 5)$."

Advanced: Answer with a sentence and help guide discussion.

Try It

1. $5(3x + 5)$
2. $4(y - 5)$
3. $12(3c + 2d)$
4. $\frac{1}{2}(n - 1)$
5. $\frac{3}{4}(p - 2)$
6. $2.5(2 + q)$

Extra Example 2

Factor $\frac{1}{5}$ out of $\frac{1}{5}x - \frac{4}{5}$. $\frac{1}{5}(x - 4)$

Extra Example 3

Factor −4 out of $-12r - 20$. $-4(3r + 5)$

Try It

7. $-5(d-6)$
8. $-4(2k+3)$

ELL Support

Allow students to work in pairs to complete Self-Assessment for Concepts & Skills Exercises 9–14. Have students display their answers for your review. After pairs have worked on their descriptions for Exercise 15, have each pair present their answer to another pair. Pairs should compare their descriptions and reach agreement on a final description. Then have each group present their final description to the class.

Self-Assessment for Concepts & Skills

9. $8(2n-3)$
10. $14(3a+b)$
11. $\frac{1}{10}(k-7)$
12. $3.5(12+h)$
13. $-8(4d-7)$
14. $-12(2k-10)$
15. *Sample answer:* When using the Distributive Property to simplify an expression, multiplication is used. For example,
$$5(2x+3) = 5(2x) + 5(3) = 10x + 15.$$
When factoring an expression, division is used. For example,
$$9x - 6 = 3\left(\frac{9x}{3} - \frac{6}{3}\right) = 3(3x-2).$$

Laurie's Notes

EXAMPLE 3

- This example looks at factoring out a negative number. If students are comfortable with the two directions of the Distributive Property identified in the last two examples, then they should be able to discuss the role of the negative factor in this example.
- As a prompt, write: $-4p + 10 = -2(\_\_\_\_ + \_\_\_\_)$.
- Ask, "−2 times what is $-4p$?" $2p$ "−2 times what is 10?" −5
- Fill in the blanks, $-4p + 10 = -2(2p + (-5))$, which can be written as $-2(2p - 5)$.

Try It

- Have students complete the exercises on whiteboards.

Formative Assessment Tip

Misconception Check

This technique gives students the opportunity to think about their own understanding of a concept or process. Write a worked-out problem on the board that demonstrates a common misconception, a mistake that students often make about a concept or process. Ask students if they agree or disagree with the solution and to explain why. Allow time for students to think about the problem independently and write an explanation. Then ask volunteers to share their explanations with the class. Listening to the thinking of others may solidify or modify their own beliefs.

Self-Assessment for Concepts & Skills

- Identify the reasons for incorrect answers for Exercises 9–14. Are the errors computational? Do students complete Exercises 9–12 with ease but struggle with Exercises 13 and 14? Are the negative numbers the issue? Make sure students are aware of the reasons for their mistakes.
- Exercise 15 asks students to explain the relationship between using the Distributive Property to simplify an expression and to factor an expression. Students' responses will provide information about their level of understanding.
- **Misconception Check:** "Do you agree or disagree with this statement? Explain."
  Factor −4 out of $-16f + 44$.
  $-16f + 44 = -4(4f + 11)$
  Sample answer: disagree; A positive 4 was factored out of the second term in the parentheses instead of a negative 4. The correct answer is $-4(4f - 11)$.
- If time permits, students can write their own *Misconception Checks.* Have each student write a worked-out problem on an index card that has at least one error. Then have students exchange cards to find the errors.

The Success Criteria Self-Assessment chart can be found in the *Student Journal* or online at *BigIdeasMath.com.*

EXAMPLE 3 Factoring Out a Negative Number

Factor -2 out of $-4p + 10$.

Write each term as a product of -2 and another factor.

$-4p = -2 \cdot 2p$ — Think: $-4p$ is -2 times what?

$10 = -2 \cdot (-5)$ — Think: 10 is -2 times what?

Use the Distributive Property to factor out -2.

$-4p + 10 = -2 \cdot 2p + (-2) \cdot (-5)$ — Rewrite the expression.

$= -2[2p + (-5)]$ — Distributive Property

$= -2(2p - 5)$ — Simplify.

So, $-4p + 10 = -2(2p - 5)$.

Try It

7. Factor -5 out of $-5d + 30$.
8. Factor -4 out of $-8k - 12$.

Self-Assessment for Concepts & Skills

Solve each exercise. Then rate your understanding of the success criteria in your journal.

FACTORING OUT THE GCF **Factor the expression using the GCF.**

9. $16n - 24$
10. $42a + 14b$

FACTORING OUT A RATIONAL NUMBER **Factor out the coefficient of the variable term.**

11. $\frac{1}{10}k - \frac{7}{10}$
12. $42 + 3.5h$

FACTORING OUT A NEGATIVE NUMBER **Factor out the indicated number.**

13. Factor -8 out of $-32d + 56$.
14. Factor -12 out of $-24k + 120$.

15. **WRITING** Describe the relationship between using the Distributive Property to simplify an expression and to factor an expression. Give an example to justify your answer.

EXAMPLE 4 Modeling Real Life

A rectangular landing platform for a rocket is 60 yards wide and has an area of $(60x + 3600)$ square yards. Write an expression that represents the perimeter (in yards) of the platform.

Factor the width of 60 yards out of the given area expression to find an expression that represents the length (in yards) of the platform.

$$60x + 3600 = 60 \cdot x + 60 \cdot 60 \quad \text{Rewrite the expression.}$$

$$= 60(x + 60) \quad \text{Distributive Property}$$

So, the length (in yards) of the platform can be represented by $x + 60$. Use the perimeter formula to write an expression that represents the perimeter of the platform.

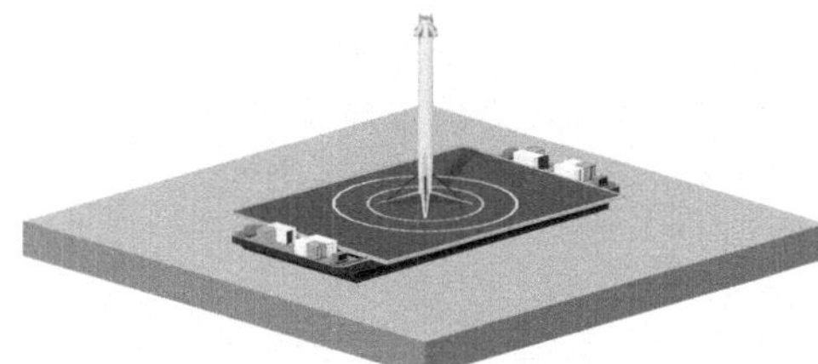

$$P = 2\ell + 2w \quad \text{Perimeter of a rectangle}$$

$$= 2(x + 60) + 2(60) \quad \text{Substitute for } \ell \text{ and } w.$$

$$= 2x + 120 + 120 \quad \text{Multiply.}$$

$$= 2x + 240 \quad \text{Add.}$$

So, an expression that represents the perimeter (in yards) of the platform is $2x + 240$.

Self-Assessment for Problem Solving

Solve each exercise. Then rate your understanding of the success criteria in your journal.

16. An organization drills 3 wells to provide access to clean drinking water. The cost (in dollars) to drill and maintain the wells for n years is represented by $34{,}500 + 540n$. Write and interpret an expression that represents the cost to drill and maintain one well for n years.

17. A photograph is 16 inches long and has an area of $(16x + 96)$ square inches. A custom-made frame is 2 inches wide and costs \$0.50 per square inch. Write an expression that represents the cost of the frame.

Laurie's Notes

EXAMPLE 4

- Ask a volunteer to read the problem aloud. Give students a minute to think about what the question is asking. Students need to recognize that the question has two parts. Sometimes, students struggle with knowing what interim result(s) are needed to solve the problem.
- ? Ask, "What is the question asking?" To find the perimeter "What do you need to find first?" the length
- **Hint:** Repeatedly modeling these questions will help students learn to verbalize their thinking when they are working independently.
- Many students will stop after finding the length of the platform. This problem emphasizes the need to check the answer for reasonableness.
- Remind students to include units in the answer.
- **Another Method:** Show students that they can factor 2 out of the perimeter formula before substituting ℓ and w.

$P = 2\ell + 2w$	Perimeter of a rectangle
$= 2(\ell + w)$	Distributive Property
$= 2(x + 60 + 60)$	Substitute for ℓ and w.
$= 2(x + 120)$	Add.
$= 2x + 240$	Distributive Property

Extra Example 4

A rectangular dog run is 12 meters long and has an area of $(12x + 48)$ square meters. Write an expression that represents the perimeter (in meters) of the dog run. $(2x + 32)$ meters

Self-Assessment for Problem Solving

- Allow time in class for students to practice using the problem-solving plan. Remember, some students may only be able to complete the first step.
- Have students work with a partner to write the verbal models.

The Success Criteria Self-Assessment chart can be found in the *Student Journal* or online at *BigIdeasMath.com*.

Self-Assessment for Problem Solving

16. $11{,}500 + 180n$; The initial cost of putting in one well is \$11,500 and the maintenance cost each year is \$180.

17. $(2x + 52)$ dollars

Closure

- Match the algebraic expression on the left with its factored form on the right.

1. $12x + 6$ C	**A.** $-6(2x - 1)$
2. $12x - 6$ B	**B.** $6(2x - 1)$
3. $-12x - 6$ D	**C.** $6(2x + 1)$
4. $-12x + 6$ A	**D.** $-6(2x + 1)$

Learning Target

Factor algebraic expressions.

Success Criteria

- Identify the greatest common factor of terms, including variable terms.
- Use the Distributive Property to factor algebraic expressions.
- Write a term as a product involving a given factor.

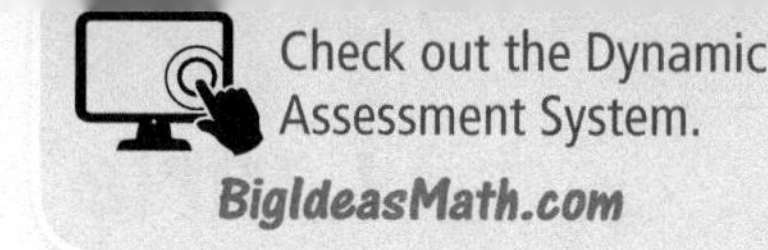
Check out the Dynamic Assessment System.
BigIdeasMath.com

Review & Refresh

1. $8k - 40$
2. $27 - 9d$
3. $\frac{1}{2}g + 1\frac{1}{2}$
4. $2\frac{1}{3}$
5. -10.3
6. $-2\frac{1}{8}$
7. 2
8. -3
9. -8

Concepts, Skills, & Problem Solving

10. *Sample answer:* $3(0.75x + 1)$; Factor out 3 from each area. Because 3 is the width of the smaller rectangles, the two lengths are $0.75x$ and 1.
11. *Sample answer:* $\frac{2}{3}\left(\frac{5}{4}m + n\right)$; Factor out $\frac{2}{3}$ from each area. Because $\frac{2}{3}$ is the width of the smaller rectangles, the two lengths are $\frac{5}{4}m$ and n.
12. $3(3b + 7)$
13. $16(2z - 3)$
14. $2(4x + 1)$
15. $3(y - 8)$
16. $14(p - 2)$
17. $2(3 + 8k)$
18. $7(3 - 2d)$
19. $4(5z - 2)$
20. $5(3w + 13)$
21. $4(9a + 4b)$
22. $7(3m - 7n)$
23. $3(4 + 3g - 10h)$
24. $\frac{1}{7}(a + 1)$
25. $\frac{1}{3}(b - 1)$
26. $\frac{3}{8}(d + 2)$
27. $2.2(x + 2)$
28. $1.5(y - 4)$
29. $0.8(w + 4.5)$
30. $\frac{3}{8}(10 + x)$
31. $4\left(h - \frac{3}{4}\right)$
32. $0.15(c - 0.48)$
33. $\frac{3}{8}\left(z + \frac{8}{3}\right)$
34. $6\left(s - \frac{1}{8}\right)$
35. $\frac{5}{2}\left(k - \frac{4}{5}\right)$

Assignment Guide and Concept Check

Scaffold assignments to support all students in their learning progression. The suggested assignments are a starting point. Continue to assign additional exercises and revisit with spaced practice to move every student toward proficiency.

Level	Assignment 1	Assignment 2
Emerging	3, 5, 6, 9, 10, 13, 14, 15, 24, 26, 28, 36, 38, 39	30, 31, 32, 37, 41, 42, 45, 46, 48
Proficient	3, 5, 6, 9, 11, 16, 17, 20, 25, 27, 30, 36, 39, 40	31, 32, 34, 37, 42, 43, 45, 46, 48
Advanced	3, 5, 6, 9, 11, 18, 20, 22, 30, 32, 34, 36, 42, 43	23, 35, 37, 44, 46, 47, 48

- Assignment 1 is for use after students complete the Self-Assessment for Concepts & Skills.
- Assignment 2 is for use after students complete the Self-Assessment for Problem Solving.
- The red exercises can be used as a concept check.

Review & Refresh Prior Skills

Exercises 1–3 Using the Distributive Property
Exercises 4–6 Subtracting Rational Numbers
Exercises 7–9 Evaluating Expressions

Common Errors

- **Exercises 12–23** Students may factor out a common factor but not the *greatest* common factor. For example, students might say that $32z - 48 = 2(16z - 24)$. While this is a true statement, it does not use the GCF. Students should realize that $16z$ and 24 still have the common factor of 8.
- **Exercise 30** Students may factor out the constant instead of the coefficient of the variable term. Remind students that the variable term does not have to be the first term in the expression.

C.4 Practice

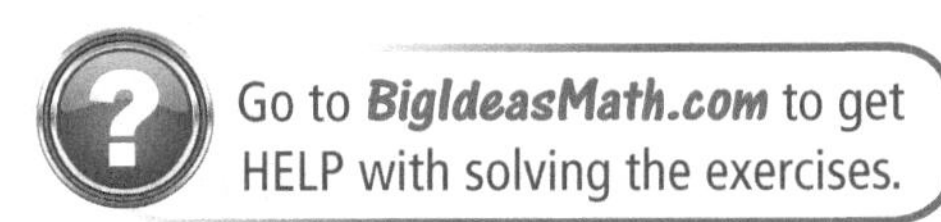
Go to BigIdeasMath.com to get HELP with solving the exercises.

Review & Refresh

Simplify the expression.

1. $8(k - 5)$
2. $-4.5(-6 + 2d)$
3. $-\frac{1}{4}(3g - 6 - 5g)$

Find the difference. Write fractions in simplest form.

4. $\frac{2}{3} - \left(-\frac{5}{3}\right)$
5. $-4.7 - 5.6$
6. $-4\frac{3}{8} - \left(-2\frac{1}{4}\right)$

Evaluate the expression when $x = 4$, $y = -6$, and $z = -3$.

7. $y \div z$
8. $\frac{4y}{2x}$
9. $\frac{3x - 2y}{z}$

Concepts, Skills, & Problem Solving

FINDING DIMENSIONS **The model shows the area (in square units) of each part of a rectangle. Use the model to find the missing values that complete the expression. Explain your reasoning.** (See Exploration 1, p. 609.)

10. $2.25x + 3 = \square(\square + \square)$

? ?

? | 2.25x | 3

11. $\frac{5}{6}m + \frac{2}{3}n = \square(\square + \square)$

? ?

? | $\frac{5}{6}m$ | $\frac{2}{3}n$

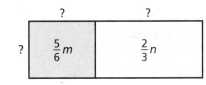

FACTORING OUT THE GCF **Factor the expression using the GCF.**

12. $9b + 21$
13. $32z - 48$
14. $8x + 2$
15. $3y - 24$
16. $14p - 28$
17. $6 + 16k$
18. $21 - 14d$
19. $20z - 8$
20. $15w + 65$
21. $36a + 16b$
22. $21m - 49n$
23. $12 + 9g - 30h$

FACTORING OUT A RATIONAL NUMBER **Factor out the coefficient of the variable term.**

24. $\frac{1}{7}a + \frac{1}{7}$
25. $\frac{1}{3}b - \frac{1}{3}$
26. $\frac{3}{8}d + \frac{3}{4}$
27. $2.2x + 4.4$
28. $1.5y - 6$
29. $0.8w + 3.6$
30. $\frac{15}{4} + \frac{3}{8}x$
31. $4h - 3$
32. $0.15c - 0.072$
33. $\frac{3}{8}z + 1$
34. $6s - \frac{3}{4}$
35. $\frac{5}{2}k - 2$

MP YOU BE THE TEACHER Your friend factors the expression. Is your friend correct? Explain your reasoning.

36.

$$16p - 28 = 4(4p - 28)$$

37.

$$\frac{2}{3}y - \frac{14}{3} = \frac{2}{3} \cdot y - \frac{2}{3} \cdot 7$$
$$= \frac{2}{3}(y - 7)$$

FACTORING OUT A NEGATIVE NUMBER Factor out the indicated number.

38. Factor -4 out of $-8d + 20$.

39. Factor -6 out of $18z - 15$.

40. Factor -0.25 out of $7g + 3.5$.

41. Factor $-\frac{1}{2}$ out of $-\frac{1}{2}x + 6$.

42. Factor -1.75 out of $-14m - 5.25n$.

43. Factor $-\frac{1}{4}$ out of $-\frac{1}{2}x - \frac{5}{4}y$.

44. **MP STRUCTURE** A rectangle has an area of $(4x + 12)$ square units. Write three multiplication expressions that can represent the product of the length and the width of the rectangle.

45. **MP MODELING REAL LIFE** A square wrestling mat has a perimeter of $(12x - 32)$ feet. Explain how to use the expression to find the length (in feet) of the mat. Justify your answer.

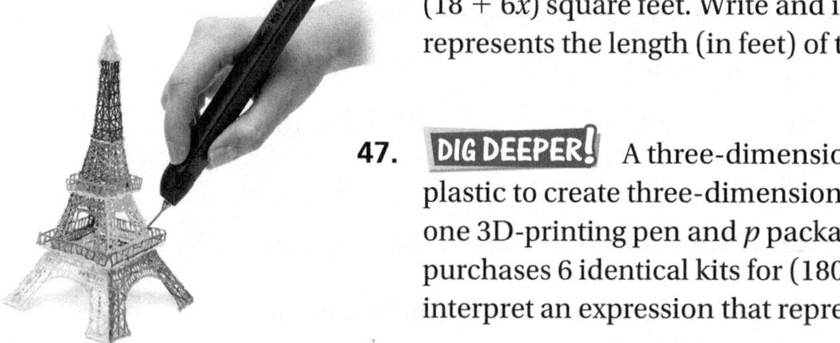

46. **MP MODELING REAL LIFE** A table is 6 feet long and 3 feet wide. You extend the length of the table by inserting two identical table *leaves*. The extended table is rectangular with an area of $(18 + 6x)$ square feet. Write and interpret an expression that represents the length (in feet) of the extended table.

47. **DIG DEEPER!** A three-dimensional printing pen uses heated plastic to create three-dimensional objects. A kit comes with one 3D-printing pen and p packages of plastic. An art club purchases 6 identical kits for $(180 + 58.5p)$ dollars. Write and interpret an expression that represents the cost of one kit.

48. **MP STRUCTURE** The area of the trapezoid is $\left(\frac{3}{4}x - \frac{1}{4}\right)$ square centimeters. Write two different pairs of expressions that represent the possible base lengths (in centimeters). Justify your answers.

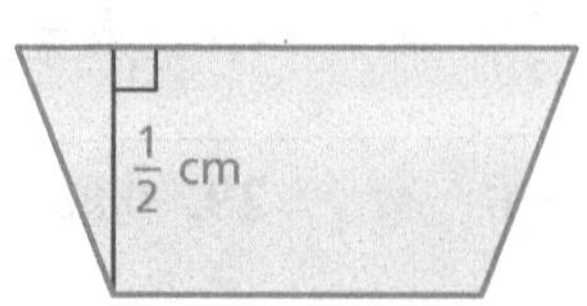

Common Errors

- **Exercises 38–43** Students may factor out the negative number from the first term but forget to factor out the negative from the second term. Remind students to factor *both* terms by the negative number.

Mini-Assessment

Factor the expression using the GCF.

1. $21w + 28$ $7(3w + 4)$
2. $9x - 15$ $3(3x - 5)$
3. Factor $\frac{1}{3}$ out of $\frac{1}{3}p - \frac{2}{3}$. $\frac{1}{3}(p - 2)$
4. Factor -6 out of $-12y - 42$. $-6(2y + 7)$
5. Your family rents a car for 4 days. The rental company charges a daily fee and an additional charge per mile driven. The total cost of the rental is $(104 + 2m)$ dollars. Write and interpret an expression that represents the cost per day. $(26 + 0.5m)$ dollars; The rental company charges \$26 per day and \$0.50 per mile.

Section Resources

Surface Level	Deep Level
Resources by Chapter • Extra Practice • Reteach • Puzzle Time Student Journal • Self-Assessment • Practice Differentiating the Lesson Tutorial Videos Skills Review Handbook Skills Trainer	Resources by Chapter • Enrichment and Extension Graphic Organizers Dynamic Assessment System • Section Practice
Transfer Level	
Dynamic Assessment System • End-of-Chapter Quiz	Assessment Book • End-of-Chapter Quiz

Concepts, Skills, & Problem Solving

36. no; Your friend did not factor a 4 out from the second term; $16p - 28 = 4(4p - 7)$

37. yes; Your friend factored out the $\frac{2}{3}$ properly from the sum and correctly rewrote the expression.

38. $-4(2d - 5)$ **39.** $-6\left(-3z + \frac{5}{2}\right)$

40. $-0.25(-28g - 14)$

41. $-\frac{1}{2}(x - 12)$

42. $-1.75(8m + 3n)$

43. $-\frac{1}{4}(2x + 5y)$

44. *Sample answer:* $4(x + 3)$; $12\left(\frac{1}{3}x + 1\right)$; $2(2x + 6)$

45. *Sample answer:* Because the mat is a square, all sides are the same length. The perimeter is $12x - 32$, and to find the dimension of each side, divide each term by 4. The length of each side is $3x - 8$ and $4(3x - 8) = 12x - 32$.

46. $6 + 2x$; The length of the extended table is the length of the original table, 6 feet, plus the lengths of the two leaves that are each x feet.

47. $30 + 9.75p$; For each kit, the pen costs \$30 and each package of plastic costs \$9.75.

48. *Sample answer:* $2x - 1$ and x, $2x$ and $x - 1$;

$$A = \frac{1}{2}h(b_1 + b_2)$$

$$\frac{3}{4}x - \frac{1}{4} = \frac{1}{2}\left(\frac{1}{2}\right)(b_1 + b_2)$$

$$\frac{1}{4}(3x - 1) = \frac{1}{4}(b_1 + b_2)$$

So, the sum of the bases is $3x - 1$.

Skills Needed

Exercise 1

- Converting Measures
- Factoring Out a Rational Number

Exercise 2

- Adding Linear Expressions
- Finding Percents

ELL Support

You may want to review the multiple meanings of the word *runway*. In Exercise 1, runway relates to flying and planes, but it can also relate to modeling and fashion. Students may be familiar with either meaning.

Using the Problem-Solving Plan

1. $10{,}560x + 26{,}928$
2. $-500t + 12{,}500$; 60%

Performance Task

The *STEAM Video Performance Task* provides the opportunity for additional enrichment and greater depth of knowledge as students explore the mathematics of the chapter within a context tied to the chapter STEAM Video. The performance task and a detailed scoring rubric are provided at *BigIdeasMath.com*.

Laurie's Notes

Scaffolding Instruction

- The goal of this lesson is to help students become more comfortable with problem solving. These exercises combine algebraic expressions with prior skills from other chapters. The solution for Exercise 1 is worked out below, to help you guide students through the problem-solving plan. Use the remaining class time to have students work on the other exercise.
- **Emerging:** The goal for these students is to feel comfortable with the problem-solving plan. Allow students to work in pairs to write the beginning steps of the problem-solving plan for Exercise 2. Keep in mind that some students may only be ready to do the first step.
- **Proficient:** Students may be able to work independently or in pairs to complete Exercise 2.
- Visit each pair to review their plan for the problem. Ask students to describe their plans.

Using the Problem-Solving Plan

Exercise 1

Understand the problem. You know the area of the rectangular runway in square miles and the width of the runway in miles. You want to know the perimeter of the runway in feet.

Make a plan. Factor the width of 0.05 mile out of the expression that represents the area to find an expression that represents the length of the runway. Then write an expression that represents the perimeter (in miles) of the runway. Finally, use a measurement conversion to write the expression in terms of feet.

Solve and check. Use the plan to solve the problem. Then check your solution.

- Factor the width of 0.05 mile out of the expression.

  $0.05x + 0.125 = 0.05(x + 2.5)$

  So, the length of the runway is $(x + 2.5)$ miles.

- Write an expression that represents the perimeter (in miles).

$P = 2\ell + 2w$	Write formula for perimeter of a rectangle.
$= 2(x + 2.5) + 2(0.05)$	Substitute $x + 2.5$ for ℓ and 0.05 for w.
$= 2x + 5 + 0.1$	Distributive Property
$= 2x + 5.1$	Simplify.

  So, the perimeter of the runway is $(2x + 5.1)$ miles.

- Convert $(2x + 5.1)$ miles to feet.

  $(2x + 5.1)\cancel{\text{mi}} \cdot \frac{5280 \text{ ft}}{1 \cancel{\text{mi}}} = (2x + 5.1)\,5280 = 10{,}560x + 26{,}928$

  So, the perimeter of the runway is $(10{,}560x + 26{,}928)$ feet.

- **Check:** Substitute $(x + 2.5)$ miles in the area formula to verify the length.

  $\text{Area} = \ell w$

  $0.05x + 0.125 = (x + 2.5)(0.05)$

  $= 0.05x + 0.125$ ✓

Connecting Concepts

Using the Problem-Solving Plan

1. The runway shown has an area of $(0.05x + 0.125)$ square miles. Write an expression that represents the perimeter (in feet) of the runway.

Understand the problem.

You know the area of the rectangular runway in square miles and the width of the runway in miles. You want to know the perimeter of the runway in feet.

Make a plan.

Factor the width of 0.05 mile out of the expression that represents the area to find an expression that represents the length of the runway. Then write an expression that represents the perimeter (in miles) of the runway. Finally, use a measurement conversion to write the expression in terms of feet.

Solve and check.

Use the plan to solve the problem. Then check your solution.

2. The populations of two towns after t years can be modeled by $-300t + 7000$ and $-200t + 5500$. What is the combined population of the two towns after t years? The combined population of the towns in Year 10 is what percent of the combined population in Year 0?

Performance Task

Chlorophyll in Plants

At the beginning of this chapter, you watched a STEAM Video called "Tropic Status." You are now ready to complete the performance task related to this video, available at ***BigIdeasMath.com***. Be sure to use the problem-solving plan as you work through the performance task.

Chapter Review

Review Vocabulary

Write the definition and give an example of each vocabulary term.

like terms, *p. 592*
simplest form, *p. 592*
linear expression, *p. 598*
factoring an expression, *p. 610*

Graphic Organizers

You can use an **Example and Non-Example Chart** to list examples and non-examples of a concept. Here is an Example and Non-Example Chart for ***like terms***.

Like Terms

Examples	Non-Examples
2 and −3	y and 4
$3x$ and $-7x$	$3x$ and $3y$
x^2 and $6x^2$	$4x$ and $-2x^2$
y and $5y$	$2y$ and 5

Choose and complete a graphic organizer to help you study the concept.

1. simplest form
2. equivalent expressions
3. linear expression
4. Distributive Property
5. factoring an expression

"Here is my Example and Non-Example Chart about things that scare cats."

Review Vocabulary

- As a review of the chapter vocabulary, have students revisit the vocabulary section in their *Student Journals* to fill in any missing definitions and record examples of each term.

Graphic Organizers

Sample answers:

1. Simplest Form

Examples	Non-Examples
$6x + 8$	$3n - 8n$
$\frac{1}{2}a - 18$	$4y - 7 + 12y$
$0.9 - 6.6m$	$-7.6 + 4.5b - 10$
$10c - 17 + 19d$	$\frac{1}{2}g - 3h - \frac{2}{3}g + 9h$

2. Equivalent Expressions

Examples	Non-Examples
$3x + 4x$ and $7x$	$3x + 4$ and $7x$
$\frac{1}{2}(b + 8)$ and $\frac{1}{2}b + 4$	$\frac{1}{2}(b + 8)$ and $\frac{1}{2}b + 8$
$9h - 5 + 8h$ and $17h - 5$	$9h - 5 + 8h$ and $h - 5$
$-2.6m - 4.1m$ and $-6.7m$	$2.6m - 4.1m$ and $1.5m$

3. Linear Expression

Examples	Non-Examples
$-5x$	$2x^2$
$\frac{1}{4}x + 8$	$-4x + x^2$
$2 - 3x$	$0.8x^5 - 2$
$6x + 7y$	$\frac{4}{5}x^4 - x$
$8.3x - 4.4y$	$2\frac{1}{6}x^7$

4–5. Answers at *BigIdeasMath.com.*

List of Organizers

Available at *BigIdeasMath.com*

Definition and Example Chart

Example and Non-Example Chart

Four Square

Information Frame

Summary Triangle

About this Organizer

An **Example and Non-Example Chart** can be used to list examples and non-examples of a concept. Students write examples of the concept in the left column and non-examples in the right column. This organizer can be used to assess students' understanding of two concepts that have subtle, but important differences. Blank Example and Non-Example Charts can be included on tests or quizzes for this purpose.

Chapter Self-Assessment

1. Terms: z, 8, $-4z$;
   Like terms: z and $-4z$
2. Terms: $3n$, 7, $-n$, -3;
   Like terms: $3n$ and $-n$, 7 and -3
3. Terms: $10x^2$, $-y$, 12, $-3x^2$;
   Like terms: $10x^2$ and $-3x^2$
4. $-4h$
5. $3.5r - 7$
6. $-6m$
7. $9y + 2$
8. $\frac{9}{20}x + 12$
9. $\frac{1}{2}y + 6$
10. *Sample answer:*
    $3x^2 + 2x^2 - 10 + 2$;
    $3x^2 + 2x^2 - 10 + 2$
    $= (3x^2 + 2x^2) + (-10 + 2)$
    $= 5x^2 - 8$
11. $7.1x$, where x is the number of each sandwich sold; *Sample answer:* The earnings for each type of sandwich is $\$2.25x$, $\$1.55x$, $\$2x$, and $\$1.3x$. The earnings for all the sandwiches is
    $2.25x + 1.55x + 2x + 1.3x$
    $= 7.1x$ dollars.
12. a. $32.67x$; It costs \$32.67 to buy one brush, one can of paint, and one paint roller. You buy x of each.

    b. \$98.01

Chapter Self-Assessment

The Success Criteria Self-Assessment chart can be found in the *Student Journal* or online at *BigIdeasMath.com.*

ELL Support

Allow students to work in pairs to complete Exercises 1–9 of the Chapter Self-Assessment. After pairs complete these exercises, check for understanding by having each pair display their answers on a whiteboard for your review. Have pairs complete Exercises 10–12. Then group two pairs to discuss their answers and come to an agreement on each answer. Monitor discussions and provide support. Use similar techniques to check the remaining sections of the Chapter Self-Assessment.

Common Errors

- **Exercises 1–3** When identifying and writing terms, make sure students include the sign of the term. Students may find it helpful to write the original problem using addition.
- **Exercises 5 and 7–9** The subtraction operation can confuse students. Tell students to write the original problem using addition and then use the Commutative Property.

Chapter Self-Assessment

As you complete the exercises, use the scale below to rate your understanding of the success criteria in your journal.

1	2	3	4
I do not understand.	I can do it with help.	I can do it on my own.	I can teach someone else.

C.1 Algebraic Expressions (pp. 591–596)

Learning Target: Simplify algebraic expressions.

Identify the terms and like terms in the expression.

1. $z + 8 - 4z$

2. $3n + 7 - n - 3$

3. $10x^2 - y + 12 - 3x^2$

Simplify the expression.

4. $4h - 8h$

5. $6.4r - 7 - 2.9r$

6. $2m - m - 7m$

7. $6y + 9 + 3y - 7$

8. $\frac{3}{5}x + 19 - \frac{3}{20}x - 7$

9. $\frac{2}{3}y + 14 - \frac{1}{6}y - 8$

10. Write an expression with 4 different terms that is equivalent to $5x^2 - 8$. Justify your answer.

11. Find the earnings for selling the same number of each type of sandwich. Justify your answer.

	Turkey	Ham
Pretzel Roll	2.25	1.55
Bagel	2.00	1.30

12. You buy the same number of brushes, rollers, and paint cans.

a. Write and interpret an expression in simplest form that represents the total amount of money you spend on painting supplies.

b. How much do you spend when you buy one set of supplies for each of 3 painters?

C.2 Adding and Subtracting Linear Expressions (pp. 597–602)

Learning Target: Find sums and differences of linear expressions.

Find the sum.

13. $(c - 4) + (3c + 9)$

14. $(5z + 4) + (3z - 6)$

15. $(-2.1m - 5) + (3m - 7)$

16. $\left(\frac{5}{4}q + 1\right) + (q - 4) + \left(-\frac{1}{4}q + 2\right)$

Find the difference.

17. $(x - 1) - (3x + 2)$

18. $(4y + 3) - (2y - 9)$

19. $\left(\frac{1}{2}h + 7\right) - \left(\frac{3}{2}h + 9\right)$

20. $(4 - 3.7b) - (-5.4b - 4) - (1.2b + 1)$

21. A basket holds n apples. You pick $(2n - 3)$ apples, and your friend picks $(n + 4)$ apples. How many apples do you and your friend pick together? How many baskets do you need to carry all the apples? Justify your answer.

22. Greenland has a population of x people. Barbados has a population of about 4500 more than 5 times the population of Greenland. Find and interpret the difference in the populations of these two countries.

C.3 The Distributive Property (pp. 603–608)

Learning Target: Apply the Distributive Property to generate equivalent expressions.

Simplify the expression.

23. $2(a - 3)$

24. $-3(4x - 10)$

25. $-2.5(8 - b)$

26. $-7(1 - 3d - 5)$

27. $9(-3w - 6.2 + 2w)$

28. $\frac{3}{4}\left(8g - \frac{1}{4} - \frac{2}{3}g\right)$

29. Mars has m moons. The number of moons of Pluto is one more than twice the number of moons of Mars. The number of moons of Neptune is one less than 3 times the number of moons of Pluto. Write and interpret a simplified expression that represents the number of moons of Neptune.

Common Errors

- **Exercises 17–20** Students may forget to subtract each term in the parentheses. Remind students to rewrite the problem so that *adding the opposite* is obvious.
- **Exercises 23–28** Students may forget to distribute to each term in the parentheses, especially when there are more than two terms. Tell students to write the expression in the parentheses on their papers and draw arrows from the number being distributed to each term.

Chapter Self-Assessment

13. $4c + 5$

14. $8z - 2$

15. $0.9m - 12$

16. $2q - 1$

17. $-2x - 3$

18. $2y + 12$

19. $-h - 2$

20. $0.5b + 7$

21. $3n + 1$; 4 baskets; *Sample answer:* One basket can hold n apples. There is a total of $(3n + 1)$ apples. $3n + 1 = n + n + n + 1$. Three baskets would hold all the apples but 1, so a 4th basket is needed to carry all the apples.

22. $4x + 4500$; The difference in population between Barbados and Greenland is 4500 more than 4 times the population of Greenland.

23. $2a - 6$

24. $-12x + 30$

25. $-20 + 2.5b$

26. $28 + 21d$

27. $-9w - 55.8$

28. $5\frac{1}{2}g - \frac{3}{16}$

29. $6m + 2$; The number of moons of Neptune is two more than 6 times the number of moons of Mars.

Chapter Self-Assessment

30. $3q + 21$

31. $2m - 18$

32. $1.5n - 3.2$

33. $-\frac{4}{15}d - 8$

34. $\left(\frac{9}{5}(C + 5) + 32\right) - \left(\frac{9}{5}C + 32\right)$

$= \frac{9}{5}C + 41 - \frac{9}{5}C - 32$

$= 9$

35. $6(3a - 2)$

36. $2(b + 4)$

37. $3(3 - 5x)$

38. $\frac{1}{4}\left(y + \frac{3}{2}\right)$

39. $1.7(j - 2)$

40. $-5(p - 4)$

41. $-\frac{3}{4}(-2x + 3y)$

42. $2.50

43. $2x + 20$

44. *Sample answer:* The blocks have square bases, so the perimeter is 4 times the length of one side, or $P = 12x - 9 = 4(3x - 2.25)$. Each side is $(3x - 2.25)$ inches. The wall is 7 blocks long, so the length of the wall is $7(3x - 2.25)$
$= (21x - 15.75)$ inches.

Common Errors

- **Exercises 35–37** Students may factor out a common factor but not the *greatest* common factor. For example, students might say that $18a - 12 = 2(9a - 6)$. While this is a true statement, it does not use the GCF. Students should realize that $9a$ and 6 still have the common factor of 3.
- **Exercises 40 and 41** Students may factor out the negative number from the first term but forget to factor out the negative from the second term. Remind students to factor *both* terms by the negative number.

Chapter Resources

Surface Level	Deep Level
Resources by Chapter • Extra Practice • Reteach • Puzzle Time Student Journal • Practice • Chapter Self-Assessment Differentiating the Lesson Tutorial Videos Skills Review Handbook Skills Trainer Game Library	Resources by Chapter • Enrichment and Extension Graphic Organizers Game Library
Transfer Level	
STEAM Video Dynamic Assessment System • Chapter Test	Assessment Book • Chapter Tests A and B • Alternative Assessment • STEAM Performance Task

Simplify the expression.

30. $3(2 + q) + 15$

31. $\frac{1}{8}(16m - 8) - 17$

32. $-1.5(4 - n) + 2.8$

33. $\frac{2}{5}(d - 10) - \frac{2}{3}(d + 6)$

34. The expression for degrees Fahrenheit is $\frac{9}{5}C + 32$, where C represents degrees Celsius. The temperature today is 5 degrees Celsius more than yesterday. Write and simplify an expression for the difference in degrees Fahrenheit for these two days.

C.4 Factoring Expressions (pp. 609–614)

Learning Target: Factor algebraic expressions.

Factor the expression using GCF.

35. $18a - 12$

36. $2b + 8$

37. $9 - 15x$

Factor out the coefficient of the variable term.

38. $\frac{1}{4}y + \frac{3}{8}$

39. $1.7j - 3.4$

40. $-5p + 20$

41. Factor $-\frac{3}{4}$ out of $\frac{3}{2}x - \frac{9}{4}y$.

42. You and 4 friends are buying tickets for a concert. The cost to buy one ticket is c dollars. If you buy all the tickets together, there is a discount and the cost is $(5c - 12.5)$ dollars. How much do you save per ticket when you buy the tickets together?

43. The rectangular pupil of an octopus is estimated to be 20 millimeters long with an area of $(20x - 200)$ square millimeters. Write an expression that represents the perimeter (in millimeters) of the octopus pupil.

44. A building block has a square base that has a perimeter of $(12x - 9)$ inches. Explain how to use the expression to find the length (in inches) of the wall shown.

Practice Test

1. Identify the terms and like terms in $4x + 9x^2 - 2x + 2$.

Simplify the expression.

2. $8x - 5 + 2x$

3. $2.5w - 3y + 4w$

4. $\frac{5}{7}x + 15 - \frac{9}{14}x - 9$

5. $(3j + 11) + (8j - 7)$

6. $(2r - 13) - (-6r + 4)$

7. $-2(4 - 3n)$

8. $3(5 - 2n) + 9n$

9. $\frac{1}{3}(6x + 9) - 2$

10. $\frac{3}{4}(8p + 12) + \frac{3}{8}(16p - 8)$

11. $-2.5(2s - 5) - 3(4.5s - 5.2)$

Factor out the coefficient of the variable term.

12. $6n - 24$

13. $\frac{1}{2}q + \frac{5}{2}$

14. $-4x + 36$

15. Find the earnings for giving a haircut and a shampoo to m men and w women. Justify your answer.

	Women	Men
Haircut	\$45	\$15
Shampoo	\$12	\$7

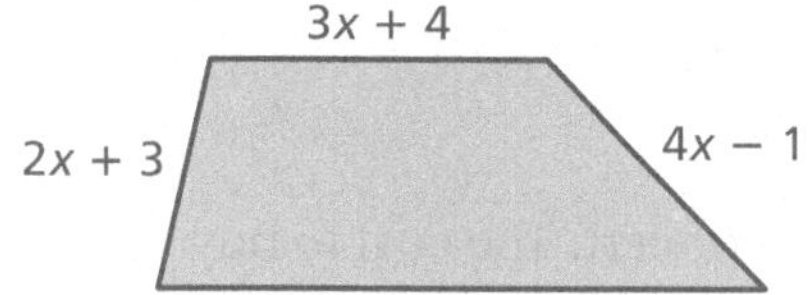

16. The expression $15x + 11$ represents the perimeter of the trapezoid. What is the length of the fourth side? Explain your reasoning.

17. The maximum number of charms that will fit on a bracelet is $3\left(d - \frac{2}{3}\right)$, where d is the diameter (in centimeters) of the bracelet.

   a. Write and interpret a simplified expression that represents the maximum number of charms on a bracelet.

   b. What is the maximum number of charms that fit on a bracelet that has a diameter of 6 centimeters?

18. You expand a rectangular garden so the perimeter is now twice the perimeter of the old garden. The expression $12w + 16$ represents the perimeter of the new garden, where w represents the width of the old garden.

   a. Write an expression that represents the perimeter of the old garden. Justify your answer.

   b. Write an expression that represents the area of the old garden.

Practice Test Item References

Practice Test Questions	Section to Review
1, 2, 3, 4, 15	C.1
5, 6, 16	C.2
7, 8, 9, 10, 11, 17	C.3
12, 13, 14, 18	C.4

Test-Taking Strategies

Remind students to quickly look over the entire test before they start so that they can budget their time. On tests, it is really important for students to **Stop** and **Think**. When students hurry on a test dealing with positive and negative numbers, they often make "sign" errors.

Common Errors

- **Exercise 1** When identifying and writing terms, make sure students include the sign of the term. Students may find it helpful to write the original problem using addition.
- **Exercises 2–4** The subtraction operation can confuse students. Tell students to write the original problem using addition and then use the Commutative Property.
- **Exercises 6 and 11** Students may forget to subtract each term in the parentheses. Remind students to rewrite the problem so that *adding the opposite* is obvious.
- **Exercises 8–11** Students may forget to distribute to each term in the parentheses, especially when there are more than two terms. Tell students to write the expression in the parentheses on their papers and draw arrows from the number being distributed to each term.
- **Exercise 14** Students may factor out the negative number from the first term but forget to factor out the negative from the second term. Remind students to factor *both* terms by the negative number.

Practice Test

1. Terms: $4x$, $9x^2$, $-2x$, 2; Like terms: $4x$ and $-2x$
2. $10x - 5$
3. $6.5w - 3y$
4. $\frac{1}{14}x + 6$
5. $11j + 4$
6. $8r - 17$
7. $-8 + 6n$
8. $15 + 3n$
9. $2x + 1$
10. $12p + 6$
11. $-18.5s + 28.1$
12. $6(n - 4)$
13. $\frac{1}{2}(q + 5)$
14. $-4(x - 9)$
15. $57w + 22m$;
    $(45 + 12)w + (15 + 7)m$
    $= 57w + 22m$
16. $6x + 5$; *Sample answer:* The perimeter of the trapezoid is the sum of the 3 known sides and the base. The sum of the 3 sides is $9x + 6$. The base is $(15x + 11) - (9x + 6) = 6x + 5$.
17. **a.** $3d - 2$; The maximum number of charms on a bracelet is two less than 3 times the diameter of the bracelet.

    b. 16 charms
18. **a.** $6w + 8$;
    $$\text{old garden} = \frac{1}{2}(\text{new garden}) = \frac{1}{2}(12w + 16) = 6w + 8$$

    b. $2w^2 + 4w$

Test-Taking Strategies

Available at *BigIdeasMath.com*
After Answering Easy Questions, Relax
Answer Easy Questions First
Estimate the Answer
Read All Choices before Answering
Read Question before Answering
Solve Directly or Eliminate Choices
Solve Problem before Looking at Choices
Use Intelligent Guessing
Work Backwards

About this Strategy

When taking a timed test, it is often best to skim the test and answer the easy questions first. Read each question carefully and thoroughly. Be careful that you record your answer in the correct position on the answer sheet.

Cumulative Practice

1. C
2. -9
3. G
4. B

Item Analysis

1. **A.** The student finds $(3.7 - 5 - 2.3)x$ instead of $3.7x - 5 - 2.3x$.

   B. The student adds $3.7x$ and $2.3x$ instead of subtracting $2.3x$ from $3.7x$.

   C. Correct answer

   D. The student finds $3.7x - 5 - 2.3$ instead of $3.7x - 5 - 2.3x$.

2. Gridded Response: Correct answer: -9

   Common error: The student substitutes -6 for c and 0 for d to get 0.

3. **F.** The student adds -38 and -14.

   G. Correct answer

   H. The student adds 38 and -14.

   I. The student adds 38 and 14.

4. **A.** The student finds the temperature of the first thermometer.

   B. Correct answer

   C. The student finds the median low temperature of the week.

   D. The student finds the range of the positive temperatures.

Cumulative Practice

Test-Taking Strategy
Answer Easy Questions First

x mummies are added to (x + 2) mummies.
How many mummies are there?
Ⓐ 2x + 2 Ⓑ 1 million
Ⓒ 11 Ⓓ 0

Tests about mummies get me all wound up.

"Scan the test and answer the easy questions first. Because *x* must be in the expression, A is correct."

1. What is the simplified form of the expression?

$$3.7x - 5 - 2.3x$$

A. $-3.6x$

B. $6x - 5$

C. $1.4x - 5$

D. $3.7x - 7.3$

2. What is the value of the expression when $c = 0$ and $d = -6$?

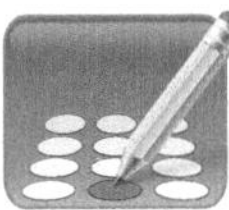

$$\frac{cd - d^2}{4}$$

3. What is the value of the expression?

$$-38 - (-14)$$

F. -52 **G.** -24

H. 24 **I.** 52

4. The daily low temperatures for a week are shown.

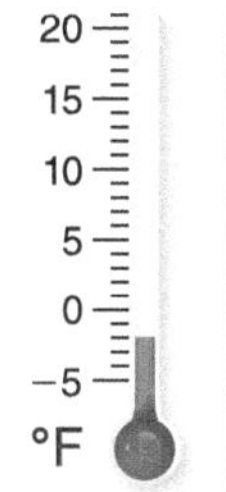

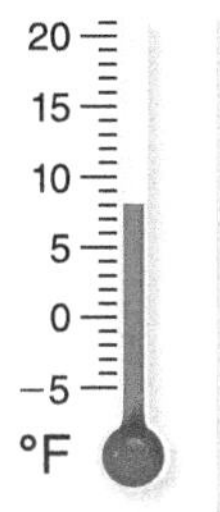

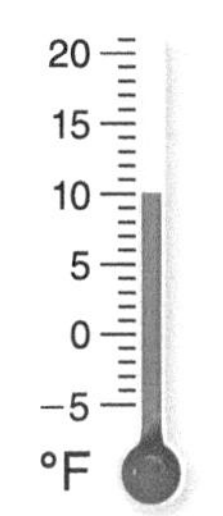

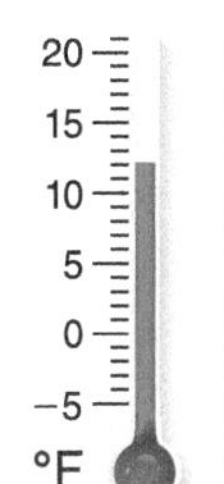

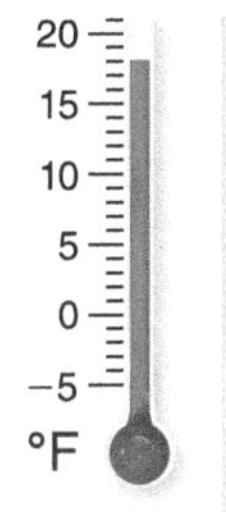

What is the mean low temperature of the week?

A. $-2°F$ **B.** $6°F$

C. $8°F$ **D.** $10°F$

5. You and a friend collect seashells on a beach. After h minutes, you have collected $(11 + 2h)$ seashells and your friend has collected $(5h - 2)$ seashells. How many total seashells have you and your friend collected?

F. $7h + 9$

G. $3h - 13$

H. $16h$

I. $7h + 13$

6. What is the value of the expression?

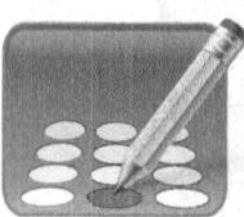

$$-0.28 \div (-0.07)$$

7. Which list is ordered from least to greatest?

A. $-\left|\frac{3}{4}\right|, -\frac{1}{2}, \left|\frac{3}{8}\right|, -\frac{1}{4}, \left|-\frac{7}{8}\right|$

B. $-\frac{1}{2}, -\frac{1}{4}, \left|\frac{3}{8}\right|, -\left|\frac{3}{4}\right|, \left|-\frac{7}{8}\right|$

C. $\left|-\frac{7}{8}\right|, \left|\frac{3}{8}\right|, -\frac{1}{4}, -\frac{1}{2}, -\left|\frac{3}{4}\right|$

D. $-\left|\frac{3}{4}\right|, -\frac{1}{2}, -\frac{1}{4}, \left|\frac{3}{8}\right|, \left|-\frac{7}{8}\right|$

8. Which number is equivalent to the expression shown?

$$-2\frac{1}{4} - \left(-8\frac{3}{8}\right)$$

F. $-10\frac{5}{8}$

G. $-10\frac{1}{3}$

H. $6\frac{1}{8}$

I. $6\frac{1}{2}$

9. What is the simplified form of the expression?

$$7x - 2(3x + 6)$$

A. $15x + 30$

B. $x - 12$

C. $13x + 12$

D. $-11x$

Item Analysis (continued)

5. F. Correct answer

   G. The student finds the difference instead of the sum.

   H. The student thinks the first expression is $11h + 2$ instead of $11 + 2h$.

   I. The student adds 11 and 2 instead of 11 and -2.

6. **Gridded Response:** Correct answer: 4
   Common error: The student incorrectly thinks that the quotient of two negative numbers is a negative number and gets -4.

7. A. The student finds the opposite of $\frac{3}{8}$ instead of the absolute value of $\frac{3}{8}$.

   B. The student finds $\left| -\frac{3}{4} \right|$ instead of $-\left| \frac{3}{4} \right|$.

   C. The student orders the values from greatest to least.

   D. Correct answer

8. F. The student finds the sum of $-2\frac{1}{4}$ and $-8\frac{3}{8}$ instead of the difference.

   G. The student finds the sum of the integers, the sum of the numerators, and the sum of the denominators.

   H. Correct answer

   I. The student finds the difference of the integers, the difference of the numerators, and the difference of the denominators.

9. A. The student does not follow the correct order of operations; incorrectly subtracting 2 from $7x$ to get $5(3x + 6)$.

   B. Correct answer

   C. The student finds $7x + 2(3x + 6)$ instead of $7x - 2(3x + 6)$.

   D. The student incorrectly adds $3x$ and 6 to get $7x - 2(9x)$.

Cumulative Practice

5. F
6. 4
7. D
8. H
9. B

Cumulative Practice

10. H

11. Part A: $16w + 68$; You and your friend currently have \$68 and save \$16 per week.

Part B: \$228; you; After 10 weeks, you have \$116 saved and your friend has \$112 saved. You saved \$4 more than your friend.

12. B

Item Analysis (continued)

10. **F.** The student does not recognize that 6 is a factor of $72m$ and 60.

G. The student does not recognize that 4 is a factor of $72m$ and 60.

H. Correct answer

I. The student does not recognize that 12 is a factor of $72m$ and 60.

11. **4 points** The student's work and explanations demonstrate a thorough understanding of writing, simplifying, interpreting, and evaluating algebraic expressions. In Part A, the student correctly writes the expression $68 + 16w$, or $16w + 68$. The student states that you and your friend have \$68 and will save an additional \$16 every week. In Part B, the student correctly finds the cost of the bike is \$228 and you will pay \$4 more than your friend. The student provides accurate work with clear and complete explanations.

3 points The student's work and explanations demonstrate an essential but less than thorough understanding of writing, simplifying, interpreting, and evaluating algebraic expressions.

2 points The student's work and explanations demonstrate a partial but limited understanding of writing, simplifying, interpreting, and evaluating algebraic expressions.

1 point The student's work and explanations demonstrate a very limited understanding of writing, simplifying, interpreting, and evaluating algebraic expressions.

0 points The student provides no response, a completely incorrect or incomprehensible response, or a response that demonstrates insufficient understanding of writing, simplifying, interpreting, and evaluating algebraic expressions.

12. **A.** The student finds $3 \div x^2 - y$ instead of $3 + x^2 \div y$.

B. Correct answer

C. The student does not follow the correct order of operations; dividing before evaluating the exponent.

D. The student does not follow the correct order of operations; subtracting before dividing.

10. Which expression is *not* equivalent to the expression?

$$72m - 60$$

F. $6(12m - 10)$

G. $4(18m - 15)$

H. $12m$

I. $12(6m - 5)$

11. You want to buy a bicycle with your friend. You have \$43.50 saved and plan to save an additional \$7.25 every week. Your friend has \$24.50 saved and plans to save an additional \$8.75 every week.

Part A Simplify and interpret an expression that represents the amount of money you and your friend save after w weeks.

Part B After 10 weeks, you and your friend use all of the money and buy the bike. How much does the bike cost? Who pays more towards the cost of the bike? Explain your reasoning.

12. Your friend evaluated $3 + x^2 \div y$ when $x = -2$ and $y = 4$.

$$3 + x^2 \div y = 3 + (-2^2) \div 4$$
$$= 3 - 4 \div 4$$
$$= 3 - 1$$
$$= 2$$

What should your friend do to correct his error?

A. Divide 3 by 4 before subtracting.

B. Square -2, then divide.

C. Divide -2 by 4, then square.

D. Subtract 4 from 3 before dividing.

D Ratios and Proportions

Chapter Learning Target:
Understand ratios and proportions.

Chapter Success Criteria:

- I can write and interpret ratios.
- I can describe ratio relationships and proportional relationships.
- I can represent equivalent ratios.
- I can model ratio relationships and proportional relationships to solve real-life problems.

Laurie's Notes

Chapter D Overview

The study of ratios and proportions in this chapter builds upon and connects to prior work with rates and ratios in Chapter 3. Students should have an understanding of how ratios are represented and how ratio tables are used to find equivalent ratios. Tape diagrams and double number lines were also used to represent and solve problems involving equivalent ratios.

The first two lessons integrate computations with rational numbers as students extend their understanding of ratios and explore rates and unit rates. Students who are not secure with computations involving rational numbers should find working with ratio tables helpful. They recognize that you can think differently about a problem and the steps you take may not be the same as your partner, yet you get the same result.

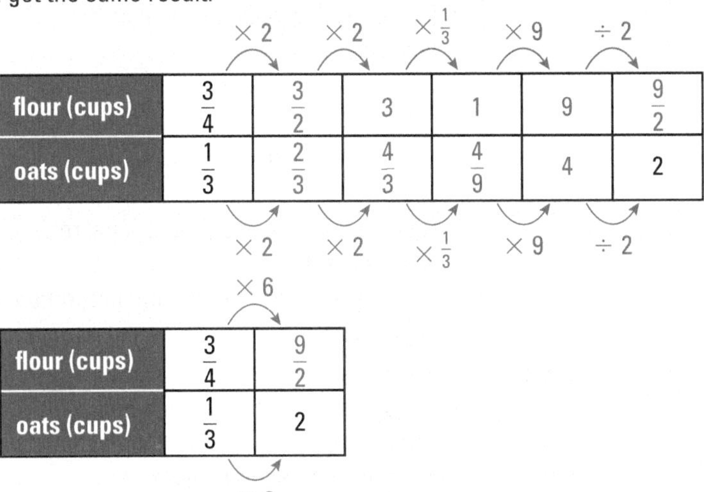

	$\times 2$	$\times 2$	$\times \frac{1}{3}$	$\times 9$	$\div 2$

flour (cups)	$\frac{3}{4}$	$\frac{3}{2}$	3	1	9	$\frac{9}{2}$
oats (cups)	$\frac{1}{3}$	$\frac{2}{3}$	$\frac{4}{3}$	$\frac{4}{9}$	4	2

	$\times 2$	$\times 2$	$\times \frac{1}{3}$	$\times 9$	$\div 2$

$\times 6$

flour (cups)	$\frac{3}{4}$	$\frac{9}{2}$
oats (cups)	$\frac{1}{3}$	2

$\times 6$

When students write ratios $a : b$ in the form $\frac{a}{b}$, they often mistakenly think of it as a fraction and wonder why you can add constant amounts in the ratio table but the same operation doesn't work with addition of fractions. They need to understand that they are not adding fractions. The equivalent ratios represent a proportional relationship, which is not the same as adding fractions.

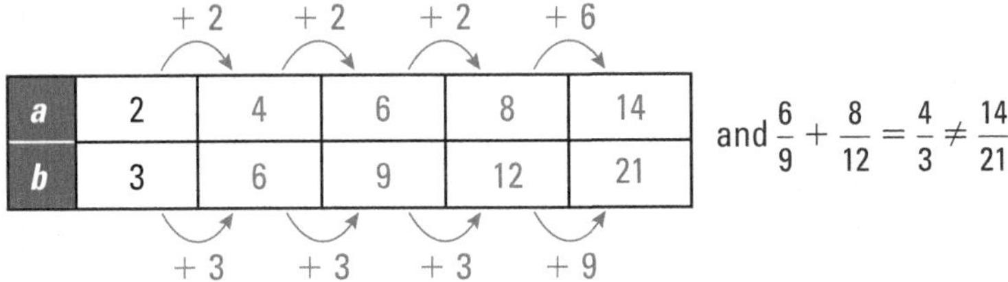

	$+2$	$+2$	$+2$	$+6$

a	2	4	6	8	14
b	3	6	9	12	21

	$+3$	$+3$	$+3$	$+9$

and $\frac{6}{9} + \frac{8}{12} = \frac{4}{3} \neq \frac{14}{21}$

The next three lessons are about writing, solving, and graphing proportions. Three methods for solving proportions are introduced: mental math, the Multiplication Property of Equality, and the Cross Products Property. Recognizing when you might use each method is reasoning you want to hear from students. Although slope is not mentioned explicitly, graphing proportional relationships enables students to see the connection between the constant of proportionality and equivalent ratios.

The last lesson uses proportions to work with scale drawings.

Suggested Pacing

Chapter Opener	1 Day
Section 1	1 Day
Section 2	1 Day
Section 3	2 Days
Section 4	2 Days
Section 5	2 Days
Section 6	1 Day
Connecting Concepts	1 Day
Chapter Review	1 Day
Chapter Test	1 Day
Total Chapter D	13 Days
Year-to-Date	150 Days

Chapter Learning Target

Understand ratios and proportions.

Chapter Success Criteria

- Write and interpret ratios.
- Describe ratio relationships and proportional relationships.
- Represent equivalent ratios.
- Model ratio relationships and proportional relationships to solve real-life problems.

Chapter D Learning Targets and Success Criteria

Section	Learning Target	Success Criteria
D.1 Ratios and Ratio Tables	Understand ratios of rational numbers and use ratio tables to represent equivalent ratios.	• Write and interpret ratios involving rational numbers. • Use various operations to create tables of equivalent ratios. • Use ratio tables to solve ratio problems.
D.2 Rates and Unit Rates	Understand rates involving fractions and use unit rates to solve problems.	• Find unit rates for rates involving fractions. • Use unit rates to solve rate problems.
D.3 Identifying Proportional Relationships	Determine whether two quantities are in a proportional relationship.	• Determine whether ratios form a proportion. • Explain how to determine whether quantities are proportional. • Distinguish between proportional and nonproportional situations.
D.4 Writing and Solving Proportions	Use proportions to solve ratio problems.	• Solve proportions using various methods. • Find a missing value that makes two ratios equivalent. • Use proportions to represent and solve real-life problems.
D.5 Graphs of Proportional Relationships	Represent proportional relationships using graphs and equations.	• Determine whether quantities are proportional using a graph. • Find the unit rate of a proportional relationship using a graph. • Create equations to represent proportional relationships.
D.6 Scale Drawings	Solve problems involving scale drawings.	• Find an actual distance in a scale drawing. • Explain the meaning of scale and scale factor. • Use a scale drawing to find the actual lengths and areas of real-life objects.

Progressions

Through the Grades		
Grade 6	**Grade 7**	**Grade 8**
• Understand ratios and describe ratio relationships. • Understand unit rates and rates. • Use ratio and rate reasoning to solve real-world and mathematical problems. • Compare ratios using tables. • Use ratio reasoning to convert measurement units. • Graph ordered pairs in all four quadrants of the coordinate plane. • Draw polygons in the coordinate plane given vertices and find lengths of sides.	• Find unit rates associated with ratios of fractions, areas, and other quantities in like or different units. • Decide whether two quantities are proportional using ratio tables and graphs. • Identify the constant of proportionality in tables, graphs, equations, diagrams, and verbal descriptions. • Represent proportional relationships with equations. • Explain what a point (x, y) means on a proportional graph in context, particularly (0, 0) and $(1, r)$, where r is the unit rate. • Use proportionality to solve multistep ratio problems. • Use scale drawings to compute actual lengths and areas and reproduce a scale drawing at a different scale.	• Graph and compare proportional relationships, interpreting the unit rate as the slope. • Use similar triangles to explain why the slope is the same between any two points on a line. Derive $y = mx$ and $y = mx + b$. • Understand that $y = mx + b$ is a linear function and recognize nonlinear functions. • Interpret the rate of change and the initial value of a function. • Verify the properties of translations, reflections, and rotations. • Understand that figures are similar when they can be related by a sequence of translations, reflections, rotations, and dilations.

Through the Chapter						
Standard	**D.1**	**D.2**	**D.3**	**D.4**	**D.5**	**D.6**
Compute unit rates associated with ratios of fractions, including ratios of lengths, areas and other quantities measured in like or different units.	●	★				
Decide whether two quantities are in a proportional relationship, e.g., by testing for equivalent ratios in a table or graphing on a coordinate plane and observing whether the graph is a straight line through the origin.			●		★	
Identify the constant of proportionality (unit rate) in tables, graphs, equations, diagrams, and verbal descriptions of proportional relationships.		●	●		★	
Represent proportional relationships by equations.					★	
Explain what a point (x, y) on the graph of a proportional relationship means in terms of the situation, with special attention to the points (0, 0) and $(1, r)$ where r is the unit rate.					★	
Use proportional relationships to solve multistep ratio and percent problems.	●	●		●		
Solve problems involving scale drawings of geometric figures, including computing actual lengths and areas from a scale drawing and reproducing a scale drawing at a different scale.						★

Key

▲ = preparing ★ = complete ● = learning ■ = extending

STEAM Video

1. 120 ft^2
2. *Sample answer:* The walls are 16.5 feet high and 20 feet long.

Performance Task

Sample answer: Add white paint.

Mathematical Practices

Students have opportunities to develop aspects of the mathematical practices throughout the chapter. Here are some examples.

1. **Make Sense of Problems and Persevere in Solving Them**
   D.6 Math Practice note, *p. 661*
2. **Reason Abstractly and Quantitatively**
   D.3 Exercise 42, *p. 646*
3. **Construct Viable Arguments and Critique the Reasoning of Others**
   D.5 Exercise 20, *p. 659*
4. **Model with Mathematics**
   D.2 Exercise 26, *p. 638*
5. **Use Appropriate Tools Strategically**
   D.2 Math Practice note, *p. 633*
6. **Attend to Precision**
   D.1 Math Practice note, *p. 627*
7. **Look for and Make Use of Structure**
   D.4 Exercise 56, *p. 654*
8. **Look for and Express Regularity in Repeated Reasoning**
   D.1 Math Practice note, *p. 630*

Laurie's Notes

STEAM Video

Before the Video

- To introduce the STEAM Video, read aloud the first paragraph of Painting a Large Room and discuss the question with your students.
- ? "What colors of paints can you mix to make green paint?"

During the Video

- The video shows Alex and Enid painting a wall.
- ? Pause the video at 1:35 and ask, "What is a proportion?" an equation that states that two ratios are equivalent
- ? "Why do they use proportions when making the paint color?" So the color stays the same.
- Watch the remainder of the video.

After the Video

- Have students work with a partner to answer Questions 1 and 2.
- As students discuss and answer the questions, listen for understanding of proportions.

Performance Task

- Use this information to spark students' interest and promote thinking about real-life problems.
- ? Ask, "Given any color of paint, how can you make the paint slightly lighter in color?"
- After completing the chapter, students will have gained the knowledge needed to complete "Mixing Paint."

STEAM Video

Painting a Large Room

Shades of paint can be made by mixing other paints. What colors of paints can you mix to make green paint?

Watch the STEAM Video "Painting a Large Room." Then answer the following questions.

1. Enid estimates that they need 2 gallons of paint to apply two coats to the wall shown. How many square feet does she expect $\frac{1}{2}$ gallon of paint will cover?

2. Describe a room that requires $5\frac{1}{2}$ gallons of paint to apply one coat of paint to each of the four walls.

Performance Task

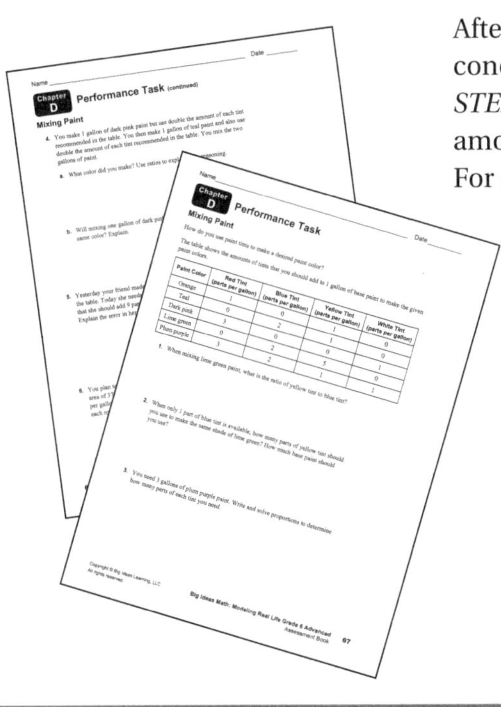
Chapter D Performance Task (continued)
Mixing Paint

Chapter D Performance Task
Mixing Paint

Mixing Paint

After completing this chapter, you will be able to use the concepts you learned to answer the questions in the *STEAM Video Performance Task*. You will be given the amounts of each tint used to make different colors of paint. For example:

Plum Purple Paint

3 parts red tint per gallon

2 parts blue tint per gallon

1 part yellow tint per gallon

1 part white tint per gallon

You will be asked to solve various ratio problems about mixing paint. Given any color of paint, how can you make the paint slightly lighter in color?

Getting Ready for Chapter

Chapter Exploration

The Meaning of a Word ▶ Rate

When you rent snorkel gear at the beach, you should pay attention to the rental **rate**. The rental rate is in dollars per hour.

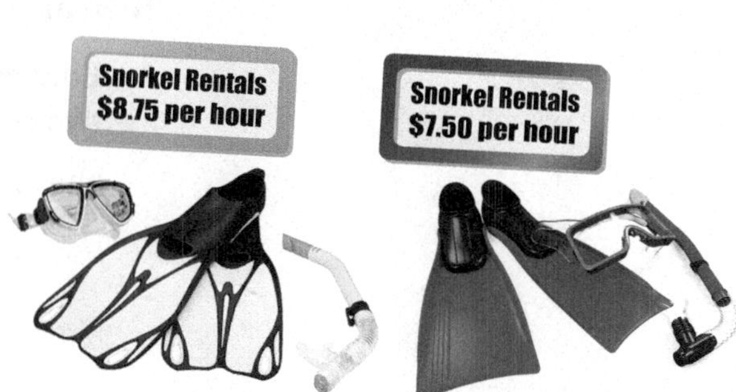

1. **Work with a partner. Complete each step.**
   - Match each description with a rate.
   - Match each rate with a fraction.
   - Give a reasonable value for each fraction. Then give an unreasonable value.

Description	Rate	Fraction
Your speed in the 100-meter dash	Dollars per hour	$\frac{\square \text{ inches}}{\text{year}}$
The hourly wage of a worker at a fast-food restaurant	Inches per year	$\frac{\square \text{ pounds}}{\text{square foot}}$
The average annual rainfall in a rain forest	Pounds per square foot	$\frac{\$\square}{\text{hour}}$
The amount of fertilizer spread on a lawn	Meters per second	$\frac{\square \text{ meters}}{\text{second}}$

2. **Work with a partner.** Describe a situation to which the given fraction can apply. Show how to rewrite each expression as a division problem. Then simplify and interpret your result.

   a. $\dfrac{\frac{1}{2}\text{ cup}}{4\text{ fluid ounces}}$ **b.** $\dfrac{2\text{ inches}}{\frac{3}{4}\text{ second}}$ **c.** $\dfrac{\frac{3}{8}\text{ cup sugar}}{\frac{3}{4}\text{ cup flour}}$ **d.** $\dfrac{\frac{5}{6}\text{ gallon}}{\frac{2}{3}\text{ second}}$

Vocabulary

The following vocabulary terms are defined in this chapter. Think about what each term might mean and record your thoughts.

proportional constant of proportionality scale drawing

Check out the digital flash cards.
BigIdeasMath.com

Laurie's Notes

Chapter Exploration

- Students found unit rates and solved rate problems in Chapter 3. This exploration reviews the language and notation associated with rates.
- After pairs complete Exercise 1, have each pair compare their answers with another pair. Discuss any discrepancies as a class.
- Exercise 2 reviews students' work with complex fractions from a prior chapter. You may need to remind students of how to simplify a complex fraction before pairs work on the problems.

  Example: $\frac{5}{\frac{4}{5}} = 5 \div \frac{4}{5} = \frac{5}{1} \cdot \frac{5}{4} = \frac{25}{4}$, or $6\frac{1}{4}$

- **Popsicle Sticks:** Solicit responses for each part in Exercise 2. Although the numeric values should be the same, students may have different contexts and interpretations. Ask several students to share with the class.

Vocabulary

- These terms represent some of the vocabulary that students will encounter in Chapter D. Discuss the terms as a class.
- Where have students heard the term *proportional* outside of a math classroom? In what contexts? Students may not be able to write the actual definition, but they may write phrases associated with *proportional*.
- Allowing students to discuss these terms now will prepare them for understanding the terms as they are presented in the chapter.
- When students encounter a new definition, encourage them to write in their *Student Journals*. They will revisit these definitions during the Chapter Review.

ELL Support

Students may know the word *scale* as an instrument for measuring weight. Explain that a scale is also a ratio used to compare measurements. The scale gives the ratio that compares the measurements of the drawing with the actual measurements. A scale drawing represents an object using a scale. The drawing and the scale provide a proportional description of the object.

Topics for Review

- Area
- Converting Measures
- Coordinate Plane
- Equations in Two Variables
- Graphing Ordered Pairs
- Identifying Equivalent Fractions
- Identifying Patterns in Tables
- Operations on Fractions and Decimals
- Perimeter
- Rates
- Ratio Tables
- Ratios
- Simplifying Fractions
- Solving Equations
- Unit Rates

Chapter Exploration

1. Your speed in the 100-meter dash; Meters per second; *Sample answer:* $\frac{8 \text{ meters}}{\text{second}}$; $\frac{80 \text{ meters}}{\text{second}}$

   The amount of fertilizer spread on a lawn; Pounds per square foot; *Sample answer:* $\frac{0.006 \text{ pound}}{\text{square foot}}$; $\frac{150 \text{ pounds}}{\text{square foot}}$

   The hourly wage of a worker at a fast food restaurant; Dollars per hour; *Sample answer:* $\frac{\$10}{\text{hour}}$; $\frac{\$1000}{\text{hour}}$

   The average annual rainfall in a rain forest; Inches per year; *Sample answer:* $\frac{100 \text{ inches}}{\text{year}}$; $\frac{5 \text{ inches}}{\text{year}}$

2. **a.** *Sample answer:* mixing orange juice and cranberry juice in a drink; $\frac{1}{2} \div 4$; $\frac{1}{8}$; There is $\frac{1}{8}$ cup of orange juice per fluid ounce of cranberry juice.

   b. *Sample answer:* speed an insect travels; $2 \div \frac{3}{4}$; $\frac{8}{3}$; The insect travels $2\frac{2}{3}$ inches per second.

   c–d. See Additional Answers.

Check out the
Dynamic Classroom.
BigIdeasMath.com

Laurie's Notes

Learning Target

Understand ratios of rational numbers and use ratio tables to represent equivalent ratios.

Success Criteria

- Write and interpret ratios involving rational numbers.
- Use various operations to create tables of equivalent ratios.
- Use ratio tables to solve ratio problems.

Warm Up

Cumulative, vocabulary, and prerequisite skills practice opportunities are available in the *Resources by Chapter* or at *BigIdeasMath.com*.

ELL Support

Explain to students that in this lesson, the word *table* does not refer to a piece of furniture. It refers to a type of chart in which ratios are listed. You may want to point to a ratio table and say, "ratio table" to clarify.

Exploration 1

a. *Sample answer:* 9 : 15, 1 : 15, 9 : 5

b. *Sample answer:* 4.5 : 7.5; 0.5 : 7.5; 4.5 : 2.5; yes; The ratios are equivalent.

Exploration 2

a. See Additional Answers.

b. yes; yes; *Sample answer:* The values of the ratios are the same.

c. yes; *Sample answer:* The operations generate equivalent ratios.

Preparing to Teach

- **Look for and Make Use of Structure:** Students worked with ratios in Chapter 3. In this lesson, they will extend their work with ratios to include fractions, making connections to their recent work with fractions.
- **Construct Viable Arguments and Critique the Reasoning of Others:** In the explorations, students will communicate their conclusions to others and justify their thinking.

Motivate

? "Can you think of any situation where it might be important to make a comparison of amounts?" Answers will vary. If students are struggling to think of any, ask about a sporting event or perhaps a recipe.

? "What if a recipe for fruit punch calls for 2 cups of mix for every 3 cups of water, does this situation model a comparison? Explain." Yes, it compares the amount of mix to the amount of water, 2 : 3.

? "How can you triple the recipe?" Use 6 cups of mix and 9 cups of water.

? "Why is it important to keep the comparisons the same?" *Sample answer:* So the fruit punch tastes the same.

- The **value of the ratio**, $\frac{2}{3}$, describes the multiplicative relationship or answers the question "The amount of mix is how many times the amount of water?"

Exploration 1

- In part (a), students can identify **ratios** between any of the ingredients. For example, one student may write 9 : 15 for stewed tomatoes to chicken broth and another might write 9 : 1 for chopped spinach to chopped chicken. It would be helpful to have students write the ratios in words as well as numbers.
- In part (b), guide students to compare the multiplicative relationships (the values of the ratios) using the same ratios as in part (a).

Exploration 2

- Allow students to experiment with finding **equivalent ratios** to complete the **ratio tables**. Remind them that each ratio in a table must have the same multiplicative relationship. Encourage students to use different operations.
- After they complete the tables, discuss which strategies they used for different operations.

? "Can you use the same strategy for addition as for multiplication?" No, for multiplication you multiply each part of the ratio by the same number, $(5 \times 2) : (1 \times 2)$. For addition, you add the ratio or a multiple of the ratio to the original ratio, $(5 + 5) : (1 + 1)$ or $(5 + 10) : (1 + 2)$.

- Have students use *Think-Pair-Share* to discuss part (c).
- By the end of this exploration, students should realize that the strategies they used for ratios involving whole numbers also work for ratios involving fractions.

D.1 Ratios and Ratio Tables

Learning Target: Understand ratios of rational numbers and use ratio tables to represent equivalent ratios.

Success Criteria:
- I can write and interpret ratios involving rational numbers.
- I can use various operations to create tables of equivalent ratios.
- I can use ratio tables to solve ratio problems.

EXPLORATION 1 Describing Ratio Relationships

Work with a partner. Use the recipe shown.

Chicken Soup

stewed tomatoes	9 ounces	chopped spinach	9 ounces
chicken broth	15 ounces	grated parmesan	5 tablespoons
chopped chicken	1 cup		

a. Identify several ratios in the recipe.

b. You halve the recipe. Describe your ratio relationships in part (a) using the new quantities. Is the relationship between the ingredients the same as in part (a)? Explain.

EXPLORATION 2 Completing Ratio Tables

Work with a partner. Use the ratio tables shown.

x	5			
y	1			

x	$\frac{1}{4}$			
y	$\frac{1}{2}$			

Math Practice

Communicate Precisely

How can you determine whether the ratios in each table are equivalent?

a. Complete the first ratio table using multiple operations. Use the same operations to complete the second ratio table.

b. Are the ratios in the first table equivalent? the second table? Explain.

c. Do the strategies for completing ratio tables of whole numbers work for completing ratio tables of fractions? Explain your reasoning.

D.1 Lesson

Key Vocabulary
ratio, *p. 628*
value of a ratio, *p. 628*
equivalent ratios, *p. 629*
ratio table, *p. 629*

Key Idea

Ratios

Words A **ratio** is a comparison of two quantities. The **value of the ratio** a to b is the number $\frac{a}{b}$, which describes the multiplicative relationship between the quantities in the ratio.

Examples 2 snails *to* 6 fish

$\frac{1}{2}$ cup of milk *for every* $\frac{1}{4}$ cup of cream

Algebra The ratio of a to b can be written as $a : b$.

Reading

Recall that phrases indicating ratios include *for each*, *for every*, and *per*.

EXAMPLE 1 Writing and Interpreting Ratios

Flubber Ingredients

cold water	3/2 cups
hot water	4/3 cups
glue	2 cups
borax	3 teaspoons

You make *flubber* using the ingredients shown.

a. Write the ratio of cold water to glue.

The recipe uses $\frac{3}{2}$ cups of water per 2 cups of glue.

So, the ratio of cold water to glue is $\frac{3}{2}$ to 2, or $\frac{3}{2}$: 2.

b. Find and interpret the value of the ratio in part (a).

The value of the ratio $\frac{3}{2}$: 2 is

$$\frac{\frac{3}{2}}{2} = \frac{3}{2} \div 2$$

$$= \frac{3}{2} \cdot \frac{1}{2}$$

$$= \frac{3}{4}.$$

So, the multiplicative relationship is $\frac{3}{4}$.

The amount of cold water in the recipe is $\frac{3}{4}$ the amount of glue.

Try It

1. You mix $\frac{2}{3}$ teaspoon of baking soda with 3 teaspoons of salt. Find and interpret the value of the ratio of baking soda to salt.

Multi-Language Glossary at BigIdeasMath.com

Laurie's Notes

Scaffolding Instruction

- Students have explored the first two success criteria. Now they will formalize their understanding of ratio tables to solve ratio problems.
- **Emerging:** Students may be able to write and simplify ratios, but they struggle with interpreting ratios, interpreting multiplicative relationships, or finding equivalent ratios. They will benefit from guided instruction for the Key Idea and examples.
- **Proficient:** Students have made the connection between ratios and fractions. They also understand the terminology. Have these students review the Key Idea before completing the Self-Assessment exercises.

Key Idea

- Remind students of the definition for **ratio**. The **value of the ratio** describes the multiplicative relationship.
- Point out the Reading note.

EXAMPLE 1

- **Teaching Strategy:** Be sure that students read ratio problems carefully. Order matters when writing a ratio. Writing $2 : \frac{3}{2}$ would be incorrect. Encourage students to write the ratio in words first, cold water : glue.
- Students can check their division using a model.

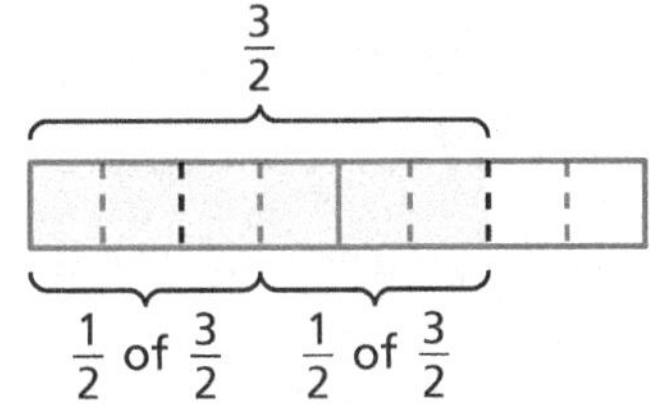

Try It

- Have students complete the exercise independently and then check with a neighbor.

ELL Support

After demonstrating Example 1, have students work in groups to complete Try It Exercise 1. Provide students with questions to guide their work: What is the ratio of baking soda to salt? What steps do you take to find the multiplicative relationship of the ratio? Describe the relationship of baking soda and salt using what you find. Expect students to perform according to their language levels.

Beginner: Write the steps and provide one-word answers.

Intermediate: Use phrases or simple sentences such as, "The ratio is two-thirds to three."

Advanced: Use detailed sentences and help guide discussion.

Scaffold instruction to support all students in their learning. Learning is individualized and you may want to group students differently as they move in and out of these levels with each skill and concept. Student self-assessment and feedback help guide your instructional decisions about how and when to layer support for all students to become proficient learners.

Teaching Strategy

Students need to understand that the order of the quantities in a problem determines the order of the ratio.

Example: There are 11 girls and 12 boys in a class. Write the ratio of boys to girls. 12 : 11

The ratio 11 : 12 is *not* correct because it does not reflect the order described in the problem. Encourage students to write the desired ratio in words and then replace the words with the appropriate numbers (boys : girls → 12 : 11).

Extra Example 1

There are 12 dogs and 15 cats at a pet store.

a. Write the ratio of cats to dogs. 5 : 4

b. Find and interpret the value of the ratio in part (a). $\frac{5}{4}$; The number of cats at the pet store is $\frac{5}{4}$ the number of dogs.

Try It

1. $\frac{2}{9}$; The amount of baking soda is $\frac{2}{9}$ the amount of salt.

Extra Example 2

Find the missing values in the ratio table. Then write the equivalent ratios.

Time (hours)	6	3		21
Money (dollars)	27		67.5	

13.5, 15, 94.5; 6 : 27, 3 : 13.5, 15 : 67.5, 21 : 94.5

Try It

2. 10, 8; $\frac{5}{2}$: 4; 10 : 16; 5 : 8

3. 2.25, 3; 0.4 : 0.75; 1.2 : 2.25; 1.6 : 3

Self-Assessment
for Concepts & Skills

4. 24; The amount of jojoba oil is 24 times the amount of essential oil.

5. 12, $\frac{7}{12}$; $\frac{3}{2}:\frac{1}{12}$; $12:\frac{2}{3}$; $\frac{21}{2}:\frac{7}{12}$

Laurie's Notes

Discuss

- Define **equivalent ratios**. Give examples such as 1 : 2, 2 : 4, and 3 : 6.
- Discuss the two methods for finding equivalent ratios.
- **Common Error:** Students may add or subtract the same quantity to each number in the ratio. For example, students may say that 1 : 2 and 3 : 4 are equivalent. Make it very clear that the numbers you add or subtract must be in the same ratio. The ratio 1 : 2 is equivalent to 3 : 6. It is *not* equivalent to 3 : 4.

EXAMPLE 2

- Read the problem and write the ratio table. Ask students for assistance in filling in the table.

? "How can you find the number of cups per quart?" *Sample answer:* Divide each number in the second column by 3 to find there are 4 cups per quart.

? "How can you find the number of quarts per cup?" *Sample answer:* Divide each number in the ratio 4 : 1 by 4 to find there is $\frac{1}{4}$ quart per cup.

? "Can you think of any other methods?" Have student share different ideas.

? "Do you think the same strategies apply to ratio tables involving decimals?" yes Students will verify this conjecture in Try It Exercise 3.

Try It

- Have students complete the tables on whiteboards. Discuss any discrepancies.

Self-Assessment for Concepts & Skills

- Have students solve the problems independently and then discuss their answers with a partner.

Thumbs Up: Ask students to assess their understanding of the first two success criteria.

ELL Support

Allow students to work in pairs for extra support and to practice language. Monitor discussions and provide support as needed. Have each pair display their answers on a whiteboard for your review.

The Success Criteria Self-Assessment chart can be found in the *Student Journal* or online at *BigIdeasMath.com*.

Two ratios that describe the same relationship are **equivalent ratios**. The values of equivalent ratios are equivalent. You can find and organize equivalent ratios in a **ratio table** by:

- adding or subtracting quantities in equivalent ratios.
- multiplying or dividing each quantity in a ratio by the same number.

EXAMPLE 2 Completing A Ratio Table

Find the missing values in the ratio table. Then write the equivalent ratios.

Cups	3	12	15	
Quarts	$\frac{3}{4}$			$\frac{5}{4}$

You can use a combination of operations to find the missing values.

$\times 4$ $+3$ $\div 3$

Cups	3	12	15	5
Quarts	$\frac{3}{4}$	3	$\frac{15}{4}$	$\frac{5}{4}$

$\times 4$ $+\frac{3}{4}$ $\div 3$

Notice that you obtain the third column by adding the values in the first column to the values in the second column.

$3 + 12 = 15$

$\frac{3}{4} + 3 = \frac{15}{4}$

The equivalent ratios are $3 : \frac{3}{4}$, $12 : 3$, $15 : \frac{15}{4}$, and $5 : \frac{5}{4}$.

Try It **Find the missing values in the ratio table. Then write the equivalent ratios.**

2.

Kilometers	$\frac{5}{2}$		5
Hours	4	16	

3.

Gallons	0.4	1.2	1.6
Days	0.75		

Self-Assessment for Concepts & Skills

Solve each exercise. Then rate your understanding of the success criteria in your journal.

4. **WRITING AND INTERPRETING RATIOS** You include $\frac{1}{2}$ tablespoon of essential oils in a solution for every 12 tablespoons of jojoba oil. Find and interpret the value of the ratio of jojoba oil to essential oils.

5. MP **NUMBER SENSE** Find the missing values in the ratio table. Then write the equivalent ratios.

Pounds	$\frac{3}{2}$		$\frac{21}{2}$
Years	$\frac{1}{12}$	$\frac{2}{3}$	

EXAMPLE 3 Modeling Real Life

You mix $\frac{1}{2}$ cup of yellow paint for every $\frac{3}{4}$ cup of blue paint to make 15 cups of green paint. How much yellow paint do you use?

Math Practice

Maintain Oversight

What value are you trying to obtain in the ratio table to solve the problem? How can you find the soltution using only one operation?

Method 1: The ratio of yellow paint to blue paint is $\frac{1}{2}$ to $\frac{3}{4}$. Use a ratio table to find an equivalent ratio in which the total amount of yellow paint and blue paint is 15 cups.

	Yellow (cups)	Blue (cups)	Total (cups)	
	$\frac{1}{2}$	$\frac{3}{4}$	$\frac{1}{2}+\frac{3}{4}=\frac{5}{4}$	
$\times 4$	2	3	5	$\times 4$
$\times 3$	6	9	15	$\times 3$

So, you use 6 cups of yellow paint.

Method 2: You can use the ratio of yellow paint to blue paint to find the fraction of the green paint that is made from yellow paint. You use $\frac{1}{2}$ cup of yellow paint for every $\frac{3}{4}$ cup of blue paint, so the fraction of the green paint that is made from yellow paint is

$$\frac{\frac{1}{2}}{\frac{1}{2}+\frac{3}{4}} = \frac{\frac{1}{2}}{\frac{5}{4}} = \frac{1}{2} \cdot \frac{4}{5} = \frac{2}{5}.$$

(yellow → numerator; green → denominator)

So, you use $\frac{2}{5} \cdot 15 = 6$ cups of yellow paint.

Self-Assessment for Problem Solving

Solve each exercise. Then rate your understanding of the success criteria in your journal.

6. **DIG DEEPER!** A satellite orbiting Earth travels $14\frac{1}{2}$ miles every 3 seconds. How far does the satellite travel in $\frac{3}{4}$ minute?

7. An engine runs on a mixture of 0.1 quart of oil for every 3.5 quarts of gasoline. You make 3 quarts of the mixture. How much oil and how much gasoline do you use?

Laurie's Notes

EXAMPLE 3

- Ask a volunteer to read the problem. Then ask another student to explain what the problem is asking.

? "How much green paint do you want to make?" 15 cups

- Point out that the ratio table shows the total number of cups of green paint for each combination of yellow paint and blue paint listed.
- Supply the thinking behind the multiplications used in the ratio table: multiply by 4 first so there is a whole number of cups of green paint and then multiply by 3 so there are 15 cups of green paint.
- **Look for and Express Regularity in Repeated Reasoning:** Discuss the Math Practice note. As students become more familiar with using ratio tables, they should be more able to find shortcuts to the solution.
- Encourage students to think about different ways of finding the solution using a ratio table. Have them try their methods to see whether the results provide insight to the next steps.
- **Model with Mathematics:** Method 2 shows a different approach. You could model the paint mixture with a tape diagram.

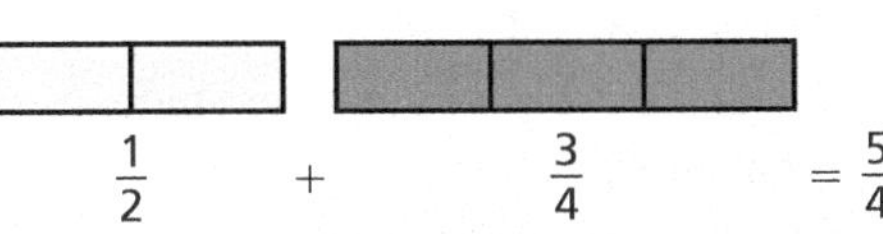

- Every $\frac{5}{4}$ cups of green paint are made up of $\frac{1}{2} = \frac{2}{4}$ cup of yellow paint and $\frac{3}{4}$ cup of blue paint. In other words, every 5 parts of green paint are made up of 2 parts yellow and 3 parts blue. So, $\frac{2}{5}$ of the green paint is made up of yellow paint and $\frac{3}{5}$ is made up of blue paint. Point out that these fractions have a sum of 1, as should be expected.
- Find $\frac{2}{5}$ of 15 to answer the question.
- **Connection:** After going through Method 2, refer back to the ratio table in Method 1 and show that $\frac{2}{5}$ of each total listed is made up of yellow paint.

Self-Assessment for Problem Solving

- The goal for all students is to feel comfortable with the problem-solving plan. It is important for students to problem-solve in class, where they may receive support from you and their peers. Keep in mind that some students may only be ready for the first step.
- Have students read the problems and then discuss problem-solving strategies with a partner before solving independently.

The Success Criteria Self-Assessment chart can be found in the *Student Journal* or online at *BigIdeasMath.com*.

Closure

- Distribute blank *Response Cards*. "Explain how to find equivalent ratios using addition, multiplication, and division."

Extra Example 3

You mix $\frac{1}{2}$ cup of red paint for every $\frac{1}{4}$ cup of blue paint to make 12 cups of purple paint. How much red paint do you use? 8 cups

Self-Assessment for Problem Solving

6. 217.5 mi

7. $\frac{1}{12}$ qt of oil, $2\frac{11}{12}$ qt of gasoline

Learning Target

Understand ratios of rational numbers and use ratio tables to represent equivalent ratios.

Success Criteria

- Write and interpret ratios involving rational numbers.
- Use various operations to create tables of equivalent ratios.
- Use ratio tables to solve ratio problems.

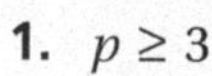

Review & Refresh

1. $p \geq 3$

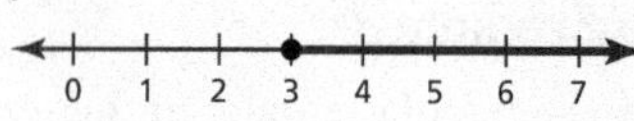

2. $n < -4$

3. $d \geq -7$

4. $\frac{1}{6}$

5. 0.84

6. $-2\frac{7}{9}$

7. D

Concepts, Skills, & Problem Solving

8. *Sample answer:*

x	4	8	2	6
y	10	20	5	15

yes; The values of the ratios are $\frac{2}{5}$.

9. *Sample answer:*

x	$\frac{4}{5}$	8	2	$\frac{14}{5}$
y	$\frac{1}{2}$	5	$\frac{5}{4}$	$\frac{7}{4}$

yes; The values of the ratios are $\frac{8}{5}$.

10. $4:2$; 2; The amount of club soda is 2 times the amount of white grape juice.

11. $\frac{1}{2}:3$; $\frac{1}{6}$; The amount of mint leaves is $\frac{1}{6}$ the amount of chopped watermelon.

12. $2:\frac{3}{4}$; $2\frac{2}{3}$; The amount of white grape juice is $2\frac{2}{3}$ the amount of sugar.

13. $\frac{3}{4}:\frac{1}{2}$; $1\frac{1}{2}$; The amount of lime juice is $1\frac{1}{2}$ the amount of mint leaves.

14. no; $\frac{1}{2} \div \frac{1}{5} = \frac{5}{2}$

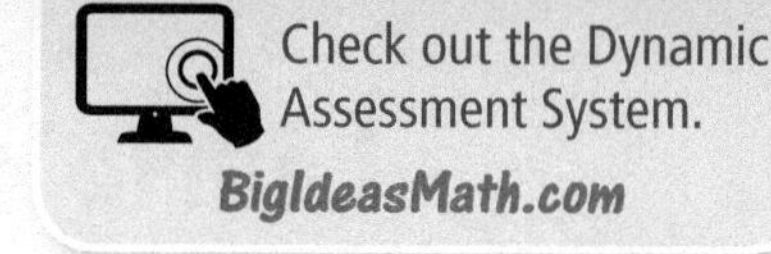
Check out the Dynamic Assessment System.
BigIdeasMath.com

Assignment Guide and Concept Check

Scaffold assignments to support all students in their learning progression. The suggested assignments are a starting point. Continue to assign additional exercises and revisit with spaced practice to move every student toward proficiency.

Level	Assignment 1	Assignment 2
Emerging	3, 5, 6, 7, 8, 10, 11, 14, 15, 16	9, 12, 13, 17, 18, 19, 20, 21, 22, 23
Proficient	3, 5, 6, 7, 9, 12, 13, 14, 16, 18	17, 19, 20, 21, 22, 23, 24
Advanced	3, 5, 6, 7, 9, 12, 13, 14, 16, 18	19, 20, 21, 22, 23, 24

- Assignment 1 is for use after students complete the Self-Assessment for Concepts & Skills.
- Assignment 2 is for use after students complete the Self-Assessment for Problem Solving.
- The red exercises can be used as a concept check.

Review & Refresh Prior Skills

Exercises 1–3 Solving a Two-Step Inequality
Exercises 4–6 Dividing Rational Numbers
Exercise 7 Interpreting a Tape Diagram

D.1 Practice

Go to *BigIdeasMath.com* to get HELP with solving the exercises.

Review & Refresh

Solve the inequality. Graph the solution.

1. $4p + 7 \geq 19$
2. $14 < -6n - 10$
3. $-3(2 + d) \leq 15$

Find the quotient. Write fractions in simplest form.

4. $\frac{2}{9} \div \frac{4}{3}$
5. $10.08 \div 12$
6. $-\frac{5}{6} \div \frac{3}{10}$

7. Which ratio can be represented by the tape diagram?

 A. 3 : 4 B. 4 : 5
 C. 4 : 9 D. 8 : 12

Quantity 1
Quantity 2

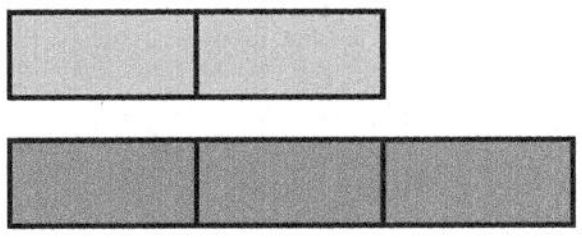

Concepts, Skills, & Problem Solving

OPEN-ENDED Complete the ratio table using multiple operations. Are the ratios in the table equivalent? Explain. (See Exploration 2, p. 627.)

8.

x	4			
y	10			

9.

x	$\frac{4}{5}$			
y	$\frac{1}{2}$			

Fruit Punch Ingredients

chopped watermelon	3 cups
sugar	3/4 cup
mint leaves	1/2 cup
white grape juice	2 cups
lime juice	3/4 cup
club soda	4 cups

WRITING AND INTERPRETING RATIOS Find the ratio. Then find and interpret the value of the ratio.

10. club soda : white grape juice
11. mint leaves : chopped watermelon
12. white grape juice to sugar
13. lime juice to mint leaves

14. **MP YOU BE THE TEACHER** You have blue ribbon and red ribbon in the ratio $\frac{1}{2} : \frac{1}{5}$. Your friend finds the value of the ratio. Is your friend correct? Explain your reasoning.

The value of the ratio is

$$\frac{\frac{1}{2}}{\frac{1}{5}} = \frac{1}{2} \div \frac{1}{5} = \frac{1}{10}.$$

COMPLETING A RATIO TABLE **Find the missing values in the ratio table. Then write the equivalent ratios.**

15.

Calories	20		10	90
Miles	$\frac{1}{6}$	$\frac{2}{3}$		

16.

Meters	8	4		
Minutes	$\frac{1}{3}$		$\frac{1}{4}$	$\frac{5}{12}$

17.

Feet	$\frac{1}{24}$		$\frac{1}{8}$	
Inches	$\frac{1}{2}$	1		$\frac{1}{4}$

18.

Tea (cups)	3.75			
Milk (cups)	1.5	1	3.5	2.5

19. **CRITICAL THINKING** Are the two statements equivalent? Explain your reasoning.

- The ratio of boys to girls is 2 to 3.
- The ratio of girls to boys is 3 to 2.

20. **MP MODELING REAL LIFE** A city dumps plastic *shade balls* into a reservoir to prevent water from evaporating during a drought. It costs \$5760 for 16,000 shade balls. How much does it cost for 12,000 shade balls?

21. **MP MODELING REAL LIFE** An oil spill spreads 25 square meters every $\frac{1}{6}$ hour. What is the area of the oil spill after 2 hours?

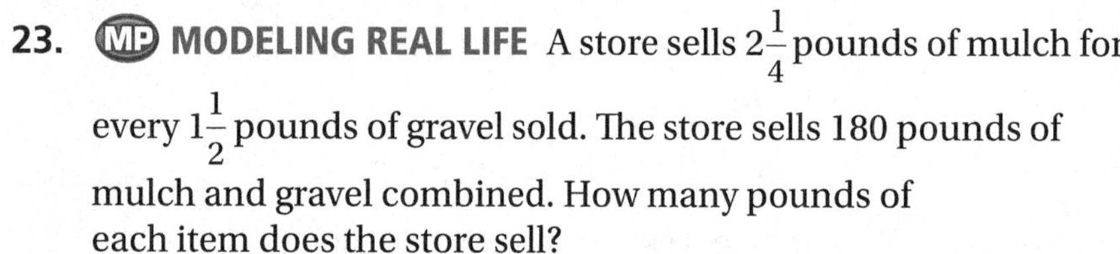

22. **MP MODELING REAL LIFE** You mix 0.25 cup of juice concentrate for every 2 cups of water to make 18 cups of juice. How much juice concentrate do you use? How much water do you use?

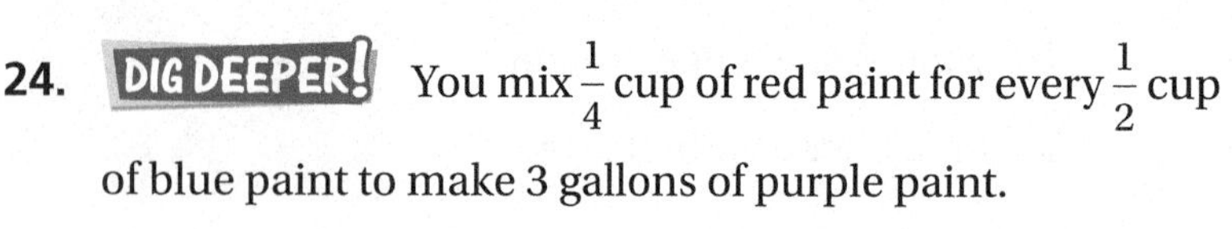

23. **MP MODELING REAL LIFE** A store sells $2\frac{1}{4}$ pounds of mulch for every $1\frac{1}{2}$ pounds of gravel sold. The store sells 180 pounds of mulch and gravel combined. How many pounds of each item does the store sell?

24. **DIG DEEPER!** You mix $\frac{1}{4}$ cup of red paint for every $\frac{1}{2}$ cup of blue paint to make 3 gallons of purple paint.

a. How much red paint do you use? How much blue paint do you use?

b. You decide that you want to make a lighter purple paint. You make the new mixture by adding $\frac{1}{4}$ cup of white paint for every $\frac{1}{4}$ cup of red paint and $\frac{1}{2}$ cup of blue paint. How much red paint, blue paint, and white paint do you use to make $1\frac{1}{2}$ gallons of the lighter purple paint?

Common Errors

- **Exercises 15–18** Students may add or subtract the same amount to each number in the ratio, saying, for example, that 2 : 3 and 4 : 5 are equivalent. Make it very clear that the numbers you add or subtract must be in the same ratio. You cannot add or subtract the same number, as when multiplying or dividing.
- **Exercises 21–23** Students may have difficulty simplifying the complex fractions that result in the solutions of these exercises. A quick review of complex fractions may be helpful. Be sure to point out that a fraction bar means division, so they can rewrite the complex fraction as *numerator ÷ denominator.*

Mini-Assessment

1. You mix $\frac{1}{4}$ cup of crisp wheat cereal with $1\frac{1}{2}$ cups of crisp rice cereal. Find and interpret the value of the ratio of crisp wheat cereal to crisp rice cereal.
   $\frac{1}{6}$; The amount of crisp wheat cereal is $\frac{1}{6}$ the amount of crisp rice cereal.

Find the missing values in the ratio table. Then write the equivalent ratios.

2.

Quarts	0.8	2.4	
Minutes	2		8

6, 3.2; 0.8 : 2, 2.4 : 6, 3.2 : 8

3.

Miles	$\frac{5}{3}$		5
Hour	6	3	

$\frac{5}{6}$, 18; $\frac{5}{3}$: 6, $\frac{5}{6}$: 3, 5 : 18

4. You mix 0.5 cup of lemon juice for every 3 cups of water to make 14 cups of lemonade. How much lemon juice do you use? How much water do you use?
   2 cups of lemon juice; 12 cups of water

Section Resources

Surface Level	Deep Level
Resources by Chapter • Extra Practice • Reteach • Puzzle Time Student Journal • Self-Assessment • Practice Differentiating the Lesson Tutorial Videos Skills Review Handbook Skills Trainer	Resources by Chapter • Enrichment and Extension Graphic Organizers Dynamic Assessment System • Section Practice

Concepts, Skills, & Problem Solving

15. 80, $\frac{1}{12}$, $\frac{3}{4}$; $20 : \frac{1}{6}$; $80 : \frac{2}{3}$; $10 : \frac{1}{12}$; $90 : \frac{3}{4}$

16. $\frac{1}{6}$, 6, 10; $8 : \frac{1}{3}$; $4 : \frac{1}{6}$; $6 : \frac{1}{4}$; $10 : \frac{5}{12}$

17. $\frac{1}{12}$, $1\frac{1}{2}$, $\frac{1}{48}$; $\frac{1}{24} : \frac{1}{2}$; $\frac{1}{12} : 1$; $\frac{1}{8} : 1\frac{1}{2}$; $\frac{1}{48} : \frac{1}{4}$

18. 2.5, 8.75, 6.25; 3.75 : 1.5; 2.5 : 1; 8.75 : 3.5; 6.25 : 2.5

19. yes; There are 2 boys for every 3 girls.

20. \$4320

21. 300 m^2

22. 2 cups of juice concentrate; 16 cups of water

23. 108 pounds of mulch; 72 pounds of gravel

24. a. 1 gallon of red paint; 2 gallons of blue paint

    b. $\frac{3}{8}$ gallon of red paint, $\frac{3}{4}$ gallon of blue paint, $\frac{3}{8}$ gallon of white paint

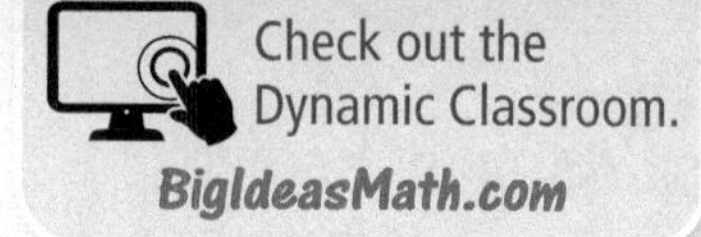
Check out the
Dynamic Classroom.
BigIdeasMath.com

Learning Target

Understand rates involving fractions and use unit rates to solve problems.

Success Criteria

- Find unit rates for rates involving fractions.
- Use unit rates to solve rate problems.

Warm Up

Cumulative, vocabulary, and prerequisite skills practice opportunities are available in the *Resources by Chapter* or at *BigIdeasMath.com*.

ELL Support

Explain to students that in this lesson, the word *degree* does not refer to a measurement of temperature. It refers to the measurement of an angle. Tell students that the arrows on a clock are called hands and point out the angle formed by the clock hands. Explain that the distance between hands can be measured in degrees and in a circle there are 360°. You may want to illustrate 180°, 90°, and 45° using portions of a circle.

Exploration 1

a. 90°; *Sample answer:* $90° : \frac{1}{4}$ h

b. yes; *Sample answer:* Double the quantities.

c. 360° : 1 h; *Sample answer:* Multiply the quantities by 2.5.

d.

75°; 30°; *Sample answer:* The hour hand moves 30° per hour.

Laurie's Notes

Preparing to Teach

- In Chapter 3, students used reasoning about multiplication and division to solve rate problems. Now they will extend their understanding to find and use unit rates involving rational numbers.
- **Look for and Make Use of Structure:** In working with rates, students will make connections to their work with fractions and ratios.

Motivate

- **Model:** In an area visible to students, set a wind-up toy in motion. If a toy is not available, ask a student to walk across the room at a constant speed.
- ? "How fast is the toy (or student) moving?" Answers will vary.
- ? "How do you measure the **rate** that the toy (or student) is moving?" *Sample answer:* in feet per second "Which two pieces of information do you need to find the *rate*?" the distance the toy (or student) travels and the time
- Provide a measuring tape and stopwatch. Ask volunteers to compute the rate.
- Discuss why you might use a convenient unit of time (i.e., 5 seconds) versus trying to use a convenient unit of distance (i.e., 10 feet).
- Write the information measured on the board in words and as a numerical rate.
- ? "In what real-life situations are rates used?" *Sample answer:* driving speed
- "Compare rates to ratios." Rates are ratios, but they have two different units.

Exploration 1

- Students have measured angles in a prior course, but they may need quick review for measures from 180° to 360°. The use of protractors may be helpful. Angles allow students to work with rates involving fractions within a context that is familiar. Students will use angles and circles in the next course.
- In part (a), you want students to focus on just the 15-minute change in time, looking for 90° for 15 minutes and then writing the rate as $90° : \frac{1}{4}$ hour. By the end of the exploration, they should be able to calculate the degrees for any time elapsed.
- In part (b), students should realize that the minute hand moves at a constant rate, so they can use the rate for 15 minutes to find the angle for 30 minutes. Remind students to be consistent with the units of measure. If they use minutes in part (a), they should use minutes in part (b).
- In part (c), students find a unit rate (degrees per hour). They should be able to use the rate to find the degrees moved by the minute hand in $2\frac{1}{2}$ hours.
- Part (d) can be approached in a variety of ways. For the first question, students may measure the angle directly, or they might multiply the degrees that the hour hand moves in 1 hour (the **unit rate**) by 2.5: $\frac{360°}{12} \cdot 2.5 = 75°$.
- For the second question, students may use the degrees for 15 minutes (90°) and reason that the minute hand moves 30° in 5 minutes, which is equivalent to a one-hour change for the hour hand.
- After completing part (d), have students share and discuss their reasoning.

D.2 Rates and Unit Rates

Learning Target: Understand rates involving fractions and use unit rates to solve problems.

Success Criteria:
- I can find unit rates for rates involving fractions.
- I can use unit rates to solve rate problems.

EXPLORATION 1 Writing Rates

Work with a partner.

a. How many degrees does the minute hand on a clock move every 15 minutes? Write a rate that compares the number of degrees moved by the minute hand to the number of hours elapsed.

Math Practice

Recognize Usefulness of Tools

Can you use a protractor to find the number of degrees the minute hand moves in 15 minutes? in 1 hour?

b. Can you use the rate in part (a) to determine how many degrees the minute hand moves in $\frac{1}{2}$ hour? Explain your reasoning.

c. Write a rate that represents the number of degrees moved by the minute hand every hour. How can you use this rate to find the number of degrees moved by the minute hand in $2\frac{1}{2}$ hours?

d. Draw a clock with hour and minute hands. Draw another clock that shows the time after the minute hand moves 900°. How many degrees does the hour hand move in this time? in one hour? Explain your reasoning.

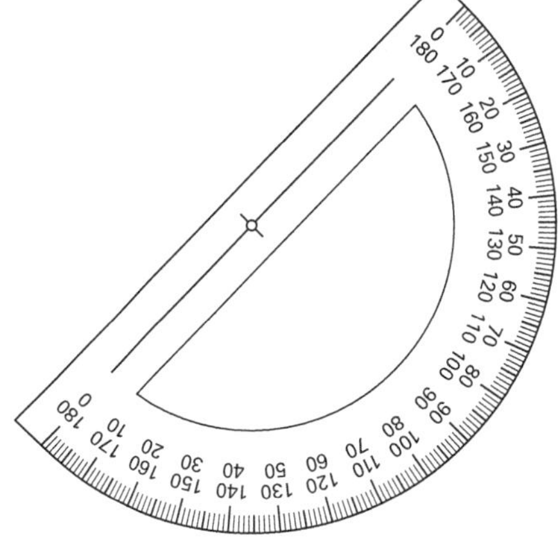

D.2 Lesson

Key Vocabulary
rate, *p. 634*
unit rate, *p. 634*
equivalent rates, *p. 634*

Key Idea

Rates and Unit Rates

Words A **rate** is a ratio of two quantities using different units. A **unit rate** compares a quantity to one unit of another quantity. **Equivalent rates** have the same unit rate.

Numbers You pay \$350 for every $\frac{1}{4}$ ounce of gold.

\$350	\$350	\$350	\$350
$\frac{1}{4}$ oz	$\frac{1}{4}$ oz	$\frac{1}{4}$ oz	$\frac{1}{4}$ oz

Rate: \$350 : $\frac{1}{4}$ oz

Unit Rate: \$1400 : 1 oz

Algebra Rate: a units : b units Unit rate: $\frac{a}{b}$ units : 1 unit

EXAMPLE 1 Finding Unit Rates

A nutrition label shows that every $\frac{1}{4}$ cup of tuna has $\frac{1}{2}$ gram of fat.

a. How many grams of fat are there for every cup of tuna?

There is $\frac{1}{2}$ gram of fat for every $\frac{1}{4}$ cup of tuna. Find the unit rate.

There are $\frac{\frac{1}{2}}{\frac{1}{4}} = 2$ grams of fat for every cup of tuna.

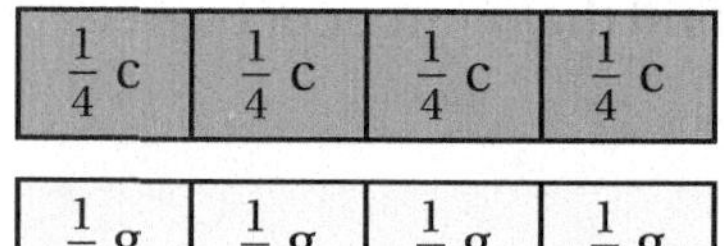

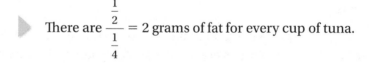

b. How many cups of tuna are there for every gram of fat?

There is $\frac{1}{4}$ cup of tuna for every $\frac{1}{2}$ gram of fat. Find the unit rate.

There is $\frac{\frac{1}{4}}{\frac{1}{2}} = \frac{1}{2}$ cup of tuna per gram of fat.

Try It

1. There is $\frac{1}{4}$ gram of fat for every $\frac{1}{3}$ tablespoon of powdered peanut butter. How many grams of fat are there for every tablespoon of the powder?

Multi-Language Glossary at BigIdeasMath.com

Laurie's Notes

Scaffolding Instruction

- In the exploration, students investigated rates. Now they will find unit rates involving fractions and use them to solve rate problems.
- **Emerging:** Students may struggle with understanding the difference between ratios, rates, and unit rates. They will benefit from guided instruction for the Key Idea and examples.
- **Proficient:** Students easily change units of measure to create **equivalent rates**. They can solve problems involving rates. Students should review the Key Idea and then proceed to the Self-Assessment exercises.

Key Idea

- Review the Key Idea. Ask students to give examples of a **rate** and a **unit rate**.
- ? Ask, "What is the difference between a rate and a unit rate?" *Sample answer:* Rates compare any two quantities of different units. A unit rate compares a quantity to just 1 unit of the other quantity.

EXAMPLE 1

- Read the directions for both parts (a) and (b), but do not reveal the solutions. Ask students to explain the problem.
- ? "What does the tape diagram represent?" Each $\frac{1}{4}$ cup of tuna has $\frac{1}{2}$ gram of fat.
- ? "Can you use the tape diagram to solve the problem? Explain." Yes, the diagram shows that there are 2 grams of fat in 1 cup of tuna and there is $\frac{1}{2}$ cup of tuna for every gram of fat.
- Work through each solution as shown.

Try It

- Ask several students to share their answer and reasoning.
- **Construct Viable Arguments and Critique the Reasoning of Others:** There are several ways in which students may explain their reasoning. Take time to hear a variety of approaches.

ELL Support

After demonstrating Example 1, have students work in groups to complete Try It Exercise 1. Provide students with questions to guide their work: What is the ratio of fat to powdered peanut butter? What steps do you take to find the unit rate? What is the answer? Expect students to perform according to their language levels.

Beginner: Write the steps and provide one-word answers.

Intermediate: Use phrases or simple sentences such as, "The ratio is one-fourth to one-third."

Advanced: Use detailed sentences and help guide discussion.

Scaffold instruction to support all students in their learning. Learning is individualized and you may want to group students differently as they move in and out of these levels with each skill and concept. Student self-assessment and feedback help guide your instructional decisions about how and when to layer support for all students to become proficient learners.

Extra Example 1

A nutrition label shows that every $\frac{1}{2}$ cup of cereal has $\frac{1}{3}$ gram of protein.

a. How many grams of protein are there for every cup of cereal? $\frac{2}{3}$ grams of protein

b. How many cups of cereal are there for every gram of protein? $1\frac{1}{2}$ cups of cereal

Try It

1. $\frac{3}{4}$ g

Laurie's Notes

Extra Example 2

A car travels 12 miles every $\frac{1}{4}$ hour. How far does the car travel in 3 hours?
144 miles

Try It

2. no; *Sample answer:* The rates are equivalent.

ELL Support

Proceed as described in Laurie's Notes for Self-Assessment for Concepts & Skills Exercises 3 and 4. You may want to have two pairs share their answers and come to agreement before discussing the answers as a class. Continue to allow students to work in pairs for Exercises 5–7. Have each pair display their answers on a whiteboard for your review.

Self-Assessment for Concepts & Skills

3. A rate $a : b$ is a unit rate when $b = 1$.
4. Unit rates are easier to compare.
5. $\$0.11 : 1$ oz
6. $\frac{5}{6}$ gal : 1 mi
7. $\frac{5}{8}$, 15, $\frac{4}{15}$, 1; $\frac{15}{4}$ g : 1 c, $\frac{4}{15}$ c : 1g

EXAMPLE 2

- Read the problem. Ask a student to explain what the question is asking.
- Work through the problem as shown. Point out that multiplying the first column by 2 is equivalent to dividing by $\frac{1}{2}$.
- Ask students to show other ways to solve the problem. Some students may set up the complex fraction: $\frac{9}{\frac{1}{2}}$, or divide both parts of the rate by $\frac{1}{2}$ and then multiply by 24.

? "Why do you multiply by 24?" To convert from 1 hour to 1 day.

? "Could you have just multiplied by 48? Explain." Yes, multiplying by 2 to convert $\frac{1}{2}$ hour to 1 hour and then multiplying by 24 to convert 1 hour to 1 day is equivalent to multiplying by 48.

- Remind students to always re-read the question and check for reasonableness.

Formative Assessment Tip

Visitor Explanation

This technique simulates what it would look like if a visitor were to enter your classroom during the middle of a lesson or activity. Could your students explain what they are doing and why they are doing it? The learning target and success criteria should have been made known to students at the beginning of the lesson.

Visitor Explanation lets you know whether students understand the learning target or the success criteria related to the lesson. Are students simply following directions or are they aware of the goal for today's lesson? Students are more engaged and their learning improves when the learning target or purpose of the lesson or activity is understood.

This technique is best used when students are actively engaged in an exploration, activity, or problem. It can be done as a *Think-Pair-Share* or as a *Writing Prompt*.

Try It

- **Visitor Explanation:** Ask, "If a visitor entered the room right now, how would you explain what you are doing and why you are doing it?" Students should practice explanations with partners. Solicit responses.

Self-Assessment for Concepts & Skills

- Have students *Turn and Talk* for Exercises 3 and 4. Circulate and listen to discussions. If students are struggling, discuss these as a class.
- Students should complete Exercises 5–7 independently.

The Success Criteria Self-Assessment chart can be found in the *Student Journal* or online at *BigIdeasMath.com*.

EXAMPLE 2 Using a Unit Rate to Solve a Rate Problem

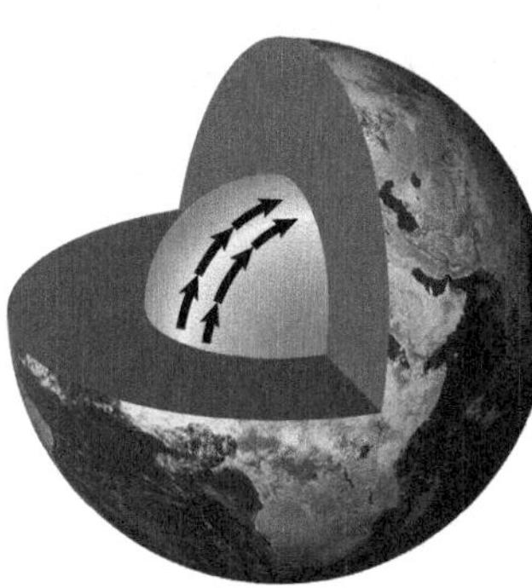

A scientist estimates that a jet of liquid iron in the Earth's core travels 9 feet every $\frac{1}{2}$ hour. How far does the liquid iron travel in 1 day?

The ratio of feet to hours is $9 : \frac{1}{2}$. Using a ratio table, divide the quantity by $\frac{1}{2}$ to find the unit rate in feet per hour. Then multiply each quantity by 24 to find the distance traveled in 24 hours, or 1 day.

× 2 × 24

Distance (feet)	9	18	432
Time (hours)	$\frac{1}{2}$	1	24

× 2 × 24

So, the liquid iron travels about 432 feet in 1 day.

Try It

2. **WHAT IF?** The scientist later states that the iron travels 3 feet every 10 minutes. Does this change your answer in Example 2? Explain.

Self-Assessment for Concepts & Skills

Solve each exercise. Then rate your understanding of the success criteria in your journal.

3. **VOCABULARY** How can you tell when a rate is a unit rate?
4. **WRITING** Explain why rates are usually written as unit rates.

Find the unit rate.

5. \$1.32 for 12 ounces
6. $\frac{1}{4}$ gallon for every $\frac{3}{10}$ mile
7. **MP USING TOOLS** Find the missing values in the ratio table. Then write the unit rate of grams per cup and the unit rate of cups per gram.

Grams	$\frac{5}{2}$		1	$\frac{15}{4}$	
Cups	$\frac{2}{3}$	$\frac{1}{6}$			4

EXAMPLE 3 Modeling Real Life

You hike up a mountain trail at a rate of $\frac{1}{4}$ mile every 10 minutes. You hike 5 miles every 2 hours on the way down the trail. How much farther do you hike in 3 hours on the way down than in 3 hours on the way up?

Because 10 minutes is $\frac{1}{6}$ of an hour, the ratio of miles to hours on the way up is $\frac{1}{4} : \frac{1}{6}$. On the way down, the ratio is $5 : 2$. Use ratio tables to find how far you hike in 3 hours at each rate.

Find the unit rate for each part of the hike.

Find the distance you hike in 3 hours on each part of the hike.

Hiking Up	
Distance (miles)	Time (hours)
$\frac{1}{4}$	$\frac{1}{6}$
$\frac{3}{2}$	1
$\frac{9}{2}$	3

Hiking Down	
Distance (miles)	Time (hours)
5	2
$\frac{5}{2}$	1
$\frac{15}{2}$	3

So, you hike $\frac{15}{2} - \frac{9}{2} = \frac{6}{2} = 3$ miles farther in 3 hours on the way down than you hike in 3 hours on the way up.

Check Your rate on the way down is $\frac{5}{2} - \frac{3}{2} = \frac{2}{2} = 1$ mile per hour faster than your rate on the way up. So, you hike 3 miles farther in 3 hours on the way down than you hike in 3 hours on the way up. ✓

Self-Assessment for Problem Solving

Solve each exercise. Then rate your understanding of the success criteria in your journal.

8. Two people compete in a five-mile go-kart race. Person A travels $\frac{1}{10}$ mile every 15 seconds. Person B travels $\frac{3}{8}$ mile every 48 seconds. Who wins the race? What is the difference of the finish times of the competitors?

9. **DIG DEEPER!** A bus travels 0.8 mile east every 45 seconds. A second bus travels 0.55 mile west every 30 seconds. The buses start at the same location. Use two methods to determine how far apart the buses are after 15 minutes. Explain your reasoning.

Laurie's Notes

EXAMPLE 3

- Ask a student to read the problem and another to explain what the question is asking.
- ? "Why do you need to convert 10 minutes to $\frac{1}{6}$ of an hour?" So the rates in both tables use the same units.
- Notice that the distances for 1 hour verify that you hike faster downhill than uphill.
- ? "What are two different ways of finding the third row of the downhill table?" Add the first and second rows or multiply the second row by 3.
- ? After completing the tables, ask, "What is the question?" How much farther do you hike in 3 hours on the way down than in 3 hours on the way up?
- Remind students to always re-read the question and write a sentence to answer the question.

Self-Assessment for Problem Solving

- Allow time in class for students to practice using the problem-solving plan. Remember, some students may only be able to complete the first step.
- Have students work with a partner to read and interpret the problems. Then have students solve the problems independently and discuss their answers with a partner.

The Success Criteria Self-Assessment chart can be found in the *Student Journal* or online at *BigIdeasMath.com.*

Closure

- **Writing:** Explain how to change a rate to a unit rate.

Extra Example 3

You and your friend compete in a 30-mile bike race. You bike at a rate of 3.75 miles every 30 minutes. Your friend bikes 18.75 miles every 3 hours. Who wins the race? What is the difference of the finish times? you; 0.8 hour

Self-Assessment for Problem Solving

8. Person B; 110 sec

9. 32.5 mi; *Sample answer:* Combine the rates of each bus first then find the number of miles, or find the number of miles for each bus and then add.

Learning Target

Understand rates involving fractions and use unit rates to solve problems.

Success Criteria

- Find unit rates for rates involving fractions.
- Use unit rates to solve rate problems.

Review & Refresh

1. $\frac{3}{2}, \frac{4}{3}, \frac{4}{9}; \frac{3}{4}:\frac{1}{3}; \frac{3}{2}:\frac{2}{3}; 3:\frac{4}{3}; 1:\frac{4}{9}$
2. $\frac{3}{2}, \frac{3}{2}, 10; \frac{1}{4}:\frac{1}{2}; \frac{3}{4}:\frac{3}{2}; \frac{3}{2}:3; 5:10$
3. >
4. <
5. =

Concepts, Skills, & Problem Solving

6. $240°; \frac{360°}{\text{h}} \times \frac{2}{3}\text{h} = 240°$
7. $210°; \frac{360°}{\text{h}} \times \frac{7}{12}\text{h} = 210°$
8. $450°; \frac{360°}{\text{h}} \times \frac{5}{4}\text{h} = 450°$
9. 60 mi : 1 h
10. 32 mi : 1 gal
11. $\frac{1}{10}$ lb : 1 day
12. $5\frac{1}{3}$ g : 1 serving
13. $2.40 : 1 lb
14. $0.80 : 1 can
15. 54 words : 1 min
16. $\frac{1}{2}$ kg : 1 ft
17. $2\frac{1}{2}$ oz : 1 pt
18. 8.7 m : 1 h
19. $75, 100, \frac{2}{3}; 25:\frac{1}{3}; 50:\frac{2}{3}; 75:1; 100:\frac{4}{3}$
20. $\frac{16}{3}, \frac{1}{4}, 3; \frac{4}{3}:\frac{1}{3}; \frac{16}{3}:1; 16:3$
21. 2.2 million people per year

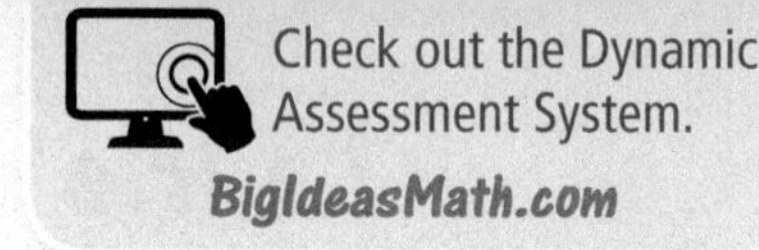
Check out the Dynamic Assessment System.
BigIdeasMath.com

Assignment Guide and Concept Check

Scaffold assignments to support all students in their learning progression. The suggested assignments are a starting point. Continue to assign additional exercises and revisit with spaced practice to move every student toward proficiency.

Level	Assignment 1	Assignment 2
Emerging	2, 4, 5, 6, 9, 11, 13, 17, 19	14, 18, 20, 21, 22, 23, 25, 28
Proficient	2, 4, 5, 7, 10, 12, 14, 16, 19	17, 18, 20, 21, 22, 23, 25, 26, 28
Advanced	2, 4, 5, 8, 12, 14, 16, 18, 20	23, 24, 25, 26, 27, 28

- Assignment 1 is for use after students complete the Self-Assessment for Concepts & Skills.
- Assignment 2 is for use after students complete the Self-Assessment for Problem Solving.
- The red exercises can be used as a concept check.

Review & Refresh Prior Skills

Exercises 1 and 2 Completing a Ratio Table
Exercises 3–5 Comparing Rational Numbers

Common Errors

- **Exercises 9–18** Students may find the unit rate but forget to include the units. Remind students that the units are necessary for understanding a unit rate, or any rate.

D.2 Practice

Go to *BigIdeasMath.com* to get HELP with solving the exercises.

Review & Refresh

Find the missing values in the ratio table. Then write the equivalent ratios.

1.

Flour (cups)	$\frac{3}{4}$		3	1
Oats (cups)	$\frac{1}{3}$	$\frac{2}{3}$		

2.

Pages	$\frac{1}{4}$	$\frac{3}{4}$		5
Minutes	$\frac{1}{2}$		3	

Copy and complete the statement using <, >, or =.

3. $\frac{9}{2}$ ▢ $\frac{8}{3}$

4. $-\frac{8}{15}$ ▢ $\frac{10}{18}$

5. $\frac{-6}{24}$ ▢ $\frac{-2}{8}$

Concepts, Skills, & Problem Solving

WRITING RATES **Find the number of degrees moved by the minute hand of a clock in the given amount of time. Explain your reasoning.** (See Exploration 1, p. 633.)

6. $\frac{2}{3}$ hour

7. $\frac{7}{12}$ hour

8. $1\frac{1}{4}$ hours

FINDING UNIT RATES **Find the unit rate.**

9. 180 miles in 3 hours

10. 256 miles per 8 gallons

11. $\frac{1}{2}$ pound : 5 days

12. 4 grams for every $\frac{3}{4}$ serving

13. $9.60 for 4 pounds

14. $4.80 for 6 cans

15. 297 words in 5.5 minutes

16. $\frac{1}{3}$ kilogram: $\frac{2}{3}$ foot

17. $\frac{5}{8}$ ounce per $\frac{1}{4}$ pint

18. $21\frac{3}{4}$ meters in $2\frac{1}{2}$ hours

MP **USING TOOLS** **Find the missing values in the ratio table. Then write the equivalent ratios.**

19.

Calories	25	50		
Servings	$\frac{1}{3}$		1	$\frac{4}{3}$

20.

Oxygen (liters)	4	$\frac{4}{3}$		16
Time (minute)	$\frac{3}{4}$		1	

21. MP **PROBLEM SOLVING** In January 2012, the U.S. population was about 313 million people. In January 2017, it was about 324 million. What was the average rate of population change per year?

22. MP **MODELING REAL LIFE** You can sand $\frac{4}{9}$ square yard of wood in $\frac{1}{2}$ hour. How many square yards can you sand in 3.2 hours? Justify your answer.

MP **REASONING** **Tell whether the rates are equivalent. Justify your answer.**

23. 75 pounds per 1.5 years
38.4 ounces per 0.75 year

24. $7\frac{1}{2}$ miles for every $\frac{3}{4}$ hour
$\frac{1}{2}$ mile for every 3 minutes

25. MP **PROBLEM SOLVING** The table shows nutritional information for three beverages.

Beverage	Serving Size	Calories	Sodium
Whole milk	1 c	146	98 mg
Orange juice	1 pt	210	10 mg
Apple juice	24 fl oz	351	21 mg

   a. Which has the most calories per fluid ounce?

   b. Which has the least sodium per fluid ounce?

26. MP **MODELING REAL LIFE** A shuttle leaving Earth's atmosphere travels 15 miles every 2 seconds. When entering the Earth's atmosphere, the shuttle travels $2\frac{3}{8}$ miles per $\frac{1}{2}$ second. Find the difference in the distances traveled after 15 seconds when leaving and entering the atmosphere.

27. **RESEARCH** Fire hydrants are one of four different colors to indicate the rate at which water comes from the hydrant.

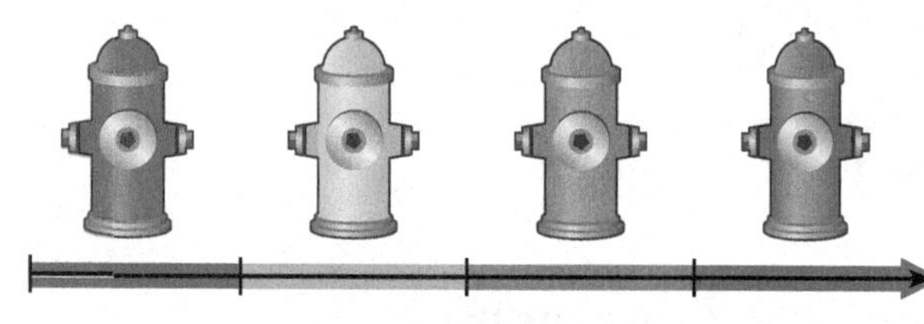

   a. Use the Internet to find the ranges of rates indicated by each color.

   b. Research why a firefighter needs to know the rate at which water comes out of a hydrant.

28. **DIG DEEPER!** You and a friend start riding bikes toward each other from opposite ends of a 24-mile biking route. You ride $2\frac{1}{6}$ miles every $\frac{1}{4}$ hour. Your friend rides $7\frac{1}{3}$ miles per hour.

   a. After how many hours do you meet?

   b. When you meet, who has traveled farther? How much farther?

Mini-Assessment

Find the unit rate.

1. 165 miles in 3 hours 55 miles per hour
2. $9.60 for 8 cans $1.20 per can
3. $\frac{3}{4}$ cup per $\frac{3}{5}$ gram $1\frac{1}{4}$ cups per gram
4. You can weed $2\frac{2}{3}$ square yards in $\frac{1}{2}$ hour. How many square yards can you weed in 4 hours? $21\frac{1}{3}$ square yards

Section Resources

Surface Level	Deep Level
Resources by Chapter • Extra Practice • Reteach • Puzzle Time Student Journal • Self-Assessment • Practice Differentiating the Lesson Tutorial Videos Skills Review Handbook Skills Trainer	Resources by Chapter • Enrichment and Extension Graphic Organizers Dynamic Assessment System • Section Practice

Concepts, Skills, & Problem Solving

22. $2.8\overline{4}\ \text{yd}^2$;
$\frac{4}{9}\ \text{yd}^2 \div \frac{1}{2}\ \text{h} = \frac{8}{9}\ \text{yd}^2$ per h,
$\frac{8}{9}\ \text{yd}^2$ per h $\times$ 3.2 h $= 2.8\overline{4}\ \text{yd}^2$
23. no; $75 \div 1.5 = 50$ lb per yr;
$38.4 \div 0.75 = 51.2$ lb per yr
24. yes; $7.5 \div \frac{3}{4} = 10$ mi per h;
$\frac{1}{2} \div 3\left(\frac{1}{60}\right) = 10$ mi per h
25. **a.** whole milk
b. orange juice
26. 41.25 mi
27. **a.** Blue: more than 1500 gallons per minute
Green: 1000–1499 gallons per minute
Yellow: 500–999 gallons per minute
Red: less than 500 gallons per minute
b. *Sample answer:* If a firefighter pumps water out at too high a rate, the pipes in the ground could burst.
28. **a.** 1.5 h
b. you; 2 mi

Check out the
Dynamic Classroom.
BigIdeasMath.com

Learning Target

Determine whether two quantities are in a proportional relationship.

Success Criteria

- Determine whether ratios form a proportion.
- Explain how to determine whether quantities are proportional.
- Distinguish between proportional and nonproportional situations.

Warm Up

Cumulative, vocabulary, and prerequisite skills practice opportunities are available in the *Resources by Chapter* or at *BigIdeasMath.com*.

ELL Support

Clarify the meaning of the word *relationship* by explaining that the mother of Sam's mother is Sam's grandmother. If necessary, draw a family tree to clarify and discuss other family relationships. Point out that ratios describe relationships between quantities. Explain that the square feet in the exploration refer to a two-dimensional measurement, not the shape of someone's feet.

Exploration 1

a. 180 min;
$(9 \text{ ft} \times 25 \text{ ft}) \times \frac{40 \text{ min}}{50 \text{ ft}^2} = 180 \text{ min}$

b. *Sample answer:* Proportional quantities have an equivalent ratio of one quantity to another quantity.

c. no; *Sample answer:* The unit rates are not equivalent.

d. 48 min; *Sample answer:* Four hours of work divided among five people is $\frac{4}{5}$ hour, or 48 minutes per person.

Laurie's Notes

Preparing to Teach

- Students have written and simplified ratios. Now they will compare ratios to determine whether two quantities are in a proportional relationship.
- **Construct Viable Arguments and Critique the Reasoning of Others:** To develop an understanding of proportions, ask students to explain their reasoning. A **proportion** is an equation stating that two ratios are equivalent. Explanations offered by students need to be connected to this definition.

Motivate

- Ask for two volunteers. Hand 8 square tiles to Student A and 4 square tiles to Student B.
- Make up a story as to why Student A starts with more than Student B.
- ? "What is the ratio of Student A's tiles to Student B's tiles?" 2 : 1
- ? "What is the ratio of Student B's tiles to Student A's tiles?" 1 : 2
- ? "If I give 2 more tiles to Student A, how many more should I give Student B so that the ratio stays the same? Explain your reasoning." 1; *Sample answer:* Student B has half as many as Student A, so you need to give Student B half as many tiles each time.
- Hand each student 2 more tiles.
- ? "Is the ratio of Student A's tiles to Student B's tiles still 2 : 1? Explain." No, the ratio is $10 : 6 = 5 : 3 \neq 2 : 1$.
- Ask additional questions if time permits.

Exploration 1

- For part (a), make sure students remember how to find the area of the mural. The question is similar to other rate problems they have solved. Listen to students' methods; they may use equivalent rates or a table. If students do not mention using a table, draw one on the board and leave some of the cells blank for students to fill in.

Area (square feet)	50	25	100	200	225
Time (minutes)	40	20	80	160	180

- ? **Think-Alouds:** Refer to the table and say, "In part (b), the problem is asking…" Ask Partner A to think aloud for Partner B to hear what the problem is asking for.
- ? You may need to give students a hint: "What do you know about the quantities in the table?" The ratios are equivalent. Allow time for partners to discuss and then have them share their definitions for **proportional** with the class.
- It is important for students share their explanations for part (c). They should recognize that the ratios are not equivalent, so x and y are *not* proportional.
- Listen to discussions of part (d). Select several pairs with different strategies to share their ideas with the class.

D.3 Identifying Proportional Relationships

Learning Target: Determine whether two quantities are in a proportional relationship.

Success Criteria:
- I can determine whether ratios form a proportion.
- I can explain how to determine whether quantities are proportional.
- I can distinguish between proportional and nonproportional situations.

EXPLORATION 1 Determining Proportional Relationships

Work with a partner.

a. You can paint 50 square feet of a surface every 40 minutes. How long does it take you to paint the mural shown? Explain how you found your answer.

b. The number of square feet you paint is *proportional* to the number of minutes it takes you. What do you think it means for a quantity to be *proportional* to another quantity?

c. Assume your friends paint at the same rate as you. The table shows how long it takes you and different numbers of friends to paint a fence. Is x proportional to y in the table? Explain.

Painters, x	1	2	3	4
Hours, y	4	2	$\frac{4}{3}$	1

Math Practice

Look for Patterns
How can the table in part (c) help you answer the question in part (d)?

d. How long will it take you and four friends to paint the fence? Explain how you found your answer.

D.3 Lesson

Key Vocabulary
proportion, *p. 640*
cross products, *p. 641*
proportional, *p. 642*

Key Idea

Proportions

Words A **proportion** is an equation stating that the values of two ratios are equivalent.

Numbers Equivalent ratios: 2 : 3 and 4 : 6

Proportion: $\frac{2}{3} = \frac{4}{6}$

EXAMPLE 1 Determining Whether Ratios Form a Proportion

Tell whether the ratios form a proportion.

a. 6 : 4 and 8 : 12

When you are determining whether ratios form a proportion, you are checking whether the ratios are equivalent.

Compare the values of the ratios.

$$\frac{6}{4} = \frac{6 \div 2}{4 \div 2} = \frac{3}{2}$$

$$\frac{8}{12} = \frac{8 \div 4}{12 \div 4} = \frac{2}{3}$$

The values of the ratios are *not* equivalent.

Because $\frac{3}{2} \neq \frac{2}{3}$, the ratios 6 : 4 and 8 : 12 do *not* form a proportion.

b. 10 : 40 and 2.5 : 10

Compare the values of the ratios.

$$\frac{10}{40} = \frac{10 \div 10}{40 \div 10} = \frac{1}{4}$$

The values of the ratios are equivalent.

$$\frac{2.5}{10} = \frac{2.5 \times 10}{10 \times 10} = \frac{25}{100} = \frac{25 \div 25}{100 \div 25} = \frac{1}{4}$$

Because $\frac{1}{4} = \frac{1}{4}$, the ratios 10 : 40 and 2.5 : 10 form a proportion.

Try It **Tell whether the ratios form a proportion.**

1. 1 : 2 and 5 : 10
2. 4 : 6 and 18 : 24
3. 4.5 to 3 and 6 to 9
4. $\frac{1}{2}$ to $\frac{1}{4}$ and 8 to 4

Multi-Language Glossary at BigIdeasMath.com

Laurie's Notes

Scaffolding Instruction

- Students should have a basic understanding of the success criteria from the exploration. Now they will formalize their understanding and use **cross products** to tell whether ratios form a proportion.
- **Emerging:** Students have a general understanding of how equivalent ratios can be used to identify proportional relationships, but they need more practice with the processes. These students will benefit from guided instruction for the examples.
- **Proficient:** Students understand the relationship between equivalent ratios and proportions. They should review the Key Ideas and vocabulary before completing Try It Exercises 5–8. Then have students check their understanding with the Self-Assessment exercises.

Key Idea

- Write the definition for a **proportion** on the board.
- ? Ask, "How can you determine whether two ratios form a proportion?" *Sample answer:* If the ratios are equivalent, they form a proportion.
- **FYI:** Without units associated with the numeric values, students think of proportions as fractions.
- If students are comfortable with writing equivalent fractions and simplifying fractions, they will generally have a good sense about working with proportions.

EXAMPLE 1

- The strategy shown in this example is to write the ratios as fractions in simplest form.
- ? "What is the relationship between $\frac{2}{3}$ and $\frac{3}{2}$?" They are reciprocals.
- After completing part (b), you may want to write the proportion $\frac{10}{40} = \frac{2.5}{10}$ on the board.
- Discuss some alternate strategies for part (b). Students may not realize that they could have divided $\frac{2.5}{10}$ by 2.5 to obtain $\frac{1}{4}$. Point out that they could have multiplied the quantities in the second ratio by 4 to obtain the other ratio, which means the ratios are equivalent.

Try It

- Students should work independently and then check their answers with a neighbor.

Scaffold instruction to support all students in their learning. Learning is individualized and you may want to group students differently as they move in and out of these levels with each skill and concept. Student self-assessment and feedback help guide your instructional decisions about how and when to layer support for all students to become proficient learners.

Extra Example 1

Tell whether the ratios form a proportion.

a. 10 : 18 and 45 : 81 yes

b. 15 : 12 and 6 : 3 no

Try It

1. yes
2. no
3. no
4. yes

Laurie's Notes

Key Ideas

- Write the Key Ideas on the board.
- ? Ask, "Which number should b and d not be equal to? Why not?"
  Zero, because it would lead to division by zero, which cannot be done.
- Have students use the Cross Products Property to verify each of their answers for Try It Exercises 1–4.
- Discuss the push-pin note. It shows why the Cross Products Property is true.
- Students should realize that a given ratio relationship, such as 2 meters per second, represents a **proportional** relationship. All of the ratios relating the quantities are equivalent due to the ratio language used in the statement.

EXAMPLE 2

- Work through each part as shown. Ask students to supply the justification for each step.

Try It

- Have students complete the exercises independently on whiteboards.
- Ask several students to explain their strategies.

ELL Support

After demonstrating Example 2, have students practice language by working in pairs to complete Try It Exercises 5 and 6. Have one student ask the other, "What are the ratios? What are the cross products? Are they equal?" Have students alternate roles.

Beginner: Write the steps and provide one-word answers.

Intermediate: Use phrases or simple sentences such as, "The ratios are six to two and twelve to one."

Advanced: Use detailed sentences such as, "The cross products are not equal, so six to two and twelve to one do not form a proportion."

Extra Example 2

Tell whether the ratios form a proportion.

a. 6 : 8 and 10 : 12 no

b. 5 : 4 and 15 : 12 yes

Try It

5. no

6. yes

Key Ideas

Cross Products

In the proportion $\frac{a}{b} = \frac{c}{d}$, the products $a \cdot d$ and $b \cdot c$ are called **cross products**.

Cross Products Property

Words The cross products of a proportion are equal.

Numbers

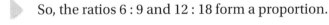

$\frac{2}{3} = \frac{4}{6}$

$2 \cdot 6 = 3 \cdot 4$

Algebra

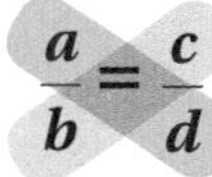

$ad = bc$,
where $b \neq 0$ and $d \neq 0$

You can use the Multiplication Property of Equality to show that the cross products are equal.

$\frac{a}{b} = \frac{c}{d}$

$\cancel{b}d \cdot \frac{a}{\cancel{b}} = b\cancel{d} \cdot \frac{c}{\cancel{d}}$

$ad = bc$

EXAMPLE 2 Using Cross Products

Tell whether the ratios form a proportion.

a. 6 : 9 and 12 : 18

Use the Cross Products Property to determine whether the ratios form a proportion.

$\frac{6}{9} \stackrel{?}{=} \frac{12}{18}$	Determine whether the values of the ratios are equivalent.
$6 \cdot 18 \stackrel{?}{=} 9 \cdot 12$	Find the cross products.
$108 = 108$	The cross products are equal.

So, the ratios 6 : 9 and 12 : 18 form a proportion.

b. 2 : 3 and 4 : 5

Use the Cross Products Property to determine whether the ratios form a proportion.

$\frac{2}{3} \stackrel{?}{=} \frac{4}{5}$	Determine whether the values of the ratios are equivalent.
$2 \cdot 5 \stackrel{?}{=} 3 \cdot 4$	Find the cross products.
$10 \neq 12$	The cross products are *not* equal.

So, the ratios 2 : 3 and 4 : 5 do *not* form a proportion.

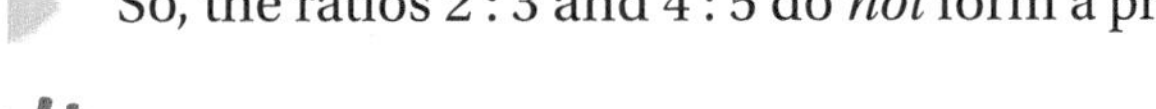

Try It **Tell whether the ratios form a proportion.**

5. 6 : 2 and 12 : 1

6. 8 : 12 and $\frac{2}{3}$: 1

Two quantities are **proportional** when all of the ratios relating the quantities are equivalent. These quantities are said to be in a *proportional relationship.*

EXAMPLE 3 Determining Whether Two Quantities are Proportional

Tell whether x and y are proportional.

x	y
$\frac{1}{2}$	3
1	6
$\frac{3}{2}$	9
2	12

Compare the values of the ratios x to y.

$$\frac{\frac{1}{2}}{3} = \frac{1}{6} \qquad \frac{1}{6} \qquad \frac{\frac{3}{2}}{9} = \frac{1}{6} \qquad \frac{2}{12} = \frac{1}{6}$$

The values of the ratios are equivalent.

So, x and y are proportional.

Math Practice

Construct Arguments

Can you use the values of the ratios y to x in Example 3? Explain.

Try It Tell whether x and y are proportional.

7.

x	1	2	3	4
y	2	4	6	8

8.

x	2	4	6	8	10
y	4	2	1	$\frac{1}{2}$	$\frac{1}{4}$

Self-Assessment for Concepts & Skills

Solve each exercise. Then rate your understanding of the success criteria in your journal.

PROPORTIONS Tell whether the ratios form a proportion.

9. 4 : 14 and 12 : 40

10. 9 : 3 and 45 : 15

11. VOCABULARY Explain how to determine whether two quantities are proportional.

12. WHICH ONE DOESN'T BELONG? Which ratio does *not* belong with the other three? Explain your reasoning.

4 : 10 | 2 : 5

3 : 5 | 6 : 15

Laurie's Notes

EXAMPLE 3

- Copy the table of values. Students may see x and y as ordered pairs or see the table as a vertical ratio table.

? "How can you decide whether x and y are proportional?" *Sample answer:* Determine whether each ratio $x : y$ is equivalent. You could have students check some of the cross products as well.

Try It

- **Construct Viable Arguments and Critique the Reasoning of Others:** Students may use different strategies for Exercises 7 and 8. Ask several students to explain their reasoning.

◉ "Write an example of two ratios that are equivalent. Explain how you know they are equal."

◉ "Write an example of two ratios that are *not* equivalent. Explain how you know they are not equal."

Self-Assessment for Concepts & Skills

- Have students use *Think-Pair-Share* for Exercises 9–12.

ELL Support

Allow students to work in pairs. To check comprehension of Exercises 9 and 10, ask if the ratios form a proportion and have students use a thumbs up for *yes* and a thumbs down for *no*. For Exercises 11 and 12, have students work in groups to discuss and draft their explanations. Then have groups share their explanations with the class.

The Success Criteria Self-Assessment chart can be found in the *Student Journal* or online at *BigIdeasMath.com*.

Extra Example 3

Tell whether x and y are proportional.

x	y
$\frac{1}{2}$	4
1	8
$\frac{3}{2}$	12
2	16

yes

Try It

7. yes

8. no

Self-Assessment for Concepts & Skills

9. no

10. yes

11. Two quantities are proportional if their ratios are equivalent.

12. 3 : 5; The others are equivalent to 2 : 5.

Laurie's Notes

Extra Example 4

You run the first 3 laps around the gym in 1.5 minutes. You complete 24 laps in 18 minutes. How long does it take you to run 8 laps? about 5 minutes

EXAMPLE 4

- Ask students to read the problem and then select a student to explain the question.
- Ask students if they expect this situation to be exactly proportional. They should realize that your speed is likely to decrease over time.
- Remind students that the quantities in the ratios need to be in the same order.
- Work through the problem as shown. When students realize that they cannot use ratio reasoning, ask them for ideas as to how they can answer the question.
- Work through the rest of the problem and continue to probe for other methods. Students may estimate that it takes you about 8 minutes to swim 10 laps because you swim 20 laps in 16 minutes; however, you swam your first 4 laps faster so it should take a little less than 8 minutes to swim 10 laps.

Self-Assessment for Problem Solving

13. 15 cloves of garlic; $\frac{3}{2} = \frac{x}{10}$, $x = 15$

14. a. yes; The ratios relating the quantities are equivalent.

b. no; *Sample answer:* A runner's speed is too variable to determine the time with certainty.

Self-Assessment for Problem Solving

- Students may benefit from trying the exercises independently and then working with peers to refine their work. It is important to provide time in class for problem solving, so that students become comfortable with the problem-solving plan.
- Remind students to read the problem carefully so they understand the question. They may need to read the problem more than one time.

The Success Criteria Self-Assessment chart can be found in the *Student Journal* or online at *BigIdeasMath.com.*

Learning Target

Determine whether two quantities are in a proportional relationship.

Success Criteria

- Determine whether ratios form a proportion.
- Explain how to determine whether quantities are proportional.
- Distinguish between proportional and nonproportional situations.

Formative Assessment Tip

3-2-1

This technique provides a structured way for students to reflect on their learning, typically at the conclusion of a lesson or chapter. Students are asked to respond to three writing prompts: giving 3 responses to the first prompt, 2 responses to the second prompt, and 1 response to the third prompt. All 6 responses relate to what students have learned during the lesson or chapter. Collect and review student responses to help you plan instruction for the next day.

Closure

- **3-2-1:** Ask students to write 3 new things (concepts, skills, or procedures) that they learned so far in this chapter, 2 things they are struggling with, and 1 thing that will help them tomorrow.
- The next day, begin class by sharing positive responses and clarifying any questions or misunderstandings.

EXAMPLE 4 Modeling Real Life

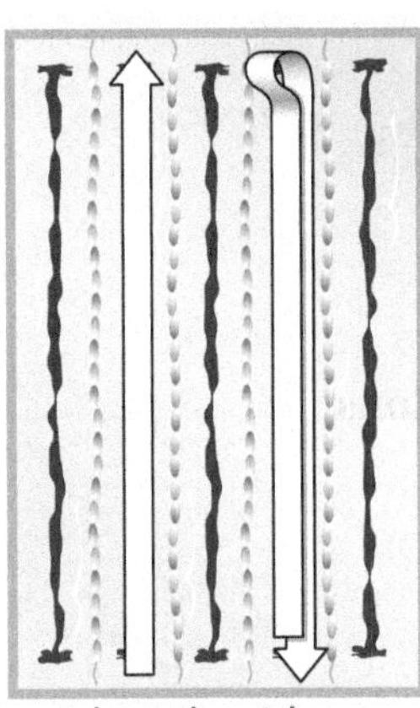
1 length 1 lap

You swim for 16 minutes and complete 20 laps. You swam your first 4 laps in 2.4 minutes. How long does it take you to swim 10 laps?

Compare unit rates to determine whether the number of laps is proportional to your time. If it is, then you can use ratio reasoning to find the time it takes you to swim 10 laps.

2.4 minutes for every 4 laps: $\frac{2.4}{4} = 0.6$ minute per lap

16 minutes for every 20 laps: $\frac{16}{20} = 0.8$ minute per lap

The number of laps is *not* proportional to the time. So, you *cannot* use ratio reasoning to determine the time it takes you to swim 10 laps.

Because you slowed down after your first 4 laps, you can estimate that you swim 10 laps in more than

$$\frac{0.6 \text{ minute}}{1 \text{ lap}} \cdot 10 \text{ laps} = 6 \text{ minutes},$$

but less than

$$\frac{0.8 \text{ minute}}{1 \text{ lap}} \cdot 10 \text{ laps} = 8 \text{ minutes}.$$

So, you can estimate that it takes you about 7 minutes to swim 10 laps.

Self-Assessment for Problem Solving

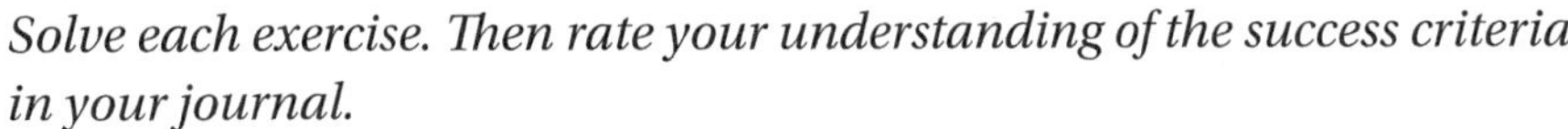

Solve each exercise. Then rate your understanding of the success criteria in your journal.

13. After making 20 servings of pasta, a chef has used 30 cloves of garlic. The chef used 6 cloves to make the first 4 servings. How many cloves of garlic are used to make 10 servings? Justify your answer.

14. **DIG DEEPER!** A runner completes a 25-mile race in 5 hours. The runner completes the first 7.5 miles in 1.5 hours.

a. Do these rates form a proportion? Justify your answer.

b. Can you determine, with certainty, the time it took the runner to complete 10 miles? Explain your reasoning.

D.3 Practice

Go to *BigIdeasMath.com* to get HELP with solving the exercises.

Review & Refresh

Find the unit rate.

1. 30 inches per 5 years
2. 486 games every 3 seasons
3. 8750 steps every 1.25 hours
4. 3.75 pints out of every 5 gallons

Add or subtract.

5. $-28 + 15$
6. $-6 + (-11)$
7. $-10 - 8$
8. $-17 - (-14)$

Solve the equation.

9. $\frac{x}{6} = 25$
10. $8x = 72$
11. $150 = 2x$
12. $35 = \frac{x}{4}$

Concepts, Skills, & Problem Solving

MP **REASONING** **You can paint 75 square feet of a surface every 45 minutes. Determine how long it takes you to paint a wall with the given dimensions.** (See Exploration 1, p. 639.)

13. 8 ft $\times$ 5 ft
14. 7 ft $\times$ 6 ft
15. 9 ft $\times$ 9 ft

PROPORTIONS **Tell whether the ratios form a proportion.**

16. 1 to 3 and 7 to 21
17. 1 : 5 and 6 : 30
18. 3 to 4 and 24 to 18
19. 3.5 : 2 and 14 : 8
20. 24: 30 and $3 : \frac{7}{2}$
21. $\frac{21}{2} : 3$ and 16 : 6
22. 0.6 : 0.5 and 12 : 10
23. 2 to 4 and 11 to $\frac{11}{2}$
24. $\frac{5}{8} : \frac{2}{3}$ and $\frac{1}{4} : \frac{1}{3}$

IDENTIFYING PROPORTIONAL RELATIONSHIPS **Tell whether *x* and *y* are proportional.**

25.

x	1	2	3
y	7	8	9

26.

x	2	4	6
y	5	10	15

27.

x	0.25	0.5	0.75
y	4	8	12

28.

x	$\frac{2}{3}$	1	$\frac{4}{3}$
y	$\frac{7}{10}$	$\frac{3}{5}$	$\frac{1}{2}$

Assignment Guide and Concept Check

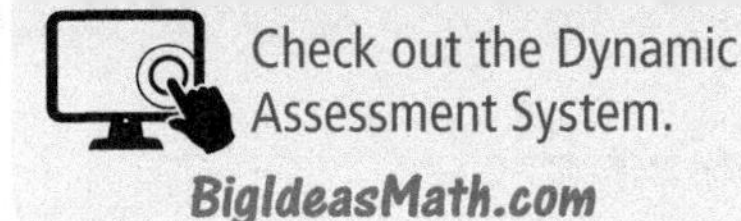

Check out the Dynamic Assessment System.
BigIdeasMath.com

Scaffold assignments to support all students in their learning progression. The suggested assignments are a starting point. Continue to assign additional exercises and revisit with spaced practice to move every student toward proficiency.

Level	Assignment 1	Assignment 2
Emerging	4, 8, 12, 13, 16, 17, 19, 25, 27, 29, 30, 31, 33	20, 22, 24, 28, 34, 35, 36, 37, 38, 39, 44
Proficient	4, 8, 12, 14, 18, 20, 22, 26, 27, 29, 30, 32, 34	24, 28, 35, 37, 38, 39, 40, 41, 42, 43, 44
Advanced	4, 8, 12, 15, 20, 22, 24, 27, 28, 29, 30, 34, 35	38, 39, 40, 41, 42, 43, 44, 45, 46, 47, 48

- Assignment 1 is for use after students complete the Self-Assessment for Concepts & Skills.
- Assignment 2 is for use after students complete the Self-Assessment for Problem Solving.
- The red exercises can be used as a concept check.

Review & Refresh Prior Skills

Exercises 1–4 Finding Unit Rates
Exercises 5 and 6 Adding Integers
Exercises 7 and 8 Subtracting Integers
Exercises 9–12 Solving an Equation

Review & Refresh

1. 6 in. : 1 yr
2. 162 games : 1 season
3. 7000 steps : 1 h
4. 0.75 pt : 1 gal
5. −13
6. −17
7. −18
8. −3
9. $x = 150$
10. $x = 9$
11. $x = 75$
12. $x = 140$

Concepts, Skills, & Problem Solving

13. 24 min
14. 25.2 min
15. 48.6 min
16. yes
17. yes
18. no
19. yes
20. no
21. no
22. yes
23. no
24. no
25. no
26. yes
27. yes
28. no

Concepts, Skills, & Problem Solving

29. no; $\frac{8}{3} \neq \frac{9}{4}$

30. no; $\frac{8}{18} \neq \frac{1}{3}$

31. yes

32. no

33. no

34. yes

35. yes

36. yes; Both can do 45 sit-ups per minute.

37. you: 1.1 beats per second
friend: 1.2 beats per second
No, the rates are not equivalent.

38. no; Your friend earns more money per hour.

39. yes; The value of the ratio of height to base for both triangles is $\frac{4}{5}$.

40. **a.** x and y, x and z, y and z

b. 30 pitches

Common Errors

- **Exercises 31–35** Students may mix up the rates and incorrectly find that they are not proportional. For example, they might write $\frac{7\text{ inches}}{9\text{ hours}} \stackrel{?}{=} \frac{54\text{ hours}}{42\text{ inches}}$. Remind students about writing a rate and help them identify which unit goes in the numerator.

MP YOU BE THE TEACHER **Your friend determines whether x and y are proportional. Is your friend correct? Explain your reasoning.**

29.

x	8	9
y	3	4

$$\frac{8+1}{3+1} = \frac{9}{4}$$

The values of the ratios x to y are equal. So, x and y are proportional.

30.

x	2	4	8
y	6	12	18

$$\frac{2}{6} = \frac{1}{3} \qquad \frac{4}{12} = \frac{1}{3}$$

The values of the ratios x to y are equal. So, x and y are proportional.

PROPORTIONS **Tell whether the rates form a proportion.**

31. 7 inches in 9 hours; 42 inches in 54 hours

32. 12 players from 21 teams; 15 players from 24 teams

33. 385 calories in 3.5 servings; 300 calories in 3 servings

34. 4.8 laps every 8 minutes; 3.6 laps every 6 minutes

35. $\frac{3}{4}$ pound for every 5 gallons; $\frac{4}{5}$ pound for every $5\frac{1}{3}$ gallons

36. **MP MODELING REAL LIFE** You do 90 sit-ups in 2 minutes. Your friend does 126 sit-ups in 2.8 minutes. Do these rates form a proportion? Explain.

37. **MP MODELING REAL LIFE** Find the heart rates of you and your friend. Do these rates form a proportion? Explain.

	Heartbeats	Seconds
You	22	20
Friend	18	15

38. **MP PROBLEM SOLVING** You earn \$56 walking your neighbor's dog for 8 hours. Your friend earns \$36 painting your neighbor's fence for 4 hours. Are the pay rates equivalent? Explain.

39. **GEOMETRY** Are the heights and bases of the two triangles proportional? Explain.

$h = 12$ cm, $b = 15$ cm

$h = 8$ cm, $b = 10$ cm

40. **MP REASONING** A pitcher coming back from an injury limits the number of pitches thrown in bullpen sessions as shown.

Session Number, x	Pitches, y	Curveballs, z
1	10	4
2	20	8
3	30	12
4	40	16

a. Which quantities are proportional?

b. How many pitches that are *not* curveballs will the pitcher likely throw in Session 5?

41. **MP STRUCTURE** You add the same numbers of pennies and dimes to the coins shown. Is the new ratio of pennies to dimes proportional to the original ratio of pennies to dimes? If so, illustrate your answer with an example. If not, show why with a counterexample.

a.

b.

42. **MP REASONING** You are 13 years old, and your cousin is 19 years old. As you grow older, is your age proportional to your cousin's age? Explain your reasoning.

43. **MP MODELING REAL LIFE** The shadow of the moon during a solar eclipse travels 2300 miles in 1 hour. In the first 20 minutes, the shadow traveled $766\frac{2}{3}$ miles. How long does it take for the shadow to travel 1150 miles? Justify your answer.

44. **MP MODELING REAL LIFE** In 60 seconds, a car in a parade travels 0.2 mile. The car traveled the last 0.05 mile in 12 seconds. How long did it take for the car to travel 0.1 mile? Justify your answer.

45. **OPEN-ENDED** Describe (a) a real-life situation where you expect two quantities to be proportional and (b) a real-life situation where you do *not* expect two quantities to be proportional. Explain your reasoning.

46. **MP PROBLEM SOLVING** A specific shade of red nail polish requires 7 parts red to 2 parts yellow. A mixture contains 35 quarts of red and 8 quarts of yellow. Is the mixture the correct shade? If so, justify your answer. If not, explain how you can fix the mixture to make the correct shade of red.

47. **MP LOGIC** The quantities x and y are proportional. Use each of the integers 1–5 to complete the table. Justify your answer.

x	10		6	
y				0.5

48. **CRITICAL THINKING** Ratio A and Ratio B form a proportion. Ratio B and Ratio C also form a proportion. Do Ratio A and Ratio C form a proportion? Justify your answer.

Mini-Assessment

Tell whether the ratios form a proportion.

1. 4 : 12 and 5 : 15 yes
2. 8 : 4 and 12 : 8 no
3. 14 : 17 and 42 : 51 yes
4. 16 : 12 and 26 : 22 no
5. You can complete 40 push-ups in 2 minutes. Your friend can complete 57 push-ups in 3 minutes. Do these rates form a proportion? Explain.
   No, the rates are not equivalent: $\frac{\text{40 push-ups}}{\text{2 minutes}} = \frac{\text{20 push-ups}}{\text{1 minute}}$ and $\frac{\text{57 push-ups}}{\text{3 minutes}} = \frac{\text{19 push-ups}}{\text{1 minute}}$.

Section Resources

Surface Level	Deep Level
Resources by Chapter • Extra Practice • Reteach • Puzzle Time Student Journal • Self-Assessment • Practice Differentiating the Lesson Tutorial Videos Skills Review Handbook Skills Trainer	Resources by Chapter • Enrichment and Extension Graphic Organizers Dynamic Assessment System • Section Practice
Transfer Level	
Dynamic Assessment System • Mid-Chapter Quiz	Assessment Book • Mid-Chapter Quiz

Concepts, Skills, & Problem Solving

41. **a.** no; *Sample answer:* Adding two pennies and two dimes to the coins will give a ratio of 5 pennies : 4 dimes. This ratio is not equivalent to 3 pennies : 2 dimes.

b. yes; *Sample answer:* Adding two pennies and two dimes to the coins will give a ratio of 6 pennies : 6 dimes. This ratio is equivalent to 4 pennies : 4 dimes.

42. no; The ratios are not equivalent; $\frac{13}{19} \neq \frac{14}{20} \neq \frac{15}{21}$ etc.

43. 30 min; $\frac{60}{2300} = \frac{x}{1150}$, $x = 30$

44. about 27 sec; *Sample answer:* Because the quantities are not proportional, estimate the time. $\frac{60}{0.2} \div 10 = 30$ seconds, $\frac{12}{0.05} \div 10 = 24$ seconds, $\frac{30 + 24}{2} = \frac{54}{2} = 27$

45. **a.** *Sample answer:* Machines at a factory that produce an output of a certain amount per unit of time.

b. *Sample answer:* Running 10 laps during gym class. The time it takes to run each lap is rarely exactly the same.

46. no; Add 2 more quarts of yellow.

47.

x	10	4	6	1
y	5	2	3	0.5

$\frac{10}{5} = \frac{4}{2} = \frac{6}{3} = \frac{1}{0.5}$

48. yes; Because Ratio *A* is equivalent to Ratio *B*, Ratios *A* and *B* simplify to the same ratio. Because Ratio *B* is equivalent to Ratio *C*, Ratios *B* and *C* simplify to the same ratio. Ratios *A* and *C* simplify to the same ratio, so they are equivalent.

Check out the
Dynamic Classroom.
BigIdeasMath.com

Learning Target

Use proportions to solve ratio problems.

Success Criteria

- Solve proportions using various methods.
- Find a missing value that makes two ratios equivalent.
- Use proportions to represent and solve real-life problems.

Warm Up

Cumulative, vocabulary, and prerequisite skills practice opportunities are available in the *Resources by Chapter* or at *BigIdeasMath.com*.

ELL Support

Review the methods learned in the previous lessons for determining equivalent ratios, creating ratio tables, finding unit rates, and identifying proportional relationships. Then present the exploration and compare the methods that students use.

Exploration 1

a. *Sample answer:* Determine the value of the ratio of miles to minutes, then multiply by 90 minutes.

b. yes; *Sample answer:* To find the value of x, set up the proportion $\frac{50}{40} = \frac{x}{90}$ and solve to get $x = 112.5$ miles.

c. 120 mi

d. Answers will vary. Some possibilities are using the unit rate and solving by proportions.

Laurie's Notes

Preparing to Teach

- Students have compared ratios using proportions and the Cross Product Property. Now they will write and solve proportions using different strategies.
- **Make Sense of Problems and Persevere in Solving Them:** Mathematically proficient students use a ratio table as a tool to show relationship between different quantities.

Motivate

- **Management Tip:** You may want to cut several lengths of string prior to this activity so all students can join in.
- Ask for a volunteer. Say, "I can estimate the distance around your neck without actually measuring your neck!"
- Use the string to measure the distance around the student's wrist.
- Two times this length will be approximately the distance around his or her neck. Have the student verify this length by measuring the distance around his or her own neck.
- **Write:** $\frac{\text{distance around wrist}}{\text{distance around neck}} = \frac{1}{2}$.
- Write a new proportion substituting the distance around the wrist. For example, $\frac{8.5 \text{ inches}}{x \text{ inches}} = \frac{1}{2}$.
- **Solve:** The distance around the neck is two times 8.5 inches, or 17 inches.

Exploration 1

- For part (a), give students time to read the problem and table.
- Ask, "How was the table created?" *Sample answer:* The miles the train travels were written in the first row and the corresponding times (in minutes) were written in the second row.
- Allow students to brainstorm how they can find the value of x.
- As students are working on parts (b) and (c), circulate and make note of the different methods they use.
- Select several students to present their different strategies to the class. Make a list on a board so students understand that there are several methods they could use (proportions, mental math, cross products, etc.).
- After students have shared their results and methods with other groups, point out a very simple method.

The train travels 30 miles every 30 minutes $\left(\frac{1}{2} \text{ hour}\right)$, or 1 mile every minute, so the train travels 120 miles in 120 minutes (2 hours).

D.4 Writing and Solving Proportions

Learning Target: Use proportions to solve ratio problems.

Success Criteria:
- I can solve proportions using various methods.
- I can find a missing value that makes two ratios equivalent.
- I can use proportions to represent and solve real-life problems.

EXPLORATION 1 Solving a Ratio Problem

Work with a partner. A train travels 50 miles every 40 minutes. To determine the number of miles the train travels in 90 minutes, your friend creates the following table.

Miles	50	x
Minutes	40	90

a. Explain how you can find the value of x.

b. Can you use the information in the table to write a proportion? If so, explain how you can use the proportion to find the value of x. If not, explain why not.

c. How far does the train below travel in 2 hours?

Math Practice

Use Equations
What equation can you use to find the answer in part (c)?

30 miles every $\frac{1}{2}$ hour

d. Share your results in part (c) with other groups. Compare and contrast methods used to solve the problem.

D.4 Lesson

You can solve proportions using various methods.

EXAMPLE 1 Solving a Proportion Using Mental Math

Solve $\frac{3}{2} = \frac{x}{8}$.

Step 1: Think: The product of 2 and what number is 8?

$$\frac{3}{2} = \frac{x}{8}$$

$$2 \times ? = 8$$

Step 2: Because the product of 2 and 4 is 8, multiply the numerator by 4 to find x.

$$3 \times 4 = 12$$

$$\frac{3}{2} = \frac{x}{8}$$

$$2 \times 4 = 8$$

The solution is $x = 12$.

Try It **Solve the proportion.**

1. $\frac{5}{8} = \frac{20}{d}$ **2.** $\frac{7}{z} = \frac{14}{10}$ **3.** $\frac{21}{24} = \frac{x}{8}$

EXAMPLE 2 Solving a Proportion Using Multiplication

Solve $\frac{5}{7} = \frac{x}{21}$.

$\frac{5}{7} = \frac{x}{21}$ Write the proportion.

$21 \cdot \frac{5}{7} = 21 \cdot \frac{x}{21}$ Multiplication Property of Equality

$15 = x$ Simplify.

The solution is $x = 15$.

Try It **Solve the proportion.**

4. $\frac{w}{6} = \frac{6}{9}$ **5.** $\frac{12}{10} = \frac{a}{15}$ **6.** $\frac{y}{10} = \frac{3}{5}$

Laurie's Notes

Scaffolding Instruction

- In the exploration, students discussed various methods of solving proportions. They will continue this work in the lesson.
- **Emerging:** Students may be able to create a ratio table but may struggle to write and/or solve the proportion. Students will benefit from close examination of the examples.
- **Proficient:** Students can write and solve proportions using a variety of methods (including tables). Students should review Examples 4 and 5 before proceeding to the Self-Assessment exercises.

Discuss

◉ Ask students to write and solve a proportion for the situation.
A stadium holds approximately 45,000 people during a baseball game. If the ratio of season ticket holders to all tickets is 1 : 3, approximately how many season ticket holders are there? 15,000 season ticket holders

EXAMPLE 1

- **Reason Abstractly and Quantitatively:** This example has no context. The focus is on the process and how mental math is used in solving the proportion.
- When finished, present the following problems to assess if students can distinguish when mental math is a reasonable approach.
  - Tell whether you can easily use mental math to solve these problems.

    a. $\frac{3}{7} = \frac{x}{27}$ 7 is not a factor of 27, so mental math is not an easy approach.

    b. $\frac{3}{7} = \frac{27}{x}$ 3 is a factor of 27, so mental math can be used.

Try It

- **Whiteboards:** Have students complete the exercises independently.

EXAMPLE 2

- The Multiplication Property of Equality works because the variable is in the numerator.

? "Why do you multiply by 21?" Because x is divided by 21.

- If this same problem had been $\frac{7}{5} = \frac{21}{x}$, you could not solve by multiplying both sides of the equation by $\frac{1}{21}$ because that would simplify to $\frac{1}{15} = \frac{1}{x}$ and you still have not isolated x. Be sure students understand this.

? "Can you use another strategy, such as mental math, to solve this problem?" yes Listen for the idea of equivalent fractions.

Try It

- **Think-Pair-Share:** Students should read each exercise independently and then work in pairs to complete the exercises. Then have each pair compare their answers with another pair and discuss any discrepancies.
- Ask students to share their strategies.

Formative Assessment Tip

Whiteboards

Whiteboards can be used to provide individual responses, or used with small groups to encourage student collaboration and consensus on a problem or solution method. Whiteboards can be used at the beginning of class for the Warm Up or throughout the lesson to elicit student responses.

Unlike writing on scrap paper (individual response) or chart paper (group response), responses can be erased and modified easily. As understanding progresses, responses can reflect this growth.

Use whiteboards for more than quick responses. Sizeable whiteboards can be used to communicate thinking, providing evidence of how a problem was solved. When students display their whiteboards in the front of the room, classmates can critique their reasoning or methods of solution.

Extra Example 1

Solve $\frac{8}{5} = \frac{n}{15}$. $n = 24$

Try It

1. $d = 32$
2. $z = 5$
3. $x = 7$

Extra Example 2

Solve $\frac{c}{12} = \frac{5}{3}$. $c = 20$

Try It

4. $w = 4$
5. $a = 18$
6. $y = 6$

Extra Example 3

Solve each proportion.

a. $\frac{u}{6} = \frac{3}{4}$ $u = 4.5$

b. $\frac{4}{13} = \frac{12}{h}$ $h = 39$

Try It

7. $x = 8$
8. $y = 2.5$
9. $z = 15$

Extra Example 4

Find the value of x so that the ratios 5 : 6 and 4 : x are equivalent. $x = 4.8$

Try It

10. $x = 3$
11. $x = 20$
12. $x = 7.5$

Laurie's Notes

EXAMPLE 3

- ? "How are parts (a) and (b) different?" *Sample answer:* In part (a), the variable is in the numerator and in part (b), the variable is in the denominator. Part (b) involves one numerator that is a factor of the other numerator.
- ? "Can you easily use the Multiplication Property of Equality to solve both proportions? Explain." No, using the Multiplication Property of Equality would be difficult in part (b) because the variable is in the denominator
- **Make Sense of Problems and Persevere in Solving Them:** As you work through the problems with students, share with them the wisdom of analyzing the problem first to decide what method makes the most sense.
- **Common Error:** Students sometimes confuse the multiplication of fractions and the Cross Products Property.

Try It

- **Think-Pair-Share:** Students should read each exercise independently and then work in pairs to complete the exercises. Then have each pair compare their answers with another pair and discuss any discrepancies.
- Ask students to share their strategies. Although Example 3 was solved using the Cross Products Property, some students may solve Exercises 7 and 8 by using mental math and recognizing equivalent fractions.

EXAMPLE 4

- Ask students to read and analyze the problem to decide which method makes the most sense. They should realize that mental math is not convenient because 8 is not a factor of 20.
- Work through the problem as shown.

Try It

- **Neighbor Check:** Have students work independently and then have their neighbors check their work. Have students discuss any discrepancies.

ELL Support

After demonstrating Example 4, have students practice language by working in pairs to complete Try It Exercises 10–12. Have one student ask another, "What proportion do you write? By what number do you multiply each side? What is your answer?" Have students alternate roles.

Beginner: Write the steps and/or use one-word answers.

Intermediate: Use simple sentences such as, "The proportion is two-fourths equals x divided by six."

Advanced: Use detailed sentences such as, "To find the value of x, write the proportion two-fourths equals x divided by six."

EXAMPLE 3 Solving a Proportion Using Cross Products

Solve each proportion.

a. $\frac{x}{8} = \frac{7}{10}$

$x \cdot 10 = 8 \cdot 7$	Cross Products Property
$10x = 56$	Multiply.
$x = 5.6$	Divide each side by 10.

The solution is $x = 5.6$.

b. $\frac{9}{y} = \frac{3}{17}$

$9 \cdot 17 = y \cdot 3$	Cross Products Property
$153 = 3y$	Multiply.
$51 = y$	Divide each side by 3.

The solution is $y = 51$.

Try It **Solve the proportion.**

7. $\frac{2}{7} = \frac{x}{28}$ **8.** $\frac{12}{5} = \frac{6}{y}$ **9.** $\frac{40}{z+1} = \frac{15}{6}$

EXAMPLE 4 Writing and Solving a Proportion

Find the value of x so that the ratios 3 : 8 and x : 20 are equivalent.

For the ratios to be equivalent, the values of the ratios must be equal. So, find the value of x for which $\frac{3}{8}$ and $\frac{x}{20}$ are equal by solving a proportion.

$\frac{3}{8} = \frac{x}{20}$	Write a proportion.
$20 \cdot \frac{3}{8} = 20 \cdot \frac{x}{20}$	Multiplication Property of Equality
$7.5 = x$	Simplify.

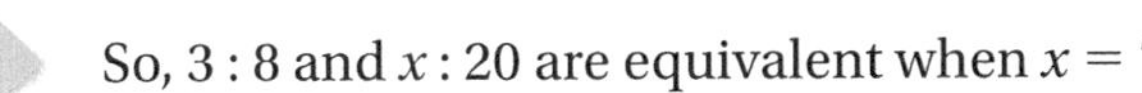

So, 3 : 8 and x : 20 are equivalent when $x = 7.5$.

Try It **Find the value of x so that the ratios are equivalent.**

10. 2 : 4 and x : 6 **11.** x : 5 and 8 : 2 **12.** 4 to 3 and 10 to x

EXAMPLE 5 Writing a Proportion

A chef increases the amounts of ingredients in a recipe to make a proportional recipe. The new recipe has 6 cups of black beans. Which proportion can be used to find the number x of cups of water in the new recipe?

Black Bean Soup

1.5 cups black beans
0.5 cup salsa
2 cups water
1 tomato
2 teaspoons seasoning

A. $\frac{2}{1.5} = \frac{6}{x}$ **B.** $\frac{1.5}{6} = \frac{x}{2}$

C. $\frac{1.5}{2} = \frac{x}{6}$ **D.** $\frac{1.5}{2} = \frac{6}{x}$

In the original recipe, the ratio of cups of black beans to cups of water is 1.5 : 2. In the new recipe, the ratio is 6 : x.

For the new recipe to be proportional to the original recipe, these ratios must be equivalent. So, the values of the ratios must be equal, $\frac{1.5}{2} = \frac{6}{x}$.

The correct answer is **D**.

Try It

13. Write a proportion that can be used to find the number of tomatoes in the new recipe.

Self-Assessment for Concepts & Skills

Solve each exercise. Then rate your understanding of the success criteria in your journal.

SOLVING A PROPORTION Solve the proportion.

14. $\frac{5}{12} = \frac{b}{36}$

15. $\frac{6}{p} = \frac{42}{35}$

16. WRITING AND SOLVING A PROPORTION Find the value of x so that the ratios x : 9 and 5 : 6 are equivalent.

17. DIFFERENT WORDS, SAME QUESTION Which is different? Find "both" answers.

Solve $\frac{3}{x} = \frac{12}{8}$.

Find x so that 3 : x and 12 : 8 are equivalent.

Find x so that 3 : 12 and x : 8 are equivalent.

Solve $\frac{12}{x} = \frac{3}{8}$.

Laurie's Notes

EXAMPLE 5

- You may want to organize the information in a table to help students write the proportion correctly.
- ? "When creating a table or writing the ratios, should the order be black beans to water or water to black beans?" Either order will work, but you need to be consistent.

Try It

- **Think-Pair-Share:** Students should read the exercise independently and then work in pairs to complete the exercise. Then have each pair compare their answer with another pair and discuss any discrepancies.

Self-Assessment for Concepts & Skills

- **One-Minute Card:** List at least three different ways to solve a proportion.
- Have students use two different methods to solve Exercise 14.
- **Neighbor Check:** Have students work independently and then have their neighbors check their work. Have students discuss any discrepancies.

ELL Support

Laurie's Notes suggest using a *Neighbor Check* after students work independently. Allow students to work in pairs for extra support. Then have pairs discuss their answers with another pair. Have each pair display their answers on a whiteboard for your review. Have each group of four explain their answer to Exercise 17 to the class.

The Success Criteria Self-Assessment chart can be found in the *Student Journal* or online at *BigIdeasMath.com*.

Extra Example 5

The chef increases the amounts of ingredients in the recipe in Example 5 to make a proportional recipe. The new recipe has 3 cups of salsa. Which proportion can be used to find the number w of cups of water in the new recipe?

A. $\frac{w}{3} = \frac{0.5}{2}$ **B.** $\frac{3}{w} = \frac{0.5}{2}$

C. $\frac{w}{0.5} = \frac{3}{2}$ **D.** $\frac{0.5}{3} = \frac{w}{2}$

B

Try It

13. $\frac{1.5}{1} = \frac{6}{x}$

Self-Assessment for Concepts & Skills

14. $b = 15$

15. $p = 5$

16. $x = 7.5$

17. Solve $\frac{12}{x} = \frac{3}{8}$; $x = 32$; $x = 2$

Extra Example 6

You buy 8 mangoes for \$10. How much do 20 mangoes cost? \$25

Self-Assessment for Problem Solving

18. between 175 and 350; $\frac{35}{3} = \frac{x}{15}, x = 175; \frac{35}{3} = \frac{x}{30}, x = 350$

19. $\frac{1}{2}$ mi per min; $\frac{x}{12} = \frac{x+3}{18}, x = 6$

Learning Target

Use proportions to solve ratio problems.

Success Criteria

- Solve proportions using various methods.
- Find a missing value that makes two ratios equivalent.
- Use proportions to represent and solve real-life problems.

Laurie's Notes

EXAMPLE 6

- Ask a volunteer to read the problem.
- Explain that 50 gallons of blood for every 2 heartbeats is the same as saying the ratio of gallons of blood to heartbeats is 50 : 2. Make students aware that ratios can be indicated in different ways.
- Make sure students understand that a single ratio determines a proportional relationship. When a problem states that there are a units for every *b* units, the quantities are proportional.
- Ask a student to explain what the problem is asking. It is important to provide many opportunities for students to analyze and explain a problem.
- After solving the problem as shown, ask if the proportion could have been written another way $\left(\frac{50}{2} = \frac{1000}{x}\right)$.

? Discuss the Another Method note and ask, "Which method do you prefer and why?" Answers will vary.

? "Would you want to use a double number line to solve this problem?" Students should recognize that while a double number line could be used, it is not an efficient method for this situation.

◉ "Will you always use the same method to solve ratio problems? Why or why not?" no Listen for understanding that some methods are more efficient than others for certain ratio problems.

Self-Assessment for Problem Solving

- Have students work with a partner and use a Four Square to complete these exercises. Until students become comfortable with the problem-solving plan, they may only be ready to complete the first square.
- **Popsicle Sticks:** Select students to share their work and reasoning.

The Success Criteria Self-Assessment chart can be found in the *Student Journal* or online at *BigIdeasMath.com.*

Closure

- Write and solve 3 proportions. One should use mental math to solve, one should use the Multiplication Property of Equality, and one should use the Cross Products Property.

EXAMPLE 6 Modeling Real Life

A titanosaur's heart pumped 50 gallons of blood for every 2 heartbeats. How many heartbeats did it take to pump 1000 gallons of blood?

Understand the problem.

You are given the rate at which a titanosaur's heart pumped blood. Because all of the rates you can write using this relationship are equivalent, the amount of blood pumped is proportional to the number of heartbeats. You are asked to find how many heartbeats it took to pump 1000 gallons of blood.

Make a plan.

The ratio of heartbeats to gallons of blood is 2 : 50. The number x of heartbeats for every 1000 gallons of blood can be represented by the ratio x : 1000. Use a proportion to find the value of x for which $\frac{2}{50}$ and $\frac{x}{1000}$ are equal.

Solve and check.

$\frac{2}{50} = \frac{x}{1000}$ Write a proportion.

$40 = x$ Multiply each side by 1000.

So, it took 40 heartbeats to pump 1000 gallons of blood.

Another Method
You can use a ratio table to solve the problem.

	× 20	
Heartbeats	2	40
Blood (gallons)	50	1000
	× 20	

✓

Self-Assessment for Problem Solving

Solve each exercise. Then rate your understanding of the success criteria in your journal.

18. You burn 35 calories every 3 minutes running on a treadmill. You want to run for at least 15 minutes, but no more than 30 minutes. What are the possible numbers of calories that you will burn? Justify your answer.

19. DIG DEEPER! Two boats travel at the same speed to different destinations. Boat A reaches its destination in 12 minutes. Boat B reaches its destination in 18 minutes. Boat B travels 3 miles farther than Boat A. How fast do the boats travel? Justify your answer.

D.4 Practice

Go to **BigIdeasMath.com** to get HELP with solving the exercises.

Review & Refresh

Tell whether x and y are proportional.

1.

x	4	6	8
y	6	8	10

2.

x	$\frac{2}{5}$	$\frac{4}{5}$	4
y	3	6	30

Plot the ordered pair in a coordinate plane.

3. $A(-5, -2)$
4. $B(-3, 0)$
5. $C(-1, 2)$
6. $D(1, 4)$

7. Which expression is equivalent to $(3w - 8) - 4(2w + 3)$?

   A. $11w + 4$ **B.** $-5w - 5$ **C.** $-5w + 4$ **D.** $-5w - 20$

Concepts, Skills, & Problem Solving

SOLVING A RATIO PROBLEM **Determine how far the vehicle travels in 3 hours.** (See Exploration 1, p. 647.)

8. A helicopter travels 240 miles every 2 hours.
9. A motorcycle travels 25 miles every 0.5 hour.
10. A train travels 10 miles every $\frac{1}{4}$ hour.
11. A ferry travels 45 miles every $1\frac{1}{2}$ hours.

SOLVING A PROPORTION **Solve the proportion. Explain your choice of method.**

12. $\frac{1}{4} = \frac{z}{20}$
13. $\frac{3}{4} = \frac{12}{y}$
14. $\frac{35}{k} = \frac{7}{3}$
15. $\frac{b}{36} = \frac{5}{9}$
16. $\frac{x}{8} = \frac{3}{12}$
17. $\frac{3}{4} = \frac{v}{14}$
18. $\frac{15}{8} = \frac{45}{c}$
19. $\frac{35}{28} = \frac{n}{12}$
20. $\frac{a}{6} = \frac{15}{2}$
21. $\frac{y}{9} = \frac{44}{54}$
22. $\frac{4}{24} = \frac{c}{36}$
23. $\frac{20}{16} = \frac{d}{12}$
24. $\frac{10}{7} = \frac{8}{k}$
25. $\frac{5}{n} = \frac{16}{32}$
26. $\frac{9}{10} = \frac{d}{6.4}$
27. $\frac{2.4}{1.8} = \frac{7.2}{k}$

28. **MP YOU BE THE TEACHER** Your friend solves the proportion $\frac{m}{8} = \frac{15}{24}$. Is your friend correct? Explain your reasoning.

$$\frac{m}{8} = \frac{15}{24}$$
$$m \cdot 24 = 8 \cdot 15$$
$$m = 5$$

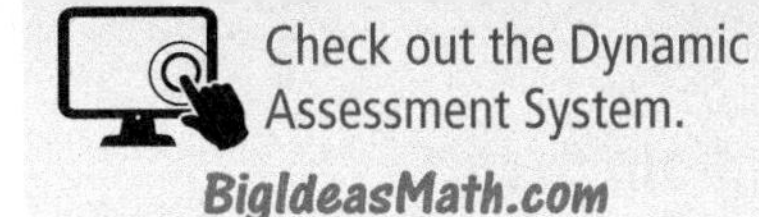
Check out the Dynamic
Assessment System.
BigIdeasMath.com

Assignment Guide and Concept Check

Scaffold assignments to support all students in their learning progression. The suggested assignments are a starting point. Continue to assign additional exercises and revisit with spaced practice to move every student toward proficiency.

Level	Assignment 1	Assignment 2
Emerging	2, 5, 7, 9, 12, 13, 15, 28, 30, 34, 40	24, 26, 29, 32, 35, 38, 41, 42, 44, 52, 56
Proficient	2, 5, 7, 10, 16, 20, 24, 28, 29, 32, 36, 40	26, 37, 38, 43, 44, 45, 46, 49, 53, 56
Advanced	2, 5, 7, 11, 24, 26, 28, 29, 32, 37, 39, 40	43, 45, 46, 48, 50, 54, 55, 56, 57

- Assignment 1 is for use after students complete the Self-Assessment for Concepts & Skills.
- Assignment 2 is for use after students complete the Self-Assessment for Problem Solving.
- The red exercises can be used as a concept check.

Review & Refresh Prior Skills

Exercises 1 and 2 Identifying Proportional Relationships
Exercises 3–6 Plotting Ordered Pairs
Exercise 7 Simplifying Expressions

Common Errors

- **Exercises 12, 15–17, 19–23, and 26** When using the Multiplication Property of Equality, students may multiply by the denominator of the fraction without the variable. Remind students that they are trying to isolate the variable, so they want to multiply both sides by the denominator of the fraction with the variable. Give students an example without a fraction on the other side of the equation to remind them of the process.
- **Exercises 12–27** When using the Cross Products Property, students may divide instead of multiply when finding the cross products, or they may multiply across the numerators and the denominators as if they were multiplying fractions. Remind students that the ratios have an equal sign between them, not a multiplication sign.

Review & Refresh

1. no
2. yes

3–6.

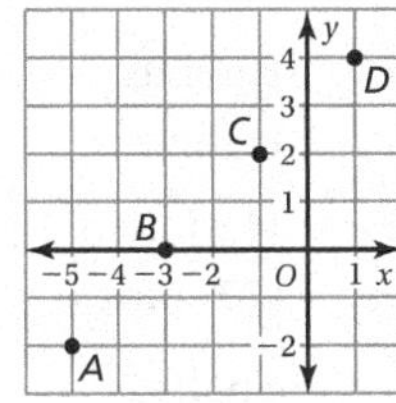
y
x
O
A
B
C
D

7. D

Concepts, Skills, & Problem Solving

8. 360 mi
9. 150 mi
10. 120 mi
11. 90 mi

12–27. Explanations will vary.

12. $z = 5$
13. $y = 16$
14. $k = 15$
15. $b = 20$
16. $x = 2$
17. $v = 10.5$
18. $c = 24$
19. $n = 15$
20. $a = 45$
21. $y = 7\frac{1}{3}$
22. $c = 6$
23. $d = 15$
24. $k = 5.6$
25. $n = 10$
26. $d = 5.76$
27. $k = 5.4$
28. yes; $\frac{5}{8} = \frac{15}{24}$

Concepts, Skills, & Problem Solving

29. yes; Both cross products give the equation $3x = 60$.

30. $\dfrac{12 \text{ points}}{14 \text{ shots}} = \dfrac{18 \text{ points}}{w \text{ shots}}$

31. $\dfrac{n \text{ winners}}{85 \text{ entries}} = \dfrac{34 \text{ winners}}{170 \text{ entries}}$

32. $\dfrac{15 \text{ miles}}{2.5 \text{ hours}} = \dfrac{m \text{ miles}}{4 \text{ hours}}$

33. $\dfrac{100 \text{ meters}}{x \text{ seconds}} = \dfrac{200 \text{ meters}}{22.4 \text{ seconds}}$

34. $x = 32$

35. $x = 16$

36. $x = 10$

37. $x = 1$

38. $x = 2$

39. $x = 4$

40. $\dfrac{1}{200} = \dfrac{19.5}{x}$; Dimensions for the model are in the numerators and the corresponding dimensions for the actual space shuttle are in the denominators.

41. 3 trombones

42. 25 seventh-grade dancers

Common Errors

- **Exercises 30–33** Students may write half of the proportion using rows and the other half using columns. They will have forgotten to include one of the values. Remind students that they need to pick a method for writing proportions with tables and be consistent throughout the problem.

29. **MP NUMBER SENSE** Without solving, determine whether $\frac{x}{4} = \frac{15}{3}$ and $\frac{x}{15} = \frac{4}{3}$ have the same solution. Explain your reasoning.

WRITING A PROPORTION **Use the table to write a proportion.**

30.

	Game 1	Game 2
Points	12	18
Shots	14	w

31.

	May	June
Winners	n	34
Entries	85	170

32.

	Today	Yesterday
Miles	15	m
Hours	2.5	4

33.

	Race 1	Race 2
Meters	100	200
Seconds	x	22.4

WRITING AND SOLVING A PROPORTION **Find the value of x so that the ratios are equivalent.**

34. $1:8$ and $4:x$

35. 4 to 5 and x to 20

36. $3:x$ and $12:40$

37. x to 0.25 and 6 to 1.5

38. $x:\frac{5}{2}$ and $8:10$

39. $\frac{7}{4}$ to 14 and x to 32

40. **WRITING A PROPORTION** Your science teacher has a photograph of the space shuttle *Atlantis*. Every 1 centimeter in the photograph represents 200 centimeters on the actual shuttle. Which of the proportions can you use to find the actual length x of *Atlantis*? Explain.

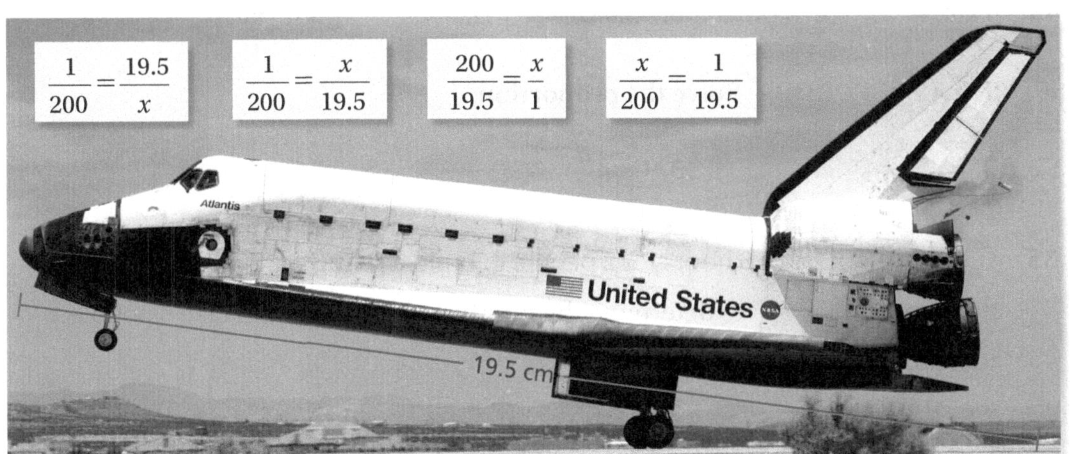

41. **MP MODELING REAL LIFE** In an orchestra, the ratio of trombones to violas is 1 to 3. There are 9 violas. How many trombones are in the orchestra?

42. **MP MODELING REAL LIFE** A dance team has 80 dancers. The ratio of seventh-grade dancers to all dancers is 5 : 16. Find the number of seventh-grade dancers on the team.

43. MP **MODELING REAL LIFE** There are 144 people in an audience. The ratio of adults to children is 5 to 3. How many are adults?

44. MP **PROBLEM SOLVING** You have $50 to buy T-shirts. You can buy 3 T-shirts for $24. Do you have enough money to buy 7 T-shirts? Justify your answer.

45. MP **PROBLEM SOLVING** You buy 10 vegetarian pizzas and pay with $100. How much change do you receive?

46. MP **MODELING REAL LIFE** A person who weighs 120 pounds on Earth weighs 20 pounds on the Moon. How much does a 93-pound person weigh on the Moon?

47. MP **PROBLEM SOLVING** Three pounds of lawn seed covers 1800 square feet. How many bags are needed to cover 8400 square feet?

48. MP **MODELING REAL LIFE** There are 180 white lockers in a school. There are 3 white lockers for every 5 blue lockers. How many lockers are in the school?

CONVERTING MEASURES **Use a proportion to complete the statement. Round to the nearest hundredth if necessary.**

49. 6 km ≈ ▢ mi

50. 2.5 L ≈ ▢ gal

51. 90 lb ≈ ▢ kg

SOLVING A PROPORTION **Solve the proportion.**

52. $\frac{2x}{5} = \frac{9}{15}$

53. $\frac{5}{2} = \frac{d-2}{4}$

54. $\frac{4}{k+3} = \frac{8}{14}$

55. MP **LOGIC** It takes 6 hours for 2 people to build a swing set. Can you use the proportion $\frac{2}{6} = \frac{5}{h}$ to determine the number of hours h it will take 5 people to build the swing set? Explain.

56. MP **STRUCTURE** The ratios $a : b$ and $c : d$ are equivalent. Which of the following equations are proportions? Explain your reasoning.

$\frac{b}{a} = \frac{d}{c}$ $\frac{a}{c} = \frac{b}{d}$ $\frac{a}{d} = \frac{c}{b}$ $\frac{c}{a} = \frac{d}{b}$

57. **CRITICAL THINKING** Consider the proportions $\frac{m}{n} = \frac{1}{2}$ and $\frac{n}{k} = \frac{2}{5}$. What is $\frac{m}{k}$? Explain your reasoning.

Mini-Assessment

Solve the proportion.

1. $\frac{x}{12} = \frac{3}{8}$ $x = 4.5$
2. $\frac{6}{11} = \frac{9}{m}$ $m = 16.5$
3. $\frac{6}{12} = \frac{c}{36}$ $c = 18$
4. You can buy 4 DVDs for $48. Write a proportion that gives the cost c of buying 6 DVDs. $\frac{4 \text{ DVDs}}{\$48} = \frac{6 \text{ DVDs}}{c}$
5. There are 36 pencils packed in 3 boxes. How many pencils are packed in 5 boxes? 60 pencils

Section Resources

Surface Level	Deep Level
Resources by Chapter • Extra Practice • Reteach • Puzzle Time Student Journal • Self-Assessment • Practice Differentiating the Lesson Tutorial Videos Skills Review Handbook Skills Trainer	Resources by Chapter • Enrichment and Extension Graphic Organizers Dynamic Assessment System • Section Practice

Concepts, Skills, & Problem Solving

43. 90 adults

44. no; $\frac{3}{24} = \frac{7}{x}$, $x = \$56$

45. $15

46. 15.5 lb

47. 4 bags

48. 480 lockers

49. about 3.72

50. about 0.65

51. about 40.5

52. $x = 1.5$

53. $d = 12$

54. $k = 4$

55. no; The relationship is not proportional. It should take more people less time to build the swing set.

56. $\frac{b}{a} = \frac{d}{c}$, $\frac{a}{c} = \frac{b}{d}$, $\frac{c}{a} = \frac{d}{b}$,

Sample answer: $\frac{a}{b} = \frac{c}{d}$, so $ad = cb$. Find which equations yield the same cross products.

57. $\frac{1}{5}$; $\frac{m}{k} = \frac{\frac{n}{2}}{\frac{5n}{2}} = \frac{n}{2} \bullet \frac{2}{5n} = \frac{1}{5}$

Check out the
Dynamic Classroom.
BigIdeasMath.com

Learning Target

Represent proportional relationships using graphs and equations.

Success Criteria

- Determine whether quantities are proportional using a graph.
- Find the unit rate of a proportional relationship using a graph.
- Create equations to represent proportional relationships.

Warm Up

Cumulative, vocabulary, and prerequisite skills practice opportunities are available in the *Resources by Chapter* or at *BigIdeasMath.com*.

ELL Support

Visual representations are especially helpful for students with limited language. Explain that a graph is a drawing of the values listed in a table. Carefully point out the relationship between the titles in the table and the labels for the axes. Demonstrate how to plot the data in the table by naming an ordered pair and determining its location.

Exploration 1

a. See Additional Answers.

b. 2 drops of red per drop of blue; *Sample answer:* The point (1, 2) represents the unit rate.

c. Multiply x by 2 to get y; $y = 2x$

Laurie's Notes

Preparing to Teach

- In Chapter 3, students plotted pairs of values from ratio tables in the coordinate plane. Plotting rational numbers in the coordinate plane is part of analyzing proportional relationships. Later, this skill will be important for studying linear equations and graphs of functions.
- The examples throughout this lesson do not distinguish between discrete and continuous data graphically, but you can ask students what numbers make sense. In drawing a line through the data, students observe that the linear relationship passes through the origin.
- **Make Sense of Problems and Persevere in Solving Them:** In this lesson, students will represent proportional relationships using graphs and equations.

Motivate

? Some states have returnable bottle laws. "If you receive \$0.05 for each bottle, how much money do you receive for 4 bottles? 10 bottles?" \$0.20; \$0.50

? "What is the unit rate?" \$0.05 per bottle

- Have students make a table to show the relationship between the number x of bottles collected and the amount y of money received.
- Then have students make a quick sketch of the ordered pairs.
- Observe that (0, 0) is on the graph and the ordered pairs lie on a line.

? "Why might a graph be useful?" *Sample answer:* If the graph is precise, the amounts can be read directly from the graph. There is no need to recalculate for each situation.

Exploration 1

- Remind students how to identify coordinates.
- **Attend to Precision:** Have students use grid paper instead of freehand sketches. Grid paper is available online at *BigIdeasMath.com*.
- In part (a), if students are confused about which graph represents a proportional relationship, remind them to reference the tables and then look at the characteristics of the graphs to make a conjecture.
- Allow time for partners to discuss and complete parts (b) and (c).
- For part (b), encourage students to focus on the point $(1, y)$ to see that the unit rate is y drops of red per 1 drop of blue.
- For part (c), you may need to remind students that the multiplicative relationship is the ratio $\frac{y}{x}$ in simplest form. In this case, $\frac{2}{1}$. If $\frac{y}{x} = \frac{2}{1}$, then in solving for y, the equation is $y = 2x$.

D.5 Graphs of Proportional Relationships

Learning Target: Represent proportional relationships using graphs and equations.

Success Criteria:
- I can determine whether quantities are proportional using a graph.
- I can find the unit rate of a proportional relationship using a graph.
- I can create equations to represent proportional relationships.

EXPLORATION 1 Representing Relationships Graphically

Work with a partner. The tables represent two different ways that red and blue food coloring are mixed.

Mixture 1

Drops of Blue, *x*	Drops of Red, *y*
1	2
2	4
3	6
4	8

Mixture 2

Drops of Blue, *x*	Drops of Red, *y*
0	2
2	4
4	6
6	8

a. Represent each table in the same coordinate plane. Which graph represents a proportional relationship? How do you know?

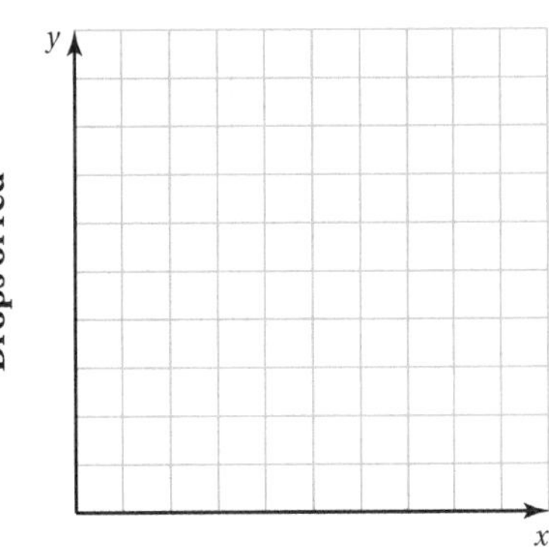

Math Practice

Use a Graph
How is the graph of the proportional relationship different from the other graph?

b. Find the unit rate of the proportional relationship. How is the unit rate shown on the graph?

c. What is the multiplicative relationship between x and y for the proportional relationship? How can you use this value to write an equation that relates y and x?

D.5 Lesson

Key Vocabulary
constant of proportionality, p. 656

The equation $y = kx$ can also be written as $\frac{y}{x} = k$. So, k is equal to the value of the ratio $y : x$.

Key Idea

Graphs of Proportional Relationships

Words Two quantities x and y are proportional when $y = kx$, where k is a number and $k \neq 0$. The number k represents the multiplicative relationship between the quantities and is called the **constant of proportionality**.

Graph The graph of $y = kx$ is a line that passes through the origin.

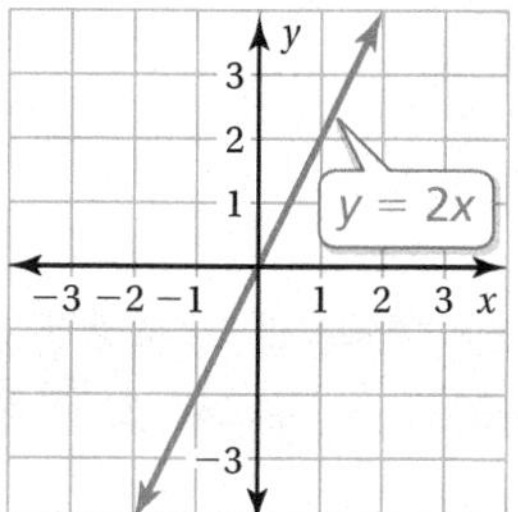

EXAMPLE 1 Determining Whether Two Quantities are Proportional

Tell whether x and y are proportional. Explain your reasoning.

a.

x	1	2	3	4
y	−2	0	2	4

Plot the points. Draw a line through the points.

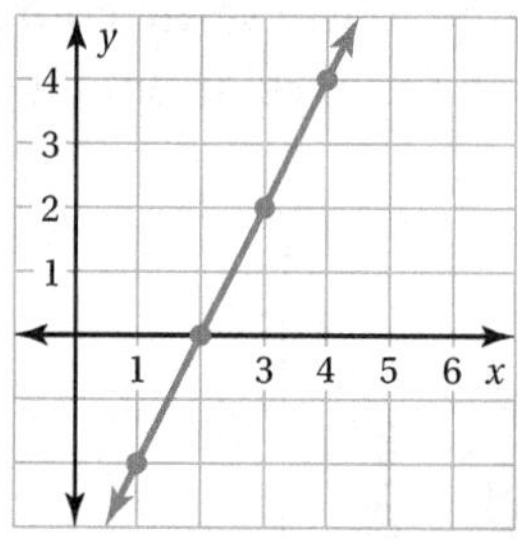

The line does *not* pass through the origin. So, x and y are not proportional.

b.

x	0	2	4	6
y	0	2	4	6

Plot the points. Draw a line through the points.

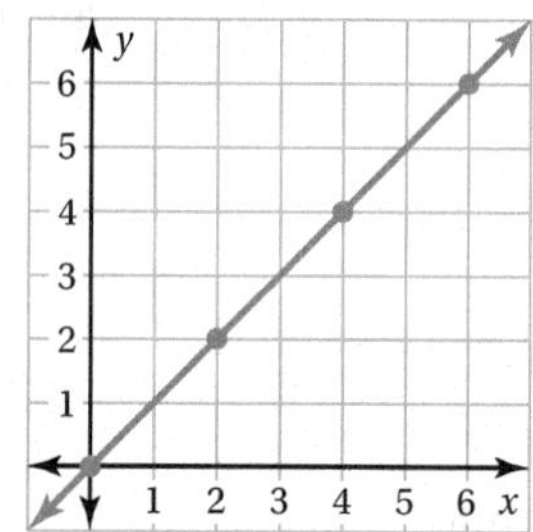

The line passes through the origin. So, x and y are proportional.

Try It **Tell whether x and y are proportional. Explain your reasoning.**

1.

x	y
0	−2
1	1
2	4
3	7

2.

x	y
1	4
2	8
3	12
4	16

3.

x	y
−2	4
−1	2
0	0
1	2

Laurie's Notes

Scaffolding Instruction

- In the exploration, students represented relationships graphically and identified proportional relationships. Now they will formalize their understanding to determine whether quantities are proportional and create equations to represent proportional relationships.
- **Emerging:** Students should be able to plot points in the coordinate plane, but they may struggle to interpret the graph. They will benefit from guided instruction for the Key Idea and examples.
- **Proficient:** Students can create and interpret graphs. They should review the Key Idea and push-pin notes for the precise vocabulary. Then have students complete Try It Exercise 4 and the Self-Assessment exercises.

Scaffold instruction to support all students in their learning. Learning is individualized and you may want to group students differently as they move in and out of these levels with each skill and concept. Student self-assessment and feedback help guide your instructional decisions about how and when to layer support for all students to become proficient learners.

Key Idea

- Write the Key Idea on the board. Remind students throughout the lesson that k is the **constant of proportionality**.
- The equation $y = kx$ can be confusing to students. They see three variables. Remind them that this is the *general form*. The variables y and x will remain in the final equation, but k will be replaced by a number.

? "Why should $k \neq 0$?" *Sample answer:* $y = kx$ can be rewritten as $\frac{y}{k} = x$. Division by zero is undefined, so $k \neq 0$.

- Mention a key feature of this graph: it passes through the origin.

◉ "Is it possible to have a constant rate of change and not have a proportional relationship?" yes; *Sample answer:* The points may lie in a line, but the graph may not pass through the origin. Refer students to the exploration.

EXAMPLE 1

- Write the table of values and plot the ordered pairs for each part.
- **Connection:** When two variables vary proportionally, you can also say that they vary directly.
- Remind students that they can check whether the quantities are proportional using equivalent ratios or cross products.
- **Extension:** "Write an equation that relates x and y from part (b)." $y = x$

Extra Example 1

Tell whether x and y are proportional. Explain your reasoning.

a.

x	0	3	6	9
y	0	1	2	3

Yes, because the line passes through the origin.

b.

x	1	2	3	4
y	−1	0	1	2

No, because the line does not pass through the origin.

Try It

- **Think-Pair-Share:** Students should read each exercise independently and then work in pairs to complete the exercises. Then have each pair compare their answers with another pair and discuss any discrepancies.

ELL Support

After demonstrating Example 1, have students practice language by working in pairs to complete Try It Exercises 1–3. Have pairs discuss questions as they complete the exercises: How do you locate x? y? Does the line pass through the origin? What does that mean?

Beginner: Draw the graphs and use one-word answers.

Intermediate: Use phrases or simple sentences such as, "Start at the origin and move left two units."

Advanced: Use detailed sentences such as, "If the line passes through the origin, then the relationship is proportional."

Try It

1. no; The line does not pass through the origin.
2. yes; The line passes through the origin.
3. no; The points do not lie on a line.

Extra Example 2

The graph shows the distance that you walk. Find your rate in feet per second.

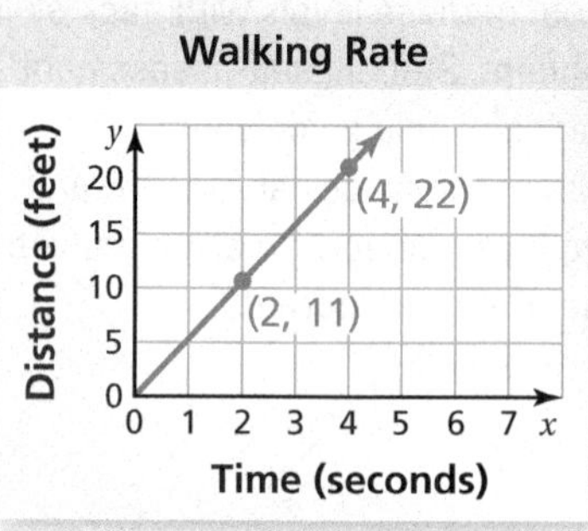

5.5 feet per second

Try It

4. no; *Sample answer:* The unit rate is still $\frac{1}{2}$ mile per minute because $\frac{\frac{1}{4}}{\frac{1}{2}} = \frac{1}{2}$.

Self-Assessment for Concepts & Skills

5. yes; The line passes through the origin.

6. (0, 0): traveling 0 inches in 0 seconds; (1, 1.5): traveling 1.5 inches in 1 second; (3, 4.5): traveling 4.5 inches in 3 seconds; 1.5 inches per second

Laurie's Notes

EXAMPLE 2

- Have students read the problem.
- ? "What information do you need to find the speed of the subway car?" how much time it takes to travel a given distance "Where can you find that information?" any point on the graph
- Students worked with unit rates in Section D.2. Review the push-pin note, which relates unit rates to proportional relationships.
  - ? "Why does the point (1, k) indicate the unit rate is k : 1?" *Sample answer:* If $x = 1$, then $\frac{y}{x} = k$ is equivalent to $\frac{y}{1} = k$, or $y = k$. So, $y : x$ is equivalent to $k : 1$.
  - The value of k indicates the steepness of the line. The greater the value, the steeper the line. This is called the *slope of the line.* Students will study slope in the next course.
- Finish working through the problem as shown.
- **Extension:** "Identify the constant of proportionality from the unit rate and write an equation of the line." $k = \frac{1}{2}$; $y = \frac{1}{2}x$

Try It

- Have students use *Think-Pair-Share* to complete the exercise. Be sure students understand the reasoning: the speed is the same for any point on the line.
- Ask each group to use a different point to support their answer.

Self-Assessment for Concepts & Skills

"How can you identify a proportional relationship from a graph?" The graph must be a line that passes through the origin.

- Students should work independently and then discuss their answers with the class.

ELL Support

Allow students to work in groups to discuss and solve the exercises. Monitor discussions and provide support as needed. Discuss the answers as a class by having each group share their answers.

The Success Criteria Self-Assessment chart can be found in the *Student Journal* or online at *BigIdeasMath.com.*

EXAMPLE 2 Finding a Unit Rate from a Graph

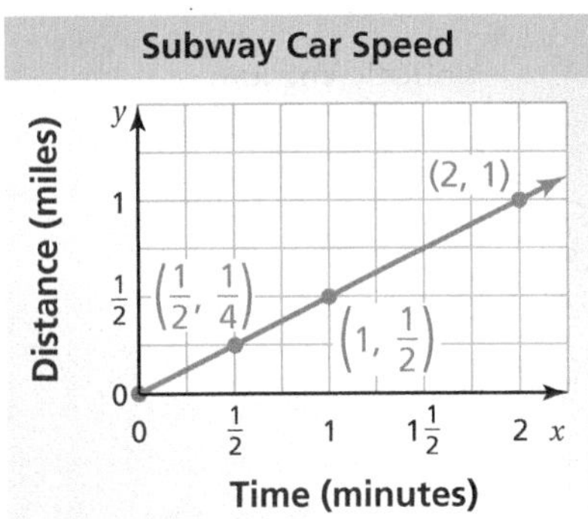

The graph shows the speed of a subway car. Find the speed in miles per minute.

The graph is a line through the origin, so time and distance are proportional. To find the speed in miles per minute, use a point on the graph to find the unit rate.

One Way: Use the point (2, 1) to find the speed.

The point (2, 1) indicates that the subway car travels 1 mile every 2 minutes. So, the unit rate is

$\frac{1}{2}$ mile per minute.

The speed of the subway car is $\frac{1}{2}$ mile per minute.

Another Way: Use the point $\left(1, \frac{1}{2}\right)$ to find the speed.

The point $\left(1, \frac{1}{2}\right)$ indicates that the subway car travels $\frac{1}{2}$ mile every 1 minute. This is the unit rate.

The speed of the subway car is $\frac{1}{2}$ mile per minute.

On the graph of a proportional relationship, the point $(1, k)$ indicates the unit rate, $k : 1$, and the constant of proportionality, k. This value is a measure of the steepness, or slope, of the line.

Try It

4. **WHAT IF?** Does your answer change when you use the point $\left(\frac{1}{2}, \frac{1}{4}\right)$ to find the speed of the subway car? Explain your reasoning.

Self-Assessment for Concepts & Skills

Solve each exercise. Then rate your understanding of the success criteria in your journal.

5. **IDENTIFYING A PROPORTIONAL RELATIONSHIP** Use the graph shown to tell whether x and y are proportional. Explain your reasoning.

6. **FINDING A UNIT RATE** Interpret each plotted point in the graph. Then identify the unit rate, if possible.

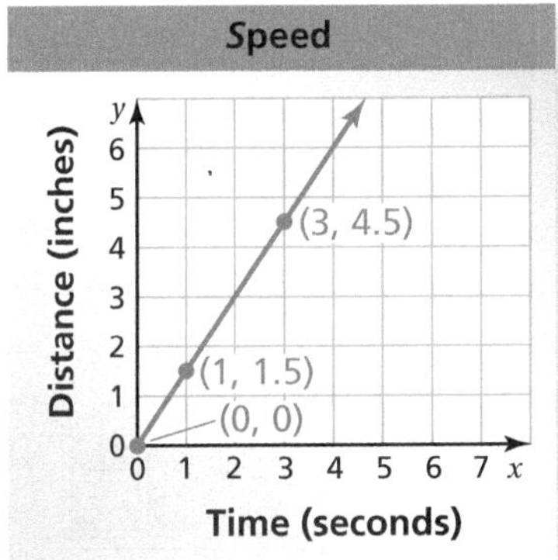

EXAMPLE 3 Modeling Real Life

The graph shows the area y (in square feet) that a robotic vacuum cleans in x minutes. Find the area cleaned in 10 minutes.

Robotic Vacuum

Area (square feet)

Time (minutes)

(2, 32)

$\left(\frac{3}{2}, 24\right)$

(1, 16)

$\left(\frac{1}{2}, 8\right)$

The graph is a line through the origin, so x and y are proportional. You can write an equation to represent the relationship between area and time.

Because the graph passes through the point (1, 16), the unit rate is 16 square feet per minute and the constant of proportionality is $k = 16$. So, an equation of the line is $y = 16x$. Substitute to find the area cleaned in 10 minutes.

$y = 16x$ Write the equation.

$= 16(10)$ Substitute 10 for x.

$= 160$ Multiply.

So, the vacuum cleans 160 square feet in 10 minutes.

Self-Assessment for Problem Solving

Solve each exercise. Then rate your understanding of the success criteria in your journal.

7. The table shows the temperature y (in degrees Fahrenheit), x hours after midnight.

Hours, x	0	0.5	1	1.5
Temperature, y (°F)	42	44	46	48

a. Describe a proportional relationship between time and temperature shown by the table. Explain your reasoning.

b. Find the temperature 3.5 hours after midnight.

8. **DIG DEEPER!** Show how you can use a proportional relationship to plan the heights of the vertical supports of a waterskiing ramp. Then explain how increasing the steepness of the ramp affects the proportional relationship.

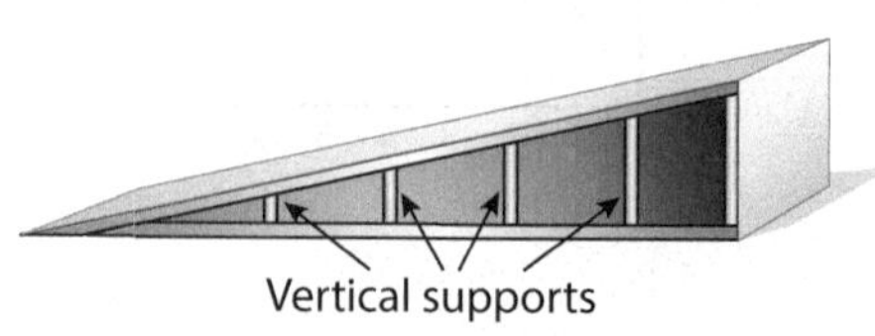

Laurie's Notes

EXAMPLE 3

- Ask students to interpret a point on the graph. For instance, $\left(\frac{1}{2}, 8\right)$ means that in $\frac{1}{2}$ minute, the robotic vacuum can clean 8 square feet.
- **Model with Mathematics:** Ask students to explain why the graph represents a ratio relationship and to identify the unit rate. Plotting the ordered pairs confirms that x and y are proportional.

? "What is the constant of proportionality?" 16

? "What is the equation of the line?" $y = 16x$

- Students can use the equation to find the area cleaned for any amount of time.

Self-Assessment for Problem Solving

- The goal for all students is to feel comfortable with the problem-solving plan. It is important for students to problem-solve in class, where they may receive support from you and their peers. Keep in mind that some students may only be ready for the first step.
- Students should answer Exercise 7 independently.
- Exercise 8 presents a challenge that should be worked on as a group or assigned as a project to more proficient students.

The Success Criteria Self-Assessment chart can be found in the *Student Journal* or online at *BigIdeasMath.com*.

Formative Assessment Tip

Muddiest Point

This technique is the opposite of *Point of Most Significance*. Students are asked to reflect on the most difficult or confusing point in the lesson. Their reflections are often collected at the end of the lesson so that the following day's instruction can address any confusion, however, this technique may be used at any time. It is important for teachers to know whether there was a point in the lesson that was confusing so that the lesson can be modified. Share with students what you learned from their reflections. Students will take reflections more seriously when they see that you value and use them.

Closure

- **Muddiest Point:** Ask students to reflect on the most confusing part of the lesson. Collect their written comments so that they can be addressed the next day.

Extra Example 3

The graph shows the area y (in square yards) that a power paint sprayer can paint in x minutes. Find the area painted in 8 minutes.

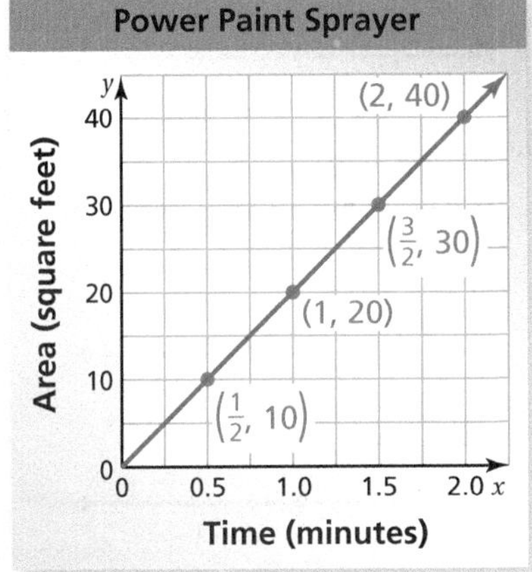

160 square feet

Self-Assessment for Problem Solving

7. **a.** 4°F per h; The temperature increases by 4°F each hour starting at 42°F.

   b. 56°F

8. See Additional Answers.

Learning Target

Represent proportional relationships using graphs and equations.

Success Criteria

- Determine whether quantities are proportional using a graph.
- Find the unit rate of a proportional relationship using a graph.
- Create equations to represent proportional relationships.

Review & Refresh

1. $x = 28$
2. $x = 27$
3. $x = 1\frac{1}{3}$
4. 9
5. -7
6. -13
7. 11
8. $x > -6$

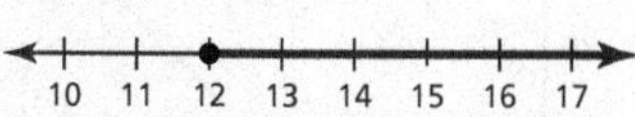

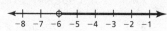

9. $p \geq 12$

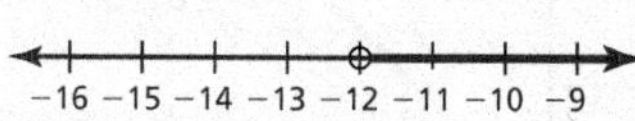

10. $n > -12$

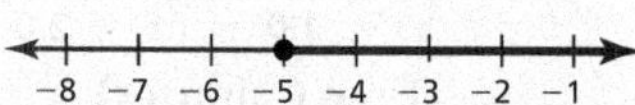

11. $w \geq -5$

Concepts, Skills, & Problem Solving

12.

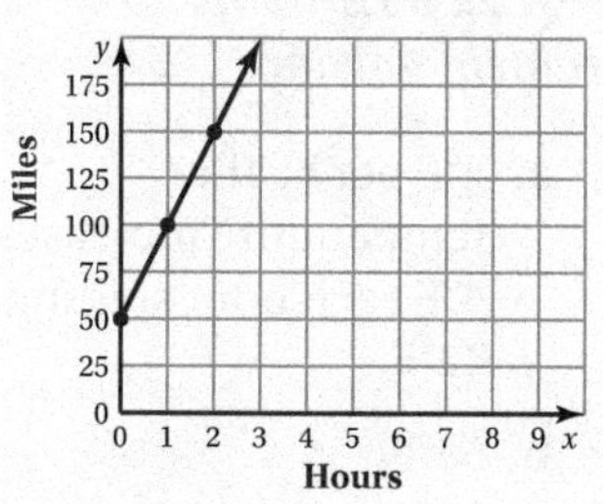

Miles
Hours

no; The line does not pass through the origin.

13. See Additional Answers.
14. yes; The line passes through the origin.
15. no; The line does not pass through the origin.
16. no; The line does not pass through the origin.
17. yes; The line passes through the origin.
18. no; The line does not pass through the origin.
19. yes; The line passes through the origin.
20. no; The line does not pass through the origin, so x and y are not proportional.

Check out the Dynamic Assessment System.
BigIdeasMath.com

Assignment Guide and Concept Check

Scaffold assignments to support all students in their learning progression. The suggested assignments are a starting point. Continue to assign additional exercises and revisit with spaced practice to move every student toward proficiency.

Level	Assignment 1	Assignment 2
Emerging	3, 7, 10, 12, 14, 15, 20, 21, 23	16, 18, 22, 24, 27, 30, 31, 33
Proficient	3, 7, 10, 12, 16, 17, 20, 21, 23	18, 19, 22, 24, 25, 28, 30, 31, 32, 33
Advanced	3, 7, 10, 13, 18, 19, 20, 22, 24	25, 26, 28, 29, 30, 31, 32, 33, 34

- Assignment 1 is for use after students complete the Self-Assessment for Concepts & Skills.
- Assignment 2 is for use after students complete the Self-Assessment for Problem Solving.
- The red exercises can be used as a concept check.

Review & Refresh Prior Skills

Exercises 1–3 Writing and Solving a Proportion
Exercises 4–7 Dividing Integers
Exercises 8–11 Solving an Inequality

Common Errors

- **Exercises 14–19** Students may immediately state that the table does not show a proportional relationship because (0, 0) is not listed. Encourage students to plot the points and then draw a line through the points to see if the graph is a line that passes through the origin.

D.5 Practice

Go to *BigIdeasMath.com* to get HELP with solving the exercises.

Review & Refresh

Find the value of x so that the ratios are equivalent.

1. $2:7$ and $8:x$
2. 3 to 2 and x to 18
3. $9:x$ and $54:8$

Find the quotient, if possible.

4. $36 \div 4$
5. $42 \div (-6)$
6. $-39 \div 3$
7. $-44 \div (-4)$

Solve the inequality. Graph the solution.

8. $-\frac{x}{3} < 2$
9. $\frac{1}{3}p \geq 4$
10. $-8 < \frac{2}{3}n$
11. $-2w \leq 10$

Concepts, Skills, & Problem Solving

REPRESENTING RELATIONSHIPS GRAPHICALLY **Represent the table graphically. Does the graph represent a proportional relationship? How do you know?** (See Exploration 1, p. 655.)

12.

Hours, x	Miles, y
0	50
1	100
2	150

13.

Cucumbers, x	Tomatoes, y
2	4
3	6
4	8

IDENTIFYING A PROPORTIONAL RELATIONSHIP **Tell whether x and y are proportional. Explain your reasoning.**

14.

x	1	2	3	4
y	2	4	6	8

15.

x	−2	−1	0	1
y	0	2	4	6

16.

x	−1	0	1	2
y	−2	−1	0	1

17.

x	3	6	9	12
y	2	4	6	8

18.

x	1	2	3	4
y	3	4	5	6

19.

x	1	3	5	7
y	0.5	1.5	2.5	3.5

20. MP **YOU BE THE TEACHER** Your friend uses the graph to determine whether x and y are proportional. Is your friend correct? Explain your reasoning.

The graph is a line, so x and y are proportional.

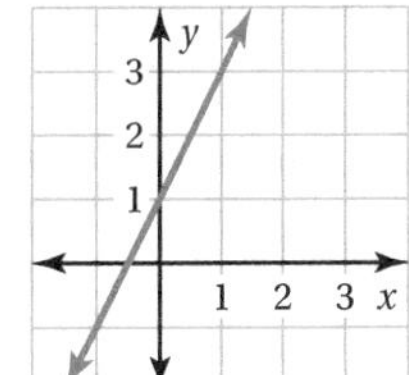

FINDING A UNIT RATE **Interpret each plotted point in the graph. Then identify the unit rate.**

21.

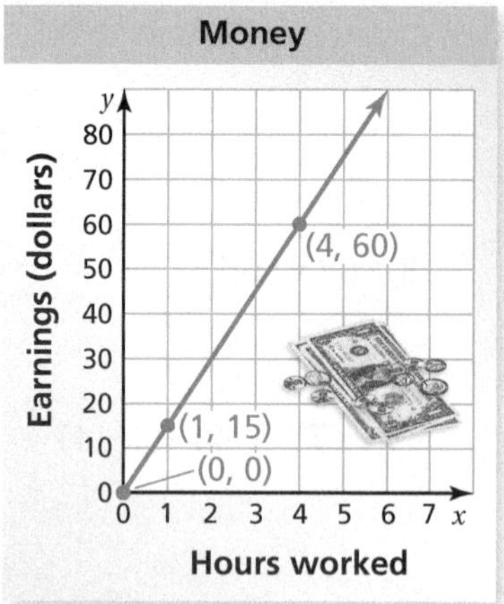

22.

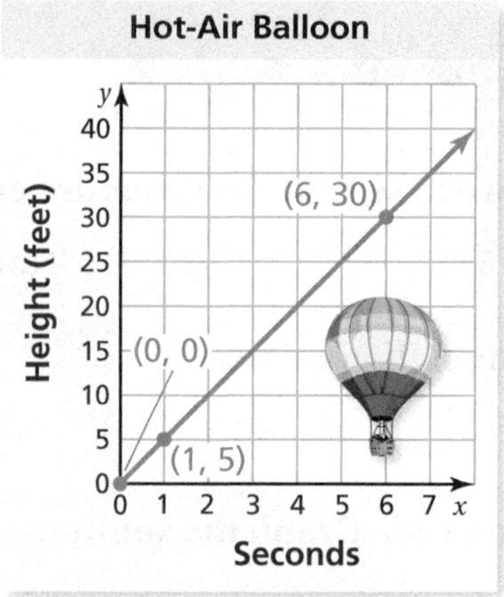

IDENTIFYING A PROPORTIONAL RELATIONSHIP **Tell whether x and y are proportional. If so, identify the constant of proportionality. Explain your reasoning.**

23. $x - y = 0$ **24.** $\frac{x}{y} = 2$ **25.** $8 = xy$ **26.** $x^2 = y$

WRITING AN EQUATION **The variables x and y are proportional. Use the values to find the constant of proportionality. Then write an equation that relates x and y.**

27. When $y = 72$, $x = 3$. **28.** When $y = 20$, $x = 12$. **29.** When $y = 45$, $x = 40$.

30. MP **MODELING REAL LIFE** The table shows the profit y for recycling x pounds of aluminum. Find the profit for recycling 75 pounds of aluminum.

Aluminum (lb), x	10	20	30	40
Profit, y	\$4.50	\$9.00	\$13.50	\$18.00

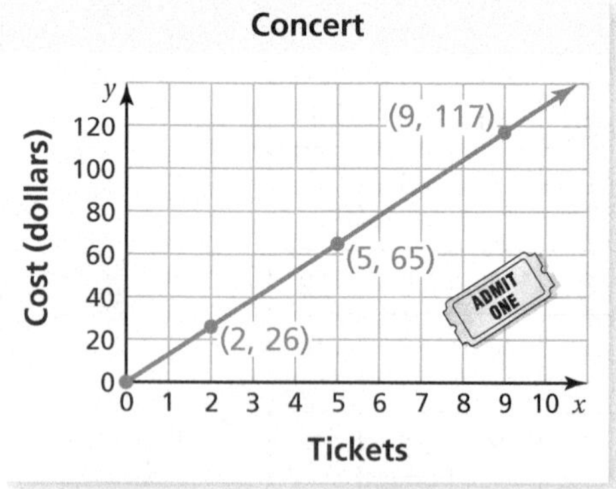

31. MP **MODELING REAL LIFE** The graph shows the cost of buying concert tickets. Tell whether x and y are proportional. If so, find and interpret the constant of proportionality. Then find the cost of 14 tickets.

32. MP **REASONING** The graph of a proportional relationship passes through (12, 16) and (1, y). Find y.

33. MP **PROBLEM SOLVING** The amount of chlorine in a swimming pool is proportional to the volume of water. The pool has 2.5 milligrams of chlorine per liter of water. How much chlorine is in the pool?

34. **DIG DEEPER!** A vehicle travels 250 feet every 3 seconds. Find the value of the ratio, the unit rate, and the constant of proportionality. How are they related?

Common Errors

- **Exercises 23–25** Students may try to determine whether x and y are proportional without solving for y. Remind students to solve for y first.
- **Exercise 26** Students may say that x and y are proportional because the graph goes through (0, 0). Ask students if the graph will be linear.
- **Exercises 27–29** Students may not grasp how to write the equation. Remind students that the equation of a proportional relationship is $y = kx$, so they can substitute the values of x and y to find k.

Mini-Assessment

Tell whether x and y are proportional. Explain your reasoning.

1.

x	2	4	6
y	2	3	4

no; The line does not pass through the origin.

2.

x	2	4	6
y	3	6	9

yes; The line passes through the origin.

Tell whether x and y are proportional. If so, identify the constant of proportionality. Explain your reasoning.

3. $xy = 4$ no; The equation cannot be written as $y = kx$.
4. $x = \frac{1}{9}y$ yes; $k = 9$; The equation can be written as $y = kx$.
5. The graph shows the cost of buying grapes. Find the cost of buying 12 pounds of grapes.
$30

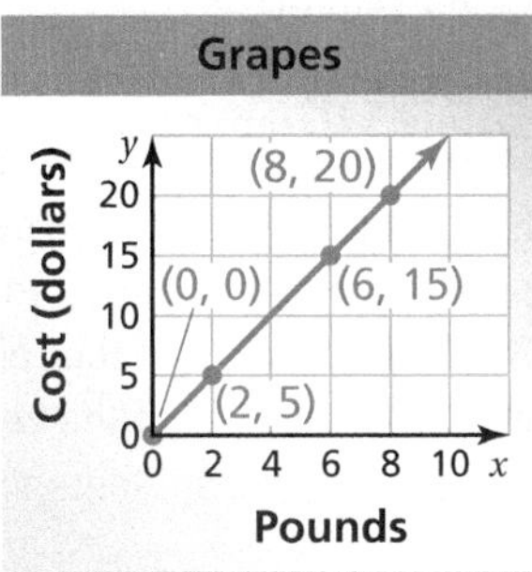

Section Resources

Surface Level	Deep Level
Resources by Chapter • Extra Practice • Reteach • Puzzle Time Student Journal • Self-Assessment • Practice Differentiating the Lesson Tutorial Videos Skills Review Handbook Skills Trainer	Resources by Chapter • Enrichment and Extension Graphic Organizers Dynamic Assessment System • Section Practice

Concepts, Skills, & Problem Solving

21. (0, 0): You earn $0 for working 0 hours; (1, 15): You earn $15 for working 1 hour; (4, 60): You earn $60 for working 4 hours; $15 : 1 h
22. (0, 0): The balloon rises 0 feet in 0 seconds; (1, 5): The balloon rises 5 feet in 1 second; (6, 30): The balloon rises 30 feet in 6 seconds; 5 ft : 1 sec
23. yes; $k = 1$; The equation can be written as $y = kx$.
24. yes; $k = \frac{1}{2}$; The equation can be written as $y = kx$.
25. no; The equation cannot be written as $y = kx$.
26. no; The equation cannot be written as $y = kx$.
27. $k = 24$; $y = 24x$
28. $k = \frac{5}{3}$; $y = \frac{5}{3}x$
29. $k = \frac{9}{8}$; $y = \frac{9}{8}x$
30. $33.75
31. yes; $k = 13$; The cost of 1 ticket is $13; $182
32. $y = \frac{4}{3}$
33. about 76,000 mg
34. $\frac{250}{3}$; $\frac{250}{3} : 1$; $\frac{250}{3}$; *Sample answer:* They all involve $\frac{250}{3}$.

Check out the
Dynamic Classroom.
BigIdeasMath.com

Learning Target

Solve problems involving scale drawings.

Success Criteria

- Find an actual distance in a scale drawing.
- Explain the meaning of scale and scale factor.
- Use a scale drawing to find the actual lengths and areas of real-life objects.

Warm Up

Cumulative, vocabulary, and prerequisite skills practice opportunities are available in the *Resources by Chapter* or at *BigIdeasMath.com*.

ELL Support

Remind students that a scale compares measurements and a scale drawing represents an object using a scale. Review the relationship between a scale drawing and the object it represents.

Exploration 1

a. The ratio of the lengths is 1 cm : 4 m.

b. *Sample answer:* The ratio of the areas is $1\text{ cm}^2 : 16\text{ m}^2$.

c. no; *Sample answer:* The ratios are not equivalent.

d. *Sample answer:* 1 cm : 8 m

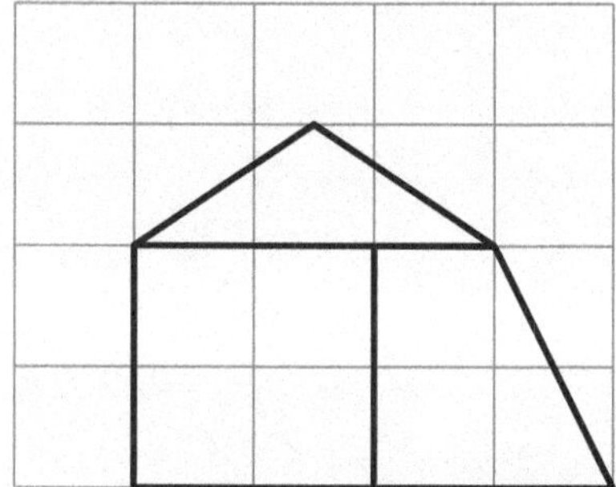

The shape is the same but the size changes.

Laurie's Notes

Preparing to Teach

- In this lesson, students will apply what they learned about proportions to scale drawings.
- **Attend to Precision:** Mathematically proficient students understand that precision in measurement and in labeling units is important.
- **Look for and Make Use of Structure:** Students will use the structure of mathematics to break down and solve complex problems.

Motivate

- It may be helpful to have some items that have scales written on them, such as maps, model cars, blueprints, floor plans, etc.
- ? Ask, "Have you ever heard of **scale drawings** or something built to **scale**?" Have students share their ideas.
- ? "Have you ever built a **scale model** of a car?" Answers will vary.
- ? "What do you think 'built to scale' means?" *Sample answer:* The dimensions of the model are proportional to the dimensions of the actual object.
- ? "Why are scale drawings important?" *Sample answer:* They can be used to represent objects that are not convenient to draw at actual size.
- Say, "In this lesson, you will create scale drawings and use them to find actual lengths."

Exploration 1

- For part (a), students will need to organize their responses. If they redraw the picture using grid paper, they can write their answers on or above the lines.
- Students should see the relationships as ratios and write them as such. For example, the ratio of the vertical lengths is 4 centimeters : 16 meters.
- For part (b), ask students to describe the relationship without calculating the areas.
- ? "Describe the relationship between the area of one square in the drawing and the actual area of one square." 1 square centimeter to 16 square meters "Is that relationship the same for the entire area? Explain." Yes, the entire area of the zoo is 16 times the entire area of the drawing.
- In part (c), students should compare the ratio in part (a), 1 : 4, with the ratio in part (b), 1 : 16. In explaining the difference between the ratios, it may be helpful for students to compute the values of the ratios and see $\frac{1}{16}$ as $\left(\frac{1}{4}\right)^2$.
- Allow time for students to explain their ideas to their partners. Use *Popsicle Sticks* to select students to present their explanations.
- In part (d), it is important for students to get a preliminary idea of similarity, but without using that terminology. Students should notice that the side lengths are different but proportional, the areas are different but proportional, and the angle measures are the same. Overall, the shapes are the same, but the sizes are different. Some students may need to find the actual dimensions to make these conclusions.

D.6 Scale Drawings

Learning Target: Solve problems involving scale drawings.

Success Criteria:
- I can find an actual distance in a scale drawing.
- I can explain the meaning of scale and scale factor.
- I can use a scale drawing to find the actual lengths and areas of real-life objects.

EXPLORATION 1 Creating a Scale Drawing

Work with a partner. Several sections in a zoo are drawn on 1-centimeter grid paper as shown. Each centimeter in the drawing represents 4 meters.

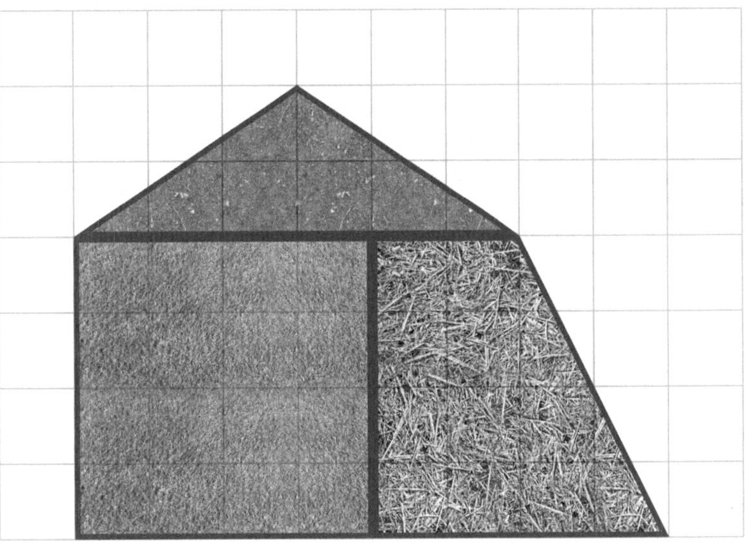

a. Describe the relationship between the lengths of the fences in the drawing and the actual side lengths of the fences.

b. Describe the relationship between the areas of the sections in the drawing and the actual areas of the sections.

c. Are the relationships in parts (a) and (b) the same? Explain your reasoning.

d. Choose a different distance to represent each centimeter on a piece of 1-centimeter grid paper. Then create a new drawing of the sections in the zoo using the distance you chose. Describe any similarities or differences in the drawings.

Math Practice

Analyze Givens
How does the information given about the drawing shown help you create an accurate drawing in part (d)?

D.6 Lesson

Key Vocabulary
scale drawing, *p. 662*
scale model, *p. 662*
scale, *p. 662*
scale factor, *p. 663*

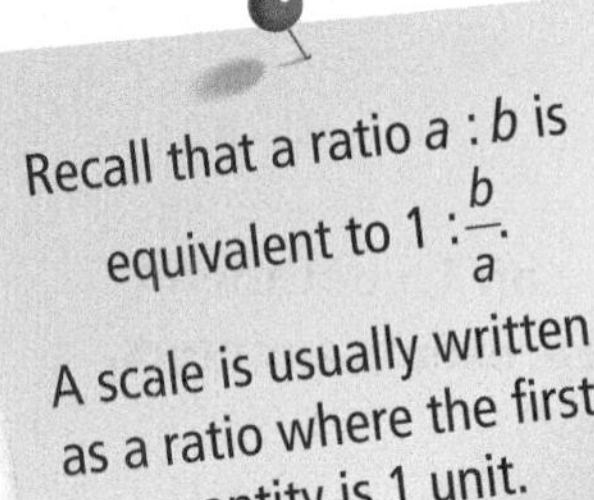

Recall that a ratio $a : b$ is equivalent to $1 : \frac{b}{a}$.
A scale is usually written as a ratio where the first quantity is 1 unit.

Key Idea

Scale Drawings and Models

A **scale drawing** is a proportional, two-dimensional drawing of an object. A **scale model** is a proportional, three-dimensional model of an object.

Scale

The measurements in scale drawings and models are proportional to the measurements of the actual object. The **scale** gives the ratio that compares the measurements of the drawing or model with the actual measurements.

1 in. : 10 mi

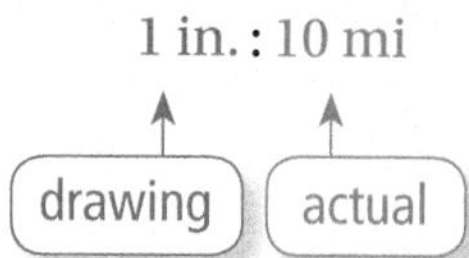

EXAMPLE 1 Finding an Actual Distance

What is the actual distance *d* between Cadillac and Detroit?

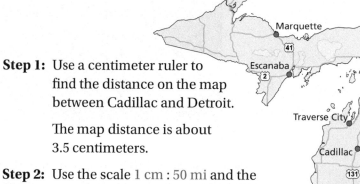

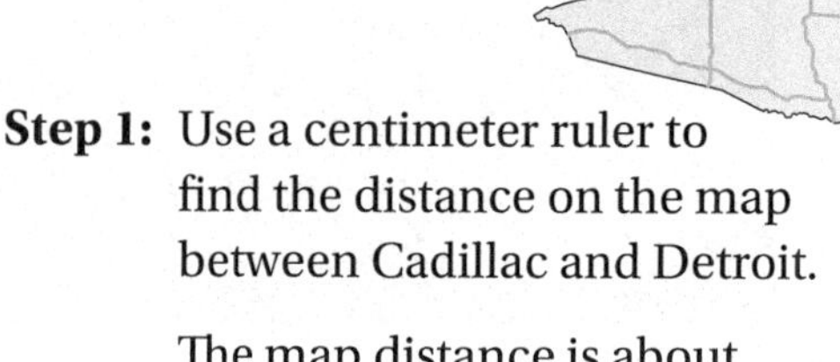

Step 1: Use a centimeter ruler to find the distance on the map between Cadillac and Detroit.

The map distance is about 3.5 centimeters.

Step 2: Use the scale 1 cm : 50 mi and the ratio 3.5 cm : d mi to write and solve a proportion.

$$\frac{1}{50} = \frac{3.5}{d}$$

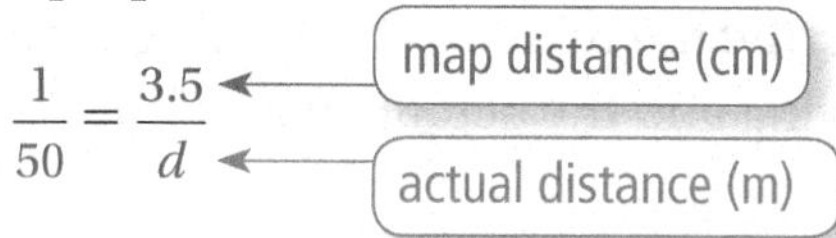

$d = 50 \cdot 3.5$ Cross Products Property

$d = 175$ Multiply.

So, the distance between Cadillac and Detroit is about 175 miles.

Another Method
You can use a ratio table.

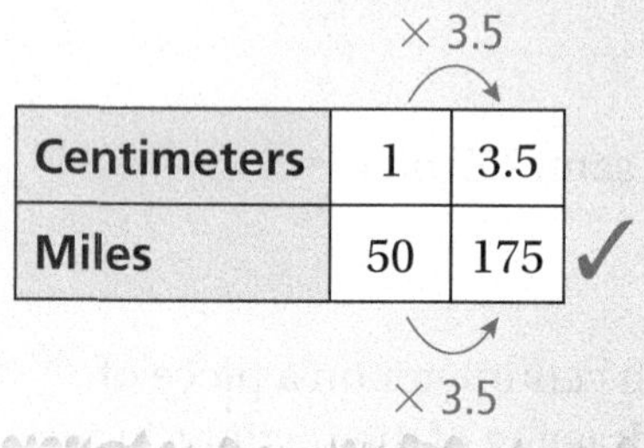

Centimeters	1	3.5
Miles	50	175

× 3.5

Try It

1. What is the actual distance between Traverse City and Marquette?

Multi-Language Glossary at *BigIdeasMath.com*

Laurie's Notes

Scaffolding Instruction

- Students explored finding an actual distance in a scale drawing. Now they will extend their understanding to find actual lengths and areas of real-life objects and to explain the meanings of scale and **scale factor**.
- **Emerging:** Students may understand that scale drawings are proportional to real-life objects but struggle with using the scale. Students will benefit from guided instruction for the Key Idea and examples.
- **Proficient:** Students can apply their knowledge of proportions to scale drawings. Have them review the Key Idea before proceeding to the Self-Assessment exercises.

Key Idea

- Explain that when drawings or objects are proportional to an object, the measurements in the **scale drawing** or **scale model** are proportional to the measurements in the actual drawing or actual object.
- **Note:** A scale drawing is a two-dimensional representation of an object, not the three-dimensional object itself. This can be clarified by asking students to imagine a picture that is exactly the same size as a three-dimensional object. A scale drawing is a proportional drawing of that picture.
- Review the definition for **scale** and the push-pin note.
- "How can you use a scale drawing to find the actual length of an object?" *Sample answer:* Write and solve a proportion using the scale and a ratio of the lengths: scale $= \frac{\text{drawing length}}{\text{actual length}}$.

EXAMPLE 1

- Use centimeter rulers to measure the distance from Cadillac to Detroit.
- **Use Appropriate Tools Strategically:** Students might use the wrong measuring tool, measure in inches instead of centimeters, or they may confuse centimeters with millimeters.
- "What is the map distance from Cadillac to Detroit?" 3.5 centimeters
- Set up the proportion using the language, "1 centimeter is to 50 miles as 3.5 centimeters is to what?"
- Point out that you can use the Cross Products Property only because both numerators are the same unit (cm) and both denominators are the same unit (mi). If the units were not the same in the numerators and were the same in the denominators, this could not be done.
- A quick way to explain this to students is to use a simple problem: If the scale is 1 centimeter : 5 feet, then 2 centimeters would be what actual distance? 10 feet
- **Attend to Precision:** Encourage students to write the units when they write the initial proportion. This ensures that the proportion has been set up correctly. When the numeric answer has been found, label with the correct units of measure.
- **Check for Reasonableness:** If the map distance is 3.5 centimeters, the actual distance should be 3.5 times the scale distance of 50 miles. Three times 50 miles is 150 miles, so about 175 miles seems reasonable.

Try It

- Have students solve the problem on whiteboards. Ask them to write the units for the two quantities before writing a proportion.

Scaffold instruction to support all students in their learning. Learning is individualized and you may want to group students differently as they move in and out of these levels with each skill and concept. Student self-assessment and feedback help guide your instructional decisions about how and when to layer support for all students to become proficient learners.

Extra Example 1

Using the map from Example 1, what is the actual distance *d* between Detroit and Marquette? about 350 miles

ELL Support

After demonstrating Example 1, have students practice language by working in groups to complete Try It Exercise 1. Provide guiding questions: What are the steps? What is the scale? What is the proportion? What is the answer? Expect students to perform according to their proficiency levels.

Beginner: Write out the problem and use one-word answers.

Intermediate: Use phrases or simple sentences to answer the guiding questions.

Advanced: Use detailed sentences and help guide discussion.

Try It

1. about 150 mi

Extra Example 2

A scale drawing of a fashion designer's shirt is 5 centimeters long. The actual shirt is 1 meter long.

a. What does 1 centimeter represent in the drawing? What is the scale? 0.5 meter; 1 centimeter : 0.5 meter

b. What is the scale factor of the drawing? $\frac{1}{50}$

Try It

2. $\frac{1}{200}$

Self-Assessment

for Concepts & Skills

3. *Sample answer:* The scale compares the measurements of the drawing with the actual measurements. The scale factor describes the multiplicative relationship between the dimensions of a scale drawing and the actual dimensions.

4. about 128 ft

5. $\frac{1}{8}$

6. **a.** The scale factor is greater than 1.

b. The scale factor is less than 1.

Laurie's Notes

Discuss

- Write and discuss the definition for **scale factor**.
- Connect the definition to the exploration. For instance, in the exploration, the scale used was 1 centimeter : 4 meters. Because 4 meters is equal to 400 centimeters, the scale factor would be 1 centimeter : 400 centimeters, or 1 : 400.

EXAMPLE 2

- **FYI:** The Sergeant Floyd Monument is located in Sioux City, Iowa. It memorializes Sgt. Charles Floyd, the only man who died on the Lewis and Clark Expedition. The monument is the nation's first nationally registered historical landmark.
- Read the problem. Because the height of the model and the height of the actual monument are proportional, students can use the ratio of the model height to the actual height to find the scale.

? "How can you find the scale factor when you know the scale?" Write the scale with the same units and simplify.

? "What conversion factor can you use?" 1 foot = 12 inches

- Work through the rest of the problem as shown.

? "What would the constant of proportionality be?" $\frac{1}{120}$ The scale factor and the constant of proportionality are equivalent.

Try It

? "Is the actual item larger or smaller than the scale model? Explain." larger; 1 millimeter represents 20 centimeters.

Self-Assessment for Concepts & Skills

- Have students use *Fist of Five* to indicate their understanding of the first two success criteria.
- Students should work independently on these problems and then complete a *Neighbor Check*.

ELL Support

Allow students to work in pairs to practice language as they work on the exercises. Check comprehension of Exercises 4 and 5 by having each pair display their answers on a whiteboard for your review. Discuss their ideas about Exercises 3 and 6 as a class.

The Success Criteria Self-Assessment chart can be found in the *Student Journal* or online at *BigIdeasMath.com*.

A scale can be written without units when the units are the same. The value of this ratio is called the **scale factor**. The scale factor describes the multiplicative relationship between the dimensions of a scale drawing or scale model and the dimensions of the actual object.

EXAMPLE 2 Finding a Scale Factor

A scale model of the Sergeant Floyd Monument is 10 inches tall. The actual monument is 100 feet tall.

a. What does 1 inch represent in the model? What is the scale?

The ratio of the model height to the actual height is 10 in. : 100 ft. Divide each quantity by 10 to determine the number of feet represented by 1 inch in the model.

$$\div 10 \quad 10 \text{ in.} : 100 \text{ ft} \quad \div 10$$
$$1 \text{ in.} : 10 \text{ ft}$$

In the model, 1 inch represents 10 feet. So, the scale is 1 in. : 10 ft.

b. What is the scale factor of the model?

Write the scale with the same units. Use the fact that 1 ft = 12 in.

$$10 \text{ ft} = 10 \cancel{\text{ft}} \times \frac{12 \text{ in.}}{1 \cancel{\text{ft}}} = 120 \text{ in.}$$

The scale is 1 in. : 120 in., or 1 : 120. So, the scale factor is $\frac{1}{120}$.

Try It

2. A drawing has a scale of 1 mm : 20 cm. What is the scale factor of the drawing?

Self-Assessment for Concepts & Skills

Solve each exercise. Then rate your understanding of the success criteria in your journal.

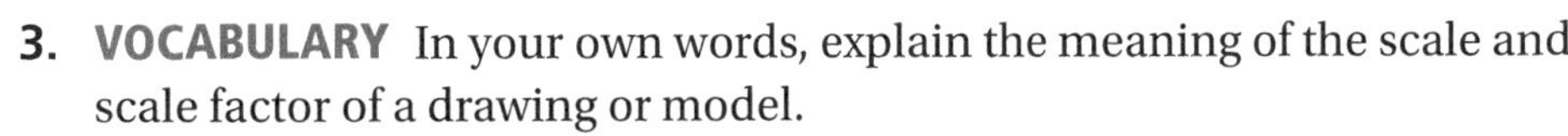

h

1 cm : 32 ft

3. **VOCABULARY** In your own words, explain the meaning of the scale and scale factor of a drawing or model.

4. **FINDING AN ACTUAL DISTANCE** Consider the scale drawing of Balanced Rock in Arches National Park. What is the actual height of the structure?

5. **FINDING A SCALE FACTOR** A drawing has a scale of 3 in. : 2 ft. What is the scale factor of the drawing?

6. MP **REASONING** Describe the scale factor of a model that is (a) larger than the actual object and (b) smaller than the actual object.

EXAMPLE 3 Modeling Real Life

1 cm : 2 mm

The scale drawing of a square computer chip helps you see the individual components on the chip.

a. Find the perimeter and the area of the computer chip in the scale drawing.

When measured using a centimeter ruler, the scale drawing of the computer chip has a side length of 4 centimeters.

So, the perimeter of the computer chip in the scale drawing is $4(4) = 16$ centimeters, and the area is $4^2 = 16$ square centimeters.

b. Find the actual perimeter and area of the computer chip.

Multiplying each quantity in the scale by 4 shows that the actual side length of the computer chip is 8 millimeters.

1 cm : 2 mm
×4 ×4
4 cm : 8 mm

So, the actual perimeter of the computer chip is $4(8) = 32$ millimeters, and the actual area is $8^2 = 64$ square millimeters.

c. Compare the side lengths of the scale drawing with the actual side lengths of the computer chip.

Find the scale factor. Use the fact that 1 cm = 10 mm.

Because the scale can be written as 10 mm : 2 mm, or 10 : 2, the scale factor is $\frac{10}{2} = 5$.

So, the side lengths of the scale drawing are 5 times the actual side lengths of the computer chip.

Self-Assessment for Problem Solving

Solve each exercise. Then rate your understanding of the success criteria in your journal.

Scale: 1 ft : 11.2 ft

7. A scale drawing of the Parthenon is shown. Find the actual perimeter and area of the rectangular face of the Parthenon. Then recreate the scale drawing with a scale factor of 0.2. Find the perimeter and area of the rectangular face in your drawing.

8. **DIG DEEPER!** You are in charge of creating a billboard advertisement that is 16 feet long and 8 feet tall. Choose a product. Create a scale drawing of the billboard using words and a picture. What is the scale factor of your design?

Laurie's Notes

Formative Assessment Tip

3-Read Modeling
This technique helps students make sense of word problems by focusing their attention on understanding the situation rather than finding the answer. The *problem stem* (the word problem without the question) is read three times with a different goal each time. First, read the problem stem to the class and ask, "What is this situation about?" Second, lead students in a choral read or have students read the problem stem to a partner. Then ask, "What quantities and units are involved?" Third, ask students to think about what is missing while they choral or partner read. Then ask, "What mathematical questions could you ask about this situation?" After each question is shared, ask, "Can this question be answered with the given information?" Discuss why or why not. Then have students work in groups to solve a question based on the problem stem. You can assign a specific question or allow groups to choose.

EXAMPLE 3

- **3-Read Modeling:** Read the problem stem and scale drawing.
- **Construct Viable Arguments and Critique the Reasoning of Others:** "Is the actual chip larger or smaller than the chip in the scale drawing? Explain." smaller; 1 centimeter represents only 2 millimeters.
- Measure to find the side length of the chip in the scale drawing.
- To find the actual perimeter and area of the chip, you can begin by setting up and solving a proportion to find the side length of the actual chip. Be careful to label units and use precise language. As shown in the solution, the numerator of each ratio is a drawing distance and the denominator of each ratio is an actual distance.
- Some students will want to bypass the step of writing the proportion and use mental math. Remind them that they are practicing a *process* that will enable them to solve more difficult problems that they may not be able to solve using mental math.
- **Attend to Precision:** Work slowly through part (c). Remind students that when finding the scale factor, it is necessary to have the same units in the numerator and in the denominator.

Self-Assessment for Problem Solving

- Allow time in class for students to practice using the problem-solving plan. Remember, some students may only be able to complete the first step.
- Have students use *Think-Pair-Share* to solve these problems. It is important for students to spend time working independently first.

The Success Criteria Self-Assessment chart can be found in the *Student Journal* or online at *BigIdeasMath.com*.

Closure

- **Exit Ticket:** A common model train scale is called the HO Scale, where the scale factor is 1 : 87. If the diameter of a wheel on a model train is 0.3 inch, what is the diameter of the actual wheel? 26.1 inches

Extra Example 3

The scale drawing of a miniature glass mosaic tile helps you see the detail on the tile.

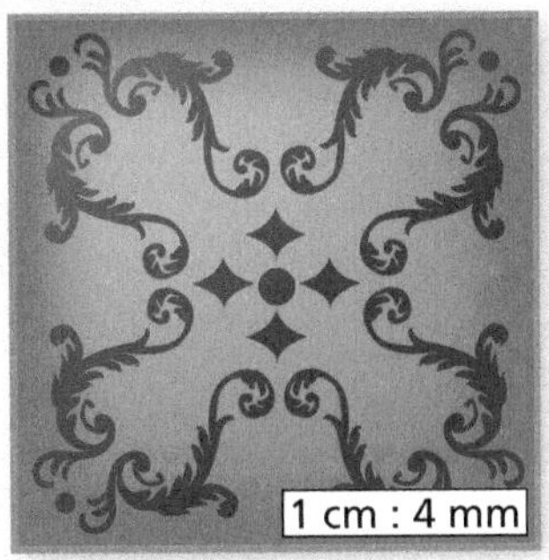

a. Find the perimeter and the area of the tile in the scale drawing. 16 cm; 16 cm^2

b. Find the actual perimeter and area of the tile. 64 mm, 256 mm^2

c. Compare the side lengths of the scale drawing with the actual side lengths of the tile. The side lengths of the scale drawing are 2.5 times the actual side lengths of the mosaic tile.

Self-Assessment for Problem Solving

7. 291.2 ft, 4515.84 ft^2; 58.24 ft, 180.6336 ft^2
8. Answers will vary.

Learning Target

Solve problems involving scale drawings.

Success Criteria

- Find an actual distance in a scale drawing.
- Explain the meaning of scale and scale factor.
- Use a scale drawing to find the actual lengths and areas of real-life objects.

Review & Refresh

1. no; The line does not pass through the origin.
2. yes; The line passes through the origin.
3. $13p$
4. $3d - 9$
5. $\frac{3}{20}b + 4$
6. $c < -3$
7. $7 + z > 5$
8. $6m \geq 30$

Concepts, Skills, & Problem Solving

9. *Sample answer:*

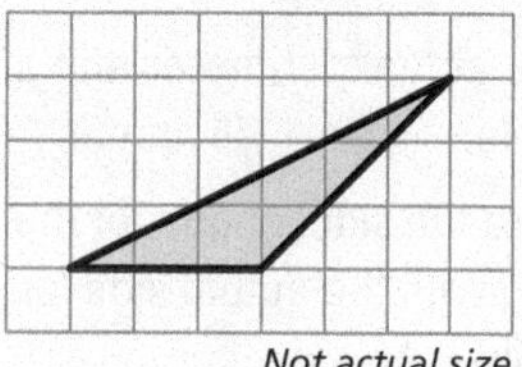

Not actual size

10. *Sample answer:*

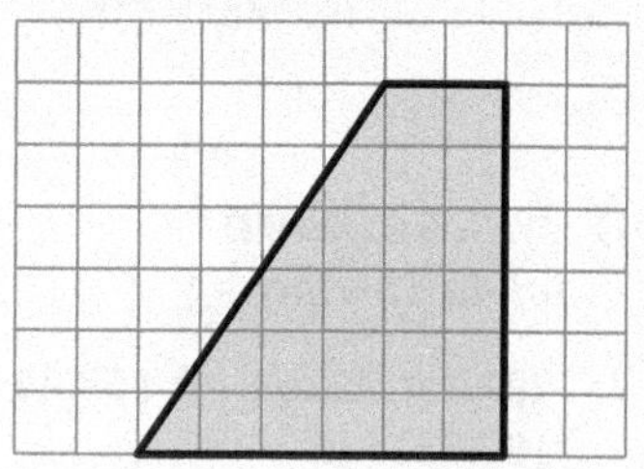

Not actual size

11. 100 mi
12. 50 mi
13. 200 mi
14. 110 mi
15. 75 in.
16. 15 in.
17. 3.84 m
18. 21.6 yd
19. 17.5 mm

Assignment Guide and Concept Check

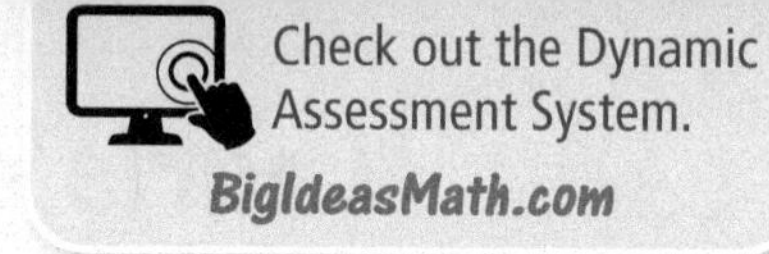
Check out the Dynamic Assessment System.
BigIdeasMath.com

Scaffold assignments to support all students in their learning progression. The suggested assignments are a starting point. Continue to assign additional exercises and revisit with spaced practice to move every student toward proficiency.

Level	Assignment 1	Assignment 2
Emerging	2, 5, 8, 9, 11, 12, 15, 16, 17	18, 19, 20, 21, 22, 23, 25
Proficient	2, 5, 8, 10, 12, 13, 15, 16, 17	18, 19, 20, 21, 22, 23, 24, 25
Advanced	2, 5, 8, 10, 13, 14, 17, 18, 19	20, 21, 22, 23, 24, 25, 26, 27

- Assignment 1 is for use after students complete the Self-Assessment for Concepts & Skills.
- Assignment 2 is for use after students complete the Self-Assessment for Problem Solving.
- The red exercises can be used as a concept check.

Review & Refresh Prior Skills

Exercises 1 and 2 Identifying a Proportional Relationship
Exercises 3–5 Simplifying Algebraic Expressions
Exercises 6–8 Writing an Inequality

Common Errors

- **Exercises 11–14** When measuring with a centimer ruler, students may not start at zero on the ruler. As a result, they will get an incorrect distance. Ask students to estimate the distance before measuring so they can check the reasonableness of their measurements.
- **Exercises 15–19** Students may mix up the proportion values when solving for the missing dimension. Remind students that the model dimension is in the numerator and the actual dimension is in the denominator.

D.6 Practice

Go to *BigIdeasMath.com* to get HELP with solving the exercises.

Review & Refresh

Tell whether x and y are proportional. Explain your reasoning.

1.

x	10	9	8	7
y	5	4	3	2

2.

x	6	12	18	24
y	7	14	21	28

Simplify the expression.

3. $7p + 6p$
4. $8 + 3d - 17$
5. $-2 + \frac{2}{5}b - \frac{1}{4}b + 6$

Write the word sentence as an inequality.

6. A number c is less than -3.
7. 7 plus a number z is more than 5.
8. The product of a number m and 6 is no less than 30.

Concepts, Skills, & Problem Solving

CREATING A SCALE DRAWING **Each centimeter on the 1-centimeter grid paper represents 8 inches. Create a proportional drawing of the figure that is larger or smaller than the figure shown.** (See Exploration 1, p. 661.)

9.

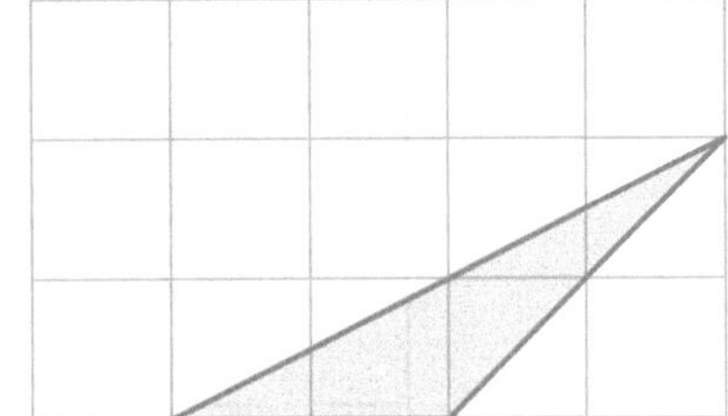

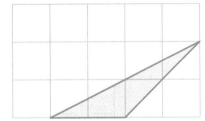

10.

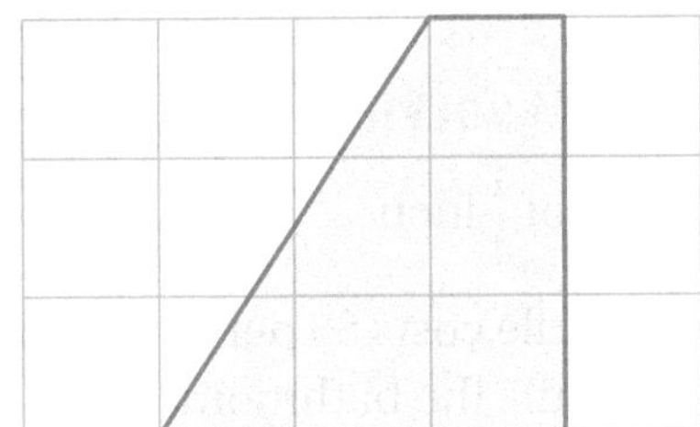

FINDING AN ACTUAL DISTANCE **Use the map in Example 1 to find the actual distance between the cities.**

11. Kalamazoo and Ann Arbor
12. Lansing and Flint
13. Grand Rapids and Escanaba
14. Saginaw and Alpena

USING A SCALE **Find the missing dimension. Use the scale 1 : 12.**

	Item	Model	Actual
15.	Mattress	Length: 6.25 in.	Length: ___ in.
16.	Corvette	Length: ___ in.	Length: 15 ft
17.	Water tower	Depth: 32 cm	Depth: ___ m
18.	Wingspan	Width: 5.4 ft	Width: ___ yd
19.	Football helmet	Diameter: ___ mm	Diameter: 21 cm

FINDING A SCALE FACTOR **Use a centimeter ruler to find the scale and the scale factor of the drawing.**

20. 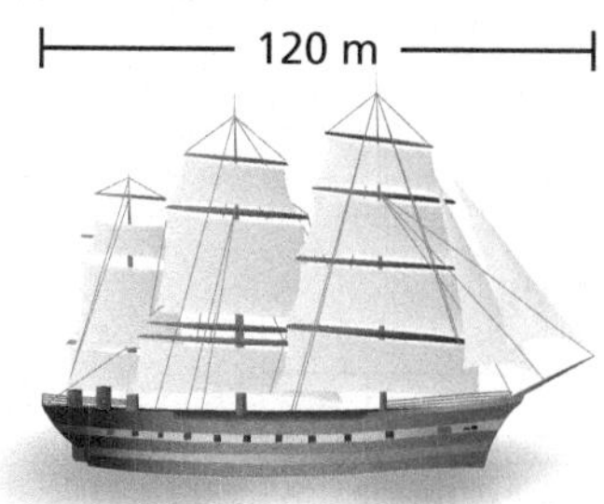

21. 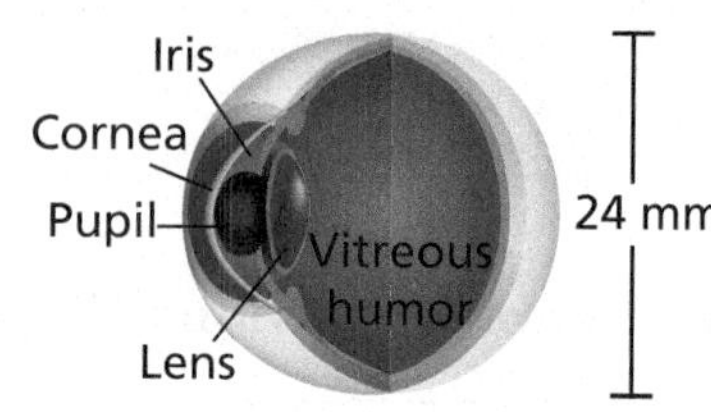

22. **CRITICAL THINKING** You know the length and the width of a scale model. What additional information do you need to know to find the scale of the model? Explain.

23. **MP MODELING REAL LIFE** Central Park is a rectangular park in New York City.

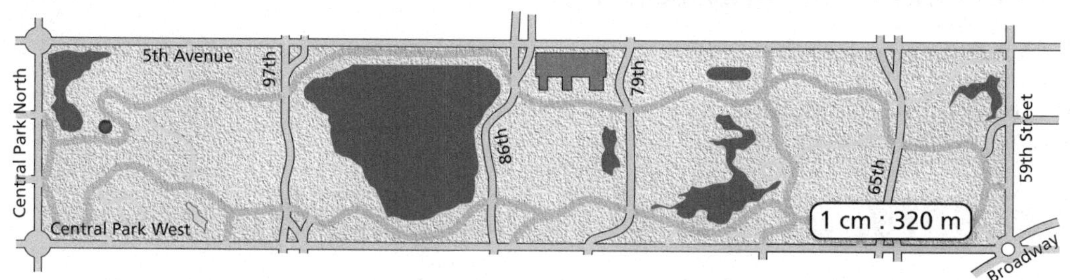

a. Find the perimeter and the area of the scale drawing of Central Park.

b. Find the actual perimeter and area of Central Park.

24. **MP PROBLEM SOLVING** In a blueprint, each square has a side length of $\frac{1}{4}$ inch.

Reduced Drawing of Blueprint

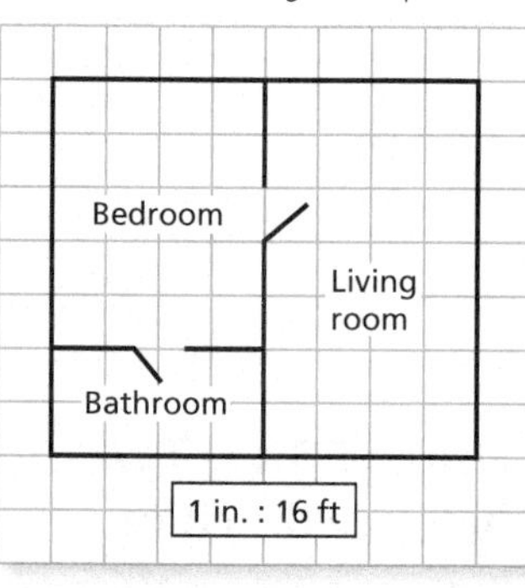

a. Ceramic tile costs $5 per square foot. How much does it cost to tile the bathroom?

b. Carpet costs $18 per square yard. How much does it cost to carpet the bedroom and living room?

REPRODUCING A SCALE DRAWING **Recreate the scale drawing so that it has a scale of 1 cm : 4 m.**

25. 

1 cm : 8 m

26. 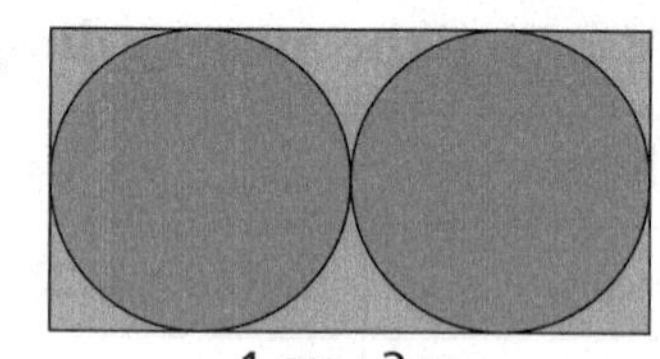

1 cm : 2 m

27. **DIG DEEPER!** Make a conjecture about the relationship between the scale factor of a drawing and the quotients $\frac{\text{drawing perimeter}}{\text{actual perimeter}}$ and $\frac{\text{drawing area}}{\text{actual area}}$. Explain your reasoning.

Common Errors

- **Exercise 24** Students may count the squares in the blueprint of the bathroom and use that as the area of the bathroom. Remind students that they need the actual length and width of each room to find the actual area.

Mini-Assessment

Find the missing dimension. Use the scale 1 : 6.

	Model	Actual
1.	12 in.	72 in.
2.	3 ft	18 ft
3.	20 cm	120 cm
4.	2 yd	12 yd

5. A fish in an aquarium is 4 feet long. A scale model of the fish is 2 inches long. What is the scale factor? $\frac{1}{24}$

Section Resources

Surface Level	Deep Level
Resources by Chapter • Extra Practice • Reteach • Puzzle Time Student Journal • Self-Assessment • Practice Differentiating the Lesson Tutorial Videos Skills Review Handbook Skills Trainer	Resources by Chapter • Enrichment and Extension Graphic Organizers Dynamic Assessment System • Section Practice
Transfer Level	
Dynamic Assessment System • End-of-Chapter Quiz	Assessment Book • End-of-Chapter Quiz

Concepts, Skills, & Problem Solving

20. 1 cm : 30 m; $\frac{1}{30}$

21. 1 cm : 10 mm; 1

22. the length or width of the actual item

23. **a.** 30 cm; 31.25 cm^2

b. 9600 m; 3,200,000 m^2

24. **a.** \$640

b. \$1536

25. See Additional Answers.

26.

27. The value of the ratio of the perimeters is the scale factor and the value of the ratio of the areas is the square of the scale factor. *Sample answer:* If 2 similar figures have a scale of $a : b$, then the ratio of their perimeters is $a : b$ and the ratio of their areas is $a^2 : b^2$.

Skills Needed

Exercise 1

- Identifying Proportional Relationships
- Solving an Equation
- Writing an Equation

Exercise 2

- Finding the Volume of a Rectangular Prism
- Identifying Proportional Relationships

Exercise 3

- Creating a Scale Drawing
- Drawing a Polygon in a Coordinate Plane

ELL Support

Discuss the word *turnpike.* Students may know the word *turn*, but they are less likely to know the word *pike.* Discuss their meanings. Point out that when they are combined, they refer to a type of highway where money is charged for its use.

Using the Problem-Solving Plan

1. 55 mi
2. yes; *Sample answer:* Using the formula for volume, $V = 400h$.
3. 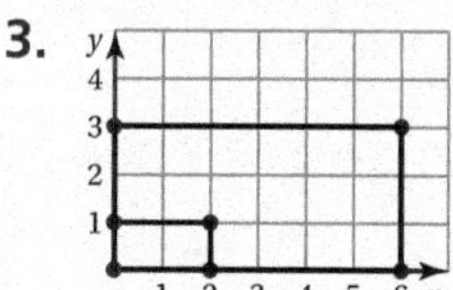

Performance Task

The *STEAM Video Performance Task* provides the opportunity for additional enrichment and greater depth of knowledge as students explore the mathematics of the chapter within a context tied to the chapter STEAM Video. The performance task and a detailed scoring rubric are provided at *BigIdeasMath.com.*

Laurie's Notes

Scaffolding Instruction

- The goal of this lesson is to help students become more comfortable with problem solving. These exercises combine ratios and proportions with prior skills from other chapters and courses. The solution for Exercise 1 is worked out below, to help you guide students through the problem-solving plan. Use the remaining class time to have students work on the other exercises.
- **Emerging:** The goal for these students is to feel comfortable with the problem-solving plan. Allow students to work in pairs to write the beginning steps of the problem-solving plan for Exercise 2. Keep in mind that some students may only be ready to do the first step.
- **Proficient:** Students may be able to work independently or in pairs to complete Exercises 2 and 3.
- Visit each pair to review their plan for each problem. Ask students to describe their plans.

Using the Problem-Solving Plan

Exercise 1

Understand the problem. The table shows the tolls for traveling several different distances on a turnpike. You have \$8.25 to pay the toll. You are asked to find how far you can travel on the turnpike with \$8.25 for tolls.

Make a plan. First, determine the relationship between x and y and write an equation to represent the relationship. Then use the equation to determine the distance you can travel.

Solve and check. Use the plan to solve the problem. Then check your solution.

- Determine the relationship between x and y.

  $\frac{3.75}{25} = 0.15 \quad \frac{4.50}{30} = 0.15 \quad \frac{5.25}{35} = 0.15 \quad \frac{6.00}{40} = 0.15$

  So, x and y are proportional.

- Write an equation to represent the relationship.

  $y = 0.15x$

- Determine the distance you can travel.

  $y = 0.15x$ Equation

  $8.25 = 0.15x$ Substitute 8.25 for y.

  $\frac{8.25}{0.15} = \frac{0.15x}{0.15}$ Division Property of Equality

  $55 = x$ Simplify.

  So, you can travel 55 miles on the turnpike.

- **Check:** Substitute 55 for x to verify the cost.

  $y = 0.15(55)$

  $y = 8.25$ ✓

D Connecting Concepts

Using the Problem-Solving Plan

1. The table shows the toll y (in dollars) for traveling x miles on a turnpike. You have \$8.25 to pay your toll. How far can you travel on the turnpike?

Distance, x (miles)	25	30	35	40
Toll, y (dollars)	3.75	4.50	5.25	6.00

Understand the problem.

The table shows the tolls for traveling several different distances on a turnpike. You have \$8.25 to pay the toll. You are asked to find how far you can travel on the turnpike with \$8.25 for tolls.

Make a plan.

First, determine the relationship between x and y and write an equation to represent the relationship. Then use the equation to determine the distance you can travel.

Solve and check.

Use the plan to solve the problem. Then check your solution.

2. A company uses a silo in the shape of a rectangular prism to store bird seed. The base of the silo is a square with side lengths of 20 feet. Are the height and the volume of the silo proportional? Justify your answer.

3. A rectangle is drawn in a coordinate plane as shown. In the same coordinate plane, create a scale drawing of the rectangle that has a vertex at $(0, 0)$ and a scale factor of 3.

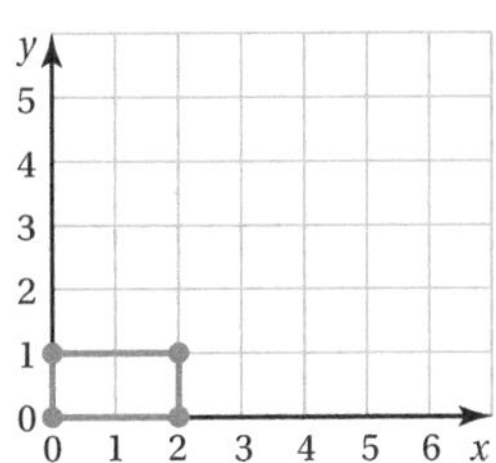

Performance Task

Mixing Paint

At the beginning of this chapter, you watched a STEAM Video called "Painting a Large Room." You are now ready to complete the performance task related to this video, available at ***BigIdeasMath.com***. Be sure to use the problem-solving plan as you work through the performance task.

D Chapter Review

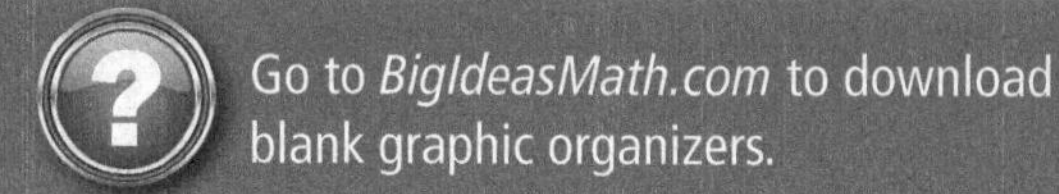

Review Vocabulary

Write the definition and give an example of each vocabulary term.

ratio, *p. 628*
value of a ratio, *p. 628*
equivalent ratios, *p. 629*
ratio table, *p. 629*
rate, *p. 634*
unit rate, *p. 634*
equivalent rates, *p. 634*
proportion, *p. 640*
cross products, *p. 641*
proportional, *p. 642*
constant of proportionality, *p. 656*
scale drawing, *p. 662*
scale model, *p. 662*
scale, *p. 662*
scale factor, *p. 663*

Graphic Organizers

You can use an **Example and Non-Example Chart** to list examples and non-examples of a concept. Here is an Example and Non-Example Chart for *scale factor*.

Scale factor

Examples	Non-Examples
$\frac{5}{1}$	1 cm : 2 mm
$\frac{1}{200}$	1 mm : 20 cm
$\frac{1}{1}$	12 in. : 1 ft
$\frac{3}{2}$	3 mi : 2 in.

Choose and complete a graphic organizer to help you study the concept.

1. ratio
2. equivalent ratios
3. rate
4. unit rate
5. equivalent rates
6. proportion
7. cross products
8. proportional
9. scale

"What do you think of my Example & Non-Example Chart for popular cat toys?"

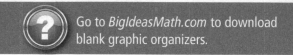

Review Vocabulary

- As a review of the chapter vocabulary, have students revisit the vocabulary section in their *Student Journals* to fill in any missing definitions and record examples of each term.

Graphic Organizers

Sample answers:

1. Ratio

Examples	Non-Examples
2 : 3	14
6 dogs to 2 cats	8 tigers
$\frac{1}{4}$ to $\frac{5}{6}$	−24
7 tablespoons : 6 cups	2.75

2. Equivalent Ratios

Examples	Non-Examples
2 : 3 and 4 : 6	2 : 3 and 4 : 5
7 to 3 and 21 to 9	7 to 3 and 11 to 9
$\frac{1}{3}$ to $\frac{4}{5}$ and 1 to $\frac{12}{5}$	$\frac{1}{3}$ to $\frac{4}{5}$ and 1 to 4
2.75 : 2 and 1.375 : 1	2.75 : 2 and 0.75 : 1

3. Rate

Examples	Non-Examples
\$15 : 2 hours	4 : 5
125 words in 2.5 minutes	$\frac{2}{3}$ to $\frac{1}{2}$
$\frac{5}{6}$ liter for every $2\frac{1}{2}$ ounces	4 cups : 3 cups
27.2 meters per hour	6 pints to 8 pints

4. Unit Rate

Examples	Non-Examples
\$7.50 : 1 hour	\$15 : 2 hours
50 words in 1 minute	125 words in 2.5 minutes
$\frac{1}{3}$ liter for every 1 ounce	$\frac{5}{6}$ liter for every $2\frac{1}{2}$ ounces
27.2 meters per hour	54.4 meters per 2 hours

5–9. Answers at *BigIdeasMath.com*.

List of Organizers

Available at *BigIdeasMath.com*
Definition and Example Chart
Example and Non-Example Chart
Four Square
Information Frame
Summary Triangle

About this Organizer

An **Example and Non-Example Chart** can be used to list examples and non-examples of a concept. Students write examples of the concept in the left column and non-examples in the right column. This organizer can be used to assess students' understanding of two concepts that have subtle, but important differences. Blank Example and Non-Example Charts can be included on tests or quizzes for this purpose.

Chapter Self-Assessment

1. $\frac{1}{2}:2$; The amount of salt is $\frac{1}{4}$ the amount of flour.
2. $\frac{3}{4}:2$; The amount of water is $\frac{3}{8}$ the amount of flour.
3. $\frac{1}{2}:\frac{3}{4}$; The amount of salt is $\frac{2}{3}$ the amount of water.
4. $\frac{9}{2}$, 6, 1; $\frac{3}{2}:\frac{1}{2}$; 3 : 1; $\frac{9}{2}:\frac{3}{2}$; 6 : 2
5. 180, 2.25, 1.5; 45 : 0.75; 135 : 2.25; 180 : 3; 90 : 1.5
6. $4
7. 28.9 mi : 1 gal
8. 2.4 revolutions : 1 sec
9. 95,040 ft^2; $\frac{23{,}760}{\frac{1}{2}} = 47{,}520$, $47{,}520 \times 2 = 95{,}040$
10. yes; $\frac{60}{2.5(12)} = \frac{30}{15}$
11. no; $\frac{2.56}{8} = 0.32$, $\frac{0.48}{6} = 0.08$

Chapter Self-Assessment

The Success Criteria Self-Assessment chart can be found in the *Student Journal* or online at *BigIdeasMath.com.*

ELL Support

Allow students to work in pairs to complete the first section of the Chapter Self-Assessment. Once pairs have finished, check for understanding by having each pair display their answers on a whiteboard for your review. If sections include discussion questions, students may benefit from grouping two pairs and having them reach an agreement. Monitor discussions and provide support. You can use a thumbs up or down signal to check answers to *yes* or *no* questions. Provide graph paper for graphing exercises. Use these techniques as appropriate.

Common Errors

- **Exercises 1–3** Students may have difficulty simplifying the complex fractions that result in the solutions of these exercises. A quick review of complex fractions may be helpful. Be sure to point out that a fraction bar means division, so they can rewrite the complex fraction as *numerator ÷ denominator.*
- **Exercises 4 and 5** Students may add or subtract the same amount to each number in the ratio, saying, for example, that 2 : 3 and 4 : 5 are equivalent. Make it very clear that the numbers you add or subtract must be in the same ratio. You cannot add or subtract the same number, as when multiplying or dividing.
- **Exercises 7–9** Students may find the unit rate but forget to include the units. Remind students that the units are necessary for understanding a unit rate, or any rate.

Chapter Self-Assessment

As you complete the exercises, use the scale below to rate your understanding of the success criteria in your journal.

1	2	3	4
I do not understand.	I can do it with help.	I can do it on my own.	I can teach someone else.

D.1 Ratios and Ratio Tables (pp. 627–632)

Learning Target: Understand ratios of rational numbers and use ratio tables to represent equivalent ratios.

Write the ratio. Then find and interpret the value of the ratio.

1. salt: flour
2. water to flour
3. salt to water

Modeling Clay

Ingredients:
2 cups flour $\frac{1}{2}$ cup salt $\frac{3}{4}$ cup water

Find the missing values in the ratio table. Then write the equivalent ratios.

4.

Flour (cups)	$\frac{3}{2}$	3		
Milk (cups)	$\frac{1}{2}$		$\frac{3}{2}$	2

5.

Miles	45	135		90
Hours	0.75		3	

6. The cost for 16 ounces of cheese is \$3.20. What is the cost for 20 ounces of cheese?

D.2 Rates and Unit Rates (pp. 633–638)

Learning Target: Understand rates involving fractions and use unit rates to solve problems.

Find the unit rate.

7. 289 miles on 10 gallons
8. $6\frac{2}{5}$ revolutions in $2\frac{2}{3}$ seconds
9. You can mow 23,760 square feet in $\frac{1}{2}$ hour. How many square feet can you mow in 2 hours? Justify your answer.

Tell whether the rates are equivalent. Justify your answer.

10. 60 centimeters every 2.5 years
    30 centimeters every 15 months
11. \$2.56 per $\frac{1}{2}$ pound
    \$0.48 per 6 ounces

D.3 Identifying Proportional Relationships (pp. 639–646)

Learning Target: Determine whether two quantities are in a proportional relationship.

Tell whether the ratios form a proportion.

12. 4 to 9 and 2 to 3

13. 12 : 22 and 18 : 33

14. $\frac{1}{2} : 2$ and $\frac{1}{4} : \frac{1}{10}$

15. 3.2 to 8 and 1.2 to 3

16. Tell whether x and y are proportional.

x	1	3	6	8
y	4	12	24	32

17. You can type 250 characters in 60 seconds. Your friend can type 375 characters in 90 seconds. Do these rates form a proportion? Explain.

D.4 Writing and Solving Proportions (pp. 647–654)

Learning Target: Use proportions to solve ratio problems.

Solve the proportion. Explain your choice of method.

18. $\frac{3}{8} = \frac{9}{x}$

19. $\frac{x}{4} = \frac{2}{5}$

20. $\frac{5}{12} = \frac{y}{15}$

21. $\frac{s+1}{4} = \frac{4}{8}$

Use the table to write a proportion.

22.

	Game 1	Game 2
Penalties	6	8
Minutes	12	m

23.

	Concert 1	Concert 2
Songs	15	18
Hours	2.5	h

24. Find the value of x so that the ratios 8 : 20 and 6 : x are equivalent.

25. Swamp gas consists primarily of methane, a chemical compound consisting of a 1 : 4 ratio of carbon to hydrogen atoms. If a sample of methane contains 1564 hydrogen atoms, how many carbon atoms are present in the sample?

Common Errors

- **Exercise 17** Students may mix up the rates and incorrectly find that they are not proportional. For example, they might write $\frac{\text{250 characters}}{\text{60 seconds}} \stackrel{?}{=} \frac{\text{90 seconds}}{\text{375 characters}}$. Remind students about writing a rate and help them identify which unit goes in the numerator.
- **Exercises 18–21** When using the Cross Products Property, students may divide instead of multiply when finding the cross products, or they may multiply across the numerators and the denominators as if they were multiplying fractions. Remind students that the ratios have an equal sign between them, not a multiplication sign.
- **Exercises 19–21** When using the Multiplication Property of Equality, students may multiply by the denominator of the fraction without the variable. Remind students that they are trying to isolate the variable, so they want to multiply both sides by the denominator of the fraction with the variable. Give students an example without a fraction on the other side of the equation to remind them of the process.
- **Exercises 22 and 23** Students may write half of the proportion using rows and the other half using columns. They will have forgotten to include one of the values. Remind students that they need to pick a method for writing proportions with tables and be consistent throughout the problem.

Chapter Self-Assessment

12. no

13. yes

14. no

15. yes

16. yes

17. yes; $\frac{250}{60} = \frac{375}{90}$

18–21. Explanations will vary.

18. $x = 24$

19. $x = 1.6$

20. $y = 6.25$

21. $s = 1$

22. $\frac{\text{8 penalties}}{\text{6 penalties}} = \frac{m\text{ minutes}}{\text{12 minutes}}$

23. $\frac{\text{15 songs}}{\text{2.5 hours}} = \frac{\text{18 songs}}{h\text{ hours}}$

24. $x = 15$

25. 391 carbon atoms

Chapter Self-Assessment

26. yes; The line passes through the origin.

27. $(0, 0): 0$ visits in 0 months; $(3, 150): 150$ visits in 3 months; $(4, 200): 200$ visits in 4 months; 50 visits per month

28. no; The equation cannot be written as $y = kx$.

29. yes; $k = 1$; The equation can be written as $y = kx$.

30. yes; $k = \frac{1}{20}$; The equation can be written as $y = kx$.

31. no; The equation cannot be written as $y = kx$.

32. $k = 8$; $y = 8x$

33. 4.5 in.

34. 75 ft

35. 1 cm : 5 in.; $\frac{1}{12.7}$

36. 1 cm : 3 in.; $\frac{1}{7.62}$

37. 160 ft

Common Errors

- **Exercise 26** Students may immediately state that the table does not show a proportional relationship because (0, 0) is not listed. Encourage students to plot the points and then draw a line through the points to see if the graph is a line that passes through the origin.
- **Exercises 28–31** Students may try to determine whether x and y are proportional without solving for y. Remind students to solve for y first.
- **Exercise 32** Students may not grasp how to write the equation. Remind students that the equation of a proportional relationship is $y = kx$, so they can substitute the values of x and y to find k.
- **Exercises 35 and 36** When measuring with a centimeter ruler, students may not start at zero on the ruler. As a result, they will get an incorrect distance. Ask students to estimate the distance before measuring so they can check the reasonableness of their measurements.
- **Exercise 37** Students may mix up the proportion values when solving for the missing dimension. Remind students that the model dimension is in the numerator and the actual dimension is in the denominator.

Chapter Resources

Surface Level	Deep Level
Resources by Chapter • Extra Practice • Reteach • Puzzle Time Student Journal • Practice • Chapter Self-Assessment Differentiating the Lesson Tutorial Videos Skills Review Handbook Skills Trainer Game Library	Resources by Chapter • Enrichment and Extension Graphic Organizers Game Library
Transfer Level	
STEAM Video Dynamic Assessment System • Chapter Test	Assessment Book • Chapter Tests A and B • Alternative Assessment • STEAM Performance Task

D.5 Graphs of Proportional Relationships (pp. 655–660)

Learning Target: Represent proportional relationships using graphs and equations.

26. Tell whether x and y are proportional. Explain your reasoning.

x	-3	-1	1	3
y	6	2	-2	-6

27. The graph shows the number of visits your website received over the past 6 months. Interpret each plotted point in the graph. Then identify the unit rate.

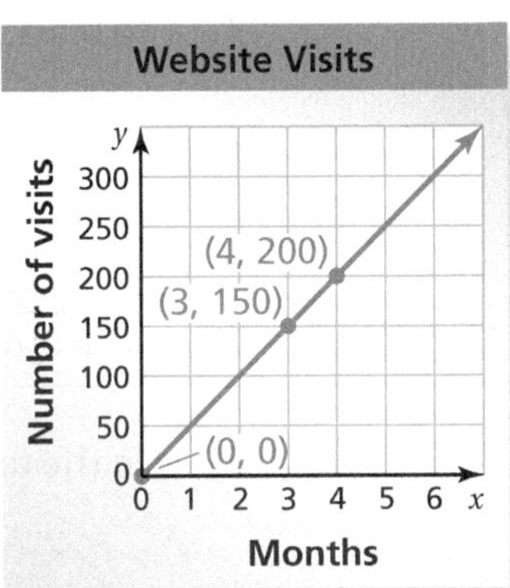

Tell whether x and y are proportional. If so, identify the constant of proportionality. Explain your reasoning.

28. $x + y = 6$ **29.** $y - x = 0$ **30.** $\frac{x}{y} = 20$ **31.** $x = y + 2$

32. The variables x and y are proportional. When $y = 4$, $x = \frac{1}{2}$. Find the constant of proportionality. Then write an equation that relates x and y.

D.6 Scale Drawings (pp. 661–666)

Learning Target: Solve problems involving scale drawings.

Find the missing dimension. Use the scale factor 1 : 20.

	Item	Model	Actual
33.	Basketball player	Height: ____ in.	Height: 90 in.
34.	Dinosaur	Length: 3.75 ft	Length: ____ ft

Use a centimeter ruler to find the scale and the scale factor of the drawing.

35. 30 in.

36. 7.5 in.

37. A scale model of a lighthouse has a scale of 1 in. : 8 ft. The scale model is 20 inches tall. How tall is the lighthouse?

D Practice Test

Find the unit rate.

1. 84 miles in 12 days

2. $2\frac{2}{5}$ kilometers in $3\frac{3}{4}$ minutes

Tell whether the ratios form a proportion.

3. 1 to 0.4 and 9 to 3.6

4. $2:\frac{8}{3}$ and $\frac{2}{3}:6$

Tell whether x and y are proportional. Explain your reasoning.

5.

x	2	4	6	8
y	10	20	30	40

6.

x	1	3	5	7
y	3	7	11	15

7. Use the table to write a proportion.

	Monday	Tuesday
Gallons	6	8
Miles	180	m

Solve the proportion.

8. $\frac{x}{8} = \frac{9}{4}$

9. $\frac{17}{4} = \frac{y}{6}$

Tell whether x and y are proportional. If so, identify the constant of proportionality. Explain your reasoning.

10. $xy - 11 = 5$

11. $\frac{y}{x} = 8$

12. A recipe calls for $\frac{2}{3}$ cup flour for every $\frac{1}{2}$ cup sugar. Write the ratio of sugar to flour. Then find and interpret the value of the ratio.

13. The graph shows the number of cycles of a crosswalk signal during the day and during the night.

a. Write equations that relate x and y for both the day and night periods.

b. Find how many more cycles occur during the day than during the night for a six-hour period.

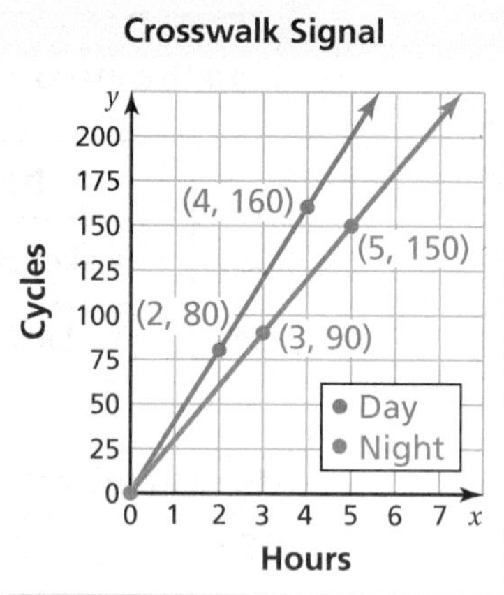

14. An engineer is using computer-aided design (CAD) software to design a component for a space shuttle. The scale of the drawing is 1 cm : 60 in. The actual length of the component is 12.75 feet. What is the length of the component in the drawing?

15. A specific shade of green glaze is made of 5 parts blue glaze to 3 parts yellow glaze. A glaze mixture contains 25 quarts of blue glaze and 9 quarts of yellow glaze. How can you fix the mixture to make the specific shade of green glaze?

Practice Test Item References

Practice Test Questions	Section to Review
12	D.1
1, 2	D.2
3, 4, 5, 6	D.3
7, 8, 9, 15	D.4
5, 6, 10, 11, 13	D.5
14	D.6

Test-Taking Strategies

Remind students to quickly look over the entire test before they start so that they can budget their time. Some students may have difficulty distinguishing between such concepts as ratios, rates, unit rates, and proportions, so encourage students to jot down definitions on the back of the test before they start. Students should use the **Stop** and **Think** strategy to ensure that they understand what is being asked before they write their answers.

Common Errors

- **Exercises 1 and 2** Students may find the unit rate but forget to include the units. Remind students that the units are necessary for understanding a unit rate.
- **Exercise 7** Students may write half of the proportion using rows and the other half using columns. They will have forgotten to include one of the values. Remind students that they need to pick a method for writing proportions with tables and be consistent throughout the problem.
- **Exercises 8 and 9** When using the Multiplication Property of Equality, students may multiply by the denominator of the fraction without the variable. Remind students that they are trying to isolate the variable, so they want to multiply both sides by the denominator of the fraction with the variable. Give students an example without a fraction on the other side of the equation to remind them of the process.
- **Exercises 8 and 9** When using the Cross Products Property, students may divide instead of multiply when finding the cross products, or they may multiply across the numerators and the denominators as if they were multiplying fractions. Remind students that the ratios have an equal sign between them, not a multiplication sign.
- **Exercises 10 and 11** Students may try to determine whether x and y are proportional without solving for y. Remind students to solve for y first.
- **Exercise 13** Students may not grasp how to write the equation. Remind students that the equation of a proportional relationship is $y = kx$, so they can substitute the values of x and y to find k.

Practice Test

1. 7 mi : 1 day
2. $\frac{16}{25}$ km : 1 min
3. yes
4. no
5. yes; The line passes through the origin.
6. no; The line does not pass through the origin.
7. $\frac{8 \text{ gallons}}{6 \text{ gallons}} = \frac{m \text{ miles}}{180 \text{ miles}}$
8. $x = 8$
9. $y = 25.5$
10. no; The equation cannot be written as $y = kx$.
11. yes; $k = 8$; The equation can be written as $y = kx$.
12. 3 : 4; The amount of sugar in the recipe is $\frac{3}{4}$ the amount of flour.
13. **a.** day: $y = 40x$; night: $y = 30x$

    b. 60 more cycles
14. 2.55 cm
15. Add 6 quarts of yellow.

Test-Taking Strategies

Available at *BigIdeasMath.com*

After Answering Easy Questions, Relax

Answer Easy Questions First

Estimate the Answer

Read All Choices before Answering

Read Question before Answering

Solve Directly or Eliminate Choices

Solve Problem before Looking at Choices

Use Intelligent Guessing

Work Backwards

About this Strategy

When taking a multiple-choice test, be sure to read each question carefully and thoroughly. Look closely for words that change the meaning of the questions, such as *not, never, all, every,* and *always.*

Cumulative Practice

1. A
2. G
3. B
4. 12
5. H
6. B

Item Analysis

1. **A.** Correct answer

B. The student thinks the price of the 4 pencils is the unit price.

C. The student multiplies 0.80 and 4.

D. The student divides 4 by 0.80.

2. **F.** The student adds -5 instead of subtracting.

G. Correct answer

H. The student adds $3x$ and $(2x - 5)$ instead of subtracting.

I. The student subtracts $3x$ from $(2x - 5)$ instead of subtracting $(2x - 5)$ from $3x$.

3. **A.** The student finds the fraction of -12.5 instead of -1.25.

B. Correct answer

C. The student finds the fraction of -0.125 instead of -1.25.

D. The student does not include the negative sign.

4. **Gridded Response**: Correct answer: 12

Common error: The student incorrectly multiplies the numerators and multiplies the denominators instead of finding the cross products to get an answer of 27.

5. **F.** The student subtracts 3 from 7 instead of adding.

G. The student does not realize that the inequality sign calls for a closed circle.

H. Correct answer

I. The student thinks the inequality symbol means *less than* instead of *greater than.*

6. **A.** The student adds $\frac{2}{3}$ to 24 instead of 6.

B. Correct answer

C. The student adds 12 to 24 instead of 6.

D. The student doubles 24 because each value in the *y*-column is twice the previous value.

D Cumulative Practice

Test-Taking Strategy
Read Question before Answering

What is **NOT** the ratio of human years to dog years?

Ⓐ $\frac{1}{7}$ Ⓑ 1:7 Ⓒ 1 to 7 Ⓓ 7

Newton the senior citizen

"Be sure to read the question before choosing your answer. You may find a word that changes the meaning."

1. The school store sells 4 pencils for \$0.80. What is the unit cost of a pencil?

A. \$0.20 **B.** \$0.80

C. \$3.20 **D.** \$5.00

2. What is the simplified form of the expression?

$$3x - (2x - 5)$$

F. $x - 5$ **G.** $x + 5$

H. $5x - 5$ **I.** $-x - 5$

3. Which fraction is equivalent to -1.25?

A. $-12\frac{1}{2}$ **B.** $-1\frac{1}{4}$

C. $-\frac{125}{1000}$ **D.** $1\frac{1}{4}$

4. What is the value of x for the proportion $\frac{8}{12} = \frac{x}{18}$?

5. What inequality is represented by the graph?

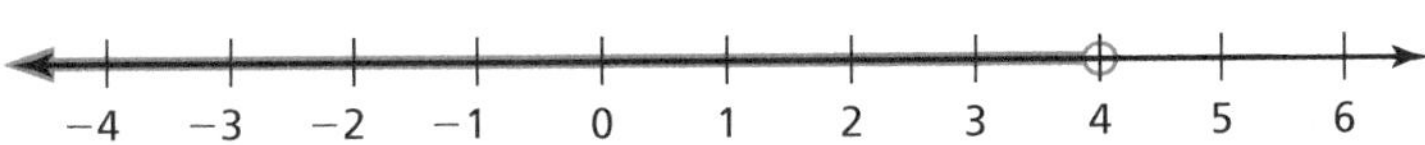

F. $x - 3 < 7$ **G.** $x + 6 \leq 10$

H. $-5 + x < -1$ **I.** $x - 8 > -4$

6. What is the missing value in the ratio table?

x	$\frac{2}{3}$	$\frac{4}{3}$	$\frac{8}{3}$	$\frac{10}{3}$
y	6	12	24	

A. $24\frac{2}{3}$ **B.** 30

C. 36 **D.** 48

7. Which expression shows factoring $12x + 54$ using the GCF?

F. $2(6x + 27)$ **G.** $3(4x + 18)$

H. $6(2x + 9)$ **I.** $12\left(x + \frac{9}{2}\right)$

8. The distance traveled by a high-speed train is proportional to the number of hours traveled. Which of the following is *not* a valid interpretation of the graph?

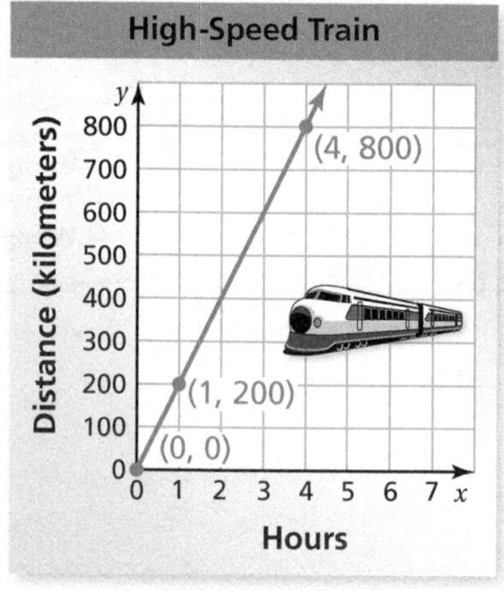

A. The train travels 0 kilometers in 0 hours.

B. The unit rate is 200 kilometers per hour.

C. After 4 hours, the train is traveling 800 kilometers per hour.

D. The train travels 800 kilometers in 4 hours.

9. Which graph represents a number that is at most -2?

F. 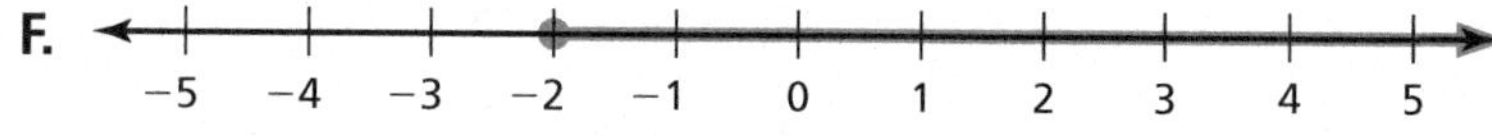

G. 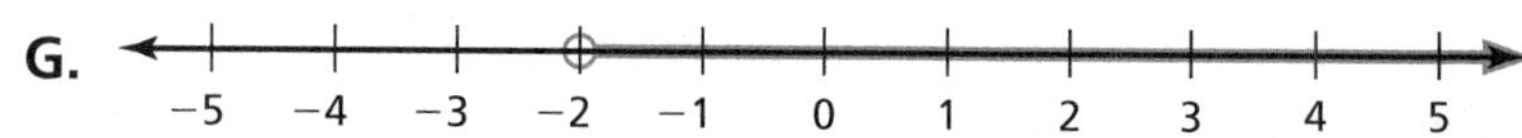

H. 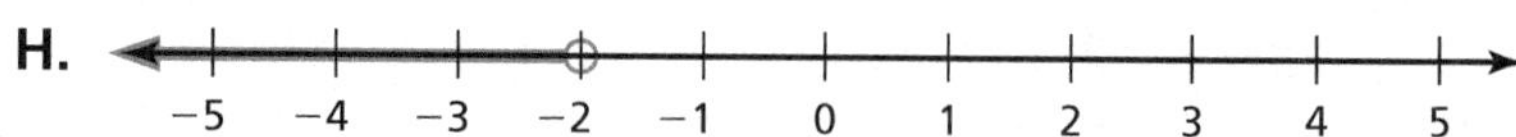

I. 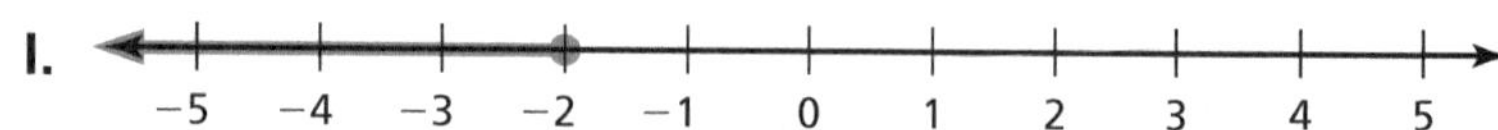

Item Analysis (continued)

7. **F.** The student factors out a common factor but not the *greatest* common factor.

   G. The student factors out a common factor but not the *greatest* common factor.

   H. Correct answer

   I. The student factors out the coefficient of the variable term instead of the greatest common factor.

8. **A.** The student misinterprets the information in the graph.

   B. The student misinterprets the information in the graph.

   C. Correct answer

   D. The student misinterprets the information in the graph.

9. **F.** The student thinks *at most* means *more than.*

   G. The student thinks *at most* means *more than* and excludes −2.

   H. The student excludes −2.

   I. Correct answer

Cumulative Practice

7. H
8. C
9. I

Cumulative Practice

10. *Part A* 90 mi; 1 inch represents 20 miles, so 4.5 inches is $4.5 \times 20 = 90$ miles.

Part B $3\frac{1}{4}$ in.; 1 inch represents 20 miles, so 65 miles is $65 \div 20 = 3.25$ inches.

11. 7

12. D

13. H

Item Analysis (continued)

10. **2 points** The student's work and explanations demonstrate a thorough understanding of working with scale drawings. In Part A, the student correctly determines that the actual distance is 90 miles. In Part B, the student correctly determines that the distance on the map should be $3\frac{1}{4}$ inches. The student provides clear and complete work and explanations.

1 point The student's work and explanations demonstrate a partial but limited understanding of working with scale drawings. The student shows some correct work and explanation.

0 points The student provides no response, a completely incorrect or incomprehensible response, or a response that demonstrates insufficient understanding of working with scale drawings.

11. **Gridded Response:** Correct answer: 7
Common error: The student thinks the quotient of two negative numbers is negative and gets an answer of -7.

12. **A.** The student adds 8 to 30 because $18 - 10 = 8$.

B. The student adds 12 to 30 because $30 - 18 = 12$.

C. The student thinks the amount being added to y is being increased by 4 each time.

D. Correct answer

13. **F.** The student thinks $8 + (-3) = -5$, so the student returns to start and then adds 2.

G. The student adds -2 instead of adding 2 for the last move.

H. Correct answer

I. The student adds 8, 3, and 2 instead of adding 8, -3, and 2.

10. A map of the state where your friend lives has the scale $\frac{1}{2}$ in. : 10 mi.

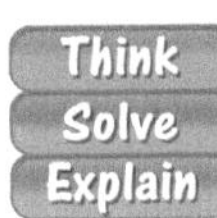

Part A Your friend measured the distance between her town and the state capital on the map. Her measurement was $4\frac{1}{2}$ inches. Based on your friend's measurement, what is the actual distance (in miles) between her town and the state capital? Show your work and explain your reasoning.

Part B Your friend wants to mark her favorite campsite on the map. She knows that the campsite is 65 miles north of her town. What distance on the map (in inches) represents an actual distance of 65 miles? Show your work and explain your reasoning.

11. What is the value of the expression $-56 \div (-8)$?

12. The quantities x and y are proportional. What is the missing value in the table?

x	y
$\frac{5}{7}$	10
$\frac{9}{7}$	18
$\frac{15}{7}$	30
4	

A. 38 B. 42

C. 46 D. 56

13. To begin a board game, you place a playing piece at START. On your first three turns, you move ahead 8 spaces, move back 3 spaces, and then move ahead 2 spaces. How many spaces are you from START?

F. 2 G. 3

H. 7 I. 13

E Percents

Chapter Learning Target:
Understand fractions, decimals, and percents.

Chapter Success Criteria:

- I can rewrite fractions, decimals, and percents.
- I can compare and order fractions, decimals, and percents.
- I can use the percent proportion or percent equation to find a percent, a part, or a whole.
- I can apply percents to solve real-life problems.

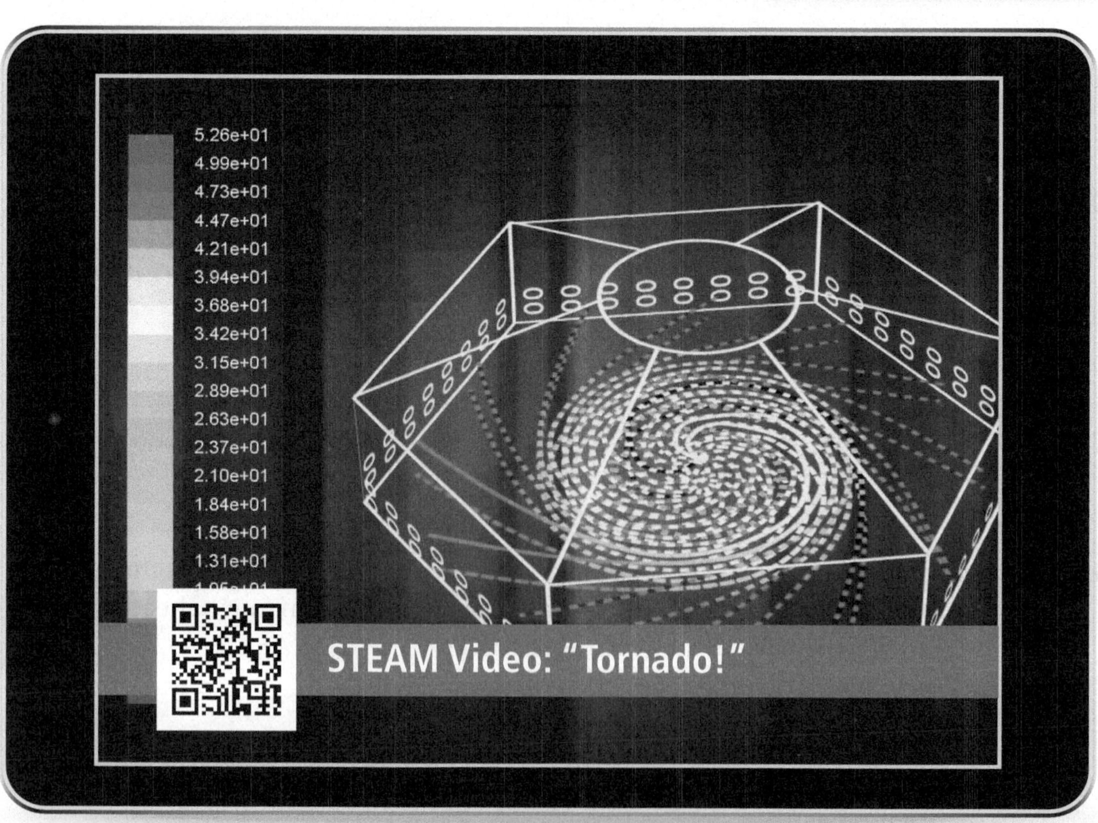

Laurie's Notes

Chapter E Overview

Percents are used to describe proportional relationships and to solve many application problems. To solve these problems, students must be able to write percents as decimals or fractions. Understanding these equivalent representations and converting between them is how the chapter begins.

To help students make sense of percent problems, percent bar models are used throughout the chapter. A percent bar model is similar to a tape diagram and provides a way for students to visualize the relationship between quantities. For many students, it provides the sense-making that may be missing when they write a proportion or equation to solve a problem. Each of the following strategies can be used to solve the problem: What number is 40% of 25?

Percent Proportion	Percent Equation	Percent Bar Model
$\frac{a}{w} = \frac{p}{100}$	$a = p\% \cdot w$	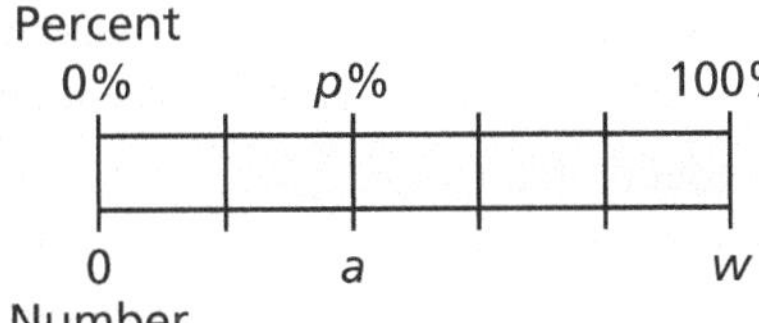
$\frac{a}{25} = \frac{40}{100}$	$a = \frac{40}{100} \cdot 25$	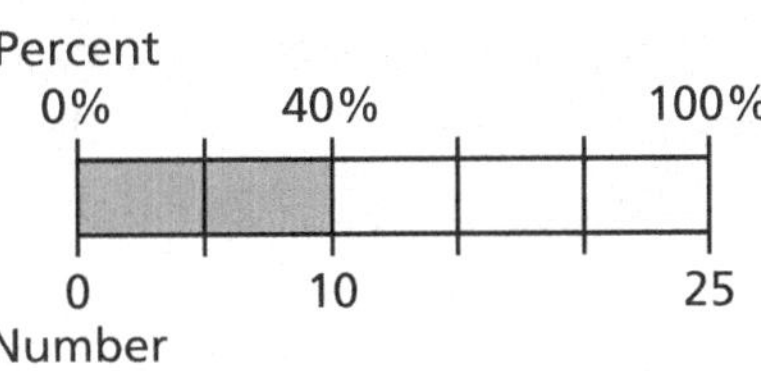

Ratio tables and double number lines are additional displays that can be used to show proportional relationships.

The second half of the chapter focuses on applications of percents: percent of increase or decrease, discounts, markups, and simple interest. Percent of change problems can be challenging for students. Finding the *amount* of change between two quantities is quite different than finding the *percent* of change between two quantities. Students may not even realize that these are two different concepts. Discount applications are very common and students should spend time using mental math strategies to estimate reasonable solutions. This is where percent bar models can be very helpful. The last lesson is on simple interest.

In all of the application problems, students are really working to understand the context and then applying mathematical skills to solve the problem. Even when the context is familiar, students need to be able to identify what the whole and the part are in terms of the information they know. The part is not always less!

Suggested Pacing

Chapter Opener	1 Day
Section 1	1 Day
Section 2	1 Day
Section 3	1 Day
Section 4	1 Day
Section 5	1 Day
Section 6	1 Day
Connecting Concepts	1 Day
Chapter Review	1 Day
Chapter Test	1 Day
Total Chapter E	10 Days
Year-to-Date	160 Days

Chapter Learning Target

Understand fractions, decimals, and percents.

Chapter Success Criteria

- Rewrite fractions, decimals, and percents.
- Compare and order fractions, decimals, and percents.
- Use the percent proportion or percent equation to find a percent, a part, or a whole.
- Apply percents to solve real-life problems.

Chapter E Learning Targets and Success Criteria

Section	Learning Target	Success Criteria
E.1 Fractions, Decimals, and Percents	Rewrite fractions, decimals, and percents using different representations.	• Write percents as decimals and decimals as percents. • Write fractions as decimals and percents. • Compare and order fractions, decimals, and percents.
E.2 The Percent Proportion	Use the percent proportion to find missing quantities.	• Write proportions to represent percent problems. • Solve a proportion to find a percent, a part, or a whole.
E.3 The Percent Equation	Use the percent equation to find missing quantities.	• Write equations to represent percent problems. • Use the percent equation to find a percent, a part, or a whole.
E.4 Percents of Increase and Decrease	Find percents of change in quantities.	• Explain the meaning of percent of change. • Find the percent of increase or decrease in a quantity. • Find the percent error of a quantity.
E.5 Discounts and Markups	Solve percent problems involving discounts and markups.	• Use percent models to solve problems involving discounts and markups. • Write and solve equations to solve problems involving discounts and markups.
E.6 Simple Interest	Understand and apply the simple interest formula.	• Explain the meaning of simple interest. • Use the simple interest formula to solve problems.

Progressions

Through the Grades		
Grade 6	**Grade 7**	**Grade 8**
• Find percent as a rate per 100; solve problems involving finding the whole, given a part and the percent. • Understand ordering of rational numbers. • Identify equivalent expressions. • Write and solve one-step equations.	• Use proportionality to solve multistep percent problems. Solve percent problems involving percents of increase and decrease, and simple interest. • Compare fractions, decimals, and percents.	• Understand that numbers that are not rational are irrational. • Compare irrational numbers using rational approximations.

Through the Chapter						
Standard	**E.1**	**E.2**	**E.3**	**E.4**	**E.5**	**E.6**
Use proportional relationships to solve multistep ratio and percent problems.		●	●	●	●	★
Solve multi-step real-life and mathematical problems posed with positive and negative rational numbers in any form (whole numbers, fractions, and decimals), using tools strategically. Apply properties of operations to calculate with numbers in any form; convert between forms as appropriate; and assess the reasonableness of answers using mental computation and estimation strategies.	●	●	●	●	●	★

Key

▲ = preparing ★ = complete

● = learning ■ = extending

STEAM Video

1. *Sample answer:*
   most: central and south;
   least: west and northeast
2. 94%

Performance Task

Sample answer: The percent of tornados in each state allows one to see which states have the highest risks of a tornado occurring.

Mathematical Practices

Students have opportunities to develop aspects of the mathematical practices throughout the chapter. Here are some examples.

1. **Make Sense of Problems and Persevere in Solving Them**
   E.1 Math Practice note, *p. 679*
2. **Reason Abstractly and Quantitatively**
   E.5 Exercise 33, *p. 708*
3. **Construct Viable Arguments and Critique the Reasoning of Others**
   E.3 Exercises 21 and 22, *p. 695*
4. **Model with Mathematics**
   E.6 Math Practice note, *p. 710*
5. **Use Appropriate Tools Strategically**
   E.2 Exercises 9–14, *p. 689*
6. **Attend to Precision**
   E.4 Exercise 23, *p. 702*
7. **Look for and Make Use of Structure**
   E.6 Math Practice note, *p. 709*
8. **Look for and Express Regularity in Repeated Reasoning**
   E.6 Exercise 39, *p. 714*

Laurie's Notes

STEAM Video

Before the Video

- To introduce the STEAM Video, read aloud the first paragraph of Tornado! and discuss the question with your students.
- ? "How can you use a percent to describe the portion of tornadoes in the United States that occur in your state?"

During the Video

- The video shows Robert and Tory discussing tornadoes.
- ? Pause the video at 0:41 and ask, "What makes the wind tunnel at WindEEE different than traditional wind tunnels?" It simulates the air swirling, rising, and falling. Traditional wind tunnels only simulate the air going in one direction.
- Watch the remainder of the video.

After the Video

- ? "What is the difference between a tornado *watch* and a tornado *warning*?" A tornado watch means that a tornado is possible, and a tornado warning means that a tornado has been spotted.
- Have students work with a partner to answer Questions 1 and 2.
- As students discuss and answer the questions, listen for understanding of finding percents.

Performance Task

- Use this information to spark students' interest and promote thinking about real-life problems.
- ? Ask, "Why is it helpful to know the percent of tornadoes that occur in each state?"
- After completing the chapter, students will have gained the knowledge needed to complete "Tornado Alley."

STEAM Video

Tornado!

More tornadoes occur each year in the United States than in any other country. How can you use a percent to describe the portion of tornadoes in the United States that occur in your state?

Watch the STEAM Video "Tornado!" Then answer the following questions.

1. The map below shows the average annual number of tornadoes in each state. Which regions have the most tornadoes? the fewest tornadoes?

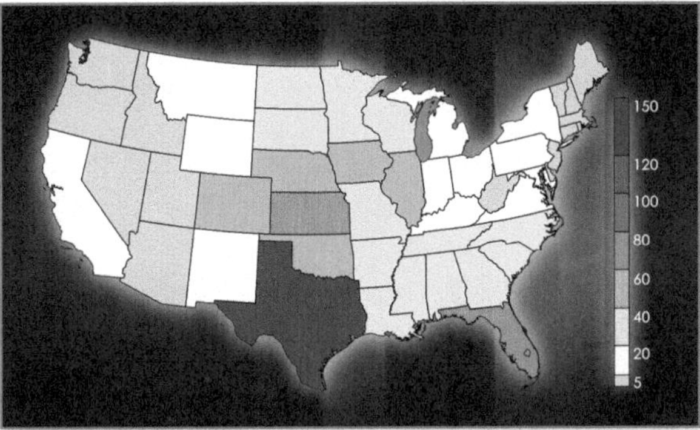

2. Robert says that only Alaska, Hawaii, and Rhode Island average less than 1 tornado per year. What percent of states average *more* than 1 tornado per year?

Performance Task

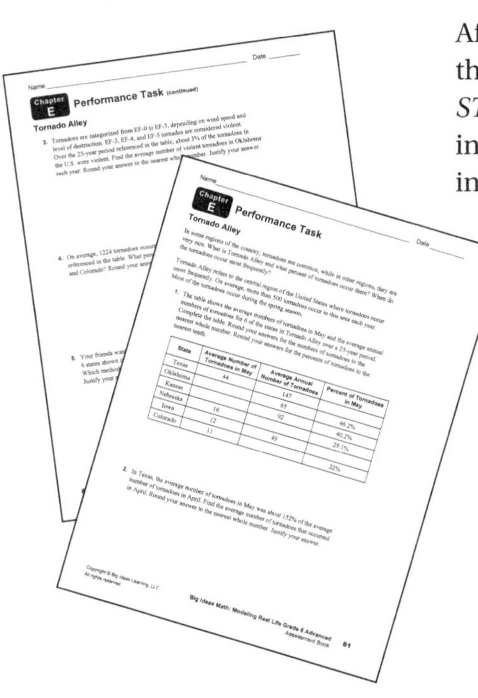

Name _____ Date _____

Chapter E **Performance Task** (continued)

Tornado Alley

3. Tornadoes are categorized from EF-0 to EF-5, depending on wind speed and level of destruction. EF-3, EF-4, and EF-5 tornados are considered violent. Over the 25-year period referenced in the table, about 3% of the tornadoes in the U.S. were violent. Find the average number of violent tornadoes in Oklahoma each year. Round your answer to the nearest who... Justify your answer.

4. On average, 1224 tornadoes occur... referenced in the table. What per... and Colorado? Round your ans...

5. Your friends wa... 6 states shown... Which method... Justify your...

Name _____ Date _____

Chapter E **Performance Task**

Tornado Alley

In some regions of the country, tornadoes are common, while in other regions, they are very rare. What is Tornado Alley and what percent of tornadoes occur there? When do the tornadoes occur most frequently?

Tornado Alley refers to the central region of the United States where tornadoes occur most frequently. On average, more than 500 tornadoes occur in this area each year. Most of the tornadoes occur during the spring season.

1. The table shows the average numbers of tornadoes in May and the average annual numbers of tornadoes for 6 of the states in Tornado Alley over a 25-year period. Complete the table. Round your answers for the numbers of tornadoes to the nearest whole number. Round your answers for the percents of tornadoes to the nearest tenth.

State	Average Number of Tornadoes in May	Average Annual Number of Tornadoes	Percent of Tornadoes in May
Texas	44	147	
Oklahoma		65	46.2%
Kansas		92	40.2%
Nebraska	16		29.1%
Iowa	12	49	
Colorado	11		22%

2. In Texas, the average number of tornadoes in May was about 152% of the average number of tornadoes in April. Find the average number of tornadoes that occurred in April. Round your answer to the nearest whole number. Justify your answer.

Copyright © Big Ideas Learning, LLC
All rights reserved.

Big Ideas Math: Modeling Real Life Grade 6 Advanced
Assessment Book 81

Tornado Alley

After completing this chapter, you will be able to use the concepts you learned to answer the questions in the *STEAM Video Performance Task*. You will be given information about the average annual numbers of tornadoes in several states over a 25-year period. For example:

Texas: 147

Kansas: 92

Oklahoma: 65

Iowa: 49

You will be asked to solve various percent problems about tornadoes. Why is it helpful to know the percent of tornadoes that occur in each state?

Getting Ready for Chapter 

Chapter Exploration

Work with a partner. Write the percent of the model that is shaded. Then write the percent as a decimal.

1. 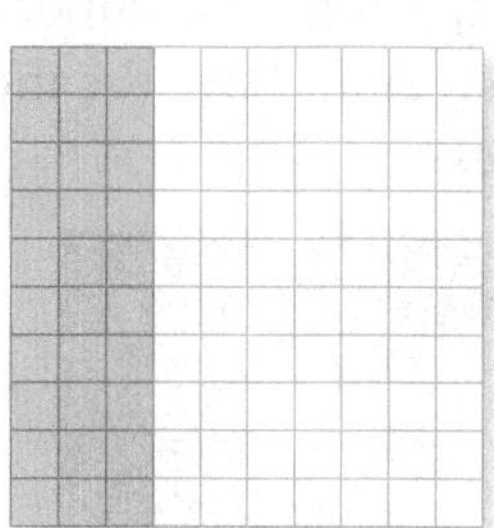

$\square\,\% = \dfrac{\square}{\square}$ ← per ← cent

$= \dfrac{\square}{\square}$ Simplify.

$= \square$ Write the fraction as a decimal.

2. 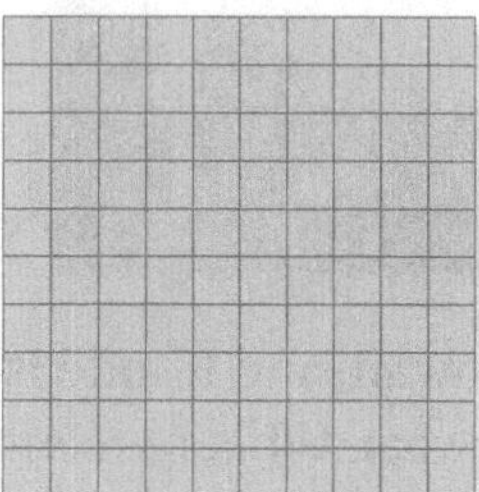

3. 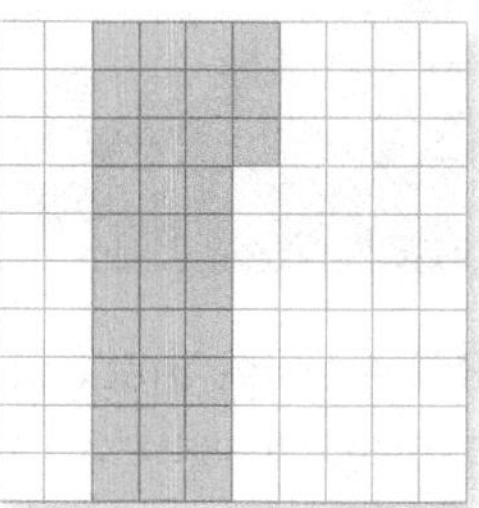

4. 

5. 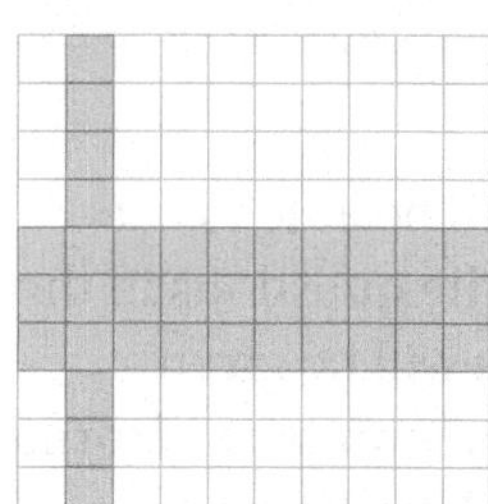

6. 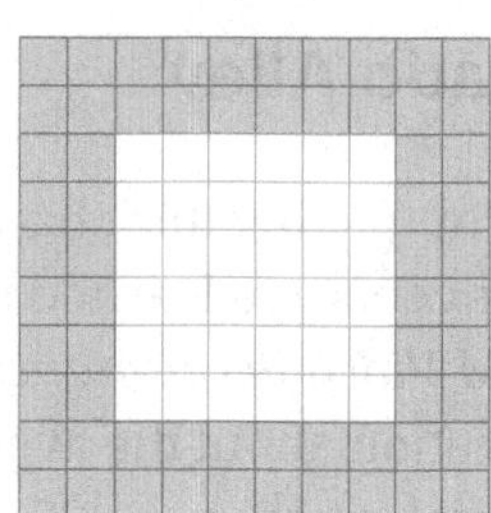

7. 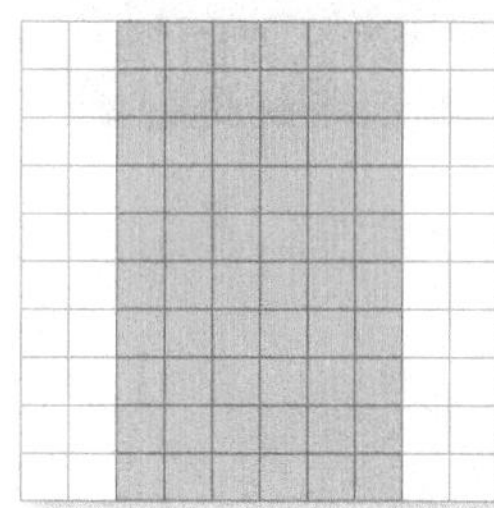

8. **WRITE A PROCEDURE** Work with a partner. Write a procedure for rewriting a percent as a decimal. Use examples to justify your procedure.

Vocabulary

The following vocabulary terms are defined in this chapter. Think about what each term might mean and record your thoughts.

percent of change	percent of decrease	discount
percent of increase	percent error	markup

Laurie's Notes

Check out the digital flash cards. **BigIdeasMath.com**

Chapter Exploration

- This exploration reviews writing and modeling percents and decimals from Chapter 4.
- Work through Exercise 1 with students.
- ? Ask, "How many squares are shaded?" 30 "How many total squares are in the model?" 100
- ? "What percent of the model is shaded?" 30% "What fraction of the model is shaded?" $\frac{30}{100} = \frac{3}{10}$ "What is $\frac{3}{10}$ as a decimal?" 0.3
- Have pairs complete Exercises 2–7 and then compare their answers with another pair. Discuss any discrepancies as a class.
- Have pairs complete Exercise 8.
- **Popsicle Sticks:** Solicit responses for Exercise 8. Have students display their examples under a document camera or at the board.

Vocabulary

- These terms represent some of the vocabulary that students will encounter in Chapter E. Discuss the terms as a class.
- Where have students heard the word *discount* outside of a math classroom? In what contexts? Students may not be able to write the actual definition, but they may write phrases associated with *discount*.
- Allowing students to discuss these terms now will prepare them for understanding the terms as they are presented in the chapter.
- When students encounter a new definition, encourage them to write in their *Student Journals*. They will revisit these definitions during the Chapter Review.

ELL Support

Point out that several of the vocabulary terms include the word *percent*. Explain that *percent* comes from the Latin language and means "by the hundred." The root word *cent* means "100" and the prefix *per–* means "by." Students whose native language is derived from Latin will likely know words for 100 that are similar, such as *cent* in French and *cein* in Spanish. Explain that when you work with percents in math, you are working with values as they relate to 100. Follow up with discussion of the terms *percent of change, percent of increase, percent of decrease*, and *percent error*.

Topics for Review

- Comparing and Ordering Integers
- Ratios
- Solving Proportions
- Writing Decimals as Fractions and Percents
- Writing Fractions as Decimals
- Writing Fractions as Percents
- Writing Percents as Fractions

Chapter Exploration

1. $30\% = \frac{30}{100} = \frac{3}{10} = 0.3$
2. $100\% = 1$
3. $33\% = 0.33$
4. $50\% = 0.5$
5. $37\% = 0.37$
6. $64\% = 0.64$
7. $60\% = 0.6$
8. *Sample answer:* 1. Write as a percent, 2. Write the percent as a fraction and simplify, 3. Write the fraction as a decimal;

   $30\% = \frac{30}{100} = \frac{3}{10} = 0.3,$

   $55\% = \frac{55}{100} = \frac{11}{20} = 0.55$

Check out the Dynamic Classroom.
BigIdeasMath.com

Learning Target

Rewrite fractions, decimals, and percents using different representations.

Success Criteria

- Write percents as decimals and decimals as percents.
- Write fractions as decimals and percents.
- Compare and order fractions, decimals, and percents.

Warm Up

Cumulative, vocabulary, and prerequisite skills practice opportunities are available in the *Resources by Chapter* or at *BigIdeasMath.com*.

ELL Support

Explain that when you represent something, you show it. The representation of a value is the way you show the value (by writing). Representations of the same value vary when you use fractions, decimals, and percents. Clarify the meaning of the word *vary*, as students may think you are saying "very." Demonstrate the same value as a fraction, decimal, and percent using $\frac{1}{2}$, 0.5, and 50%.

Exploration 1

a. 7%; *Sample answer:* convert both to decimals, $0.07 > 0.05$

b. 0.37; *Sample answer:* convert both to decimals, $0.37 > 0.\overline{3}$

c. $\frac{5}{8}$; *Sample answer:* convert both to decimals, $0.625 > 0.375$

d–e. See Additional Answers.

Exploration 2

Check students' work.

Laurie's Notes

Preparing to Teach

- Students have previously worked with decimals, fractions, and percents.
- **Reason Abstractly and Quantitatively:** In this lesson, students will convert between different representations of a number so that numbers may be compared. Mathematically proficient students would reason that $\frac{6}{11} > 0.48$ because $\frac{6}{11} > \frac{1}{2}$ and $\frac{1}{2} > 0.48$.

Motivate

- Write each number on an index card: $\frac{1}{10}$, $\frac{13}{20}$, $\frac{4}{5}$, 0.18, 0.45, 0.5, 35%, 60%, 85%.
- Hand out the 9 cards. Ask the 3 students holding fraction cards to stand in order (least to greatest). Then ask the 3 students holding decimal cards and the 3 students holding percent cards to do the same.
- Have each group of students describe the strategies for ordering themselves.
- Now ask all 9 students to order themselves.
- Discuss strategies used when all 3 forms are used in the same problem.

Exploration 1

- It might be helpful to review repeating decimals from Section B.3.
- Remind students of the conversion triangle. Today they will work with all 3 forms.
- Students may be able to use number sense in their comparisons. In part (c), they may reason that $\frac{5}{8} > \frac{1}{2}$ and $0.375 < \frac{1}{2}$, so $\frac{5}{8} > 0.375$.

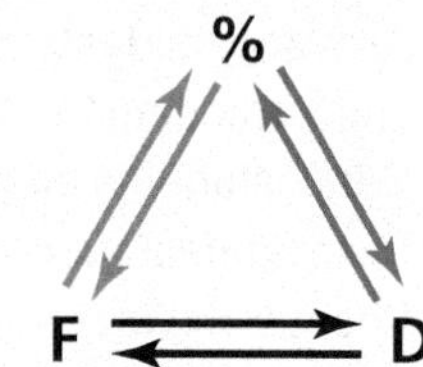
%
F
D

? "Which fractions in the exploration are repeating decimals?" Listen for knowledge that thirds and sixths are repeating decimals.

- **Common Error:** Students who do not have a good understanding of how to convert a fraction to a decimal may take simple fractions such as $\frac{1}{20}$ and write 1.20 or 0.120. For $\frac{1}{3}$, they write 1.3 or 0.13.

Exploration 2

- **Make Sense of Problems and Persevere in Solving Them:** Point out the Math Practice note. Before students begin the exploration, they should share strategies for ordering numbers. Listen for key understanding, such as looking for numbers greater than or less than a certain number or converting all numbers to decimals.
- You may need to guide students to choose reasonable numbers. You might suggest ranges for the numbers, such as 0% to 100% and 0 to 1.
- This is an opportunity for students to review conversion skills. It also provides an informal assessment to help guide instruction in the sections ahead.

E.1 Fractions, Decimals, and Percents

Learning Target: Rewrite fractions, decimals, and percents using different representations.

Success Criteria:
- I can write percents as decimals and decimals as percents.
- I can write fractions as decimals and percents.
- I can compare and order fractions, decimals, and percents.

EXPLORATION 1 Comparing Numbers in Different Forms

Work with a partner. Determine which number is greater. Explain your method.

a. 7% sales tax or $\frac{1}{20}$ sales tax

b. 0.37 cup of flour or $\frac{1}{3}$ cup of flour

c. $\frac{5}{8}$-inch wrench or 0.375-inch wrench

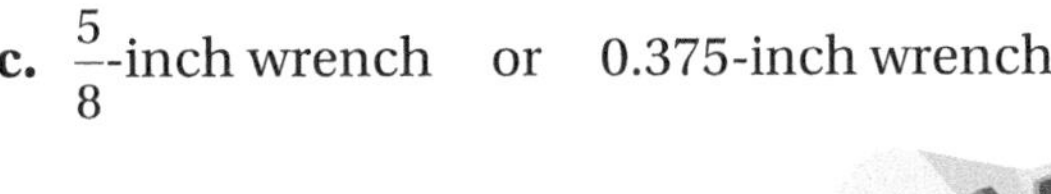

d. $12\frac{3}{5}$ dollars or 12.56 dollars

e. $5\frac{5}{6}$ fluid ounces or 5.6 fluid ounces

Toothpaste

EXPLORATION 2 Ordering Fractions, Decimals, and Percents

Work with a partner and follow the steps below.

- Write five different numbers on individual slips of paper. Include at least one decimal, one fraction, and one percent.
- On a separate sheet of paper, create an answer key that shows your numbers written from least to greatest.
- Exchange slips of paper with another group and race to order the numbers from least to greatest. Then exchange answer keys to check your orders.

Math Practice

Make a Plan

Make a plan to order the numbers. How might having a plan help you to order numbers quickly?

E.1 Lesson

Key Ideas

Writing Percents as Decimals

Words Remove the percent symbol. Then divide by 100, which moves the decimal point two places to the left.

Numbers $82\% = 82.\% = 0.82$ $2.\overline{45}\% = 02.\overline{45}\% = 0.02\overline{45}$

Remember

Bar notation indicates one or more repeating digits.

Writing Decimals as Percents

Words Multiply by 100, which moves the decimal point two places to the right. Then add a percent symbol.

Numbers $0.47 = 0.47 = 47\%$ $0.\overline{2} = 0.222\ldots = 22.\overline{2}\%$

EXAMPLE 1 Converting Between Percents and Decimals

Write each percent as a decimal or each decimal as a percent. Use a model to represent each number.

a. $61\% = 61.\% = 0.61$

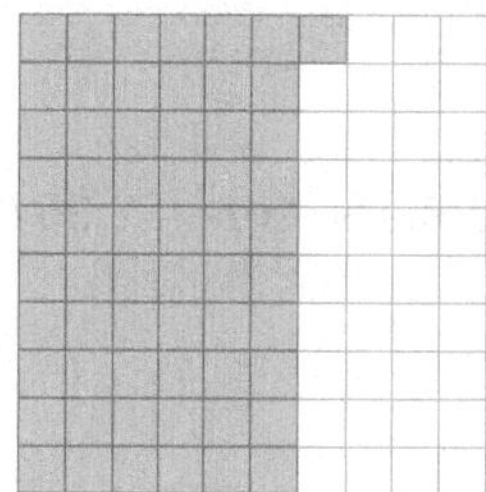

b. $8\% = 08.\% = 0.08$

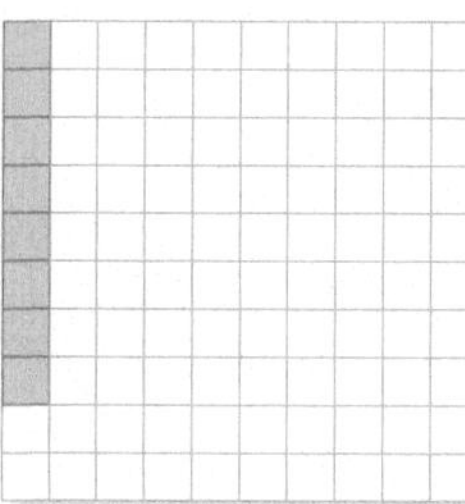

c. $0.27 = 0.27 = 27\%$

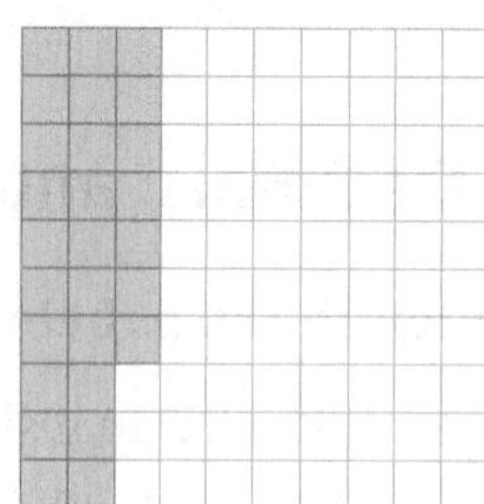

d. $0.\overline{3} = 0.333\ldots = 33.\overline{3}\%$

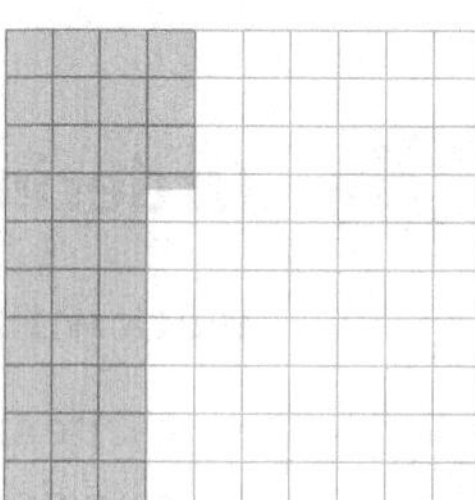

Try It **Write the percent as a decimal or the decimal as a percent. Use a model to represent the number.**

1. 39% **2.** $12.\overline{6}\%$ **3.** 0.05 **4.** 1.25

Laurie's Notes

Scaffolding Instruction

- In the exploration, students reviewed converting fractions, decimals, and percents. They also reviewed how to order numbers in all three forms. Now students will extend their understanding of comparing and ordering to less common fractions, decimals, and percents (including repeating decimals).
- **Emerging:** Students may lack confidence in moving between the three forms of numbers and will benefit from guided instruction for the examples.
- **Proficient:** Students move between the three forms with ease and order numbers accurately. After reviewing the Key Ideas, students should complete the Try It exercises and then proceed to the Self-Assessment exercises.

Key Ideas

◉ "Write a percent between 75% and 90%. Write the percent as a fraction and decimal." *Sample answer:* 85%, $\frac{17}{20}$, 0.85

- To reinforce the meaning behind moving the decimal point, say, "82 percent, 82 per one hundred, or 82 hundredths."
- **Connection:** Dividing by 100 is equivalent to multiplying by 0.01. The decimal point moves 2 places to the left. Multiplying by 100 is equivalent to dividing by 0.01. The decimal point moves 2 places to the right.
- Tell students that they can convert between repeating decimals and percents in the same as they did with terminating decimals and percents.

EXAMPLE 1

- Work through each part with students.
- Remind students that when moving the decimal point, it may be necessary to place one or more zeros in the number, as in part (b). Have students show the multiplication by 0.01.
- The models help students visualize the numbers. Explain that the models for repeating decimals, are not expected to be exact, but they should demonstrate understanding.

Try It

- **Think-Pair-Share:** Students should read each exercise independently and then work in pairs to complete the exercises. Then have each pair compare their answers with another group and discuss any discrepancies.
- Remind students that the model for Exercise 2 will be an approximation.

ELL Support

After demonstrating Example 1, have students work in groups to complete Try It Exercises 1–4. Provide them with guiding questions: Is the number a decimal or a percent? To which form must you change it? How do you make the change? Expect students to perform according to their language levels.

Beginner: Write the steps and provide one-word answers.

Intermediate: Use simple sentences such as, "Change it to a decimal."

Advanced: Use detailed sentences and help guide discussion.

Scaffold instruction to support all students in their learning. Learning is individualized and you may want to group students differently as they move in and out of these levels with each skill and concept. Student self-assessment and feedback help guide your instructional decisions about how and when to layer support for all students to become proficient learners.

Extra Example 1

Write each percent as a decimal or each decimal as a percent. Use a model to represent each number.

a. 56% 0.56

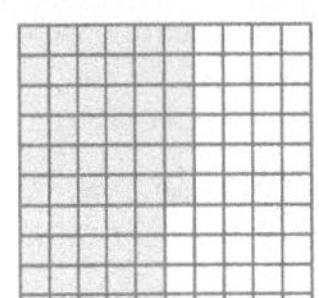

b. 5% 0.05

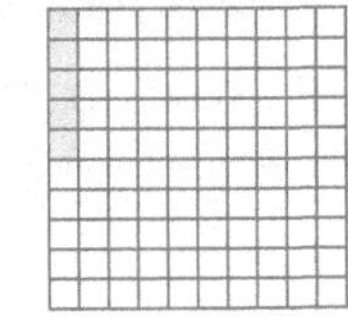

c. 0.77 77%

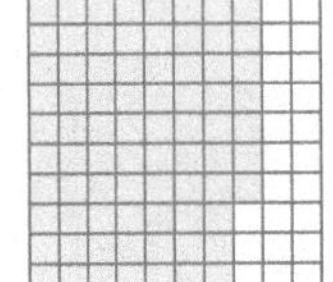

d. $0.\overline{6}$ $66.\overline{6}\%$

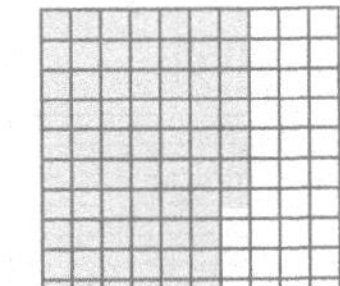

Try It

1. 0.39

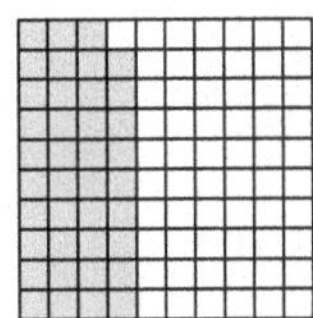

2. 0.126

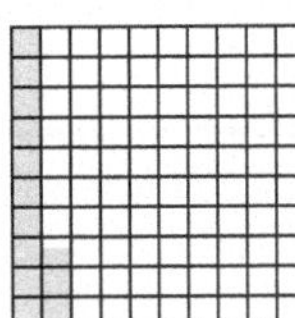

3. 5%

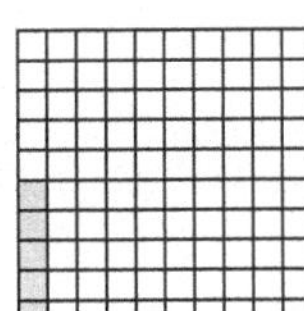

4. See Additional Answers.

Extra Example 2

Write each fraction as a decimal and a percent.

a. $\frac{13}{20}$ 0.65; 65%

b. $\frac{13}{9}$ $1.\overline{4}$; $144.\overline{4}$%

Try It

5. 0.625, 62.5%
6. $0.1\overline{6}$, $16.\overline{6}$%
7. $3.\overline{6}$, $366.\overline{6}$%
8. 0.003, 0.3%

Self-Assessment for Concepts & Skills

9. 0.46

10. $0.\overline{6}$

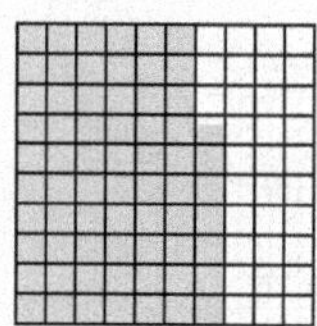

11. 18%

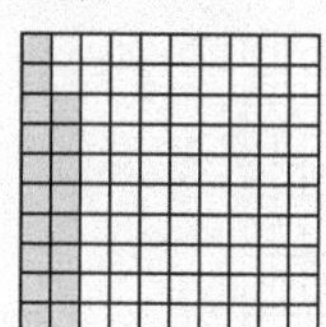

12. See Additional Answers.
13. 0.7, 70%
14. $0.\overline{5}$, $55.\overline{5}$%
15. 0.0035, 0.35%
16. $1.1\overline{3}$, $113.\overline{3}$%

Laurie's Notes

EXAMPLE 2

- Work through both parts as shown.
- ? "How will you decide whether to write an equivalent fraction or use long division when writing a fraction as a decimal?" *Sample answer:* If the fraction can be written as an equivalent fraction with a denominator of 100, use equivalent fractions. Otherwise, use long division.
- You may want to point out that only denominators composed of factors of 2 and 5 will terminate.
- If students need help converting fractions to decimals, you may want to review long division from Section B.3.

Try It

- **Think-Pair-Share:** Students should read each exercise independently and then work in pairs to complete the exercises. Then have each pair compare their answers with another group and discuss any discrepancies.

Self-Assessment for Concepts & Skills

- **Neighbor Check:** Have students work independently and then have their neighbors check their work. Have students discuss any discrepancies.
- Using *Partner Speaks*, have students explain how to convert decimals, fractions, and percents.

ELL Support

Allow students to work in pairs for extra support and to practice language. After completing the exercises, have pairs display their answers on whiteboards for your review.

The Success Criteria Self-Assessment chart can be found in the *Student Journal* or online at *BigIdeasMath.com.*

EXAMPLE 2 Writing Fractions as Decimals and Percents

Remember

For a fraction with a denominator of 100, $\frac{n}{100} = n\%$.

Write each fraction as a decimal and a percent.

a. $\frac{4}{5}$

$$\frac{4}{5} = \frac{4 \times 20}{5 \times 20} = \frac{80}{100} = 80\% = 0.8$$

So, $\frac{4}{5}$ can be written as 0.8 or 80%.

b. $\frac{15}{11}$

Use long division to divide 15 by 11.

$$\frac{15}{11} = 1.\overline{36}$$

$$\begin{array}{r} 1.3636 \\ 11\overline{)15.0000} \\ -\underline{11} \\ 40 \\ -\underline{33} \\ 70 \\ -\underline{66} \\ 40 \\ -\underline{33} \\ 70 \\ -\underline{66} \\ 4 \end{array}$$

Write $1.\overline{36}$ as a percent.

$$1.\overline{36} = 1.3636\ldots = 136.\overline{36}\%$$

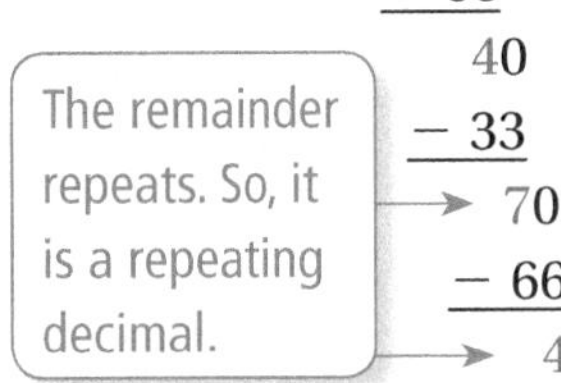

The remainder repeats. So, it is a repeating decimal.

So, $\frac{15}{11}$ can be written as $1.\overline{36}$ or $136.\overline{36}\%$.

Try It **Write the fraction as a decimal and a percent.**

5. $\frac{5}{8}$ **6.** $\frac{1}{6}$ **7.** $\frac{11}{3}$ **8.** $\frac{3}{1000}$

Self-Assessment for Concepts & Skills

Solve each exercise. Then rate your understanding of the success criteria in your journal.

CONVERTING BETWEEN PERCENTS AND DECIMALS **Write the percent as a decimal or the decimal as a percent. Use a model to represent the number.**

9. 46% **10.** $66.\overline{6}\%$ **11.** 0.18 **12.** $2.\overline{3}$

WRITING FRACTIONS AS DECIMALS AND PERCENTS **Write the fraction as a decimal and a percent.**

13. $\frac{7}{10}$ **14.** $\frac{5}{9}$

15. $\frac{7}{2000}$ **16.** $\frac{17}{15}$

EXAMPLE 3 Modeling Real Life

An ice rink is open December through February. The table shows the attendance each month as a portion of the total attendance. How many times more guests visit the ice rink in the busiest month than in the least busy month?

Month	December	January	February
Portion of Guests	0.72	$\frac{3}{25}$	16%

Write $\frac{3}{25}$ and 16% as decimals.

January: $\frac{3}{25} = \frac{12}{100} = 0.12$ **February:** $16\% = 16.\% = 0.16$

The busiest month was December, the second busiest month was February, and the least busy month was January. So, divide 0.72 by 0.12.

$$0.12\overline{)0.72} \longrightarrow 12\overline{)72.} \quad 6. \quad -72 \quad 0$$

Multiply each number by 100.

So, 6 times more guests visit the ice rink in the busiest month than in the least busy month.

Self-Assessment for Problem Solving

Solve each exercise. Then rate your understanding of the success criteria in your journal.

17. An astronaut spends 53% of the day working, 0.1 of the day eating, $\frac{3}{10}$ of the day sleeping, and the rest of the day exercising. Order the events by duration from least to greatest. Justify your answer.

18. **DIG DEEPER!** A band plays one concert in Arizona, one concert in California, and one concert in Georgia. In California, the band earned $\frac{3}{2}$ the profit that they earned in Arizona. Of the total profit earned by the band, 32% is earned in Arizona. How many times more money did the band earn at the most profitable concert than at the least profitable concert? Justify your answer.

Laurie's Notes

EXAMPLE 3

- Ask a student to read the problem. Then ask another to explain what the question is asking.
- Ask students to review the table. Allow time for them to think before asking volunteers to explain what it represents.
- Some students may want to just start doing anything. They need to take time to think about the process.

? **Teaching Strategy:** "What is your plan? What do you need to do to answer the question?" *Sample answer:* Write the numbers in the same form.

- **Another Method:** You could convert all of the numbers to percents and then compare the numbers.
- Remind students to check that they have answered the question and to write a summary sentence.

Self-Assessment for Problem Solving

- Encourage students to use a Four Square to complete these exercises. Until students become comfortable with the problem-solving plan, they may only be ready to complete the first square.
- Students should work independently on the first two squares of each exercise. Then each student should compare his or her squares with a neighbor's squares and discuss any discrepancies. Have students complete the last two squares of each exercise independently.
- Have students use *Fist of Five* to indicate their understanding of the success criteria.

The Success Criteria Self-Assessment chart can be found in the *Student Journal* or online at *BigIdeasMath.com*.

Closure

- Complete the table of common fractions, decimals, and percents.

Fraction	$\frac{1}{4}$	$\frac{3}{10}$	$\frac{1}{2}$	$\frac{2}{5}$	$\frac{1}{20}$	$\frac{3}{20}$	$\frac{7}{10}$	$\frac{3}{4}$	$\frac{1}{5}$	1
Decimal	0.25	0.3	0.5	0.4	0.05	0.15	0.7	0.75	0.2	1
Percent	25%	30%	50%	40%	5%	15%	70%	75%	20%	100%

Teaching Strategy

The Math Practice note on page 679 tells students to make a plan. It is important to encourage students to think before they leap. Often students want to just jump in and start doing anything rather than carefully considering the problem and making a plan. Remind students to "work smarter, not harder."

Extra Example 3

A beach store is open June through August. The table shows the profit each month as a portion of the total profit. How many times more money did the store earn in the most profitable month than in the least profitable month?

Month	June	July	August
Portion of Profit	0.18	54%	$\frac{7}{25}$

3 times more

Self-Assessment for Problem Solving

17. exercising, eating, sleeping, working;
$0.07 < 0.1 < 0.3 < 0.53$

18. See Additional Answers.

Learning Target

Rewrite fractions, decimals, and percents using different representations.

Success Criteria

- Write percents as decimals and decimals as percents.
- Write fractions as decimals and percents.
- Compare and order fractions, decimals, and percents.

Review & Refresh

1. 4.5 in. 2. 75 ft
3. $10p - 12$ 4. $-7n - 3$ 5. D

Concepts, Skills, & Problem Solving

6. $4\frac{2}{5}$; *Sample answer:* convert both to decimals, $4.4 > 4.3$
7. $\frac{5}{6}$; *Sample answer:* convert both to decimals, $0.8\overline{3} > 0.82$
8. 0.26

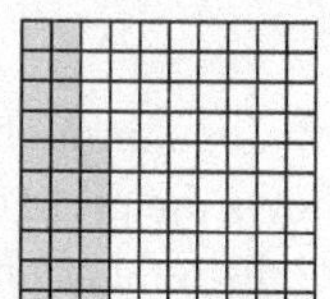

9. 63%

10. 0.09

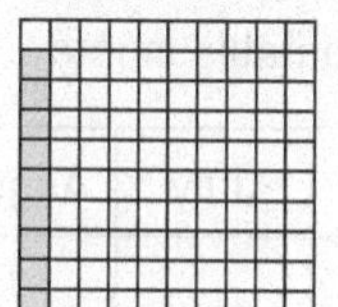

11. 60%

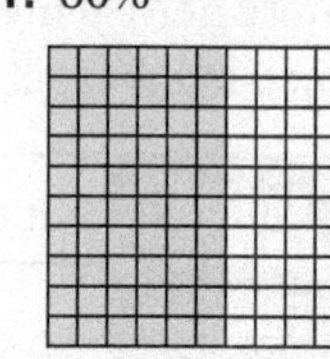

12. 0.447

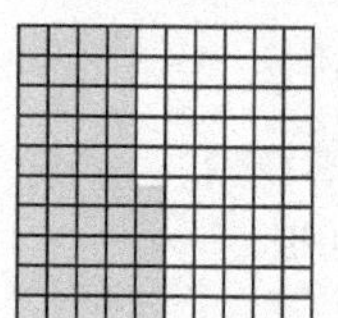

13. 0.55

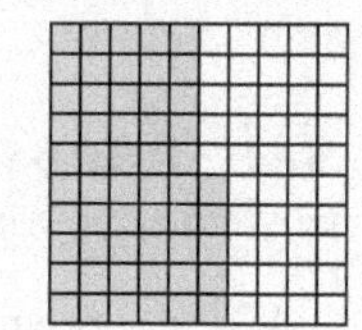

14. $0.39\overline{2}$

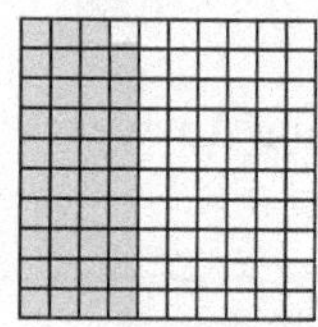

15–19. See Additional Answers.
20. no; When converting a percent to a decimal, move the decimal 2 places to the left.
21. 0.29, 29% 22. 0.75, 75%
23. 0.875, 87.5% 24. $0.\overline{6}$, $66.\overline{6}\%$
25. $0.\overline{7}$, $77.\overline{7}\%$ 26. 2.4, 240%
27. 4.5, 450% 28. 0.001, 0.1%
29. $2.8\overline{3}$, $283.\overline{3}\%$ 30. $0.\overline{27}$, $27.\overline{27}\%$
31. $0.00\overline{13}$, $0.\overline{13}\%$ 32. $2.\overline{4}$, $244.\overline{4}\%$

Check out the Dynamic Assessment System.
BigIdeasMath.com

Assignment Guide and Concept Check

Scaffold assignments to support all students in their learning progression. The suggested assignments are a starting point. Continue to assign additional exercises and revisit with spaced practice to move every student toward proficiency.

Level	Assignment 1	Assignment 2
Emerging	2, 4, 5, 6, 8, 9, 14, 15, 20, 21, 22, 24, 26, 33	16, 17, 19, 28, 32, 34, 35, 36, 37, 38, 39, 40, 41, 43
Proficient	2, 4, 5, 6, 13, 15, 16, 20, 25, 26, 28, 29, 33	17, 19, 30, 31, 34, 35, 36, 37, 38, 39, 40, 41, 43
Advanced	2, 4, 5, 6, 16, 17, 19, 20, 26, 30, 31, 32, 33	34, 35, 36, 37, 38, 40, 41, 42, 43, 44

- Assignment 1 is for use after students complete the Self-Assessment for Concepts & Skills.
- Assignment 2 is for use after students complete the Self-Assessment for Problem Solving.
- The red exercises can be used as a concept check.

Review & Refresh Prior Skills

Exercises 1 and 2 Using a Scale
Exercises 3 and 4 Simplifying Expressions
Exercise 5 Solving a Two-Step Inequality

Common Errors

- **Exercises 8, 10, 12–14, 16, and 19** Students may write the percent as a fraction using the wrong denominator, or try to remove the decimal point when writing it over 100. For example, a student may write $\frac{775}{100}$ instead of $\frac{77.5}{100}$. Ask students how many percents are in one whole (100). Remind students that the denominator represents the whole and the denominator will always be 100. Tell students that the number to the left of the percent symbol will be the numerator.
- **Exercises 9, 11, 15, 17, and 18** Students may move the decimal point the wrong way, forget to place zeros as placeholders, or move the decimal point too many places. Remind students that when writing a decimal as a percent, they need to multiply the decimal by 100 and then add the percent symbol.
- **Exercises 21–32** Students may not know when it is appropriate to use an equivalent fraction to write a fraction as a percent. Brainstorm some denominators that are easily rewritten as denominators of 100, such as 4, 5, 10, 20, and 25.

E.1 Practice

Go to *BigIdeasMath.com* to get HELP with solving the exercises.

Review & Refresh

Find the missing dimension. Use the scale 1 : 15.

	Item	Model	Actual
1.	Figure skater	Height: ___ in.	Height: 67.5 in.
2.	Pipe	Length: 5 ft	Length: ___ ft

Simplify the expression.

3. $2(3p - 6) + 4p$

4. $5n - 3(4n + 1)$

5. What is the solution of $2n - 4 > -12$?

A. $n < -10$ **B.** $n < -4$ **C.** $n > -2$ **D.** $n > -4$

Concepts, Skills, & Problem Solving

COMPARING NUMBERS IN DIFFERENT FORMS **Determine which number is greater. Explain your method.** (See Exploration 1, p. 679.)

6. $4\frac{2}{5}$ tons or 4.3 tons

7. 82% success rate or $\frac{5}{6}$ success rate

CONVERTING BETWEEN PERCENTS AND DECIMALS **Write the percent as a decimal or the decimal as a percent. Use a model to represent the number.**

8. 26%

9. 0.63

10. 9%

11. 0.6

12. 44.7%

13. 55%

14. $39.\overline{2}\%$

15. 3.554

16. 123%

17. 0.041

18. 0.122

19. $49.\overline{92}\%$

20. MP **YOU BE THE TEACHER** Your friend writes $4.\overline{8}\%$ as a decimal. Is your friend correct? Explain your reasoning.

$4.\overline{8}\% = 4.888\ldots\% = 488.\overline{8}$

WRITING FRACTIONS AS DECIMALS AND PERCENTS **Write the fraction as a decimal and a percent.**

21. $\frac{29}{100}$

22. $\frac{3}{4}$

23. $\frac{7}{8}$

24. $\frac{2}{3}$

25. $\frac{7}{9}$

26. $\frac{12}{5}$

27. $\frac{9}{2}$

28. $\frac{1}{1000}$

29. $\frac{17}{6}$

30. $\frac{3}{11}$

31. $\frac{1}{750}$

32. $\frac{22}{9}$

MP PRECISION **Order the numbers from least to greatest.**

33. 66.1%, 0.66, $\frac{2}{3}$, 0.667

34. $\frac{2}{9}$, 21%, $0.2\overline{1}$, $\frac{11}{50}$

MATCHING **Tell which letter shows the graph of the number.**

35. $\frac{7}{9}$

36. 0.812

37. $\frac{5}{6}$

38. 79.5%

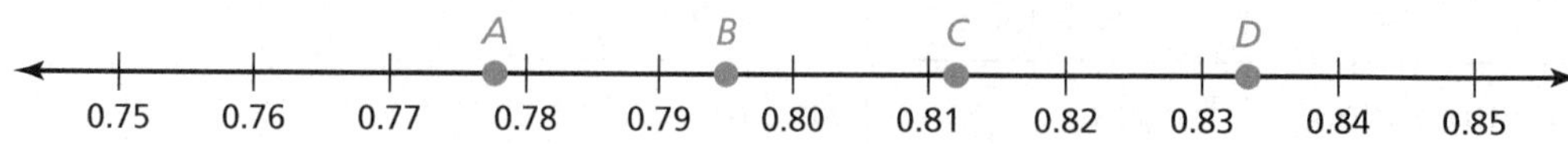

39. **MP PROBLEM SOLVING** The table shows the portion of students in each grade that participate in School Spirit Week. Order the grades by portion of participation from least to greatest.

Grade	Participation
6	0.64
7	$\frac{3}{5}$
8	65%

40. **MP MODELING REAL LIFE** The table shows the portion of gold medals that were won by the United States in five summer Olympic games. In what year did the United States win the least portion of gold medals? the greatest portion? Justify your answers.

Year	2000	2004	2008	2012	2016
Portion of Gold Medals Won	$12.\overline{3}\%$	$\frac{36}{301}$	$0.\overline{12}$	$\frac{23}{150}$	$\frac{46}{307}$

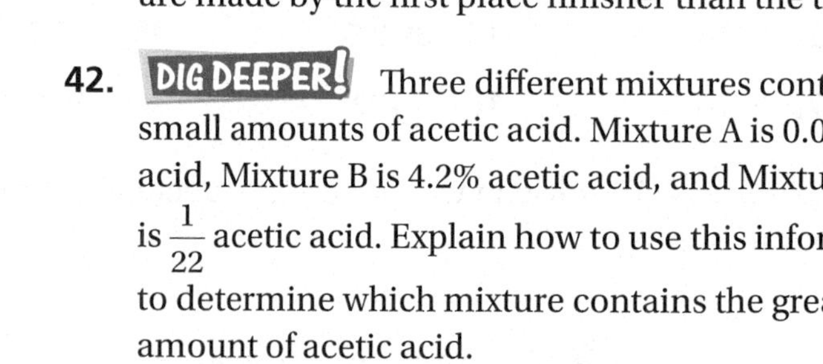

41. **MP PROBLEM SOLVING** You, your friend, and your cousin have a basketball competition where each person attempts the same number of shots. You make 70% of your shots, your friend makes $\frac{7}{9}$ of her shots, and your cousin makes $0.7\overline{2}$ of his shots. How many times more shots are made by the first place finisher than the third place finisher?

42. **DIG DEEPER!** Three different mixtures contain small amounts of acetic acid. Mixture A is 0.036 acetic acid, Mixture B is 4.2% acetic acid, and Mixture C is $\frac{1}{22}$ acetic acid. Explain how to use this information to determine which mixture contains the greatest amount of acetic acid.

43. **MP MODELING REAL LIFE** Over 44% of the 30 students in a class read a book last month. What are the possible numbers of students in the class who read a book last month? Justify your answer.

44. **MP NUMBER SENSE** Fill in the blanks using each of the numbers 0–7 exactly once, so that the percent, decimal, and fraction below are ordered from least to greatest. Justify your answer.

$\square\square.\square\%$ $\quad$ $\square.\square\square$ $\quad$ $\frac{\square}{\square}$

Common Errors

- **Exercises 33 and 34** Students may try to order the numbers without converting them or will only convert them mentally and do so incorrectly. Tell them that it is necessary to convert all the numbers to one form and that they should write out the steps to make sure that they are converting correctly.
- **Exercises 33 and 34** Students may try to round the numbers that have repeating decimals and incorrectly order the numbers. Remind them that even though you often round repeating decimals, the decimal is actually less than or greater than the rounded decimal. For example, $0.\overline{6}$ is less than 0.667, but greater than 0.666.

Mini-Assessment

1. Write 12% as a decimal. 0.12
2. Write 2.25 as a percent. 225%
3. Write $\frac{5}{11}$ as a decimal and a percent. $0.\overline{45}$; $45.\overline{45}$%
4. Order the numbers from least to greatest.
   0.334, $\frac{1}{3}$, 33.3%, 0.33
   0.33, 33.3%, $\frac{1}{3}$, 0.334
5. You, your friend, and your cousin have a soccer competition where each person attempts the same number of shots. You make 84% of your shots, your friend makes 0.72 of his shots, and your cousin makes $\frac{9}{11}$ of her shots. How many times more shots are made by the first place finisher than the third place finisher? $1.1\overline{6}$ times more

Section Resources

Surface Level	Deep Level
Resources by Chapter • Extra Practice • Reteach • Puzzle Time Student Journal • Self-Assessment • Practice Differentiating the Lesson Tutorial Videos Skills Review Handbook Skills Trainer	Resources by Chapter • Enrichment and Extension Graphic Organizers Dynamic Assessment System • Section Practice

Concepts, Skills, & Problem Solving

33. 0.66, 66.1%, $\frac{2}{3}$, 0.667
34. 21%, $0.2\overline{1}$, $\frac{11}{50}$, $\frac{2}{9}$
35. A
36. C
37. D
38. B
39. Grade 7, Grade 6, Grade 8
40. 2004; 2012; $0.1196 < 0.\overline{12} < 0.12\overline{3} < 0.1498 < 0.15\overline{3}$
41. $1.\overline{1}$ times more shots
42. *Sample answer:* Convert all mixture amounts into decimals; $0.0\overline{45} > 0.042 > 0.036$; Mixture C contains the greatest amount of acetic acid.
43. 14 or more students; $0.44 \times 30 = 13.2$. Because 13.2 is a decimal and over 44% of students read a book last month, round the value up to 14.
44. *Sample answer:* 14.5%, 0.32, $\frac{6}{7}$

Check out the
Dynamic Classroom.
BigIdeasMath.com

Learning Target

Use the percent proportion to find missing quantities.

Success Criteria

- Write proportions to represent percent problems.
- Solve a proportion to find a percent, a part, or a whole.

Warm Up

Cumulative, vocabulary, and prerequisite skills practice opportunities are available in the *Resources by Chapter* or at *BigIdeasMath.com*.

ELL Support

Remind students that a ratio is a comparison of two quantities and a proportion is an equation stating that the values of two ratios are equivalent. A proportion can be used to describe the relationship between a scale drawing and the object it represents. When a ratio is represented by a percent, it can be written as the percent compared to 100.

Exploration 1

a. 50%; 15; percents of 30

20%; 60%; 30; 60; percents of 75

$33\frac{1}{3}\%$; $66\frac{2}{3}\%$; 24; 48; 72; percents of 72

b. 15; 20%; 72

c. See Additional Answers.

d. *Sample answer:* 40% of 75 is what number?; 30

Laurie's Notes

Preparing to Teach

- Students should know how to solve simple percent problems and how to use ratio tables. They will build upon this understanding to write and solve percent proportions.
- **Reason Abstractly and Quantitatively:** In this lesson, students use the concept of a proportion to solve different types of percent problems. The percent bar models and ratio tables help build students' reasoning with visual and numeric displays.

Motivate

- Share with students that sometimes their thinking can get "scrambled up" while solving percent problems, so an egg model is a good way to introduce the lesson!

? Use an egg carton to help students visualize a few simple percent problems.
  - "What is 75% of 12?" 9
  - "3 is what percent of 12?" 25%
  - "12 is 50% of what number?" 24

Exploration 1

- **Use Appropriate Tools Strategically:** If students have an understanding of fractional parts of a whole, the percent bar model is an effective tool for estimating an answer or judging the reasonableness of an answer.
- The length of the bar is 100%, the whole. Percents near 50% are about $\frac{1}{2}$ of the whole.
- Students should be able to judge percents near 25% $\left(\frac{1}{4}\right)$ and 75% $\left(\frac{3}{4}\right)$.
- When students have finished part (a), draw each model on the board and have volunteers share their answers. Students should recognize that the models show percents of 30, 75, and 72.
- Have students complete the remaining parts with their partners.
- When discussing part (b), remind students that these are approximations. Check for reasonableness in their approximations. For example, 40% is closer to 50% than 25%.
- Part (c) may take more time. Students may have difficulty determining how to use a proportion. Remind them that $\frac{\text{part}}{\text{whole}} = \text{percent}$.
- After pairs have answered part (c), discuss their ideas as a class. Have several pairs share their examples on the board or under a document camera.
- Ask several students to share their questions in part (d) with the class.

E.2 The Percent Proportion

Learning Target: Use the percent proportion to find missing quantities.

Success Criteria:
- I can write proportions to represent percent problems.
- I can solve a proportion to find a percent, a part, or a whole.

EXPLORATION 1 Using Percent Models

Work with a partner.

a. Complete each model. Explain what each model represents.

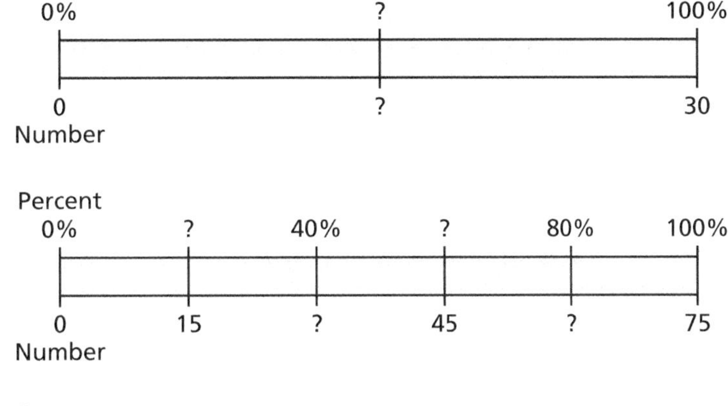

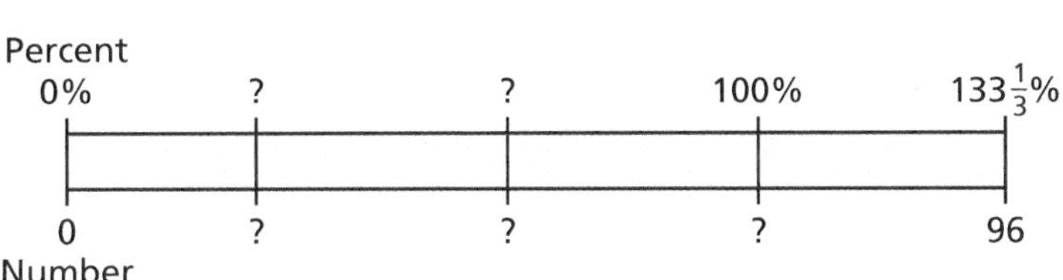

> **Math Practice**
>
> **Use a Model**
> What quantities are given in each model? How can you use these quantities to answer the questions in part (b)?

b. Use the models in part (a) to answer each question.

- What number is 50% of 30?
- 15 is what percent of 75?
- 96 is $133\frac{1}{3}\%$ of what number?

c. How can you use ratio tables to check your answers in part (b)? How can you use proportions? Provide examples to support your reasoning.

d. Write a question different from those in part (b) that can be answered using one of the models in part (a). Trade questions with another group and find the solution.

Key Idea

The Percent Proportion

Words You can represent "a is p percent of w" with the proportion

$$\frac{a}{w} = \frac{p}{100}$$

where a is part of the whole w, and $p\%$, or $\frac{p}{100}$, is the percent.

Numbers 3 out of 4 is 75%.

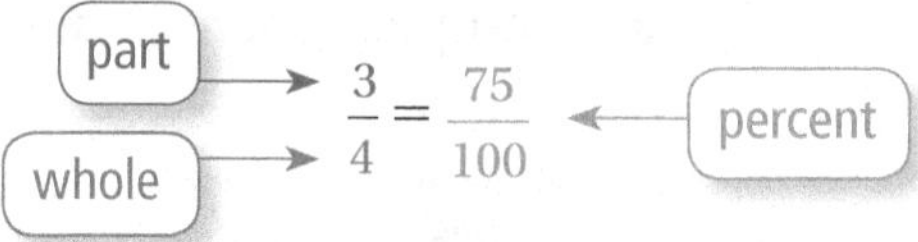

$$\frac{3}{4} = \frac{75}{100}$$

In percent problems, the word *of* is usually followed by the whole.

EXAMPLE 1 Finding a Percent

What percent of 15 is 12?

$\frac{a}{w} = \frac{p}{100}$ Write the percent proportion.

$\frac{12}{15} = \frac{p}{100}$ Substitute 12 for a and 15 for w.

$100 \cdot \frac{12}{15} = 100 \cdot \frac{p}{100}$ Multiplication Property of Equality

$80 = p$ Simplify.

So, 80% of 15 is 12.

Math Practice

Use a Table

Show how to use a ratio table to find the percent.

Check Use a model to check your answer.

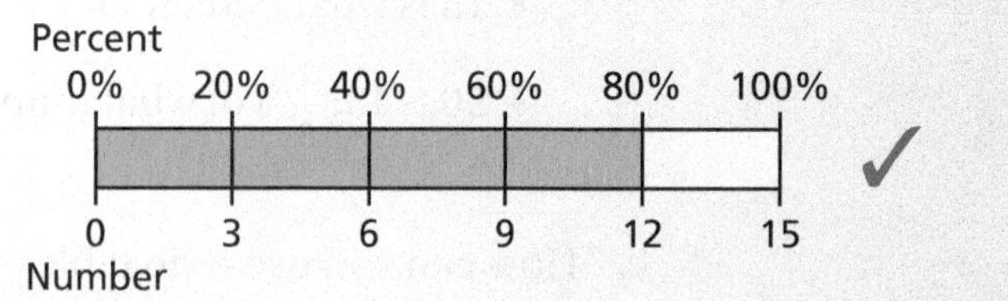

Try It **Write and solve a proportion to answer the question.**

1. What percent of 5 is 3?
2. 24 is what percent of 20?

Laurie's Notes

Scaffolding Instruction

- In the exploration, students developed their number sense by using percent bar models to find percents of wholes and missing percents. They will now use the percent proportion to solve three types of percent problems.
- **Emerging:** Students may still be developing their confidence in converting between fractions, decimals, and percents. Visual representations of the percent problems will support their understanding. Working through each example and making sense of the models is necessary.
- **Proficient:** Students may be confident using a percent bar model to represent a percent problem. Can they use an equation to represent the problem? After reviewing the Key Idea, have students self-assess using the Try It and Self-Assessment exercises.

Key Idea

- Students may need to review the meaning of the vocabulary: *part, whole*, and *percent*. Use the percent bar models from the exploration to demonstrate.
- Begin each example by establishing which variable you are asked to find in the proportion and which variables are given.
- **Reason Abstractly and Quantitatively:** In all of the examples, draw a percent bar model off to the side to help student reasoning. The model helps students estimate and consider the reasonableness of the answers.

EXAMPLE 1

? "Which variable are you asked to find?" p "Which variables are given?" a and w

? "What is the whole?" 15 "What is the part?" 12

? "Is 12 more or less than 50% of 15?" more than

- Set up the percent proportion, substitute the known quantities, and solve.

? "What other strategies could be used to solve the proportion?" *Sample answer:* Simplify $\frac{12}{15} = \frac{4}{5}$, write $\frac{4}{5}$ as a fraction with 100 in the denominator $\left(\frac{80}{100}\right)$, and then write $\frac{80}{100}$ as a percent.

- Point out the Math Practice note. Students need to be familiar with both tables and percent bar models. Because the part and the whole are known and the problem is asking for the percent, you want the whole to be 100. Remind students that although they may be able to solve the problem without making a percent bar model or a ratio table, they are learning a process.

Try It

- Have students solve these exercises on whiteboards before sharing with the class.

Scaffold instruction to support all students in their learning. Learning is individualized and you may want to group students differently as they move in and out of these levels with each skill and concept. Student self-assessment and feedback help guide your instructional decisions about how and when to layer support for all students to become proficient learners.

Extra Example 1

What percent of 20 is 8? 40%

ELL Support

After demonstrating Example 1, have students work in groups to complete Try It Exercises 1 and 2. Provide students with questions to guide their work: How do you write a proportion? How do you solve the proportion? What are the steps? Expect students to perform according to their language levels.

Beginner: Write the steps and provide one-word answers.

Intermediate: Use phrases or simple sentences such as, "Write the percent proportion $\frac{a}{w} = \frac{p}{100}$."

Advanced: Use detailed sentences and help guide discussion.

Try It

1. $\frac{3}{5} = \frac{p}{100}$; $p = 60$
2. $\frac{24}{20} = \frac{p}{100}$; $p = 120$

Extra Example 2

What number is 45% of 80? 36

Try It

3. $\frac{a}{60} = \frac{80}{100}$; $a = 48$

4. $\frac{a}{40.5} = \frac{10}{100}$; $a = 4.05$

Extra Example 3

210% of what number is 84? 40

Try It

5. $\frac{4}{w} = \frac{0.1}{100}$; $w = 4000$

6. $\frac{\frac{1}{2}}{w} = \frac{25}{100}$; $w = 2$

ELL Support

Allow students to work in pairs on the Self-Assessment for Concepts & Skills exercises. Have two pairs present their answers to one another. Encourage questions and discussion. Monitor discussions and provide support.

Self-Assessment for Concepts & Skills

7. $\frac{54}{120} = \frac{p}{100}$; $p = 45$

8. See Additional Answers.

9. $\frac{15}{50} = \frac{p}{100}$; All of the proportions represent $\frac{15}{30} = \frac{50}{100}$ except $\frac{15}{50} = \frac{p}{100}$.

Laurie's Notes

EXAMPLE 2

- Before working through the problem, ask students to guess the answer. Students may think the question is "What is half of 200?" 100
- ? "Are you looking for the whole or the part?" the part
- Draw a percent bar model with 200 as the whole. Divide into 10 parts and label the corresponding percents and amounts.
- ? "What percent does each section represent?" 10%
- ? "What amount does each section represent?" 20
- ? "How can you find 0.5%?" *Sample answer:* Divide the first section into 10 parts, each representing 1%, and then divide that into 2 parts.
- Ask students to reconsider their estimates and make changes if necessary.
- Set up the percent proportion, substitute the known quantities, and solve.
- Refer back to the percent bar model to confirm that the answer makes sense.
- Have students compare the answer to their estimates. Discuss any questions.

Try It

- Have students solve these exercises on whiteboards.

EXAMPLE 3

- ? "Are you looking for the whole or the part? Explain." 30 is the part, so you are looking for the whole.
- ? "Will the answer be more or less than 30? Explain." less than; 30 is more than 100% of the whole. The whole is the number associated with the 100%, which is not obvious to all students.
- **Model:** Begin by drawing a percent bar model to represent 100% of the whole.

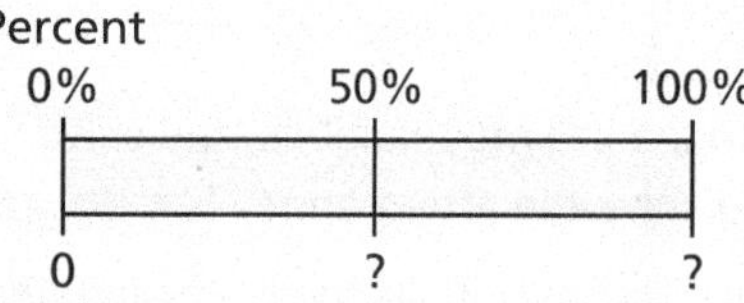

Because you are finding 150% of a number, extend the model to 150%.

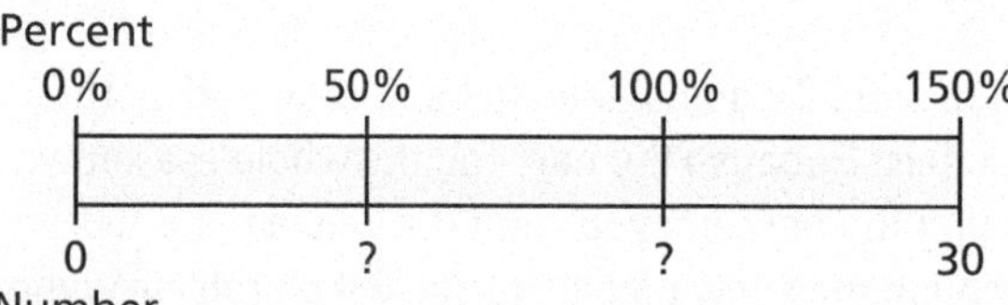

- Set up the percent proportion, substitute the known quantities, and solve. Refer back to the percent bar model to confirm that the answer makes sense.

Self-Assessment for Concepts & Skills

- "What are the three components of a percent proportion?" part, whole, and percent
- **Neighbor Check:** Have students work independently and then have their neighbors check their work. Have students discuss any discrepancies.

The Success Criteria Self-Assessment chart can be found in the *Student Journal* or online at *BigIdeasMath.com.*

EXAMPLE 2 Finding a Part

What number is 0.5% of 200?

$\frac{a}{w} = \frac{p}{100}$ Write the percent proportion.

$\frac{a}{200} = \frac{0.5}{100}$ Substitute 200 for w and 0.5 for p.

$a = 1$ Multiply each side by 200.

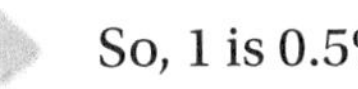

So, 1 is 0.5% of 200.

Try It **Write and solve a proportion to answer the question.**

3. What number is 80% of 60?

4. 10% of 40.5 is what number?

EXAMPLE 3 Finding a Whole

150% of what number is 30?

$\frac{a}{w} = \frac{p}{100}$ Write the percent proportion.

$\frac{30}{w} = \frac{150}{100}$ Substitute 30 for a and 150 for p.

$3000 = 150w$ Cross Products Property

$20 = w$ Divide each side by 150.

So, 150% of 20 is 30.

Try It **Write and solve a proportion to answer the question.**

5. 0.1% of what number is 4?

6. $\frac{1}{2}$ is 25% of what number?

Self-Assessment for Concepts & Skills

Solve each exercise. Then rate your understanding of the success criteria in your journal.

7. USING THE PERCENT PROPORTION Write and solve a proportion to determine what percent of 120 is 54.

8. MP CHOOSE TOOLS Use a model to find 60% of 30.

9. WHICH ONE DOESN'T BELONG? Which proportion at the left does *not* belong with the other three? Explain your reasoning.

$\frac{15}{w} = \frac{50}{100}$	$\frac{15}{50} = \frac{p}{100}$
$\frac{15}{30} = \frac{p}{100}$	$\frac{a}{30} = \frac{50}{100}$

EXAMPLE 4 Modeling Real Life

The bar graph shows the strengths of tornadoes that occurred in a state in a recent year. What percent of the tornadoes were EF1s?

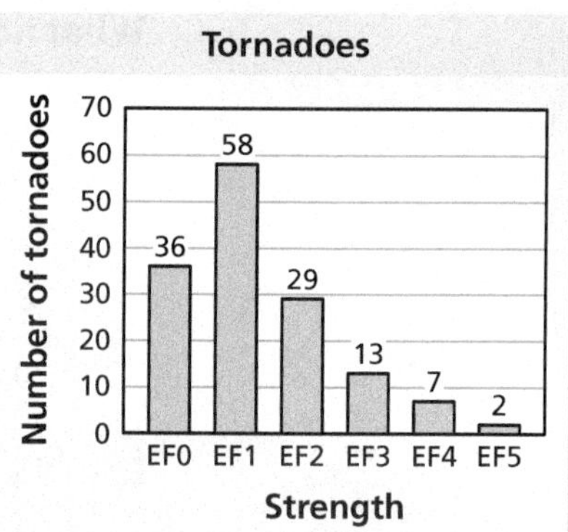

Understand the problem.

You are given a bar graph that shows the number of tornadoes in each strength category. You are asked to find the percent of the tornadoes that were EF1s.

Make a plan.

The total number of tornadoes, 145, is the whole, and the number of EF1 tornadoes, 58, is the part. Use the percent proportion to find the percent of the tornadoes that were EF1s.

Solve and check.

$$\frac{a}{w} = \frac{p}{100}$$ Write the percent proportion.

$$\frac{58}{145} = \frac{p}{100}$$ Substitute 58 for a and 145 for w.

$$100 \cdot \frac{58}{145} = 100 \cdot \frac{p}{100}$$ Multiplication Property of Equality

$$40 = p$$ Simplify.

So, 40% of the tornadoes were EF1s.

Check Reasonableness

The number of EF1 tornadoes, 58, is less than half the total number of tornadoes, 145. So, the percent of the tornadoes that were EF1s should be less than 50%. Because 40% < 50%, the answer is reasonable. ✓

Self-Assessment for Problem Solving

Solve each exercise. Then rate your understanding of the success criteria in your journal.

10. An arctic woolly-bear caterpillar lives for 7 years and spends 90% of its life frozen. How many days of its life is the arctic woolly-bear frozen?

Day	Pictures Uploaded
Monday	2
Tuesday	2
Wednesday	4
Thursday	1
Friday	8

11. DIG DEEPER! The table shows the numbers of pictures you upload to a social media website for 5 days in a row. How many total pictures do you upload during the week when 32% of the total pictures are uploaded on Saturday and Sunday?

Laurie's Notes

EXAMPLE 4

- Give students time to read the problem and the bar graph.

? "What is the problem asking?" What percent of the tornadoes were EF1s?

? "What do you need to know to solve the problem?" the total number of tornadoes (145) and the number that were EF1s (58)

- Discuss the plan. It might help to have students write the problem as a sentence, "58 is what percent of 145?"

? "Will the answer be more or less than 50%? Explain." less than; Half of 145 is about 72 and 58 < 72.

- It is very important to model this thinking process so that students begin to ask themselves the same questions.
- Set up the percent proportion, substitute the known quantities, solve and check for reasonableness.
- Students may want to solve or check using a percent bar model.

Self-Assessment for Problem Solving

- Students may benefit from trying the exercises independently and then working with peers to refine their work. It is important to provide time in class for problem solving, so that students become comfortable with the problem-solving plan.
- Encourage students to draw percent bar models or make ratio tables.
- Students should show all of their work, including the sentence, "The part is what percent of the whole?"
- Have students share their results.

The Success Criteria Self-Assessment chart can be found in the *Student Journal* or online at *BigIdeasMath.com*.

Closure

Flashcards: Divide students into groups of three. Assign each student in a group a different type of percent problem to write: find the part, find the whole, or find the percent. Tell students to solve their problems on the backs of the cards. There should be no talking during this time. Have students pass their cards to the left, solve the problem, and then pass to the left again. All three students should solve all three problems.

Extra Example 4

Using the bar graph from Example 4, what percent of the tornadoes were EF2s? 20%

Self-Assessment for Problem Solving

10. about 2300 days

11. 25 pictures

Formative Assessment Tip

Flashcards

This technique allows students to compare solutions or ways of thinking about different problems. Each student writes a problem on the front of an index card, and then solves the problem on the back. Students must show their work. Students exchange cards, but do not look at the backs of the cards they receive. Students then solve the problems on the fronts of the cards they received. After answering, each student checks his or her answer with the answer on the back. Students return the cards to the original owners and work together to correct any errors.

Learning Target

Use the percent proportion to find missing quantities.

Success Criteria

- Write proportions to represent percent problems.
- Solve a proportion to find a percent, a part, or a whole.

Review & Refresh

1. 0.42, 42%
2. 0.007, 0.7%
3. $1.\overline{4}$, $144.\overline{4}\%$
4. $0.6\overline{21}$, $62.1\overline{21}\%$
5. 3
6. −0.6
7. −2.5
8. B

Concepts, Skills, & Problem Solving

9. 16
10. 25%
11. 50
12. 84
13. 40%
14. 64
15. $\frac{12}{25} = \frac{p}{100}$; $p = 48$
16. $\frac{14}{56} = \frac{p}{100}$; $p = 25$
17. $\frac{9}{w} = \frac{25}{100}$; $w = 36$
18. $\frac{36}{w} = \frac{0.9}{100}$; $w = 4000$
19. $\frac{a}{124} = \frac{75}{100}$; $a = 93$
20. $\frac{a}{90} = \frac{110}{100}$; $a = 99$
21. $\frac{a}{40} = \frac{0.4}{100}$; $a = 0.16$
22. $\frac{72}{45} = \frac{p}{100}$; $p = 160$
23. yes; Your friend wrote and solved the correct percent proportion.
24. 21 students
25. $6000

Assignment Guide and Concept Check

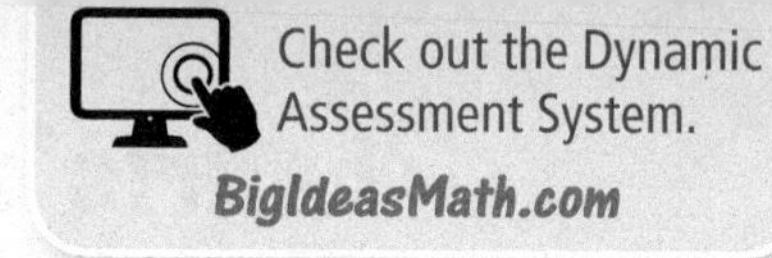
Check out the Dynamic Assessment System.
BigIdeasMath.com

Scaffold assignments to support all students in their learning progression. The suggested assignments are a starting point. Continue to assign additional exercises and revisit with spaced practice to move every student toward proficiency.

Level	Assignment 1	Assignment 2
Emerging	4, 7, 8, 9, 11, 13, 15, 16, 17, 18, 23	19, 20, 21, 22, 24, 25, 26, 28, 30, 31, 32, 35
Proficient	4, 7, 8, 10, 12, 14, 17, 18, 19, 20, 23	21, 22, 24, 25, 27, 28, 30, 31, 32, 33, 35
Advanced	4, 7, 8, 10, 12, 14, 18, 20, 21, 22, 23	25, 27, 29, 31, 32, 33, 34, 35, 36

- Assignment 1 is for use after students complete the Self-Assessment for Concepts & Skills.
- Assignment 2 is for use after students complete the Self-Assessment for Problem Solving.
- The red exercises can be used as a concept check.

Review & Refresh Prior Skills

Exercises 1–4 Writing Fractions as Decimals and Percents
Exercises 5–7 Evaluating Expressions
Exercise 8 Solving an Equation

For Your Information

- **Exercise 25** Students may get confused by the word *commission.* Tell students that commission is a fee or percentage paid to a sales representative or an agent for services provided.

Common Errors

- **Exercises 9–22** Students may not know what number to substitute for each variable. Remind students that the word *is* means "equals" and *of* means "to multiply." Tell students to write the question and then write the meaning of each word or phrase underneath.

E.2 Practice

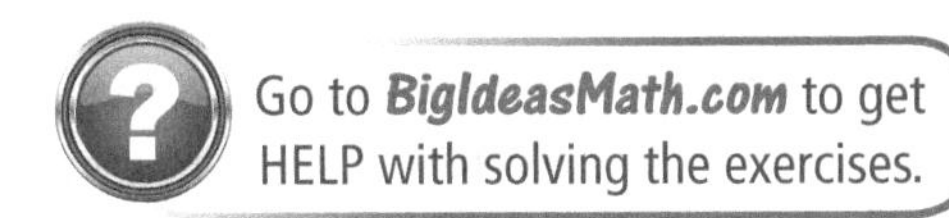
Go to BigIdeasMath.com to get HELP with solving the exercises.

Review & Refresh

Write the fraction as a decimal and a percent.

1. $\frac{42}{100}$
2. $\frac{7}{1000}$
3. $\frac{13}{9}$
4. $\frac{41}{66}$

Evaluate the expression when $a = -15$ and $b = -5$.

5. $a \div b$
6. $\frac{b + 14}{a}$
7. $\frac{b^2}{a + 5}$
8. What is the solution of $9x = -1.8$?

   A. $x = -5$ **B.** $x = -0.2$ **C.** $x = 0.2$ **D.** $x = 5$

Concepts, Skills, & Problem Solving

MP CHOOSE TOOLS **Use a model to answer the question. Use a proportion to check your answer.** (See Exploration 1, p. 685.)

9. What number is 20% of 80?
10. 10 is what percent of 40?
11. 15 is 30% of what number?
12. What number is 120% of 70?
13. 20 is what percent of 50?
14. 48 is 75% of what number?

USING THE PERCENT PROPORTION **Write and solve a proportion to answer the question.**

15. What percent of 25 is 12?
16. 14 is what percent of 56?
17. 25% of what number is 9?
18. 36 is 0.9% of what number?
19. 75% of 124 is what number?
20. 110% of 90 is what number?
21. What number is 0.4% of 40?
22. 72 is what percent of 45?

$$\frac{a}{w} = \frac{p}{100}$$
$$\frac{34}{w} = \frac{40}{100}$$
$$w = 85$$

23. MP YOU BE THE TEACHER Your friend uses the percent proportion to answer the question below. Is your friend correct? Explain your reasoning.

    "40% of what number is 34?"

PRESIDENTIAL YOUTH FITNESS AWARD

24. MP MODELING REAL LIFE Of 140 seventh-grade students, 15% earn the Presidential Youth Fitness Award. How many students earn the award?
25. MP MODELING REAL LIFE A salesperson receives a 3% commission on sales. The salesperson receives $180 in commission. What is the amount of sales?

USING THE PERCENT PROPORTION **Write and solve a proportion to answer the question.**

26. 0.5 is what percent of 20?

27. 14.2 is 35.5% of what number?

28. $\frac{3}{4}$ is 60% of what number?

29. What number is 25% of $\frac{7}{8}$?

30. MP **MODELING REAL LIFE** You are assigned 32 math exercises for homework. You complete 75% of the exercises before dinner. How many exercises do you have left to do after dinner?

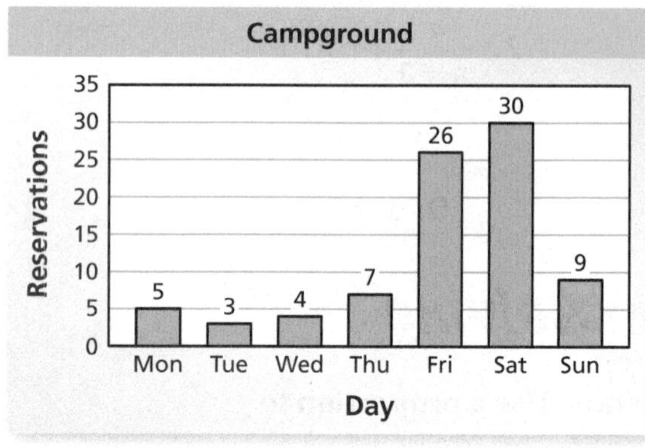

31. MP **MODELING REAL LIFE** Your friend earns $10.50 per hour, which is 125% of her hourly wage last year. How much did your friend earn per hour last year?

32. MP **MODELING REAL LIFE** The bar graph shows the numbers of reserved campsites at a campground for one week. What percent of the reservations were for Friday or Saturday?

33. MP **PROBLEM SOLVING** Your friend displays the results of a survey that asks several people to vote on a new school mascot.

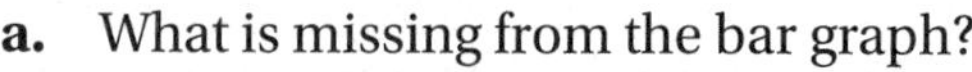

a. What is missing from the bar graph?

b. What percent of the votes does the least popular mascot receive? Explain your reasoning.

c. There are 124 votes total. How many votes does tiger receive?

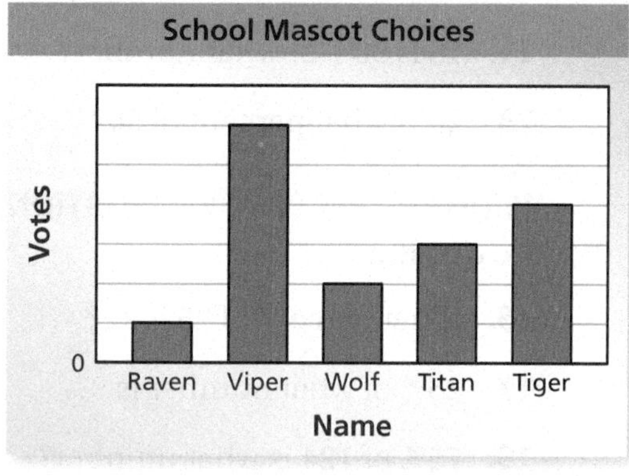

34. DIG DEEPER! A quarterback throw 33 passes in the first three quarters of a football game. The ratio of complete passes to incomplete passes during the first three quarters is 6 : 5. He completes every pass in the fourth quarter and 62.5% of his passes for the entire game. How many passes does the quarterback throw in the fourth quarter? Justify your answer.

35. MP **REASONING** 20% of a number is x. What is 100% of the number? Assume $x > 0$.

36. MP **STRUCTURE** Answer each question. Assume $x > 0$.

a. What percent of $8x$ is $5x$?

b. What is 65% of $80x$?

Common Errors

- **Exercise 33** Students may struggle with this problem because there is no vertical scale. Tell students to think of the bars as a model. This will get them heading in the right direction.

Mini-Assessment

Write and solve a proportion to answer the question.

1. What percent of 35 is 28? $\frac{28}{35} = \frac{p}{100}$; $p = 80$
2. What number is 28% of 50? $\frac{a}{50} = \frac{28}{100}$; $a = 14$
3. 160% of what number is 144? $\frac{144}{w} = \frac{160}{100}$; $w = 90$
4. 0.15% of what number is 10.5? $\frac{10.5}{w} = \frac{0.15}{100}$; $w = 7000$
5. You earn 80% on a test. You answer 44 questions correctly. How many questions are on the test? 55 questions

Section Resources

Surface Level	Deep Level
Resources by Chapter • Extra Practice • Reteach • Puzzle Time Student Journal • Self-Assessment • Practice Differentiating the Lesson Tutorial Videos Skills Review Handbook Skills Trainer	Resources by Chapter • Enrichment and Extension Graphic Organizers Dynamic Assessment System • Section Practice

Concepts, Skills, & Problem Solving

26. $\frac{0.5}{20} = \frac{p}{100}$; $p = 2.5$
27. $\frac{14.2}{w} = \frac{35.5}{100}$; $w = 40$
28. $\frac{\frac{3}{4}}{w} = \frac{60}{100}$; $w = 1\frac{1}{4}$
29. $\frac{a}{\frac{7}{8}} = \frac{25}{100}$; $a = \frac{7}{32}$
30. 8 exercises
31. $8.40
32. $66\frac{2}{3}\%$
33. **a.** a scale along the vertical axis

    b. 6.25%; *Sample answer:* Although you do not know the actual number of votes, you can visualize each bar as a model with the horizontal lines breaking the data into equal parts. The sum of all the parts is 16. Raven has the least parts with 1, which is 100% ÷ 16 = 6.25%.

    c. 31 votes
34. 7 passes; $\frac{18 + x}{33 + x} = \frac{62.5}{100}$; $x = 7$
35. $5x$
36. **a.** 62.5%

    b. $52x$

Check out the
Dynamic Classroom.
BigIdeasMath.com

Learning Target

Use the percent equation to find missing quantities.

Success Criteria

- Write equations to represent percent problems.
- Use percent equation to find a percent, a part, or a whole.

Warm Up

Cumulative, vocabulary, and prerequisite skills practice opportunities are available in the *Resources by Chapter* or at *BigIdeasMath.com*.

ELL Support

Tell students that in this lesson, they will use the percent equation to find a percent, a part, or a whole. Point out that a percent describes the size of a part when the whole is 100.

Exploration 1

a. Person A: 20%, Person B: 25%, Person C: 15%, Person D: 40%; *Sample answer:* Use the percent proportion, division, or ratio tables.

b. part = percent × whole; *Sample answer:* Multiplying both sides of the equation by the "whole" provides the equation part = percent × whole.

c. Person A: 30, Person B: 24, Person C: 24, Person D: 42

d. *Sample answer:* Use a proportion to solve; I prefer the percent equation because it is a more efficient method to solve the problem.

Laurie's Notes

Preparing to Teach

- Students know how to solve percent problems using the percent proportion. Now they will use the percent equation to solve percent problems.
- **Construct Viable Arguments and Critique the Reasoning of Others:** Mathematically proficient students are able to explain their reasoning in a way in which others can understand. They are able to compare different solution methods and analyze benefits of each, or why different methods might be used for certain types of problems.

Motivate

- Do a quick review of benchmark percents.
- Write the different forms of each benchmark on index cards.
  Examples: 5%, 0.05, $\frac{1}{20}$; 12.5%, 0.125, $\frac{1}{8}$; 25%, 0.25, $\frac{1}{4}$; 30%, 0.3, $\frac{3}{10}$; $33\frac{1}{3}$%, $0.\overline{3}$, $\frac{1}{3}$; 40%, 0.4, $\frac{2}{5}$; 50%, 0.5, $\frac{1}{2}$; 75%, 0.75, $\frac{3}{4}$; 100%, 1.00, 1
- **Teaching Tip:** Laminate the cards for future use.
- Distribute the cards so that each student has one card. If the number of students is not a multiple of 3, make one or two duplicate cards.
- Without speaking, students should walk around and find the other forms equivalent to their numbers.
- Debrief by having each group display their three representations.
- Then have students with the percent cards order themselves in a line. Ask students with the fraction and decimal cards to do the same. Compare the lines.

Exploration 1

- **FYI:** Students will be using different methods to solve the percent problems. It is important to make time for students to share different strategies versus having only one method presented.

? "Before finding the percents in part (a), what do you need to know?" the total number of students

- There are several ways in which students can find the percent of students who voted for each of the four candidates. Methods include:
  - Write a fraction and then write the percent.
  - Write a proportion and solve.
  - Change the fraction to a decimal and then to a percent.
- When students have finished part (a), ask several students to explain their methods and then give students time to answer part (b).

? "How many students voted? Explain." 120; Half (or 50%) of the students have voted and there are 60 in the circle graph, so 100% would be 120 students.

- There are several ways in which students can find the number of students who voted for each of the four candidates. Methods include:
  - Mental math
  - Write a proportion and solve.
  - Multiply.
- **Extension:** Have students explore whether voting patterns changed from the first 60 voters to the last 60 voters.

E.3 The Percent Equation

Learning Target: Use the percent equation to find missing quantities.

Success Criteria:
- I can write equations to represent percent problems.
- I can use the percent equation to find a percent, a part, or a whole.

EXPLORATION 1 Using Percent Equations

Work with a partner.

a. The circle graph shows the number of votes received by each candidate during a school election. So far, only half of the students have voted. Find the percent of students who voted for each candidate. Explain your method.

Votes Received by Each Candidate

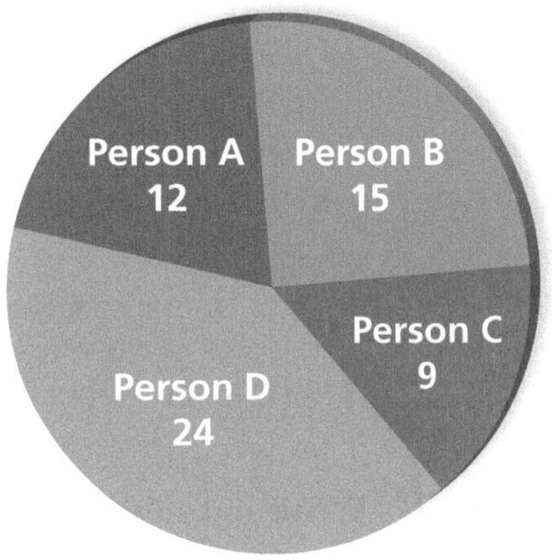

b. You have learned that $\frac{\text{part}}{\text{whole}} = \text{percent}$. Solve the equation for the "part." Explain your reasoning.

Math Practice

Use Equations
How does the equation you wrote in part (b) compare to the percent proportion? Explain.

c. The circle graph shows the final results of the election after every student voted. Use the equation you wrote in part (b) to find the number of students who voted for each candidate.

Final Results

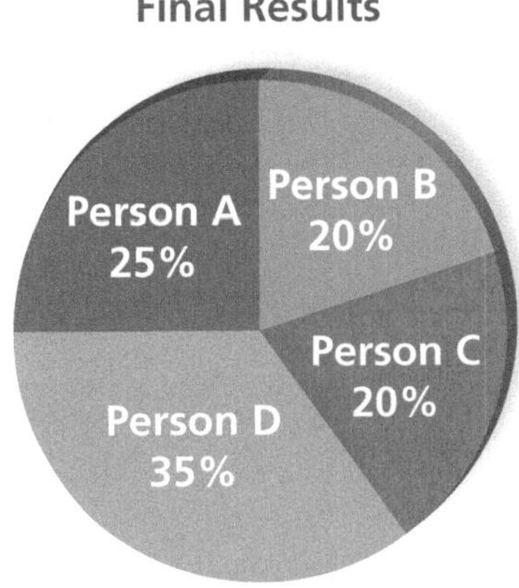

d. Use a different method to check your answers in part (c). Which method do you prefer? Explain.

E.3 Lesson

Key Idea

The Percent Equation

Words To represent "a is p percent of w," use an equation.

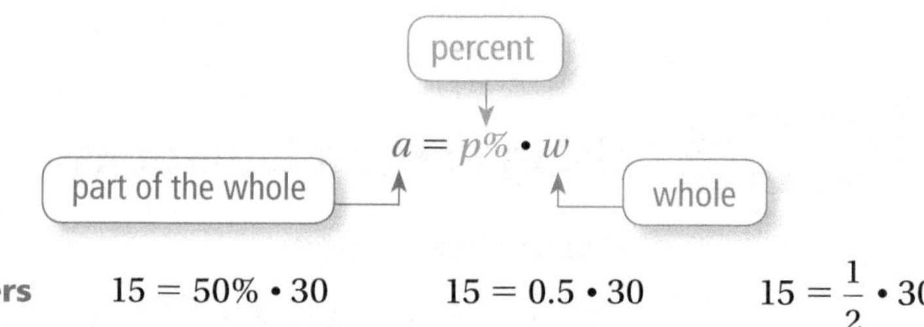

Numbers $15 = 50\% \cdot 30$ $15 = 0.5 \cdot 30$ $15 = \frac{1}{2} \cdot 30$

EXAMPLE 1 Finding a Part of a Number

What number is 24% of 50? **Estimate**

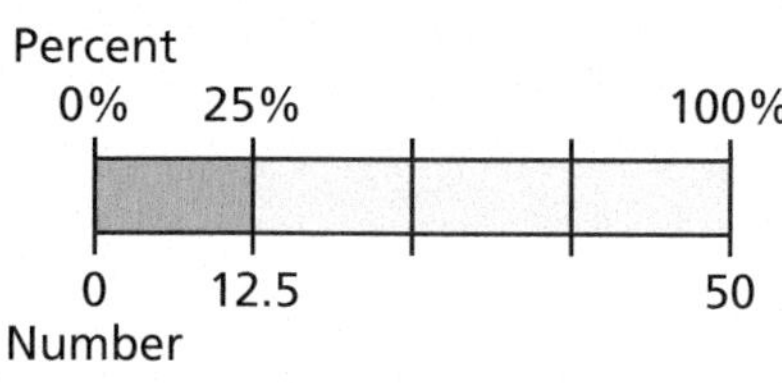

$a = p\% \cdot w$ Write the percent equation.

$= \frac{24}{100} \cdot 50$ Substitute $\frac{24}{100}$ for $p\%$ and 50 for w.

$= 12$ Simplify.

So, 12 is 24% of 50. **Reasonable?** $12 \approx 12.5$

Common Error

Remember to convert a percent to a fraction or a decimal when using the percent equation. For Example 1, write 24% as $\frac{24}{100}$.

Try It **Write and solve an equation to answer the question.**

1. What number is 10% of 20?
2. What number is 150% of 40?

EXAMPLE 2 Finding a Percent

9.5 is what percent of 25?

$a = p\% \cdot w$ Write the percent equation.

$9.5 = p\% \cdot 25$ Substitute 9.5 for a and 25 for w.

$\frac{9.5}{25} = \frac{p\% \cdot 25}{25}$ Division Property of Equality

$0.38 = p\%$ Simplify.

Because 0.38 equals 38%, 9.5 is 38% of 25.

Laurie's Notes

Scaffolding Instruction

- In the exploration, students solved the equation $\frac{\text{part}}{\text{whole}}$ = percent for the "part." Now they will use the percent equation to solve percent problems.
- **Emerging:** Students may still be developing confidence in understanding and solving the percent equation. Going through each example and making sense of the problems is necessary.
- **Proficient:** Students can solve percent problems with a model or an equation. After reviewing the Key Idea, students should complete the Try It exercises and then move on to the Self-Assessment exercises.

Scaffold instruction to support all students in their learning. Learning is individualized and you may want to group students differently as they move in and out of these levels with each skill and concept. Student self-assessment and feedback help guide your instructional decisions about how and when to layer support for all students to become proficient learners.

Key Idea

- **Connection:** Students should know how to find a percent of a number by multiplying. The percent equation builds upon this idea to find the missing percent or the unknown whole. When you know two of the three quantities in this equation, you can solve for the third.
- **Teaching Strategy:** The equation is not something students should just memorize. They should be able to derive the equation based on their understanding of percents and proportions.
- **Reason Abstractly and Quantitatively:** In all of the examples, draw a percent bar model off to the side to help build students' reasoning. The model helps students estimate and consider the reasonableness of the answer.

Teaching Strategy

Whenever possible, encourage students to make sense of problems rather than just memorize and apply a process. As they proceed through their mathematics courses, many processes will be presented. If students simply memorize the processes, they will quickly forget or confuse them. If students understand the basis of a problem, then they can recreate the method as needed.

EXAMPLE 1

- Another way to phrase this question is "24% of 50 is what number?"
- **Estimate:** 24% is close to 25%, and 25% is $\frac{1}{4}$.

? "What is $\frac{1}{4}$ of 50?" 12.5

Try It

- Students should solve these problems on whiteboards.

Extra Example 1

What number is 73% of 200? 146

ELL Support

After demonstrating Example 1, have students practice language by working in pairs to complete Try It Exercises 1 and 2. Have one student ask the other, "What is the percent equation? What fraction or decimal do you substitute for *p*%? What do you substitute for *w*? What is the solution?"

Beginner: Write the steps and state the numbers.

Intermediate: Use phrases or simple sentences such as, "*a* equals ten-hundredths times twenty."

Advanced: Use detailed sentences such as, "The percent equation is *a* equals ten-hundredths times twenty."

Try It

1. $a = 0.1 \cdot 20$; 2
2. $a = 1.5 \cdot 40$; 60

EXAMPLE 2

- Read the example as "9.5 is a part of 25."

? "Is 9.5 more or less than half of 25?" less than

- Draw a percent bar model and explain that it represents 25. Draw the half mark (50%) and ask how much that would represent. 12.5
- Now draw the quarter mark (25%) and ask how much that would represent. 6.25 Through this process, students should recognize that 9.5 is between 25% and 50% of 25.
- **Common Error:** Students may forget to convert the decimal to a percent.

Extra Example 2

36.4 is what percent of 40? 91%

Laurie's Notes

Try It

3. $3 = p\% \cdot 600$; 0.5%
4. $18 = p\% \cdot 20$; 90%

Extra Example 3

18 is 15% of what number? 120

Try It

5. $8 = 0.8 \cdot w$; 10
6. $90 = 1.8 \cdot w$; 50

Self-Assessment for Concepts & Skills

7. A part of the whole is equal to a percent times the whole.
8. $14 = p\% \cdot 70$; 20%
9. $a = 0.36 \cdot 85$; 30.6
10. $9 = 0.12 \cdot w$; 75
11. $108 = p\% \cdot 72$; 150%
12. 55 is 20% of what number?; 275; 11

Try It

- Students should solve these problems on whiteboards. Then check answers as a class.

EXAMPLE 3

- This type of problem, finding a whole, is a bit harder. Knowing fractional equivalents is extremely helpful in developing a sense about the size of the answer.
- ? "What is the part?" 39 "So, 39 is a part of something."
- ? "How big of a part is it, approximately?" about half
- **Construct Viable Arguments and Critique the Reasoning of Others:** Help students reason that if 39 is half of something, the whole must be about 80. Only at this point does it make sense to translate what is known into an equation: 39 is 52% of some number.
- **Common Error:** Students may divide 39 by 52 and ignore the decimals completely.

Try It

- Encourage students to sketch the percent bar model and record the information they know. Ask several students to put their work on the board.
- Ask, "What percent problem is suggested by $12 = \frac{1}{4}w$?" *Sample answer:* 12 is 25% of what number?

Self-Assessment for Concepts & Skills

- **Neighbor Check:** For Exercises 8–11, have students write the equation and then compare with a neighbor. Have students discuss any discrepancies. Students should solve the equations independently and then have their neighbors check their solutions.

ELL Support

Allow students to work in pairs for extra support and to practice language. After completing Exercises 8–11, have pairs display their answers on whiteboards for your review. Discuss the answers for Exercises 7 and 12 as a class.

The Success Criteria Self-Assessment chart can be found in the *Student Journal* or online at *BigIdeasMath.com*.

Try It **Write and solve an equation to answer the question.**

3. 3 is what percent of 600?

4. 18 is what percent of 20?

EXAMPLE 3 Finding a Whole

39 is 52% of what number?

$a = p\% \cdot w$ Write the percent equation.

$39 = 0.52 \cdot w$ Substitute 39 for a and 0.52 for $p\%$.

$\dfrac{39}{0.52} = \dfrac{0.52 \cdot w}{0.52}$ Division Property of Equality

$75 = w$ Simplify.

So, 39 is 52% of 75.

Math Practice

Use a Table
Show how to use a ratio table to find the whole.

Try It **Write and solve an equation to answer the question.**

5. 8 is 80% of what number?

6. 90 is 180% of what number?

Self-Assessment *for Concepts & Skills*

Solve each exercise. Then rate your understanding of the success criteria in your journal.

7. **VOCABULARY** Write the percent equation in words.

USING THE PERCENT EQUATION **Write and solve an equation to answer the question.**

8. 14 is what percent of 70?

9. What number is 36% of 85?

10. 9 is 12% of what number?

11. 108 is what percent of 72?

12. **DIFFERENT WORDS, SAME QUESTION** Which is different? Find "both" answers.

What number is 20% of 55?	55 is 20% of what number?
20% of 55 is what number?	0.2 • 55 is what number?

EXAMPLE 4 Modeling Real Life

8th Street Cafe

DATE: MAY04 12:45PM
TABLE: 29
SERVER: JANE

Food Total	**27.50**
Tax	**1.65**
Subtotal	**29.15**

TIP: ____________

TOTAL: ____________

Thank You

You are paying for lunch and receive the bill shown.

a. Find the percent of sales tax on the food total.

Answer the question: $1.65 is what percent of $27.50?

$a = p\% \cdot w$	Write the percent equation.
$1.65 = p\% \cdot 27.50$	Substitute 1.65 for a and 27.50 for w.
$0.06 = p\%$	Divide each side by 27.50.

 Because 0.06 equals 6%, the percent of sales tax is 6%.

b. You leave a 16% tip on the food total. Find the total amount you pay for lunch.

Answer the question: What tip amount is 16% of $27.50?

$a = p\% \cdot w$	Write the percent equation.
$= 0.16 \cdot 27.50$	Substitute 0.16 for $p\%$ and 27.50 for w.
$= 4.40$	Multiply.

The amount of the tip is $4.40.

 So, you pay a total of $29.15 + $4.40 = $33.55.

Self-Assessment for Problem Solving

Solve each exercise. Then rate your understanding of the success criteria in your journal.

13. **DIG DEEPER!** A school offers band and chorus classes. The table shows the percents of the 1200 students in the school who are enrolled in band, chorus, or neither class. How many students are enrolled in both classes? Explain.

Class	Enrollment
Band	34%
Chorus	28%
Neither	42%

14. Water Tank A has a capacity of 550 gallons and is 66% full. Water Tank B is 53% full. The ratio of the capacity of Water Tank A to Water Tank B is 11 : 15.

a. How much water is in each tank?

b. What percent of the total volume of both tanks is filled with water?

Laurie's Notes

EXAMPLE 4

- Work through the problem as shown.
- ? "In addition to paying for what you ordered (food and drink), what other costs are there when you eat at a restaurant?" sales tax and tip
- Remind students that $0.06 = p\%$ does not answer the question. Writing a summary sentence helps students ensure they have answered the question.
- ? "Does 4.40 answer the question? Explain." No, \$4.40 is the amount of the tip. The question asks for the total amount you pay for lunch.
- ? "Is \$4.40 a reasonable amount for a tip? Explain. Draw a percent bar model to support your conclusion." Yes, the bill is approximately \$30. 10% of \$30 is \$3 and 20% of \$30 is \$6. 16% is about halfway between 10% and 20%, so \$4.40 is reasonable.

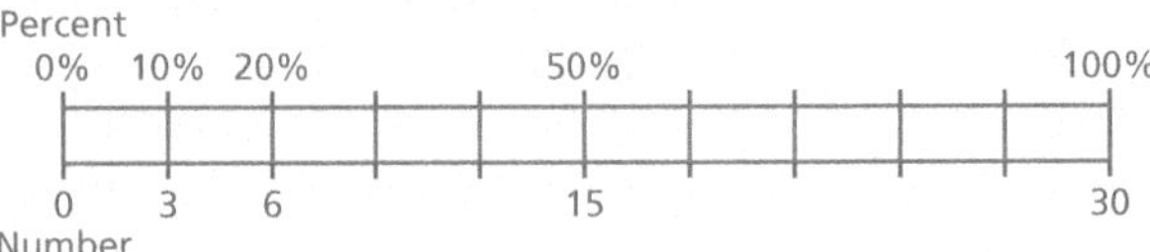

Self-Assessment for Problem Solving

- The goal for all students is to feel comfortable with the problem-solving plan. It is important for students to problem-solve in class, where they may receive support from you and their peers. Keep in mind that some students may only be ready for the first step.
- Mathematically proficient students use their reasoning skills to make sense of contextual problems and then use their computational skills to solve them. The quantities and operations have meanings that are evident in students' work.
- **Make Sense of Problems and Persevere in Solving Them:** Be sure students understand the context for each exercise before they make a plan. If students are confused about what they need to find, have them ask, "What can I find?" Remind students that the first answer they need to find may not be the answer to the question.
- Have students work in pairs or groups. One student reads the problem and the other interprets it. Students switch roles for Exercise 14.
- If students are struggling with Exercise 13, suggest creating a third column labeled "Students." Making a table for Exercise 14 may be helpful.

The Success Criteria Self-Assessment chart can be found in the *Student Journal* or online at *BigIdeasMath.com*.

Closure

- **Exit Ticket**: Use the percent equation to answer the question: 12 is what percent of 48? Support your answer with a percent bar model. 25%;

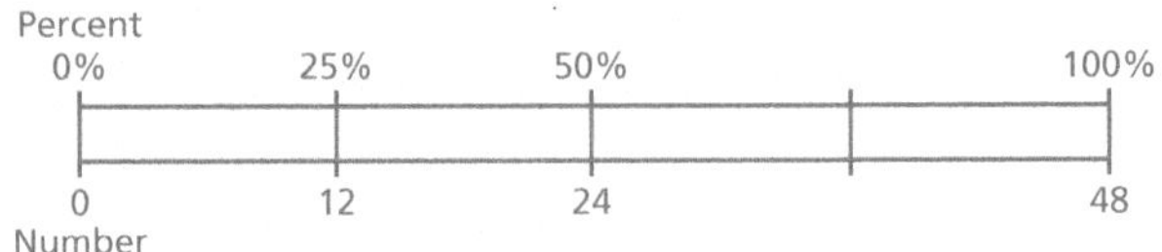

Extra Example 4

Your total cost for dinner is \$18.50 for food and \$1.48 for tax.

a. Find the percent of sales tax on the food total. 8%

b. You leave an 18% tip on the food total. Find the total amount you pay for dinner. \$23.31

Self-Assessment for Problem Solving

13. 48 students;
$100\% - 42\% = 58\%$,
$34\% + 28\% = 62\%$,
$62\% - 58\% = 4\%$,
$a = 0.04 \cdot 1200$

14. **a.** Tank A: 363 gal;
Tank B: 397.5 gal

b. 58.5%

Learning Target

Use the percent equation to find missing quantities.

Success Criteria

- Write equations to represent percent problems.
- Use percent equation to find a percent, a part, or a whole.

Review & Refresh

1. $\frac{30}{100} = \frac{9}{w}$; $w = 30$
2. $\frac{42}{80} = \frac{p}{100}$; $p = 52.5$
3. $\frac{p}{100} = \frac{20}{36}$; $p = 55.\overline{5}$
4. $\frac{a}{80} = \frac{120}{100}$; $a = 96$
5. 14
6. 2
7. $4\frac{1}{10}$
8. 11.8
9. A

Concepts, Skills, & Problem Solving

10. 36%
11. 40%
12. 24%
13. $a = 0.2 \cdot 150$; 30
14. $45 = p\% \cdot 60$; 75%
15. $35 = 0.35 \cdot w$; 100
16. $a = 0.008 \cdot 150$; 1.2
17. $29 = p\% \cdot 20$; 145%
18. $12 = 0.005 \cdot w$; 2400
19. $51 = p\% \cdot 300$; 17%
20. $102 = 1.2 \cdot w$; 85
21. yes; The percent was converted to a decimal and multiplied by the "whole".
22. no; 30 is the "part" in the equation.

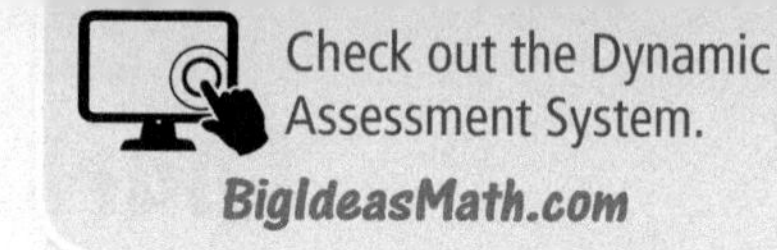
Check out the Dynamic Assessment System.
BigIdeasMath.com

Assignment Guide and Concept Check

Scaffold assignments to support all students in their learning progression. The suggested assignments are a starting point. Continue to assign additional exercises and revisit with spaced practice to move every student toward proficiency.

Level	Assignment 1	Assignment 2
Emerging	4, 7, 8, 9, 10, 13, 14, 15, 16, 21, 22	17, 18, 19, 20, 23, 24, 25, 26, 29
Proficient	4, 7, 8, 9, 11, 15, 16, 17, 18, 21, 22	19, 20, 23, 24, 25, 26, 27, 28, 29, 30
Advanced	4, 7, 8, 9, 12, 16, 18, 19, 20, 21, 22	25, 26, 27, 28, 29, 30, 31, 32, 33

- Assignment 1 is for use after students complete the Self-Assessment for Concepts & Skills.
- Assignment 2 is for use after students complete the Self-Assessment for Problem Solving.
- The red exercises can be used as a concept check.

Review & Refresh Prior Skills

Exercises 1–4 Using the Percent Proportion
Exercises 5–8 Finding Distance on a Number Line
Exercise 9 Writing a Proportion

Common Errors

- **Exercises 13–20** Students may not know what number to substitute for each variable. Remind students that the word *is* means "equals" and *of* means "to multiply." Tell students to write the question and then write the meaning of each word or phrase underneath.

E.3 Practice

Review & Refresh

Write and solve a proportion to answer the question.

1. 30% of what number is 9?
2. 42 is what percent of 80?
3. What percent of 36 is 20?
4. What number is 120% of 80?

Find the distance between the two numbers on a number line.

5. -4 and 10
6. $-\frac{2}{3}$ and $\frac{4}{3}$
7. $-5\frac{2}{5}$ and $-1\frac{3}{10}$
8. -4.3 and 7.5

9. There are 160 people in a grade. The ratio of boys to girls is 3 to 5. Which proportion can you use to find the number x of boys?

   A. $\frac{3}{8} = \frac{x}{160}$ **B.** $\frac{3}{5} = \frac{x}{160}$ **C.** $\frac{5}{8} = \frac{x}{160}$ **D.** $\frac{3}{5} = \frac{160}{x}$

Concepts, Skills, & Problem Solving

USING PERCENT EQUATIONS **The circle graph shows the number of votes received by each candidate during a school election. Find the percent of students who voted for the indicated candidate.** (See Exploration 1, p. 691.)

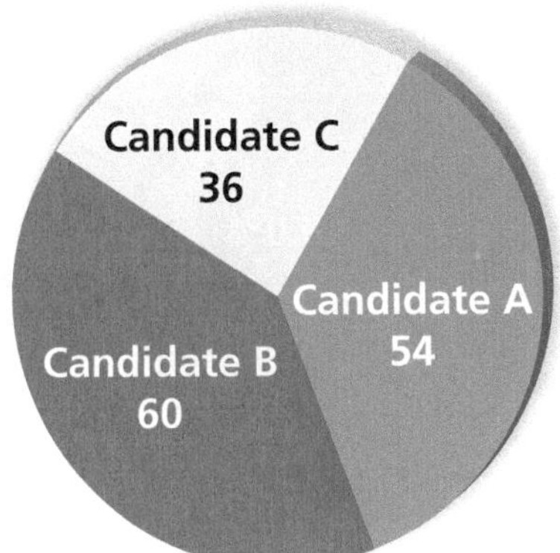

10. Candidate A
11. Candidate B
12. Candidate C

USING THE PERCENT EQUATION **Write and solve an equation to answer the question.**

13. 20% of 150 is what number?
14. 45 is what percent of 60?
15. 35% of what number is 35?
16. 0.8% of 150 is what number?
17. 29 is what percent of 20?
18. 0.5% of what number is 12?
19. What percent of 300 is 51?
20. 120% of what number is 102?

MP YOU BE THE TEACHER **Your friend uses the percent equation to answer the question. Is your friend correct? Explain your reasoning.**

21. What number is 35% of 20?

$$a = p\% \cdot w$$
$$= 0.35 \cdot 20$$
$$= 7$$

22. 30 is 60% of what number?

$$a = p\% \cdot w$$
$$= 0.6 \cdot 30$$
$$= 18$$

23. **MP MODELING REAL LIFE** A salesperson receives a 2.5% commission on sales. What commission does the salesperson receive for $8000 in sales?

24. **MP MODELING REAL LIFE** Your school raised 125% of its fundraising goal. The school raised $6750. What was the goal?

25. **MP MODELING REAL LIFE** The sales tax on the model rocket shown is $1.92. What is the percent of sales tax?

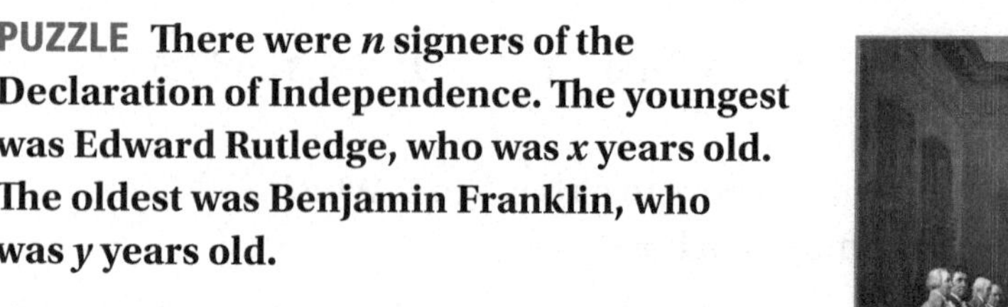

PUZZLE There were *n* signers of the Declaration of Independence. The youngest was Edward Rutledge, who was *x* years old. The oldest was Benjamin Franklin, who was *y* years old.

26. x is 25% of 104. What was Rutledge's age?

27. 7 is 10% of y. What was Franklin's age?

28. n is 80% of y. How many signers were there?

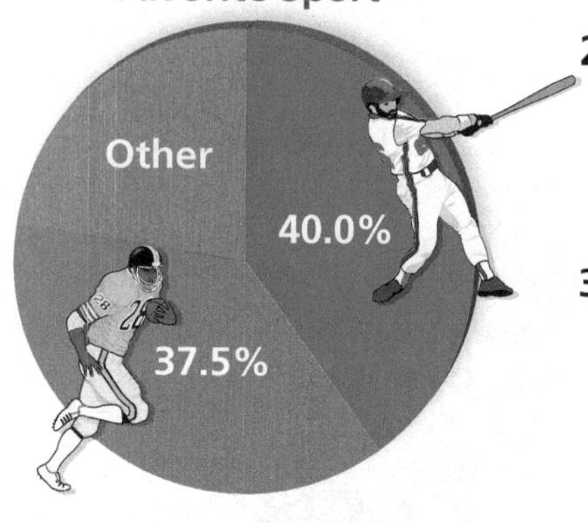

29. **MP LOGIC** How can you tell whether a percent of a number will be *greater than, less than,* or *equal to* the number? Give examples to support your answer.

30. **MP PROBLEM SOLVING** In a survey, a group of students is asked their favorite sport. Eighteen students choose "other" sports.
   a. How many students participate in the survey?
   b. How many choose football?

31. **TRUE OR FALSE?** Tell whether the statement is *true* or *false*. Explain your reasoning.

If W is 25% of Z, then $Z : W$ is $75 : 25$.

32. **DIG DEEPER!** At a restaurant, the amount of your bill before taxes and tip is $18.53. A 6% sales tax is applied to your bill, and you want to leave at least a 20% tip, but have only five-dollar bills. You plan to use any change you receive as part of the tip. What is the minimum percent that you can tip? Explain your reasoning.

33. **MP REASONING** The table shows your test results in a math class. What score do you need on the last test to earn 90% of the total points on the tests?

Test Score	Point Value
83%	100
91.6%	250
88%	150
?	300

Common Errors

- **Exercise 30** Students may not realize that the sum of the parts of a circle graph equals 100%.

Mini-Assessment

Write and solve an equation to answer the question.

1. 52 is what percent of 80? $52 = p\% \cdot 80\%; p = 65$
2. 28 is 35% of what number? $28 = 0.35 \cdot w; w = 80$
3. What number is 25% of 92? $a = 0.25 \cdot 92; a = 23$
4. What percent of 250 is 60? $60 = p\% \cdot 250; p = 24$
5. A new laptop computer costs \$800. The sales tax on the computer is \$48. What is the percent of sales tax? 6%

Section Resources

Surface Level	Deep Level
Resources by Chapter • Extra Practice • Reteach • Puzzle Time Student Journal • Self-Assessment • Practice Differentiating the Lesson Tutorial Videos Skills Review Handbook Skills Trainer	Resources by Chapter • Enrichment and Extension Graphic Organizers Dynamic Assessment System • Section Practice
Transfer Level	
Dynamic Assessment System • Mid-Chapter Quiz	Assessment Book • Mid-Chapter Quiz

Concepts, Skills, & Problem Solving

23. \$200
24. \$5400
25. 8%
26. 26 years old
27. 70 years old
28. 56 signers
29. If the percent is less than 100%, the percent of a number is less than the number; 50% of 80 is 40; If the percent is equal to 100%, the percent of a number is equal to the number; 100% of 80 is 80; If the percent is greater than 100%, the percent of a number is greater than the number; 150% of 80 is 120.
30. **a.** 80 students

    b. 30 students
31. false; If W is 25% of Z, then $Z : W$ is $100 : 25$, because Z represents the whole.
32. about 28.9%; *Sample answer:* The total with tax is \$19.64. \$25 − \$19.64 is a tip of \$5.36, which is about 28.9% of the original amount.
33. 92%

Check out the
Dynamic Classroom.
BigIdeasMath.com

Learning Target

Find percents of change in quantities.

Success Criteria

- Explain the meaning of percent of change.
- Find the percent of increase or decrease in a quantity.
- Find the percent error of a quantity.

Warm Up

Cumulative, vocabulary, and prerequisite skills practice opportunities are available in the *Resources by Chapter* or at *BigIdeasMath.com.*

ELL Support

Explain that *increase* and *decrease* have opposite meanings. Both come from the Latin root word *crescere*, which means "to grow." When the prefix *in–* is added, it means "to grow larger." The prefix *de–* means "away from." When *de–* is added to the root word, it means "to grow smaller."

Exploration 1

a. 880 salmon

b. about 360 salmon

c. 12%

d. *Sample answer:* The population of a city increases by 5% every year.

Laurie's Notes

Preparing to Teach

- Students should be able to find the percent of a number, round decimal values, and convert between fractions, decimals, and percents. These are necessary skills for finding **percents of change** and **percent error**.
- **Use Appropriate Tools Strategically:** Use of calculators allows students to draw important conclusions. When there is a repeated percent change (increase or decrease), the percent remains constant while the amount changes.

Motivate

- Talk about light-emitting diode (LED) bulbs. LED bulbs use at least 75% less energy than incandescent light bulbs (**percent of decrease**) and last up to 2500% longer (**percent of increase**). LEDs are also much cooler and made with epoxy lenses, not glass.
- LED bulbs are more expensive than incandescent bulbs, but they produce considerable savings due to their longevity and reduction in energy use.

Exploration 1

- Ask a student to read the information.
- **FYI:** Electric turbines in the dams generate electricity. These turbines are what affect the survival rate of the young salmon.

? "What percent of salmon makes it through each dam?" about 88%

? "What percent of salmon does not make it through each dam?" about 12%

- Discuss the general concept of fewer salmon at the second dam than at the first dam.
- In part (b), students should organize their data. Encourage them to make a table and/or represent the information in a bar graph.

Dam	0	1	2	3	4	5	6	7	8
Salmon	1000	880	774	681	599	527	464	408	359

- Remind students to round their answers to a whole number of salmon at each dam.
- **Use Appropriate Tools Strategically:** Use of a calculator will help facilitate the computation, so that students can focus on how the numbers are changing.
- **Look for and Make Use of Structure:** Have students read and discuss the Math Practice note. Then have students describe any other patterns they observe in the table or the bar graph.
- **Big Idea:** Each entry in the table or bar in the graph is 12% less than the previous entry or bar. The *amount* of decrease is changing, but the *percent* is not.

E.4 Percents of Increase and Decrease

Learning Target: Find percents of change in quantities.

Success Criteria:
- I can explain the meaning of percent of change.
- I can find the percent of increase or decrease in a quantity.
- I can find the percent error of a quantity.

EXPLORATION 1 Exploring Percent of Change

Work with a partner.

Each year in the Columbia River Basin, adult salmon swim upriver to streams to lay eggs.

To go up the river, the adult salmon use fish ladders. But to go down the river, the young salmon must pass through several dams.

At one time, there were electric turbines at each of the eight dams on the main stem of the Columbia and Snake Rivers. About 88% of the young salmon pass through a single dam unharmed.

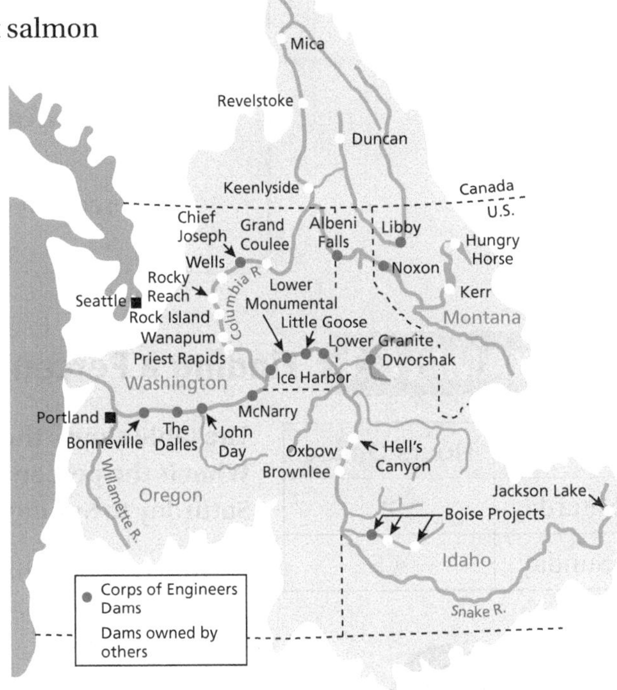

Math Practice

Check Progress

As the number of dams increases, what should be true about the number of young salmon that pass through unharmed?

a. One thousand young salmon pass through a dam. How many pass through unharmed?

b. One thousand young salmon pass through the river basin. How many pass through all 8 dams unharmed?

c. By what percent does the number of young salmon *decrease* when passing through a single dam?

d. Describe a similar real-life situation in which a quantity *increases* by a constant percent each time an event occurs.

E.4 Lesson

Key Vocabulary 
percent of change, p. 698
percent of increase, p. 698
percent of decrease, p. 698
percent error, p. 700

A **percent of change** is the percent that a quantity changes from the original amount.

$$\text{percent of change} = \frac{\text{amount of change}}{\text{original amount}}$$

 **Key Idea**

Percents of Increase and Decrease

When the original amount increases, the percent of change is called a **percent of increase**.

$$\text{percent of increase} = \frac{\text{new amount} - \text{original amount}}{\text{original amount}}$$

When the original amount decreases, the percent of change is called a **percent of decrease**.

$$\text{percent of decrease} = \frac{\text{original amount} - \text{new amount}}{\text{original amount}}$$

EXAMPLE 1 Finding a Percent of Increase

Day	Hours Online
Saturday	2
Sunday	4.5

The table shows the numbers of hours you spent online last weekend. What is the percent of change in your time spent online from Saturday to Sunday?

The time spent online Sunday is greater than the time spent online Saturday. So, the percent of change is a percent of increase.

$$\text{percent of increase} = \frac{\text{new amount} - \text{original amount}}{\text{original amount}}$$

$$= \frac{4.5 - 2}{2} \quad \text{Substitute.}$$

$$= \frac{2.5}{2} \quad \text{Subtract.}$$

$$= 1.25, \text{ or } 125\% \quad \text{Write as a percent.}$$

So, your time spent online increased 125% from Saturday to Sunday.

Try It **Find the percent of change. Round to the nearest tenth of a percent if necessary.**

1. 10 inches to 25 inches
2. 57 people to 65 people

Multi-Language Glossary at BigIdeasMath.com

Laurie's Notes

Scaffolding Instruction

- Students have used a table and/or graph to determine the percent of decrease. Now they will use a percent of change formula to find percents of change in quantities.
- **Emerging:** Students have a general understanding of **percent of increase** and **percent of decrease**, but they need help formalizing the process. They will benefit from guided instruction for the examples.
- **Proficient:** Students can calculate the percent of increase and the percent of decrease. They should review the Key Ideas before completing the Try It and Self-Assessment exercises.

Key Idea

- Explain the difference between *amount* of change and *percent* of change. Refer to the exploration.
- Use the salmon example to help identify vocabulary:

  original amount = 1000,

  amount of change (between Dam 1 and Dam 2) = 120,

  percent of change $= \frac{120}{1000} = 12\%$ decrease.

EXAMPLE 1

? "Did the online use increase or decrease from Saturday to Sunday?" increase

? "How much did the online use increase from Saturday to Sunday?" 2.5 hours

- Have students write the equation, substitute the values, and then simplify. The original amount is 2. The new amount is 4.5. Because the number of hours increased, you are finding a percent of increase.

  percent of increase $= \frac{4.5 - 2}{2} = 1.25 = 125\%$

- **Common Error:** Students think the answer is 1.25. This decimal must still be converted to a percent. This often happens when the percent answer is greater than 100%.
- Remind students to check for reasonableness. They can use number sense to recognize that the number of hours more than doubled, so the percent of increase should be greater than 100%.

Try It

- In Exercise 1, the length has more than doubled, so the percent of increase is greater than 100%.
- In Exercise 2, the number of people has not doubled, so the percent of increase is less than 100%.

Scaffold instruction to support all students in their learning. Learning is individualized and you may want to group students differently as they move in and out of these levels with each skill and concept. Student self-assessment and feedback help guide your instructional decisions about how and when to layer support for all students to become proficient learners.

Extra Example 1

Find the percent of change from 40 hours to 50 hours. 25% increase

ELL Support

After demonstrating Example 1, have students practice language by working in pairs to complete Try It Exercises 1 and 2. Have one student ask another, "Which quantity is the new amount? the original amount? How do you find the percent of increase? What is your answer?" Have students alternate roles.

Beginner: Write or state the numbers.

Intermediate: Use simple sentences such as, "The new amount is twenty-five inches."

Advanced: Use detailed sentences such as, "To find the percent of increase, subtract the original amount from the new amount. Then divide by the original amount and write as a percent."

Try It

1. 150% increase
2. about 14.0% increase

Extra Example 2

Find the percent of change from 20 days to 12 days. 40% decrease

Try It

3. decrease of about 44.4%

Self-Assessment
for Concepts & Skills

4. *Sample answer:* The quantity increases or decreases by *n*% compared to the original amount.
5. 5 bonus points added to 50 points; *Sample answer:* The original amount is smaller for 50 points, making the percent of change a larger amount.
6. increase; 200%
7. decrease; 30%

Laurie's Notes

EXAMPLE 2

? "How much did the number of home runs change each year?" decrease of 8, increase of 18, decrease of 8

? "What is the original amount?" 28

? "What is the new amount?" 20

- Students should now use the percent of decrease formula.
- This problem involves a number of skills: reading a bar graph, using the percent of decrease formula, converting a fraction to a decimal, and converting a decimal to a percent.
- **Attend to Precision:** The answer is rounded to the nearest tenth of a percent. Have students discuss whether they think this is appropriate for the problem context.

? "Is the percent change from 2015 to 2016 more or less than 100%? How do you know?" more than; The number of home runs more than doubled, so the increase is greater than 100%.

Try It

- Encourage students to write the percent of decrease in words before substituting the numbers. This will help them understand the formula.

Self-Assessment for Concepts & Skills

- Vocabulary is very important throughout this chapter. Students should not only recognize and understand the terms, but they need to read each problem carefully to decide how to begin.
- **Neighbor Check:** Have students work independently and then have their neighbors check their work. Have students discuss any discrepancies.
- **Thumbs Up:** Ask students to assess their understanding of percent of change.

ELL Support

Allow students to work in pairs for extra support. Then have each pair discuss their answers with another pair. Have each group of four explain their answers to Exercises 4 and 5 to the class. Have pairs display their answers to Exercises 6 and 7 on whiteboards for your review.

The Success Criteria Self-Assessment chart can be found in the *Student Journal* or online at *BigIdeasMath.com.*

EXAMPLE 2 Finding a Percent of Decrease

The bar graph shows a softball player's home run totals. What was the percent of change from 2016 to 2017?

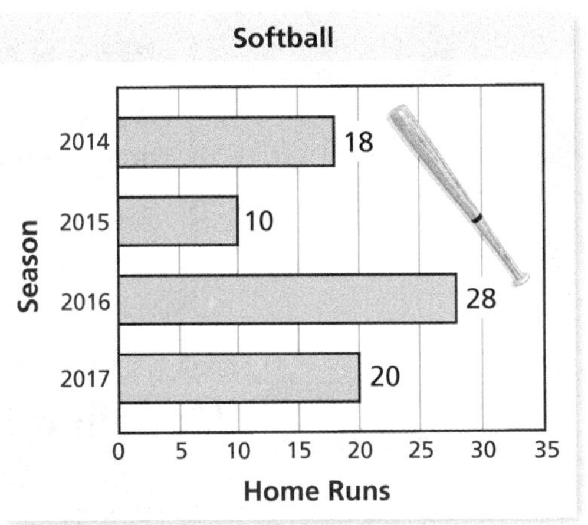

The number of home runs decreased from 2016 to 2017. So, the percent of change is a percent of decrease.

$$\text{percent of decrease} = \frac{\text{original amount} - \text{new amount}}{\text{original amount}}$$

$$= \frac{28 - 20}{28} \qquad \text{Substitute.}$$

$$= \frac{8}{28} \qquad \text{Subtract.}$$

$$\approx 0.286, \text{ or } 28.6\% \qquad \text{Write as a percent.}$$

So, the number of home runs decreased about 28.6% from 2016 to 2017.

Try It

3. In Example 2, what was the percent of change from 2014 to 2015?

Self-Assessment for Concepts & Skills

Solve each exercise. Then rate your understanding of the success criteria in your journal.

4. **VOCABULARY** What does it mean for a quantity to change by $n\%$?

5. MP **NUMBER SENSE** Without calculating, determine which situation has a greater percent of change. Explain.

- 5 bonus points added to 50 points
- 5 bonus points added to 100 points

FINDING A PERCENT OF CHANGE **Identify the percent of change as an *increase* or a *decrease*. Then find the percent of change.**

6. 8 feet to 24 feet

7. 300 miles to 210 miles

Key Idea

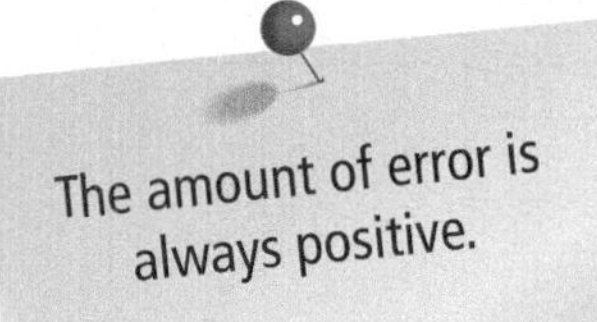

Percent Error

A **percent error** is the percent that an estimated amount differs from the actual amount.

$$\text{percent error} = \frac{\text{amount of error}}{\text{actual amount}}$$

EXAMPLE 3 Modeling Real Life

You fill bags with about 16 ounces of homemade dog treats. The acceptable percent error when filling a bag is 5%. Tell whether each bag is acceptable.

Bag A: 15 ounces

Bag B: 16.5 ounces

Find the percent error for each bag.

Bag A: The amount of error is $16 - 15 = 1$ ounce.

$$\text{percent error} = \frac{\text{amount of error}}{\text{actual amount}}$$

$$= \frac{1}{16}$$

$$= 0.0625, \text{ or } 6.25\%$$

Bag B: The amount of error is $16.5 - 16 = 0.5$ ounce.

$$\text{percent error} = \frac{\text{amount of error}}{\text{actual amount}}$$

$$= \frac{0.5}{16}$$

$$= 0.03125, \text{ or } 3.125\%$$

Because $6.25\% > 5\%$, Bag A is not acceptable. Because $3.125\% < 5\%$, Bag B is acceptable.

Self-Assessment for Problem Solving

Solve each exercise. Then rate your understanding of the success criteria in your journal.

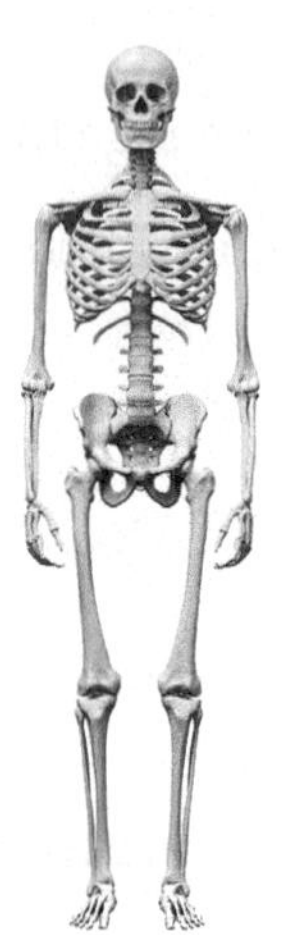

8. In one round of a game, you are asked how many bones are in a human body. If the percent error of your answer is at most 5%, you earn two points. If the percent error is at most 10%, but greater than 5%, you earn one point. You guess 195 bones. The correct answer is 206 bones. How many points do you earn?

9. **DIG DEEPER!** The manager of a restaurant offers a 20% decrease in price to tennis teams. A cashier applies a 10% decrease and then another 10% decrease. Is this the same as applying a 20% decrease? If so, justify your answer. If not, explain how to achieve a 20% decrease after first applying a 10% decrease.

Laurie's Notes

Key Idea

- Write the Key Idea.
- **Percent error** is really an application of percent of change. The percent error compares the amount of error to the actual amount.
- An estimate can be too high or too low when compared to the actual, but generally percent error is referred to as a positive amount.

EXAMPLE 3

- **Use Appropriate Tools Strategically:** Calculators are an appropriate tool for this problem.
- ? "What is meant by the amount of error?" *Sample answer:* the difference between what you want and what you have
- Work through each percent error calculation as shown.
- ? **Extension:** "Based on your calculations for the two bags, would 15.5 ounces be acceptable? Explain." Yes, because the amount of error for 15.5 ounces (0.5 ounce) is the same as the amount of error for 16.5 ounces.

Self-Assessment for Problem Solving

- Allow time in class for students to practice using the problem-solving plan. Remember, some students may only be able to complete the first step.
- These exercises assess students' understanding of the last two success criteria.
- **Think-Pair-Share:** Students should read each exercise independently and then work in pairs to complete the exercises. Students should take turns reading and interpreting the problems. Circulate and evaluate students' understanding. Have pairs share their results with the class.

The Success Criteria Self-Assessment chart can be found in the *Student Journal* or online at *BigIdeasMath.com*.

Formative Assessment Tip

Writing Prompt

This technique asks students to give feedback at the end of the lesson, activity, or learning experience. The *Writing Prompt* allows you to collect feedback in a short period of time (two minutes) on student learning.

Used at the end of the class, a *Writing Prompt* is similar to an *Exit Ticket*. The written responses give students time to reflect on their learning, how well they believe they understand the concept or skill, and where they are still uncertain. It is important to share responses with students on the following day, and let them know how you have adjusted the lesson based on their responses. Students need to know that you value their feedback, and that instruction will be modified accordingly. Students will take the *Writing Prompt* more seriously if it is valued and used.

Closure

- **Writing Prompt:** To find the percent of change...

Extra Example 3

A company fills cans with about 11 ounces of vegetable soup. The acceptable percent error when filling a can is 4%. Tell whether each can is acceptable.

Can A: 10.75 ounces

Can B: 11.5 ounces

Can A is acceptable; Can B is not acceptable.

Self-Assessment for Problem Solving

8. 1 point
9. no; *Sample answer:* If the total bill is \$100, then a 10% decrease would subtract \$10 from the bill. To achieve a 20% decrease, subtract another \$10 from the bill (10% of the original total).

Learning Target

Find percents of change in quantities.

Success Criteria

- Explain the meaning of percent of change.
- Find the percent of increase or decrease in a quantity.
- Find the percent error of a quantity.

Review & Refresh

1. $a = 0.25 \cdot 64$; 16
2. $39.2 = p \cdot 112$; 35%
3. $5 = 0.05 \cdot w$; 100
4. $18 = 0.32 \cdot w$; 56.25
5. $-\frac{2}{7}$
6. -0.696
7. $\frac{1}{3}$

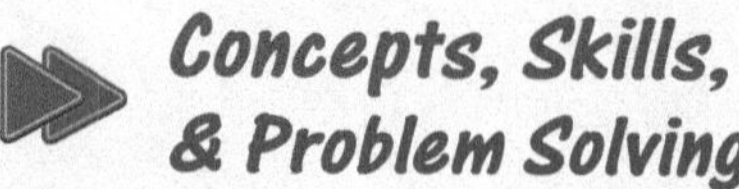

Concepts, Skills, & Problem Solving

8. 25%
9. 20%
10. 38%
11. 6%
12. increase; 200%
13. decrease; 66.7%
14. decrease; 30%
15. increase; 225%
16. increase; 140%
17. decrease; 12.5%
18. increase; 176.3%
19. decrease; 37.5%
20. no; The denominator should be 18, which is the original amount.
21. 12.5% decrease
22. 25%

Check out the Dynamic
Assessment System.
BigIdeasMath.com

Assignment Guide and Concept Check

Scaffold assignments to support all students in their learning progression. The suggested assignments are a starting point. Continue to assign additional exercises and revisit with spaced practice to move every student toward proficiency.

Level	Assignment 1	Assignment 2
Emerging	1, 2, 3, 6, 7, 8, 13, 15, 16, 20, 25	18, 19, 21, 22, 23, 24, 28, 31, 33
Proficient	1, 2, 3, 6, 7, 10, 12, 14, 16, 20, 24	18, 19, 21, 22, 23, 27, 28, 29, 30, 31, 33
Advanced	1, 2, 3, 6, 7, 11, 14, 16, 18, 20, 26	23, 27, 28, 29, 30, 31, 33, 34, 35, 36

- Assignment 1 is for use after students complete the Self-Assessment for Concepts & Skills.
- Assignment 2 is for use after students complete the Self-Assessment for Problem Solving.
- The red exercises can be used as a concept check.

Review & Refresh Prior Skills

Exercises 1–4 Using the Percent Equation
Exercises 5–7 Adding Rational Numbers

Common Errors

- **Exercises 12–19** Students may mix up where to place the numbers in the formula to find percent of change. When they do not put the numbers in the correct places, they might find a negative number in the numerator. First, emphasize that students must know if it is increasing or decreasing before they start the problem. Next, tell students the number in the denominator is the original or starting number given. Finally, the numerator should never have a negative answer. If students get a negative number, it is because they found the wrong difference. The numerator is always the greater number minus the lesser number.

E.4 Practice

Go to BigIdeasMath.com to get
HELP with solving the exercises.

Review & Refresh

Write and solve an equation to answer the question.

1. What number is 25% of 64?
2. 39.2 is what percent of 112?
3. 5 is 5% of what number?
4. 18 is 32% of what number?

Find the sum. Write fractions in simplest form.

5. $\frac{4}{7} + \left(-\frac{6}{7}\right)$
6. $-4.621 + 3.925$
7. $-\frac{5}{12} + \frac{3}{4}$

Concepts, Skills, & Problem Solving

EXPLORING PERCENT CHANGE **You are given the percent of salmon that pass through a single dam unharmed. By what percent does the number of salmon decrease when passing through a single dam?** (See Exploration 1, p. 697.)

8. 75%
9. 80%
10. 62%
11. 94%

FINDING A PERCENT OF CHANGE **Identify the percent of change as an *increase* or a *decrease*. Then find the percent of change. Round to the nearest tenth of a percent if necessary.**

12. 12 inches to 36 inches
13. 75 people to 25 people
14. 50 pounds to 35 pounds
15. 24 songs to 78 songs
16. 10 gallons to 24 gallons
17. 72 paper clips to 63 paper clips
18. 16 centimeters to 44.2 centimeters
19. 68 miles to 42.5 miles

20. MP **YOU BE THE TEACHER** Your friend finds the percent increase from 18 to 26. Is your friend correct? Explain your reasoning.

$$\frac{26 - 18}{26} \approx 0.31 = 31\%$$

21. MP **MODELING REAL LIFE** Last week, you finished Level 2 of a video game in 32 minutes. Today, you finish Level 2 in 28 minutes. What is the percent of change?

22. MP **MODELING REAL LIFE** You estimate that a baby pig weighs 20 pounds. The actual weight of the baby pig is 16 pounds. Find the percent error.

23. **MP PRECISION** A researcher estimates that a fossil is 3200 years old. Using *carbon-14 dating*, a procedure used to determine the age of an object, the researcher discovers that the fossil is 3600 years old.

a. Find the percent error.

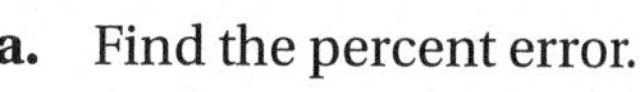

b. What other estimate gives the same percent error? Explain your reasoning.

FINDING A PERCENT OF CHANGE **Identify the percent of change as an *increase* or a *decrease*. Then find the percent of change. Round to the nearest tenth of a percent if necessary.**

24. $\frac{1}{4}$ to $\frac{1}{2}$

25. $\frac{4}{5}$ to $\frac{3}{5}$

26. $\frac{3}{8}$ to $\frac{7}{8}$

27. $\frac{5}{4}$ to $\frac{3}{8}$

28. **CRITICAL THINKING** Explain why a change from 20 to 40 is a 100% increase, but a change from 40 to 20 is a 50% decrease.

29. **MP MODELING REAL LIFE** The table shows population data for a community.

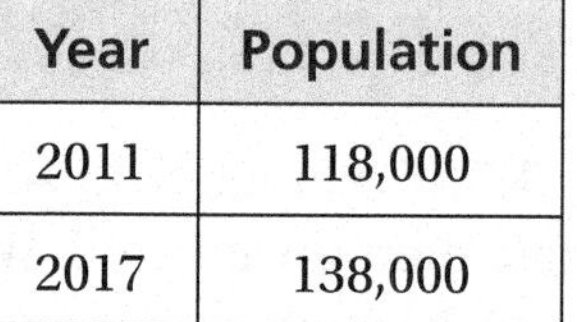

Year	Population
2011	118,000
2017	138,000

a. What is the percent of change from 2011 to 2017?

b. Predict the population in 2023. Explain your reasoning.

30. **GEOMETRY** Suppose the length and the width of the sandbox are doubled.

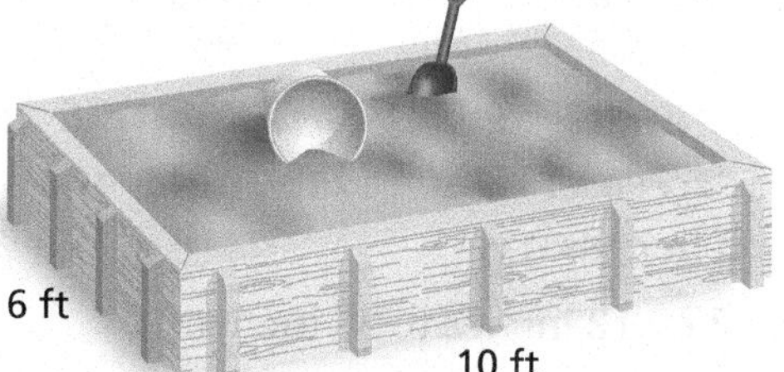

a. Find the percent of change in the perimeter.

b. Find the percent of change in the area.

31. **MP MODELING REAL LIFE** A company fills boxes with about 21 ounces of cereal. The acceptable percent error in filling a box is 2.5%. Box A contains 20.4 ounces of cereal and Box B contains 21.5 ounces of cereal. Tell whether each box is an acceptable weight.

32. **MP PRECISION** Find the percent of change from June to September in the mile-run times shown.

33. **CRITICAL THINKING** A number increases by 10% and then decreases by 10%. Will the result be *greater than*, *less than*, or *equal to* the original number? Explain.

34. **MP PROBLEM SOLVING** You want to reduce your daily calorie consumption by about 9%. You currently consume about 2100 calories per day. Use mental math to estimate the number of calories you should consume in one week to meet your goal. Explain.

35. **DIG DEEPER!** Donations to an annual fundraiser are 15% greater this year than last year. Last year, donations were 10% greater than the year before. The amount raised this year is $10,120. How much was raised two years ago?

36. **MP REASONING** Forty students are in the science club. Of those, 45% are girls. This percent increases to 56% after more girls join the club. How many more girls join?

Mini-Assessment

Identify the percent of change as an *increase* or a *decrease*. Then find the percent of change.

1. 15 meters to 36 meters increase; 140%
2. 20 songs to 70 songs increase; 250%
3. 90 people to 45 people decrease; 50%
4. Yesterday, it took 40 minutes to drive to school. Today, it took 32 minutes to drive to school. What is the percent of change in the time to drive to school? 20% decrease
5. You estimate that a box contains 141 envelopes. The actual number of envelopes is 150. Find the percent error. 6%

Section Resources

Surface Level	Deep Level
Resources by Chapter • Extra Practice • Reteach • Puzzle Time Student Journal • Self-Assessment • Practice Differentiating the Lesson Tutorial Videos Skills Review Handbook Skills Trainer	Resources by Chapter • Enrichment and Extension Graphic Organizers Dynamic Assessment System • Section Practice

Concepts, Skills, & Problem Solving

23. **a.** $11.\overline{1}\%$

b. 4000 years old; *Sample answer:* The amount of the error and the original amount are the same, giving the same percent of error.

24. decrease; 100%

25. decrease; 25%

26. increase; 133.3%

27. decrease; 70%

28. Increasing 20 to 40 is the same as increasing 20 by 20. So, it is a 100% increase. Decreasing 40 to 20 is the same as decreasing 40 by one-half of 40. So, it is a 50% decrease.

29. **a.** about 16.95% increase

b. 161,391 people; *Sample answer:* The percent of change for the 6-year span is a 16.95% increase. The population in 2017 is 138,000, so
$138{,}000 \times 0.1695 = 23{,}391$ increase in population for 2023.
$138{,}000 + 23{,}391 = 161{,}391$ people

30. **a.** 100% increase

b. 300% increase

31. Box B is acceptable, Box A is unacceptable

32. about 24.52% decrease

33. less than; *Sample answer:* Let x represent the number. A 10% increase is equal to $x + 0.1x$, or $1.1x$. A 10% decrease of this new number is equal to $1.1x - 0.1(1.1x)$, or $0.99x$. Because $0.99x < x$, the result is less than the original number.

34. about 13,300 calories; $0.10 \times 2000 = 200$ calorie decrease per day, $2100 - 200 = 1900$ calories per day, $1900 \times 7 = 13{,}300$ calories per week.

35. \$8000 **36.** 10 girls

Check out the
Dynamic Classroom.
BigIdeasMath.com

Laurie's Notes

Learning Target

Solve percent problems involving discounts and markups.

Success Criteria

- Use percent models to solve problems involving discounts and markups.
- Write and solve equations to solve problems involving discounts and markups.

Warm Up

Cumulative, vocabulary, and prerequisite skills practice opportunities are available in the *Resources by Chapter* or at *BigIdeasMath.com*.

ELL Support

Explain that *discount* and *markup* are opposites that are related to the words *decrease* and *increase*. A discount is a decrease in price. A markup is an increase in price. When a store has a sale, it decreases prices. When a store buys merchandise, it pays one price and then increases that price to make money when it sells the merchandise. The increase is called a markup.

Exploration 1

a–c. See Additional Answers.

Preparing to Teach

- Students have used the percent equation to solve percent problems. Now they will use the percent equation to find discounts and markups.
- **Reason Abstractly and Quantitatively:** Percent applications are abundant. The percent bar model helps students visualize the problem and check the reasonableness of the answer.

Motivate

- **Story Time:** "A store buys an electronic keyboard for $100 and marks it up 50%. The store has a 50% off sale. You purchase the electronic keyboard. What do you pay?" $75 "Did the store lose money?" yes
- Show a newspaper circular that advertises a discount (sale).
- Explain that today's lesson will help students become wiser consumers as they learn about **discounts** and **markups**.

Exploration 1

- Explain that sale items involve a *percent* discount and the *amount* of discount. If possible, use the newspaper circular to make this distinction.
- The percent bar models are divided into 10 equal parts. Dollar amounts for items are shown on the bars.
- Discuss how the missing dollar amounts can be computed. Students can use mental math to find 10% and multiply by the correct amount.
- **Big Idea:** When you *save* 40% ($18), you *pay* 60% ($27). Starting at $45 in the first model, move 40% to the left and that is the savings.
- **Extension:** Determine the amount you save *and* the price paid.

? "How do you decide the best buy?" Listen for the lowest final price instead of the greatest savings because the original prices may vary.

- **Connection:** In part (b), finding the original price is the same as finding the whole. $22.40 is the part.

? "What percent does $22.40 represent of the original price?" 70%

? "How does the percent bar model help you think about the original price?" Students might describe the $22.40 as 70% or about $\frac{2}{3}$ of the original price. So, another $\frac{1}{3}$ has to be added on to find the original price.

- Use the percent equation: $22.40 is 70% of what number?

? "Why is 70% used instead of 30%?" Because $22.40 is the part and it is 70% of the whole, or the original price.

? "In part (c), what percent does the selling price represent of $22.40?" 160%

- Another way to phrase the question is: 160% of $22.40 is what number?

? "Why is 160% used instead of 60%?" Because the selling price is the part and it is 160% of the whole, or $22.40.

◉ Students are beginning to work on the first success criterion.

E.5 Discounts and Markups

Learning Target: Solve percent problems involving discounts and markups.

Success Criteria:
- I can use percent models to solve problems involving discounts and markups.
- I can write and solve equations to solve problems involving discounts and markups.

EXPLORATION 1 Comparing Discounts

Work with a partner.

a. The same pair of earrings is on sale at three stores. Which store has the best price? Use the percent models to justify your answer.

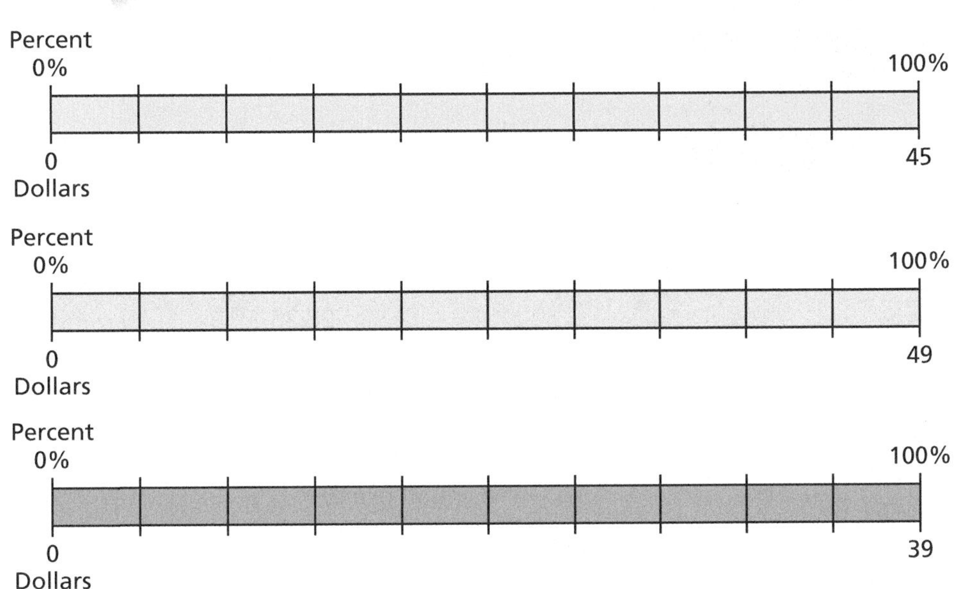

b. You buy the earrings on sale for 30% off at a different store. You pay $22.40. What was the original price of the earrings? Use the percent model to justify your answer.

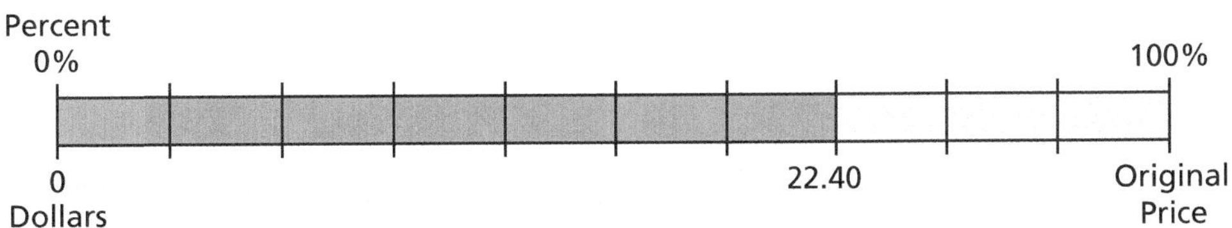

Math Practice

Communicate Precisely

Explain to your partner why 30% of the original price in part (b) is not the same as 30% of what you paid.

c. You sell the earrings in part (b) to a friend for 60% more than what you paid. What is the selling price? Use a percent model to justify your answer.

E.5 Lesson

Key Vocabulary
discount, *p. 704*
markup, *p. 704*

Key Ideas

Discounts

A **discount** is a decrease in the original price of an item.

Markups

To make a profit, stores charge more than what they pay. The increase from what the store pays to the selling price is called a **markup**.

EXAMPLE 1 **Finding a Sale Price**

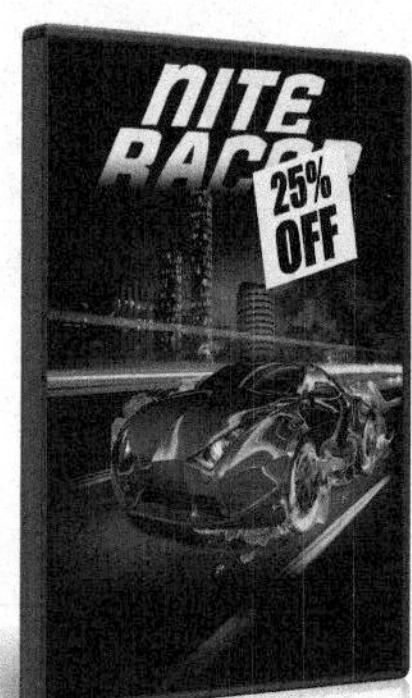

The original price of a video game is $35. What is the sale price?

Method 1: First, find the discount. The discount is 25% of $35.

$a = p\% \cdot w$ — Write the percent equation.

$= 0.25 \cdot 35$ — Substitute 0.25 for $p\%$ and 35 for w.

$= 8.75$ — Multiply.

Next, find the sale price.

Sale price	=	Original price	−	Discount
	=	35	−	8.75
	= 26.25			

So, the sale price is $26.25.

For an item with an original price of p, the price after a 25% discount is $p - 0.25p$, or $0.75p$. So, a 25% discount is the same as paying 75% of the original price.

Method 2: Use the fact that the sale price is 100% − 25% = 75% of the original price.

Find the sale price.

Sale price = 75% of $35

$= 0.75 \cdot 35$

$= 26.25$

So, the sale price is $26.25.

Check

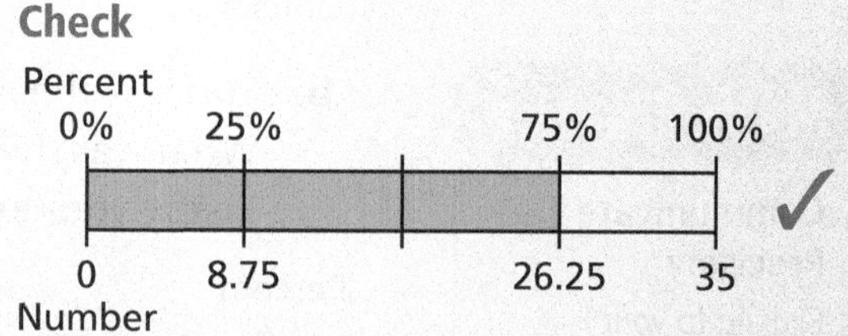

Try It

1. The original price of a skateboard is $50. The skateboard is on sale for 20% off. What is the sale price?

Multi-Language Glossary at BigIdeasMath.com

Laurie's Notes

Scaffolding Instruction

- Students explored using percent bar models to solve problems involving discounts and markups. Now they will use the percent equation to find discounts and markups. You want students to discover that they can find the selling price after a 25% discount by multiplying by 0.75 (one step) or by multiplying by 0.25 and then subtracting the result from the original price (two steps).
- **Emerging:** Students sometimes struggle with this concept. Reinforce by constantly saying, "25% off the original price is the same as paying 75% of the original price." Students will benefit from guided instruction.
- **Proficient:** Students can find discounts, markups, and original prices using a variety of methods. They should review the Key Ideas and complete the Try It exercises before moving on to the Self-Assessment exercises.

Key Ideas

- Discuss each concept using examples from the exploration.
- Use the following to help students understand the vocabulary.

wholesale price + markup = retail price (or selling price)

wholesale price	markup	retail price (or selling price)
↑	↑	↑
what a store pays	increase in price	price you pay

- **FYI:** Some students may choose to use the percent proportion instead of the percent equation. Although they are equivalent methods, all examples in this lesson are solved using the percent equation.

EXAMPLE 1

- Two methods are shown, work through each method. In the first method, you multiply to find the amount of discount and then subtract to find the sale price. In the second method, you subtract first to find the percent of the original price you will pay and then use the percent equation to find the sale price.
- **Connection:** The amount of discount is a *part* of the *whole* original price. The percent equation is used to find the amount of the discount.
- **Common Error:** Students find the discount or the amount saved ($8.75) instead of the sale price ($26.25). Remind students to always check that they have answered the question.
- Discuss the push-pin note. Try other discounts (e.g., 30%) and ask what percent you are paying (70%).

? "Why is the percent bar model divided into 4 parts?" Because the discount is 25%, or $\frac{1}{4}$.

Try It

- Have students work in pairs. Select two pairs that used different methods to share their work at the board.

Scaffold instruction to support all students in their learning. Learning is individualized and you may want to group students differently as they move in and out of these levels with each skill and concept. Student self-assessment and feedback help guide your instructional decisions about how and when to layer support for all students to become proficient learners.

Extra Example 1

The original price of a T-shirt is $15. The T-shirt is on sale for 35% off. What is the sale price? $9.75

ELL Support

After demonstrating Example 1, have students practice language by working in pairs to complete Try It Exercise 1. Have one student ask another, "What is the value of *p*%? *w*? What is the percent equation? What is the sale price?" Have students alternate roles.

Beginner: Write or state the numbers.

Intermediate: Use simple sentences such as, "*p* percent is twenty hundredths."

Advanced: Use detailed sentences such as, "To find the sale price, subtract the discount from the original price."

Try It

1. $40

Laurie's Notes

Extra Example 2

The discount on a package of athletic socks is 15%. It is on sale for $17. What is the original price of the package of athletic socks? $20

Try It

2. $20

Self-Assessment
for Concepts & Skills

3. *Sample answer:* Multiply the original price by $100\% - 15\% = 85\%$ to find the sale price.
4. $21
5. $56
6. $48
7. $90

EXAMPLE 2

? "What is the percent equation?" $a = p\% \cdot w$

? "What do you know in this problem?" 33 is the part and 60% is the percent.

- Some students may want to use a ratio table to solve. Have them share their tables.

Example:

÷ 3 → × 2 → + 60

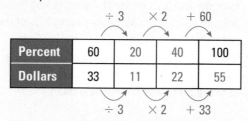

Percent	60	20	40	100
Dollars	33	11	22	55

÷ 3 → × 2 → + 33

- **Common Error:** Students multiply 33 by 60% (or 40%). Students need to remember that 33 is a *part* of the original price, not the *whole*.
- Remind students to always check for reasonableness.

Try It

- **Neighbor Check:** Have students work independently and then have their neighbors check their work. Have students discuss any discrepancies.

? **Extension:** "Is a 25% discount followed by a 10% discount the same as a 35% discount? Explain." No, the sale price for an item discounted 25% followed by a 10% discount would be $0.75(0.9) = 0.675$, or 67.5% of the original price. The sale price for an item discounted 35% would be 65% of the original price.

Self-Assessment for Concepts & Skills

- Have students work with a partner.
- **Writing Prompt:** Explain two ways to find the sale price for an item marked 30% off. 1) Find the amount of discount and subtract from the original price. 2) Find the percent of the original price and multiply the percent by the original price.

ELL Support

As Laurie's Notes suggest, allow students to work in pairs. Discuss answers to Exercise 3 as a class. Check comprehension of Exercises 4–7 by having each pair display their equations and answers on a whiteboard for your review.

The Success Criteria Self-Assessment chart can be found in the *Student Journal* or online at *BigIdeasMath.com.*

EXAMPLE 2 Finding an Original Price

What is the original price of the cleats?

The sale price is $100\% - 40\% = 60\%$ of the original price.

Answer the question:

33 is 60% of what number?

$a = p\% \cdot w$	Write the percent equation.
$33 = 0.6 \cdot w$	Substitute 33 for a and 0.6 for $p\%$.
$55 = w$	Divide each side by 0.6.

So, the original price of the cleats is $55.

Check

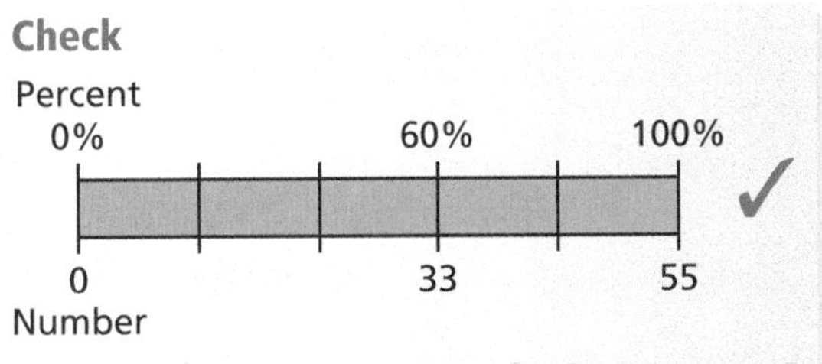

Try It

2. The discount on a DVD is 50%. It is on sale for $10. What is the original price of the DVD?

Self-Assessment for Concepts & Skills

Solve each exercise. Then rate your understanding of the success criteria in your journal.

3. **WRITING** Describe how to find the sale price of an item that has a 15% discount.

FINDING A SALE PRICE Find the sale price. Use a percent model to check your answer.

4. A portable table tennis set costs $30 before a 30% discount.
5. The original price of an easel is $70. The easel is on sale for 20% off.

FINDING AN ORIGINAL PRICE Find the original price. Use a percent model to check your answer.

6. A bracelet costs $36 after a 25% discount.
7. The discount on a toy robot is 40%. The toy robot is on sale for $54.

EXAMPLE 3 Modeling Real Life

A store pays $70 for a bicycle. What is the selling price when the markup is 20%?

Method 1: First, find the markup. The markup is 20% of $70.

$$a = p\% \cdot w$$
$$= 0.20 \cdot 70$$
$$= 14$$

Next, find the selling price.

$$\text{Selling price} = \text{Cost to store} + \text{Markup}$$
$$= 70 + 14$$
$$= 84$$

So, the selling price is $84.

Method 2: Use a ratio table. The selling price is 120% of the cost to the store.

Percent	Dollars
100%	$70
20%	$14
120%	$84

(÷ 5, then × 6 on each column)

So, the selling price is $84.

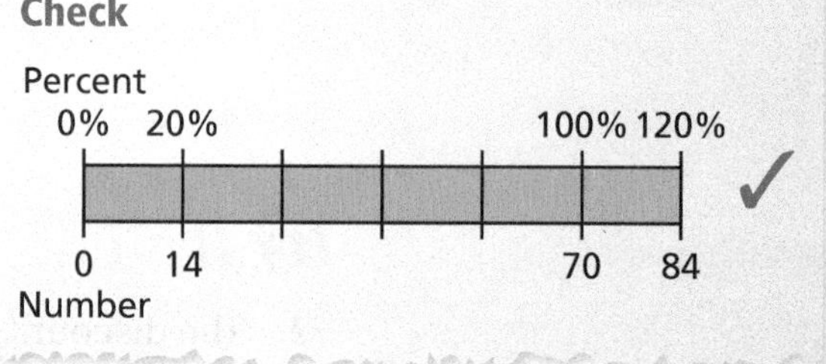

Self-Assessment for Problem Solving

Solve each exercise. Then rate your understanding of the success criteria in your journal.

8. You have two coupons for a store. The first coupon applies a $15 discount to a single purchase, and the second coupon applies a 10% discount to a single purchase. You can only use one coupon on a purchase. When should you use each coupon? Explain.

9. A store sells memory cards for $25 each.

   a. The markup for each memory card is 25%. How much did the store pay for 50 memory cards?

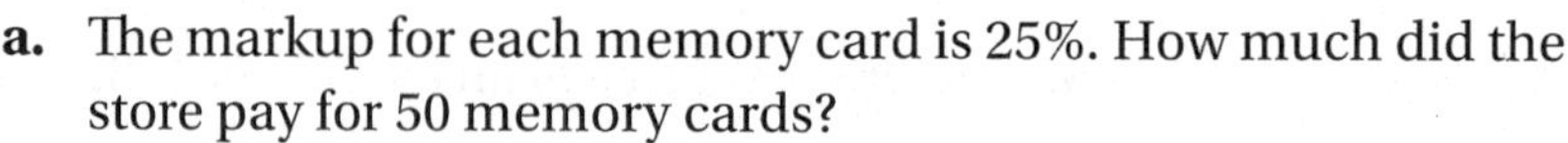

   b. The store offers a discount when a customer buys two or more memory cards. A customer pays $47.50 for two memory cards. What is the percent of discount?

   c. How much does a customer pay for three memory cards if the store increases the percent of discount in part (b) by 2%?

Laurie's Notes

EXAMPLE 3

- Work through the problem as shown. Encourage students to use mental math to find 20% of $70: 10% of 70 is 7, so 20% of 70 is 2(7), or 14.
- Two steps are used in Method 1: Find 20% of $70 and then add this amount to the original amount of $70.

? "Can this problem be solved in one step? Explain." Yes, 120% of $70 = $84.

- "Explain why 120% makes sense." You pay 100% of the store's cost plus an additional 20% markup for a total of 120%.
- Method 2 uses the fact that the selling price is 120% of what the store paid. Make sure students understand this. The ratio table shows the division and multiplication to get to 120% and that this is also the sum of the first two rows, which is comparable to the procedure in Method 1.
- Also show students how to use a proportion, $\frac{a}{70} = \frac{120}{100}$ and a one-step percent equation, $a = 1.2(70)$.
- Discuss the percent bar model in the Check note.
- **Common Error:** Students find the markup ($14) instead of the selling price ($84).
- **Reason Abstractly and Quantitatively:** Now go back and ask students what other ways they can solve the previous examples. Deep understanding results from considering different ways in which to solve problems.

Self-Assessment for Problem Solving

- Encourage students to use a Four Square to complete these exercises. Until students become comfortable with the problem-solving plan, they may only be ready to complete the first square.
- **Think-Pair-Share:** Students should work independently before working with a partner. Then have each pair compare their answers with another pair.

Have students use *Thumbs Up* to indicate their understanding of solving percent problems involving discounts and markups.

The Success Criteria Self-Assessment chart can be found in the *Student Journal* or online at *BigIdeasMath.com*.

Closure

? **Entry Ticket:** "The original price of a book is $10. The book is on sale for 50% off. If the store is offering an additional 50% discount, will they give you the book for free? Explain." No, the sale price for a book discounted 50% followed by another 50% discount would be 0.5(0.5) = 0.25, or 25% of the original price ($2.50).

Have extra tickets available for students who forget their *Entry Tickets* the next day. Those students can complete their *Entry Tickets* at the back of the room before going to their seats.

Extra Example 3

A store pays $15 for a baseball cap. What is the selling price when the markup is 60%? $24

Self-Assessment for Problem Solving

8. *Sample answer:* Use the $15 coupon for any item under $150. Use the 10% coupon for any item above $150.
9. a. $1000

   b. 5%

   c. $69.75

Formative Assessment Tip

Entry Ticket

This technique is similar to *Exit Ticket.* You pose a short problem, or ask a question, at the end of class. Students write their responses on tickets as part of their homework. Students give you their *Entry Tickets* as they enter your class the next day. Because they are short responses, you can read them quickly to decide if you need to answer any questions or clear up any misconceptions.

Learning Target

Solve percent problems involving discounts and markups.

Success Criteria

- Use percent models to solve problems involving discounts and markups.
- Write and solve equations to solve problems involving discounts and markups.

Review & Refresh

1. increase; 25%
2. decrease; 55.$\overline{5}$%
3. decrease; 66.$\overline{6}$%
4. increase; 44.74%
5. $-\frac{2}{21}$
6. −9.5116
7. $6\frac{3}{8}$

Concepts, Skills, & Problem Solving

8–9. See Additional Answers

10. \$64
11. \$35.70
12. \$24
13. \$76.16
14. \$27.92
15. \$53.33
16. \$60
17. \$450
18. \$200
19. \$172.40
20. 25%
21. 20%
22. 35%
23. \$55
24. \$128
25. \$175

Check out the Dynamic Assessment System.
BigIdeasMath.com

Assignment Guide and Concept Check

Scaffold assignments to support all students in their learning progression. The suggested assignments are a starting point. Continue to assign additional exercises and revisit with spaced practice to move every student toward proficiency.

Level	Assignment 1	Assignment 2
Emerging	4, 6, 7, 8, 11, 13, 15, 21, 23, 26	14, 18, 22, 25, 27, 28, 29
Proficient	4, 6, 7, 9, 12, 14, 16, 20, 24, 26	18, 22, 25, 27, 28, 29, 30, 31, 33
Advanced	4, 6, 7, 9, 14, 18, 22, 25, 26	27, 28, 29, 30, 31, 32, 33

- Assignment 1 is for use after students complete the Self-Assessment for Concepts & Skills.
- Assignment 2 is for use after students complete the Self-Assessment for Problem Solving.
- The red exercises can be used as a concept check.

Review & Refresh Prior Skills

Exercises 1–4 Finding a Percent of Change
Exercises 5–7 Multiplying Rational Numbers

Common Errors

- **Exercises 10–14** Students may write the discount amount as the sale price instead of subtracting it from the original price. When students copy the table, ask them to add another column titled "Discount Amount." Remind them to subtract the discount amount from the original price.
- **Exercises 15–19** Students may use the percent of discount instead of the percent of the original price of the item. Remind students that there is an extra step in the problem. They should subtract the percent of discount from 100% to find the percent of the original price of the item.
- **Exercises 20–22** Students may find the percent of the original price of the item instead of the percent of discount. Remind students that there is an extra step in the problem. They should subtract the percent of the original price of the item from 100% to find the percent of discount.
- **Exercises 23–25** Students may find the markup and not the selling price. Remind students that they must add the markup to the cost to obtain the selling price.

E.5 Practice

Go to **BigIdeasMath.com** to get HELP with solving the exercises.

Review & Refresh

Identify the percent of change as an *increase* or a *decrease*. Then find the percent of change. Round to the nearest tenth of a percent if necessary.

1. 16 meters to 20 meters
2. 9 points to 4 points
3. 15 ounces to 5 ounces
4. 38 staples to 55 staples

Find the product. Write fractions in simplest form.

5. $\frac{4}{7}\left(-\frac{1}{6}\right)$
6. $-1.58(6.02)$
7. $-3\left(-2\frac{1}{8}\right)$

Concepts, Skills, & Problem Solving

COMPARING DISCOUNTS **The same item is on sale at two stores. Which one is the better price? Use percent models to justify your answer.** (See Exploration 1, p. 703.)

8. 60% off \$60 or 55% off \$50
9. 85% off \$90 or 70% off \$65

MP USING TOOLS **Copy and complete the table.**

	Original Price	Percent of Discount	Sale Price
10.	\$80	20%	
11.	\$42	15%	
12.	\$120	80%	
13.	\$112	32%	
14.	\$69.80	60%	
15.		25%	\$40
16.		5%	\$57
17.		80%	\$90
18.		64%	\$72
19.		15%	\$146.54
20.	\$60		\$45
21.	\$82		\$65.60
22.	\$95		\$61.75

FINDING A SELLING PRICE **Find the selling price.**

23. Cost to store: \$50
Markup: 10%
24. Cost to store: \$80
Markup: 60%
25. Cost to store: \$140
Markup: 25%

26. MP **YOU BE THE TEACHER** A store pays \$60 for an item. Your friend finds the selling price when the markup is 20%. Is your friend correct? Explain your reasoning.

0.2(\$60) = \$12

So, the selling price is \$12.

27. MP **STRUCTURE** The scooter is being sold at a 10% discount. The original price is shown. Which methods can you use to find the new sale price? Which method do you prefer? Explain.

- Multiply \$42.00 by 0.9.
- Multiply \$42.00 by 0.1, then subtract from \$42.00.
- Multiply \$42.00 by 0.9, then add to \$42.00.
- Multiply \$42.00 by 0.9, then subtract from \$42.00.

28. MP **NUMBER SENSE** The original price of an item is p dollars. Is the price of the item with an 18% markup the same as multiplying the original price by 1.18? Use two expressions to justify your answer.

29. MP **PROBLEM SOLVING** You are shopping for a video game system.

a. At which store should you buy the system?

b. Store A has a weekend sale. What discount must Store A offer for you to buy the system there?

Store	Cost to Store	Markup
A	\$162	40%
B	\$155	30%
C	\$160	25%

30. DIG DEEPER! A pool manager balances the pH level of a pool. The price of a bucket of chlorine tablets is \$90, and the price of a pH test kit is \$11. The manager uses a coupon that applies a 40% discount to the total cost of the two items. How much money does the pool manager pay for each item?

31. MP **PRECISION** You buy a pair of jeans at a department store.

a. What is the percent of discount to the nearest percent?

b. What is the percent of sales tax to the nearest tenth of a percent?

c. The price of the jeans includes a 60% markup. After the discount, what is the percent of markup to the nearest percent?

Department Store

Jeans	39.99
Discount	-10.00
Subtotal	29.99
Sales Tax	1.95
Total	31.94

Thank You

32. **CRITICAL THINKING** You buy a bicycle helmet for \$22.26, which includes 6% sales tax. The helmet is discounted 30% off the selling price. What is the original price?

33. MP **REASONING** A drone that costs \$129.50 is discounted 40%. The next month, the sale price is discounted an additional 60%. Is the drone now "free"? If so, explain. If not, find the sale price.

Mini-Assessment

Find the price, percent of discount or markup, or cost to store.

1. Original price: $50

   Percent of discount: 15%

   Sale price: ?

   $42.50

2. Original price: $35

   Percent of discount: ?

   Sale price: $31.50

   10%

3. Cost to store: $75

   Percent of markup: ?

   Selling price: $112.50

   50%

4. Cost to store: ?

   Percent of markup: 15%

   Selling price: $85.10

   $74

5. The discount on a bicycle is 20%. It is on sale for $89.90. What is the original price of the bicycle? $112.38

Section Resources

Surface Level	Deep Level
Resources by Chapter • Extra Practice • Reteach • Puzzle Time Student Journal • Self-Assessment • Practice Differentiating the Lesson Tutorial Videos Skills Review Handbook Skills Trainer	Resources by Chapter • Enrichment and Extension Graphic Organizers Dynamic Assessment System • Section Practice

Concepts, Skills, & Problem Solving

26. no; The selling price is 120% of the cost to the store, or 1.2 • $60.

27. "Multiply $42 by 0.9" and "Multiply $42 by 0.1, then subtract from $42." The first method is easier because it is only one step.

28. yes; $p \cdot 1.18 = 1.18p$;
$p + 0.18p = 1.18p$

29. **a.** Store C

b. at least 11.82%

30. $54 for chlorine tablets and $6.60 for pH test kit

31. **a.** 25%

b. 6.5%

c. 20%

32. $30

33. no; $31.08

Learning Target

Understand and apply the simple interest formula.

Success Criteria

- Explain the meaning of simple interest.
- Use the simple interest formula to solve problems.

Warm Up

Cumulative, vocabulary, and prerequisite skills practice opportunities are available in the *Resources by Chapter* or at *BigIdeasMath.com*.

ELL Support

Students may know the word *interest* from everyday life. Point out that it has a special meaning in math. It describes the amount of money paid or earned for using or lending money. You may want to explain what simple interest means as opposed to compound interest.

Exploration 1

a. *Sample answer:* Every year the balance increases by $9.

b. The amount of interest each year is determined by multiplying the original amount, $150, by the simple interest rate, 6%.

c. *Sample answer:* Multiply the initial amount, interest rate, and the period of time together.

d. 10%; $300

Laurie's Notes

Preparing to Teach

- Students have solved percent problems in a variety of ways. Now they will explore simple interest.
- **Model with Mathematics:** Percent applications are abundant in the financial world. Interest rates are stated as percents and students need to understand how interest is paid or charged to consumers.

Motivate

- **Story Time:** Tell students that you just saw an ad for the latest smart phone and you really want to buy it. "It's only $400, but unfortunately I have a few other bills this month and can't afford $400 all at once."
- ? "What can I do?" Students may suggest that you borrow money from a bank or get a payment plan.
- ? "Will a bank or the cell phone company just give me $400?" Hopefully, students will know that there is a fee you have to pay to borrow the money.

Discuss

- **Financial Literacy:** You want students to have some understanding of the cost of borrowing money or the ability to earn money when it is deposited in a bank, not to become trained loan officers.
- **Discuss:** When you *deposit* money, you should *earn* money. When you *borrow* money, you should *pay* money. Interest earned/owed is influenced by how much money is involved (**principal**), the **interest** rate, and the amount of time.
- Students should assume that deposits are made at the beginning of the interest period in all banking problems, unless otherwise stated.

Exploration 1

- In this situation, the principal stays the same for each year's calculation. Interest paid is *not* being compounded.
- **Demonstrate:** After one year, you earn $\$150(0.06) = 9.00$, which is added to the initial amount (the principal).
- Students should recognize that the same amount is added each year. They can determine the amount of interest earned in 6 years by multiplying the amount of interest earned in one year by 6.
- **Look for and Express Regularity in Repeated Reasoning:** In part (c), students may be able to create a verbal model for simple interest.

  Amount of **simple interest** = (Initial amount)(interest rate)(time)
- In part (d), students should observe that each year $15 of interest is earned.
- They can use the percent of change formula to find the interest rate.

$$\text{Percent of change} = \frac{\text{amount of change}}{\text{original amount}} = \frac{15}{150} = 0.1 = 10\%$$

- Students can use their answers in part (c) to find the simple interest earned in 10 years ($150) and then add it to the initial amount to find the balance after 10 years ($300).
- **Popsicle Sticks:** Select several students to share their answers for each part.
- ◉ Students are beginning to work on both success criteria.

E.6 Simple Interest

Learning Target: Understand and apply the simple interest formula.

Success Criteria:
- I can explain the meaning of simple interest.
- I can use the simple interest formula to solve problems.

EXPLORATION 1 Understanding Simple Interest

Work with a partner. You deposit \$150 in an account that earns 6% *simple interest per year*. You do not make any other deposits or withdrawals. The table shows the balance of the account at the end of each year.

Years	Balance
0	\$150
1	\$159
2	\$168
3	\$177
4	\$186
5	\$195
6	\$204

a. Describe any patterns you see in the account balance.

b. How is the amount of interest determined each year?

c. How can you find the amount of simple interest earned when you are given an initial amount, an interest rate, and a period of time?

d. You deposit \$150 in a different account that earns simple interest. The table shows the balance of the account each year. What is the interest rate of the account? What is the balance after 10 years?

Years	0	1	2	3
Balance	\$150	\$165	\$180	\$195

Math Practice

Look for Patterns

How does the pattern in the balances help you find the simple interest rate?

Key Vocabulary
interest, *p. 710*
principal, *p. 710*
simple interest, *p. 710*

Interest is money paid or earned for using or lending money. The **principal** is the amount of money borrowed or deposited.

Key Idea

Simple Interest

Words **Simple interest** is money paid or earned only on the principal.

Algebra $I = Prt$

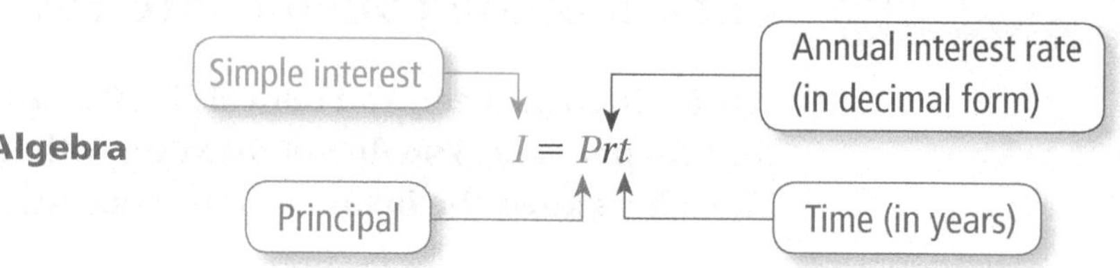

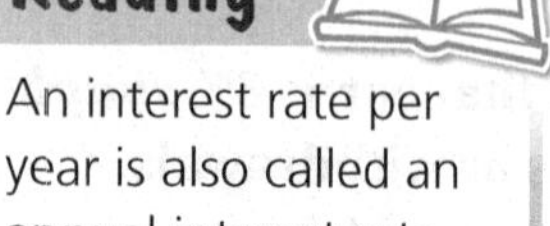

Reading

An interest rate per year is also called an annual interest rate.

EXAMPLE 1 Finding a Balance

You deposit \$500 in a savings account. The account earns 3% simple interest per year. What is the balance after 3 years?

To find the balance, calculate the interest and add it to the principal.

$I = Prt$	Write the simple interest formula.
$= 500(0.03)(3)$	Substitute 500 for *P*, 0.03 for *r*, and 3 for *t*.
$= 45$	Multiply.

The interest earned is \$45 after 3 years.

So, the balance is \$500 + \$45 = \$545 after 3 years.

Math Practice

Use a Formula
Write a formula that you can use to find the total balance *B* of an account. Explain your reasoning.

Try It

1. What is the balance of the account after 9 months?

EXAMPLE 2 Finding an Annual Interest Rate

You deposit \$1000 in an account. The account earns \$100 simple interest in 4 years. What is the annual interest rate?

$I = Prt$	Write the simple interest formula.
$100 = 1000(r)(4)$	Substitute 100 for *I*, 1000 for *P*, and 4 for *t*.
$100 = 4000r$	Simplify.
$0.025 = r$	Divide each side by 4000.

So, the annual interest rate of the account is 0.025, or 2.5%.

Laurie's Notes

Scaffolding Instruction

- Students have explored simple interest. Now they will use the simple interest formula to solve various interest problems.
- **Emerging:** Students may be able to compute the interest for one year but struggle with how it applies to longer periods of time. They will benefit from guided instruction for the Key Idea and examples.
- **Proficient:** Students can solve simple interest problems. They should review the definitions and Key Idea before completing the Try It and Self-Assessment exercises.

Key Idea

- Discuss the vocabulary used in simple interest problems: **interest**, money paid or earned, **principal**, amount of money borrowed or deposited, balance, interest rate, annual.
- **Representation:** Write the formula in words first.
  Simple interest = (Principal)(Annual interest rate)(Time)
- Explain that the interest rate is written as a decimal and the time is written in terms of years. When time is given in months, remember to express it as a fraction of a year or as a decimal. For example, 9 months $= \frac{9}{12} = 0.75$ year.

EXAMPLE 1

- There are two parts to the problem: calculate the interest earned and then determine the balance (the amount in the account).
- ? "What operation is performed in writing *Prt*?" multiplication
- ? "In calculating 500(0.03)(3), what order is the multiplication performed?" Order doesn't matter, because multiplication is commutative.
- **Explain:** The balance is the original principal *plus* the interest earned.
- ? **Reason Abstractly and Quantitatively:** If time permits, ask, "What would the balance be if the interest rate had been 6% instead of 3%?" $590 Doubling the interest rate doubles the amount earned. This can be shown in the equation: $I = 500(0.06)(3) = 500(0.03)(2)(3)$.

Try It

- Have students work with a partner.

EXAMPLE 2

- This example uses the Division Property of Equality to solve for the interest rate.
- ? "Why does $1000(r)(4) = 4000r$?" Commutative Property of Multiplication
- **Common Error:** Students divide 4000 by 100 instead of 100 by 4000.
- ? "How do you write a decimal as a percent?" Multiply by 100 (move the decimal point two places to the right). Then write the percent symbol.

Scaffold instruction to support all students in their learning. Learning is individualized and you may want to group students differently as they move in and out of these levels with each skill and concept. Student self-assessment and feedback help guide your instructional decisions about how and when to layer support for all students to become proficient learners.

Extra Example 1

You deposit $200 in a savings account. The account earns 2% simple interest per year. What is the balance after 5 years? $220

ELL Support

After demonstrating Example 1, have students practice language by working in pairs to complete Try It Exercise 1. Have one student ask another, "What is the simple interest formula? What is the value of *P*? *r*? *t*? What is the answer?" Have students alternate roles.

Beginner: Write or state the numbers.

Intermediate: Use simple sentences such as, "*P* is five hundred."

Advanced: Use detailed sentences such as, "To find the simple interest, multiply the principal amount, interest rate, and number of years."

Try It

1. $511.25

Extra Example 2

You deposit $700 in an account. The account earns $224 simple interest in 8 years. What is the annual interest rate? 4%

Try It

2. 2%

Extra Example 3

Using the diagram in Example 3, how long does it take an account with a principal of $400 to earn $36 in interest?

6 years

Try It

3. 2.5 yr

Self-Assessment for Concepts & Skills

4. *Sample answer:* Simple interest is money paid or earned only on the principal.
5. $23.20
6. 15%
7. about 5.5 years

Laurie's Notes

Try It

- **Neighbor Check:** Have students work independently and then have their neighbors check their work. Have students discuss any discrepancies.
- Check accuracy of decimals in students' work.

EXAMPLE 3

- Discuss the diagram.
- ? "Why would a bank offer different interest rates for different principals?" Students may not understand that banks are using deposited money to loan to other people. Banks also base decisions about interest rates on the borrower's credit score.
- Work through the problem as shown.
- ? "What is 6.25 as a mixed number?" $6\frac{1}{4}$
- **Connection:** Students may wonder why anyone would want to know how long it takes to earn $100 in interest. Use an example of depositing money for a future purchase (car, house, college education).

Try It

- **Neighbor Check:** Have students work independently and then have their neighbors check their work. Have students discuss any discrepancies.
- Check accuracy of decimals in students' work.

Self-Assessment for Concepts & Skills

- These exercises assess students' understanding of the success criteria. Students have several opportunities to demonstrate their understanding of simple interest and how to use the simple interest formula to solve problems.
- Vocabulary is important throughout this chapter. Students should not only recognize and understand the terms, but they need to read problems with context carefully to make decisions about their solution methods.

ELL Support

Allow students to work in pairs. Monitor discussions and provide support as needed. Have pairs share their answers to Exercise 4 and discuss as a class. Check comprehension of Exercises 5–7 by having each pair display their equations and answers on a whiteboard for your review.

The Success Criteria Self-Assessment chart can be found in the *Student Journal* or online at *BigIdeasMath.com*.

Try It

2. You deposit \$350 in an account. The account earns \$17.50 simple interest in 2.5 years. What is the annual interest rate?

EXAMPLE 3 Finding an Amount of Time

A bank offers three savings accounts. The simple annual interest rate is determined by the principal. How long does it take an account with a principal of \$800 to earn \$100 in interest?

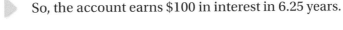

The diagram shows that the interest rate for a principal of \$800 is 2%.

$I = Prt$	Write the simple interest formula.
$100 = 800(0.02)(t)$	Substitute 100 for I, 800 for P, and 0.02 for r.
$100 = 16t$	Simplify.
$6.25 = t$	Divide each side by 16.

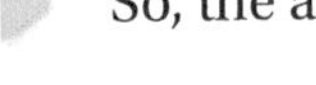

So, the account earns \$100 in interest in 6.25 years.

Try It

3. In Example 3, how long does it take an account with a principal of \$10,000 to earn \$750 in interest?

Self-Assessment for Concepts & Skills

Solve each exercise. Then rate your understanding of the success criteria in your journal.

4. **VOCABULARY** Explain the meaning of simple interest.

USING THE SIMPLE INTEREST FORMULA **Use the simple interest formula.**

5. You deposit \$20 in a savings account. The account earns 4% simple interest per year. What is the balance after 4 years?

6. You deposit \$800 in an account. The account earns \$360 simple interest in 3 years. What is the annual interest rate?

7. You deposit \$650 in a savings account. How long does it take an account with an annual interest rate of 5% to earn \$178.25 in interest?

EXAMPLE 4 Modeling Real Life

You borrow \$600 to buy a violin. The simple annual interest rate is 15%. You pay off the loan after 2 years of equal monthly payments. How much is each payment?

Understand the problem.

You are given the amount and simple annual interest rate of a loan that you pay back in 2 years. You are asked to find the monthly payment.

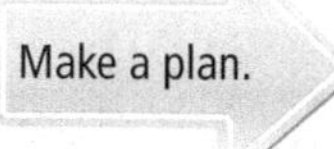

Use the simple interest formula to find the interest you pay on the loan. Then divide the total amount you pay by the number of months in 2 years.

Solve and check.

$I = Prt$	Write the simple interest formula.
$= 600(0.15)(2)$	Substitute 600 for P, 0.15 for r, and 2 for t.
$= 180$	Multiply.

You pay \$600 + \$180 = \$780 for the loan.

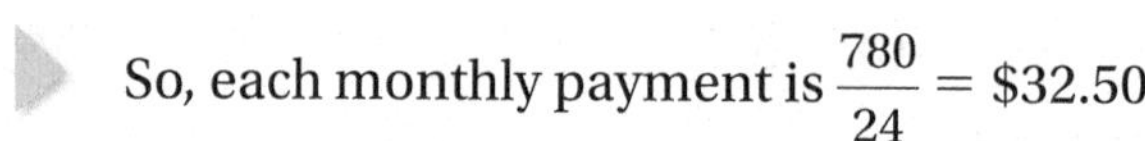

So, each monthly payment is $\frac{780}{24} = \$32.50$.

Look Back When you substitute 600 for P and 0.15 for r, you obtain $I = 90t$. This indicates that you pay \$90 in interest each year. So, in 2 years you pay 2(90) = \$180 in interest. ✓

Self-Assessment for Problem Solving

Solve each exercise. Then rate your understanding of the success criteria in your journal.

8. You want to deposit \$1000 in a savings account for 3 years. One bank adds a \$100 bonus to your principal and offers a 2% simple annual interest rate. Another bank does not add a bonus, but offers 6% simple interest per year. Which bank should you choose? Explain.

9. Your cousin borrows \$1125 to repair her car. The simple annual interest rate is 10%. She makes equal monthly payments of \$25. How many years will it take to pay off the loan?

10. **DIG DEEPER!** You borrow \$900 to buy a laptop. You plan to pay off the loan after 5 years of equal monthly payments. After 10 payments, you have \$1200 left to pay. What is the simple annual interest rate of your loan?

Laurie's Notes

EXAMPLE 4

- Remind students that the simple interest formula is used to calculate interest *earned* when you *deposit* money and to calculate interest *owed* when you *borrow* money.
- **Discuss:** There are three parts to the problem.
  1. Calculate the interest owed.
  2. Determine the total cost you must pay back for the loan.
  3. Determine the monthly payment.
- **Explain:** Simple interest is only one type of interest. Typical loans use *compound* interest, which will be studied in future courses.

Self-Assessment for Problem Solving

- Students may benefit from trying the exercises independently and then working with peers to refine their work. It is important to provide time in class for problem solving, so that students become comfortable with the problem-solving plan.
- **Make Sense of Problems and Persevere in Solving Them:** Some students may see real-life problems as too complicated and want to go back to simpler problems. Build their confidence by explaining that those problems are the building blocks. Reassure them that they are capable of learning the next step. Problems in real life will be in context. Encourage students to apply the skills and reasoning they have developed through the examples to solve real-life problems.
- **Think-Pair-Share:** Have groups share their work and discuss the reasonableness of their answers. It is important to maintain a classroom culture in which mistakes are viewed as opportunities for learning.

The Success Criteria Self-Assessment chart can be found in the *Student Journal* or online at *BigIdeasMath.com*.

Formative Assessment Tip

Creating Context
Students create their own contexts to represent a particular problem. Students should solve the problems on the backs of their papers and check their answers for reasonableness. Then students trade papers and identify any revisions that should be made. Collect and review each real-life problem. Identify problems that work well, problems that need more information, and problems that may be misleading.
Another way to provide feedback is to have a class discussion about ways to revise or improve each real-life problem. The process of writing and revising real-life problems enhances students' ability to problem-solve.

Closure

- **Creating Context:** Have students work in pairs to write a real-life problem that can be modeled by $I = 1000(0.05)(11)$.

Extra Example 4

You borrow \$300 to buy a guitar. The simple annual interest rate is 12%. You pay off the loan after 4 years of equal monthly payments. How much is each payment? \$9.25

Self-Assessment for Problem Solving

8. 6% interest; 1st bank: $I = (1000 + 100) \cdot 0.02 \cdot 3 = \$66$, 2nd bank: $I = 1000 \cdot 0.06 \cdot 3 = \$180$
9. 6 years
10. 12%

Learning Target

Understand and apply the simple interest formula.

Success Criteria

- Explain the meaning of simple interest.
- Use the simple interest formula to solve problems.

Review & Refresh

1. $9.60
2. $3.15
3. $x < -3$

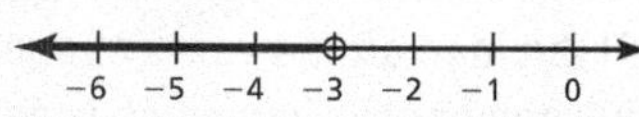

4. $b \geq 1$

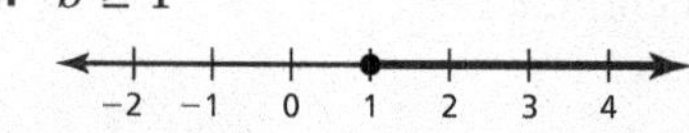

5. $w \leq -9$

−12 −11 −10 −9 −8 −7 −6

Concepts, Skills, & Problem Solving

6. 5%; $60
7. 8%; $315
8. a. $60

   b. $660
9. a. $300

   b. $1800
10. a. $105

    b. $455
11. a. $292.50

    b. $2092.50
12. a. $51.06

    b. $976.06
13. a. $1722.24

    b. $6922.24
14. no; The time should be in terms of years, not months.
15. 3%
16. 7.5%
17. 4%
18. 12%
19. 2 yr
20. 8 yr
21. 1.5 yr
22. 2.5 yr

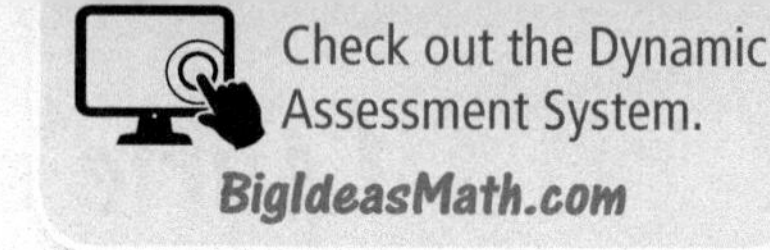

Assignment Guide and Concept Check

Scaffold assignments to support all students in their learning progression. The suggested assignments are a starting point. Continue to assign additional exercises and revisit with spaced practice to move every student toward proficiency.

Level	Assignment 1	Assignment 2
Emerging	2, 5, 6, 9, 11, 14, 15, 17, 19, 21, 23	12, 18, 22, 24, 25, 27, 30, 32, 34, 36, 40
Proficient	2, 5, 7, 8, 10, 14, 16, 18, 20, 22, 23	12, 24, 25, 26, 28, 30, 32, 34, 35, 36, 40
Advanced	2, 5, 7, 10, 12, 14, 16, 18, 20, 22, 23	24, 28, 32, 33, 34, 35, 36, 37, 38, 39, 40

- Assignment 1 is for use after students complete the Self-Assessment for Concepts & Skills.
- Assignment 2 is for use after students complete the Self-Assessment for Problem Solving.
- The red exercises can be used as a concept check.

Review & Refresh Prior Skills

Exercises 1 and 2 Finding the Selling Price

Exercises 3–5 Solving an Inequality

Common Errors

- **Exercises 8–13 and 19–22** Students may forget to change the percent to a decimal. Remind students that before they can put the percent into the formula, they must change the percent to a decimal or a fraction.
- **Exercises 11 and 13** Students may not change months into years and calculate a much greater interest amount. Remind students that the simple interest formula is for *years* and that the time must be changed to years.
- **Exercises 17 and 18** Students may not change months into years and calculate a much lower interest rate. Remind students that the simple interest formula is for *years* and that the time must be changed to years.

E.6 Practice

Go to BigIdeasMath.com to get
HELP with solving the exercises.

Review & Refresh

Find the selling price.

1. A store pays $8 for a pool noodle. The markup is 20%.
2. A store pays $3 for a magazine. The markup is 5%.

Solve the inequality. Graph the solution.

3. $x + 5 < 2$
4. $b - 2 \geq -1$
5. $w + 6 \leq -3$

Concepts, Skills, & Problem Solving

UNDERSTANDING SIMPLE INTEREST **The table shows the balance of an account each year. What is the interest rate of the account? What is the balance after 10 years?** (See Exploration 1, p. 709.)

6.

Years	Balance
0	$40
1	$42
2	$44
3	$46

7.

Years	Balance
0	$175
1	$189
2	$203
3	$217

FINDING INTEREST EARNED **An account earns simple annual interest. (a) Find the interest earned. (b) Find the balance of the account.**

8. $600 at 5% for 2 years
9. $1500 at 4% for 5 years
10. $350 at 3% for 10 years
11. $1800 at 6.5% for 30 months
12. $925 at 2.3% for 2.4 years
13. $5200 at 7.36% for 54 months

14. MP YOU BE THE TEACHER Your friend finds the simple interest earned on $500 at 6% for 18 months. Is your friend correct? Explain your reasoning.

$I = (500)(0.06)(18)$
$= \$540$

FINDING AN ANNUAL INTEREST RATE **Find the annual interest rate.**

15. $I = \$24, P = \$400, t = 2$ years
16. $I = \$562.50, P = \$1500, t = 5$ years
17. $I = \$54, P = \$900, t = 18$ months
18. $I = \$160, P = \$2000, t = 8$ months

FINDING AN AMOUNT OF TIME **Find the amount of time.**

19. $I = \$30, P = \$500, r = 3\%$
20. $I = \$720, P = \$1000, r = 9\%$
21. $I = \$54, P = \$800, r = 4.5\%$
22. $I = \$450, P = \$2400, r = 7.5\%$

23. **FINDING AN ACCOUNT BALANCE** A savings account earns 5% simple interest per year. The principal is \$1200. What is the balance after 4 years?

24. **FINDING AN ANNUAL INTEREST RATE** You deposit \$400 in an account. The account earns \$18 simple interest in 9 months. What is the annual interest rate?

25. **FINDING AN AMOUNT OF TIME** You deposit \$3000 in a CD (certificate of deposit) that earns 5.6% simple annual interest. How long will it take to earn \$336 in interest?

FINDING AN AMOUNT PAID **Find the amount paid for the loan.**

26. \$1500 at 9% for 2 years

27. \$2000 at 12% for 3 years

28. \$2400 at 10.5% for 5 years

29. \$4800 at 9.9% for 4 years

USING THE SIMPLE INTEREST FORMULA **Copy and complete the table.**

	Principal	Annual Interest Rate	Time	Simple Interest
30.	\$12,000	4.25%	5 years	
31.		6.5%	18 months	\$828.75
32.	\$15,500	8.75%		\$5425.00
33.	\$18,000		54 months	\$4252.50

34. **MP MODELING REAL LIFE** A family borrows money for a rainforest tour. The simple annual interest rate is 12%. The loan is paid after 3 months. What is the total amount paid for the tour?

Rainforest Tour

Tickets	\$940
Food	\$170
Supplies	\$120

35. **MP MODELING REAL LIFE** You deposit \$5000 in an account earning 7.5% simple interest per year. How long will it take for the balance of the account to be \$6500?

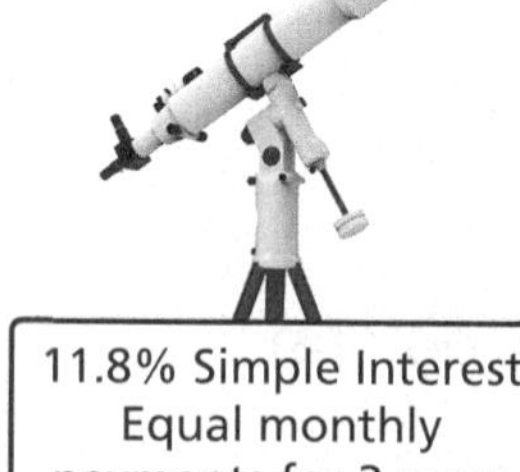

11.8% Simple Interest
Equal monthly
payments for 2 years

36. **MP MODELING REAL LIFE** You borrow \$1300 to buy a telescope. What is the monthly payment?

37. **MP REASONING** How many years will it take for \$2000 to double at a simple annual interest rate of 8%? Explain how you found your answer.

38. **DIG DEEPER!** You take out two loans. After 2 years, the total interest for the loans is \$138. On the first loan, you pay 7.5% simple annual interest on a principal of \$800. On the second loan, you pay 3% simple annual interest. What is the principal for the second loan?

39. **MP REPEATED REASONING** You deposit \$500 in an account that earns 4% simple annual interest. The interest earned each year is added to the principal to create a new principal. Find the total amount in your account after each year for 3 years.

40. **MP NUMBER SENSE** An account earns r% simple interest per year. Does doubling the initial principal have the same effect on the total interest earned as doubling the amount of time? Justify your answer.

Common Errors

- **Exercises 26–29** Students may only find the amount of interest paid for the loan. Remind students that the total amount paid on a loan is the sum of the principal and the interest.

Mini-Assessment

1. You deposit $1300 in a savings account. The account earns 4.5% simple interest per year. What is the balance after 3 years? $1475.50
2. You deposit $600 in an account. The account earns $45 simple interest in 2 years. What is the annual interest rate? 3.75%
3. You borrow $800 to buy new furniture. The simple annual interest rate is 3%. The loan is paid after 3 years. What is the total amount paid for the loan? $872
4. You borrow $600 to buy a canoe. The simple annual interest rate is 5%. You pay off the loan after 4 years of equal monthly payments. How much is each payment? $15

Section Resources

Surface Level	Deep Level
Resources by Chapter • Extra Practice • Reteach • Puzzle Time Student Journal • Self-Assessment • Practice Differentiating the Lesson Tutorial Videos Skills Review Handbook Skills Trainer	Resources by Chapter • Enrichment and Extension Graphic Organizers Dynamic Assessment System • Section Practice
Transfer Level	
Dynamic Assessment System • End-of-Chapter Quiz	Assessment Book • End-of-Chapter Quiz

Concepts, Skills, & Problem Solving

23. $1440
24. 6%
25. 2 yr
26. $1770
27. $2720
28. $3660
29. $6700.80
30. $2550
31. $8500
32. 4 yr
33. 5.25%
34. $1266.90
35. 4 yr
36. $66.95
37. 12.5 yr; Substitute $2000 for P, $2000 for I, 0.08 for r, and solve for t.
38. $300
39. Year 1 = $520
Year 2 = $540.80
Year 3 = $562.43
40. yes; doubling principal: $I = (2P)rt = 2Prt$; doubling time: $I = Pr(2t) = 2Prt$; $2Prt = 2Prt$

Skills Needed

Exercise 1

- Completing a Ratio Table
- Using the Percent Equation

Exercise 2

- Adding Rational Numbers
- Writing Fractions as Decimals and Percents

Exercise 3

- Finding a Percent of Change
- Finding a Unit Rate

ELL Support

Many students who are new to the country may not be familiar with the game of hockey. You might want to discuss basics of how it is played.

Using the Problem-Solving Plan

1. Blazers: 3 goals; Hawks: 4 goals
2. *Sample answer:* $\frac{4}{5} + \left(-\frac{2}{4}\right)$; $\frac{4}{5} + \left(-\frac{2}{4}\right) = \frac{3}{10}$, $\frac{4}{5} \times 0.375 = 0.3 = \frac{3}{10}$
3. 37.1% increase

Performance Task

The *STEAM Video Performance Task* provides the opportunity for additional enrichment and greater depth of knowledge as students explore the mathematics of the chapter within a context tied to the chapter STEAM Video. The performance task and a detailed scoring rubric are provided at *BigIdeasMath.com.*

Laurie's Notes

Scaffolding Instruction

- The goal of this lesson is to help students become more comfortable with problem solving. These exercises combine solving percent problems with prior skills from other chapters. The solution for Exercise 1 is worked out below, to help you guide students through the problem-solving plan. Use the remaining class time to have students work on the other exercises.
- **Emerging:** The goal for these students is to feel comfortable with the problem-solving plan. Allow students to work in pairs to write the beginning steps of the problem-solving plan for Exercise 2. Keep in mind that some students may only be ready to do the first step.
- **Proficient:** Students may be able to work independently or in pairs to complete Exercises 2 and 3.
- Visit each pair to review their plan for each problem. Ask students to describe their plans.

Using the Problem-Solving Plan

Exercise 1

Understand the problem. You know that 55 shots are taken in a hockey game and that the Blazers take 6 shots for every 5 shots taken by the Hawks. You also know the percent of successful shots for each team.

Make a plan. Use a ratio table to determine the number of shots taken by each team. Then use the percent equation to determine the number of successful shots for each team.

Solve and check. Use the plan to solve the problem. Then check your solution.

- Use a ratio table to determine the number of shots taken by each team.

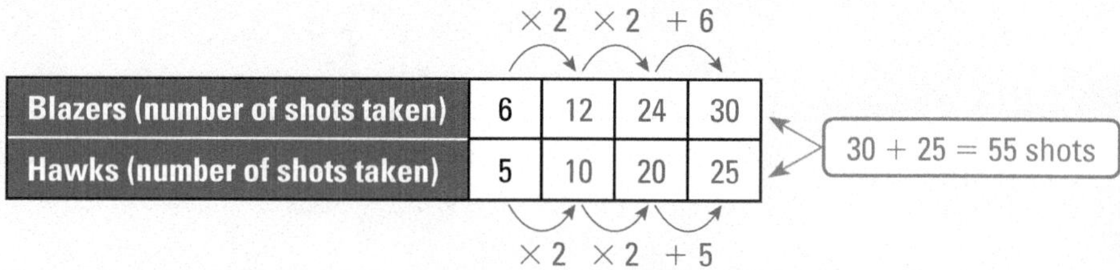

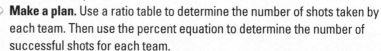

Blazers (number of shots taken)	6	12	24	30
Hawks (number of shots taken)	5	10	20	25

So, the Blazers take 30 shots and the Hawks take 25 shots.

- Determine the number of successful shots for each team.

Blazers:		Hawks:
$a = p\% \cdot w$	Write the percent equation.	$a = p\% \cdot w$
$a = 0.10 \cdot 30$	Substitute values for $p\%$ and w.	$a = 0.16 \cdot 25$
$a = 3$	Multiply.	$a = 4$

The Blazers score 3 goals and the Hawks score 4 goals.

- **Check:** Verify the number of shots taken by each team using proportions.

Blazers:

$\frac{6}{11} = \frac{x}{55}$

$11x = 330$

$x = 30$ ✓

Hawks:

$\frac{5}{11} = \frac{x}{55}$

$11x = 275$

$x = 25$ ✓

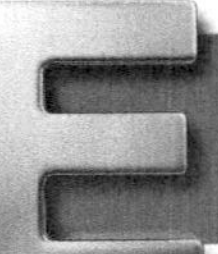

Connecting Concepts

Using the Problem-Solving Plan

1. The table shows the percent of successful shots for each team in a hockey game. A total of 55 shots are taken in the game. The ratio of shots taken by the Blazers to shots taken by the Hawks is 6 : 5. How many goals does each team score?

Team	Percent of Successful Shots
Blazers	10%
Hawks	16%

Understand the problem. You know that 55 shots are taken in a hockey game and that the Blazers take 6 shots for every 5 shots taken by the Hawks. You also know the percent of successful shots for each team.

Make a plan. Use a ratio table to determine the number of shots taken by each team. Then use the percent equation to determine the number of successful shots for each team.

Solve and check. Use the plan to solve the problem. Then check your solution.

2. Fill in the blanks with positive numbers so that the sum of the fractions is 37.5% of the first fraction. Justify your answer.

$$\frac{\square}{5} + \left(-\frac{\square}{4}\right)$$

3. The graph shows the distance traveled by a motorcycle on a dirt road. After turning onto a paved road, the motorcycle travels $\frac{1}{5}$ mile every $\frac{1}{4}$ minute. Find the percent of change in the speed of the motorcycle. Round to the nearest tenth of a percent if necessary.

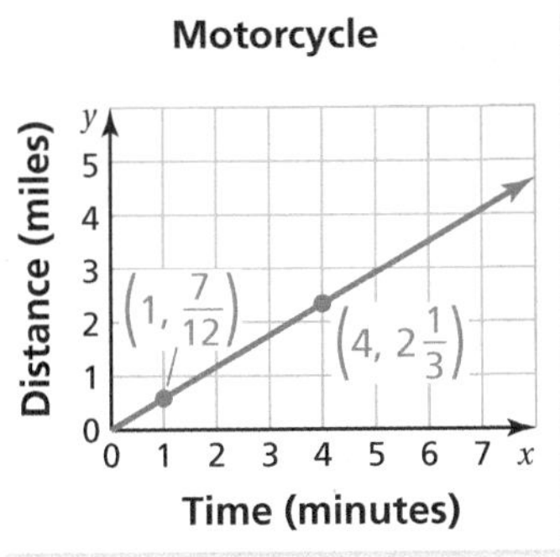

Performance Task

Tornado Alley

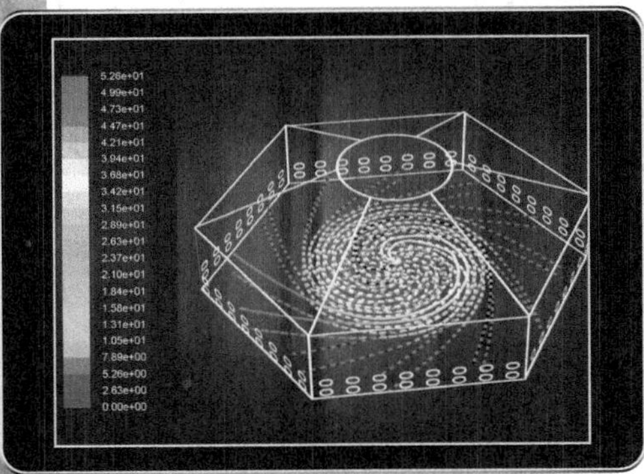

At the beginning of this chapter, you watched a STEAM Video called "Tornado!" You are now ready to complete the performance task related to this video, available at ***BigIdeasMath.com***. Be sure to use the problem-solving plan as you work through the performance task.

Chapter Review

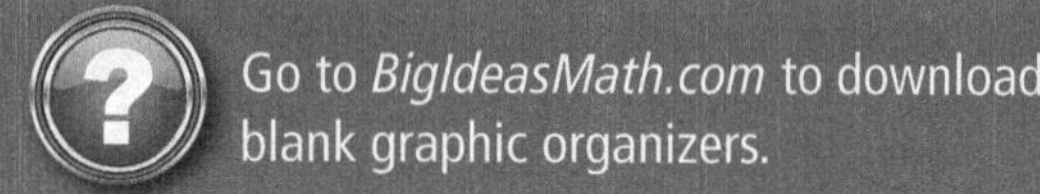
Go to BigIdeasMath.com to download
blank graphic organizers.

Review Vocabulary

Write the definition and give an example of each vocabulary term.

percent of change, *p. 698*
percent of increase, *p. 698*
percent of decrease, *p. 698*
percent error, *p. 700*
discount, *p. 704*
markup, *p. 704*
interest, *p. 710*
principal, *p. 710*
simple interest, *p. 710*

Graphic Organizers

You can use a **Summary Triangle** to explain a concept. Here is an example of a Summary Triangle for ***writing a percent as a decimal***.

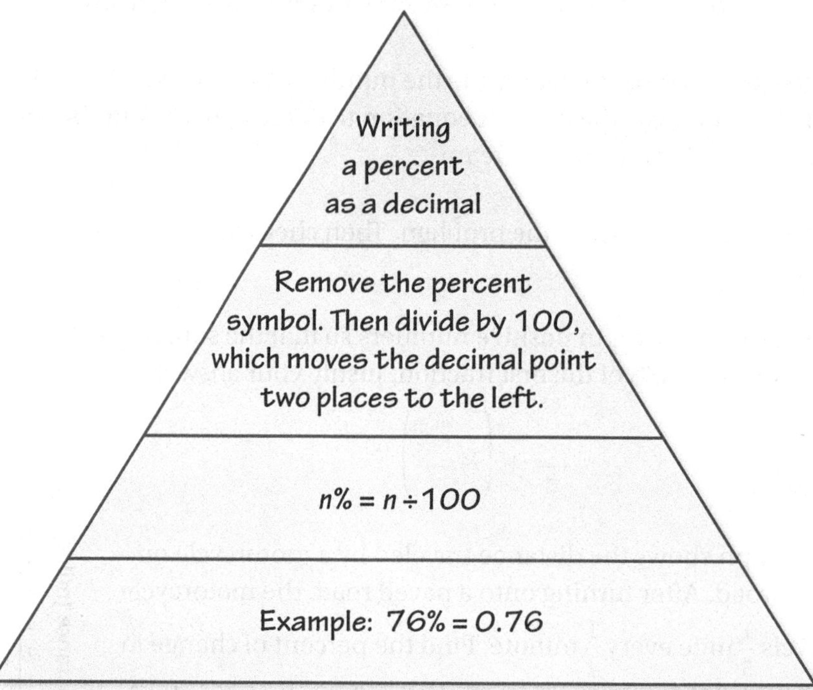
Writing
a percent
as a decimal
Remove the percent
symbol. Then divide by 100,
which moves the decimal point
two places to the left.
n% = n ÷ 100
Example: 76% = 0.76

Choose and complete a graphic organizer to help you study the concept.

1. writing a decimal as a percent
2. comparing and ordering fractions, decimals, and percents
3. the percent proportion
4. the percent equation
5. percent of change
6. discount
7. markup

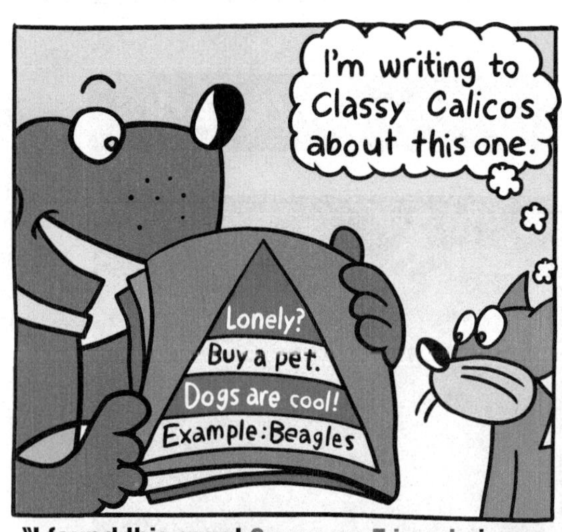
I'm writing to
Classy Calicos
about this one.
Lonely?
Buy a pet.
Dogs are cool!
Example: Beagles

"I found this great Summary Triangle in my *Beautiful Beagle Magazine*."

Review Vocabulary

- As a review of the chapter vocabulary, have students revisit the vocabulary section in their *Student Journals* to fill in any missing definitions and record examples of each term.

Graphic Organizers

Sample answers:

1.

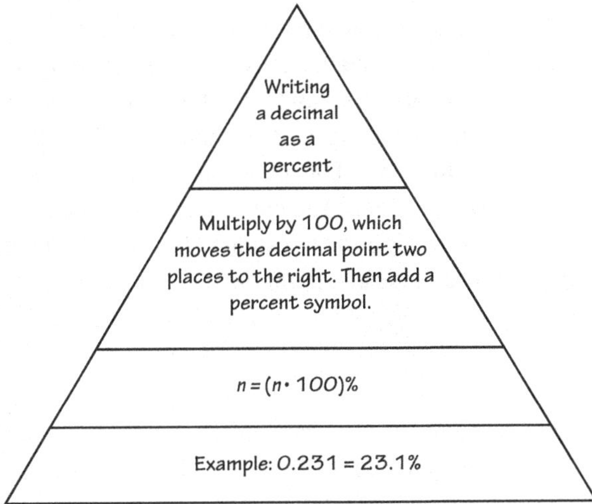

Writing a decimal as a percent
Multiply by 100, which moves the decimal point two places to the right. Then add a percent symbol.
$n = (n \cdot 100)\%$
Example: $0.231 = 23.1\%$

2.

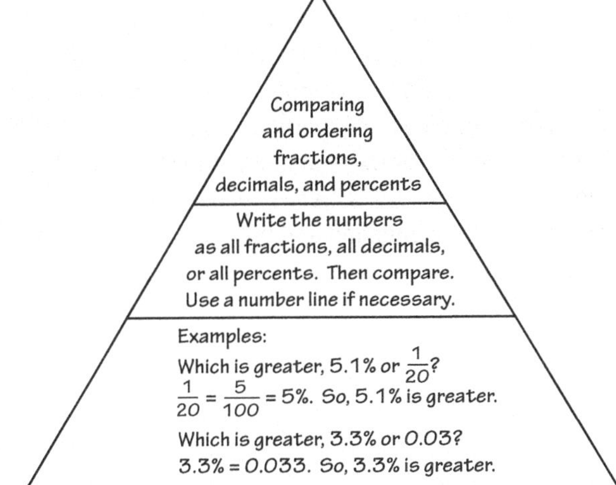

Comparing and ordering fractions, decimals, and percents
Write the numbers as all fractions, all decimals, or all percents. Then compare. Use a number line if necessary.
Examples:
Which is greater, 5.1% or $\frac{1}{20}$?
$\frac{1}{20} = \frac{5}{100} = 5\%$. So, 5.1% is greater.
Which is greater, 3.3% or 0.03?
3.3% = 0.033. So, 3.3% is greater.

3.

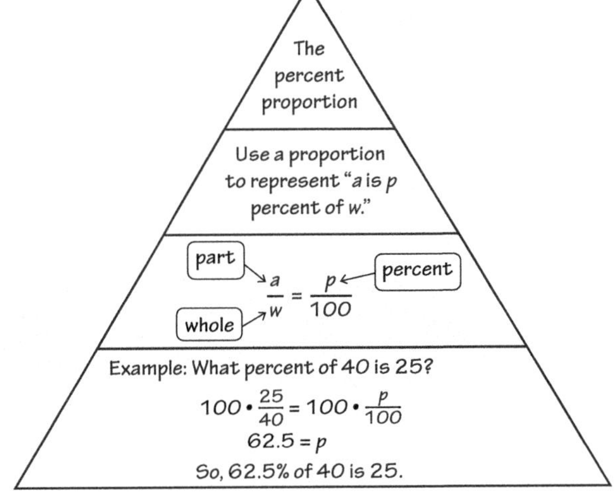

The percent proportion
Use a proportion to represent "a is p percent of w."
part
percent
whole
$\frac{a}{w} = \frac{p}{100}$
Example: What percent of 40 is 25?
$100 \cdot \frac{25}{40} = 100 \cdot \frac{p}{100}$
$62.5 = p$
So, 62.5% of 40 is 25.

4–7. Answers at *BigIdeasMath.com*.

List of Organizers

Available at *BigIdeasMath.com*
Definition and Example Chart
Example and Non-Example Chart
Four Square
Information Frame
Summary Triangle

About this Organizer

A **Summary Triangle** can be used to explain a concept. Typically, the Summary Triangle is divided into 3 or 4 parts. Students write related categories in the middle part(s). Related categories may include: procedure, explanation, description, definition, theorem, or formula. In the bottom part, students write an example to illustrate the concept. A Summary Triangle can be used as an assessment tool, in which students complete the missing parts. Students may also place their Summary Triangles on note cards to use as a quick study reference.

Chapter Self-Assessment

1. 0.74

2. 0.02

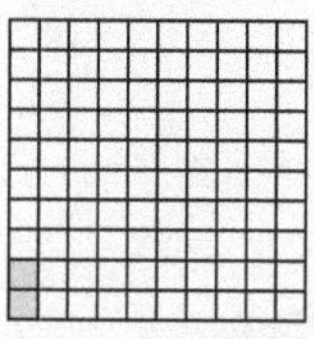

3. See Additional Answers.
4. 17%

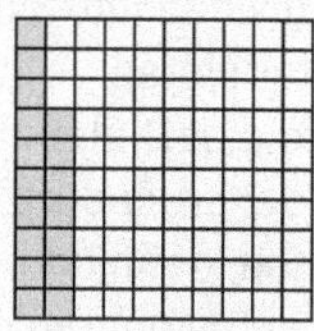

5. See Additional Answers.
6. 7.9%

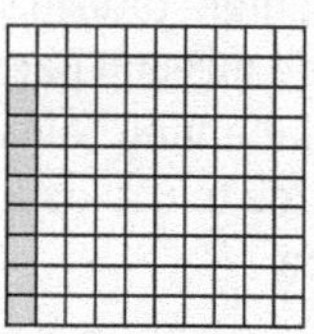

7. 0.85, 85%
8. 0.375, 37.5%
9. $1.\overline{5}$, $155.\overline{5}\%$
10. gold, orange, white, blue; $0.1 < 0.11875 < 0.15625 < 0.625$
11. $\frac{18}{60} = \frac{p}{100}$; $p = 30$
12. $\frac{40}{32} = \frac{p}{100}$; $p = 125$
13. $\frac{a}{70} = \frac{70}{100}$; $a = 49$
14. $\frac{\frac{3}{4}}{w} = \frac{75}{100}$; $w = 1$
15. 147.9 million km^2

Chapter Self-Assessment

The Success Criteria Self-Assessment chart can be found in the *Student Journal* or online at *BigIdeasMath.com*.

ELL Support

Allow students to work in pairs to complete the first section of the Chapter Self-Assessment. Once pairs have finished, check for understanding by asking them to display their answers on whiteboards for your review. For sections that include discussion questions, students may benefit from grouping two pairs and having them reach a consensus for the answers. Monitor discussions and provide support. You can use a thumbs up or down signal to check answers to *yes* or *no* questions. Use these and other techniques for the remaining sections as appropriate.

Common Errors

- **Exercises 4–6** Students may move the decimal point the wrong way, forget to place zeros as placeholders, or move the decimal point too many places. Remind students that when writing a decimal as a percent, they need to multiply the decimal by 100 and then add the percent symbol.
- **Exercise 10** Students may try to order the numbers without converting them or will only convert them mentally and do so incorrectly. Tell them that it is necessary to convert all the numbers to one form and that they should write out the steps to make sure that they are converting correctly.
- **Exercises 11–14** Students may not know what number to substitute for each variable. Remind students that the word *is* means "equals" and *of* means "to multiply." Tell students to write the question and then write the meaning of each word or phrase underneath.

Chapter Self-Assessment

As you complete the exercises, use the scale below to rate your understanding of the success criteria in your journal.

1	2	3	4
I do not understand.	I can do it with help.	I can do it on my own.	I can teach someone else.

E.1 Fractions, Decimals, and Percents (pp. 679–684)

Learning Target: Rewrite fractions, decimals, and percents using different representations.

Write the percent as a decimal or the decimal as a percent. Use a model to represent the number.

1. 74% **2.** 2% **3.** 221%

4. 0.17 **5.** $4.\overline{3}$ **6.** 0.079

Write the fraction as a decimal and a percent.

7. $\frac{17}{20}$ **8.** $\frac{3}{8}$ **9.** $\frac{14}{9}$

10. For school spirit day, 11.875% of your class wears orange shirts, $\frac{5}{8}$ of your class wears blue shirts, 0.15625 of your class wears white shirts, and the rest of your class wears gold shirts. Order the portions of shirts of each color from least to greatest. Justify your answer.

E.2 The Percent Proportion (pp. 685–690)

Learning Target: Use the percent proportion to find missing quantities.

Write and solve a proportion to answer the question.

11. What percent of 60 is 18?

12. 40 is what percent of 32?

13. What number is 70% of 70?

14. $\frac{3}{4}$ is 75% of what number?

15. About 29% of the Earth's surface is covered by land. The total surface area of the Earth is about 510 million square kilometers. What is the area of the Earth's surface covered by land?

E.3 The Percent Equation (pp. 691–696)

Learning Target: Use the percent equation to find missing quantities.

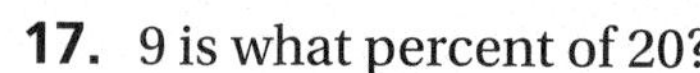

Write and solve an equation to answer the question.

16. What number is 24% of 25?

17. 9 is what percent of 20?

18. 60.8 is what percent of 32?

19. 91 is 130% of what number?

20. 85% of what number is 10.2?

21. 83% of 20 is what number?

22. 15% of the parking spaces at a school are handicap spaces. The school has 18 handicap spaces. How many parking spaces are there in total?

23. Of the 25 students on a field trip, 16 bring cameras. What percent of the students bring cameras?

E.4 Percents of Increase and Decrease (pp. 697–702)

Learning Target: Find percents of change in quantities.

Identify the percent of change as an *increase* or a *decrease*. Then find the percent of change. Round to the nearest tenth of a percent if necessary.

24. 6 yards to 36 yards

25. 120 meals to 52 meals

26. You estimate that a jar contains 68 marbles. The actual number of marbles is 60. Find the percent error.

27. The table shows the numbers of skim boarders at a beach on Saturday and Sunday. What was the percent of change in boarders from Saturday to Sunday?

Day	Number of Skim Boarders
Saturday	12
Sunday	9

Common Errors

- **Exercises 16–21** Students may not know what number to substitute for each variable. Remind students that the word *is* means "equals" and *of* means "to multiply." Tell students to write the question and then write the meaning of each word or phrase underneath.
- **Exercises 24 and 25** Students may mix up where to place the numbers in the formula to find percent of change. When they do not put the numbers in the correct places, they might find a negative number in the numerator. First, emphasize that students must know if it is increasing or decreasing before they start the problem. Next, tell students the number in the denominator is the original or starting number given. Finally, the numerator should never have a negative answer. If students get a negative number, it is because they found the wrong difference. The numerator is always the greater number minus the lesser number.

Chapter Self-Assessment

16. $a = 0.24 \cdot 25$; 6

17. $9 = p\% \cdot 20$; 45%

18. $60.8 = p\% \cdot 32$; 190%

19. $91 = 1.3 \cdot w$; 70

20. $10.2 = 0.85 \cdot w$; 12

21. $a = 0.83 \cdot 20$; 16.6

22. 120 parking spaces

23. 64%

24. increase; 500%

25. decrease; 56.7%

26. about 13.3%

27. 25% decrease

Chapter Self-Assessment

28. $42.50

29. $93.75

30. $30

31. **a.** $62.50

b. $66.25

32. **a.** $36

b. $336

33. **a.** $280

b. $2280

34. 1.7%

35. 7.1%

36. 3 years

37. 6 years

38. 4%

39. **a.** Bank A: $261; Bank B: $179.25

b. *Sample answer:* A person would choose Bank A if they wanted a short term loan. A person would choose Bank B if they wanted lower monthly payments.

Common Errors

- **Exercise 28** Students may write the discount amount as the sale price instead of subtracting it from the original price. Remind them to subtract the discount amount from the original price.
- **Exercises 29 and 30** Students may use the percent of discount instead of the percent of the original price of the item. Remind students that there is an extra step in the problem. They should subtract the percent of discount from 100% to find the percent of the original price of the item.
- **Exercise 31** Students may find the markup and not the selling price. Remind students that they must add the markup to the cost to obtain the selling price.
- **Exercises 32, 33, 36, and 37** Students may forget to change the percent to a decimal. Remind students that before they can put the percent into the formula, they must change the percent to a decimal or a fraction.

Chapter Resources

Surface Level	Deep Level
Resources by Chapter • Extra Practice • Reteach • Puzzle Time Student Journal • Practice • Chapter Self-Assessment Differentiating the Lesson Tutorial Videos Skills Review Handbook Skills Trainer Game Library	Resources by Chapter • Enrichment and Extension Graphic Organizers Game Library
Transfer Level	
STEAM Video Dynamic Assessment System • Chapter Test	Assessment Book • Chapter Tests A and B • Alternative Assessment • STEAM Performance Task

E.5 Discounts and Markups *(pp. 703–708)*

Learning Target: Solve percent problems involving discounts and markups.

Find the sale price or original price.

28. Original price: \$50
Discount: 15%
Sale price: ?

29. Original price: ?
Discount: 20%
Sale price: \$75

30. What is the original price of the tennis racquet?

31. A store pays \$50 for a pair of shoes. The markup is 25%.

a. What is the selling price for the shoes?

b. What is the total cost for a person to buy the shoes including a 6% sales tax?

E.6 Simple Interest *(pp. 709–714)*

Learning Target: Understand and apply the simple interest formula.

An account earns simple interest. (a) Find the interest earned. (b) Find the balance of the account.

32. \$300 at 4% for 3 years

33. \$2000 at 3.5% for 4 years

Find the annual interest rate.

34. $I = \$17$, $P = \$500$, $t = 2$ years

35. $I = \$426$, $P = \$1200$, $t = 5$ years

Find the amount of time.

36. $I = \$60$, $P = \$400$, $r = 5\%$

37. $I = \$237.90$, $P = \$1525$, $r = 2.6\%$

38. You deposit \$100 in an account. The account earns \$2 simple interest in 6 months. What is the annual interest rate?

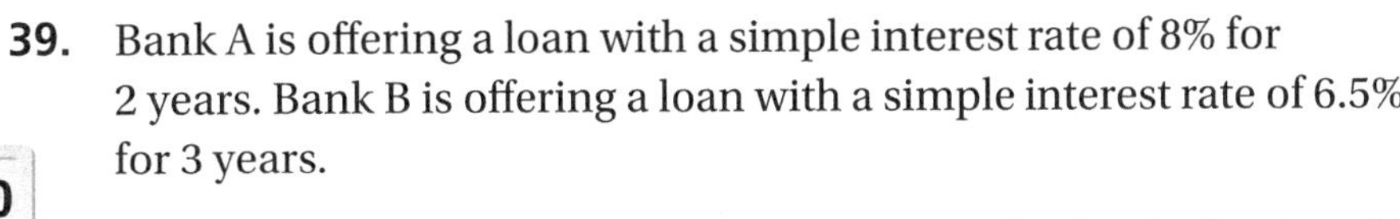

39. Bank A is offering a loan with a simple interest rate of 8% for 2 years. Bank B is offering a loan with a simple interest rate of 6.5% for 3 years.

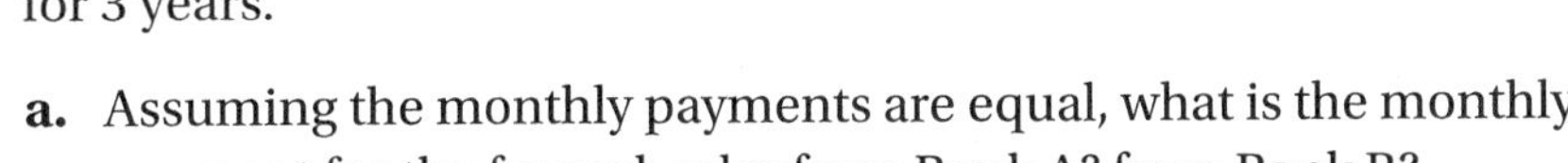

a. Assuming the monthly payments are equal, what is the monthly payment for the four wheeler from Bank A? from Bank B?

b. Give reasons for why a person might choose Bank A and why a person might choose Bank B for a loan to buy the four wheeler. Explain your reasoning.

Practice Test

Write the percent as a decimal, or the decimal as a percent. Use a model to represent the number.

1. 0.96%
2. 3%
3. $25.\overline{5}\%$
4. $0.\overline{6}$
5. 7.88
6. 0.58

Order the numbers from least to greatest.

7. 86%, $\frac{15}{18}$, 0.84, $\frac{8}{9}$, $0.\overline{86}$
8. 91.6%, 0.91, $\frac{11}{12}$, 0.917, 9.2%

Write and solve a proportion or equation to answer the question.

9. What percent of 28 is 21?
10. 64 is what percent of 40?
11. What number is 80% of 45?
12. 0.8% of what number is 6?

Identify the percent of change as an *increase* or a *decrease*. Then find the percent of change. Round to the nearest tenth of a percent if necessary.

13. 4 strikeouts to 10 strikeouts
14. \$24 to \$18

Find the sale price or selling price.

15. Original price: \$15
    Discount: 5%
    Sale price: ?
16. Cost to store: \$5.50
    Markup: 75%
    Selling price: ?

An account earns simple interest. Find the interest earned or the principal.

17. Interest earned: ?
    Principal: \$450
    Interest rate: 6%
    Time: 8 years
18. Interest earned: \$27
    Principal: ?
    Interest rate: 1.5%
    Time: 2 years

19. You spend 8 hours each weekday at school. (a) Write the portion of a weekday spent at school as a fraction, a decimal, and a percent. (b) What percent of a week is spent at school if you go to school 4 days that week? Round to the nearest tenth.

20. Research indicates that 90% of the volume of an iceberg is below water. The volume of the iceberg above the water is 160,000 cubic feet. What is the volume of the iceberg below water?

21. You estimate that there are 66 cars in a parking lot. The actual number of cars is 75.
    a. Find the percent error.
    b. What other estimate gives the same percent error? Explain your reasoning.

Practice Test Item References

Practice Test Questions	Section to Review
1, 2, 3, 4, 5, 6, 7, 8, 19	E.1
9, 10, 11, 12, 20	E.2
9, 10, 11, 12, 20	E.3
13, 14, 21	E.4
15, 16	E.5
17, 18	E.6

Test-Taking Strategies

Remind students to quickly look over the entire test before they start so that they can budget their time. Remind them that the test includes fractions, decimals, and percents and that they need to read the problems carefully. Students need to use the **Stop** and **Think** strategy before they write their answers. Students need to remember to think of the different representations of each number as they work through the test, such as 0.5, $\frac{1}{2}$, and 50%.

Common Errors

- **Exercises 4–6** Students may move the decimal point the wrong way, forget to place zeros as placeholders, or move the decimal point too many places. Remind students that when writing a decimal as a percent, they need to multiply the decimal by 100 and then add the percent symbol.
- **Exercises 7 and 8** Students may try to order the numbers without converting them or will only convert them mentally and do so incorrectly. Tell them that it is necessary to convert all the numbers to one form and that they should write out the steps to make sure that they are converting correctly.
- **Exercises 7 and 8** Students may try to round the numbers that have repeating decimals and incorrectly order the numbers. Remind them that even though you often round repeating decimals, the decimal is actually less than or greater than the rounded decimal.
- **Exercises 9–12** Students may not know what number to substitute for each variable. Remind students that the word *is* means "equals" and *of* means "to multiply." Tell students to write the question and then write the meaning of each word or phrase underneath.
- **Exercise 15** Students may write the discount amount as the sale price instead of subtracting it from the original amount. Remind them to subtract the discount amount from the original price.
- **Exercises 17 and 18** Students may forget to change the percent to a decimal. Remind students that before they can put the percent into the formula, they must change the percent to a decimal or a fraction.

Practice Test

1. 0.0096

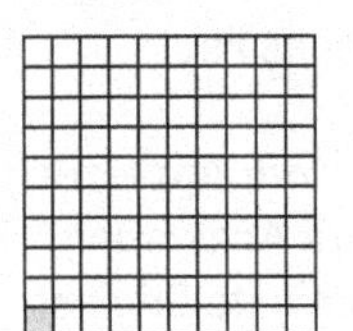

2. 0.03

3. $0.2\overline{5}$

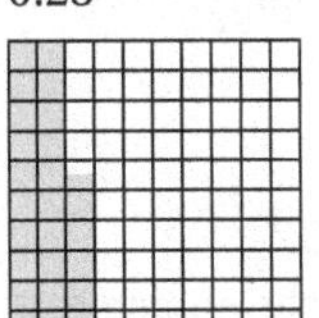

4. $66.\overline{6}\%$

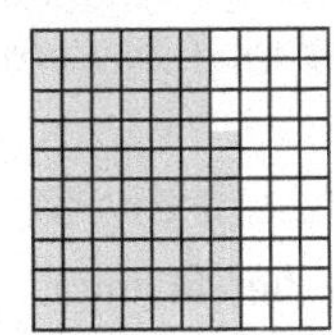

5. See Additional Answers.

6. 58%

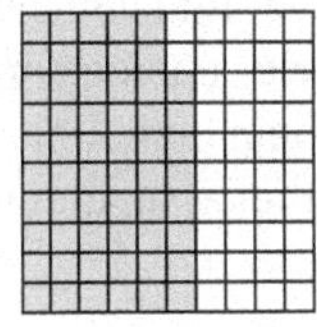

7. $\frac{15}{18}$, 0.84, 86%, $0.8\overline{6}$, $\frac{8}{9}$

8. 9.2%, 0.91, 91.6%, $\frac{11}{12}$, 0.917

9. 75%

10. 160%

11. 36

12. 750

13. increase; 150%

14. decrease; 25%

15. $14.25

16. $9.63

17. $216

18. $900

19. **a.** $\frac{1}{3}$, $0.\overline{3}$, $33.\overline{3}\%$

b. about 19.0%

20. 1,440,000 ft^3

21. **a.** 12%

b. 84 cars; To get the same percent error, the amount of error needs to be the same. Because your estimate was 9 cars below the actual number, an estimate of 9 cars above the actual number will give the same percent error.

Test-Taking Strategies

Available at *BigIdeasMath.com*
After Answering Easy Questions, Relax
Answer Easy Questions First
Estimate the Answer
Read All Choices before Answering
Read Question before Answering
Solve Directly or Eliminate Choices
Solve Problem before Looking at Choices
Use Intelligent Guessing
Work Backwards

About this Strategy

When taking a multiple-choice test, be sure to read each question carefully and thoroughly. It is also very important to read each answer choice carefully. Do not pick the first answer that you think is correct! If two answer choices are the same, eliminate them both. Unless the question states otherwise, there can only be one answer.

Cumulative Practice

1. C
2. −8
3. F
4. D
5. I

Item Analysis

1. **A.** The student finds 30% of \$8.50 but does not subtract this amount from \$8.50.

   B. The student thinks that 30% is equivalent to \$3.00 and subtracts this amount from \$8.50.

   C. Correct answer

   D. The student thinks that 30% is equivalent to \$0.30 and subtracts this amount from \$8.50.

2. **Gridded Response:** Correct answer: −8

   Common error: The student multiplies by −2 instead of dividing by −2 and gets −32.

3. **F.** Correct answer

   G. The student computes the area in square meters but then uses the given scale factor, which is for length, not area.

   H. The student reverses the relationship between the actual park and the scale model. The student also computes the area in square meters but then uses the given scale factor, which is for length, not area.

   I. The student reverses the relationship between the actual park and the scale model.

4. **A.** The student chooses a proportion that will find what percent 17 is of 43.

   B. The student chooses a proportion that will find 43% of 17.

   C. The student chooses a proportion that will find 17% of 43.

   D. Correct answer

5. **F.** The student thinks that 0.09 is 0.9.

   G. The student thinks that 70% is equivalent to 70.

   H. The student orders the numbers using either the numerator or the nonzero digit.

   I. Correct answer